MAXIMUM SECURITY

THIRD EDITION

Anonymous

SAMS

201 West 103rd St., Indianapolis, Indiana, 46290 USA

Maximum Security, Third Edition

Copyright © 2001 by Sams Publishing

International Standard Book Number: 0-672-31871-7

Library of Congress Catalog Card Number: 00-109549

Printed in the United States of America

First Printing: May 2001

04   03   02   01   4   3   2   1

Trademarks

Warning and Disclaimer

Inside Front Cover Illustration by J. Norman Scott, ApeOEvil@aol.com.

ACQUISITIONS EDITOR
Shelley Johnston Markanday

DEVELOPMENT EDITORS
Heather Goodell
Scott Meyers

MANAGING EDITOR
Charlotte Clapp

PROJECT EDITOR
Carol Bowers

COPY EDITORS
Mary Ellen Stephenson
Margaret Berson

INDEXER
Johnna VanHoose Dinse

PROOFREADER
Tony Reitz

TECHNICAL EDITORS
Robert Blader
Billy Barron

TEAM COORDINATOR
Amy Patton

MEDIA DEVELOPER
Dan Scherf

INTERIOR DESIGNER
Anne Jones

COVER DESIGNER
Anne Jones

PAGE LAYOUT
Stacey Richwine-DeRome

Contents at a Glance

Table of Contents

About the Lead Author

Anonymous is a self-described UNIX and Perl fanatic, who lives in southern California with his wife, Michelle, and a half-dozen computers. He currently runs an Internet security consulting company and is at work building one of the world's largest computer security archives. He also moonlights doing contract programming for several Fortune 500 firms.

About the Contributing Authors

Craig Balding is a full-time security practitioner, employed by one of the largest banking and finance companies in the world. In addition to heading up UNIX security, he is responsible for IDS strategy, technical e-business security assessments, and penetration testing. He has worked with UNIX for some eight years, in multivendor environments across diverse sectors. He has been at the sharp end, working on high-end, mission-critical UNIX servers and multiterabyte databases.

Billy Barron (bbbarron@delphis.com) is a principal Java/OO consultant for Delphi Consultants, LLC (http://www.delphis.com/). He founded the Java Metroplex User Group (JavaMUG at http://www.javamug.org/) and was the first Webmaster in the Dallas/Fort Worth area. He has co-authored and tech-edited numerous books including *Web Programming Unleashed*, *Tricks of the Internet Gurus*, *Maximum Java 1.1*, *Web Commerce Unleashed*, *Creating Web Applets with Java*, and *Internet Unleashed*.

Robert Blader has worked for more than 15 years at the Naval Surface Warfare Center. For nearly 3 years, he has worked in the Information Systems Security Office, which performs intrusion detection and risk management for systems and networks on the base, as well as security training and forensics. For 10 years prior to that, he worked as a systems administrator for the Trident missile project. He has contributed to SANS GIAC courses and *SysAdmin* magazine. He holds a bachelor's degree in computer science from Long Island University

Chad Cook is co-founder and chief security architect of Zetari Inc., where he is responsible for product security, software design, and development. Prior to starting Zetari Inc., he was a senior member of the Internet security consulting firm @stake, where he worked in research and development and on client solutions. He has developed new security technologies and published papers on numerous security topics, including secure product design, vulnerability analysis, and encryption. He has 10 years of experience in the Internet Security field with emphasis on secure product architecture, network and operating system security, and the research and development of new security technologies with companies including BBN, GTE, and Infolibria.

Jonathan Feldman is the author of *Sams Teach Yourself Network Troubleshooting* and Que's *Network+ Exam Guide*. He is a contributing editor with *Network Computing* magazine, where he writes a column and frequently contributes technical workshops. He enjoys living in Savannah, Georgia, working as chief technical manager for Chatham County, where he handles the practical and political aspects of network security on a daily basis. In his copious spare time, he enjoys running, cooking, and playing the guitar, but not all at the same time. He can be reached at `jf@feldman.org`.

David Harley (`harley@sherpasoft.org.uk`) learned his trade managing security for the Imperial Cancer Research Fund. He now occupies a senior management post in the UK's National Health Service Information Authority. He also works with TruSecure (formerly ICSA), the WildList Organization, and the European Institute for Computer Anti-virus Research. He maintains a number of virus- and security-related information resources at `sherpasoft.org.uk` and `macvirus.com`, and a security alert verification service at `security-sceptic.org.uk`. He writes regularly for *Virus Bulletin* and is a frequent speaker at security conferences. His book *Viruses Revealed* (with Robert Slade and Urs Gattiker) is due for publication in late 2001. He lives in London with his 11-year-old daughter.

Joe Jenkins is a system administrator/security consultant with NoWalls, Inc. (`http://www.nowalls.inc`). He has been dealing with network security since 1993, conducting in-depth security audits and consulting on various aspects of intrusion detection, perimeter defense, and policy. He routinely writes for online security magazines, notably *SecurityFocus*, and has also worked as a programmer and hardware engineer.

L.J. Locher began working with mainframe and personal computers in the mid-1980s, and has since been employed as a network administrator, programmer, and security consultant for mainframe systems and PC LANs. Now a full-time author and editor, L.J. has contributed to numerous books and articles for various publishers including Microsoft Press and *Windows 2000* magazine.

Toby Miller is a security engineer for Advanced Systems Development. He holds a bachelor's degree in Computer Information Systems and is working towards his master's degree. He is a contributing author for *Intrusion Signatures and Analysis* (New Riders). He also is the author of many papers published for securityfocus.com and the SANS Institute, and works as an MCP and a GIAC analyst.

Brooke Paul began working in information technology as a systems and network administrator at the University of California. Due to the loose nature of university security at the time, he experienced several security incidents within his first few months on the job. He quickly learned about the limitations of TCP/IP security and the lack of security in most vendors' default operating system configurations. Taking this as a challenge, he began working on improving the security of the systems and networks under his care. He now works as an information technology and security consultant and frequently publishes articles about security in technology trade magazines.

Nicholas Raba goes by the handle Freaky. He originally started writing by creating an underground printed publication and from there created the Web site Freaks Macintosh Archives. He loves security, and MacOS just so happened to be the niche category he chose to specialize in. He created `SecureMac.com` and ever since has been writing security articles covering all aspects of the MacOS for that Web site and various magazines. He has also given speeches for Defcon 7 and Defcon 8 on Macintosh Hacking/Security. He says, "Thanks to Rie, who pushed me to contribute to this book." You can reach him with any questions/comments about Macintosh security at `nick@staticusers.net`.

Greg Shipley is a native Chicagoan. He was introduced to the world of computers through a dangerous fixation with video games and taught himself assembly on his Commodore 64. After spending a number of years studying computer science, he moved into the world of network engineering and Internet security. Today, he serves as the CTO for Neohapsis, a U.S.–based information security consultancy. When he's not immersed in the seas of corporate security storms, he's busy at work performing product testing in the Neohapsis/Network Computing Chicago lab. He would like to send his greetings to the people of Molokai, as they helped him gain some much-needed perspective during the early stages of this book.

Gregory B. White, Ph.D., joined SecureLogix in March 1999. He serves as the Vice President of Professional Services. Before joining SecureLogix, he was the deputy head of the Computer Science department and an associate professor of computer science at the United States Air Force Academy in Colorado Springs, Colorado. While at the Academy, Dr. White was instrumental in the development of two courses on computer security and information warfare. He also ensured that security was taught throughout the computer science curriculum. During his two tours at the Academy, he authored a number of papers on security and information warfare and is a co-author for two textbooks on computer security.

Tell Us What You Think!

As the reader of this book, *you* are our most important critic and commentator. We value your opinion and want to know what we're doing right, what we could do better, what areas you'd like to see us publish in, and any other words of wisdom you're willing to pass our way.

You can fax or write me directly to let me know what you did or didn't like about this book—as well as what we can do to make our books stronger.

Please note that I cannot help you with technical problems related to the topic of this book, and that due to the high volume of mail I receive, I might not be able to reply to every message.

When you write, please be sure to include this book's title and author as well as your name and phone or fax number. I will carefully review your comments and share them with the author and editors who worked on the book.

E-mail: webdev@samspublishing.com

Mail: Mark Taber
            Associate Publisher
            Sams Publishing
            201 West 103rd Street
            Indianapolis, IN 46290 USA

Setting the Stage

PART
I

IN THIS PART

Why This Book Was Written

IN THIS CHAPTER

Sams published *Maximum Security* because there is a real need. In the remaining paragraphs, I'd like to explore that need.

Thousands of institutions, businesses, and individuals go online every day. This phenomenon— which has been given a dozen different names—is commonly called the *Internet explosion*. That explosion has drastically changed the Internet's composition.

A decade ago, personnel with at least basic security knowledge maintained most servers. That fact didn't prevent break-ins, of course, but they occurred rarely in proportion to the number of potential targets.

Today, Internet servers are established by average folks, many of whom have little security experience. The number of viable targets is now staggering and that number grows daily. However, despite this critical situation, corporate America urges citizens onward. The Internet is safe, they say, so don't worry about a thing. Is that true? No.

Marketing folks are lying through their teeth. Either that, or they have absolutely no idea what they're talking about. The truth is, the Internet is not secure—not even moderately so.

What makes the situation even more dire is that authorities in the computer industry often assist Madison Avenue in snowing the public. They make extraordinary claims about their security products, leading the average consumer to believe that all is well. The reality is harsher than that, I'm afraid: Each month, hackers or crackers break yet another industry-standard security mechanism.

Maximum Security is a tool that can be used to start fixing the problem. Whether you use this book as a kick-start, a roadmap, or simply a reference guide, it should be handy to anyone having to deal with information security issues. We've taken special care in this revision to not only provide information that is relevant today, but information that will continue to be relevant in the years that follow. Some of the material will obviously become dated over time, but much of the methodology presented is timeless.

Our additions build upon the original author's foundation, taking many of his concepts one step further. It is our hope that we've taken his hard work to the next level, and provided the masses with the tools necessary to help address the information security industry's current nightmare.

The Need for Information Security

So what's the big deal? Why is this information security problem supposedly so large? Although I could talk about hacking trends, the increasing number of Web defacements, the round-the-clock compromises of government agencies and organizations, the theft of corporate secrets, and so on, I'd rather approach this from a more down-to-earth level. Why should we care?

Well, let me first ask whether your organization's data is valuable. Personnel data, social security numbers, credit card numbers, salary information, contact lists, marketing strategies, research and development efforts, intellectual property, earnings reports, and financial forecasts—are these of any value?

Next, let's take a look at some of the systems today that rely on computers:

- Transportation systems
- Personal and corporate financial records and systems
- Credit card processing systems
- Automatic Teller Machines (ATMs)
- The public telephone network
- Emergency communication, such as 911 calls
- Air traffic control systems
- Systems responsible for storing and transporting healthcare data
- Power systems
- Generic payment processing systems
- Ticketing systems

Now, let's say that I, as a "black hat" hacker, can attack and compromise any of these systems. What can I do? Well, I could go look up healthcare records on anyone. I could steal money from your bank account—or a series of bank accounts. I could steal credit cards. I could monkey with the phone system, and turn your home phone into a pay phone—or maybe just disconnect it. I could issue myself travel tickets, or turn the power off in your neighborhood. I could use the information on your spending patterns and your cell phone to track your movements and daily routines. In short, I could be a real pain in the ass.

Or, I could start doing far worse. I could use obtained information to assume your identity, get credit cards under your name, and thrash your credit rating while spending tens of thousands of dollars. I could bring e-commerce–based "dot com" startups to their knees during the holiday seasons, resulting in the loss of millions of dollars for both employees and shareholders. I could alter healthcare records resulting in eventual harm or death to my victims. I could cripple air traffic control systems, or attempt to stage in-flight collisions.

Although I don't know of any single individual that has pulled off all these stunts, most of them have already been attempted or successfully executed individually. Read that again—most of these have already happened.

Still not convinced?

Okay, let's pull back a second and assume that you aren't employed by a massive hospital, airport, or living in a strategic missile silo. Let's assume that you work for a Global 1000 (but this could easily apply to much smaller organizations). Now imagine I am a disgruntled employee, and I have it out for you. I trojan a bunch of your internal systems to launch automated and distributed denial of service attacks on your key database and production servers. I introduce hidden agents to attach to your databases at intermittent times, and corrupt random records. I order the cancellation of a few of your key WAN links. And I coordinate all of this fun to begin on the exact same day.

The result? Your organization is brought down globally—to a standstill—for at least a few days. You then face continued challenges for months to come, as you hunt down all the little demons I have left behind. Would this, perhaps, cause a problem?

Convinced yet?

Whether you see yourself as a target or not, by the time you finish this book, you'll realize that everyone is a target. It's that simple. You are either part of the problem, or part of the solution—there are no neutral bystanders in this war. Learn how to protect yourself, and hope that we never see such an attack occur.

The Root of the Problem

The simple truth is we face many challenges when attempting to secure enterprise environments. Most of the problems we face, however, can be grouped into the following categories:

- Network and host misconfigurations
- Operating system and application flaws
- Deficiencies in vendor QA efforts and response
- Lack of qualified people in the field

Let's briefly examine some examples in detail.

Network and Host Misconfigurations

One of the biggest drivers behind security breaches is the misconfigurations of the targets. This can bring down any site at any time, regardless of the security measures taken. (For example, when the Justice Department server was cracked, DOJ was running a firewall. As they discovered, a misconfigured firewall might as well be no firewall at all.)

Misconfiguration can occur at any point along the distribution chain, all the way from the factory to your office. For example, certain network utilities, when enabled, open serious security holes. Many software products ship with these utilities enabled. The resulting risks remain until you deactivate or properly configure the utility in question.

A good example would be network-printing utilities. These might be enabled in a fresh install, leaving the system insecure. It's up to you to disable those utilities. However, in order to disable them, you first have to know of their existence.

Seasoned network administrators laugh about this. After all, how could anyone be unaware of utilities running on their box? The answer is simple: Think of your favorite word processor. Just how much do you know about it? If you routinely write macros in a word-processing environment, you are an advanced user, one member of a limited class. In contrast, most people use only the basic functions of word processors: text, tables, spell check, and so forth. There is certainly nothing wrong with this approach. Nevertheless, most word processors have more advanced features, which are often missed by casual users.

NOTE

There is an often-quoted axiom in computing publishing circles, and it goes like this: "Eighty percent of the people use only twenty percent of a program's capabilities."

For example, how many readers that used DOS-based WordPerfect knew that it included a command-line screen-capture utility? It was called Grab. It grabbed the screen in any DOS-based program. At the time, that functionality was unheard of in word processors. The Grab program was extremely powerful when coupled with a sister utility called Convert, which was used to transform other graphic file formats into `*.wpg` files, a format suitable for importation into a WordPerfect document. Both utilities were called from a command line in the `C:\WP` directory. Neither were directly accessible from within the WordPerfect environment. Despite the power these two utilities possessed, they were not well known.

Similarly, users might know little about the inner workings of their favorite operating system. For most, the cost of acquiring such knowledge far exceeds the value. Oh, they pick up tidbits over the years—perhaps they read computer periodicals that feature occasional tips and tricks, or perhaps they learn because they are required to at their job or another official position where extensive training is offered. No matter how they acquire the knowledge, nearly everyone knows something cool about their operating system.

Keeping up with the times is difficult, though. The software industry is a dynamic environment, and users are generally two years behind development. This lag in the assimilation of new technology only contributes to the security problem. When an operating system development team materially alters its product, many users are suddenly left knowing less. Microsoft Windows 95 is a good example. When it was released, 95 had new support for all sorts of different protocols—protocols with which the average Windows user wasn't familiar (and migrating to a Registry-based system was quite a leap). It is possible (and probable) that users can be unaware of obscure network utilities.

That's one scenario. Utilities and services are enabled, and this fact is unknown to the user. These services, while enabled, can foster security holes of varying magnitude. When a machine configured in this manner is connected to the Net, it is a hack waiting to happen.

Such problems are easily remedied. The solution is to turn off (or properly configure) the offending utility or service. Typical examples of this type of problem include the following:

- Network printing utilities
- Remote system-configuration utilities
- File-sharing utilities
- Default passwords
- Sample CGI programs and scripts

Of the examples listed, default services (i.e. file sharing, printing, or Web-based sample scripts) with known vulnerabilities are the most common. There is also the reverse situation. Instead of being unaware of active services that threaten your security, you might be unaware of inactive utilities that could strengthen your security.

Many operating systems have built-in security features. These features can be quite effective when enabled, but remain worthless until you activate them. Again, it boils down to knowledge. If you're lacking in knowledge, you are bound to suffer needlessly.

But, unfortunately, it doesn't end there. There are other problems facing the modern network administrator. For instance, certain security utilities are simply impractical. Consider security programs that administrate file-access privileges and restrict user access depending on security level, time of day, and so forth. Perhaps your small network cannot operate with fluidity and efficiency if advanced access restrictions are enabled. If so, you must take that chance, perhaps implementing other security procedures to compensate. In essence, these issues are the basis of security theory: You must balance the risks against practical security measures, based on the sensitivity of your network data.

You'll notice that most network security problems arise, however, from a lack of education. For that reason, education is a recurring theme throughout this book.

NOTE

Education issues are entirely within your control. That is, you can eliminate these problems by providing yourself or your associates with adequate education. (Put another way, crackers are most effective at gaining entry into networks where such knowledge is lacking.)

Operating System and Application Flaws

As if the complexity surrounding advanced security features combined with the fact that operating systems are shipping with dozens of enabled services weren't enough of a problem, we face an additional challenge: vulnerabilities introduced by flawed programming. Unfortunately, these forces are well beyond your control. That's too bad because here's a fact: Vendor failure is one of the most common sources of security problems. Anyone who subscribes to a bug or security mailing list (such as BUGTRAQ) knows this. Every day, bugs or programming weaknesses are found in network software. Every day, these are posted to the Internet in advisories or warnings. Unfortunately, not all users read such advisories.

System flaws needn't be classified into many subcategories here. It's sufficient to say that a system flaw is any flaw that causes a program to do the following:

- Work improperly (under either normal or extreme conditions)
- Allow crackers to exploit that weakness (or improper operation) to damage or gain control of a system

There are two primary types of system flaws. The first type, which I call a *primary* flaw, is a flaw nested within your operating system's security structure. It's a flaw inherent within a security-related program. By exploiting it, a cracker obtains one-step, unauthorized access to the system or its data.

The Netscape Secure Sockets Layer Flaw

In January 1996, two students in the Computer Science department at the University of California, Berkeley, highlighted a serious flaw in the Netscape Navigator encryption scheme. Their findings were published in *Dr. Dobb's Journal*. The article, "Randomness and the Netscape Browser," was written by Ian Goldberg and David Wagner. In it, Goldberg and Wagner explain that Netscape's implementation of a cryptographic protocol called Secure Sockets Layer (SSL) was inherently flawed. This flaw would allow secure communications intercepted on the WWW to be cracked. This is an excellent example of a primary flaw.

Conversely, there are secondary flaws. A *secondary* flaw is any flaw arising in a program that, although totally unrelated to security, opens a security hole elsewhere on the system. In other words, the programmers were charged with making the program functional, not secure. No one (at the time the program was designed) imagined cause for concern, nor did they imagine that such a flaw could arise.

Secondary flaws are far more common than primary flaws, particularly on platforms that have not traditionally been security oriented. An example of a secondary security flaw is any flaw within a program that requires special access privileges in order to complete its tasks (in other words, a program that must run with root or superuser privileges). If that program can be attacked, the cracker can work through that program to gain special, privileged access to files and services.

Whether primary or secondary, system flaws are especially dangerous to the Internet community when they emerge in programs that are used on a daily basis, such as FTP, DNS, SSH, or Telnet. These mission-critical applications form the heart of the Internet and cannot be suddenly taken away, even if a security flaw exists within them.

To understand this concept, imagine if Microsoft Word were discovered to be totally insecure. Would people stop using it? Of course not. Millions of offices throughout the world rely on Word. However, there is a vast difference between a serious security flaw in Microsoft Word and a serious security flaw in the Apache Web server. The serious flaw in Apache would place hundreds of thousands of servers (and therefore, millions of accounts) at risk. Because of the Internet's size and the services it now offers, flaws inherent within its security structure are of international concern.

To understand the true scope of this problem, take a look at just some of the vulnerabilities discovered in services during 1999 and 2000 that have allowed "root" or "administrative" level compromises:

- The wu-ftpd FTP daemon shipped in many BSD and Linux distributions
- The University of Washington imapd daemon
- ISC's Bind (an implementation of DNS)
- Numerous services found in Sun Solaris
- Microsoft's IIS
- The Linuxconf configuration utility
- SSH (Secure Shell)

…and that's just a small sample. At the time of this writing, based on the Security Alert Consensus (SAC, a weekly vulnerability newsletter put out by SANS, Network Computing, and Neohapsis), there are new vulnerabilities being discovered at the rate of 10–30 *per week*. We will go into the entire process of vulnerability research and publication in greater detail in Part III, "Hacking 101: The Tricks of the Trade." For now, know that when a flaw is discovered within sendmail, FTP, DNS, SSH, or other indispensable elements of the Internet, programmers develop *patches* (small programs or source code) to temporarily solve the problem. These patches are distributed to the world at large, along with detailed advisories. This brings us to vendor response.

Deficiencies in Vendor QA Efforts and Response

Two summers ago I found myself sitting in on a meeting between Microsoft officials and one of their larger clients. During this meeting the topic of the hidden flight simulator in Excel came up. The client wanted to know what a flight simulator was doing in a spreadsheet program. They wanted to know how much room it was taking up in the program, in memory, and on their workstations. But above all else, they wanted to know how it had gotten past Microsoft's QA/QC efforts. A few lines of code is one thing, but an entire flight simulator is quite another. Microsoft's response? That they knew it was in there all along, and that this "Easter egg" was just something they let their programmers in Redmond do for fun. "It's part of the development culture," the Microsoft representatives said.

> **NOTE**
>
> If you weren't aware of the embedded gift in your Microsoft Excel application, fire up a copy of MS Excel that shipped in Office 97. Press F5 (to go to a location), type **X97:L97**, and then click OK. Press the Tab key. Then hold down Ctrl and Shift at the same time, and simultaneously click the "chart wizard" button once—it's the one with the colorful bar graphs. Violà—instant flight simulator.

The first word that came out of my mouth began with a "B" and ended with a "T." But what else was Microsoft going to say? Whoops? Sorry? We missed the few thousand lines of extra code that just happened to be a mini video game?

So in the spring of 2000 when "rain forest puppy," an infamous and clever member of the underground reported that the phrase "Netscape Engineers are Weenies" had been used as a key and served as a pseudo back door into servers running FrontPage 98 extensions, I couldn't wait to hear Microsoft's excuse for this one. Was this part of the development culture as well? Back doors and cheap shots at the competition's development staff?

It turns out Microsoft initially admitted to the existence of the egg that was all over their face, but then quickly masked it with an even bigger problem that was released a bit later. Check out the updated advisory at `http://www.microsoft.com/technet/security/bulletin/ms00-025.asp`— at no point is there any mention of the word "weenie," back doors, or other such shenanigans. Microsoft has appeared to have swept this one under the carpet as well.

> **NOTE**
>
> One more thing I'd like to note about the Excel "Easter egg" story. When MS offered this client the "We knew about it" excuse, this client demanded a list of other back doors and Easter eggs MS supposedly knew about. MS agreed—and then never delivered on its promise. Makes you wonder, huh?

So if the largest software vendor in the world can't control what is entering its code, is there any hope for the rest of the industry? The simple fact of the matter is that many software companies don't have adequate quality control/quality assurance programs in place. Microsoft is an easy target as it has SO MANY software products in the marketplace, but the truth is that a lot of companies are guilty of this as well. Who winds up ultimately paying for these oversights? We do—the consumers. We're the ones who get hammered when these oversights get used for breaching our networks. However, the vendors claim that their customers want more features, not more security. If that's not the case I encourage the readers of this book to make their voices heard. Tell your vendors how you really feel.

Let's take a look at a few of specific examples of oversights and their impact on the scene.

Allaire's ColdFusion Problems

The beginning of 1999 was a great time for Allaire. Their product, ColdFusion, had taken the industry by storm in giving Web developers some powerful but easy tools for designing Web sites that interacted with database back-ends. In the spring of 1999, however, rain forest puppy reported a number of problems with the CGI sample scripts Allaire shipped with ColdFusion. Remote attackers could leverage these scripts to execute code on the vulnerable machines, retrieve protected files, and ultimately compromise the targeted machine. A few months later, the L0pht reported more problems. Although administrators probably shouldn't have been installing sample scripts on production servers to begin with, ignorance had prevailed once again. Soon black hat hackers all over the planet were hacking ColdFusion servers at an alarming rate, and Allaire had a major public relations issue on its hands.

Allaire was slow to react, as this was its first exposure to the harshness known as the information security community. Eventually Allaire released advisories urging customers to remove the scripts and patch their servers, but the damage was done. Hundreds upon hundreds of machines had already been hit, and the trend continued throughout the rest of the year.

Eventually the chaos subsided, and attackers moved on with more popular attack trends. Allaire has since then beefed up its internal security efforts, released new, more secure versions of ColdFusion, solicited third-party application reviews, and launched an awareness heightening campaign within its user base. Allaire is now one of the most pro-active vendors out there when it comes to security. However, Allaire has been paying for its sins ever since. In June 2000 when SANS (System Administration, Networking, and Security) released its report on the Top 10 vulnerabilities found on the Net today, Allaire's ColdFusion problem had crept up once again—it was on the charts because it had been a BIG problem. Even though the vulnerabilities had been addressed for close to a year, people remembered them. The simple fact of the matter was that the vulnerability hit the security scene really hard, and organizations were hurt pretty badly by it. Vulnerable servers based on older versions of ColdFusion still creep up once in a while, and administrators who suffered through the siege of 1999 were slow to forgive.

Fortunately, Allaire learned from its mistakes and its customers will benefit from this. However, the people who were hacked because of ColdFusion's earlier problems paid the price of this education.

Microsoft PPTP

Another example that wasn't exploited en masse but is definitely flawed is Microsoft Corporation's implementation of Point-to-Point Tunneling Protocol (PPTP). PPTP is a protocol that's used to build Virtual Private Networks (VPNs) over the Internet. VPNs enable secure, encrypted traffic between corporate link-points, thus eliminating the need for leased lines. (Through VPNs, corporations can use the Internet as their global leased line.)

Microsoft's implementation of PPTP had been lauded as one of the most solid security measures you could employ. In fact, it even won an award or two in consumer computing magazines, Microsoft's PPTP had been written up as an industry standard solution. That's great.

One month before the second edition of this book went to press, Microsoft's PPTP was broken by two well-respected encryption authorities, Bruce Schneier and Mudge. The press release rocked the security world. Here's a portion of that release:

> Doesn't Microsoft know better? You'd think they would. The mistakes they made are not subtle; they're "kindergarten cryptographer" mistakes. The encryption is used in a way that completely negates its effectiveness. The documentation claims 128-bit keys, even though nothing remotely close to that key length is actually used. Passwords are protected by hash functions so badly that most can be easily recovered. And the control channel is so sloppily designed that anyone can cause a Microsoft PPTP server to go belly up.
>
> —Frequently Asked Questions, Microsoft's PPTP Implementation. Counterpane Technologies. `http://www.counterpane.com/pptp-faq.html`

That doesn't sound as if Microsoft's version of PPTP is very secure, does it? Researchers found five separate flaws in the implementation, including holes in password hashing, authentication, and encryption. In short, they discovered that Microsoft's implementation of PPTP was a disaster.

I am willing to bet that you never saw that advisory. If you didn't, you're like information officers in companies all over the country. They believe that the products they're using are secure. After all, Microsoft is a big, well-established company. If they say their products are secure, it must be true.

That's the mindset of the average network manager these days, and thousands of companies are at risk because of it.

> **NOTE**
>
> Mistakes of this sort are made all the time. Here's an amusing example. It was discovered a while ago that the encryption scheme in Microsoft Windows NT could be effectively turned off. The attack is now known as the "You Are Now in France" attack. It works like this: France did not allow private citizens access to strong encryption. If Windows NT interpreted that your location was France, the operating system's strong encryption was disabled. Not very secure, is it?

The bottom line is this: You're on your own. That is, it's up to you to take measures to secure your data. Don't count on any vendor to do it for you. If you do, you're setting yourself up for a serious fall.

Vendor Response

Vendor response has traditionally been good, but this shouldn't give you a false sense of security. Vendors are in the business of selling software. To them, there is nothing fascinating about someone discovering a hole in the system. At best, a security hole represents a loss of revenue or prestige. Accordingly, vendors quickly issue assurances to allay users' fears, but actual corrective action can sometimes be long in coming.

The reasons for this can be complex, and often the vendor is not to blame. Sometimes, immediate corrective action just isn't feasible, such as in the following cases:

- When the affected application is comprehensively tied to the operating system
- When the application is widely in use or is a standard
- When the application is third-party software and that third party has poor support, has gone out of business, or is otherwise unavailable

In these instances, a patch (or other solution) can provide temporary relief. However, for this system to work effectively, all users must know that the patch is available. Notifying the public would seem to be the vendor's responsibility and, to be fair, vendors post such patches to security groups and mailing lists. However, vendors might not always take the extra step of informing the general public. In many cases, it just isn't cost effective.

Once again, this issue breaks down to knowledge. Users who have up-to-date knowledge of their network utilities, of holes, and of patches are well prepared. Users without such knowledge tend to be victims. That, more than any other reason, is why we wrote this book. In a nutshell, security education is the best policy.

Lack of Qualified People in the Field

So if we didn't have vendors and programmers putting out buggy code, operating systems shipping with every possible service enabled and running by default, sample scripts installed everywhere, and a slew of misconfigurations and mistakes being made, we'd still have one major problem—not enough people have information security experience. IT managers are having a hard enough time these days finding competent network engineers, system administrators, and programmers, much less security professionals.

Making matters worse, you can't get training that will instantly make you an information security specialist. You have to take it in steps. First, become competent with routers, switches, and firewalls. Learn the ins and outs of UNIX and Windows NT. Learn the basics surrounding cryptography and programming, and obtain a SOLID understanding of TCP/IP. And then you can BEGIN to learn the intricacies surrounding security, incident response, and other late night and stressful activities.

Excited yet?

The lack of personnel contributes to misguided or absent information security programs within organizations. Policies remain incomplete or nonexistent. Companies operate without a threat identification effort. Machines go unpatched, development efforts go awry, logs go unmonitored, and users remain uneducated. In short, we find ourselves living in the world that we exist in today.

It doesn't have to be like this, however. If administrators and users held up their areas of responsibility from a security standpoint, we wouldn't be needing fleets of all-encompassing infosec gurus. We're hoping for the day when security practices are as common as running system backups—part of any good system administrator's job. Unfortunately, we believe that day is a ways off.

The funniest part about this crazy field is that most of us who are considered information security professionals got here by accident. However, as time goes on, it continues to get easier to exchange knowledge and learn at a quicker pace. More books are coming out, more conferences exist, more papers are being written, information security portals and sites continue to improve, and the security mailing lists that exist on the net are only getting better. Security-related certifications like the CISSP and the SANS GIAC programs are starting to crank out more and more qualified people. In short, it's getting easier to learn as there is a lot more out there then there was even two to three years ago.

Suffice it to say, however, that there will be a shortage of good security people for quite some time.

Why Education in Security Is Important

Traditionally, security folks have attempted to obscure security information from the average user. As such, security specialists occupy positions of prestige in the computing world. They are regarded as high priests of arcane and recondite knowledge that is unavailable to normal folks. There was a time when this approach had merit. After all, users should only be afforded such information on a need-to-know basis. However, the average American has now achieved need-to-know status.

Today, we all need at least some education in network security. We hope that this book, which is both a cracker's manual and an Internet security reference, will force into the foreground issues that need to be discussed. Moreover, we wrote this book to increase awareness of security within the general public.

Whether you really need to be concerned depends on your station in life. If you're a merchant, the answer is straightforward: In order to conduct commerce on the Net, you must have assurances about data security. No one will buy your services on the Internet unless they feel safe doing so, which brings us to the consumer's point of view. If crackers are capable of capturing sensitive financial data, why buy over the Internet? Of course, there stands between the consumer and the merchant yet another individual concerned with data security: the software vendor who supplies the tools to facilitate that commerce. These parties (and their reasons for security) are obvious. However, there are some less conspicuous reasons.

Privacy is one concern. The Internet represents the first real evidence that an Orwellian society can be established. Every user should be aware that nonencrypted communication across the Internet is totally insecure. Although the Internet is a wonderful resource for research or recreation, it is not your friend (at least, not if you have anything to hide).

Finally, there are still other reasons to promote security education. We'd like to focus on these briefly.

The Corporate Sector

For the moment, set aside dramatic scenarios like industrial espionage and international spy rings. These situations are exciting for purposes of discussion, and they do indeed happen, but their incidence is rare in relation to general data security threats. Instead, let's focus on a simple example case of a common corporate application: an e-commerce initiative.

Modern day e-commerce applications have many components, but usually they are split into three primary areas: front-end Web pages, middle-tier applications, and back-end databases. Database access might ultimately require the use of one or more languages to get the data from the database to the actual Web page. We've seen scenarios that were pretty complex.

In one scenario, we observed a six-part process. From the moment the user clicked a Submit button, a series of operations was undertaken:

1. The variable search terms submitted by the user were extracted and parsed by a Perl script.
2. The Perl script fed these variables to an intermediate program designed to interface with a proprietary database package.
3. The proprietary database package returned the result, passing it back to a Perl script that formatted the data into HTML.

That single process touches network administrators who provision the connectivity between the machines, system administrators who maintain the machines, database administrators who configure and maintain the database, and application developers who write the programs and scripts. It doesn't take a rocket scientist to realize that this can get incredibly complex, fairly quickly. Each stage of the operation boasts potential security holes.

While some organizations might even have an information security officer (most don't), it's not practical to expect that individual to be able to keep everything locked down single handedly. Worse, the chances of all of these groups (system administrators, network administrators, database administrators, and application developers) all performing their tasks in a secure manner is a long-shot, at best.

Managers are sometimes quick to deny (or restrict) funding for security within their corporation. They see this cost as unnecessary, largely because they don't understand the dire nature of the alternative. The reality is this: One or more talented crackers could—in minutes or hours—destroy several years of data entry.

Education is an economical way for companies to achieve at least minimal security. What they spend now in time and effort might save many times that amount later.

The Schools

Although those of us in the field love to pound on the vendors for sloppy programming, consider this: Colleges and universities are not helping the situation. I've spoken at a number of universities, and I often ask whether or not any of the students' professors have ever spoken to them about buffer overflows, bounds checking, or general data scrubbing techniques in class.

The answers I get point to a unanimous "No"—rarely are these subjects addressed in class. I've asked this question at colleges and universities across the nation. The answers are almost always the same.

So although we have a shortage of talented people in the field, the next generation of programmers we are bringing up in the schools are not being trained in the previous generations' mistakes. At least not in the area of security, anyway.

The Government

Folklore and common sense both suggest that the U.S. government agencies know something more, something special about computer security. Unfortunately, this simply isn't true (with the notable exception of the National Security Agency). As you will learn, government agencies routinely fail in their quest for security.

In the following chapters, we examine various reports that demonstrate the poor security now maintained by U.S. government servers. The sensitivity of data accessed by hackers is amazing.

These arms of the U.S. government (and their attending institutions) hold some of the most personal data on Americans. More importantly, these folks hold sensitive data related to national security. At the minimum, this information needs to be protected.

It's not just the U.S. government that needs to bone up on network security. The rest of the world is also at risk. A good case in point is the incident that occurred in India a few years ago. At the height of tensions between India and Pakistan (each country loudly proclaiming themselves a nuclear state), a curious thing happened. Crackers—some of them a mere 15-years-old—broke into a nuclear research facility in India and intercepted private email between nuclear physicists there. Not satisfied with that hack, the teenagers went a step further. On June 8, 1998, Bill Pietrucha of *NewsBytes* reported this:

> A group of teenage hackers, more accurately known as crackers, who broke into India's Bhabha Atomic Research Center (BARC) yesterday have set their sights on doing the same to Pakistan, *Newsbytes* has learned. The group, which calls itself MilW0rm, consists of about a half dozen teens, aged 15 to 18, from around the world. MilW0rm members include a former member of the Enforcer hacker group, which broke into U.S. military and National Aeronautics and Space Administration (NASA) networks earlier this year. Officials at India's BARC earlier today confirmed the break-in to *Newsbytes*.

Extraordinary, right? That's not the end of the story. Only 24 hours later, those same teenagers penetrated a nuclear facility in Turkey.

Many people were amused by the teenagers' antics, but there's a darker underside to their activity. At one point, one of the young crackers joked that it would be "funny" if they had forged an email message from India to Pakistan warning that India was about to undertake a first strike. Now, although no one receiving such a message would take action until they had confirmed it through other sources, the point was not missed: As we ease into the 21st century, information warfare has become more than amusing armchair discussion—it has become a reality.

Are you scared yet? If so, it's time to allay your fears a bit and tell you a bedtime story. It's a brief insight into the mind of an attacker.

From the Eye of the Beholder

Our bedtime story, from the eyes of the intruder, goes something like this:

I power up my Linux-based firewall while rummaging through my diagrams. While looking for the legal pad that I use to track my progress, I hear my firewall start dialing, and the familiar hiss of my modem negotiating the baud rate. Although I have DSL in my apartment, I prefer to mask my midnight escapades as much as possible by using hacked out ISP accounts. The phone company has records, sure, but that's just one more hop that any potential pursuer of mine will have to negotiate. Besides, I've hacked a dozen ISPs locally and rarely use the same one in the same month.

The modem connects and syncs, and my firewall rule set kicks into place. I'm up. I power on my other machines: a few simple Pentium-based boxes a local company was getting rid of, and a fresh set of Pentium III machines I just built the other day. I left off last night with an R&D network I found somewhere in Holland—I think. Heck, it doesn't matter where it is anyway as long at it's useful. It was pretty open when I got there, but a little hard to find. Thank God for ARIN.

My eventual target is a manufacturer of cell phone software. Although I know little about cell phones, my curiosity was sparked a few months ago. These guys appear to be a worthy challenge. But I haven't actually started knocking on their doors yet. You see, I need a buffer zone—a little padding. I figure if I can bounce off of a dozen organizations or so, even if they do catch my attacks, they'll never find me. They might trace me back through the first three or four organizations, but I'll be long gone before they get anywhere close. So where was I...oh yeah...that R&D network.

I fire up nmap, and pump my output into whisker looking for vulnerable CGI sample scripts. My results come back in about 30 seconds. It appears that these bozos haven't patched their IIS servers yet. They are still vulnerable to that RDS/MDAC hole. I snicker as I fire up my msadcpl exploit script—I can't believe that the RDS/MDAC problem in IIS has been out for over a year now, and they still haven't patched it. Too bad for them.

After two minutes, I'm in and discover that one of the machines is an NT domain controller. Jackpot. There are more than a thousand accounts in this domain alone. Assuming I can crack them, the owners will have a hard time locking me out with access to that many user accounts. I initiate a backup copy of the NT SAM, download it, and move on.

From there I start poking at a data warehousing company because I know they have a ton of HP/UX and Solaris machines. I prefer UNIX machines, but will settle for NT when I have to. I launch into my reconnaissance phase again using whisker and nmap. What does this data warehousing company handle? Healthcare data was it? Ah, who cares. More accounts. More territory. More padding.

I ponder for a second on whether or not legal precedence will be set if the second company sues the first for negligence. But then I realize—not my problem. The thought leaves my head as quickly as it entered. I turn the shadowed password hashes and the NT SAM over to my Pentium IIIs running John the Ripper. I grab some RedBull and vodka, and head out to the clubs—the password cracking session might take a few hours. My day is coming...I just need to give my Pentium III clusters some more time to chew on those passwords. After all, time is on my side.

Who am I?

It doesn't matter who I am, what age I am, or where I am working from. You can't classify me because I am not of one type. Instead, you should be worrying about how close I am to you, how I am going to get at your data, use your systems, and what I am going to do when I own your network.

How to Use This Book

IN THIS CHAPTER

How to Use This Book? Duh!

Most computer books have the infamous "How to Use This Book" chapter. If you're like me, you probably never read them. After all, the best way to use a book is to read it, so what more needs to be said? Well, you might be surprised.

This book is structured very differently from your average computer title. In fact, it's structured so differently that there really are different ways to use this book. This chapter, therefore, briefly discusses ways to maximize your usage of *Maximum Security*.

This Book's General Structure

Maximum Security contains more than 1,000 URLs or Internet addresses. These URLs house important security information, including the following:

- Freely available tools
- Commercial security tools
- White papers or technical reports
- Security advisories
- Source code for exploits
- Security patches

We designed *Maximum Security* this way to provide you with supplemental information. Thus, you're getting more than just hundreds of pages of my rhetoric. You're getting a roadmap to online sources of Internet security information.

The links take you places that maintain security information which is constantly being updated. Ideally, when you're finished, you will never buy another general Internet security book. Instead, you'll know where to find the very latest security information online. This book has also been designed to teach you underlying information security *methodology*. Although some of the material in this book will obviously be dated over time, the techniques this book teaches are not time critical.

For these reasons, *Maximum Security* has many advantages over its competitors. True, you can read *Maximum Security* cover to cover to gain a solid, basic understanding of Internet security. However, the book's real purpose is to provide you with

1. Internet security tools
2. A roadmap for securing your environment

Methods of Using This Book

There are three basic ways to use this book:

- To learn the basics of information security
- To secure a computing environment
- For heavy-duty security research

Each approach is slightly different. Let's quickly cover these now.

Learning the Basics of Information Security

If you bought *Maximum Security* to learn the basics of information security, you can rejoice. The book is well suited to that purpose. To gain the maximum benefit, read the book cover to cover. If you encounter online references, it might be wise to stop reading the book, and download the referenced document. Not all the external references are pivotal to understanding information security principles, but they aren't superfluous either.

Information security is slowly moving from a black art to a more calculated science. However, the field is, for the most part, very young. Because of this, it is dotted with true experts and amazing phonies, with most people treading the middle ground. If you finish this book and truly grasp most of what has been discussed, you will be ahead of the curve—no doubts about that. And, by the time you're done, the fourth edition of *Maximum Security* should be released. However, we would recommend against downloading source code unless you are already familiar with the basics of C, makefiles, compilers, and so on. Chances are, if you're entirely new to information security, you probably don't need even one-tenth of the programs mentioned in this book.

Using This Book to Secure a Computing Environment

If you've bought *Maximum Security* to secure a network, you'll really dig this third edition. You'll note that we've made a lot of additions in this revision that focus on corporate environments and attack strategies. When you spot the various Notes and Tips spread throughout the chapters don't skip them—read them! Learn from our experiences—and our mistakes! Although you will definitely benefit from reading the entire book, there are some parts that will be more relevant then others. Part II, "Security Concepts," is a must-read. Part IV, "The Defender's Toolkit," can be used for reference when you start evaluating and looking for tools to help you. Finally, Part VI, "Platforms and Security," is where you'll want to focus a lot of your time—this is where you'll find a lot of the low-level guts of how to lock systems down.

> **NOTE**
>
> You might spend some time downloading tools mentioned in this book. To save you some time, on the CD-ROM you'll find that many of the tools mentioned are linked into HTML pages. Load these into your browser and you'll be good to go.

Using This Book for Heavy-Duty Security Research

If you bought *Maximum Security* to do serious research, you'll want to take a completely different approach in reading it. The majority of the additional links, product, and vendor information is located at the ends of the chapters. This should allow people looking specifically for additional resources easier access to the information, while simultaneously removing the "yellow pages" feel of the older versions of this book.

There is a ton of references to third-party tools, and we've borrowed on some of my experiences from running the Network Computing Magazine Chicago Lab to add additional commercial products. (Earlier editions didn't list as many of the commercial tools.)

Feed these URLs to a personal spider or a utility like WGET, and you can pull down every external source we've referenced. Enjoy.

The Book's Parts

This section describes the book's various parts and the subjects treated in them.

Part I: "Setting the Stage"

Part I sets the stage and assists new readers in understanding the current climate in the information security scene. It also introduces some of the problems we face, and why we face them. Topics include the following:

- Why this book was written
- Why you need security

Part II: "Security Concepts"

Part II addresses the basics of information security, provides a roadmap for how to get started in cleaning up an environment, and provides some background on the Internet's early development. Topics include the following:

- Some of the pillars of information security strategies
- A brief tour of the underground

- A primer on TCP/IP
- Poor security on the Internet and the reasons for it
- Internet warfare as it relates to individuals and networks
- Definitions of hacking and cracking
- A brief look at who is vulnerable, and why

Part III: "Hacking 101: The Tricks of the Trade"

Part III examines the hacking scene in greater detail. It covers the contents of a hacker's toolbox. It familiarizes you with Internet munitions, or weapons. It covers the proliferation of such weapons, who creates them, who uses them, how they work, and how you can benefit from them. It also gives you a first-hand look at exploiting vulnerabilities, as well as drilling into some of the top problems the Net faced in 1999 and 2000. Some of the topics covered are:

- Use of exploit scripts
- The evolution of exploits and the "0-day" phenomena
- Spoofing and masking one's identity
- Dispelling some of the hacking folklore

Part IV: "The Defender's Toolkit"

Part IV examines the tools, utilities, and products used to defend your environment from hostile attacks. We examine the products and concepts of the following tools:

- Firewalls
- Vulnerability assessment tools (scanners)
- Intrusion detection systems
- Logging and auditing tools
- Password crackers
- Sniffers

Part V: "Virtual Weapons of Mass Destruction"

Part V deals with the nastiest software in the computing industry—things that are used to destroy systems and networks. In this part, we examine

- Viruses and worms
- Denial of Service (DoS) tools
- Trojan horses

Part VI: "Platforms and Security"

Part VI deals with creating strategies to protect specific machines and operating systems from hostile activity. We examine issues involving the following platforms:

- Microsoft operating systems
- UNIX
- Novell NetWare
- Cisco's IOS
- Macintosh
- VAX/VMS

Part VII: "Bringing It All Together"

Part VII deals with taking all the previous sections and tying them together to formulate a comprehensive information security strategy. It also cover some topics in greater detail, including:

- Forming policies and procedures
- Network architecture considerations
- Application development issues
- Addressing internal security
- How to mine the crazy amount of information out there

This Book's Limitations

This book is wide in scope but has several limitations. Before enumerating these shortcomings, we want to make an important point: Information security is a complex field. If you're charged with securing a network, relying solely on this book is a terrible mistake. No book has yet been written that can replace the experience, gut feeling, and basic savvy of a good system or network administrator. It is likely that no such book will ever be written. That settled, please allow us to point out this book's limitations in terms of timeliness and utility.

Timeliness

The first limitation of this book relates to timeliness.

The degree to which timeliness will affect the benefits you reap from this book depends on several factors. Many people don't use the latest and the greatest in software or hardware. Economic and administrative realities often preclude this. Thus, there are LANs with Internet connectivity that have workstations running Windows for Workgroups. Similarly, some folks are using SPARCstation 1s, running SunOS 4.1.3. Because older software and hardware exist, much of the material here will remain current. (Good examples are machines with fresh installs of an older operating system that has now been proven to contain numerous security bugs.)

Rest assured, however, that as of this writing, the information contained within this book was current. If you are unsure whether the information you need has changed, contact your vendor. With this said, however, the TECHNIQUES this book will teach you are without an expiration date. Although the holes we detail relating to Microsoft products in this book will eventually be a thing of the past, we're quite confident Microsoft will continue to provide us with new, even more elegant problems to overcome. The same goes for other vendors and software writers. The specifics will change quite a bit; the strategies will change very little. Learn the strategy, and the rest becomes footwork.

Utility

Although this book contains practical examples, it's not a how-to for cracking Internet servers. True, we provide many examples of how cracking is done and even utilities with which to accomplish that task, but this book will not make the reader a master hacker or cracker. There is no substitute for experience, and this book cannot provide that.

What this book can provide is a strong background in Internet security. A reader with little prior knowledge of the subject will come away with enough information to crack or secure their network.

Odds and Ends to Know About *Maximum Security*

Here are a few notes on this book:

- *Links and home pages.* The first edition provided readers direct links to many files, often bypassing the home pages of vendors. In this edition, we've done things a little differently. If a vendor requires that you register prior to downloading their tool, we provide the registration URL. This is only fair.

- *About all those products.* There are hundreds of products mentioned in this book, but we're not affiliated with any of them. If a product is mentioned, it's here purely because it's useful.

- *Mistakes and such.* If you find that your product has been mentioned and the information was incorrectly reported, please contact this book's Associate Publisher. In addition, we would personally like to know, so please drop us a line at maxsec@neohapsis.com.

Cool Stuff on the CD-ROM

The CD-ROM has some special tools and information, including:

- A list of all URLs from this book (just click and go)
- Bastille   a utility to tighten security on Linux and Unix machines
- Nmap   a port scanner
- Snort   an open source network intrusion detection system
- OpenSSH   a free implementation of the SSH suite of network connectivity tools
- OpenSSL   an open source toolkit implementing the Secure Sockets Layer (SSL v2/v3) and Transport Layer Security (TLS v1) protocols

These things should get you started right away.

Unfortunately, this approach of placing things on CD-ROM has its disadvantages. For example, you will need many additional tools to reap the maximum benefit from this book:

- A Web browser
- An FTP client
- Archiving utilities
- Document readers
- A compiler (if you want to compile source code)

In the next few sections, prior to discussing various methods of using this book, I'd like to provide locations where you can obtain these tools for free.

FTP Clients

Although you can download most of the files mentioned in this book via a Web browser, it might be wise to have an FTP client on hand. Table 2.1 provides locations for FTP clients for most operating systems.

Table 2.1   FTP Clients for Various Operating Systems

Client	OS	Location
EmTec FTP	OS/2	`http://www.musthave.com`
Fetch	Macintosh	`http://www.dartmouth.edu/pages/softdev/fetch.html`
FtpTool	Linux	`http://rufus.w3.org/linux/RPM/FByName.html`
Gibbon FTP	OS/2	`http://www.gibbon.com/catalog/catalog.html`
NetFinder	Macintosh	`http://www.ozemail.com.au/~pli/netfinder/`
WS_FTP	Windows	`http://www.ipswitch.com`

Archive File Formats

If you're lucky, you have a 1.5Mbps or faster connection to the Internet. Sadly, many users don't. Instead, many folks still surf using a 28.8 or 56k modem connection, and at that speed, the Internet is pathetically slow. When Webmasters provide files for download, they generally compress them, and by doing so reduce the file size. The smaller the file, the quicker it will download. These compressed files are referred to as *archives,* or *archived files.*

Archives are created using compression packages. Unfortunately, there is no universally used compression format. Therefore, files compressed on a Macintosh might be difficult to decompress on an IBM-PC compatible. Because many online references in this book are archived files, you must obtain tools that can uncompress all archive formats. Table 2.2 provides locations for various archiving tools.

TABLE 2.2 Popular Archive Utilities

Utility	Platform	Description and Location
Winzip	Windows	Winzip decompresses the following archive formats: ARC, ARJ, BinHex, gzip, LZH, MIME, TAR, UNIX compress, and Uuencode. Winzip is therefore the industry-standard archive utility on the Windows platform. It is available at `http://www.winzip.com/`.
Zip98Plus	Windows	Zip98Plus handles the following archive formats: ARC, ARJ, ARJSFX, CAB, GZIP, LHA, LHASFX, RAR, TAR, ZIP, ZIPSFX, and ZOO. Zip98Plus is available at `http://download.mycomputer.com/detail/0/69.html`.
StuffIt	Macintosh	StuffIt decompresses the following archive formats: ARC, Arj, BinHex, gzip, Macbinary, StuffIt, Uuencoded, and ZIP. StuffIt is available at `http://www.aladdinsys.com/expander/index.html`.

Text File Formats and Document Readers

When compiling this edition, we tried to favor sites that offer documents in HTML (which is a fairly universal format). However, that wasn't always possible. Thankfully, many site authors are now providing their documents in PDF, a document format invented by Adobe. PDF is architecture-neutral and to read a PDF document, all you need is the free PDF reader for your platform.

NOTE

PDF stands for *Portable Document Format*. After years of research, Adobe developed PDF to satisfy the need for a universal typesetting technique. PostScript preceded PDF and was very powerful. However, some PostScript documents require a PostScript printer. PDF remedies this problem.

You might be wondering why all technical reports and white papers aren't written in ASCII. After all, ASCII is a universally recognized standard, and easily readable on any platform. The reason is this: You cannot embed graphs, sketches, or photographs in ASCII text documents. Because many technical reports have diagrams (often of network topology), ASCII is poorly suited for this task.

You might also wonder why all technical reports or white papers aren't written in HTML (especially because anyone on the Internet can read HTML). There are several reasons. First, although HTML specifications have made great progress in recent years, most HTML packages don't adhere strictly to those standards, nor do they force HTML authors to do so. HTML doesn't always look the same from platform to platform, or even from browser to browser. Also—and this is a major factor—writing a document in HTML can require knowledge of HTML tags. Technical report authors might not have time to learn about these tags. True, WYSIWYG HTML editors exist, but even using these takes more time than simply writing out a document in your favorite word processor. (Some advances have been made with export filters. For example, PageMaker and Microsoft Word both let you export documents to HTML. Again, these filters aren't perfect, and there's no guarantee that the document will come out precisely as it was designed.)

You must be prepared to accommodate different file formats. That is easier than it sounds. Most commercial word processor manufacturers are aware of this situation. Therefore, they make readers available to the public. *Readers* are programs that will read a document written in this or that format. (For example, Adobe makes a PDF reader, and Microsoft makes a Word reader.) Readers are generally free. Table 2.3 provides a list of locations for popular word-processing readers.

TABLE 2.3 Readers for Popular Word-Processing Formats

Reader	Description and Location
Adobe Acrobat	Adobe Acrobat Reader decodes PDF files. Acrobat Reader is available for DOS, Windows, Windows 95, Windows NT, UNIX, Macintosh, and OS/2. You can get it at `http://www.adobe.com/supportservice/custsupport/download.html`.
Gsview	GSView is a utility that reads PostScript and GhostScript files (`*.PS`). GSView is available for OS/2, Windows, Windows 3.11, Windows NT, and Windows NT. Get it at `http://www.cs.wisc.edu/~ghost/`.
PowerPoint Viewer	PowerPoint Viewer is for viewing presentations generated in Microsoft PowerPoint (`*.PPT`). The PowerPoint Viewer for Windows 95 is available at `http://www.gallaudet.edu/~standard/presentation/pptvw32.exe`. PowerPoint Viewer for Windows NT is available at `http://www.gallaudet.edu/~standard/presentation/pptvw32.exe`.

Programming Languages

Many links in this book lead you to source code. *Source code* is raw programming code that when compiled or interpreted constitutes a functional computer program. To capitalize on the source code you encounter, you will need the proper compiler or interpreter. These tools and their locations are listed in Table 2.4.

TABLE 2.4 Compilers and Interpreters

Language	Description and Location
C and C++	C and C++ are popular computer programming languages commonly used for network programming. Many programs available from links in this book are written in C or C++. You can obtain a freeware C/C++ compiler from the Free Software Foundation. They provide two compilers, one for UNIX and one for DOS. The UNIX version can be downloaded from `http://www.gnu.org/software/gcc/gcc.html`. The DOS version can be downloaded from `http://www.delorie.com/djgpp/`.
Perl	The Practical Extraction and Report Language (Perl) is a popular programming language used in network programming. Perl programs can run on multiple platforms, although they are most commonly run on UNIX, Macintosh, and Windows NT. Many of the programs mentioned in this book require a Perl interpreter to function correctly. Perl is free (generally) and is available at `http://www.perl.com/pub/language/info/software.html`.

TABLE 2.4 Continued

Language	Description and Location
Java	Java is a versatile programming language developed by Sun Microsystems. Some of the programs mentioned in this book require a Java runtime environment to function correctly. Java is free, and you can get it at `http://www.javasoft.com/`.
JavaScript	JavaScript is a programming language embedded within Netscape Navigator and Netscape Communicator. JavaScript is sometimes used to generate malicious code (or legitimate security applications). JavaScript can be found in most recent versions of popular Web browsers (Netscape Communicator or Internet Explorer).
VBScript	VBScript is a scripting language developed by Microsoft Corporation. Its purpose is to manipulate Web browser environments. VBScript and VBScript documentation are available for free at `http://msdn.microsoft.com/scripting/default.htm?/scripting/vbscript/download/vbsdown.htm`.

Summary

That's it. This book was overhauled something fierce, but we believe only for the better. Have fun.

Security Concepts

PART II

IN THIS PART

Building a Roadmap for Securing Your Enterprise

IN THIS CHAPTER

This chapter will arm you with the guidelines necessary to survive the information security onslaught. The odds are stacked in this battle, and not in the favor of the defenders. If there is to be any hope of coming out of the war victorious, you need a serious strategy. This chapter is designed to give you an introduction to that strategy in the form of an information security roadmap.

Proactive Versus Reactive Models

We have a saying in the consulting field in regard to IT security spending: "The easiest client to sell security services to is the one that just got attacked." Unfortunately, the statement is as sad as it is true. The simple fact of the matter is that most organizations only react to security threats, and, often times, those reactions come after the damage has already been done. For example, patching your legacy systems after an intruder has already stolen your customer records won't help regain consumer confidence. Starting a log monitoring effort after a contractor has sent your research and development data to an overseas competitor will not bring back your competitive advantage. Convincing executives to encrypt their high-value data after their laptops have already been stolen won't reverse their earlier mistakes.

Although all these tactics are positive and encouraged courses of action, they don't stop the problems before they occur. It is for this reason alone that, when operating in a catch-up mode, security programs will only be marginally successful at best. The key to a successful information security program resides in taking a pro-active stance towards security threats, and attempting to eliminate vulnerability points before they can be used against you. By defining and organizing the information security effort beforehand, organizations stand a chance against the seemingly endless onslaught of security threats in the world today.

This is, of course, easier said then done. However, if pro-active security measures are done right, there is a light at the end of the tunnel. You'll want to perform the following tasks to launch a pro-active security program:

- Understand where the corporation's assets reside
- Reduce the number of vulnerability and exposure points
- Secure systems and infrastructure equipment
- Develop, deploy, and enforce security policies
- Develop, deploy, and enforce standardized OS configuration and lock-down documents
- Train administrators, managers, and developers on relevant areas of information security
- Implement an incident-response program
- Implement a threat-identification effort

- Implement a self-audit mechanism
- Educate, educate, educate, and educate

By getting these efforts off the ground, you can help place your organization in the driver's seat, and help reduce the amount of time you spend chasing your tail.

Benchmarking Your Current Security Posture

Security administration is not about achieving some unobtainable goal of absolute security. Instead, it's about managing risk. There will never be "absolute" security when it comes to computing environments, but there are ways to effectively minimize risk levels through reducing the number of vulnerabilities.

The first thing most people do when they inherit the responsibility of securing an environment is panic. The second thing they usually do is attempt to ascertain the current state of affairs. Understanding the state of the terrain is essential before moves can be made to secure it. This is why most security efforts begin with an assessment of some sort. Whether this assessment comes from an outside third party, or through the use of well-trained internal staff, the following areas should be investigated:

- The current state of the security policies
- The current state of security on the network
- The current state of the system security
- The current state of security of network applications
- The current state of employee awareness
- The current state of management awareness
- The current state of information security–training efforts

Often times, organizations hire outside consulting firms to assess either all of, or particular components of, the previous list. Although few organizations have all these efforts defined and operating efficiently, it's important to document the status of these efforts. Documentation can be used for a number of things later on, such as aiding in the production of status reports, benchmarking progress, gaining further security funding, and identifying areas that need the most help. Regardless of how it is done, or by whom, getting a good idea of where you presently are can help you define where you want to be headed.

This third edition of *Maximum Security* can be used to help with many of these needs. For example, Chapter 11 covers the selection of vulnerability assessment tools that can help identify system security holes. Part VI, "Platforms and Security," can help with some of the details surrounding the securing of specific operating systems. Finally, Chapter 26, "Policies, Procedures, and Enforcement," can help with policy definition efforts.

3

BUILDING A
ROADMAP FOR
SECURING YOUR
ENTERPRISE

Identifying Digital Assets

When presented with the term *asset identification*, most IT folks think of *asset management*, or *asset tracking*, in the literal sense of the term. Although tracking physical assets is important, rarely do organizations take the time to granularly identify or quantify the value associated with their digital assets. For example, an e-commerce delivery system might comprise a dozen Web servers, a few database servers, a merchant gateway, and various pieces of supporting infrastructure equipment. For example, let's say that a sample medium-sized e-commerce deployment runs around $400,000 in hardware. The machines and systems themselves have a book value that is easy enough to calculate. A little bit more difficult to identify might be the costs associated with a site-wide outage. One would have to calculate hourly or daily revenue losses, as well as the costs associated with expenses necessary to respond to the problem, and any other outage-based costs.

Drilling a little deeper into our example, let us also suppose that the customer records and the purchasing trend data for this e-commerce initiative are stored on a single, internal database server. Again, the financial value of the hardware is easy enough to identify and record. But what happens when that server is compromised, and its data is leaked to the public? There will then be some less tangible, but very important items at risk: consumer confidence, industry reputation, and perhaps even legal liability. So the value of the server, and the data on it, might be a lot higher then what was initially thought.

Why does this matter? Back to the concept of managing risks. In an ideal world, every server, network device, and piece of data would be sufficiently protected. Unfortunately, we don't live in that world. Reality states that we have to choose our battles wisely, as there are only a finite number of them that we can fight. By identifying key assets, and protecting those assets first, organizations can maximize the effectiveness of their risk mitigation efforts.

Readers should note that there have been entire books written on asset identification and data value classification, and how they relate to overall risk analysis. Although many of the areas of true risk analysis are outside the scope of this book, there are some basics areas to look at in the IT field that can help you get started. For example, the following areas are often classified as "high value":

- Payroll information
- Research and development data
- Source code
- Marketing strategies
- Financial systems
- Sales information

- Customer data
- Financial reports
- Miscellaneous proprietary data

Remember, certain data, and certain systems, are more critical than others. It is up to the security officers and the business to determine what systems and data are the most valuable. Remember to choose your battles wisely—if you can only wage war on a few fronts, make sure they are the fronts that really count.

▶ Brooke Paul, one of the contributing authors of this book, wrote an introduction to Risk Assessment for Network Computing that readers might find useful. It can be found at: `http://www.networkcomputing.com/1121/1121f3.html`

Protecting Assets

Most organizations start identifying security risks at the perimeter (usually their firewalls) and move in. Although the perimeter is important, the narrow vision of this strategy has contributed to the sad state of affairs that we face today.

There's been a long-standing holy war in the information security scene that pits the notion of the internal threat against that of the external one. Pundits on the internal threat state that the highest documented financial losses occur because of intrusions instigated by insiders. The opposing school focuses on the rising trend of external attacks. The fact of the matter is that we simply don't have enough data to prove either stance. Much of the speculation is based upon reports such as the annual CSI/FBI reports, which draw upon such a statistically small sample size that it's hard to draw any definitive conclusions.

▶ The CSI/FBI report is not available in electronic format, but you can request a hardcopy of it directly from CSI: `http://www.gocsi.com/fbi_survey.htm`

However, one thing is for certain: In only protecting your perimeter, your organization becomes primed for compromise if either

    A) Your perimeter defenses falter or

    B) An insider attacks you.

Organizations should look to defend both their perimeter and their internal assets, and should do so by creating a defense-in-depth strategy. Part IV, "The Defenders Toolkit" demonstrates a number of technologies that can aid in this quest. However, it should be noted that by not creating multiple tiers of security, organizations put themselves at risk.

Identifying and Removing Vulnerabilities

One of the most common methods of entry for intruders is through the use of known operating system and network vulnerabilities—vulnerabilities that can usually be remedied through patches or minimal configuration changes. Because of this, it is important that organizations look to implement procedures to discover, evaluate, and mitigate security vulnerabilities in a timely manner. This discovery process should be twofold:

- Use tools such as a vulnerability assessment scanner (see Chapter 11) to discover both new and old vulnerabilities.

- Identify individuals in the organization who are responsible for monitoring weekly security announcements (from SANS SAC, SF BUGTRAQ, and so on) and initiating patching efforts. Chapter 25, "Mining the Data Monster," has more information on keeping on top of the plethora of security information sources available.

▶ One of the easiest ways to stay on top of the onslaught of vulnerability announcements is to subscribe to the NWC/SANS Security Alert Consensus (SAC) newsletter. SAC supplies a summarized, customizable report of the week's vulnerability discoveries to more than 100,000 subscribers. Pulling from more than 70 sources of information, SAC is extremely thorough. You can find this information at `http://www.sans.org/nwcnews/`.

Without both efforts operating in succession, you run the risk of being open to some of the most prevalent attacks in the security scene today.

Developing Standardized Build Documents

Small to mid-sized organizations might have an assortment of platforms to support. Large organizations often have dozens. It's not uncommon to have an IT staff tasked with supporting Solaris, Windows NT, NetWare, Linux, HP/UX, AIX, AS/400, and OS/390-based systems. Each of these system types has its own set of security features, and its own set of vulnerabilities. Organizations need to be both aware of these issues as well as continue to operate the systems in a secure manner.

So how can organizations cope with the myriad of potential security nightmares? One method is to standardize the way operating systems are configured and deployed, and then keep an eye on vendor announced updates. Although production servers will have a level of customization applied to them based on function, most systems can be installed with a baseline configuration. If this configuration has been properly hardened from a security perspective, administrators will have an easier time keeping them secure.

One way to arrive at a baseline configuration is to seek a consensus among system administrators and security personnel on what a "secure" configuration of a particular OS should be. This should include necessary patches, service packs, or configuration changes that will improve the security of the target OS. It is important to remember that no operating system is secure out of the box—this is a mistake many organizations make and pay for.

Readers should read Part VI, "Platforms and Security," later in this book to learn about vulnerabilities within specific platforms and to help identify what their strategy will be for securing various platforms (UNIX, Microsoft Windows, NetWare, and so on).

Developing and Deploying Policies and Procedures

Although they have less sex appeal than cutting edge intrusion detection technology, enforced policies are the cornerstone of any strong information security practice. Security officers should think of policy as being the constitution governing the secure operation of their environment. Without approved policies, it is often extremely hard to enforce and defend security actions. Policies are sometimes your last line of defense.

Organizations should have policies that address at least the following issues:

- Acceptable usage
- Data value classification
- Data disclosure and destruction
- Roles and responsibilities
- Change control
- Disaster recovery

Perhaps the hardest part of successful policy implementation is getting upper management approval. Unfortunately, without management approval policies do not hold any weight, and are virtually unenforceable. Policies and procedures are gone over in more detail in Chapter 26.

Incident Response

The ability to respond to a security threat or incident is becoming increasingly more important in today's world. The efficiency with which an organization responds to a given threat can make the difference between a thwarted attack, and tomorrow morning's headline story. Unfortunately, organizations often don't realize this fact until it's too late. However, this short-coming can be avoided with a pro-active incident response model. Hammering out incident response (IR) policies and procedures beforehand will not only save embarrassment, but time and money as well.

Although today's information security challenges call for a defined IR strategy, the real-world need for incident response pre-dates computers by more then a century. Before taking a look at this need, let's take a brief look at the history and certification of one of the oldest security devices—the safe.

"Tan," a member of the hacker think-tank L0pht, published a paper in the late '90s on the need for a Cyber Underwriters Laboratory. He drew some interesting comparisons between the origins of the UL rating system for safes and the current challenges in the field of security certification. He begins the paper by providing a brief history of the Underwriters Laboratory:

> Underwriters Laboratories was founded in 1894 by an electrical inspector from Boston, William Henry Merrill. In 1893, Chicago authorities grew concerned over the public safety due to the proliferation of untamed DC circuits and the new, even more dangerous technology of AC circuits. These new and little-understood technologies threatened our society with frequent fires, which caused critics to question whether the technology could ever be harnessed safely. Merrill was called in and set up a one-room laboratory with $350.00 in electrical test equipment and published his first report on March 24, 1894.

> Back in Boston, insurance underwriters rejected Merrill's plans for a non-biased testing facility for certification of electrical devices. Chicago, however, embraced the idea. Merrill took advantage of the situation in Chicago to get up and running and within months had support at the national level.

> Today, UL has tested more than 12,500 products world-wide and is a internationally recognized authority on safety and technology. The UL mark of approval has come to provide an earned level of trust between customers and manufacturers and safely allowed our society to leverage hundreds of inventions that would have otherwise been unfit for public use.

▶ You can find Tan's paper at `http://www.l0pht.com/~tan/ul/CyberUL.html`.

Today, the UL labs are famous for testing many products, one of them being industrial-strength safes. Infamous cryptography expert Bruce Schneier has often pointed out that part of the UL rating for safes is based on how long it will take an attacker to break into the unit. For example, a rating of TL-15 signifies 15 minutes with the use of tools (saws, hammers, carbide-tipped drills, and so on), whereas a rating of TRTL-30 signifies 30 minutes with the use of tools (TL) and a torch (TR). Now, in the real world, these times are important because they set some level of expectation regarding how long an organization has to respond to an attack. For example, if you know that the police and your security guards will be able to detect and respond to an intruder in less than 5 minutes, a TL-15 rated safe might be sufficient for your organization. If, however, you will be thwarting skilled attackers and your response ability is closer to 20 minutes, you might be better off with a device touting a rating of TRTL-30.

Now, transferring this over to the world of information security, this method of approaching the problem has its problems. For example, Tan states in his paper:

> The first problem is that if a security system is defeated in the physical world, it is typically very obvious to those who come into work on Monday and see that the money is gone and the safe is in pieces. Detection of a cyber intrusion is typically NOT very obvious to those who come into work on Monday. Because of this fact, safe crackers have

very limited time to crack a vault. Hackers, on the other hand, have unlimited time to crack a system. Once they get in, safe crackers typically REMOVE items which then become 'missing'. Hackers typically COPY items unless their motives are political rather than financial, leaving the originals and the system intact. For cyber intrusions to become less surreptitious, intrusion detection needs to mature and become more widely deployed if 'time' is to be a meaningful factor in the process.

The author's points are extremely valid. Making matters worse, Tan assumes that you have something watching your systems, and the ability to respond to such cracking attempts if or when you detect them. Most organizations have neither.

If businesses do not have the ability to properly identify and respond to an attack, attackers will always have the upper hand. In order to be effective at thwarting intruders, security officers should

- Monitor key assets
- Consider deploying some method of intrusion detection. (See Chapter 12, "Intrusion Detection Systems (IDS).")
- Possess some type of incident response capability

In addition, at a bare minimum, organizations should look to define

- Who is responsible for responding to security threats
- What the escalation procedures are
- The "call list" for decision making should a business-critical decision need to be made

Again, pro-active measures on the IR front will save organizations both time and money.

▶ Two good primers on incident response:

Allaire's Incident Response Guide: `http://www.allaire.com/DocumentCenter/Partners/ASZ_ASWPS_Incident_Response.pdf`

The SANS Computer Security Incident Handling Step-by-Step Paper: `http://www.sansstore.org/`

Training Users and Administrators

I've run into administrators in numerous organizations who claim, "Security is not my problem—it's the problem of the security folks." As silly as this statement might sound, many old-school system and network administrators foolishly subscribe to this philosophy. This is not an easy challenge to overcome, but one you must work with, or around, to be successful. Put frankly, security is everyone's responsibility…and everyone's problem. It only takes one vulnerability, one weak link, to break the entire chain.

Unfortunately, getting this message into everyone's head is easier said then done. However, there are a few things that can help the cause:

- Make sure that the general security policies (like AUPs) are distributed to all employees.

- Embark on an awareness campaign. This will help to ensure that the general user population understands the threats, as well as help to reaffirm that there is an information security effort within the organization.

- Identify an executive sponsor who is willing to publish memos to the rest of the company stressing the importance of strong security practices. Again, if it doesn't come from the top, it's hard to enforce.

- Build responsibility matrices that clearly identify specific security responsibilities within the organization. With management backing, this can be used to drive home the point that security is everyone's duty.

Tying It All Together

As daunting as each of the tasks in this chapter might seem, the most important thing to remember is that efforts must be started to address them in unison. For example, protecting your perimeter won't help with internal intruders when your systems aren't secured. By the same token, even if your systems are secured, it will be hard to defend yourself from distributed denial of service attacks when your network security is in shambles. Finally, even if you have most of the technology problems under wraps, this won't stop your users from making damaging security blunders.

Overwhelmed yet? Don't be. Rare are the organizations that have managed to get on top of all of these issues, which is precisely why defense in-depth strategies are so popular; they help reduce single points of security failure. By building your security strategy around many of these foundational concepts, you can create tiers of protection. Your organization's overall security strength will ultimately depend on how many of these efforts get off the ground, and how successful each of them becomes.

This book can help you with many of the areas you'll need to address. Use it to help identify what you want to protect. Use it to learn about various information security technologies, and how they can make your life easier. Use it to learn about operating system security, network security, and application security. Use it to gain a holistic view of the information security landscape, and learn how to leverage this knowledge in today's technological age.

Summary

In order for organizations to operate a successful information security program, they need to combine technology with discipline. In today's world, the security scene operates at an extraordinary pace and slows down for no one. Without covering the basics and forming a pro-active security model, organizations will be caught in an endless game of catch-up—game that they will ultimately lose.

This book presents many of the foundational principles needed to operate secure computing environments. This book also explains some of the basics: how IP networks work, how vulnerabilities are exploited, and how operating systems are both exploited and protected. The next chapter focuses on one of the most fundamental components security personnel need to understand: TCP/IP.

3

BUILDING A
ROADMAP FOR
SECURING YOUR
ENTERPRISE

A Brief Primer on TCP/IP

IN THIS CHAPTER

In this chapter, you learn about various protocols (or methods of data transport) used on the Internet, including Transmission Control Protocol (TCP) and Internet Protocol (IP). This chapter is not an exhaustive treatment of TCP/IP. Instead, it is intended to ensure that you have enough understanding of TCP/IP to get maximum benefit out of the chapters that follow. Throughout this chapter, links are provided to other documents and resources from which you can find more comprehensive information on TCP/IP.

What Is TCP/IP?

TCP/IP refers to two network protocols used on the Internet: Transmission Control Protocol and Internet Protocol. However, TCP and IP are only two protocols belonging to a much larger collection of protocols called the *TCP/IP suite*.

The TCP/IP suite of networking protocols connects various operating systems and network components. It provides a standard method for moving data between systems, and is used both on the Internet as well as in the world of private networking.

Protocols within the TCP/IP suite provide data transport for all services available to today's network user. Some of those services include

- Transmission of electronic mail
- File transfers
- Instant messaging
- Access to the World Wide Web

The Open Systems Interconnection (OSI) Reference Model

The OSI Reference Model was defined to standardize discussion of various technologies involved in networking. Its seven layers represent the architecture for data communication protocols. Each layer in the OSI model specifies a particular network function. The OSI model can be thought of as a stack with each layer lying on the one below it. The services that a given layer performs are defined by the protocols at that layer. Understanding the OSI model and each layer is very helpful in conceptualizing how the different parts of TCP/IP networks and applications interact. The seven layers of the OSI model stack are

- **Layer 7 (Application).** The highest layer of the OSI model. This layer defines the way applications interact with the network and between systems.
- **Layer 6 (Presentation).** Contains protocols that are part of the operating system. This layer defines how information is formatted for display. Data encryption and translation can occur at this layer.
- **Layer 5 (Session).** Coordinates communication between endpoints. Session state is maintained at this layer for security, logging, and administrative functions.

- **Layer 4 (Transport).** Controls the flow of data between systems, defines the structure of data in messages, and performs error checking. Web browser encryption commonly occurs at this layer.
- **Layer 3 (Network).** Defines protocols for routing data between systems. This is the layer where endpoint addressing occurs; it makes sure that data arrives at the correct destination.
- **Layer 2 (Data-link or Network interface).** Defines the rules for sending and receiving information from one node to another in local network environments (that is, LANs).
- **Layer 1 (Physical or Media).** Governs hardware connections and byte-stream encoding for transmission. It is the only layer that involves a physical transfer of information between network nodes.

TCP/IP was created prior to the development of the OSI reference model, and, although TCP/IP fits within the OSI architecture, not all OSI layers are relevant when talking about TCP/IP. With respect to TCP/IP, the most important OSI layers are the application, transport, network, and data-link. Each of these layers has specific protocols associated with them, which we'll examine in detail later in this chapter. Common protocols at these layers are

- Application: Hypertext Transfer Protocol (HTTP)
- Transport: Transmission Control Protocol (TCP)
- Network: Internet Protocol (IP)
- Data-link: Address Resolution Protocol (ARP)

These protocols can be divided into two types, network and application (see Figure 4.1):

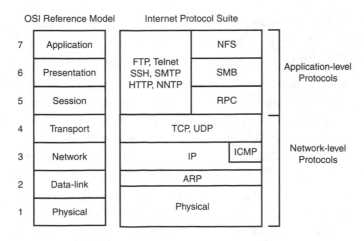

4

A BRIEF PRIMER ON TCP/IP

FIGURE 4.1
OSI and IP protocol stacks.

Network-Level Protocols

Network-level protocols manage the mechanics of data transfer, and are typically invisible to the end user. For example, the Internet Protocol (IP) provides packet delivery of information sent between the user and remote machines. It does this based on a variety of data, most notably the IP address of the two machines. Based on the IP address and other information, IP provides a "best-effort" service to route the information to its intended destination. Throughout this process, IP interacts with other network-level protocols engaged in data transport. Short of using network utilities (perhaps a sniffer or other device that reads IP datagrams), the user will never see IP's work on the network.

Application-Level Protocols

Unlike network-level protocols, application-level protocols are visible to the user. For example, Hypertext Transfer Protocol (HTTP) is an interactive protocol; you see the results of your connection and transfer as it's happening. (That information is presented in error messages and status reports on the transfer—for example, the number of bytes that have been transferred at any given moment).

The History of TCP/IP

In 1969, the Defense Advanced Research Projects Agency (DARPA) commissioned development of a network for its research centers. The chief concern was this network's capability to withstand a nuclear attack. If the Soviet Union launched a first strike, the network still had to facilitate communication. The design of this network had several other requisites, the most important of which was this: It had to operate independently of any centralized control. The prototype for this system (called ARPANET) was based in large part on research done in 1962 and 1963.

The original ARPANET worked well but was subject to periodic system crashes. Furthermore, long-term expansion of that network proved costly. A search was therefore initiated for a more reliable set of protocols; that search ended in the mid-1970s with the development of TCP/IP.

TCP/IP had two chief advantages over other protocols: It was lightweight and could be implemented at lower cost than the other choices then available. Based on these factors, TCP/IP became exceedingly popular. By 1983, TCP/IP was integrated into release 4.2 of Berkeley Software Distribution (BSD) UNIX. Its integration into commercial forms of UNIX soon followed, and TCP/IP was established as the Internet standard. It has remained so to this day. (For more on the history of the Internet, see Appendix B, "Internet 101.")

Today, TCP/IP is used for many purposes, not just for Internet communication. For example, intranets are often built using TCP/IP. In such environments, TCP/IP can offer significant advantages over other networking protocols. For example, TCP/IP works on a wide variety of hardware and operating systems. Using TCP/IP, one can quickly and easily create a heterogeneous network that links Macs, IBM compatibles, Mainframes, Sun UNIX servers, MIPS machines, and so on. Each of these can communicate with its peers using a common protocol suite. For this reason, TCP/IP has remained extremely popular since its introduction.

The RFCs

The protocols of TCP/IP suite are usually defined by documents called *Requests For Comments* (*RFCs*). The RFC approval process is managed by the Internet Engineering Steering Group (IESG) based on recommendations from the Internet Engineering Task Force (IETF). RFCs can be composed and submitted by anyone. In addition, RFCs are unlike many other networking standards in that they are freely available online and are open to comment by anyone.

▶ For complete information about The Internet Standards Process, see
  `http://info.internet.isi.edu:80/in-notes/rfc/files/rfc2026.txt`.

The IETF is primarily responsible for forming working groups focused on strategic TCP/IP issues. Standards *RFCs* are often the product of many months of discussion within these working groups, which are made up of people interested in a particular aspect of the Internet. The working groups often draft proposed RFCs and make them available for discussion. These discussions typically take place on mailing lists, which welcome input from any interested party. Not all *RFCs* specify TCP/IP standards. Some *RFCs* contain background information, some provide documentation and tips for managing a TCP/IP network, some document protocol weaknesses, and some are even completely humorous. The core RFCs that define the standards associated with TCP/IP networking are

- RFC 768: User Datagram Protocol
- RFC 791: Internet Protocol
- RFC 792: Internet Control Message Protocol
- RFC 793: Transmission Control Protocol
- RFC 1122: Requirements for Internet Hosts—Communication Layers
- RFC 1123: Requirements for Internet Hosts—Application and Support.

▶ For more complete information about Internet protocols and associated RFCs, visit an RFC archive such as that provided by the IETF at `http://www.ietf.org/rfc.html`.

Implementations of TCP/IP

The de facto standard for TCP/IP implementations has been the 4.x BSD releases, and its code has been the starting point for many other implementations. There are numerous implementations available including a number of BSD derivatives such as FreeBSD, OpenBSD, and NetBSD. In addition, the UNIX-like operating system GNU/Linux includes source code for a

4

TCP/IP implementation. Source code for non-UNIX implementations is also available. Packages for MS-DOS and Windows include WATTCP/WATT-32 and KA9Q.

How Does TCP/IP Work?

As with the OSI model, TCP/IP operates through the use of a *protocol stack*. This stack is the sum total of all protocols necessary to transfer data between two machines, as shown in Figure 4.2. (It is also the path that data takes to get out of one machine and into another.)

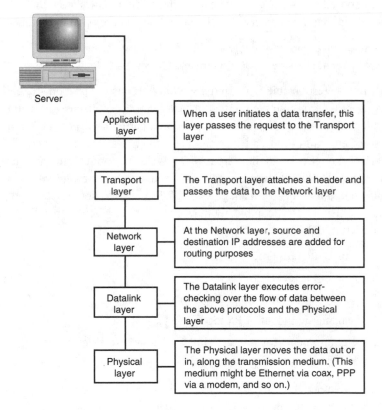

FIGURE 4.2
The TCP/IP protocol stack.

After data passes through the stack, it travels to its destination on another machine or network. There, the process is executed in reverse. (The data first meets the physical layer and subsequently travels its way up the stack.) Throughout this process, a system of error checking is employed both on the originating machine and the destination machine.

Each stack layer can send data to and receive data from its neighbor. Each layer is also associated with multiple protocols. At each tier of the stack, these protocols provide the user with various services. When two applications are communicating over a network, data passes from one application to the other by moving down the stack from the application on the transmitting system and back up the stack of the receiving system to the application running there. As information moves down the stack, information is added to the packet in the form of a header. This header information is like an envelope in which the previous layer's information is wrapped. As the packet goes up the stack, the header is processed and removed before that packet is passed on to the next layer (much like a person opening an envelope to read the letter inside).

The Individual Protocols

Data is transmitted via TCP/IP using the protocol stack. In each layer of the TCP/IP stack, individual protocols provide certain network services. These protocols can be categorized as network-level or application-level, with many individual protocols existing in each level.

Network-Level Protocols

Network-level protocols facilitate the data transport process transparently. They are invisible to the end user unless that user employs utilities to monitor system processes.

> **TIP**
>
> Sniffers are devices that can monitor network processes. A sniffer is a device—either hardware or software—that can read every packet sent across a network. Sniffers are commonly used to isolate network problems that, although invisible to the end user, are degrading network performance. As such, sniffers can read all activity occurring between network-level protocols. Moreover, sniffers can pose a tremendous security threat. You will examine sniffers in Chapter 15, "Sniffers."

Important TCP/IP network-level protocols include the following:

- Address Resolution Protocol (ARP)
- Internet Control Message Protocol (ICMP)
- Internet Protocol (IP)
- Transmission Control Protocol (TCP)
- User Datagram Protocol (UDP)

We will briefly examine each, ascending up the stack from the data-link layer to the transport layer.

▶ For more comprehensive information about protocols (or the stack in general), see *TCP/IP Illustrated, Volume 1* by W. Richard Stevens (Addison Wesley, ISBN # 0-201-63346-9).

The Address Resolution Protocol (ARP)

The Address Resolution Protocol (ARP) serves the critical purpose of mapping Internet addresses into hardware addresses and translating the network layer address (or IP address) to the data-link address. This is vital in routing information between hosts on a local network, and out onto the Internet. Before a message (or other data) is sent, it is packaged into IP packets, or blocks of information suitably formatted for Internet transport. These contain the numeric, network IP address of both the originating and destination machines. What remains is to determine the hardware, or the data-link address of the destination machine. This is where ARP makes its entrance.

An ARP request message is broadcast on a local network. If the destination IP address is active on the local network, the destination host will reply with its own hardware address. The originating machine receives this reply, and the transfer process can begin.

▶ For those readers seeking in-depth information on ARP, see RFC 826 at
`http://info.internet.isi.edu:80/in-notes/rfc/files/rfc826.txt`.

The Internet Control Message Protocol (ICMP)

The Internet Control Message Protocol provides error and control messages that are passed between two (or more) computers or hosts. It enables those hosts to share the information. In this respect, ICMP is critical for diagnosis of network problems. ICMP provides helpful messages, such as the following:

- Echo and reply messages to test for network availability
- Redirect messages to enable more efficient routing
- Time-exceeded messages to inform sources that a packet has exceeded its allocated time within the network

An ICMP packet can be of several types. The two most common are the `ICMP_ECHO_REQUEST` and `ICMP_ECHO_REPLY`. These packets are used to test network connectivity to make sure a host or network component is active and reachable.

TIP

Perhaps the most widely known ICMP implementation involves a network utility called ping. Ping is often used to determine whether a remote machine is alive. Ping's method of operation is simple: When the user pings a remote machine, a series of `ICMP_ECHO_REQUEST` packets are forwarded from the user's machine to the remote host. The remote host replies with `ICMP_ECHO_REPLY` packets. If no reply packets are received at the user's end, the ping program usually generates an error message, indicating that the remote host is down or unreachable.

▶ In-depth information about ICMP can be found in RFC 792 at
  `http://info.internet.isi.edu:80/in-notes/rfc/files/rfc792.txt`.

The Internet Protocol (IP)

The Internet Protocol provides packet delivery for all protocols within the TCP/IP suite. Thus, IP is the heart of the process by which data traverses the Internet. The IP *datagram*, or packet, is the vehicle for transmission of data on TCP/IP networks. The structure of an IP datagram is shown in Figure 4.3.

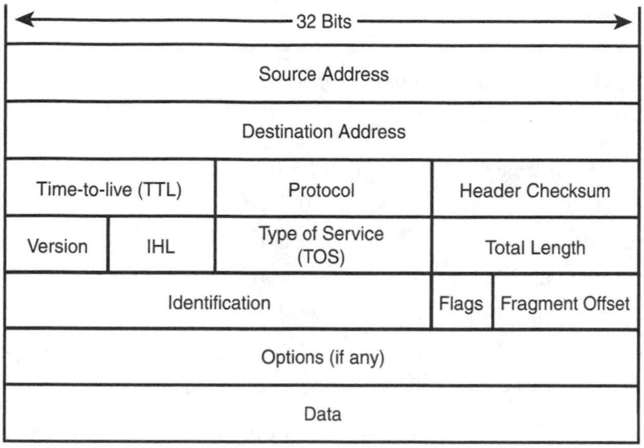

FIGURE 4.3
The IP datagram.

An IP datagram is composed of several parts. The first part, the *header*, is composed of important network information, including source and destination IP addresses. Together, these elements form a complete header. The remaining portion of a datagram contains whatever data is then being sent.

One of the important aspects of IP networking is that it can be used to transmit data using a number of protocols (that is, TCP, UDP, and so on). Each protocol serves a particular function; we'll be looking at some important ones soon. In addition, IP enables the fragmentation and reassembly of data. At the data-link layer, networks can only transmit data in discrete chunks up to a specific size, called the Maximum Transmission Unit (MTU). If the data you want to transmit is larger than the MTU that a network can transmit, the data must be broken into pieces smaller than the MTU, transmitted, and then put back together at the other end. IP provides a mechanism for fragmenting the data, tracking it, and reassembling it. Fragmentation is also important from a security perspective. In some cases, it can be manipulated to work around security measures if security isn't implemented carefully.

An IP datagram also contains a time-to-live (TTL) field. A numeric value, the TTL is decremented as the IP datagram traverses the network. When that value finally reaches zero, the datagram is discarded. This ensures that the network doesn't become clogged with datagrams that can't find their destination in a timely fashion. Many other types of packets have time-to-live limitations, and some network utilities (such as Traceroute) use the time-to-live field as a marker in diagnostic routines.

IP Network Addressing

The IP address is a unique identifier for a system on the network. It is 32 bits long and is usually represented as 4 numbers, each a byte, separated by decimal points, for example, 32.96.111.130. Each byte, or octet, in an IP address can range from 0 to 255. This representation of an IP address is called *dotted-decimal notation* and is the most common humanly readable format for working with IP addresses.

A contiguous range of IP addresses defines an IP network. This range of IP addresses is denoted by the combination of an IP address and network mask (or *netmask*). A netmask is a 32-bit value like an IP address, which, when combined with the IP address, defines address boundaries of the IP network. This requires conversion of the IP address and netmask to binary format and their combination using binary arithmetic. Note that the first address in a contiguous range of IP addresses indicates the network address. The last address in the contiguous range denotes the network broadcast address.

The network layer in TCP/IP is usually considered to be unicast. This is in contrast to the data-link layer, where ARP operates in a broadcast mode. *Unicast* indicates that IP communications occur between two endpoints in a point-to-point fashion. However, an IP datagram can be addressed to the network broadcast address. This causes the IP datagram to be received and responded to by all nodes on the IP network. Several network based denial of service attacks take advantage of this broadcast capability in IP.

▶ In-depth information on the Internet Protocol can be found in RFC 760 at
http://info.internet.isi.edu:80/in-notes/rfc/files/rfc760.txt.

The Transmission Control Protocol (TCP)

The Transmission Control Protocol (TCP) is one of the main protocols employed on the Internet. Working at the transport level in the stack, it facilitates such mission-critical tasks as file transfers and remote sessions. TCP accomplishes these tasks through a method called *reliable communication*. In this respect, TCP is more reliable than other protocols within the suite because it includes mechanisms for sequencing and acknowledgment of data transmission.

As with IP, TCP has its own packet structure (see Figure 4.4), composed of source port and destination port numbers that identify services. In addition, important parts of a TCP packet are the sequence number, flags, and checksum. The *sequence number* tracks a TCP connection and the order in which data is sent. The *flags* control the connection state, whether it is being established, in use, or being closed. There are six flags that can be used in combination to describe the state of a TCP connection. The most important for this analysis are SYN, ACK, and FIN. The *checksum* in the TCP packet ensures that the data has not been corrupted during transmission.

Source Port			Destination Port	
Sequence Number				
Acknowledgment Number				
Data Offset	Reserved	Flags	Window	
Checksum			Urgent Pointer	
Options (if any)				
Data (variable)				

FIGURE 4.4
TCP packet structure.

The TCP system relies on a virtual circuit between the requesting machine (client) and its target (server). This circuit is opened via a three-part process, often referred to as the *three-way handshake*. The process typically follows the pattern illustrated in Figure 4.5.

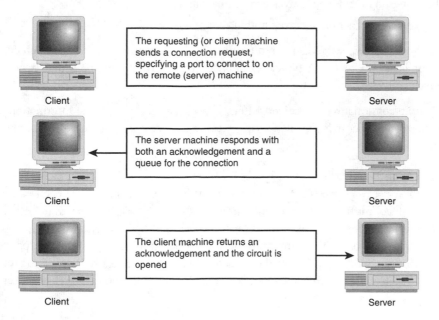

Client   The requesting (or client) machine sends a connection request, specifying a port to connect to on the remote (server) machine   Server

Client   The server machine responds with both an acknowledgement and a queue for the connection   Server

Client   The client machine returns an acknowledgement and the circuit is opened   Server

FIGURE 4.5
Establishment of TCP connection.

To establish a TCP connection, the three-way handshake must be completed as follows:

1. The client sends a TCP SYN packet to the server that it wants to establish a connection with. This is a TCP packet with only the SYN flag active. The packet also contains an initial sequence number (ISN) that will be used to track the connection.

2. The server responds with a TCP SYN packet with its own ISN. The server also acknowledges the client's TCP SYN by setting the ACK flag on this packet and using the client's ISN plus 1 as the acknowledgement number.

3. The client acknowledges the server's TCP SYN with a TCP ACK using the server's ISN plus 1.

No data is exchanged during this process, but, when it is completed, a connection is available for data transfer between the client and server. This connection provides a *full-duplex transmission path*. Full-duplex transmission enables data to travel to both machines at the same time. In this way, while a file transfer (or other remote session) is underway, any errors that arise can be forwarded to the requesting machine.

TCP also provides extensive error-checking capabilities. For each block of data sent, a checksum is calculated, and the sequence number is incremented. The two machines identify each transferred block using the sequence number. For each block successfully transferred, the receiving host sends an ACK message to the sender that the transfer was clean. Conversely, if the transfer is unsuccessful, one of two things might occur:

- The requesting machine receives error information.
- The requesting machine receives nothing.

When an error is received, the data is retransmitted unless the error is fatal, in which case, the transmission is usually halted. A typical example of a fatal error would be if the connection was dropped.

Similarly, if no confirmation is received within a specified time period, the information is also retransmitted. This process is repeated as many times as necessary to complete the transfer or remote session.

TCP Connection Termination
As you might expect, because TCP provides a protocol for establishing a connection, it also provides a protocol for terminating a connection. Establishing a TCP connection takes three steps, whereas terminating one takes four steps. Because a TCP connection is bi-directional or full-duplex, transmission in both directions of the connection must be shut down separately. This is done by using the TCP FIN packet, much as the TCP SYN packet is used to create a connection. When a client is finished using a connection, it will issue a TCP FIN packet to the

server. The server responds with a TCP ACK to acknowledge that the connection is closing. Because the connection is bi-directional, the server will also issue a TCP FIN to the client. The client will then acknowledge the server's TCP FIN, thus completing the TCP connection termination process.

▶ In-depth information about TCP can be found in RFC 793 at
`http://info.internet.isi.edu:80/in-notes/rfc/files/rfc793.txt`.

User Datagram Protocol (UDP)

The User Datagram Protocol (UDP) is a simple, connectionless transport layer protocol. In fact, it is so simple that the RFC that defines it is only three pages long. Unlike TCP, UDP provides no reliability, and, because it is connectionless, it doesn't have any mechanism for connection establishment or termination. It does provide data integrity checks via a checksum. Although it might seem that UDP is inferior to TCP, it is, in fact, much better for certain applications because it has very low overhead.

▶ In-depth information about UDP can be found in RFC 768 at
`http://info.internet.isi.edu:80/in-notes/rfc/files/rfc768.txt`.

Application Level Protocols—The Ports

Each time a machine requests services from another, it specifies a particular destination and transport method. The destination is expressed as the Internet (IP) address of the target machine, and the transport method is the transport protocol (that is, TCP or UDP). Further, the requesting machine specifies the application it is trying to reach at the destination by using a system of *ports*.

Just as machines on the Internet have unique IP addresses, each application (FTP or Telnet, for example) is assigned a unique address called a *port*. The port defines the type of service that is being requested or provided. The application in question is bound to that particular port, and, when any connection request is made to that port, the corresponding server application responds.

There are thousands of ports on the average Internet server, although often, most will not be active. For purposes of convenience and efficiency, a standard framework has been developed for port assignments. (In other words, although a system administrator can assign services to the ports of his choice, services are generally assigned to recognized ports commonly referred to as *well-known ports*.) Table 4.1 shows some commonly recognized ports and the applications typically bound to them.

TABLE 4.1   Common Ports and Their Corresponding Services or Applications

Service or Application	Port
Hypertext Transfer Protocol (HTTP)	TCP port 80
Domain Name System (DNS)	UDP and TCP port 53
Telnet	TCP port 23
File Transfer Protocol (FTP)	TCP port 20 and 21
Simple Mail Transfer Protocol (SMTP)	TCP port 25
Secure Shell (SSH)	TCP port 22

Each of the ports described in Table 4.1 are assigned to application-level protocols or services—that is, they are visible to the user, and the user can interact with them. We will examine each of these applications in the following sections.

▶ For a comprehensive list of all port assignments, visit `ftp://ftp.isi.edu/in-notes/iana/` `assignments/port-numbers`. This document is extremely informative and exhaustive in its treatment of commonly assigned port numbers.

Hypertext Transfer Protocol (HTTP)

Hypertext Transfer Protocol (HTTP) is perhaps the most renowned protocol of all because it enables users to surf the World Wide Web. Stated briefly in RFC 1945, HTTP is

> …an application-level protocol with the lightness and speed necessary for distributed, collaborative, hypermedia information systems. It is a generic, stateless, object-oriented protocol which can be used for many tasks, such as name servers and distributed object management systems, through extension of its request methods (commands). A feature of HTTP is the typing of data representation, enabling systems to be built independently of the data being transferred.

▶ RFC 1945 has been superseded by RFC 2068, which is available at `http://info.internet.isi.edu:80/in-notes/rfc/files/rfc2068.txt`. RFC 2068 is a more recent specification of HTTP.

HTTP has forever changed the nature of the Internet, primarily by bringing the Internet to the masses. Using a common browser such as Netscape Navigator or Microsoft Internet Explorer, you can monitor the process of HTTP as it occurs. Depending upon the version of HTTP the server supports, your browser will contact the server for each data element (text, graphic, sound) on a WWW page. Thus, it will first grab text, then a graphic, then a sound file, and so on. In the lower-left corner of your browser's screen is a status bar. Watch it for a few moments while it is loading a page. You will see this request/response activity occur, often at a very high speed.

HTTP typically runs on port 80 using TCP. HTTP does little to protect the confidentiality of data because documents are transmitted without encryption. Some security can be added by using HTTPS, which is HTTP transmitted over Secure Sockets Layer (SSL). HTTPS typically runs on port 443 using TCP.

Domain Name System (DNS)

The Domain Name System (DNS) provides services that translate host names to IP addresses and back again. Much as Address Resolution Protocol provides a mechanism for translating addresses between the data-link and network layers (hardware address to IP address), DNS translates addresses between the network layer and the application layer (IP address to host-names). Because IP addresses aren't exactly human friendly, the Domain Name System was developed to allow people to use human-friendly naming for systems. For example, when you enter **www.fbi.gov** into your Web browser, the name needs to be translated from that friendly format into an IP address that can be used by the network layer.

DNS has two modes of operation. The first mode is primarily for communications to clients that need names resolved to addresses. Because this is a small, easy task, transport for this mode is provided by UDP. DNS servers also must transfer large blocks of DNS records so that the workload and administration involved with resolving names to and from IP addresses can be distributed. These larger transfers (called *DNS zone transfers*) occur via TCP.

DNS is a very active area of discussion, and numerous Internet drafts and RFCs have been created to add functionality and security to DNS.

▶ The core RFCs for DNS are 1034 and 1035. You can find them at
http://info.internet.isi.edu:80/in-notes/rfc/files/rfc1034.txt and
http://info.internet.isi.edu:80/in-notes/rfc/files/rfc1035.txt.

All modern operating systems that run TCP/IP come with a DNS client (called a *resolver*) as part of the OS. A client program that enables a user to query DNS directly is often included. On UNIX and Microsoft Windows NT or 2000, the program nslookup is provided. This DNS client lets you interactively connect to a DNS server and perform various queries of the DNS data.

The most widely used DNS server is the Berkeley Internet Name Domain (BIND) DNS server. Developed and supported by the Internet Software Consortium, BIND is available for most UNIX systems as well as for Microsoft Windows NT. DNS typically runs on port 53 using UDP and TCP.

Telnet

Telnet is best described in RFC 854, the Telnet protocol specification:

> The purpose of the Telnet protocol is to provide a fairly general, bi-directional, eight-bit byte-oriented communications facility. Its primary goal is to allow a standard method of interfacing terminal devices and terminal-oriented processes to each other.

Telnet not only enables the user to log in to a remote host, it also lets that user execute commands on the host. Thus, an individual in Los Angeles can telnet to a machine in New York and begin running programs on the New York machine just as though she were in New York.

For those of you who are unfamiliar with Telnet, it operates much like the interface of a bulletin board system (BBS). Telnet is an excellent application for providing a terminal-based front-end to databases. For example, many university library catalogs can be accessed via Telnet or tn3270 (a variation that emulates an IBM 3270 terminal). Figure 4.6 shows an example of a Telnet library catalog screen.

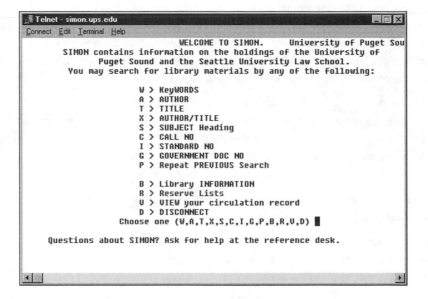

FIGURE 4.6

A sample Telnet session.

Even though GUI applications have taken the world by storm, Telnet—which is essentially a text-based application—is still incredibly popular. Telnet enables you to perform a variety of functions (retrieving mail, for example) at a minimal cost in network resources.

To use Telnet, the user issues whatever command necessary to start his Telnet client, followed by the name (or numeric IP address) of the target host. In UNIX, this is done as follows:

```
% telnet www.fbi.gov
```

This command launches a Telnet session, contacts www.fbi.gov, and requests a TCP connection on port 23. That connection request will either be honored or denied, depending on the configuration at the target host. In UNIX, the telnet command has long been a native one. In addition, Telnet has been included with Microsoft Windows distributions for more than a decade.

Telnet is a simple protocol, and offers very little in the way of security. All data transmitted during a Telnet session, including the login ID and password, are sent unencrypted. Anyone with access to a sniffer and the network between the client and server could capture critical data including your password.

Secure Shell (examined later in this chapter) provides services similar to Telnet, but adds security by encrypting the data between client and server.

Telnet typically runs on port 23 via TCP.

File Transfer Protocol (FTP)

File Transfer Protocol (FTP) is a standard method of transferring files from one system to another. Its purpose is set forth in RFC 0765 as follows:

> The objectives of FTP are 1) to promote sharing of files (computer programs and/or data), 2) to encourage indirect or implicit (via programs) use of remote computers, 3) to shield a user from variations in file storage systems among Hosts, and 4) to transfer data reliably and efficiently. FTP, though usable directly by a user at a terminal, is designed mainly for use by programs.

For more than two decades, researchers have investigated a wide variety of file-transfer methods. The development of FTP has undergone many changes in that time. Its first definition occurred in April 1971, and the full specification can be read in RFC 114.

▶ RFC 114 contains the first definition of FTP, but a more practical document might be RFC 959, found at `http://info.internet.isi.edu:80/in-notes/rfc/files/rfc959.txt`.

Mechanical Operation of FTP

File transfers using FTP can be accomplished using any suitable FTP client. Table 4.2 defines some common FTP clients, by operating system.

4

TABLE 4.2 FTP Clients for Various Operating Systems

Operating System	Clients
UNIX	Native, LLNLXDIR2.0, FTPtool, NCFTP
Microsoft Windows 95/98	Native, WS_FTP, Netload, Cute-FTP, Leap FTP, SDFTP, FTP Explorer
Microsoft Windows NT/2000	See listings for Windows 95/98
Microsoft Windows 3.x	Win_FTP, WS_FTP, CU-FTP, WSArchie
Macintosh	Anarchie, Fetch, Freetp
OS/2	Gibbon FTP, FTP-IT, Lynn's Workplace FTP

FTP file transfers occur in a client/server environment. The requesting machine starts one of the clients named in Table 4.2. This generates a request that is forwarded to the targeted FTP server (usually a host on another network). Typically, the request is sent by the client to port 21. For a connection to be established, the targeted file server must be running an FTP server.

FTPD: An FTP Server Daemon

FTPD is the standard FTP server daemon for UNIX. Its function is simple: to reply to connect requests received and to satisfy those requests for file transfers. An FTP daemon comes standard on most distributions of UNIX (for other operating systems, see Table 4.3).

TABLE 4.3 FTP Servers for Various Operating Systems

Operating System	Servers
UNIX	Native (FTPD), WUFTD
Microsoft Windows 95/98	WFTPD, Microsoft FrontPage, WAR FTP Daemon, Vermilion
Microsoft Windows NT/2000	Serv-U, OmniFSPD, Microsoft Internet Information Server
Microsoft Windows 3.x	WinQVT, Serv-U, Beames & Whitside BW Connect, WFTPD FTP Server, WinHTTPD
Macintosh	Netpresenz, FTPd
OS/2	Penguin

FTPD waits for a connection request. When such a request is received, FTPD requests the user login. The user must either provide her valid user login and password or log in anonymously (if the server allows anonymous sessions).

When logged in, the user can download files. In certain instances and if security on the server allows, the user can also upload files.

As with Telnet, FTP is an insecure protocol. It does nothing to encrypt the user ID, password, or any of the files being transferred. Secure Shell provides a more secure method of file transfer via either Secure Copy (SCP) or Secure FTP (SFTP).

FTP uses ports 20 and 21 via TCP.

Simple Mail Transfer Protocol (SMTP)

SMTP is the protocol responsible for email transmission between servers, and the sending of email from clients to servers. Its purpose is stated concisely in RFC 821:

> The objective of Simple Mail Transfer Protocol (SMTP) is to transfer mail reliably and efficiently.

SMTP is an extremely lightweight protocol. Running any SMTP-compliant client, the user sends a request to an SMTP server. The client forwards a series of instructions, indicating that it wants to send mail to a recipient somewhere on the Internet. If the SMTP allows this operation, an affirmative acknowledgment is sent back to the client machine. At that point, the session begins. The client might then forward the recipient's identity, his IP address, and the message (in text) to be sent.

Despite the simple character of SMTP, mail service has been the source of countless security holes. The configuration of an SMTP server can be complex, depending upon the options an administrator needs to support. A combination of SMTP server application bugs, and difficulty in configuration have led to numerous security holes. These security issues are covered in detail later in this book.

Most networked operating systems have SMTP servers available for use. STMP server support is included as sendmail for most UNIX distributions, or part of Internet Information Services for Microsoft Windows.

SMTP typically runs on port 25 via TCP.

▶ Further information on SMTP is available in RFC 821 `http://info.internet.isi.edu:80/in-notes/rfc/files/rfc821.txt`.

Secure Shell Protocol (SSH)

SSH is relatively new to the TCP/IP suite of protocols. Unlike the application protocols we've examined already, SSH has been widely implemented without completing the RFC process. This is largely because of the vast demand for a more secure method of providing services similar to Telnet and FTP.

There are two versions of the SSH protocol, and a number of implementations. The first widely used version of the protocol was SSH1, which was defined in an Internet draft (a pre-RFC document) in 1995. As of this writing, there is an Internet Engineering Task Force working group developing the second generation of SSH. Based upon that group's Internet drafts, a number of SSH2 implementations have been completed.

▶ Information on the IETF SSH working group, along with the latest Internet drafts, can be found at `http://www.ietf.org/html.charters/secsh-charter.html`.

SSH allows you to log in to another computer over a network, to execute commands in a remote machine (like Telnet), and to move files from one machine to another (like FTP). It provides for strong authentication and secure, encrypted communications over otherwise insecure networks. It is intended as a replacement for Telnet and other remote access protocols like rlogin, rsh, and rcp. In SSH2, there is a replacement for FTP as well, called *sftp*.

Secure Shell client implementations exist for a variety of platforms, as shown in Table 4.4.

TABLE 4.4 SSH Clients for Various Operating Systems

Operating System	*Clients*
UNIX	SSH Communications, F-Secure, OpenSSH, Lsh, MindTerm
Microsoft Windows 95/98	SSH Communications, F-Secure, PuTTY, TeraTerm, FiSSH, SecureCRT, Cygwin32, MindTerm
Microsoft Windows NT/2000	Same as 95/98
Macintosh	F-Secure, NiftyTelnet 1.1 SSH, MindTerm
OS/2	MindTerm

Secure Shell server implementations are also available, although not on as many platforms as for clients (see Table 4.5).

TABLE 4.5 SSH Servers for Various Operating Systems

Operating System	*Servers*
UNIX	SSH Communications, F-Secure, OpenSSH, Lsh
Microsoft Windows 95/98	SSH Communications, F-Secure, Cygwin32
Microsoft Windows NT/2000	Same as 95/98

IPsec, IPv6, VPNs, and Looking Ahead

The Internet Protocol discussed in this chapter is version 4. It was developed many years ago and, although it has delivered amazing potential and growth, it really wasn't designed to provide many of the services that we expect from the Internet today. Some of the limitations of IP version 4 (IPv4) that need to be addressed are

- **Limitations on IPv4 addressing.** Because of the explosive growth of the Internet, there is a critical shortage of available IP addresses. As the Internet continues to grow and more devices become Internet enabled, there will be an increased demand for new IP addresses.

- **Lack of prioritization in IPv4.** There is currently no method to prioritize particular kinds of traffic on the Internet. For example, a packet stream that provides real-time audio or video gets the same priority as a packet containing an email message. If packets are a few seconds late delivering real-time audio or video, it is very noticeable. If a few packets arrive later for a non–real-time service such as email, no one will notice.

- **Lack of security in IPv4.** The current version of IP doesn't provide for authentication or the privacy of data transmitted.

Actions have been taken over the past few years to address these issues. The lack of available IPv4 addresses has been temporarily alleviated through the use of address translation techniques, but this will only suffice for a time before addresses are completely used up. In addition, address translation is known to break certain protocols that expect valid, non-changing IP addresses on datagrams.

Prioritization technologies are available for use with IPv4, but are limited to use in local networks. These technologies will not work in the Internet environment, where a central authority is not available to manage the flow of data.

Finally, security needs to be added to the Internet if we expect to be able transmit confidential data (that is, bank accounts, medical records, personal data, and so on), and expect that no one will break into our home and business systems connected to the Internet.

A great deal of effort has been put forth in the area of IPv4 security. IP Security (IPsec) has been developed to offer security services at the IP layer. IPsec provides methods for authentication and encryption of data at the network layer, but they are not universally available. IPsec can be used today to establish Virtual Private Networks (VPNs), which are logical private networks created over the Internet. However, these extensions are not normally available to the average Internet user. In addition, the successes of IPsec extensions do not yet address some of the more unusual aspects of IPv4, such as address translation.

▶ Information on IP security can be found in RFC 2401 at `http://www.ietf.org/rfc/rfc2401.txt`. You can also visit the IP security working group's Web site at `http://www.ietf.org/html.charters/ipsec-charter.html`.

Fortunately, planning has been going on for quite some time to develop the next generation of the Internet Protocol. Enter Internet Protocol version 6 (IPv6)! IPv6 has been a very active area of discussion at the Internet Engineering Task Force, and has generated numerous RFCs over the past few years as planning for the next phase of Internet growth and services continues.

IPv6 promises to alleviate the limitation on IP addresses, add proper flow control and data prioritization, and provide security at the network layer. In addition, Ipv6 will provide nice services such as auto-configuration of networked systems, simplification of datagrams, improved performance, and greater capability for expansion. However, IPv6 is not currently widely deployed, and it will most likely be a few more years before the IPv6 standards are solidified. It will be several years beyond that when Internet providers base their services upon IPv6.

▶ Information on IP version 6 (sometimes called IPng for "next generation") can be found in RFC 2460 (`http://www.ietf.org/rfc/rfc2460.txt`) and by visiting the IP version 6 working group's Web site, `http://www.ietf.org/html.charters/ipngwg-charter.html`.

Summary

TCP/IP makes up the Internet itself. It is a complex collection of hundreds of protocols, and many more are being developed each year. Many of the primary protocols in use on the Internet have been found to have one or more security problems.

In this chapter, you learned about these relevant points about the TCP/IP protocol suite:

- The TCP/IP suite contains all protocols necessary to facilitate data transfer over the Internet.
- The TCP/IP suite provides quick, reliable networking without consuming heavy network resources.
- TCP/IP is implemented on almost all computing platforms.
- Security is lacking in TCP/IP version 4.

Now that you know a little bit about TCP/IP, let's move ahead to a more exciting subject: hackers and crackers.

Hackers and Crackers

IN THIS CHAPTER

The purpose of this chapter is to illustrate the methodology and steps a hacker or cracker employs when attacking a network. It also provides an overview of the System Administration Network Security (SANS) Top 10 vulnerabilities that crackers can exploit.

The Difference Between Hackers and Crackers

In order to understand the methodology of a hacker or cracker, one must understand what a hacker or a cracker is. Internet enthusiasts have argued the difference between hackers and crackers for many years. This chapter contains my contribution to that debate.

If I were forced to define the terms *hacker* and *cracker*, my bottom line would probably be this:

- A *hacker* is a person intensely interested in the arcane and recondite workings of any computer operating system. Hackers are most often programmers. As such, hackers obtain advanced knowledge of operating systems and programming languages. They might discover holes within systems and the reasons for such holes. Hackers constantly seek further knowledge, freely share what they have discovered, and never, ever intentionally damage data.

- A *cracker* is one who breaks into or otherwise violates the system integrity of remote machines with malicious intent. Having gained unauthorized access, crackers destroy vital data, deny legitimate users service, or cause problems for their targets. Crackers can easily be identified because their actions are malicious.

Tools of the Trade

The "tools of the trade" are the means a cracker or hacker might use to penetrate your network. Some of the tools covered are programs, and some of these tools are techniques.

Reconnaissance

When most people hear the word *reconnaissance*, they think of spies and the espionage world. Although, that community does indeed uses reconnaissance, so does the cracker community. What is reconnaissance, and why do crackers use reconnaissance? First, reconnaissance is the process of gathering information about specific target(s). When a good burglar decides to rob a house he will scope out an area to see how often neighbors, cops, and other traffic passes through. This gives the robber a good idea of the time of day he can attack. The same basic philosophy holds true for a cracker when she wants to attack a network or Web site.

When a cracker decides she wants to attack a network, there are many "recon" tools at her disposal. Let's look at a few of them and see how they work.

Social Engineering

The first and probably the most underrated tool available is social engineering. *Social engineering* involves tricking, conning, or manipulating people into providing information detrimental to a company, organization, or a person. This type of information can be used to help plan, organize, or execute an attack.

> **NOTE**
>
> Ira Winkler wrote an excellent book called *Corporate Espionage*. This book covers social engineering along with many other tactics used in obtaining information. It also talks about how to protect yourself against these types of attacks. It was published by Prima Publishing (ISBN 0-7615-0840-6). For more on Ira ,you can go to `http://www.thetrainingco.com/html/BioIraWinkler.html`.

How does social engineering work? A good example is through a help desk. Cracker A wants to attack ABC123 inc., a computer software company. Cracker A wants to find out usernames, passwords, and maybe even some security measures ABC123 has in place. Cracker A begins by calling ABC123's main number, explains to the secretary that he is new to the company, he works off-site, and he needs the help desk number in order to set up his account and password. The secretary provides him with the number. Cracker A then calls up the help desk number, explaining to the person on the phone what the situation is and asks for a username, a password, and how can he get access to the network from the outside. Help Desk Worker B happily provides this information within seconds, not once questioning his request. (Why not? Most help desk operations I have seen stress customer service. "Remember: Never anger a customer.")

That simple scenario can provide the attacker with enough information to make an attack much easier to pull off without being detected. Other techniques that are related to social engineering are

- **Dumpster Diving.** A person goes through a dumpster or trash can looking for "trash" that contains information, such as an IP address, old passwords, and quite possibly a map of the network. Although this technique is often a dirty one, it is very effective.
- **Impersonations.** A cracker pretends to be someone important and use that authority to obtain the information he is looking for.

These social engineering techniques are effective, and there are many more that are beyond the scope of this book. Keep in mind that people still use these techniques, and they are a threat to your security and your company's security.

Port Scanners and Passive Operating System Identification

This section provides a technical overview of port scanners and sniffers, along with details regarding the art of passive operating system identification.

Port scanners are programs that check a computer's TCP/IP stack for ports that are in the LISTEN state. As you learned in the previous chapter, TCP/IP combines many protocols, enabling communication on the Internet. The TCP/IP protocol suite consist of 65,535 ports. Ports 1 through 1023 are considered "well known" and, on many computer systems, only users with root/admin privileges can use these ports. Ports 1024 through 49151 are called *registered ports*, and ports 49152 through 65535 are considered dynamic and/or private ports.

▶ Find the PORT NUMBERS list online at `http://www.isi.edu/in-notes/iana/assignments/port-numbers`.

The Transmission Control Protocol is covered by RFC 793, which defines many standards that socket programmers need to follow. It also defines how TCP will react to certain packets (that is, FIN, ACK, and SYN). In order to understand port scanners and how they work, a person needs to understand RFC 793.

RFC 793 (`http://www.ietf.org/rfc/rfc0793.txt?number=793`) defines how TCP (Transmission Control Protocol) will react to the FIN, ACK, and SYN packets:

> If the state is CLOSED (that is, Transmission Control Block does not exist) then all data in the incoming segment is discarded. An incoming segment containing a RESET (RST) is discarded. An incoming segment not containing a RST causes a RST to be sent in response. The acknowledgment and sequence field values are selected to make the reset sequence acceptable to the TCP that sent the offending segment.

> If the state is LISTEN then first check for an RST, An incoming RST should be ignored. Second check for an ACK. Any acknowledgment is bad if it arrives on a connection still in the LISTEN state. An acceptable reset segment should be formed for any arriving ACK-bearing segment. Third check for a SYN, if the SYN bit is set, check the security. If the security/compartment on the incoming segment does not exactly match the security/compartment in the TCB then send a reset and return.

What this tells us is how listening and closed ports respond to certain TCP flags. Knowing this, programmers can write programs that go out and identify open and closed ports. These programs are considered port scanner(s).

Let's look at some "famous" port scanners and see what they can and cannot do.

▶ To find out more information on TCP/IP, see the RFCs online at `http://www.ietf.org/rfc/rfc0793.txt?number=793` and `http://www.ietf.org/rfc/rfc0793.txt?number=791`.

For some great information on TCP/IP fingerprinting, see the following:
`http://www.insecure.org/nmap/nmap-fingerprinting-article.html`

NMAP

NMAP is probably the *most* popular port scanner being used and actively developed today. The brainchild of Fyodor (www.insecure.org), NMAP has grown through the active participation of the open source community. NMAP allows the user many options in scanning. Listing 5.1 shows us the results of nmap –h. This is a great starting point for nmap. If you need more details on nmap, see the man page (available online at http://www.insecure.org/nmap/nmap_manpage.html).

LISTING 5.1   nmap -h Results

```
Nmap V. 2.54BETA7 Usage: nmap [Scan Type(s)] [Options] <host or net list>
Some Common Scan Types ('*' options require root privileges)
-sT TCP connect() port scan (default)
* -sS TCP SYN stealth port scan (best all-around TCP scan)
* -sU UDP port scan
-sP ping scan (Find any reachable machines)
* -sF,-sX,-sN Stealth FIN, Xmas, or Null scan (experts only)
-sR/-I RPC/Identd scan (use with other scan types)
Some Common Options (none are required; most can be combined):
* -O Use TCP/IP fingerprinting to guess remote operating system
-p <range> ports to scan. Example range: '1-1024,1080,6666,31337'
-F Only scans ports listed in nmap-services
-v Verbose. Its use is recommended. Use twice for greater effect.
-P0 Don't ping hosts (needed to scan www.microsoft.com and others)
* -Ddecoy_host1,decoy2[,...] Hide scan using many decoys
-T <Paranoid|Sneaky|Polite|Normal|Aggressive|Insane> General timing policy
-n/-R Never do DNS resolution/Always resolve [default: sometimes resolve]
-oN/-oX/-oG <logfile> Output normal/XML/grepable scan logs to <logfile>
-iL <inputfile> Get targets from file; Use '-' for stdin
* -S <your_IP>/-e <devicename> Specify source address or network interface
--interactive Go into interactive mode (then press h for help)
Example: nmap -v -sS -O www.my.com 192.168.0.0/16 '192.88-90.*.*'
```

Listing 5.1 shows us how easy NMAP is to configure and what options are available for scanning. Let's take a look at a few switches, discuss what they do, and how they can be used in reconnaissance.

The –sT switch is probably the loudest switch we will cover (not as stealthy as others). This switch tells NMAP to make a complete connection with the targeted computer. This type of scan is easy to detect and probably won't be used if an attacker is serious about performing reconnaissance on a computer system.

> **NOTE**
>
> In the summer of 2000, a group of SANS analysts put together a book about intrusion detection signatures, called *Intrusion Signatures and Analysis*. Published by New Riders (ISBN 0-7357-1063-5), this book is a great reference for anyone who wants to dig deeper into intrusion detection and attack signatures.

The -sF switch sends FIN packets to the targeted computer. How does this work? When a computer receives a FIN, it has a few options in how to react:

- If the port is in the LISTEN state, the computer will not reply.
- If the port is in the CLOSED state, the computer will respond with a RESET.
- If there has been a connection, the computer will begin breaking the connection. (Hint: We don't care about this option right now.)

The computer's response tells NMAP what ports are open when using the -sF switch. Listing 5.2 shows us the results of an -sF scan from a user standpoint.

LISTING 5.2   nmap -sF User Results

```
Starting nmap V. 2.54BETA7 ( www.insecure.org/nmap/ )
Interesting ports on (192.168.1.3):
(The 4000 ports scanned but not shown here are in state: closed)
Port    State   Service
47017/tcp       open    unknown
TCP Sequence Prediction: Class=random positive increments
Difficulty=3980866 (Good luck!)
Remote operating system guess: Linux 2.1.122 - 2.2.16
Nmap run completed -- 1 IP address (1 host up) scanned in 5 seconds
```

This scan ran against a Linux machine that had the t0rn rootkit (port 47017 is a dead give-away) running, and these are the results:

```
20:00:48.813047 > 192.168.1.5.47257 >
➡192.168.1.1.473: F 0:0(0) win 1024 (ttl 48, id 31728)
          4500 0028 7bf0 0000 3006 8b89 c0a8 0105
          c0a8 0101 b899 01d9 0000 0000 0000 0000
          5001 0400 6e1a 0000
20:00:48.813153 > 192.168.1.5.47257 >
➡192.168.1.1.663: F 0:0(0) win 1024 (ttl 48, id 56669)
```

```
        4500 0028 dd5d 0000 3006 2a1c c0a8 0105
        c0a8 0101 b899 0297 0000 0000 0000 0000
        5001 0400 6d5c 0000
20:00:48.813188 > 192.168.1.5.47257 >
➥192.168.1.1.1458: F 0:0(0) win 1024 (ttl 48, id 23854)
        4500 0028 5d2e 0000 3006 aa4b c0a8 0105
        c0a8 0101 b899 05b2 0000 0000 0000 0000
        5001 0400 6a41 0000
```

If a person was running a sniffer, they would see this code. What you don't see here are the resets being sent back by the ports being scanned. This technique is used by many crackers to perform reconnaissance against target(s). This scan is much harder to detect then the –sT switch covered earlier.

The –sS switch uses SYN packets to determine whether a port or group of ports is open. This scan is commonly referred to as the *half-open* scan. Why? Well, NMAP sends a SYN packet to a port. If the port is open, it will respond with a SYN|ACK. If NMAP receives the SYN|ACK, it will respond with a RESET. Therefore, if you send half-open packets, your chance of being detected decreases (in theory) Many crackers use this scanning technique to check for open ports because, sometimes, this activity is logged. In today's world, though, many firewalls and IDSs do log these attempts.

The final switch covered is the –sX switch, NMAP's "X-mas tree" packet, in which NMAP sets the FIN, URG, and PUSH flags. Under normal conditions, this is not a normal flag combination. Normally, a person would see a FIN, URG, and ACK but not a FIN, URG, and PUSH combination. The reason for this flag combination is simple: Crackers can bypass some firewalls and intrusion detection systems with it.

How does this relate to reconnaissance? NMAP is a great tool in performing reconnaissance. With all the switches and options available, it is difficult for a firewall administrator or IDS analyst to positively identify all the possible scans available with NMAP.

▶ Dying for more information on NMAP? See the following URL: www.insecure.org.

HPING2

Another great port scanner used today for reconnaissance is HPING2. This is probably one of my favorite tools to have because it is very configurable. Table 5.1 shows us many of the options available with HPING2.

▶ Information on HPING2 to can be found at www.kyuzz.org/antirez/hping2.html.

TABLE 5.1   HPING2 Options

Usage	HPING Host	Options
-h	--help	Show this help
-v	--version	Show version
-c	--count	Packet count
-i	--interval	Wait (uX for *X* microseconds, for example, -i u1000)
-n	--numeric	Numeric output
-q	--quiet	Quiet
-I	--interface	Interface name (otherwise, default routing interface)
-V	--verbose	Verbose mode
-D	--debug	Debugging info
-z	--bind	Bind Ctrl+Z to ttl (default to dst port)
-Z	--unbind	Unbind Ctrl+Z
		Modes
Default	default mode	TCP
-0	--rawip	RAW IP mode
-1	--icmp	ICMP mode
-2	--udp	UDP mode
-9	--listen	Listen mode
		IP
-a	--spoof	Spoof source address
-t	--ttl	ttl (default 64)
-N	--id	id (default random)
-W	--winid	Use win* id byte ordering
-r	--rel	Relativize id field (to estimate host traffic)
-f	--frag	Split packets in more frag (can pass weak acl)
-x	--morefrag	Set more fragments flag
-y	--dontfrag	Set dont fragment flag
-g	--fragoff	Set the fragment offset
-m	--mtu	Set virtual mtu; implies --frag if packet size > mtu
-o	--tos	Type of service (default 0x00); try --tos help
-G	--rroute	Includes RECORD_ROUTE option and display the route buffer
-H	--ipproto	Set the IP protocol field, only in RAW IP mode

TABLE 5.1 Continued

Usage	HPING Host	Options
		ICMP
-C	--icmptype	ICMP type (default echo request), try --icmptype help
-K	--icmpcode	ICMP code (default 0)
	--icmp-help	Display help for other ICMP options
		UDP/TCP
-s	--baseport	Base source port (default random)
-p	--destport	[+][+]<port> destination port (default 0) Ctrl+Z inc/dec
-k	--keep	Keep still source port
-w	--win	winsize (default 64)
-O	--tcpoff	Set fake TCP data offset (instead of tcphdrlen/4)
-Q	--seqnum	Show only TCP sequence number
-b	--badcksum	Send packets with a bad IP checksum
-M	--setseq	Set TCP sequence number
-L	--setack	Set TCP ack
-F	--fin	Set FIN flag
-S	--syn	Set SYN flag
-R	--rst	Set RST flag
-P	--push	Set PUSH flag
-A	--ack	Set ACK flag
-U	--urg	Set URG flag
-X	--xmas	Set X unused flag (0x40)
-Y	--ymas	Set Y unused flag (0x80)
	--tcpexitcode	Sse last tcp->th_flags as exit code
		TS
-d	--data	Data size (default is 0)
-E	--file	Data from file
-e	--sign	Add 'signature'
-j	--dump	Dump packets in hex
-J	--print	Dump printable characters
-B	--safe	Enable "safe" protocol
-u	--end	Tell you when --file reached EOF and prevent rewind
-T	--traceroute	(Implies --bind) traceroute mode

5

You can see from the help file how configurable HPING2 really is. A cracker can modify almost any byte in the TCP/IP header. This enables a cracker to really become creative with her scanning techniques in performing reconnaissance. This tool also enables the cracker to insert crafted data into the packet. This means that the cracker could insert malicious code of any kind—buffer overflows, Trojans, and so on— into a packet and use it to penetrate networks. If you don't have HPING2, I recommend downloading it and giving it a test drive.

There are many more great port scanners out there then what we have covered here. Port scanners provide the cracker with a tool that "knocks" on the door of computer networks. This also gives the cracker an idea of what operating system and services the targeted network is running. With this type of information, the cracker can then proceed to her favorite exploit toolkit and proceed to penetrate the targeted network. These tools can be and should be used by the computer professional to evaluate systems. By using these tools, a systems administrator can identify vulnerabilities before an attacker does.

Passive Operating System Identification Fingerprinting

Passive OS fingerprinting is a technique that is gaining popularity in both the cracker world as well as in the security world. Passive OS fingerprinting allows a person to identify an operating system by analyzing its TCP/IP stack. This technique is as stealth as stealth can get because all you need is a packet sniffer and some time. An attacker using a sniffer does not have to worry about sending strange packets to determine what OS he is up against.

Almost all operating systems have default settings, including settings for TCP/IP. An example of this is Linux. If you look at `/proc/sys/net/ipv4` in Listing 5.3, you'll find a wide range of settings that contain default information that the system uses in its daily task(s). Listing 5.3 shows the TCP/IP parameters in Linux.

LISTING 5.3   `/proc/sys/net/ipv4`

```
Conf
icmp_destunreach_rate
icmp_echo_ignore_all
icmp_echo_ignore_broadcasts
icmp_echoreply_rate
icmp_ignore_bogus_error_responses
icmp_paramprob_rate
icmp_timeexceed_rate
igmp_max_memberships
ip_always_defrag
ip_autoconfig
ip_default_ttl
ip_dynaddr
```

LISTING 5.3   Continued

```
ip_forward
ip_local_port_range
ip_masq_debug
ip_no_pmtu_disc
ipfrag_high_thresh
ipfrag_low_thresh
ipfrag_time
neigh
route
tcp_fin_timeout
tcp_keepalive_probes
tcp_keepalive_time
tcp_max_ka_probes
tcp_max_syn_backlog
tcp_retrans_collapse
tcp_retries1
tcp_retries2
tcp_rfc1337
tcp_sack
tcp_stdurg
tcp_syn_retries
tcp_syncookies
tcp_timestamps
tcp_window_scaling
```

Let's look at a few of these parameters and determine what they do and how they affect the operating system.

- `ip_default-ttl`: This parameter sets the default time-to-live value to 64. It can be changed on a Linux box by `echo 128 >> ip_default_ttl`.

- `ip_forward`: Although this parameter does not directly affect passive OS fingerprinting, it does have a big effect on OS security. By default, `ip_forward` is set to 0, which disables IP forwarding. Setting it to 1 enables IP forwarding.

- `ip_local_port_range`: This parameter identifies the default source port range that Linux will use. Normally, this is set to `1024-4999`. This is good information to know if you are attempting to determine whether a packet is good or bad.

- `tcp_sack`: This parameter lets the operating system know whether it supports the Selective Acknowledgment standard (RFC 2883). By default (Linux), this is set to 1 (supports this standard).

- `tcp_timestamps`: This parameter lets the operating system know whether it supports the timestamp function. By default (Linux), this is set to 1.

- `tcp_window_scaling`: This parameter lets the operating system know whether it supports the window scaling function. This option is used to decrease congestion. By default (Linux), this is set to 1.

Listing 5.3 shows only the parameters that are related to passive OS fingerprinting. Although we have only covered Linux default settings so far, every OS has its own set of default settings. A good example is the Windows platform; Windows 98, NT, and 2000 all use default TTL of 128.

▶ There is, however, a whole world using ICMP. To check this out go to `www.sys-security.com`.

Let's look at a few other operating systems and their default TCP/IP settings:

- Microsoft (98, NT)

  Packet size (just headers) = 44 bytes (default)

  SYN or SYN|ACK packets = Sets the Don't Fragment flag and the Maximum Segment Size (MSS)flag

  TTL = 128

- Microsoft (2000)

  Packet size (just headers) = 48 bytes (default)

  SYN or SYN|ACK packets = Sets the Don't Fragment (DF)flag, Maximum Segment Size (MSS)flag, two (2) NOPs, and the Selective Acknowledgment flag.

  TTL = 128

- Linux (Red Hat 6.2)

  Packet size (just headers) = 60 bytes (default)

  SYN or SYN|ACK packets = Sets the Don't Fragment (DF)flag, Maximum Segment Size (MSS)flag, NOPs, Selective Acknowledgment flag, Timestamp, Window Scaling (wscale). These hold true for initial SYN. SYN|ACK Linux responds according to the computer that made the initial SYN.

  TL = 64, on a RESET packet the TTL is 255

Knowing this, you can identify operating systems by looking at network traffic. One thing to keep in mind is that, if a sys-admin or cracker changes any of the parameters, it will throw off your analysis. Therefore, passive OS fingerprinting is not 100% accurate, but, then again, nothing is. Listing 5.4 shows two packets and will help us identify an OS, using passive fingerprinting.

LISTING 5.4   Identifying Operating Systems

```
15:59:52.533502 > my_isp.net.1100 > 134.11.235.232.www:
➥S 325233392:325233392(0) win 32120
➥<mss 1460,sackOK,timestamp 88950 0,nop,wscale 0> (DF) (ttl 64, id 505)
          4500 003c 01f9 4000 4006 0522 xxxx xxxx
          860b ebe8 044c 0050 1362 aaf0 0000 0000
          a002 7d78 7887 0000 0204 05b4 0402 080a
          0001 5b76 0000 0000 0103 0300

16:00:14.188756 >my_isp.net.1105 >
➥134.11.235.232.www: R 346737591:346737591(0) win 0 (ttl 255, id 544)
          4500 0028 0220 0000 ff06 860e xxxx xxxx
          860b ebe8 0451 0050 14aa cbb7 0000 0000
          5004 0000 973c 0000
```

In Listing 5.4, you see two packets. The first is a SYN packet, and the second is a RST packet. Looking at the SYN packet, notice some important indicators:

- The SYN has a TTL of 64.

- The SYN sets its `mss`, `sackOK`, `nop`, and `wscale parameters` and the `DF` flag. Also, pay close attention to the header size (3c = 60 bytes).

- Look at the source port as well. Port 1100 falls with in the default source port range of 1024 through 4999.

These indicators point to…LINUX. That's right, the OS we were looking at in Listing 5.4 is coming from a Linux machine. Let's take a brief look at the RST packet. First, look at the TTL (255). When Red Hat Linux sends an RST, it will use a default TTL of 255, whereas, when it is trying to establish a connection, it uses a TTL of 64. Another characteristic of Linux RST packets is their size. Normally, a Red Hat packet is 60 bytes in length. When setting the RST flag, RH Linux has a packet length of only 40 bytes.

How does OS fingerprinting and Linux tie back into reconnaissance? If a cracker uses any of the previously mentioned techniques, he can obtain very valuable information about a computer network. That type of information includes network mapping, IP addresses, patch levels, and discovery of different operating systems.

Exploits and the SANS Top 10

In this section, we will cover the exploits run by crackers. We will also look at the SANS 10 Most Critical Internet Security Threats list.

5

Exploits

Reconnaissance is vital in figuring out what is open and what is closed. The next step for a cracker is to actually break in to a computer network. Crackers do this by exploiting weaknesses in operating systems services.

There are many exploits out there; finding the right exploit can be a headache. Not all exploits are created equal. By this, I mean that most exploits are operating system dependent. Just because there is a line printer exploit for Linux doesn't mean it would work on Solaris, and vice versa.

▶ If you want to find out the latest in exploits and vulnerabilities, subscribe to the BUGTRAQ
   mailing list at `http://www.securityfocus.com/forums/bugtraq/intro.html`.

To help explain what an exploit is and looks like when it is being executed, I have included in this section the output from an exploit and some packets involved in the exploit. First, a little background on the exploit I decided to run. In late 2000, probing activity increased on port 515 (line printer port). This was related to an exploit in the Red Hat 7.0 line printer daemon. At the time of this writing, I am still seeing many probes for this service on my firewall.

▶ If you want to see the exploit I used, it can be found at `www.netcat.it`.

Here are the listings promised along with some play by play for each:

```
+++ www.netcat.it remote exploit for LPRng/lpd

+++ Exploit information
+++ Victim: 192.168.1.25
+++ Type: 0 - RedHat 7.0 - Guinesss
+++ Eip address: 0xbffff3ec
+++ Shellcode address: 0xbffff7f2
+++ Position: 300
+++ Alignment: 2
+++ Offset 0

+++ Attacking 192.168.1.25 with our format string
+++ Brute force man, relax and enjoy the ride ;>
```

From this output, we know that the exploit is attacking a Red Hat 7.0 line printer (Type 0-RedHat7.0 -Guinesess). Want to see how tcpdump views this attack?

```
18:34:19.991789 > 192.168.1.5.2894 >
➥192.168.1.25.printer: S 4221747912:4221747912(0)
➥win 32120 <mss 1460,sackOK,timestamp 4058996 0,nop,wscale 0>
➥(DF) (ttl 64, id 11263)
              4500 003c 2bff 4000 4006 8b4e c0a8 0105
              c0a8 0119 0b4e 0203 fba2 c2c8 0000 0000
              a002 7d78 8bb1 0000 0204 05b4 0402 080a
              003d ef74 0000 0000 0103 0300
```

```
18:34:19.993434 < 192.168.1.25.printer >
➥192.168.1.5.2894: S 397480959:397480959(0) ack 4221747913 win 32120
➥<mss 1460,sackOK,timestamp 393475 4058996,nop,wscale 0>
➥(DF) (ttl 64, id 3278)
            4500 003c 0cce 4000 4006 aa7f c0a8 0119
            c0a8 0105 0203 0b4e 17b1 13ff fba2 c2c9
            a012 7d78 5ee7 0000 0204 05b4 0402 080a
            0006 0103 003d ef74 0103 0300
18:34:19.993514 > 192.168.1.5.2894 > 192.168.1.25.printer: . 1:1(0)
➥ ack 1 win 32120 <nop,nop,timestamp 4058996 393475> (DF) (ttl 64, id 11264)
            4500 0034 2c00 4000 4006 8b55 c0a8 0105
            c0a8 0119 0b4e 0203 fba2 c2c9 17b1 1400
            8010 7d78 8dac 0000 0101 080a 003d ef74
            0006 0103


18:34:19.999662 < 192.168.1.25.printer > 192.168.1.5.2894: P 1:31(30)
➥ack 1 win 32120 <nop,nop,timestamp 393476 4058996> (DF) (ttl 64, id 3279)
            4500 0052 0ccf 4000 4006 aa68 c0a8 0119
            c0a8 0105 0203 0b4e 17b1 1400 fba2 c2c9
            8018 7d78 3e5b 0000 0101 080a 0006 0104
            003d ef74 6c70 643a 203a 204d 616c 666f
            726d 6564 2066 726f 6d20 6164 6472 6573
            730a
18:34:19.999686 > 192.168.1.5.2894 >
➥192.168.1.25.printer: . 1:1(0) ack 31 win 32120
➥<nop,nop,timestamp 4058997 393476> (DF) (ttl 64, id 11265)
            4500 0034 2c01 4000 4006 8b54 c0a8 0105
            c0a8 0119 0b4e 0203 fba2 c2c9 17b1 141e
            8010 7d78 8d8c 0000 0101 080a 003d ef75
            0006 0104
18:34:20.000863 < 192.168.1.25.printer >
➥192.168.1.5.2894: F 31:31(0) ack 1 win 32120
➥<nop,nop,timestamp 393476 4058997> (DF) (ttl 64, id 3280)
            4500 0034 0cd0 4000 4006 aa85 c0a8 0119
            c0a8 0105 0203 0b4e 17b1 141e fba2 c2c9
            8011 7d78 8d8b 0000 0101 080a 0006 0104
            003d ef75
18:34:20.000878 > 192.168.1.5.2894 > 192.168.1.25.printer: . 1:1(0)
➥ack 32 win 32120 <nop,nop,timestamp 4058997 393476> (DF) (ttl 64, id 11266)
            4500 0034 2c02 4000 4006 8b53 c0a8 0105
            c0a8 0119 0b4e 0203 fba2 c2c9 17b1 141f
            8010 7d78 8d8b 0000 0101 080a 003d ef75
            0006 0104
18:34:20.049095 > 192.168.1.5.2894 > 192.168.1.25.printer: P 1:424(423)
➥ ack 32 win 32120 <nop,nop,timestamp 4059002 393476> (DF) (ttl 64, id 11267)
            4500 01db 2c03 4000 4006 89ab c0a8 0105
            c0a8 0119 0b4e 0203 fba2 c2c9 17b1 141f
```

```
8018 7d78 54c5 0000 0101 080a 003d ef7a
0006 0104 4242 f0ff ffbf f1ff ffbf f2ff
ffbf f3ff ffbf 5858 5858 5858 5858 5858
5858 5858 5858 5858 252e 3137 3675 2533
3030 246e 252e 3133 7525 3330 3124 6e25
2e32 3533 7525 3330 3224 6e25 2e31 3932
```

Let's look at what is happening here. First, we see 192.168.1.5 and 192.168.1.25 attempting to make a connection using the TCP typical three-way handshake. In the next sequence of events, we see 192.168.1.5 attempting to run the exploit against 192.168.1.25. Finally, we see the 192.168.1.5 pushing 423 bytes of data to 192.168.1.25. The exploit continues this for a while until it is able to brute-force the exploit.

When this exploit worked, 192.168.1.25 provided me with a shell (not that I needed it), and I could do what ever I wanted.

Exploits are the way crackers break into systems. To protect yourself against them, you will have to update your operating system with patches. (This goes for all systems.)

The SANS Top 10

The SANS Top 10 Most Critical Internet Security Threats is a list of the most common exploits found on computer networks. What makes this list so valuable is the fact that the group System Administration Network Security provides a list of the related CVE entries (Common Vulnerabilities and Exposures), so that a person can do more research if necessary. This list was compiled by SANS with the help of many security experts and the security community.

▶ The CVE database can be found at http://www.cve.mitre.org/.

▶ To read more on the SANS Top 10, visit http://www.sans.org/topten.htm.

The first exploit listed on the Top 10 is BIND. BIND is a program used for DNS servers (to help resolve names to addresses) and is used throughout the Internet. In the past couple years, major holes have been found in many versions of BIND. It is vital for anyone who runs BIND to always keep up on the latest vulnerabilities. On Jan. 29, 2001, Network Associates Incorporated announced that it discovered more vulnerabilities relating to BIND version 4 and BIND version 8. Patches have been released and can be downloaded from your operating system vendor's Web site.

▶ If you would like to read the paper released by NAI, you can get it here: http://www.pgp.com/ aboutus/press/pr_template.asp?PR=/PressMedia/01282001-A.asp&Sel=900 or you can read the CERT advisory at http://www.cert.org/advisories/CA-2001-02.html.

The second exploit in SANS Top 10 is Vulnerable CGI programs. These have been around for years and are the main reason for most of the hack Web sites that receive mainstream attention.

Many of these CGI-BIN programs leave sample programs after installation that are vulnerable and allow a malicious user to obtain "root" access. When an attacker obtains that level of access, he can do as he pleases (include changing the Web site). I provided some links to obtain more information on CGI-BIN attacks. This list is *not* comprehensive; please dig a little further if you think you are vulnerable.

▶ More information can be found on CGI-BIN attacks from `http://www.cert.org/advisories/` `CA-1997-24.html`, `http://www.cert.org/advisories/CA-1996-11.html`, or `http://www.cert.org/advisories/CA-1997-07.html`.

The third exploit is vulnerable Remote Procedure Calls (RPCs). RPCs allow C programs to make procedure calls on other machines across the network. Most vendors provide patches to help tighten down RPC services. Nevertheless, the best policy regarding this service is, if you don't need it, then kill it. You can run `ps-ef|grep rpc`, find the Process ID (PID), and then run `kill -9 PID`. You can also disable RPC services at start upon most UNIX operating systems by changing the startup file (located at /etc/rc.d/) from an S (start up) to K (kill). You can find out what RPC programs are running by using `rpcinfo -p`.

▶ More information can be found on RPC attacks from `http://www.cert.org/incident_notes/` `IN-99-04.html`.

The fourth exploit on the SANS Top 10 list is vulnerable Remote Data Service security holes in IIS. (To be honest, I am surprised Microsoft doesn't have more vulnerabilities in the Top 10.) I can sum up dealing with this exploit really quick… Patch your IIS.

▶ More information can be found on RDS security holes from `http://www.wiretrip.net/rfp/` `p/doc.asp?id=29&iface=2`.

The fifth exploit is vulnerable sendmail and MIME attacks. These vulnerabilities are related to buffer overflows as well as pipe attacks that enable immediate root compromise. There are a couple of ways to secure these problem areas. The first is to maintain the correct patches for your sendmail/mail servers. If you do not need to run either of these services, you can disable them (follow the same procedures as spelled out for RPC).

▶ More information can be found on sendmail security holes from `http://www.cert.org/` `advisories/CA-97.05.sendmail.html`.

The sixth exploit is vulnerable sadmind and mountd. This vulnerability applies to Linux machines as well as Solaris machines.

▶ For more information on sadmind and mountd security holes, visit `http://www.cert.org/` `advisories/CA-99-16-sadmind.html` or `http://www.cert.org/advisories/CA-1998.12.` `mountd.html`.

The seventh exploit in the Top 10 is global file sharing, using NetBIOS Ports 135–139). This is probably the biggest security problem users have if they are connected to a cable modem or DSL. Most do not understand the concept of file sharing and leave file sharing enabled. Another problem is Napster. Although Napster is not listed here, it does require people to share directories and that can lead to sharing more then necessary. How do we correct it? These suggestions are from the SANS site `http://www.sans.org/topten.htm`:

A. When sharing mounted drives, ensure only required directories are shared.

B. For added security, allow sharing only to specific IP addresses because DNS names can be spoofed.

C. For Windows systems, ensure all shares are protected with strong passwords.

D. For Windows NT systems, prevent anonymous enumeration of users, groups, system configuration and Registry keys via the "null session" connection.

Block inbound connections to the NetBIOS Session Service (tcp 139) at the router or the NT host. Consider implementing the RestrictAnonymous Registry key for Internet-connected hosts in standalone or non-trusted domain environments.

The eighth exploit is weak passwords. Need I say any more? In any form of risk assessment, one of the most common vulnerabilities I see is weak passwords. When coming up with a password, remember to follow these simple guidelines:

• Make sure that the password is eight characters in length.

• Make sure that the password is a combination of numbers, special characters, and alphanumeric characters.

• Pick a password that is not in the dictionary.

▶ For more information on password strengths, visit `http://www.cert.org/tech_tips/passwd_file_protection.html`.

The ninth exploit is IMAP and POP buffer overflow vulnerabilities or incorrect configuration. Again, the best way to secure yourself from these attacks is to disable the service if you do not need it. Also, apply the latest patches (if you need to run the service).

▶ For more information on IMAP and POP security please visit `http://www.cert.org/advisories/CA-1998.09.imapd.html`, `http://www.cert.org/advisories/CA-1998.08.qpopper_vul.html`, or `http://www.cert.org/advisories/CA-1997.09.imap_pop.html`.

The final exploit in the SANS Top 10 is Default SNMP community strings set to `"public"` and `"private"`. Along with the weak passwords, this vulnerability can be controlled by basic administration.

▶ For more information on SNMP and community strings, see `http://www.cisco.com/univercd/cc/td/doc/cisintwk/ito_doc/snmp.htm#xtocid210315`.

Keep in mind that these are not the only vulnerabilities on the Web. A cracker can use any exploit he has in his bag of tricks against you and your network.

Summary

This chapter covered a variety of topics including passive OS fingerprinting, social engineering, tools, and the SANS Top 10. Hopefully, from this chapter you can grasp the thinking and the process a cracker will go through to obtain access to a network. With the world becoming one, through the Internet and cybercrime on the rise, protecting yourself and your information will become more challenging. Knowing how a hacker/cracker works can assist you in protecting yourself against these people. As Bruce Scheiner of CTO Counterpane Internet Systems says, "Security is a process, not a product." As for the products you do have, remember to apply the latest patches and disable the services you don't need.

The State of the Net: A World at War

IN THIS CHAPTER

Since 1973, Internet sites have been breached on a regular basis. Although it's difficult to compare the Internet of the late '70s and '80s with the network known as the Internet today, it is safe to say that the attack trends are not decreasing. This chapter was designed to give the reader a tour of some of the chaos that exists on the Internet today, as well as to provide some insight into what could possibly lie ahead. We will examine the fact that every type of organization in existence has been broken into, ranging from educational institutions to corporations to the U.S. Department of Defense (DoD). There is evidence that Internet-based attacks could be used to cripple organizations and government agencies for political purposes. Today, security technologies are complex, but the Internet is still easily cracked. This chapter discusses who can, and has been, broken into and why.

Hacking, Cracking, and Other Malicious Behavior

Although most people have succumbed to using the term *hacked* when they refer to an illegal intrusions, the term *cracked* might be more proper. *Cracked* refers to that condition in which the victim network has suffered an unauthorized intrusion. There are various degrees of this condition. Here are a few examples:

- The intruder gains access and nothing more (*access* being defined as simple unauthorized entry on a network that requires—at a minimum—a login and password).

- The intruder gains access and destroys, corrupts, or otherwise alters data.

- The intruder gains access and seizes control of a compartmentalized portion of the system or the whole system, perhaps denying access even to privileged users.

- The intruder does not gain access, but instead forges messages from your system. (Folks often do this to send unsolicited mail or spam.)

- The intruder does not gain access, but instead implements malicious procedures that cause that network to fail, reboot, hang, or otherwise manifest an inoperable condition, either permanently or temporarily. These type of attacks are usually classified as Denial of Service (DoS) attacks.

Modern security techniques have made cracking more difficult. However, the distance between the word *difficult* and the word *impossible* is still wide. Today, crackers have access to a wealth of security information, much of which is freely available on the Internet. The balance of knowledge between crackers and bona fide security specialists is not greatly disproportionate. In fact, it is arguable that each side possesses components that the other side lacks, which makes the balance all the more interesting.

This chapter shows that cracking is a common activity—so common that assurances from anyone that the Internet is secure should be viewed with extreme suspicion. To drive that point home, I will begin with governmental entities. After all, defense and intelligence agencies form the basis of our national security infrastructure. They, more than any other group, must be secure.

Governments at War

If I asked you who your friends were, you'd answer without hesitation. That's because human relationships are based on mutual interest and affection, simple qualities that are largely subjective. If I asked you to identify friends of the United States, again, you would answer without hesitation. In that instance, however, your answer would probably be dead wrong.

In diplomatic circles, the word *ally* describes any foreign nation that shares common territorial, ideological, or economic interests with your own. We call this or that foreign state an ally based on various treaties, a handful of assurances, and on occasion, binding contracts.

For example, we count France and Israel as allies. Each occupies a geographical region that we have interest in protecting, and each shares with us a vision of democracy. (The French stood with us against the Nazis, and we have long supported Israel in the repatriation of Jews driven from Soviet Russia.) If these nations are our friends, why are they spying on us?

In the last decade, the United States has been the target of widespread technological and industrial espionage, often perpetrated by friends and allies. In 1997, the American Society for Industrial Security identified several nations that routinely conduct industrial espionage against the United States. Of those, these nations were most prominent:

- France
- Germany
- Israel
- China
- South Korea

Four are considered U.S. allies.

CAUTION

Do you fly Air France? If so, watch what you say on the telephone. Air France has been caught intercepting electronic communications of American tourists in transit to Europe.

France's espionage activities are particularly prominent. On January 12, 1998, the *Los Angeles Times* reported that French intelligence had penetrated some 70 U.S. corporations, including

Boeing and Texas Instruments. Like most nations spying on us, France employs these generic intelligence-gathering techniques:

- Eavesdropping
- Penetrating computer networks
- Stealing proprietary information

Do you still believe that France is an ally?

You're probably shocked that I would say all this. Let me take a different angle. If you're a French, Israeli, German, or South Korean national, know this: The U.S. government spies on your countrymen 24 hours a day, 7 days a week. In fact, every industrialized country does it. That's simply the way it is; nations have their own economic and political agendas. These agendas naturally—and necessarily—have far greater priority than pacts made with allies. In other words, we can't blame France for trying.

The problem is, times have changed drastically. For 10,000 years, spying, sabotage, and warfare have all required human participation. Indeed, the spy's face has changed little throughout the ages. Whether he was a stealthy infiltrator, an agent-of-influence, or an agent provocateur, he was, above all, human.

The rules have since changed. Telecommunications and computer technology have made electronic espionage and warfare not simply fanciful notions, but hard realities. Therefore, hostile foreign nations need not send human spies anymore. Instead, they can send packets—and why not? Packets are cheaper. Packets don't drink or smoke (that we know of), they don't gamble, and they cannot be compromised by virtue of reputation, sexual indiscretion, or criminal record. Most importantly, packets are invisible (at least to folks who maintain poor security practices).

From this, it's only a small step to imagine the Internet as a superb espionage tool. Unfortunately, many government sources have been slow to recognize this. Instead, the Internet spy scenario was considered pulp fiction—wildly exaggerated fantasies of military and intelligence experts who had no war to keep them occupied and therefore turned to conjecture for amusement.

Can the Internet Be Used for Espionage?

The better question is, *how often* is the Internet used for espionage? Analysts have hotly debated for quite some time now whether the Internet could be used for spying. They can stop arguing, however, because it is already happening. For example, the Soviet Union's space shuttle program was based on American technology stolen from the Internet. Designs were acquired from various technical universities online. In fact, Robert Windrem, in "How Soviets Stole a Shuttle," says that:

> So thorough was the online acquisition, the National Security Agency learned, that the Soviets were using two East-West research centers in Vienna and Helsinki as covers to

funnel the information to Moscow, where it kept printers going "almost constantly"....Intelligence officials told NBC News that the Soviets had saved billions on their shuttle program by using online spying.

The Soviets have long recognized the Internet as a valid intelligence source. An Internet legend gained international fame by breaking a KGB spy ring that used the Internet to steal American secrets. I refer here to Clifford Stoll, an astronomer then working at a university in Berkeley, California.

Stoll set out to discover the source of a 75-cent accounting error. During his investigation, he learned that someone had broken into the university's computers. Instead of confronting the intruder, Stoll watched the activity. What he saw was disturbing.

The intruder was using Stoll's servers as a launch point. The real targets were military computers, including servers at the Pentagon. The intruder was probing for information on U.S. nuclear preparedness. Stoll recognized this for what it was: spying. He therefore contacted the Federal Bureau of Investigation. However, to Stoll's surprise, FBI agents dismissed the entire incident and refused to offer assistance. Stoll began his own investigation. What followed has since become the most well known chapter in Internet folklore.

After analyzing chained connections through the telephone system, Stoll traced the spy to Germany. His evidence would ultimately prompt the FBI, the CIA, and the West German Secret Police to get involved. In March 1989, Clifford Stoll was credited with cracking a German spy ring that stole our secrets from the Net and sold them to the KGB. (An interesting side note: The German spies received not only money, but also large amounts of cocaine for their services.)

▶ The full story can be read in *The Cuckoo's Egg: Tracking a Spy Through the Maze of Computer Espionage,* by Clifford Stoll. Mass Market Paperback, ISBN: 0-67172-688-9.

The Threat Gets More Personal

These cases are intriguing but reveal only a glimpse of what's to come. Today, hostile foreign nations are studying how to use the Internet to attack us. The new threat, therefore, is not simply espionage but all-out Internet warfare. Are we ready? Sort of.

Information warfare has been on the minds of defense officials for years. Recent studies suggest that we'll experience our first real information warfare attack within 20 years. Most hostile foreign nations are already preparing for it:

> Defense officials and information systems security experts believe that over 120 foreign countries are developing information warfare techniques. These techniques enable our enemies to seize control of or harm sensitive Defense information systems or public networks, which Defense relies upon for communications. Terrorists or other adversaries

now have the United States to launch untraceable attacks from anywhere in the world. They could infect critical systems, including weapons and command and control systems, with sophisticated computer viruses, potentially causing them to malfunction. They could also prevent our military forces from communicating and disrupt our supply and logistics lines by attacking key Defense systems.

—"Information Security: Computer Attacks at Department of Defense Pose Increasing Risks." (Testimony, 05/22/96, GAO/T-AIMD-96-92).

Most information warfare policy papers center on the importance of information warfare in a wartime situation. However, some U.S. information warfare specialists have recognized that we needn't be at war to be attacked:

The United States should expect that its information systems are vulnerable to attack. It should further expect that attacks, when they come, may come in advance of any formal declaration of hostile intent by an adversary state…This is what we have to look forward to in 2020 or sooner.

—"A Theory of Information Warfare; Preparing For 2020." Colonel Richard Szafranski, USAF.

The real question is this: If they attack, what can they do to us? The answer might surprise you.

The President's Commission on Critical Infrastructure Protection (a group studying U.S. vulnerability) has identified key resources that can be attacked via the Internet. Here are a few:

- Information and communications
- Electrical power systems
- Gas and oil transportation and storage
- Banking and finance
- Transportation
- Water supply systems
- Emergency services
- Government services

In 1998, the PCCIP delivered a report with preliminary findings. They, too, concluded that we might be attacked without warning:

Potentially serious cyber attacks can be conceived and planned without detectable logistic preparation. They can be invisibly reconnoitered, clandestinely rehearsed, and then mounted in a matter of minutes or even seconds without revealing the identity and location of the attacker.

Is the situation that critical?

Who Holds the Cards?

Technology is a strange and wonderful thing. Depending on who's using it, the same technology used to create Godzilla can also be used to create weapons of mass destruction. For this reason, technology transfer has been tightly controlled for almost five decades.

During that time, however, commercial advances have dramatically influenced the distribution of high-grade technology. Thirty years ago, for example, the U.S. government held all the cards; the average U.S. citizen held next to nothing. Today, the average American has access to technology so advanced that it starts to come close to technology currently possessed by the government.

Encryption technology is a good example. Many Americans use encryption programs to protect their personal data from prying eyes. Some of these encryption programs (such as Pretty Good Privacy) produce military-grade encryption. This is sufficiently strong that U.S. intelligence agencies have a hard time cracking it within a reasonable amount of time, and time is often of the essence.

NOTE

Encryption has already thwarted several criminal investigations. For example, in the case of famed cracker Kevin Mitnick, the prosecution had a problem: Mitnick encrypted much of his personal data. As reported by David Thomas from Online Journalism:

The encrypted data still posed a problem for the court. As is stands, government officials are holding the encrypted files and have no idea of their contents. The defense claims that information in those files may prove exculpatory, but revealing their contents to the government would violate Mitnick's Fifth Amendment protection against self-incrimination. Further, prosecutors have indicated that they will not be using the encrypted files against Mitnick, but they refuse to return the evidence because they do not know what information the files hold. Ultimately, the court sided with the prosecution. Judge Pfaelzer described Mitnick as "tremendously clever to put everyone in this position" but indicated that "as long as he (Mitnick) has the keys in his pocket, the court is going to do nothing about it."

Advanced technology has trickled down to the public. In many cases, crackers and hackers have taken this technology and rapidly improved it. Meanwhile, the government moves along more slowly, tied down by restrictive and archaic policies. As a result, the private sector has caught (and in some cases, surpassed) the government in some fields of research.

This is a matter of national concern and has sparked an angry debate. Consider the Mitnick case. Do you believe that the government is entitled to Mitnick's encryption key so it can find out what's inside those files? That's a hard question to answer. If Mitnick has a right to conceal that information, so does everybody.

In the meantime, there's a more pressing question: How does this technology trickle-down affect our readiness for an Internet attack?

Can the United States Protect the National Information Infrastructure?

From a military standpoint, there's no comparison between the United States and even a gang of third-world nations. The same is not true, however, in respect to information warfare.

In March 1997, a Swedish cracker penetrated and disabled a 911 system in Florida. Eleven counties were affected. The cracker amused himself by connecting 911 operators to one another (or simply denying service altogether).

NOTE

The Swedish case was not the first instance of crackers disrupting 911 service. In Chesterfield, New Jersey, a group dubbed the Legion of Doom was charged with similar crimes. What was their motivation? "[T]o attempt to penetrate 911 computer systems and infect them with viruses to cause havoc."

NOTE

Another disturbing case occurred in March 1997, when a Rutland, Massachusetts, teenager cracked an airport. During the attack, the airport control tower and communication facilities were disabled for six hours. (The airport fire department was also disabled.) It was reported as follows:

"Public health and safety were threatened by the outage which resulted in the loss of telephone service, until approximately 3:30 p.m., to the Federal Aviation Administration Tower at the Worcester Airport, to the Worcester Airport Fire Department, and to other related concerns such as airport security, the weather service, and various private airfreight companies. Further, as a result of the outage, both the main radio transmitter, which is connected to the tower by the loop carrier system, and a circuit which enables aircraft to send an electric signal to activate the runway lights on approach were not operational for this same period of time."

—*Transport News*, March 1998.

The introduction of advanced minicomputers has forever changed the balance of power. The average Pentium and Alpha processors are more powerful than many mainframes were five years ago. Add to this advances in Linux clustering and distributed processing solutions, and with relatively cheap hardware you can start approaching the processing power that was previously only known by a few government and research institutes.

A third-world nation could theoretically pose a threat to our national information infrastructure. Using advanced microcomputers (and some high-speed connections), a third-world nation could wage a successful information warfare campaign against the United States at costs well within its means. In fact, bona fide cyberterrorism will probably emerge in the next few years.

Furthermore, the mere availability of such advanced technology threatens our military future in the "real" world. Nations such as Russia and China have progressed slowly because they lacked access to such technology. Their missiles are less accurate because their technology base was less advanced. U.S. defense programs, however, were sufficiently advanced that even when we appeared to make concessions in the arms race, we really made no concessions at all. Here's an example: The United States only agreed to quit nuclear tests after we developed the technology to perform such tests using computer modeling.

As the United States' perceived enemies obtain more sophisticated computer technology, their weapons will become more sophisticated—but it's not simply weapons that make the difference. It's the combination of weapons, communication, and information. If our enemies can alter our information, or prevent us from accessing it, they can gain a tremendous tactical military advantage. This could make up for shortcomings in other areas. Shane D. Deichman reports the following in his paper "On Information War:"

> A key element of the information warfare environment is the participants need not possess superpower status. Any power (even those not considered nation-states) with a modicum of technology can disrupt fragile C2 networks and deny critical information services. Rather than a Mahanian "information control" strategy that attempts to dominate all segments of the information spectrum, though, a more realistic strategy for U.S. forces is one of "information denial" (that is, the denial of access to truthful information).

Perhaps a question less asked, however, is, should the U.S. government be responsible for protecting all of the U.S. infrastructure? After all, aren't the companies that operate systems like our telephone networks FOR PROFIT? Shouldn't the protection of these systems be one of their primary concerns?

You'd think so, wouldn't you? Although the U.S. government has more then its fair share of problems and tasks, organizations turning to the government to make their information security problems go away are missing the point. Information security is everyone's problem—welcome to the party.

What Would an Information Attack Look Like?

There hasn't yet been an all-out information war. The distributed denial of service attacks that hit in February 2000 definitely opened some eyes, but it's difficult to say how a full-scale attack would be conducted. Military officials aren't willing to talk specifics. We can speculate, however, as many think tanks do.

▶ In February 2000, some of the largest sites were knocked off the Internet using distributed denial of service tools. The attack made headlines in just about every news publication out there. One of the early reports can be seen at `http://www.computerworld.com/cwi/story/0,1199, NAV47_STO43010,00.html`.

Specialists from Rand Corporation, for example, have engaged in some armchair planning. They delivered a report that posed various questions about the United States' readiness and made recommendations for intensive study on the subject:

> We suggest analytical exercises to identify what cyberwar, and the different modalities of cyberwar, may look like in the early twenty-first century when the new technologies should be more advanced, reliable, and internetted than at present. These exercises should consider opponents that the United States may face in high- and low-intensity conflicts. *CYBERWAR IS COMING!*
>
> —"*International Policy Department.*" John Arquilla and David Ronfeldt, RAND. 1993. Taylor & Francis. ISBN 0-14959-339-0.

Not surprisingly, military and intelligence analysts are learning a great deal simply by studying how the Internet works (and how Americans use it).

Much current research is aimed at defining what types of threats the Internet poses to political structures. Charles Swett, an assistant for strategic assessment at the Pentagon, made strides in this area. He released a report titled "Strategic Assessment: The Internet." In it, he addressed how the Internet will influence American domestic politics. He suggested that special groups can use the Internet to network amongst themselves. He offered one example in particular:

> Another, somewhat startling, example, is a message posted on the Internet on December 16, 1994, calling for nationwide protests against the Republican Party's Contract with America. The message accuses the Contract with America of being, in effect, class war, race war, gender war, and generational war, and urges recipients to "mobilize thousands of demonstrations in local communities across the nation," "fill the jails by engaging in acts of civil disobedience," and engage in other disruptive actions.

Swett predicted that this would ultimately lead to domestic threats. However, he also suggested that these elements are vulnerable to attack:

Political groups whose operations are coordinated through the Internet will be vulnerable to having their operations disrupted by false messages inserted by opposing groups.

NOTE

Mr. Swett was more correct than he realized. What he described has already happened. In recent years, several wars have erupted on Usenet between Scientologists and their critics. These wars were attended by some fairly mysterious happenings. At one stage of a particularly ugly struggle, just when the Scientologists seemed overwhelmed by their adversaries, a curious thing happened:

And thus it was that in late 1994, postings began to vanish from alt.religion.scientology, occasionally with an explanation that the postings had been "canceled because of copyright infringement." To this day, it is not known who was behind the deployment of these "cancelbots," as they are known. Again, the CoS disclaimed responsibility, and the anti-Scientology crowd began to refer to this anonymous participant simply as the "Cancelbunny," a tongue-in-cheek reference to both the Energizer bunny and to a well-known Net inhabitant, the Cancelmoose, who has taken it upon himself (itself? themselves?) to set up a cancelbot-issuing process to deal with other kinds of spamming incidents. But whoever or whatever the Cancelbunny may be, its efforts were quickly met by the development of yet another software weapon, appropriately dubbed "Lazarus," that resurrects canceled messages (or, more accurately, simply alerts the original poster, and all other participants in the newsgroup, that a specific message has been canceled, leaving it up to the original poster to reinstate the message if he or she were not the party that issued the cancel command).

—"The First Internet War; The State of Nature and the First Internet War: Scientology, its Critics, Anarchy, and Law in Cyberspace." David G. Post. *Reason* magazine, April 1996. (© 1996 David G. Post. Permission granted to redistribute freely, in whole or in part, with this notice attached.)

Swett closed his report with several observations about monitoring general Internet traffic on a wholesale basis:

Monitoring of that traffic would need to be supported by automated filters that pass through for human analysis only those messages that satisfy certain relevance criteria.

What Swett described (though he might not have realized it) is a complex, automated, domestic intelligence system. In other words, welcome to 1984. In all probability, early attempts to use the Internet to ascertain and mold political sentiment will be directed toward a country's own people.

But that's about theoretical, domestic information warfare. What about actual Internet warfare? What are some likely targets? The Rand Corporation claims to know. In their paper "Information Warfare: A Two-Edged Sword," Rand specialists wrote

> Information war has no front line. Potential battlefields are anywhere networked systems enable access—oil and gas pipelines, for example, electric power grids, telephone switching networks. In sum, the U.S. homeland may no longer provide a sanctuary from outside attack.

For more information, see
`http://www.rand.org/publications/RRR/RRR.fall95.cyber/infor_war.html`.

In their paper, Rand authors described an imaginary attack set in the not-so-distant future. They predicted the following events:

- Electrical and telephone systems in the United States would be knocked out for hours.
- Freight and passenger trains would derail or collide.
- Oil refineries would ignite.
- Our financial system would fail, including automatic tellers.
- Well-organized domestic extremists would make strategic strikes.
- Computer-controlled weapons systems would malfunction.

Experts suggest that this could happen in a matter of hours. That's a chilling thought. Is it true? Are we really that dependent on technology, or are our government agencies fishing for funding?

The truth is that we are that dependent on technology.

The State of the Government

Throughout the Internet's history, government sites have been popular targets. One of the primary reasons this happens is because of press coverage that follows such an event. Crackers enjoy media attention, so their philosophy often times is that, if you're going to crack a site, crack one that matters.

Government sites are supposed to have better security than their commercial counterparts. Hence, the media reacts more aggressively when a government site is cracked. Likewise, crackers who successfully penetrate a government site gain greater prestige among their fellows (whether it's deserved or not).

You needn't look far to find evidence that government sites are being cracked regularly. A 1997 report filed by the Government Accounting Office (GAO) concerning the security of the nation's defense networks concluded that:

Defense may have been attacked as many as 250,000 times last year…In addition, in testing its systems, DISA [Defense Information Systems Agency] attacks and successfully penetrates Defense systems 65% of the time. According to Defense officials, attackers have obtained and corrupted sensitive information—they have stolen, modified, and destroyed both data and software. They have installed unwanted files and "back doors" which circumvent normal system protection and enable attackers unauthorized access in the future. They have shut down and crashed entire systems and networks, denying service to users who depend on automated systems to help meet critical missions. Numerous Defense functions have been adversely affected, including weapons and supercomputer research, logistics, finance, procurement, personnel management, military health, and payroll.

▶ *Information Security: Computer Attacks at Department of Defense Pose Increasing Risks* ([Chapter Report, 05/22/96, GAO/AIMD-96-84]; Chapter 0:3.2, Paragraph 1), which is the source of the preceding information, is available online at http://www.securitymanagement. com/library/000215.html.

That same report indicates that, although more than a quarter million attacks occur annually, only 1 in 500 attacks are detected and reported.

NOTE

Earlier reports indicate similar results. For example, between 1992 and 1995, DISA attacked some 38,000 defense networks. Better than 65% of those networks were successfully penetrated. Of that number (roughly 24,700), some 96% failed to detect that they were under attack. Interestingly, however, the Air Force seems to be on their toes, or at least more so than their Army counterparts: In general testing, only 1 out of every 140 attacks was detected; in an Air Force study (covering from 1992 to 1995) 1 out of every 8 incidents was detected.

Government agencies understandably try to minimize these facts, but some of the incidents are hard to obscure. For example, in 1994, crackers gained carte blanche access to a weapons-research laboratory in Rome, New York. Over a two-day period, the intruders downloaded vital national security information, including wartime-communication protocols. Such information is extremely sensitive and, if used improperly, could jeopardize the lives of American service personnel. If crackers with relatively modest equipment can access such information, hostile foreign governments (with ample computing power) could access even more.

> **NOTE**
>
> Whether some foreign governments have the technical knowledge to attack U.S. information infrastructure is debatable. (Although GAO reports indicate that some 120 nations have information warfare programs.) However, it is known that despite technology transfer restrictions, many nations are acquiring the tools necessary to make a viable attack. China, for example, acquired high-end Silicon Graphics workstations for use in 3D modeling. These were ultimately used in China's nuclear program.

This phenomenon is not new, nor have government officials done much to improve the situation. Indeed, some very high-profile government sites have been cracked in recent years. In 1996, for example, both the Central Intelligence Agency (CIA) and the Department of Justice (DoJ) were cracked.

In the CIA case, a cracker seized control on September 18, 1996, replacing the welcome banner with one that read *The Central Stupidity Agency*. Links to a hacker group in Scandinavia accompanied the new "banner." In the DoJ incident (Saturday, August 17, 1996), a photograph of Adolph Hitler was offered as the Attorney General of the United States.

While these two incidents might seem noteworthy, because of the agencies that were attacked, the truth is that hundreds, if not thousands, of government sites have been attacked in recent years. In one case, 26 government sites were hit in the same day.

▶ "Online gang defaces 26 government sites"—Government sites in the UK, United States, and Australia were all hit simultaneously by a single "Cyber Gang." Get more information at `http://www.computerworld.com/cwi/story/0,1199,NAV47_STO43010,00.html`.

Federal agencies aren't the only targets, either. In October 1996, the Florida State Supreme Court's home page was cracked. Prior to its cracking, the page was used to distribute recent court decisions. The crackers removed this information and replaced it with pornography. (The court subsequently reported an unusually high rate of hits.)

These attacks are increasing, and so far the availability of advanced security technology has had little impact. Why? It's not the technology; it's the people. (For example, the DoJ site had a firewall but it was improperly configured.) To illustrate how fragile our government sites are, I want to look at some more recent cases.

Defense Information Systems Network

In April 1998, a group dubbed the Masters of Downloading (not to be confused with the Masters of Destruction) cracked the DISN. When they were inside, the intruders stole customized software used by DISN—software not available to the public. (DISN controls vital military satellites.) As reported by Reuters news service:

> MOD members said the stolen software, known as the Defense Information Systems Network Equipment Manager (DEM), was the key to the U.S. network of military Global Positioning System (GPS) satellites—used to pinpoint missile strikes, guide troops, and assess ground conditions. `http://www.news.com/News/Item/0,4,21357,00.html`

Such vital data could prove devastating in the hands of a hostile foreign nation. DISN services include the following:

> ...the infrastructure, satellite communications (military and commercial), forward deployed telecommunications, and readily deployable assets, all of which provide the war-fighting Commanders-in-Chief (CINCs) the ability to plug in and access the full capability of the Defense Information Infrastructure from anywhere, at anytime, and in support of any mission.... `http://www.disa.mil/DISN/disns54.html`

The folks at DISN clearly need to put their house in order. At present, national security is at risk.

The United States Navy and NASA

Also in April 1998, several U.S. Navy and NASA hosts were crippled by wholesale denial of service attacks. (Though no data was lost or damaged, the hosts were unreachable and unusable for minutes or, in some cases, hours.) Many of those hosts were critical military and technological research centers. Here are a few of the victims:

- Ames Research Center
- Dryden Flight Research Center
- Goddard Space Flight Center
- The Jet Propulsion Laboratory
- Kennedy Space Center
- Langley Research Center
- Lewis Research Center
- Marshall Space Flight Center
- Moffett Airfield (California)
- NASA headquarters
- Stennis Space Center

Microsoft, the vendor responsible for the hole, posted an advisory about the vulnerability. In the advisory, Microsoft officials wrote this:

> Since March 2, 1998, there have been numerous reports of malicious network-based, denial of service attacks launched against Internet-connected systems. We were notified of these attacks, which affected some Internet-connected Microsoft Windows NT and Windows 95 systems, by customers and security alert organizations, including CIAC and CERT.

"Numerous reports" is an understatement. In fact, the attacks knocked out hundreds of hosts that served thousands of users. In addition to NASA and Navy computers, a laundry list of university hosts were downed. Here are a few:

- The University of California at Berkeley
- The University of California at Los Angeles
- The University of California at San Diego
- The University of California at Irvine
- Cornell University
- MIT
- The University of Texas at Austin
- The University of Washington
- The University of Wisconsin at Madison

The attack was a new breed of denial of service, which emerged in January 1998. To learn the mechanics of the attack, please read Chapter 16, "Denial of Service Attacks."

The Pentagon Attacks

In February 1998, key Pentagon hosts were cracked in what authorities dubbed "the most organized and systematic attack ever" on military networks. The crack was masterminded by Israeli teenager Ehud Tenebaum. He reportedly tutored two California teenagers, showing them various ways to breach the Pentagon's security. The kids from California put this knowledge to work and within days, the three broke into hundreds of networks across America.

NOTE

The Israeli teen also managed to uncover weaknesses at the Knesset, the Israeli parliament. (Little information is available on the Knesset hack, but it is known that the Knesset network was penetrated.)

The Pentagon attack was particularly disturbing because it illustrated how anyone (located anywhere) could easily cripple defense networks. It is true that the machines compromised did not contain secret or even classified information. But, ideally, none of our prized defense networks should be vulnerable to attack.

Perhaps even more disturbing was Israel's initial reaction to the attack. Israeli government officials made light of it, and praised Mr. Tenebaum for his talents at breaching American networks.

Simultaneously adding insult to injury, a team of young crackers claiming affiliation with Tenebaum threatened to down more servers if their associate were arrested. Tenebaum was ultimately placed under house arrest along with a number of his cohorts and is now being tried.

Other Cracked Government Sites

Targets like NASA, the Pentagon, and the U.S. Navy draw ample press coverage. However, lesser government sites are also cracked regularly—we just don't hear about them. In fact, it's now at a point where tracking the number of government sites cracked is almost a full-time job. For example, the second edition of *Maximum Security* listed a half-dozen or so sites that had been broken into in the late '90s. Today, dozens are broken into and reported *every month*. The numbers are simply staggering.

▶ Although I could go on listing government sites that were hacked until I'm blue in the face, there is already a great, up-to-date site that does it for me. See `http://www.attrition.org` for a massive archive of defaced Web sites. Although defacements are not always as severe as thorough break-ins, they serve as a good tell-tale that a site's security is not up to par.

Government Security

In the past, the U.S. government has blamed its problem on many people and many factors. Some of these include

- The widespread availability of automated cracking tools
- Technology advancing at an incredible rate
- Those damn kids

In reality, none of these factors are totally responsible, and these misconceptions have left their mark on the industry. However, even the government has started to come around in this realization:

Defense information networks are operating with archaic internal security policies. These policies prevent, rather than promote security. To demonstrate why, I want to refer to the GAO report I mentioned previously. In it, the government concedes

> The military services and Defense agencies have issued a number of information security policies, but they are dated, inconsistent and incomplete.

The report points to a series of defense directives as examples. It cites (as the most significant DoD policy document) Defense Directive 5200.28. This document, *Security Requirements for Automated Information Systems*, is dated March 21, 1988.

Let's examine a portion of that defense directive. Paragraph 5 of Section D in that document states

> Computer security features of commercially produced products and Government-developed or -derived products shall be evaluated (as requested) for designation as trusted computer products for inclusion on the Evaluated Products List (EPL). Evaluated products shall be designated as meeting security criteria maintained by the National Computer Security Center (NCSC) at NSA defined by the security division, class, and feature (for example, B, B1, access control) described in DoD 5200.28-STD (reference (K)).

It is within the provisions of that paragraph that the government's main problem lies. The Evaluated Products List (EPL) is a list of products that have been evaluated for security ratings, based on DoD guidelines. (The National Security Agency actually oversees the evaluation.) Products on the list can have various levels of security certification.

▶ *Security Requirements for Automated Information Systems* is available on the Internet at `http://www.c3i.osd.mil/bpr/bprcd/485x.htm`.

▶ Before you continue, you should probably briefly view the EPL for yourself. Check it out at `http://www.radium.ncsc.mil/tpep/epl/epl-by-class.html`.

The first thing you'll notice about this list is that most of the products are old. For example, examine the EPL listing for Trusted Information Systems' Trusted XENIX, a UNIX-based operating system.

▶ The listing for Trusted XENIX can be found at `http://www.radium.ncsc.mil/tpep/epl/entries/CSC-EPL-92-001-A.html`.

TIS's Trusted XENIX is endorsed and cleared as a safe system, one that meets the government's guidelines (as of September 1993). However, examine closely the platforms on which this product has been cleared. Here are a few:

- AST 386/25 and Premium 386/33
- HP Vectra 386
- NCR PC386sx
- Zenith Z-386/33

These architectures are ancient. By the time products reach the EPL, they are often pathetically obsolete. (The evaluation process is lengthy and expensive not only for the vendor, but for the

American people, who are footing the bill for all this.) Therefore, you can conclude that much of the DoD's equipment, software and security procedures are likewise obsolete.

Now add the question of internal education. Are defense personnel trained in (and implementing) the latest security techniques? No. Again, quoting the GAO report:

> Defense officials generally agreed that user awareness training was needed, but stated that installation commanders do not always understand computer security risk and thus, do not always devote sufficient resources to the problem.

In the past, there wasn't adequate funding for training. As such, the majority of defense personnel remained unskilled in even detecting an intrusion, let alone tracing the source.

This situation was allowed to spiral out of control for years. The government recently took action and although it might still be a day late, it is no longer a dollar short. Special teams have since been formed at various levels of government. Let's take a look at those teams now.

The National Infrastructure Protection Center (NIPC)

In February 1998, Attorney General Janet Reno announced the formation of the National Infrastructure Protection Center (NIPC), an investigative organization populated with personnel from the FBI's Computer Investigations and Infrastructure Threat Assessment Center (CIITAC). The NIPC tracks network intrusions and attempts to develop long-range solutions, including intrusion detection and international cooperation of police agencies.

There are some interesting articles about the CIITAC, the NIPC, and related organizations:

- **Hacking Around.** *The NewsHour with Jim Lehrer*, March 1998. `http://www.pbs.org/ newshour/bb/cyberspace/jan-june98/hackers_5-8.html`

- **U.S. to Set Up Interagency Defense Against Cyberattacks.** *Sunworld* Online, February 1998. `http://www.sun.com/sunworldonline/swol-03-1998/swol-03-if.html#2`

- **Attorney General Announces Crime Center To Tackle Cyberattacks.** Gayle Kesten, February 28, 1998. `http://www.techweb.com/wire/story/TWB19980228S0004`

- **Open Sources: NIPC's film debut.** Lewis Koch, ZDNET, May 8, 2000 `http://www. zdnet.com/intweek/stories/news/0,4164,2567603,00.html`

Summary of Government Vulnerabilities

To date, government security has been largely inadequate, and although the efforts of the PCCIP, NIPC, and CIITAC will undoubtedly improve the situation, further work is needed.

Until information security officers are properly trained, government sites will be cracked on a regular basis. Reasonable levels of security are obtainable, and, if the government cannot obtain them on its own, it must enlist private sector specialists who can.

The State of the Corporate Sector

It's clear that government servers can be successfully attacked, but what about the public sector? Is American business—big or small—immune to the cyber threat? Hardly. In fact, private sites are taken down with much greater frequency. Virtually every information security survey ever issued has reported a steep rise in incidents, and defacement mirrors such as attrition.org and defaced.alldas.de report hundreds of Web site defacements per month. Worse, while Web site defacements are publicly humiliating, most security experts agree that they are only the tip of the iceberg in terms of total incidents in the field.

Marketers who are anxious to sell electronic commerce to the public assure us that these incidents are harmless. They point out, for example, that credit card and personal data is perfectly safe. Are they right? No—not by a long shot.

Credit Card Theft Goes Cyber: The StarWave Incident

In July 1997, crackers demonstrated one of the first widely known attacks on Internet credit card data. Their targets weren't small-time firms, either. Credit card numbers of NBA and ESPN site users were captured and distributed.

StarWave was the site responsible for protecting that data. StarWave is a widely known firm that hosts many large commercial sites, including ABC News. However, in July 1997, StarWave officials were apparently unprepared for the security breach.

The cracker or crackers took the credit card numbers and mailed them to NBA and ESPN subscribers to demonstrate to those users that their credit data was unsafe. Included in the mailing was a message. The relevant portion of that message was this:

> Clearly, StarWave doesn't consider the protection of individual credit card numbers a worthwhile endeavor. (This is one of the worst implementations of security we've seen.)

StarWave officials responded quickly, explaining that the security breach was minor. They also changed system passwords and have since added an extra level of encryption. However, the fact remains: User credit card data had leaked out.

Credit Card Theft Hits Overdrive

Electronic commerce advocates originally asserted that the StarWave case was an isolated incident. In fact, at the time, many contended that few verified cases of credit card theft existed, and that the threat was relatively small. Time eventually proved them to be dead wrong.

Consider the case of Carlos Felipe Salgado. Salgado used a sniffer program (you'll learn about these in Chapter 15, "Sniffers") to steal thousands of credit card numbers off the Net. In their affidavit, FBI agents explained:

Between, on or about May 2, 1997, and May 21, 1997, within the State and Northern District of California, defendant CARLOS FELIPE SALGADO, JR., a.k.a. "Smak," did knowingly, and with intent to defraud, traffic in unauthorized access devices affecting interstate commerce, to wit, over 100,000 stolen credit card numbers, and by such conduct did obtain in excess of $1000; in violation of Title 18, United States Code, Section 1029(a)(2).

Salgado's method was one well known to crackers:

While performing routine maintenance on the Internet servers on Friday, March 28, 1997, technicians discovered that the servers had been broken into by an intruder. Investigation by technicians revealed a "packet sniffer" installed on the system. The packet sniffer program was being used to capture user IDs and passwords of the authorized users....the FBI, met "Smak" at the appointed hour and place. "Smak" delivered an encrypted CD containing over 100,000 stolen credit card numbers. After the validity of the credit card information was confirmed through decryption of the data on the CD, "Smak" was taken into custody by the FBI.

Sniffer attacks are probably the most common way to grab credit card data (and usernames and password pairs). They are so common that Jonathan Littman (a renowned author of a best-selling book on hacking) wrote this in response to the Salgado case:

Fact No. 1: This was an old fashioned attack—and it happens about as often as dogs sniff themselves. The packet sniffer that Carlos Felipe Salgado Jr., a.k.a. Smak, allegedly installed in a San Diego Internet provider's server is something hackers have been doing for years. My provider in Northern California was hacked a couple of months ago and just last week too. Guess what that hacker was about to install?

—"Take No Solace in This Sting," Jonathan Littman. ZDNET News.
`http://www.zdnet.com/zdnn/content/zdnn/0523/zdnn0007.html`

Unfortunately, these incidents were only the start. Consider the following cases:

- In 1995, thieves stole 50,000 phone card numbers from an MCI server. Those numbers were ultimately used to charge some $50 million in calls.

- In November 1996, someone lifted a server from VISA in California, netting 300,000 credit card numbers.

- In May 1997, someone lifted a hard disk from a Levi-Strauss server. The thief made away with 40,000 credit card numbers and other personal customer information.

- In January 1999, thieves stole 485,000 credit card numbers and hid them on the Web site of a U.S. government agency. Apparently the site was used to store the data, and wasn't discovered until much later.

- In January 2000, thieves stole 300,000 credit cards from CD Universe. At the time, this was the largest theft of credit cards to be publicly reported.

- In March 2000, a cracker known as "Curador" lead authorities on a global chase after lifting 26,000 some credit cards from an assortment of e-commerce sites. Curador was caught later that same month.

- In December 2000, Egghead.com reported that they had suffered a security breach that might have exposed 3.7 million credit card numbers. Egghead later reported that they didn't believe the intruder was able to access the credit cards, but the scare was definitely significant.

- In March 2001, the FBI and NIPC issued a warning that Russian and Ukrainian thieves have stolen more then 1 million credit cards.

Notice a trend here? The problem is only getting worse. These are just some of the reasons why the Internet is a dangerous place to do business. Unfortunately, the stories are only getting more and more outrageous.

The Trends

Hard statistics on security breaches are difficult to come by. However, there are a few good sources. One is the Computer Security Institute's Computer Crime and Security Survey. The CSI Survey is conducted annually, and the 1999 results are in. You can obtain those results at `http://www.gocsi.com/prelea_000321.htm`.

Briefly, the 1999 results indicate yet another increase in computer crime. For example, 90% of the respondents reported security breaches in the previous year. In 1998, that number was at 64%, and, in 1997, it was at 48%. Approximately three-quarters of all respondents suffered hard denial of service attacks, and an equal number experienced penetration by remote attackers. Of all respondents, 59% indicated that the Internet was the point of entry for intruders.

CSI's survey is not the only one that suggests an increase in Internet security breaches. Probably the most fascinating study was performed by a rather colorful and iconoclastic security researcher named Dan Farmer.

Dan Farmer's Survey

In 1996, Farmer used SATAN (a tool that automates scans for vulnerabilities) to do a generalized Internet survey. In that survey (titled *Shall We Dust Moscow? Security Survey of Key Internet Hosts and Various Semi-Relevant Reflections*), Farmer scanned some 2,200 Internet hosts. The scan's purpose was simple: Determine how many hosts were vulnerable to remote attack.

The survey was controversial because Farmer did not ask permission from his targets. In addition, Farmer didn't choose average sites as his targets. Instead, he chose banks, credit unions, government sites, and other key servers that should have superb security. Some of his findings follow:

- Farmer found that a staggering 1,700 sites (some 65% of all sites tested) were vulnerable to attacks widely known to crackers.

- Many targets had firewalls and other baseline security measures, measures that administrative personnel rely heavily on for their core security.

To view Farmer's survey, point your browser here:

```
http://www.trouble.org/survey/
```

The Ernst & Young LLP/ComputerWorld Information Security Survey

If your company has asked you to justify a security plan, you're probably looking around for more statistics. No problem; there's a lot of material out there. One good source is the Ernst & Young LLP/ComputerWorld Information Security Survey. That survey is located here:

```
http://www.ey.com/global/vault.nsf/US/2nd_Annual_Global_Information_Security_
Survey/$file/FF0157.pdf
```

The Ernst & Young survey differs a bit from others mentioned earlier. For a start, it's a survey of human beings. (Actually, it's a survey of more than 4,300 information managers.) Respondents were asked a wide variety of questions about Internet security and secure electronic commerce.

One recurring theme throughout the 1998 survey was this: Most information officers (and even administrative folks) now recognized security to be a major issue. The report indicated that, despite that fact, the majority of sites still did not employ best practices. Respondents also indicated the following:

- More than 35% did not plan on using cryptography in the future.

- More than 49% did not use firewalls.

- More than 75% did not have an incident response team in place.

If your company holds similar attitudes toward security measures, you need to get busy.

A Warning

Many companies that consider establishing a Web server feel that security is not a significant issue. For example, they might co-locate their box, and in doing so might throw both the responsibility and liability to their ISP. After all, ISPs know the lay of the land, and they never get cracked, right? Wrong. ISPs get cracked all the time.

▶ Do not to exclude universities from your sites, either. For example, in December 2000, Security Focus ran a report on the University of Washington break-in. Intruders stole more than 5,000 patient records from the University's Medical Center. See a report on this incident at `http://www.securityfocus.com/news/122`.

If you're an information officer and your firm requests Internet connectivity, be sure to cover the bases. Make it known to all concerned that security is a serious issue. Otherwise, you'll take the blame later. You should also be wary of any ISP that gives you blanket assurances. Today, even firewalls can be cracked, and cracked through the same old methods by which servers are cracked—exploitation of human error.

Summary

We've established that any site can be cracked, including the following types:

- Banks
- Credit unions
- Military servers
- Universities
- Internet service providers

Do not expect this climate to change, either. New and more effective cracking methods are surfacing, and the pace is only getting quicker. New cracking tools and viruses are being manufactured every day, and these tools—which were once toys for hackers and crackers—have now become viable weapons. These methods will be used by both hostile foreign nations seeking to destroy other countries' national information infrastructure, as well as kids who are bored and want to take down a popular Web site.

On the information warfare front, there are several key objectives, but these two are particularly prominent:

- Denying the target computer services
- Destroying the target's computer systems

Today's denial of service attacks and viruses will likely form the basis for tomorrow's information warfare arsenal. Considering that anyone, anywhere can obtain these tools, compile them, and deploy them in minutes, the immediate future looks pretty scary.

Internet Resources on Information Warfare

The following papers focus on Internet and information warfare. Most are written by folks now actively engaged in INFOWAR research.

An Analysis Of Security Incidents On The Internet. John D. Howard.
http://www.cert.org/research/JHThesis/index.html

Cyberwar and Netwar: New Modes, Old Concepts, of Conflict. John Arquilla and David Ronfeldt of the International Policy Department at RAND. http://www.rand.org/publications/RRR/RRR.fall95.cyber/cyberwar.html

Defensive Information Warfare. David S. Alberts. http://www.ndu.edu:80/ndu/inss/books/diw/index.html

Foreign Information Warfare Programs and Capabilities. John M. Deutch, Director of Central Intelligence. http://www.odci.gov/cia/public_affairs/speeches/archives/1996/dci_testimony_062596.html

From InfoWar to Knowledge Warfare: Preparing for the Paradigm Shift. Philippe Baumard. http://www.indigo-net.com/annexes/289/baumard.htm

Induced Fragility in Information Age Warfare. Bruce W. Fowler and Donald R. Peterson. http://lionhrtpub.com/orms/orms-4-97/warfare.html

Information Security: Computer Attacks at Department of Defense Pose Increasing Risks. U.S. Government Accounting Office. http://www.access.gpo.gov/cgi-bin/getdoc.cgi?dbname=gao&docid=f:ai96084.txt

Information War and the Air Force: Wave of the Future? Current Fad? Glenn Buchan. http://www.rand.org/publications/IP/IP149/

Information Warfare and International Law. Lawrence T. Greenberg, Seymour E. Goodman, and Kevin J. Soo Hoo. http://www.dodccrp.org/iwilindex.htm

Information Warfare. Brian C. Lewis. http://www.fas.org/irp/eprint/snyder/infowarfare.htm

Intelligence-Based Threat Assessments for Information Networks and Infrastructures. Kent Anderson from Global Technology Research, Inc. http://www.aracnet.com/~kea/Papers/threat_white_paper.shtml

Keeping Information Warfare in Perspective. David C. Gompert. http://www.rand.org/publications/RRR/RRR.fall95.cyber/perspective.html

Knowledge-Based Warfare: A Security Strategy for the Next Century. Lawrence E. Casper, Irving L. Halter, Earl W. Powers, Paul J. Selva, Thomas W. Steffens, and T. LaMar Willis. http://www.dtic.mil/doctrine/jel/jfq_pubs/1813.pdf

Network-Centric Warfare: Its Origin and Future. Vice Admiral Arthur K. Cebrowski, U.S. Navy, and John J. Garstka. http://www.usni.org/Proceedings/Articles98/PROcebrowski.htm

Political Aspects of Class III Information Warfare: Global Conflict and Terrorism. Matthew G. Devost. http://www.mnsinc.com/mdevost/montreal.html

The Digital Threat: United States National Security and Computers. Matthew G. Devost.
`http://www.mnsinc.com/mdevost/hackers4.html`

The Unintended Consequences of Information Age Technologies. David S. Alberts.
`http://www.ndu.edu/ndu/inss/books/uc/uchome.html`

Books on Information Warfare

Information Warfare: Chaos on the Electronic Superhighway. Winn Schwartau. (Engaging INFOWAR title by the owner of `http://www.infowar.com`.) 1996. ISBN: 1-56025-132-8.

Strategic Information Warfare: A New Face of War. Roger C. Molander, Andrew S. Riddile, and Peter A. Wilson. 1996. ISBN: 0-83302-352-7.

The Military Technical Revolution: A Structural Framework. M. J. Mazarr. 1993. ISBN: 0-89206-218-5.

The Advent of Netwar. John Arquilla and David Ronfeldt. 1996. ISBN: 0-83302-414-0.

Cyberwar: Security, Strategy, and Conflict in the Information Age. R. Thomas Goodden. 1996. ISBN: 0916159264.

Defensive Information Warfare. David S. Alberts. 1996. ISBN: 9-99600-792-8.

The First Information War: The Story of Communications, Computers, and Intelligence Systems in the Persian Gulf War. Alan D. Campen. 1992. ISBN: 0-91615-924-8.

Information Warfare: How Computers Are Fighting the New World Wars. James Adams. 1998. ISBN: 0-68483-452-9.

Introduction to Information Warfare. Edward L. Waltz. 1998. ISBN: 089006511X.

U.S. Information Warfare Jane's Special 1997–1998. Jane's Information Group.

Information Warfare and Deterrence. Gary F. Wheatley and Richard E. Hayes. 1996. ISBN: 9-99664-621-1.

What Is Information Warfare? Martin C. Libicki. 1995. ISBN: 9-99668-061-4.

Hacking 101: The Tricks of the Trade

IN THIS PART

Spoofing Attacks

IN THIS CHAPTER

In this chapter you learn about spoofing attacks—how they are performed and how you can prevent them.

What Is Spoofing?

The secret to creativity is knowing how to hide your sources.

—*Albert Einstein*

Spoofing can be summed up in a single sentence: It's a sophisticated technique of authenticating one machine to another by forging packets from a trusted source address.

From that definition, you can safely conclude that spoofing is a complicated process. However, by this chapter's end, you'll have a clear understanding of spoofing and how to prevent it.

Internet Security Fundamentals

There are two recurring themes in Internet security:

- Trust
- Authentication

Trust is the relationship between machines that are authorized to connect to one another. *Authentication* is the process those machines use to identify each other.

Trust and authentication generally have an inverse relationship. Thus, if a high level of trust exists between machines, stringent authentication is not required to make a connection. On the other hand, if little or no trust exists between machines, more rigorous authentication is required.

If you think about it, humans exercise similar rules. For example, if your best friend came to your front door, you'd let him right in. Why not? You trust him. However, if a total stranger came knocking, you would demand that he identify himself.

Methods of Authentication

Although you might not realize it, you are constantly being authenticated. For example, you might have to provide a username and password to use any of the following services:

- Your Internet connection
- FTP sites
- Telnet services and shell accounts

In fact, today, most subscription-based Web sites require a username and password. You're subjected to high levels of authentication every day. Do you know what that means? The Internet simply doesn't trust you!

Authenticating humans, therefore, involves a password scheme. (Some models employ a simple username/password scheme, whereas others can be more complex, such as challenge-response systems based on one-time passwords. The end result is the same, though—the user either has the correct password or she does not.)

Machines can be authenticated in other ways, depending on their trust relationship. For example, a machine can be authenticated by its host name or an IP source address. Using RHOSTS entries is a common procedure for setting this up.

RHOSTS

The RHOSTS system can be used to establish a relationship of trust between machines. It's described in the Solaris Manual Page:

> The /etc/hosts.equiv and .rhosts files provide the "remote authentication" database for rlogin(1), rsh(1), rcp(1), and rcmd(3N). The files specify remote hosts and users that are considered "trusted." Trusted users are allowed to access the local system without supplying a password.

> **NOTE**
>
> hosts.equiv files are essentially .rhosts configuration files for the entire system. These are set by root and apply hostwide. In contrast, .rhosts files are user-based and apply only to particular users and directories. (This is why users should be restricted from making their own .rhosts files. These open smaller holes all over the system.)

A sample .rhosts file might look like this:

```
node1.sams.hacker.net hickory
node2.sams.hacker.net dickory
node3.sams.hacker.net doc
node4.sams.hacker.net mouse
```

This file specifies that the four machines named (and the users hickory, dickory, doc, and mouse) are now trusted. These can access the local machine through the r services without being subjected to password authentication.

To complete the process (and create a two-way trust relationship), all four of the machines must also maintain rhost entries.

> **NOTE**
>
> The r services consist of the following applications:
>
> rlogin—Remote login. This works in very similar fashion to Telnet and offers a remote login session.
>
> rsh—Remote shell. This enables users to run shell commands on the remote box.
>
> rcp—Remote file copy. This enables users to copy files from local to remote machines, and vice versa.
>
> rcmd—Remote command. This enables privileged users to execute commands on remote hosts.
>
> All four r services use the /etc/hosts.equiv or .rhosts allow/deny scheme for trust purposes. No trust exists if these files are empty or don't exist, and therefore a spoofing attack (of this variety) cannot occur.

The authentication that occurs at connection time, then, is based solely on the IP source address. This is known to be a flawed model, as Steve M. Bellovin explains in his paper *Security Problems in the TCP/IP Protocol Suite:*

> If available, the easiest mechanism to abuse is IP source routing. Assume that the target host uses the reverse of the source route provided in a TCP open request for return traffic. Such behavior is utterly reasonable; if the originator of the connection wishes to specify a particular path for some reason—say, because the automatic route is dead— replies may not reach the originator if a different path is followed.

> The attacker can then pick any IP source address desired, including that of a trusted machine on the target's local network. Any facilities available to such machines become available to the attacker.

▶ *Security Problems in the TCP/IP Protocol Suite* by Steve M. Bellovin can be found on the Web at ftp://ftp.research.att.com/dist/internet_security/ipext.ps.Z.

The following points have been established for now:

1. Trust and authentication have an inverse relationship; more trust results in less stringent authentication.

2. Initial authentication is based on the source address in trust relationships.

3. IP source address authentication is unreliable because IP addresses (and most fields of an IP header) can be forged.

4. A trust relationship of some kind must exist for a spoofing attack to work.

From this, you can surmise one of the reasons why IP spoofing has achieved cult status in the cracker community. Most cracking attacks have historically relied on password schemes; crackers would steal the /etc/passwd file and crack it. They would do their dirty work after having obtained the root password (and at least one user login/password). In spoofing, however, neither a username nor a password is passed during the attack. The security breach occurs at a very discrete level.

Another reason IP spoofing has gained much notoriety is that it can be used as a key element in other forms of attack. One example of this is known as "session hijacking," which is described in the next section.

The Mechanics of a Spoofing Attack

The mere fact that source address authentication is flawed does not in itself make IP spoofing possible. Here's why: The connection process requires more than just the right IP address. It requires a complete, sustained dialog between machines.

You can more easily understand the process in steps:

- IP is responsible for packet transport. Packet transport performed by IP is unreliable, meaning that there is no absolute guarantee that packets will arrive unscathed and intact. (For example, packets can be lost, corrupted, and so forth.) The main point is this: IP merely routes the packets from point A to point B. Therefore, the first step of initiating a connection is for the packets to arrive intact to the proper host.

- After the packets do arrive, TCP takes over. TCP is more reliable and has facilities to check that packets are intact and are being transported properly. Each one is subjected to verification. For example, TCP first acknowledges receipt of a packet and then sends a message verifying that it was received and processed correctly.

TCP's process of packet error checking is done sequentially. If five packets are sent, packets 1, 2, 3, 4, and 5 are dealt with in the order they were received. Each packet is assigned a number as an identifying index. Both hosts use this number for error checking and reporting.

In his article *Sequence Number Attacks*, Rik Farrow explains the sequence number process used in the attack on Tsutomu Shimomura's computer by Kevin Mitnick:

> The sequence number is used to acknowledge receipt of data. At the beginning of a TCP connection, the client sends a TCP packet with an initial sequence number, but no acknowledgment (there can't be one yet). If there is a server application running at the other end of the connection, the server sends back a TCP packet with its own initial sequence number, and an acknowledgment: the initial sequence number from the client's packet plus one. When the client system receives this packet, it must send back its own acknowledgment: the server's initial sequence number plus one. Thus, it takes three packets to establish a TCP connection....

▶ Find *Sequence Number Attacks* by Rik Farrow online at `http://www.nwc.com/unixworld/security/001.txt.html`.

The attacker's problem can thus far be characterized as twofold. First, he must forge the source address, and, second, he must maintain a sequence dialog with the target. It is this second task that makes the attack complex. Here's why: The sequence dialog is not arbitrary. The target sets the initial sequence number, and the attacker must counter with the correct response.

This further complicates the attack and here's why: The attacker must guess the correct sequence response because he never actually receives packets from the target. In his article *A Weakness in the 4.2BSD UNIX TCP/IP Software*, Robert Morris explains

> 4.2BSD maintains a global initial sequence number, which is incremented by 128 each second and by 64 after each connection is started; each new connection starts off with this number. When a SYN packet with a forged source is sent from a host, the destination host will send the reply to the presumed source host, not the forging host. The forging host must discover or guess what the sequence number in that lost packet was, in order to acknowledge it and put the destination TCP port in the ESTABLISHED state.

▶ Find Morris's article online at `ftp://ftp.research.att.com/dist/internet_security/117.ps.Z`.

That might sound confusing, so let me illustrate the concept more clearly. Assume the following:

- The cracker knows that the hosts `207.171.0.111` and `199.171.190.9` have a trust relationship.
- He intends to penetrate `207.171.0.111`.
- To do so, he must impersonate `199.171.190.9`.
- To impersonate `199.171.190.9`, he forges that address.

The problem is that all responses from `207.171.0.111` are actually routed to `199.171.190.9` (and not the cracker's machine). Because of this, the cracker cannot see the packet traffic. He is driving blind. It is because of this inability to see the responses that this method of spoofing is known as *blind spoofing*. *Non-blind spoofing* occurs when the responses can be seen because the traffic occurs along a network segment that the attacker can watch.

The blind spoofing situation presents an even more serious obstacle. What if `199.171.190.9` responds to packets from the target while the cracker is conducting his attack? This blows the entire operation. Therefore, the cracker must perform one last, additional step prior to actually conducting the attack: He must either attempt the spoof when `199.171.190.9` is not running or put `199.171.190.9` to sleep.

> **NOTE**
>
> Killing 199.171.190.9 is simple. To do so, the cracker exposes 199.171.190.9 to a syn-flood attack. This floods the connection queues of 199.171.190.9, temporarily rendering that machine unable to process incoming connection requests. (This works because of the way connection requests are processed. Each time a connection request is received, the target attempts to complete the three-way handshake. Eventually, the target times out on that request and then attempts to process the next one. All connection requests are handled in the order they were received. Thus, if the target is flooded with hundreds of such requests, considerable time will pass before the flooded host can again process connection requests.)

At this point, it's time to recap everything presented until now.

The Ingredients of a Successful Spoofing Attack

These are the essential steps that must be taken in a spoofing attack:

1. The cracker must identify his targets.
2. He must anesthetize the host he intends to impersonate.
3. He must forge the address of the host he's impersonating.
4. He must connect to the target, masquerading as the anesthetized host.
5. He must accurately guess the correct sequence number requested by the target.

The first four steps are easy. The difficult part is guessing the correct sequence number. To do so, the cracker must execute a trial run:

- He contacts the intended target requesting connection.
- The target responds with a flurry of sequence numbers.
- The cracker logs these sequence numbers and cuts the connection.

The cracker next examines the logs of sequence numbers received from the target. In his analysis, he seeks to identify a pattern. He knows, for example, that these sequence numbers are incremented uniformly by an algorithm designed specially for this purpose. His job is to determine that algorithm, or at least determine the numeric values by which the numbers are incremented. When he knows this, he can reliably predict what sequence numbers are required for authentication.

He is now ready to perform the spoofing attack. In all, spoofing is an extraordinary technique. However, what's even more extraordinary is this: Since 1985, the security community has known that spoofing was possible.

Opening a More Suitable Hole

When the connection and authentication procedures are complete, the cracker must create a more suitable hole through which to compromise the system. (He should not be forced to spoof each time he wants to connect.) He therefore fashions a custom hole. The easiest method is to rewrite the .rhosts file so that the now-compromised system accepts connections from any source without requiring additional authentication.

Having done this, the cracker shuts down the connection and reconnects. He can now log in without a password and has control of the system.

Who Can Be Spoofed?

IP spoofing can only be implemented against certain machines running certain services. Many flavors of UNIX are viable targets. (This shouldn't give you the impression that non-UNIX systems are invulnerable to spoofing attacks. There's more on that later in this chapter.)

The following configurations and services are known to be vulnerable:

- Any device running Sun RPC
- Any network service that uses IP address authentication
- The X Window System from MIT
- The r services

To put that in perspective, consider this: Most network services use IP-based authentication, and although RPC, X, and the r services have problems inherent to UNIX-based operating systems, other operating systems are not immune.

Windows NT, for example, is vulnerable to sequence number attacks. Sessions can be high-jacked via TCP sequence number guessing. At its heart, the problem is a spoofing issue. It affects a multitude of network services, not just RPC. In fact, it even affects NetBIOS and SMB connections. Exploit code for the attack can be found here:

http://www.engarde.com/software/seqnumsrc.c

▶ Sun RPC refers to Sun Microsystems' standard of *Remote Procedure Calls*, which enable users to issue system calls that work transparently over networks. The RFC that addresses RPC, titled *RPC: Remote Procedure Call Protocol Specification*, can be found at http://www.netsys.com/rfc/rfc1057.txt.

How Common Are Spoofing Attacks?

Spoofing attacks used to be rare. However, they became far more common after January 1995. Consider this Defense Data Network advisory from July 1995:

> ASSIST has received information about numerous recent IP spoofing attacks directed against Internet sites internationally. A large number of the systems targeted in the IP spoofing attacks are name servers, routers, and other network operation systems, and the attacks have been largely successful.

▶ To view the DDN bulletin online, visit `http://csrc.ncsl.nist.gov/secalert/ddn/1995/sec-9532.txt`.

Prior to 1995, spoofing was a very grass-roots attack. Anyone trying to spoof had to have a very strong background in TCP/IP, sockets, and network programming generally. That is no longer true.

After it was demonstrated that spoofing actually worked (it was previously a theoretical notion), spoofing code immediately began surfacing. Today, prefabbed spoofing utilities are widely available. The following sections present some useful spoofing utilities.

Spoofing/Hijacking Utilities

1644

Author: Vasim V.

Language: C

Build Platform: FreeBSD

Target Platform: UNIX

Requirements: C compiler, IP header files, FreeBSD

URL: `http://www.insecure.org/sploits/ttcp.spoofing.problem.html`

Hunt

Author: Pavel Krauz

Language: C

Build Platform: Linux

Target Platform: Linux

Requirements: C compiler, Linux

URL: `http://lin.fsid.cvut.cz/~kra/index.html`

ipspoof

Author: Unknown

Language: C

Build Platform: UNIX

Target Platform: UNIX

Requirements: C compiler, IP Header Files, UNIX

URL: `http://www.rootshell.com/archive-j457nxiqi3gq59dv/199707/ipspoof.c`

Juggernaut

Author: route

Language: C

Build Platform: UNIX

Target Platform: UNIX

Requirements: C compiler, IP Header Files, UNIX

URL: `http://staff.washington.edu/dittrich/talks/qsm-sec/P50-06.txt`

rbone

Author: Unknown

Language: C

Build Platform: Linux

Target Platform: UNIX

Requirements: C compiler, IP header files, Linux

URL: `http://www.net-security.sk/network/spoof/rbone.tar.gz`

Spoofit

Author: Brecht Claerhout

Language: C

Build Platform: Linux

Target Platform: UNIX

Requirements: C compiler, IP header files, Linux 1.3 or later

URL: `http://rootshell.com/archive-j457nxiqi3gq59dv/199707/IP-spoof.txt.html`

synk4.c (Syn Flooder by Zakath)

Author: Zakath with Ultima

Language: C

Build Platform: Linux

Target Platform: UNIX

Requirements: C compiler, IP header files, Linux

URL: `http://rootshell.com/archive-j457nxiqi3gq59dv/199707/synk4.c.html`

NOTE

There's also a UDP spoofing utility available. To try it, download it from `http://www.deter.com/unix/software/arnudp.c`.

Documents Related Specifically to IP Spoofing

There are many documents online that address IP spoofing. Here are a few good ones:

A Weakness in the 4.2BSD UNIX TCP/IP Software. Robert T. Morris. Technical Report, AT&T Bell Laboratories. `ftp://research.att.com/dist/internet_security/117.ps.Z`

Sequence Number Attacks. Rik Farrow. (UnixWorld.) `http://www.nwc.com/unixworld/security/001.txt.html`

Security Problems in the TCP/IP Protocol Suite. Steve Bellovin. `ftp://research.att.com/dist/internet_security/ipext.ps.Z`

Defending Against Sequence Number Attacks. S. Bellovin; Request for Comments: 1948. AT&T Research. May 1996. `http://andrew2.andrew.cmu.edu/rfc/rfc1948.html`

A Short Overview of IP Spoofing. Brecht Claerhout. `http://rootshell.com/archive-j457nxiqi3gq59dv/199707/IP-spoof.txt.html` (An excellent freelance treatment of the subject)

Internet Holes—Eliminating IP Address Forgery. Management Analytics. `http://all.net/journal/netsec/9606.html`

Ask Woody about Spoofing Attacks. Bill Woodcock from Zocalo Engineering. `http://www.netsurf.com/nsf/v01/01/local/spoof.html`

IP-Spoofing Demystified Trust-Relationship Exploitation. route@infonexus.com (Michael Schiffman). `http://www.fc.net/phrack/files/p48/p48-14.html`

How Do I Prevent IP Spoofing Attacks?

Configuring your network to reject packets from the Net that claim to originate from a local address can thwart IP spoofing attacks. This is done at the router level. Conversely, it is also generally a good policy to reject packets originating inside of your network that claim to come from a host on the outside.

> **NOTE**
>
> Although routers are a solution to the general spoofing problem, they too operate by examining the source address. Thus, they can only protect against incoming packets that purport to originate from within your internal network. If your network (for some inexplicable reason) trusts foreign hosts, routers will not protect against a spoofing attack that purports to originate from those hosts.

There are several products that incorporate anti-spoofing technology into their general design. Here are a couple:

- **NetVision Synchronicity for Windows NT.** The Synchronicity product line incorporates concurrent management of NDS and NT objects and systems. Anti-spoofing support is built in. Check it out here: `http://www.netvision.com/products/synchronicity.html`
- **Cisco PIX Firewall.** PIX is Cisco's premier Internet BXsecurity product and is a full-fledged firewall with built-in anti-spoofing capabilities. `http://www.cisco.com/warp/public/cc/pd/fw/sqfw500`

Certain products can also test your network for vulnerability to IP spoofing. (Check Chapter 11, "Vulnerability Assessment Tools (Scanners)," for scanners that perform this diagnostic.)

> **CAUTION**
>
> If you're running a firewall, this does not automatically protect you from spoofing attacks. If you allow internal addresses access through the outside portion of the firewall, you're still vulnerable. Moreover, if your firewall runs proxies and those proxies perform their authentication based on the IP source address, you have a problem. (Essentially, this type of authentication is no different from any other form of IP-based authentication.)

Closely monitoring your network is another preventative measure. Try identifying packets that purport to originate within your network, but attempt to gain entrance at the firewall or first network interface that they encounter on your wire. The following paragraph is excerpted from Defense Information System Network Security Bulletin #95-32. This bulletin can be found online at `http://csrc.ncsl.nist.gov/secalert/ddn/1995/sec-9532.txt`.

> There are several classes of packets that you could watch for. The most basic is any TCP packet where the network portion (Class A, B, or C or a prefix and length as specified by the Classless Inter-Domain Routing (CIDR) specification) of the source and destination

addresses are the same but neither are from your local network. These packets would not normally go outside the source network unless there is a routing problem worthy of additional investigation, or the packets actually originated outside your network. The latter can occur with mobile IP testing, but an attacker spoofing the source address is a more likely cause.

As a closing note, if you can afford the resource overhead, you can also detect spoofing through logging procedures (even in real-time). Running a comparison on connections between trusted hosts is a good start. For example, assume that trusted hosts A and B have a live session. Both will show processes indicating that the session is underway. If one of them doesn't indicate activity, a spoofing attack is afoot.

Other Strange and Offbeat Spoofing Attacks

IP spoofing is only one form of spoofing. Other spoofing techniques exist, including ARP and DNS spoofing. Let's briefly examine each.

ARP Spoofing

ARP spoofing is a technique that alters the ARP cache. Here's how it works: The ARP cache contains hardware-to-IP mapping information. The key is to keep your hardware address, but to assume the IP address of a trusted host. This information is simultaneously sent to the target and the cache. From that point on, packets from the target are routed to your hardware address. (The target now "believes" that your machine is the trusted host.)

There are severe limitations to this type of attack. One is that the ruse might fail when crossing intelligent hubs and some routers. Therefore, ARP cache spoofing is reliable only under certain conditions, and even then it might be restricted to the local network segment. Moreover, cache entries expire pretty quickly. Thus, you still have to backtrack periodically and update the cache entries while implementing the attack.

Can ARP spoofing be defeated? Absolutely. There are several things that you can do. One is to write your address mappings in stone. This can, however, be an irritating prospect. Paul Buis explains in his paper *Names and Addresses*:

> Many operating systems do however have provisions for making entries in the ARP cache "static" so they do not time out every few minutes. I recommend using this feature to prevent ARP spoofing, but it requires updating the cache manually every time a hardware address changes.

▶ Get Paul Buis' paper from `http://www.cs.bsu.edu/homepages/peb/cs637/nameadd/`.

Another choice is to use ARPWATCH. ARPWATCH is a utility that watches changes in your IP/Ethernet mappings. If changes are detected, you are alerted via email. (Also, the information will be logged, which helps track down the offender.) Get ARPWATCH here:

```
ftp://ftp.ee.lbl.gov/arpwatch.tar.gz
```

NOTE

To use ARPWATCH, you need UNIX, C, and AWK. (The distribution comes in source only.)

DNS Spoofing

In *DNS spoofing*, the cracker compromises the DNS server and explicitly alters the hostname-IP address tables. These changes are written into the translation table databases on the DNS server. Thus, when a client requests a lookup, he or she is given a bogus address; this address is the IP address of a machine that is completely under the cracker's control.

The likelihood of this happening is slim, but widespread exposure could result if it does occur. The rarity of these attacks should not be taken as a comforting indicator. Earlier in this chapter, I cited a DDN advisory that documented a rash of attacks against DNS machines. Moreover, an important CIAC advisory addresses this issue:

> Although you might be willing to accept the risks associated with using these services for now, you need to consider the impact that spoofed DNS information might have.... It is possible for intruders to spoof BIND into providing incorrect name data. Some systems and programs depend on this information for authentication, so it is possible to spoof those systems and gain unauthorized access.

▶ The previous paragraph is excerpted from the CIAC advisory titled *Domain Name Service Vulnerabilities*. It can be found online at `http://ciac.llnl.gov/ciac/bulletins/g-14.shtml`.

DNS spoofing has now been automated at least on some platforms. There's a utility called Jizz, written by Nimrood (and based on code written by Johannes Erdfelt). To try it out, download it from this address:

```
http://packetstorm.securify.com/Exploit_Code_Archive/jizz.c
```

There is an interesting document that addresses a DNS spoofing technique—*Java Security: From HotJava to Netscape and Beyond*, by Drew Dean, Edward W. Felten, and Dan S. Wallach. The paper discusses a technique by which a Java applet makes repeated calls to the attacker's machine, which is, in effect, a cracked DNS server. In this way, it is ultimately possible to redirect DNS lookups from the default name server to an untrusted one. From there, the attacker might conceivably compromise the client machine or network. (This bug was fixed in 1.02.)

▶ *Java Security: From HotJava to Netscape and Beyond* is located online at `http://www.cs.`
`princeton.edu/sip/pub/oakland-paper-96.pdf`.

DNS spoofing is fairly easy to detect, however. If you suspect one of the DNS servers, poll the
other authoritative DNS servers on the network. Unless the originally affected server has been
compromised for some time, evidence will immediately surface that it has been spoofed. Other
authoritative servers will report results that vary from those given by the cracked DNS server.

Polling might not be sufficient if the originally spoofed server has been compromised for some
time. Bogus address-host name tables might have been passed to other DNS servers on the network. If you are noticing abnormalities in name resolution, you might want to employ a script
utility called DOC (domain obscenity control). As articulated in the utility's documentation:

> DOC (domain obscenity control) is a program which diagnoses misbehaving domains by
> sending queries off to the appropriate domain name servers and performing a series of
> analyses on the output of these queries.

▶ DOC is available online at `ftp://coast.cs.purdue.edu/pub/tools/unix/sysutils/doc/`
`doc.2.0.tar.Z`.

Other techniques that defeat DNS spoofing attacks include the use of reverse DNS schemes.
Under these schemes, sometimes referred to as *tests of your forwards*, the service attempts to
reconcile the forward lookup with the reverse. This technique might have limited value. In all
likelihood, the cracker has altered both the forward and reverse tables. For more information
on configuring your DNS server, see

`http://www.dns.net/dnsrd/`
`http://www.cert.org/advisories/CA-1999-14.html`

Summary

Spoofing is popular now and when done from the outside, it leaves relatively little evidence. At
a minimum, you should block apparent local requests that originate outside your network, and
as always, you should employ logging utilities. Finally, I recommend keeping up with the latest
advisories—particularly from your router vendor. New spoofing attacks tend to emerge every
few months or so.

Hiding One's Identity

IN THIS CHAPTER

If you are looking to protect your data, there are many tools available to you. The list is almost endless: digital certificates, packet filters, strong encryption, firewalls, virus utilities, virtual private networks, network appliances, and a dozen other tools. Each can offer some assurance that your Internet site and network is safe. What about more basic issues? For example, what steps can you take to secure your privacy while surfing online? As with data protection, there are also several methods available for protecting your personal privacy on the Internet. This chapter looks at these methods.

Degrees of Exposure

Unless you take steps to prevent it, your identity will eventually be exposed if you surf the Internet. That exposure will manifest in different forms and degrees, depending on many factors, including

- Your network connection
- Your browser
- Your public traffic
- The plug-ins and applications you support

These variables expose you to two different types of intelligence:

- Human intelligence
- Network intelligence

Let's examine each in turn.

Human Intelligence

Human beings spy on you. Through such spying, they can discover your identity, track your movements, or even catch you in a criminal act. Of all forms of intelligence, human intelligence is the oldest. (In fact, spies often muse that human intelligence is the world's oldest profession.)

Human intelligence comes in two flavors, collective and penetrative:

- *Collective intelligence* has as its chief objective to collect information without necessarily establishing direct contact.
- *Penetrative intelligence* has as its chief objective to establish direct contact, gain the contacted person's trust, and obtain information on an ongoing basis.

The Internet is a superb tool for collective intelligence. For example, consider your posts to Usenet. These are available to the public, to persons known and unknown. Others can track your messages closely and can learn a great deal about you by doing so. Naturally, this presents law enforcement agencies with a unique opportunity. Simply by using search engines, they can conduct collective intelligence at a whim.

This is completely different from the situation 25 years ago. To illustrate how different, let me take you back to the early 1970s. Here in America, the '70s were filled with political turmoil. Many radical organizations emerged, and some advocated violent overthrow of the government. U.S. intelligence agencies responded by conducting collective and penetrative operations. These operations were carried out by human beings. For example, to identify supporters of the Students for a Democratic Society, the FBI would send agents on foot. (These agents might have been employed by the FBI, or they might have been civilian informers. It didn't really matter which.) Such agents would mix with the crowds at political rallies and record license plate numbers, or gather names. Later, field agents would connect faces, fingerprints, and addresses to those names by running license plate files, retrieving criminal records, or questioning still other informants.

Those methods are no longer necessary. Instead, the Internet enables intelligence agencies to monitor public sentiment from the comfort of their own offices. Furthermore, they can do this without violating any law. No search warrant is required to study someone's activity on the Internet. This means that any agency can freely utilize tools and software available on the Internet to collect data on anyone. Likewise, no warrant is required before using the Internet to compile lists of people who might be involved in illegal or seditious activity. A warrant is only required when the data needed resides on private systems, such as an ISP. Obtaining a subpoena, an intelligence agency can then gain access to ISP log files, any e-mail traffic (if available), and any other digital data pertaining to the individual.

If you harbor radical political views, you should keep them to yourself. (Either that or gain a decent education in cryptography.) Here's why: Today's search engines can be used to isolate all Usenet traffic between a particular class of individuals (militia members, for example). You can bet your last dollar that Kirk Lyons (a white supremacist lawyer whose clients have been a "Who's Who" of the radical right) has been monitored closely by the FBI.

Be forewarned: Usenet is not a forum to exercise your right to free speech. Instead, it's a place where you are exposed, naked to the world. Usenet is just the beginning. Six out of every ten Web sites you visit track your movements. (Probably eight out of ten big commercial sites try to.) Advances in digital snooping make it possible for nearly anyone with a computer to become an electronic Peeping Tom.

Recently, the FBI introduced DCS1000, a system that, when plugged into a computer network, captures and tracks all network communication through that system. DCS1000 has created a large controversy with privacy advocates. One of the biggest reasons for this is simply that DCS1000 is not designed to monitor just a single individual (or select individuals) whom the FBI might be legally wiretapping. It captures all communications on the systems that the investigators plug it into. Recently, with the help of the Freedom of Information Act, about 600 documents relating to DCS1000 were released. From this information, SecurityFocus.com has put together an interesting overview:

Newly declassified documents obtained by Electronic Privacy Information Center (EPIC) under the Freedom of Information Act reveal that DCS1000 can monitor all of a target user's Internet traffic, and, in conjunction with other FBI tools, can reconstruct web pages exactly as a surveillance target saw them while surfing the web.

This is fine for tracking and monitoring illegal activities of people suspected of criminal activity, but what about all the innocent users that have unknowingly had their privacy violated? The FBI doesn't let the public know what it does with that data gathered from DCS1000.

NOTE

DCS1000 is the most recent name for the program formerly known as Carnivore.

Web Browsing and Invasion of Privacy

Before Web browsers existed, you could only access the Internet from a command-line interface. This interface was bare bones and intimidating to most people. Browsers changed that by turning the Internet into a point-and-click paradise; anyone with a mouse could easily navigate the World Wide Web. The results were phenomenal. Indeed, practically overnight, millions of users flocked to the Web.

When humanity rushed to the Web, marketing agencies took notice. This question was immediately posed: How can we use the Internet to make a buck? Companies came up with various answers, including electronic commerce. (In electronic commerce, consumers buy products or services over the Web, right from their own homes.)

From the start, there was a strong drive to develop methods of tracking not only consumer purchases but also consumer interests. Many such methods emerged by 1993, and today there are more than a dozen. In the following pages, you learn how your identity is ferreted out, bit by bit, by persons known and unknown.

Internet Architecture and Privacy

I'll begin by making a blanket statement and one you should never forget: The Internet's architecture was not designed with personal privacy in mind. In fact, there are many standard Internet utilities designed specifically for tracing and identifying users.

In a moment we'll examine some and how they work. First, however, we need to cover how user information is stored on servers.

How User Information Is Stored on Servers

There are two universal forms of identification on the Internet: your email address and your IP address. Both reveal your identity. At a minimum, both serve as good starting places for a spy.

Your email address in particular can reveal your real name. Here's why: Even if your Internet service provider uses Windows NT to host a few Web sites, almost all ISPs use UNIX as their base platform. That's because UNIX (coupled with a protocol called RADIUS) makes management of dial-up accounts very easy. (It also provides better mail support than Windows NT if you are dealing with hundreds or even thousands of accounts.)

On the UNIX system, user information is stored in a file called `passwd`, which is located in the `/etc` directory. This file contains user login names, usernames, and occasionally, user passwords (although only in encrypted form). An entry from the `passwd` file looks like this:

```
jdoe:x:65536:1:John Doe:/export/home/jdoe:/sbin/sh
```

If you examine the entry closely, you'll see that the fields are colon-delimited. Here you should be concerned with fields 1, 5, and 6. Using the entry as an example, those fields are as follows:

- `jdoe`   Your username
- `John Doe`   Your real name
- `/export/home/jdoe`   Your home directory

This information is vital, and UNIX uses it for many tasks. For example, this information is double-checked each time you log in, each time you receive mail, and each time you log out. Unfortunately, the information is also usually available to the general public through a utility called finger.

Finger

Finger is a service common to UNIX systems. Its purpose is to provide user information to remote hosts, and, like all TCP/IP services, finger is based on the client/server model.

When a UNIX system first boots, it loads nearly a dozen remote services (for example, a Web server, an FTP server, a Telnet server, and so forth). The finger server is called `fingerd`, and is commonly referred to as the *finger daemon.*

The finger daemon listens for local or remote requests for user information. When it receives such a request, it forwards whatever information is currently available on the target. (The target in this case is you.)

On UNIX, a finger request can be issued from a command prompt. The results from the finger server are then printed to the local terminal. Here's what a command-prompt finger request looks like:

```
$finger -l jdoe@john-doe.com
```

The command translates into plain English like this: "Look up jdoe and tell me everything you can about him." When a user issues such a request, the finger daemon at john-doe.com is contacted. It searches through the system for jdoe and ultimately, it returns this information:

```
Login name: jdoe                    In real life: John Doe
Directory: /                        Shell: /sbin/sh
Last login Tue May 18 19:53 on pts/22
New mail received Mon May 18 04:05:58 1997;
  unread since Mon May 18 03:20:43 1997
No Plan.
```

For years, this information was available only to UNIX and VAX/VMS users. Not any more. Today, there are *finger clients* (programs that perform finger lookups) for all platforms. Table 8.1 lists a few.

TABLE 8.1   Finger Clients for Non-UNIX, Non-Windows NT Users

Client	Platform	Location
InkFinger	Windows	http://www.inkland.f9.co.uk/ifinger/inkf122.exe
Total Finger	Windows	http://www.mrfrosty.co.uk/files/tfinger.exe
Tray Finger	Windows	ftp://ftp.igsnet.com/pub/trayfinger.exe
IPNetMonitor	Mac OS (PPC)	http://www.sustworks.com/cgibin/ftp.pl?file=IPNetMonitor_245.hqx
IPNetMonitor	Mac OS (68K)	http://www.sustworks.com/cgibin/ftp.pl?file=IPNetMonitor68K_221.sit.hqx
Gibbon Finger	OS/2	ftp://ftp.gibbon.com/pub/gcp/gcpfng10.zip
Thumb	OS/2	http://www.catherders.com/dirs/PCB/OS2LAN/THUMB10.ZIP

NOTE

Windows NT now has integrated finger support, so a third-party client is not required. To finger someone from an NT box, simply open a command prompt window and type finger_target@host.com.

These days, most system administrators deny remote finger requests to their networks, even internally. When network finger requests are allowed, they are often unrestricted and unregulated. This permits remote users to identify not only you, but everyone on the system. To do so, remote users issue the following command:

```
finger @my_target_host.com
```

The @ symbol works precisely as an asterisk does in regular expression searches. In plain English, the command says this: "Tell me about all users currently logged on."

When writing this chapter, I wanted to give you an example, so, I fingered all users at Reed College in Portland, Oregon. Here is the result from that query:

```
finger @reed.edu
[reed.edu]
Login      Name                TTY Idle     When         Office
copeland   D. Jeremy Copeland  *p1    12 Tue 19:24  Box 169     775 6945
boothbyl   Lawrence E. Boothby  p3 121d Sun 09:05
mab        Mark Bedau           p4     Tue 19:32
copeland   D. Jeremy Copeland   p6     4 Tue 19:29  Box 169     775 6945
slam       Greg (don't call me  p7  13d Wed 08:36   Box 470     or Coleman
slam       Greg (don't call me  p8  18d Fri 07:29   Box 470     or Coleman
mayer      Ray Mayer           *p9   2d Mon 16:59   (fac)
mcclellj   Joshua J McClellan   pf   4d Fri 14:45   (813)
slam       Greg (don't call me  pe   6d Wed 08:19   Box 470     or Coleman
mcclellj   Joshua J McClellan   q0   4d Fri 16:12   (813)
moored     Dustin B Moore       q2 6:32 Tue 13:05   (1172)
obonfim    Osiel Bonfim         q3 3:02 Mon 16:07
rahkolar   Rahua Rahkola        q6    46 Tue 18:34
obonfim    Osiel Bonfim         q9 2:59 Tue 09:45
mcclellj   Joshua J McClellan   qb   4d Fri 15:00   (813)
jwitte     John Witte          *qc 4:00 Tue 15:14
lillieb    Ben Lillie           r3    58 Tue 13:11  P04
szutst     Tobi A. Szuts       *r7     5 Tue 14:51  (819)
mcclard    Ron McClard         *re 1:22 Mon 10:55   (x218)
queue      Print Queue Display  qd   8d Mon 15:42
jimfix     James D. Fix        *qf    32 Tue 13:04
mcclellj   Joshua J McClellan   r6 3:50 Mon 10:47   (813)
```

It doesn't look like these folks have much privacy, does it? Well, here's a fact: 99% of listings I checked around the Internet revealed the users' real names. If you think that listing only your company name will hide your identity, think again. Take a look at the first line of the preceding output:

```
copeland D. Jeremy Copeland   *p1   12 Tue 19:24  Box 169     775 6945
```

Here, as you can see, we already have this person's full name, his login name and email address (Copeland@reed.edu), and a phone number. Using Google (http://www.google.com), I found his personal Web site at Reed College. I can also safely assume from the location of the college that he is in Portland, Oregon. A search on Worldpages (http://www.worldpages.com) gave me four individuals matching this person, all with home phone numbers and personal addresses. Not a lot of personal privacy here, is it?

In many cases, by starting with finger and ending with WorldPages, you can find someone's home address (along with a map for directions) in fewer than 30 seconds. If someone tells you that finger doesn't present a privacy issue, give them a copy of this book. Finger can bring a total stranger right to your doorstep.

Solutions for the Finger Problem

There are solutions for the finger problem. However, before you bother, you should check to see whether you are a viable target.

> **NOTE**
>
> If you use America Online, know that AOL does not allow finger requests on their users.

There are two ways to determine whether you are a viable finger target:

- Perform a finger query on yourself.
- Check the `/etc/passwd` file on your ISP's server.

To check from a shell prompt, issue either of the following commands:

```
grep your_username /etc/passwd
```

```
ypcat passwd || cat /etc/passwd | grep your_username
```

These commands will print the information in the server's `/etc/passwd` file. The output will look like this:

```
jdoe:x:65536:1:John Doe:/export/home/jdoe:/sbin/sh
```

If you are a viable finger target, there are several things you can do to minimize your exposure:

- Use the utility `chfn` to alter the finger information available to outsiders.
- If `chfn` is not available, request that the system administrator change your information.
- Cancel your current account and start a new one.

> **NOTE**
>
> You might be puzzled why I suggest canceling your account. Here's why: It was you who provided the information in the `/etc/passwd` account. You provided that information when you signed up. If you can't access `chfn` and your SA refuses to change this information, it will remain there until you cancel your account. If you cancel your account and create a new one, you can dictate what information the server has on you.

On the other hand, if you don't care about getting fingered but you simply want to know who's doing it, you need MasterPlan.

MasterPlan

MasterPlan (written by Laurion Burchall) takes a more aggressive approach by identifying who is trying to finger you. Each time a finger query is detected, MasterPlan captures the hostname and user ID of the fingering party. This information is stored in a file called `finger_log`. MasterPlan will also determine how often you are fingered, so you can detect whether someone is trying to clock you. (In *clocking,* user A attempts to discern the habits of user B via various network utilities, including finger and the r commands.)

> **TIP**
>
> The r commands consist of a suite of network utilities that can glean information about users on remote hosts.

In clocking, the snooping party uses an automated script to finger his target every *X* number of minutes or hours. Reasons for such probing can be diverse. One is to build a profile of the target: When does the user log in? How often does the user check mail? From where does the user usually log in? From these queries, a nosy party can determine other possible points on the network where you can be found.

Here's an example: A cracker I know wanted to intercept the email of a nationally renowned female journalist who covers hacking stories. This journalist had several accounts and frequently logged in to one from another. (In other words, she *chained* her connections. In this way, she was trying to keep her private email address a secret.)

By running a clocking script on the journalist, the cracker was able to identify her private, unpublished email address. He was also able to compromise her network and ultimately capture her mail. The mail consisted of discussions between the journalist and a software engineer in England. The subject matter concerned a high-profile cracking case in the news. (That mail was later distributed to crackers' groups across the Internet.)

MasterPlan can identify clocking patterns, at least with respect to finger queries. The utility is small and easy to configure. The C source is included, and the distribution is known to compile cleanly on most UNIX systems. (The exceptions are Ultrix and NeXT.) One nice amenity for Linux users is that a precompiled binary comes with most distributions. The standard distribution of MasterPlan is available at the following address:

```
ftp://ftp.netspace.org/pub/Software/Unix/masterplan.tar.Z
```

The Linux-compiled version is available at this address:

`ftp://ftp.netspace.org/pub/Software/Unix/masterplan-linux.tar.Z`

> **NOTE**
>
> MasterPlan does not prevent others from fingering you; it simply identifies those parties and how often they finger you. Unfortunately, as of this date, MasterPlan is only available for UNIX and is no longer maintained.

After you shield yourself against finger queries, you might feel that your name is safe from prying eyes. Wrong again. Finger is just the beginning. There are a dozen other ways your email address and your name reveal information about you.

Beyond Finger

Even if your provider forbids finger requests, your name is still easy to obtain. When snoops try to finger you and discover finger isn't running, they turn to your mail server. In most cases, servers accept Telnet connections to port 25 (the port that sendmail runs on). Such a connection looks like this:

`220 shell. Sendmail SMI-8.6/SMI-SVR4 ready at Wed, 19 Feb 1997 07:17:18 -0800`

If outsiders can reach the prompt, they can quickly obtain your name by issuing the following command:

`expn username`

The `expn` command expands usernames into email addresses and real names. The response will typically look like this:

`username <username@target_of_probe.com> Real Name`

The first field will report your username or user ID, followed by your email address, and finally, your "real" name.

System administrators can disable the `expn` function, but few actually do. In any event, if the `expn` function is operable, nosy individuals can still get your real name, if it is available. Again, the best policy is to remove your real name from the `passwd` file.

> **NOTE**
>
> Unfortunately, even if the `expn` function has been disabled, the snooping party can sometimes still verify the existence of your account using the `vrfy` function (if your server supports it).

As you can see, finger poses a unique privacy problem—but that's just the beginning.

Browser Security

With the rise of electronic commerce, various methods to track your movements have been developed. Three key methods are implemented through your Web browser:

- IP address and cache snooping
- Cookies
- Banner ads and Web bugs

By themselves, these techniques seem harmless enough. However, if you want to remain anonymous, you must take steps to safeguard yourself against them. Let's examine each in turn.

IP Address and Cache Snooping

Each time you visit a Web server, you leave behind a trail. This trail is recorded in different ways on different servers, but it is always recorded. A typical log entry on UNIX (running Apache) looks like this:

```
153.35.38.245 [01/May/1998:18:12:10 -0700] "GET / HTTP/1.1" 401 362
```

Note the first entry (the IP address). All Web server packages are capable of recording visitor IP addresses. However, most Web servers can also record other information, including your hostname and even your username. To see what a Web server can tell about you, visit this site:

```
http://www.agentz.com/browsers/cgitest.cgi
```

I had a friend at JetLink Internet services visit that site. Here is the information that server returned on him:

```
The host SERVER_NAME, DNS alias, or IP address is: "www.ixd.com"
The name and revision of the SERVER_SOFTWARE is: "Netscape-Enterprise/2.0a"
The name and revision of the SERVER_PROTOCOL is: "HTTP/1.0"
The SERVER_PORT number for this server is: "80"
The SERVER_ADMINistrator e-mail address is: ""
The name and revision of cgi GATEWAY_INTERFACE is: "CGI/1.1"
The extra PATH_INFO included on the URL is: ""
The actual extra PATH_TRANSLATED is: ""
The server DOCUMENT_ROOT directory is: ""
The cgi SCRIPT_NAME is: "/cgi-bin/cgi-test.cgi"
The query REQUEST_METHOD is: "GET"
The QUERY_STRING from Form GET is: ""
The CONTENT_TYPE of the Form POST data is: ""
The CONTENT_LENGTH of the Form POST data is: ""
```

```
The name of the REMOTE_HOST making the request is: "ppp-208-19-49-
➥216.isdn.jetlink.net"
The IP REMOTE_ADDRress of the remote host is: "208.19.49.216"
The authentication (AUTH_TYPE) method is: ""
The authenticated REMOTE_USER is: ""
The remote user (REMOTE_IDENT) for (rfc 931) is: ""
The MIME types that the client will (HTTP_ACCEPT):
➥"image/gif, image/x-xbitmap,
➥image/jpeg, image/pjpeg, image/png, */*"
The client's browser type (HTTP_USER_AGENT) is:
➥"Mozilla/4.04   (Win95; U)"
The page (HTTP_REFERER) that client came from:
"http://altavista.digital.com/cgi-bin/query?pg=q&text=yes&q=
➥%22test%2ecgi%22&stq=10"
The e-mail address (HTTP_FROM) of the client is: ""
```

Note that in addition to grabbing the IP address, the server also grabbed the dial-up line my friend was using:

```
The name of the REMOTE_HOST making the request is: "ppp-208-19-49-
➥216.isdn.jetlink.net"
```

However, even more importantly, the server identified the last site my friend visited:

```
The page (HTTP_REFERER) that client came from:
"http://altavista.digital.com/cgi-
bin/query?pg=q&text=yes&q=%22test%2ecgi%22&stq=10"
```

The script that captured that information is called test-cgi. It is used to capture basic environment variables, both on the server and client sides. (As it happens, test-cgi can also be a tremendous security hole, and most ISPs remove it from their servers.)

Using these logs and scripts, Webmasters can precisely pinpoint where you are, what your network address is, and where you've been. Are you uncomfortable yet? Now quickly examine cookies.

Cookies

Cookies. The word might sound inviting to you, but not to me—I very much value my privacy. In the past, many reporters have written articles about cookies, attempting to allay the public's fears. In such articles, they minimize the influence of cookies, dismissing them as harmless. Are cookies harmless? Not in my opinion.

Cookies (which Netscape calls Persistent Client State HTTP Cookies) are used to store information about you as you browse a Web page. The folks at Netscape explain it this way:

> This simple mechanism provides a powerful new tool that enables a host of new types of applications to be written for Web-based environments. Shopping applications can now

store information about the currently selected items, for fee services can send back registration information and free the client from retyping a user-id on next connection, sites can store per-user preferences on the client, and have the client supply those preferences every time that site is connected to.

▶ The article from which the previous quote is excerpted, Persistent Client State HTTP Cookies, can be found at `http://home.netscape.com/newsref/std/cookie_spec.html`.

The cookie concept is like getting your hand stamped at a dance club that serves cocktails. You can roam the club, have some drinks, dance the floor, and even go outside for a few minutes. As long as the stamp is on your hand, you will not have to pay again, nor will your access be restricted. Similarly, cookies enable Web servers to "remember" you, your password, your interests, and so on. That way, when you return, this information is automatically retrieved. The issue concerning cookies, though, isn't that the information is retrieved. The controversy is about where the information is retrieved from—your hard disk drive.

The process works like this: When you visit a Web page, the server writes a cookie to your hard disk drive. This cookie is stored in a special file.

NOTE

Windows users can find the cookies file in varying places, depending on their browser type and their version of Windows. Cookies in older distributions are kept in a file called `cookies.txt`. In newer distributions (and with Microsoft Internet Explorer), cookies are stored individually in the directory `C:\WINDOWS\COOKIES`. (On Macintosh systems, the file is called `MagicCookie`.)

8

Here are some typical entries from a cookie file:

```
www.webspan.net    FALSE    /~frys    FALSE    859881600    worldohackf
➥  2.netscape.com    TRUE    /    FALSE    946684799
➥NETSCAPE_ID
1000e010,107ea15f.adobe.com    TRUE    /    FALSE    946684799    INTERSE
➥207.171.18.182 6852855142083822www.ictnet.com    FALSE    /    FALSE
➥946684799    Apache    pm3a-4326561855491810745.microsoft.com    TRUE
➥    /    FALSE    937422000    MC1
➥GUID=260218f482a111d0889e08002bb74f65.msn.com    TRUE    /    FALSE
➥937396800    MC1    ID=260218f482a111d0889e08002bb74f65comsecltd.com
➥FALSE    /    FALSE    1293753600    EGSOFT_ID
➥207.171.18.176-3577227984.29104071
.amazon.com    TRUE    /    FALSE    858672000    session-id-time
➥855894626.amazon.com    TRUE    /    FALSE    858672000
➥    session-id    0738-6510633-772498
```

This cookie file is a real one, pulled from an associate's hard disk drive. You will see that under the GUID (field number 6), the leading numbers are an IP address. (I have added a space between the IP address and the remaining portion of the string so that you can easily identify the IP. In practice, however, the string is unbroken.) From this, you can see that setting a cookie generally involves recording your IP address.

Advocates of cookies insist that they are harmless, cannot assist in identifying the user, and are therefore benign. That is not true, as explained by D. Kristol and L. Montulli in RFC 2109:

> An origin server could create a Set-Cookie header to track the path of a user through the server. Users may object to this behavior as an intrusive accumulation of information, even if their identity is not evident. (Identity might become evident if a user subsequently fills out a form that contains identifying information.)

Today, cookies are routinely used for user authentication. This is disturbing and was immediately recognized as a problem. As expressed in RFC 2109:

> User agents should allow the user to control cookie destruction. An infrequently-used cookie may function as a "preferences file" for network applications, and a user may wish to keep it even if it is the least-recently-used cookie. One possible implementation would be an interface that allows the permanent storage of a cookie through a checkbox (or, conversely, its immediate destruction).

Despite these early warnings about cookies, mainstream Web browsers still ship with the Accept Cookies option enabled. Worse still, although most browsers have an option that warns you before accepting a cookie, this option is also disabled by default. Netscape Communicator, for example, ships this way. If you use Netscape Communicator, take a moment to go to the Edit menu and choose Preferences. After you have the Preference option window open, click Advanced.

Microsoft Internet Explorer ships in basically the same state. Think about that for a moment: How many new computer owners are aware that cookies exist? Shouldn't they at least be informed that such intelligence gathering is going on? I think so.

TIP

To disable cookies in Internet Explorer, click on Tools, and then select Internet Options from the list. A new window will open. Click the Security tab. You can change the security level to High, or click Custom Level. There you will find the options to disable cookies in Internet Explorer.

Combating Cookies

Cookies can easily be managed and defeated using *cookie cutters*. These are programs that give you control over cookies (such as viewing them, deleting them, or conditionally refusing them). Table 8.2 provides names and locations of several cookie cutters.

TABLE 8.2 Cookies Cutters, Their Platforms, and Their Locations

Cutter	Platform	Location
Cookie Pal	Windows	`http://www.kburra.com/cp1setup.exe`
Cookie Crusher	Windows	`http://www.rbaworld.com/Programs/CookieCruncher/`
Cookie Monster	MacOS	`http://www.geocities.com/Paris/1778/` `CookieMonster151.sit`
NoMoreCookies	MacOS	`ftp://ftp.zdnet.com/pub/private/sWlIB/internet/` `world_wide_web/nomcooks.hqx`
ScapeGoat	MacOS	`ftp://zdftp.zdnet.com/pub/private/sWlIB/` `internet/world_wide_web/scapegt.hqx`

NOTE

Windows and MacOS users can also make the cookies file or directory read-only. This will prevent any cookies from being written to the drive. UNIX users should delete the `cookies.txt` file and place a symbolic link there that points to `/dev/null`.

If you want to learn more about cookies, check out some of the following articles:

- *A Cookies Monster?* Stephen T. Maher, *Law Products* Magazine. `http://www.usual.com/article6.htm`

- **Cookies and Privacy FAQ.** `http://www.cookiecentral.com/n_cookie_faq.htm`

- **Are Cookie Files Public Record?** Dan Goodin, CNET. `http://www.news.com/News/Item/0,4,17170,00.html`

- **How Web Servers' Cookies Threaten Your Privacy.** Junkbusters. `http://www.junkbusters.com/ht/en/cookies.html`

- **HTTP State Management Mechanism** (RFC 2109, a document discussing the technical aspects of the cookie mechanism.) `http://www.ics.uci.edu/pub/ietf/http/rfc2109.txt`

You should also know this: Cookies and the test-cgi script are not the only ways that Webmasters grab information about you. Other, less conspicuous techniques exist. Many JavaScript and Perl scripts can "get" your IP address. This type of code also can get your browser type, your operating system, and so forth. Following is an example in JavaScript:

```
<script language=javascript>
    function Get_Browser() {
    var appName = navigator.appName;
    var appVersion = navigator.appVersion;
    document.write(appName + " " + appVersion.substring
➥(0,appVersion.indexOf(" ")));
    }
</script>
```

JavaScript will get the browser and its version. Scripts like this are used at thousands of sites across the Internet. A very popular one is the "Book 'em, Dan-O" script. This script (written in the Perl programming language) will get the time you accessed the page, your browser type and version, and your IP address.

▶ The "Book 'em, Dan-O" script was written by an individual named Spider. It is currently available for download at Matt's Script Archive at `http://worldwidemart.com/scripts/dano.shtml`.

Similar programs are available in a wide range of programming languages, including Java. You will find a Java program designed specifically for this purpose here:

`http://www.teklasoft.com/java/applets/connect/socket.html`

Banner Ads and Web Bugs

You've no doubt visited plenty of Web sites with banner advertisements. The Internet has become a marketing executive's dream come true, with nearly unlimited methods of tracking and recording information on consumers. Today, nearly every popular Web site is littered with annoying banner ads, Web bugs, and targeted marketing. The only cost is your own personal privacy. Banner ads are a necessary evil of the new Internet economy, but did you know that these innocent images can also be used to track users and transmit demographics back to the advertising companies responsible for them?

The methods vary, but it generally works like this: A user visits a popular Web site with a banner ad that has the capability to track. As the page loads, it will grab the required banner image directly off of a Web server run by the advertising company. Every time this happens, the ad server has the capability to log a great deal of information on who is loading that image. Using cookies, sophisticated JavaScript, and CGI, the unwitting visitor might be sending nothing more that her IP, or every piece of personal information she might have submitted to another Web site previously. It is also possible for the remote ad server to set a cookie on the user's computer to help it track that person in better detail.

The latest trend in violating your Web surfing privacy comes from Web bugs. A Web bug is usually a small, transparent gif, 1×1 pixels in size, that works in a similar manner to a tracking banner ad. When the page loads, the invisible Web bug loads also, triggering the same transfer of information that the banner ads can send. The biggest difference is simply stealth. You can't see or detect a Web bug, unless you look at the source for that particular Web page. Take a look at this example from the ZDNet Web site:

```
<img src="http://ads3.zdnet.com/i/g=r001&c=a56998&idx=2001.01.04.21.48.58/
http://images.zdnet.com/adverts/imp/dotclear.gif">
```

This is the HTML code to display an image on the ZDNet Web page. This, however, is no ordinary image. It's a Web bug used to track people visiting the Web site. Notice the height and width parameters, and the lack of a border or an ALT entry. This invisible image, when loaded, triggers the ad server at ZDNet to record whatever information they programmed it to retrieve. ZDNet is not alone in this behavior. I simply loaded the first Web site that came to mind, and found this Web bug.

▶ There are several good articles online about the proliferation of Web bugs and banner ads with tracking capabilities. Be sure to check out this article: Nearly Undetectable Tracking Device Raises Concerns by Stefanie Olsen at `http://news.cnet.com/news//0-1007-200-2247960.html`.

What do these companies need this information for? Why do they violate your privacy, without your permission or consent? Marketing. Marketing and selling products to consumers requires detailed demographics and statistics. With this information, the advertising companies are better able to target a specific group in order to sell them something. If you visit a lot of Web sites related to computers, for instance, you will notice that the ads you see will be designed to get you to buy computer-related products and services. Also, a high traffic Web site can make a good sum of money by enabling advertisers to post banner ads and Web bugs on their pages.

Protecting Yourself from Banner Ads and Web Bugs

Thankfully, there are many solutions for combating intrusive cookies, banner ads, and Web bugs. Today, there are several software programs that you can proxy your Web browser traffic through to block this material. A proxy is a type of software that acts as a sort of middle man between you and the Internet. Your Internet traffic flows through it, and depending on the proxy's functionality, it is sped up, filtered, or redirected. My personal favorite is the Internet Junkbuster. Junkbuster's developers have also recently released a consumer version of Junkbuster called Guidescope, which is aimed at the general public and is easy to install and use. Guidescope offers the same level of protection as Junkbuster, but it is designed to be a lot more user friendly and easier to install and maintain.

Internet Junkbuster acts as a proxy server for all your Web surfing traffic. As you load Web pages, it inspects the incoming code for common patterns used by banner ads and Web bugs. Before this code ever reaches your Web browser, it is stripped from the HTML, effectively

8

HIDING ONE'S
IDENTITY

sterilizing the privacy-invading banners and bugs. Not only does this help safeguard your privacy, but blocking banner advertisements significantly speeds up Web browsing, and you will find it is a lot easier to concentrate on the information you came to see, rather than flashy obnoxious Web advertising. Internet Junkbuster and Guidescope can also be configured to block cookies.

NOTE

If your privacy is important, you should take a few minutes to take a look at the Junkbuster Web site. They provide a great deal of information on proactively protecting yourself from invasive advertising in email, postal mail, telemarketing, and other means.

More information on Internet Junkbuster and Guidescope can be found at

`http://www.junkbusters.com`

`http://www.guidescope.com`

Your Email Address and Usenet

Earlier in this chapter, I claimed that your email address could expose you to spying on Usenet. In this section, I will prove it.

Your email address is like any other text string. If it appears on (or within the source of) a Web page, it is reachable by search engines. When a spy has your email address, it's all over but the screaming. In fact, perhaps most disturbing of all, your email address and name (after they are paired) can reveal other accounts that you might have.

To provide you with a practical example, I pondered a possible target. I was looking for someone who changed email addresses frequently and routinely used others as fronts. *Fronts* are third parties who post information for you. By using a front, you avoid being pinned down because it's the front's email address that appears, not your own.

I decided to do a bit of research on a controversial person, Kirk D. Lyons of the Southern Legal Resource Center (SLRC). This name might not be too familiar to many people right away. Mr. Lyons is an outspoken attorney with a history of defending right-wing and extremist groups. He has also been a prominent voice and an active participant in several newsworthy incidents, especially in the last 10 years. Mr. Lyons has been directly involved with issues relating to the Oklahoma Federal Building bombing and Timothy McVeigh, the Ruby Ridge incident with Randy Weaver, and the Waco stand-off, to name a few.

NOTE

The following exercise is not an invasion of Mr. Lyons' privacy. All information was obtained from publicly available databases on the Internet. Instead, this exercise is very similar to the results of an article in a June 1997 Time magazine about Internet privacy. In that article, a Time reporter tracked California Senator Dianne Feinstein. The reporter did an extraordinary job, and even managed to ascertain Senator Feinstein's Social Security number. The article, "My Week as an Internet Gumshoe," is by Noah Robischon. At the time of this writing, it is available online here: `http://www.pathfinder.com/time/magazine/1997/dom/970602/technology.my_wek.html`.

The first step in tracking an individual is to capture his or her email addresses. To find Kirk D. Lyons's email address, any garden-variety search engine will do, although `www.altavista.com` and `www.google.com` have the most malleable designs. That's where I started. (Remember that I have never met Mr. Lyons and know very little about him.)

I began my search with AltaVista (`http://www.altavista.com`). AltaVista is one of the most powerful search engines available on the Internet and is provided as a public service by CMGI, Inc. It accepts various types of queries that can be directed toward WWW pages (HTML), images and video, and other forms of digital media. I followed up using Google (`http://www.google.com`), a newer but amazingly powerful search engine. Don't let the clean, simple interface fool you. Google quickly grew out of obscurity into one of the best search engines available.

I chose AltaVista for one reason: It performs case-sensitive, exact-match regular expression searches. That means that it will match precisely what you search for. (In other words, there are no "close" matches when you request such a search. This feature enables you to narrow your results to a single page out of millions.)

In order to force such a precise search, you must enclose your search string in double-quotation marks. I began by searching the Web for this string:

```
"Kirk D. Lyons"
```

This search returned nearly 200 matches, and I started sorting them looking for anything interesting. Most of what I found were various articles and publications either about Mr. Lyons or written by him. I was able to discover an older, shared email address used by Mr. Lyons and one of his colleagues, `unreconfed@cheta.net`. Searching for just this email address yielded very little, so I turned to Usenet postings. Using `http://www.deja.com/usenet/`, I was able to search thousands of postings. I came across some by Kirk himself using the email address above. What was interesting here is that the email header information was left intact, which gives quite a bit of information:

```
Return-Path: unreconfed@cheta.net
Received: from lexington.ioa.net
  (IDENT:root@lexington.ioa.net [208.131.128.7])
  by mail.hal-pc.org (8.9.1/8.9.0) with ESMTP id DAA09388
for <abnrngrs@hal-pc.org>; Thu, 4 Nov 1999 03:23:08 -0559 (CST)
  Received: from 1861 (ppp227.arden.dialup.ioa.com [205.138.38.236])
  by lexington.ioa.net (8.9.3/8.9.3) with SMTP id EAA29654;
Thu, 4 Nov 1999 04:19:27 -0500
Message-ID: <1bed01bf26a5$a5ea0560$cb268acd@1861>
To: <Undisclosed.Recipients@lexington.ioa.net>
From: "Kirk D. Lyons or Dr. Neill H. Payne" <unreconfed@cheta.net> Subject:
HELP
```

From this, it is possible to determine who is using this address, and where they were connecting from and which service provider they were using to send the message. I can also determine that this is a dial-up account, possibly a home user account in Arden, North Carolina. Further investigation helped me discover that this individual is heavily involved in Civil War re-enactment. This led me to discover Mr. Lyons's sideline business, Different Drummer, including more detailed information including the address, phone number, fax number and email for this business.

> **Note**
>
> Google acquired Deja's Usenet archive as this book went to press. The Deja URLs redirect to `http://groups.google.com/`, however, Google has yet to make available the entire archive, as Deja had done. Check in often with the Google site to check the progress of that endeavor.

This may not seem like much information, but, in reality, it is enough that I could easily start pulling up business and tax records, property information, and other public data on Mr. Lyons. There is very little limit on how far this investigation could be taken. In just a few minutes using freely available Internet Web site based searching, I was able to gather a considerable amount of information about Mr. Lyons.

That might not initially seem very important. You are probably thinking, "So what?" However, think back to what I wrote at the beginning of this chapter. Twenty years ago, the FBI would have spent thousands of dollars (and secured a dozen wiretaps) to discover the same information.

Usenet is a superb tool for building models of human networks. (These are groups of people that think alike.) If you belong to such a group (and maintain controversial or unpopular views), do not post those views to Usenet.

Even though you can prevent your Usenet posts from being archived by making x-no-archive: yes the first line of your post, you cannot prevent others from copying the post and storing it on a Web server. By posting unpopular political views to Usenet (and inviting others of like mind to respond), you are inadvertently revealing your associations to the world.

DejaNews

As previously noted in this chapter, Google bought the Usenet archives from Deja. At press time, the entire archive was not online as it had been with Deja. However, it's quite likely that the archives will be back online eventually. Check in with http://groups.google.com/ for the status. So do not assume that your postings cannot be found one day!

To recap, assume that although your real name does not appear on Usenet postings, it does appear in the /etc/passwd file on the UNIX server that you use as a gateway to the Internet. Here are the steps someone must take to find you:

1. The snooping party sees your post to Usenet. Your email address is in plain view, but your name is not.

2. The snooping party tries to finger your address, but, as it happens, your provider prohibits finger requests.

3. The snooping party telnets to port 25 of your server. There, he issues the expn command and obtains your real name.

Having gotten that information, the snooping party next needs to find the state you live in. For this, he turns to the WHOIS service.

The WHOIS Service

The WHOIS service (centrally located at rs.internic.net) contains domain registration records of all American, non-military Internet sites. This registration database contains detailed information on each Internet site, including domain name, server addresses, technical contacts, the telephone number, and the address. Here is a WHOIS request result on the provider Netcom, a popular Northern California Internet service provider:

```
NETCOM On-Line Communication Services, Inc (NETCOM-DOM)
   3031 Tisch Way, Lobby Level
   San Jose, California 95128
   US
   Domain Name: NETCOM.COM
   Administrative Contact:
      NETCOM Network Management  (NETCOM-NM)  dns-mgr@NETCOM.COM
      (408) 983-5970
   Technical Contact, Zone Contact:
      NETCOM DNS Administration  (NETCOM-DNS)  dns-tech@NETCOM.COM
      (408) 983-5970
```

```
Record last updated on 03-Jan-97.
Record created on 01-Feb-91.
Domain servers in listed order:
NETCOMSV.NETCOM.COM          192.100.81.101
NS.NETCOM.COM                192.100.81.105
AS3.NETCOM.COM               199.183.9.4
```

Take a good look at the Netcom WHOIS information. From this, the snooping party discovers that Netcom is in California. (Note the location at the top of the WHOIS return listing, as well as the telephone points of contact for the technical personnel.)

Armed with this information, the snooping party proceeds to `http://www.worldpages.com/`. WorldPages is a massive database that houses the names, email addresses, and telephone numbers of several million Internet users.

At WorldPages, the snooping party uses your real name as a search string, specifying California as your state. Instantly, he is confronted with several matches that provide name, address, and telephone number. Here, he might run into some trouble, depending on how common your name is. If your name is John Smith, the snooping party will have to do further research. However, assume that your name is not John Smith—that your name is common, but not that common. The snooping party uncovers three addresses, each in a different California city: One is in Sacramento, one is in Los Angeles, and one is in San Diego. How does he determine which one is really you? He proceeds to the host utility.

The host utility will list all machines on a given network and their relative locations. With large networks, it is common for a provider to have machines sprinkled at various locations throughout a state. The `host` command can identify which workstations are located where. In other words, it is generally trivial to obtain a listing of workstations by city. These workstations are sometimes even named for the cities in which they are deposited. Therefore, you might see an entry such as the following:

```
chatsworth1.target_provider.com
```

Chatsworth is a city in southern California. From this entry, we can assume that `chatsworth1.target_provider.com` is located within the city of Chatsworth. What remains for the snooper is to reexamine your Usenet post.

By examining the source code of your Usenet post, he can view the path the message took. That path will look something like this:

```
news2.cais.com!in1.nntp.cais.net!feed1.news.erols.com!howland.erols.net!
➥ix.netcom.com!news
```

By examining this path, the snooping party can now determine which server was used to post the article. This information is then coupled with the value for the NNTP posting host:

```
grc-ny4-20.ix.netcom.com
```

The snooping party extracts the name of the posting server (the first entry along the path). This is almost always expressed in its name state and not by its IP address. For the snooping party to complete the process, the IP address is needed. Therefore, he telnets to the posting host. When the Telnet session is initiated, the hard, numeric IP is retrieved from DNS and printed to STDOUT. The snooping party now has the IP address of the machine that accepted the original posting. This IP address is then run against the outfile obtained by the host query. This operation reveals the city in which the machine resides.

> **TIP**
>
> If this information does not exactly match, the snooping party can employ other methods. One technique is to issue a traceroute request. When tracing the route to a machine that exists in another city, the route must invariably take a path through certain gateways. These are main switching points through which all traffic passes when going in or out of a city. Usually, these are high-level points, operated by telecommunication companies such as MCI, Sprint, and so forth. Most have city names within their addresses. Bloomington and Los Angeles are two well-known points. Thus, even if the reconciliation of the posting machine's name fails against the host outfile, a traceroute will reveal the approximate location of the machine.

Having obtained this information (and having now differentiated you from the other names), the snooping party returns to WorldPages and chooses your name. Within seconds, a graphical map of your neighborhood appears. The exact location of your home is marked on the map by a circle. The snooping party now knows exactly where you live and how to get there. From this point, he can begin to gather more interesting information about you. For example:

- The snooping party can determine your status as a registered voter and your political affiliations. He obtains this information at http://www.wdia.com/lycos/voter-records.htm.

- From federal election records online, he can determine which candidates you support and how much you have contributed. He gets this information from http://www.tray.com/fecinfo/zip.htm.

- He can also get your Social Security number and date of birth. This information is available at http://kadima.com/.

Many people minimize the seriousness of this. Their prevailing attitude is that all such information is available through other sources anyway. The problem is that the Internet brings these sources of information together. Integration of such information allows this activity to be conducted on a wholesale basis, and that's where the trouble begins.

8

HIDING ONE'S IDENTITY

As a side note, complete anonymity on the Internet is possible, but usually not achievable by legal means. Given enough time, for example, authorities could trace a message posted via anonymous remailer. (Although, if that message were chained through several remailers, the task would be far more complex.) The problem is in the design of the Internet itself. As Ralf Hauser and Gene Tsudik note in their article *On Shopping Incognito*:

> From the outset the nature of current network protocols and applications runs counter to privacy. The vast majority have one thing in common: they faithfully communicate end-point identification information. "End-point" in this context can denote a user (with a unique ID), a network address or an organization name. For example, electronic mail routinely communicates sender's [*sic*] address in the header. File transfer (e.g., FTP), remote login (e.g., Telnet), and hypertext browsers (e.g., WWW) expose addresses, host names and IDs of their users.

Then there is the question of whether users are entitled to anonymity. I believe they are. Certainly, there are plenty of legitimate reasons for allowing anonymity on the Internet. The following is excerpted from *Anonymity for Fun and Deception: The Other Side of "Community"* by Richard Seltzer:

> Some communities require anonymity for them to be effective, because without it members would not participate. This the case with Alcoholics Anonymous, AIDS support groups, drug addiction support and other mutual help organizations, particularly when there is some risk of social ostracism or even legal consequences should the identity of the members be revealed.

This is a recurring theme in the now-heated battle over Internet anonymity. Even many members of the "establishment" recognize that anonymity is an important element that might preserve free speech on the Internet—not just here, but abroad. This issue has received increased attention in legal circles. An excellent paper on the subject was written by A. Michael Froomkin, a lawyer and prominent professor. In *Anonymity and Its Enmities*, Froomkin writes

> Persons who wish to criticize a repressive government or foment a revolution against it may find remailers invaluable. Indeed, given the ability to broadcast messages widely using the Internet, anonymous email may become the modern replacement of the anonymous handbill. Other examples include corporate whistle-blowers, people criticizing a religious cult or other movement from which they might fear retaliation, and persons posting requests for information to a public bulletin board about matters too personal to discuss if there were any chance that the message might be traced back to its origin.

▶ Anonymity and Its Enmities by Professor Froomkin is an excellent source for links to legal analysis of Internet anonymity. The paper is an incredible resource, especially for journalists. It can be found on the Web at http://warthog.cc.wm.edu/law/publications/jol/froomkin.html.

However, not everyone feels that anonymity is a good thing. Some people believe that if anonymity is available on the Internet, it amounts to nothing but anarchy. A rather ironic quote, considering the source, is found in *Computer Anarchy: A Plea for Internet Laws to Protect the Innocent*, by Martha Seigel:

> People need safety and order in cyberspace just as they do in their homes and on the streets. The current state of the Internet makes it abundantly clear that general anarchy isn't working. If recognized governments don't find a way to bring order to the growing and changing Internet, chaos may soon dictate that the party is over.

You might or might not know why this quote is so incredibly ironic. The author, Martha Seigel, is no stranger to "computer anarchy." In her time, she has been placed on the Internet Blacklist of Advertisers for violating network policies against spamming the Usenet news network. The Internet Blacklist of Advertisers is intended to curb inappropriate advertising on Usenet newsgroups and via junk e-mail. It works by describing offenders and their offensive behavior, expecting that people who read it will punish the offenders in one way or another. The following is quoted from the docket listing on that Blacklist in regards to Cantor & Seigel, Ms. Seigel's law firm:

> The famous greencard lawyers. In 1994, they repeatedly sent out a message offering their services in helping to enter the U.S. greencard lottery to almost all Usenet newsgroups. (Note in passing: they charged $100 for their service, while participating in the greencard lottery is free and consists merely of sending a letter with your personal information at the right time to the right place.) When the incoming mail bombs forced their access provider to terminate their account, they threatened to sue him until he finally agreed to forward all responses to them.

▶ The Internet Blacklist can be found on the Web at `http://math-www.uni-paderborn.de/~axel/BL/blacklist.html`.

However, all this is academic. As we move toward a cashless society, anonymity might be built in to the process. In this respect, at least, list brokers (and other unsavory information collectors) had better do all their collecting now. Analysis of consumer-buying habits will likely become a thing of the past, at least with relation to the Internet. The majority of electronic payment services being developed (or already available) on the Internet include anonymity as an inherent part of their design.

▶ Several digital electronic payment systems exist today. A lot of research has been done in this area. Several companies currently developing systems are

- eCash Technologies
- Zero-Knowledge Systems
- CyberCash
- Millicent

8

HIDING ONE'S IDENTITY

What I have a hard time understanding is how these systems can provide anonymous transactions. The reason I bring this up is simply that records must be maintained, log files generated, transactions authorized, and people involved to ensure the system works. Therefore, these "anonymous" transactions really aren't—and that brings you to my warning.

A Warning

Technology is rapidly changing our society, and personal privacy is disappearing in the process. The Internet will only further facilitate that process.

Already, many banks are using biometrics for customer identification. The process is bone chilling. In order to withdraw your money, you must surrender your retina or thumbprint to a scanner that authenticates you. This technology is already being marketing for personal computers, and the sales pitch sounds enticing. After all, aren't you tired of having to enter a password every time you boot your machine or log on to the Net?

Soon, biometric authentication will be used in online electronic commerce. Before you close this book, I ask you to consider this very carefully: Imagine the climate a decade from now. Each user will have a unique, digital ID based on a cryptographic value. That value will be a 32-bit or 64-bit number derived from the physical characteristics of your face or your right hand. Without that number, you will not be able to buy or sell anything. When that time comes, remember that you read it here first.

Internet Resources

Finally, here are some good sources concerning privacy on the Internet.

Privacy & Anonymity on the Internet FAQ

Author: L. Detweiler

Content: Many sources on privacy and anonymity on the Internet; a must for users new to identity issues on the Net.

URL: `http://www.prz.tu-berlin.de/~derek/internet/sources/privacy.faq.02.html`

Anonymous Remailer FAQ

Author: Andre Bacard

Content: A not-too-technical description of anonymous remailers, how they work, and where they can be found. Bacard is also the author of *Computer Privacy Handbook* ("The Scariest Computer Book of the Year").

URL: `http://www.andrebacard.com/remail.html`

Anonymous Remailers

Author: Francis Litterio

Content: Locations of anonymous remailers on the Internet.

URL: `http://world.std.com/~franl/crypto/remailers.html`

How-To Chain Remailers with PGP Encryption

Author: Anonymous

Content: A no-nonsense tutorial on how to chain remailers, and, in doing so, send a totally anonymous message with encryption.

URL: `http://www.email.about.com/internet/email/library/weekly/aa042400a.htm`

Privacy on the Internet

Authors: David M. Goldschlag, Michael G. Reed, and Paul F. Syverson, Naval Research Laboratory Center for High Assurance Computer Systems

Content: A good primer that covers all the aspects discussed in this chapter.

URL: `http://www.itd.nrl.navy.mil/ITD/5540/projects/onion-routing/inet97/index.htm`

Anonymous Connections and Onion Routing

Author: David M. Goldschlag, Michael G. Reed, and Paul F. Syverson, Naval Research Laboratory Center For High Assurance Computer Systems

Content: PostScript presented in the proceedings of the Symposium on Security and Privacy in Oakland, CA, May 1997. A detailed analysis of anonymous connections and their resistance to tracing and traffic analysis. (Also discusses vulnerabilities of such systems; a must read.)

URL: `http://www.itd.nrl.navy.mil/ITD/5540/projects/onion-routing/OAKLAND_97.ps`

Special Report: Privacy in the Digital Age

Author: Susan Stellin

Content: CNET article containing resources on privacy on the Internet.

URL: `http://www.cnet.com/Content/Features/Dlife/Privacy/`

The Electronic Frontier Foundation

Author: N/A

Content: Comprehensive sources on electronic privacy.

Location: `http://www.eff.org/`

The Electronic Privacy Information Center (EPIC)

Author: N/A

Content: Civil liberties issues; this site is indispensable in getting legal information on privacy and anonymity on the Internet and elsewhere.

URL: `http://epic.org/`

Computer Professionals for Social Responsibility (CPSR)

Author: N/A

Content: A group devoted to discussion about ethics in computer use.

URL: `http://www.cpsr.org/`

The Anonymizer

Author: N/A

Content: A site that offers free anonymous surfing. The application acts as a middleman between you and the sites you surf. Basically, it is a more complex proxying service. It allows chaining as well, and your IP is stripped from their logs.

URL: `http://www.anonymizer.com/`

Articles and Papers and Related Web Sites

Data Spills in Banner Ads. Richard M. Smith. February 14, 2000.
`http://users.rcn.com/rms2000/privacy/banads.htm`

Nameless in Cyberspace: Anonymity on the Internet. Jonathan D. Wallace, 1996.
`http://www.cato.org/pubs/briefs/bp-054es.html`

On Shopping Incognito. R. Hauser and G. Tsudik. Second USENIX Workshop on Electronic Commerce, November 1996. `http://www.isi.edu/~gts/paps/hats96.ps.gz`

The Anonymous E-mail Conversation. Ceki Gulcu. Technical Report, Eurecom Institute. June 1995.

Control of Information Distribution and Access. Ralf C. Hauser. Technical Report, Department of Computer Science, University of Zurich. September 1995.

Internet Privacy Enhanced Mail. Stephen T. Kent. *Communications of the ACM*, Vol. 36, No. 8. August 1993.

Certified Electronic Mail. Alireza Bahreman, J. D. Tygar. 1994.
`ftp://ftp.cert.dfn.de/pub/pem/docs/CEM.ps.gz`

E-Mail Security. Dr. John A. Line. UKERNA Computer Security Workshop, 15/16. November 1994. `ftp://ftp.cert.dfn.de/pub/pem/docs/UKERNA-email-security.ps.gz`

How Companies Track Your Movements on the Internet. `http://www.privacy.net/track/` provided by `privacy.net`

Electronic Fingerprints: Computer Evidence Comes of Age. M.R. Anderson, *Government Technology Magazine.* November 1996.

Achieving Electronic Privacy. David Chaum. *Scientific America*n, pp. 96-101. August 1992.

Erased Files Often Aren't. M.R. Anderson, *Government Technology Magazine.* January 1997.

FBI Seeks Right to Tap All Net Services. M. Betts. *ComputerWorld*, Vol. XXVI, No. 23. June 8, 1992.

8

HIDING ONE'S
IDENTITY

Dispelling Some of the Myths

IN THIS CHAPTER

The explosive growth of the Internet has thrust the topic of computer security directly in the face of everyone, whether they work with computers or not. Everywhere we read about viruses, system break-ins, malicious software, and a myriad of other threats. It really comes as no surprise that there is an equal number of hoaxes, myths, and exaggerations that exist about the risks you might face every time your computer is turned on and connected to the Internet. Although you should definitely be concerned about what the risks are, it is just as important to realize when someone is trying to con you, or exaggerate the truth.

If you ever saw the movie *The Net*, you were drawn into a world where a group of crackers had erased the identity of an innocent person to protect themselves. By using the Internet, they nearly were able to destroy the victim's life without much other than a mouse click or a keystroke. What you and many others might not realize is that this scenario is extremely implausible in today's networked world. Hollywood has turned the black art of cracking into a glamorous place where anyone can control nearly every aspect of the human experience from a desktop computer. Nothing could be further from the truth.

In this chapter, I will help you understand when and where you might be vulnerable, who is actually perpetrating the attacks, why they are doing it, and what the risks are that you actually might face. In doing so maybe I can help you understand better how you are affected by Internet or network security.

When Can Attacks Occur?

I've heard it said many times, "The only secure computer is the one that is left turned off and unplugged." This is actually not far from the truth. The moment a computer system comes online and connects to any network, it becomes a potential target. This doesn't mean that the minute you connect to the Internet, you are immediately being scanned, probed, or attacked. There are several important factors that come into play. I'll cover some of these first.

How Do I Become a Hacker's Target?

The minute you link up to the Internet, you are unwittingly opening yourself up for an attack. In order to become a target, you first have to be discovered or selected by the cracker as his victim. In some cases, you might be attacked at random when someone runs software that randomly selects addresses and launches an attack. Random selection is less common than discovery or targeting. In the case of discovery, the methods used to find out who and where you are, and how vulnerable you might be, are often the same. An attacker runs a port scanner, such as nmap, feeding it a large block of IP addresses to check. The program will then report back to the end user what computers it has found in that range of addresses, what ports are open, and, in the case of nmap, what operating system the remote system is running. Using this information, the attacker now has several potential targets to choose from. With the information he received on the remote operating system and open ports, he can now narrow the scope of the attack to target vulnerabilities already known within the remote system or service. This type of probe is often carried out before any actual cracking attempt is made.

The following shows the output from nmap when scanning one of my own workstations. It also shows you just how easy it is to get a lot of information about a single machine:

```
[root@server user]# nmap -vO 10.0.0.15
Starting nmap V. 2.53 by fyodor@insecure.org ( www.insecure.org/nmap/ )
No tcp,udp, or ICMP scantype specified, assuming vanilla tcp connect() scan.
Use -sP if you really don't want to portscan (and just want to
 see what hosts are up).

Host  (10.0.0.15) appears to be up ... good.
Initiating TCP connect() scan against  (10.0.0.15)
Adding TCP port 554 (state open).
Adding TCP port 5900 (state open).
Adding TCP port 1433 (state open).
Adding TCP port 445 (state open).
Adding TCP port 1025 (state open).
Adding TCP port 427 (state open).
Adding TCP port 139 (state open).
Adding TCP port 135 (state open).
Adding TCP port 25 (state open).
Adding TCP port 5800 (state open).
The TCP connect scan took 1 second to scan 1523 ports.
For OSScan assuming that port 25 is open and port 1 is closed and neither are
firewalled
Interesting ports on  (10.0.0.15):
(The 1513 ports scanned but not shown below are in state: closed)
Port        State       Service
25/tcp      open        smtp
135/tcp     open        loc-srv
139/tcp     open        netbios-ssn
427/tcp     open        svrloc
445/tcp     open        microsoft-ds
554/tcp     open        rtsp
1025/tcp    open        listen
1433/tcp    open        ms-sql-s
5800/tcp    open        vnc
5900/tcp    open        vnc

TCP Sequence Prediction: Class=random positive increments
                        Difficulty=9491 (Worthy challenge)
Sequence numbers: B896EAF2 B897E041 B8988355 B89936FB B89A1722 B89B1A0A
Remote operating system guess: Windows 2000 RC1 through final release
Nmap run completed -- 1 IP address (1 host up) scanned in 43 seconds
[root@server user]#
```

9

DISPELLING SOME OF THE MYTHS

You can see that this machine is running Windows 2000, a Microsoft SQL database server, an e-mail server, and many other services. With this information, it becomes easy for the would-be cracker to do a little research online about vulnerabilities and exploits for your specific system or software. Often, this information also includes code or examples of methods used to exploit the weakness, making the job of the cracker that much easier. Even if the person probing your system is an unskilled cracker, he can improve his attack by employing some of the software programs freely available on the Internet. These programs will test any remote system for hundreds of known vulnerabilities automatically.

An attacker can also be someone who has preselected you as his victim. The reasons for this are varied, but they include notoriety, contempt, theft of information, or financial gain. In this scenario, the attacker doesn't need to waste any time searching large network IP blocks to find a victim; he's already got one in mind. Depending on his motivation, he will most likely do a considerable amount of research before actually engaging in any malicious activity. The type of victim you are will determine the amount of caution or stealth employed by the cracker to avoid detection. For example, if the computers you work on belong to the Central Intelligence Agency, a great deal of time and ingenuity will be used by any attacker crazy enough to attempt to penetrate the systems to begin with.

Who you are, or for whom you work, also plays an important part in why or how often you might be targeted. A home or small office user is unlikely to be specifically targeted unless there is something worth the time and effort to be gained from doing so. If you happen to be the system administrator for Microsoft, things are very different indeed. Companies such as Microsoft typically log thousands of unsuccessful attack attempts every day. There are some fairly obvious reasons for this. The first one is simply name recognition. Just about anyone to ever operate a computer knows of Microsoft. Launching a successful attack against Microsoft would bring a cracker or group of crackers some considerable bragging rights. Microsoft is also one of the wealthiest computer software companies on the planet. The monetary and intellectual worth of source code and design documentation, financial data, and business information housed on the systems at Microsoft are, no doubt, very high indeed. Some of the more shady competitors of Microsoft would likely pay a good deal of money to get their hands on information like that.

▶ In October 2000, Microsoft fell victim to hackers via the Internet. Apparently, an employee opened an e-mail inside Microsoft that had an attached Trojan, which was then used by the attacker to gain entry into MS's corporate network. Although Microsoft denies any damage was done, it is rumored that source code and other proprietary information was leaked and made public. You can read all about it at `http://www.abcnews.go.com/sections/tech/DailyNews/microsoft_hacked001027.html`

It should also be mentioned that it is possible to make yourself a target just by participating in the use of a popular network service, such as IRC (Internet Relay Chat). IRC is often the home base and the battlefield for many cracking groups, large and small. IRC network operators often must go to great lengths to keep abuse on their systems to a minimum. In retaliation, the attackers target the IRC service providers and innocent users of the service. As of late, the IRC network Undernet, one of the largest free IRC services worldwide, has been the victim of continual assaults. These have escalated to the point that the service operators are ready to pull the plug permanently.

▶ More information about the January 2001 Undernet IRC attacks can be found at `http://www.newsfactor.com/perl/story/6655.html`

Dial-Up Versus Persistent Connections

How you make your connection to the Internet plays a significant role in how easy it is to find and target you, and there are trade-offs for each method. The most popular connection methods include dial-up connections, modems or ISDN, or persistent ("always-on") connections, such as a cable modem or any type of DSL (Digital Subscriber Line).

When you use a modem to connect to an Internet Service Provider (ISP), you typically dial into a modem bank at the ISP and its systems pick an IP address for you from a pool of addresses assigned to it. This address is required to make a TCP/IP connection, and is unique for every host connecting to the Internet. The immediate benefit of this is that, every time you dial up and connect to the Internet, you have a different IP address, and this makes specifically targeting you a lot more difficult. On the downside, a dial-up connection is slow, unreliable, and, in most cases, extremely vulnerable to denial of service attacks, as you will see later in this chapter.

Dial-up connections are quickly becoming less common. With cable modems, DSL, and other high-speed Internet access technologies, anyone from almost anywhere can enjoy a very fast and considerably stable Internet connection. In most cases, these connections are considered "always-on," which indicates that every time your computer is turned on, it is connected to the Internet. This is great for end-user convenience. I certainly enjoy being able to sit down and get to work immediately online. This also puts you at considerable risk for an attacker out on the Internet to target you and attempt to break into your machine or take it offline. Many always-on connections assign you a static IP address. This is really nice for people who need to be able to connect to their computer remotely, but it also makes it really easy for your machine to be found on the Internet. It also helps make it easy to find you again later on, if the attacker decides he isn't through with you. Even if you don't have a static IP address, an always-on connection usually does not change its address often enough to be hard to find.

TIP

I used a cable modem for some time from @Home AT&T that was supposed to *automatically* change addresses every few hours. The entire time I had this connection, the address never changed, contrary to what I had been told when I purchased the service.

Which Computer Operating Systems Are Vulnerable?

Everyone that uses a computer for anything will eventually find an operating system that they are most comfortable with, and that they most enjoy using. The average computer user rarely uses system security as a basis from which to make this choice. These users are typically drawn to a particular interface, or by the available applications for the operating system. Even when security is an issue, many people are led to believe that their OS of choice is somehow more secure than another. The truth is simply that every operating system is vulnerable in one way or another. Computer users will stubbornly defend their OS over another, and most often bash the other systems available, especially where it concerns system security. It doesn't matter whether you run Windows, or Linux, or any other operating system. You are potentially vulnerable.

There are operating systems that are designed to be secure. For example, OpenBSD is an operating system built from the ground up to be the most secure operating system available. When I checked the OpenBSD Web site, the operating system had gone more than three years without a remote exploit in a standard release. Even with this record, it has had several locally exploitable vulnerabilities.

Windows users are often the target of verbal abuse and ridicule by security professionals, script kiddies, and crackers alike. Many Windows users have been driven into some sort of security paranoia, believing that people can connect to their computers, get inside, and wreak all kinds of havoc. In most cases, this is simply not true.

Consumer editions of Windows, such as Windows 95/98 and Windows Millennium Edition ship without any network services for a typical installation. This means there is nothing running on the machine that will accept outside network connections. Even Windows NT 4 Workstation or Server, and Windows 2000 Professional install with minimal or no default network services running.

Before the Windows users break out the champagne, let me bring you back down to earth. As soon as you set up any type of network connection under Windows, you are throwing the doors wide open. Windows will install several unneeded components along with a network adapter or a dial-up configuration. Services such as file and print sharing, and, in some cases, Internet connection sharing, are activated without the end user being made aware of it. Some may argue whether these services are needed, but for a standalone Internet connection, they just aren't needed.

Windows users also suffer from other glaring security problems that don't even exist on other systems. Viruses, malicious scripts, Trojans, and back doors, plus a weak TCP/IP stack implementation, make Windows extremely vulnerable to a wide variety of attacks. Also, Windows often installs File and Print Sharing over TCP/IP and NetBIOS along with its other networking components, even when you are only a dial-up user. In a normal network environment, this allows Windows users to share files and printers with other people on the same network. Many people might never use or need this feature, and they don't disable it. This can be an open door for anyone on the Internet to access the system and do his dirty work.

Some people may not consider UNIX variants such as Linux, FreeBSD, NetBSD, OpenBSD— operating systems more commonly found in servers—as desktop operating systems, but they are gaining acceptance rapidly in this area. Out of the box, UNIX systems come with all sorts of services installed, such as Telnet, FTP, and httpd (Web server service), including easily exploitable legacy daemons. It is up to you as an end user to assess security after the installation and make necessary changes. A properly secured open source operating system can provide an extremely reliable and secure alternative to expensive commercial operating systems, when properly set up and configured.

Macintosh and the Mac OS are not as popular as they were back in the mid-1980s, but they are still widely used, and Mac users are just as stubborn when defending the Mac OS. The Mac OS has grown up into a very robust and powerful operating system. Of course, it, too, has its vulnerabilities. Macs can fall victim to viruses just as easily as any Windows system. Depending on your version of the Mac OS, you can also be targeted because of weaknesses in Apple's Web Sharing and File Sharing. Unless absolutely needed, these features should be permanently disabled.

My Firewall Will Stop the Pesky Crackers!

The biggest craze in protection from attack has got to be the firewall. A firewall is a device that sits between your computer(s) and another network, such as the Internet, that can be configured to block access to services and data inside the firewall. A properly configured firewall is a great tool for defending your assets from remote attack. It is not, however, the end-all solution. A firewall also allows traffic to come through, and because of this, the hole is not completely plugged. Many firewalls also allow you the option of setting up service proxies, which gives the user the ability to allow a dangerous service through, but only through a *protected* proxy.

Recently, I did a security audit for clients who were using a high-end commercial grade firewall. They had left a Telnet proxy service running, and, through it, I was able to penetrate and map their entire network, using the firewall as my point of access. This service allows people to use a simple network Telnet client to pass directly though the firewall without authentication. The people using the system had not correctly configured the firewall, and by doing so, made it easy for anyone outside to get in. Most people don't realize that proper security requires more than just a fancy firewall. With the increase of e-mail–based viruses, Trojans, and malicious scripts, firewalls are becoming less effective. The firewall would correctly permit the e-mail traffic to come in, but, by the time anything dangerous is detected, it could be too late. For more information, see Chapter 10, "Firewalls."

What Kinds of Attackers Exist?

There are as many definitions out there for network attackers as there are for attacks. Most commonly, you will hear people refer to these individuals as hackers, crackers, script kiddies, black and white hats, and many other names. I will touch on the most common types here.

Script Kiddies—Your Biggest Threat?

The most common and prolific type of attacker today is the *script kiddie*. These people get their name from the simple fact that they are most often young, unskilled crackers who find and use scripts and utilities other skilled attackers have written and released free to anyone on the Internet. Mom and Dad got the kiddies an AOL account, and the first keyword they went looking for on a search engine was "hacking." With all the glorification of hacking in the media and on the Internet, and the relative safety of perpetrating this type of crime, young people are easily lured to this dark underworld. There are thousands of Web sites with material and information for the young, enterprising cracker to get started with.

Often, many of the attacks proliferated by script kiddies are unsuccessful, or maybe just mildly annoying to the victim. However, because of their relentless persistence, they will and often do eventually find systems that they can break into, damage, and attack more computers from. There is no love in the security community for this type of cracker. Script kiddies are more likely to attack systems and maliciously damage data than any other type of cracker. Even professional crackers speak about this group with ill will.

Black Hats—"The Dark Side"

Black hats are generally considered "The Dark Side" of the hacking community. These people are generally highly skilled with computers, programming, and network security and administration. They are the crackers who rarely get caught, who take their time and target specific systems for specific reasons. Often, these are the people who discover the vulnerabilities you and I read about, and they often will code the exploit that allows the system to be attacked or penetrated (which eventually the script kiddies get hold of and use against other unsuspecting victims).

Black hat crackers do not often talk about or boast about their skills or activities. They are generally secretive in nature. I have heard some people refer to them as the Ninja of the Internet. Black hat groups often hold cracking conferences, such as DEFCON, where they get together to share and learn from each other. A lot of security professionals love to attend these conferences also, as does the FBI. Not surprisingly, the crackers don't use their real names at these events.

White Hats—The Good Guys

On the other end of the spectrum are the white hat hackers. These are often security professionals who work very hard to help test and make available security patches, information, and software to the user community to help users become more secure. Often, companies call on white hats to help test and implement security, or to help improve it. Many white hats got their start in the security community as a black hat cracker. For whatever reason, they decided to put their skills to use to help others with system security. A lot of these people have started and continue to run professional security companies.

Operating Systems Used by Crackers

As I mentioned earlier, everyone that uses computers will most likely develop a preference for a particular operating system. In my opinion, you should use what works best for you. There are arguments good and bad for any system you might be interested in using. Here, I will explain why crackers choose to use a particular operating system. In Part VI, "Platforms and Security," you will learn more about specific platform vulnerabilities.

Windows Operating Systems

Windows is arguably the most popular operating system available these days. It is easy to use, and is installed on the majority of systems shipped in the world. Windows has been translated to multiple languages and is run by users all over the world. It certainly doesn't appeal to most users as a cracker OS, but it does get used in this arena. In most cases, script kiddie crackers used the Windows operating system. There are many cracking utilities and such written for the Windows environment. These prepackaged apps generally are not powerful enough to penetrate most systems. Most of these utilities are for mail bombing, denial of service, port scanning, and IRC (Internet Relay Chat) user attacks. Windows is of limited use to intelligent attackers, and, therefore, I only reference it briefly.

Linux/NetBSD/FreeBSD

The open source software movement has given the Internet community and computer users everywhere a plethora of robust and reliable operating systems. The most common ones you will hear of or use are Linux, FreeBSD, or NetBSD, which are popular with both the cracking underground and security professionals alike.

Open source operating systems are very popular simply because they are open source. This means that the end user has full access to the source code of the entire operating system. This allows the user to learn and understand how the system works, how to make it secure, and how to exploit its weaknesses on other computers. Another benefit of it being open source is the speed of patch releases. In most cases, the moment a security issue is released relating to an open source operating system, it will typically be fixed and patched within an hour or less of the initial announcement. This allows the end user to maintain every aspect of system security, including the ability to patch the operating system when necessary. Most crackers using open source operating systems, such as Linux, learned security exploitation techniques while securing and maintaining their own systems.

Another benefit of an open source OS is that the cracker has full access to the network protocol stacks and can manipulate packets easily and efficiently when required. This allows the user to craft very specific exploits that rely on very specific weaknesses in other systems. Most open source operating systems come with a free compiler such as gcc, which allows users to write their own code, compile it, and distribute it all over the Internet. gcc is one of the most powerful C/C++ compilers out there, and it is completely free and has been ported to several platforms.

Many of the best utilities exist and are available free for open source operating systems. Tools for scanning, packet capture and analysis, security auditing, and other related programs have been written directly for these operating systems and are not available in most cases for Windows- or Macintosh-based operating systems.

Another attraction in using open source operating systems is attitude and the perception of others. People who have never become familiar with a POSIX-compliant operating system, such as Linux or FreeBSD, are often intimidated by their complexity. Computer users taking the initiative to learn a powerful operating system such as Linux are usually looked on with respect by those afraid to venture into this territory.

OpenBSD

OpenBSD is billed as the most secure operating system freely available to anyone outside of government agencies. OpenBSD is a BSD–based (Berkeley Software Design), free, and secure version of the UNIX operating system. As I mentioned earlier, this OS has had a long history of excellent security, and, because of this, it makes an ideal operating system for a cracker. Any cracker worth his salt in the cracking community also needs to maintain his own high system security. What better operating system to use than the one with best record of security? Also,

OpenBSD is completely open source, giving the same benefits I listed for Linux, NetBSD, and FreeBSD. The same utilities for those operating systems compile and run just fine in OpenBSD. OpenBSD will also run Linux, FreeBSD, and NetBSD software, if the need arises. If you want to be as secure as possible, out-of-the-box OpenBSD wins hands down.

Is There a Typical Attack?

When it comes to being a victim of a network attack, I don't think any one incident can be described as typical. No matter the scale of the attack, being a cracker's victim is a very infuriating experience. It can feel as much of a violation as having your home broken into and robbed. There are several common attacks that anyone can experience at any time. Attacks that an average user is most likely to face in everyday computer use include denial of service, viruses, and malicious scripts or Trojans, or Web site defacement. We'll explore each of these in the following sections. (You'll also learn more about these types of attacks in Part V, "Virtual Weapons of Mass Destruction.") We'll also briefly look at insider attacks.

Denial of Service

Denial of service attacks (DoS) are the latest big news it seems in network security. A denial of service attack is the intentional overload of a network service or connection with excessive or disruptive data that causes the connection or service to fail. In the late 1990s and early 2000s, many well-known, Web-based companies and services fell victim to this type of attack. The attackers used what is now termed *distributed denial of service (DDoS) attacks*, wherein multiple coordinated machines are used in tandem to launch a denial of service attack against one host or network.

Depending on the speed of your Internet connection, you might be more susceptible than others. Because a denial of service attack relies on overloading the remote network connection, the slower the connection the victim has, the more likely it is that they can be taken offline. For example, a 56Kbs modem is an easy target for denial of service. When enough data is slammed against such a weak connection, normal network traffic cannot flow properly, often causing serious connection lag and finally disconnection.

One of the biggest problems with this type of attack is the difficulty in tracking and stopping the people perpetrating these attacks. In the case of a DDoS attack, it becomes infinitely harder to determine who is attacking you as the number of machines in the attack multiply. Also, there currently aren't many solutions to warding off this type of attack. Most companies with Internet access only host one route of access to the Internet. When enough data is thrown against this connection for an extended period of time, eventually the connection or the system hosting the connection will fail.

Usually, this type of attack does not direct damage to the affected systems. However, if this is successful against a company that relies on customers visiting their site from the Internet, then there is the obvious possibility of financial loss because of downtime, customer and staff frustration, and recovery costs.

Viruses, Trojans, and Malicious Scripts or Web Content

Almost everyone knows about computer viruses. They have been in existence nearly as long as computers and operating systems. A *virus* is a small piece of software that is designed to replicate and spread itself from one system to the next. Most known viruses are not malicious in nature. They are generally more annoying than malicious. There are some very dangerous computer viruses in existence, but you are not as likely to come across many of these. In fact, the name *virus* is now being used to categorize malicious scripts also.

These scripts, often coded in Microsoft Visual Basic, propagate from machine to machine via e-mail, or they are sometimes embedded in a Web site. When the unsuspecting visitor loads the page, the script loads and installs somewhere on the host machine without the user knowing. From there, it will usually replicate, drop its payload, and then try to e-mail everyone in your e-mail address book. Many of these viruses will automatically send everyone listed there a copy of the virus without your control or knowledge. The person receiving this will think it came legitimately from someone they know and trust, open the attachment, and start the process all over again.

In the Internet age, e-mail is the primary distribution method for malicious viruses and scripts. Outlook and Outlook Express (Microsoft e-mail clients) are probably the systems most vulnerable to this type of virus or script transmission mechanism. The best practice is to use a safe email client, and be suspicious of *any* e-mail attachment.

Back Orifice is a Trojan (for more on Trojan programs see Chapter 18) that has created quite a bit of controversy around the Net. Written and maintained by the Cult of the Dead Cow cracking group, Back Orifice demonstrated the weaknesses of Microsoft operating systems security. When it is installed on a machine, it hides itself and its process so that the host user has no idea it is running there. When it is running, the attacker just needs to run the client program and connect to the affected machine to have complete control and access to everything on the machine. You can easily see the problems that this would present. Back Orifice is often designed to seem like an innocuous piece of friendly software that a computer user could download from the Internet or receive as an email attachment. Thinking it is safe to run, the user executes the program, and it installs Back Orifice (or some other Trojan) quietly in the background while the user is distracted by some sort of cute or interesting front end.

Most known viruses and Trojans only affect Windows or Macintosh operating systems. This is due mostly to the nature of these systems. Security is often an afterthought in most consumer operating systems. Consumer operating systems like Windows do not employ filesystem- and kernel-level process security, so a virus or a Trojan can easily run freely through the system, doing anything it wants.

Web Defacement or "Tagging"

Web defacement is the electronic equivalent of spray-painted graffiti. Although this type of attack isn't usually damaging, it can be frustrating and embarrassing. If you run a high traffic Web site, and a cracker comes along and "tags" it with erroneous, belittling, or socially unacceptable content, people visiting your site will see the tag, too. If you are running a business at the site, your customers might question the integrity of your systems and go somewhere else. Obviously this could constitute a considerable loss to the business that is targeted by this attack.

Web defacement is growing in popularity, especially by small groups or cliques of crackers. It is very similar to gang behavior in most modern cities, except instead of guns and spray paint, crackers use security exploits and Web tagging to harass victims. Many times, the tag left is a greeting to fellow crackers, friends, and often a note to the system administrator telling him to tighten security. I have even looked at defacements where the attacker leaves his email address, inviting the admin to contact him to discuss the weakness in his systems.

▶ If you are interested in seeing examples of Web site defacement, attrition.org keeps an online listing of several, including the actual content of the defaced Web site, and the operating system of the affected Web server. You can view this list at `http://www.attrition.org/mirror/attrition/`.

Attacks from the Inside

Most people, especially home Internet users, will never experience or need to worry about internal attack. However, it occurs more commonly than any successful remote exploit that exists. This is often simply because the person responsible already has access, either physical or from across your network, to the targets she has chosen to attack.

Also, it takes a lot less work to perpetrate an internal attack. The attacker already knows plenty about the systems and software in place, making it that much easier to thwart security and cause problems. This method is obviously most common in an office or corporate environment. For whatever reasons, most administrators in this type of environment fail to realize the dangers or take action or precaution against this all too common scenario.

Who Gets Targeted Most Frequently?

As mentioned before, there is nothing typical when it comes to having network security compromised and being attacked. With the large number of systems on the Internet, there is no end of potential targets or victims available. There are, however, computers or systems more likely to be attacked than others, and the methods and motivation vary greatly. We'll take a look at motivation later in this chapter. Let's examine the most commonly attacked Internet targets. Hopefully, as we go along, it will become clearer to you why these targets are singled out.

Home and Small Business Internet Users

Home and small business users are just as vulnerable as any large scale dot.com. The biggest difference is that they are more likely to suffer from denial of service or virus type attacks.

The number of home and small business users with always-on connections has increased exponentially in recent years, adding to the probability of attack. Also, for this group of users, Internet or system security is routinely not an issue. Most small businesses do not employ a system administrator, nor can they afford to hire a security professional to address these issues. Home users generally fall into the casual computer users category, with little or no experience in computer security issues. Most home users feel relatively safe running an outdated virus scanner, or installing a personal firewall, which seems to be all the rage lately.

Larger Businesses and Corporations

In recent history, several prominent companies have had their system security attacked in one way or another. Companies such as Yahoo!, eBay, Nike, and Microsoft have been victimized by intrusions, denial of service, Web defacement, and theft of customer and credit card information. If companies like these are vulnerable, why do so many of us believe we are somehow immune? Several well-known network security companies have also been attacked, with varying degrees of success. Almost every day, you can read about another dot.com falling prey to crackers. It makes it hard for me to go online and feel safe about anything anymore.

Government and Military Institutions

Believe it or not, the computer systems of government and military institutions—no matter what nationality—are some of the most popular cracker targets anywhere. These are high profile systems, and, because of that, any attacker going after them faces considerable risk in doing so. In the United States, it is a federal crime to tamper with or attempt to access information systems of the U.S. government or military. Also, these are some of the best-protected systems on the planet. The U.S. Department of Defense logs thousands of attacks on its systems daily. Interestingly, some such attacks actually are successful and undetected, and, in some cases, classified material has been stolen, or government Web sites have been defaced.

Many attacks against government computers often originate from another country, making it more difficult to find and prosecute anyone involved.

Financial Institutions

When it comes to picking a target, selecting a financial institution makes more sense to me than most any other objective. I can understand someone wanting to profit from their cracking work a lot more than I can make any sense of someone wanting to cause a remote user to disconnect.

It should be noted right off that banks and other financial institutions often employ some of the best network security in the world. Financial institutions rely heavily on computer equipment and networks to manage finance, and transfer money electronically from one institution to the next. Security can never be an afterthought. When someone's money is at stake, and the institution's reputation, banks spare no expense making sure that everything is as safe and cracker-proof as possible. This doesn't mean that they have not fallen victim; they certainly have on several occasions. Financial institutions realized the need for expert security long before computers and networks came along. It is no surprise then that they work so hard to protect the financial assets of their customers.

NOTE

The majority of cracks against banks and other financial institutions are inside jobs. Because of the amount of security in place, these too are rarely successful, and the crook ends up vacationing in a federal prison.

What Is the Motivation Behind Attacks?

By now, you might be asking yourself why people do these things to begin with. What is the motivation? As with any form of crime, the attacker is meeting his own needs, for whatever reason, and the motivation varies. There are no doubt thrills associated with breaking into and gaining complete access to others' computer systems. Those who get caught often state that this rush alone is motivation enough. For now, we will take a look at the following motivations:

- Notoriety
- Maliciousness or destruction
- Making a political statement
- Financial gain and theft
- Knowledge

Notoriety, or the "Elite" Factor

Probably more common than any other motivating factor for cyber attacks is simply becoming notorious in the cracking community. This is most common with script kiddies and unskilled crackers who want to be the next Kevin Mitnick. Unfortunately, it seems that, even with all the publicity of the consequences, crackers still can't seem to stop cracking into vulnerable systems. For whatever reason, they seek fame from perpetrating some of the most ridiculous and pointless computer crimes known today. In most cases, you can find these people hanging out in obscure channels on IRC bragging to other script kiddies about how elite they are ("3l33t" in script kiddy parlance). Most of these individuals are young teenage boys with a computer, an Internet connection, and far too much free time on their hands.

On a positive note, many of them are skilled computer users, and they eventually grow out of being pranksters to becoming excellent security professionals in the white hat community. As you probably already guessed, those drawn to "The Dark Side" end up very differently indeed. Notoriety or hacker "brand-name" recognition only take you so far. Recently, a well-known 16-year-old Canadian cracker calling himself "mafiaboy" pleaded guilty on several counts of computer crime, and as such will likely be serving prison time soon.

▶ Kevin Mitnick is a well-known cracker who, in the early 1990s, was charged with 25 counts of federal computer and wire fraud violations. He spent nearly five years in federal prison, and has amassed quite a following around the world. For more information, check out http://www. kevinmitnick.com.

Maliciousness and Destruction

Most people would assume that the majority of cracking attempts are destructive in nature, but this is rarely accurate. Depending on the degree of the damage, it might be merely annoying or a complete loss. We'll take a look at a couple of common examples.

Destructive Pranks or Lack of Cause

Some people are just outright malicious. Some crackers are this way, too. They enjoy damaging or destroying things that do not belong to them. They could be best related to someone who randomly throws rocks through windows or sets buildings on fire. Often, the reasons don't make sense, or there is no obvious cause-and-effect relationship. The attacker was merely venting his anger, rage, or frustration on someone completely innocent. When similar attackers gain access to a computer, they will plant destructive viruses, delete important system files or personal documents, or just completely wipe the system's hard drive clean, rendering it useless. If the owner didn't routinely back up his data, the loss can be severe.

Disgruntled Employees

Another type of person you don't want to confront at all is a disgruntled employee. Although most people deal with on-the-job anger and frustration in a constructive and mature manner, there are those people who only know how to lash out when they are set off. If the company they work for relies heavily on computers, the computers likely will be used to vent the angry employee's frustration. I already covered insider attacks briefly in this chapter, but it gets much worse when the attacker also has a personal vendetta against the company for which he works. This can result in considerable loss for the company at stake. These days, most companies using computers also have a security policy in place, which outlines the consequences employees might face if they violate system security in any manner. Employees are routinely required to sign and agree to such policies as a condition of their employment. When anger is present, these policies naturally slip the mind of the angry worker as he systematically goes about destroying the data of his employer. I'll also revisit this charming individual in a moment when I discuss financial motivations for attacks.

Making a Political Statement

Earlier we looked at any government being a potential target for computer attack. In many cases, the reason is simply political. Often these attacks come from outside the country that is being victimized, but they also originate quite frequently from citizens of that country. Recently, many small countries in Europe and in third-world areas have been targeted over the Internet in a rash of political attacks on various governments, leaders, and military forces. During the war in Serbia, several small groups from all over the world launched cracking attacks on Serbian computer networks. Most of these failed, mostly because the communication systems of that country were quickly cut off as a result of the fighting. In January 1999, the Indonesian government was blamed for a highly organized attack against computers in Ireland, which brought down the entire East Timor virtual country domain, an Internet community of some 3000 users. Israel and Palestine have been engaging each other in a long "cyber battle" for several months. China has also fallen victim to computer crackers, mostly because of its stance on human rights issues. The new soldier is a computer with an Internet connection. The new battlefield is cyberspace. Wars are being fought there that are just as serious and politically engaging as any in history.

Financial Gain

Everybody wants more money, right? Why should crackers be any different? The digital thieves of the twenty-first century are quickly becoming the most elusive and daunting criminals in the world. The world's vast computer network is synonymous to the wild west enterprises of nineteenth century North America. With so much electronic wealth flowing from one computer to the next, it was only a matter of time before shady characters started finding ways to dip their greedy fingers into the Internet goldmine.

As stated earlier, companies dealing with finance or money in any way rely heavily on computer systems to remain in the business. Now, their customers expect that they can also access this same data from the comfort of their home via the Internet. Most banks now allow full account control from a Web browser over the Internet.

Thousands of companies have moved their ordering and inventory systems online, so that anyone can purchase these products with nothing more than a computer, an Internet connection, and a credit card number. All of this has come into existence only within the last few years, and, as such, the technology and standards driving e-commerce are far from mature, or secure. It really is a cracker's goldmine out there, if he knows where to look. The following sections look at the most common issues.

Theft or Unauthorized Transfer of Funds

Money zips all over the world electronically 24 hours a day. The digital economy is booming, but it's also fragile and prone to criminals just as any bank would be. It also seems a lot easier and safer to rob a bank with a computer than with a gun. Before the Internet existed, stealing from the electronic money stream did happen, most often by an employee with access to the proper systems. In nearly every case I have ever read about, the thief simply set up some sort of dummy account, and set up a process to transfer a portion of the e-money into the dummy account. After doing this for some period of time, the money would be withdrawn or transferred again to an accessible account. This type of theft has been very successful in many cases. Depending on how it is perpetrated, the victims often don't detect the loss of funds for some time, and usually by then it is too late. The banks have to cover such losses through insurance, the cost of which eventually trickles down to honest consumers. With the Internet, a whole new set of possibilities for theft exists. There have been cases of these illegal transfers taking place across international borders, making it difficult to ever recover the stolen funds or prosecute the crook responsible.

▶ Read more about "How to Hack a Bank" by David H. Freedman at `http://www.forbes.com/asap/2000/0403/056.html`. Mr. Freedman cites a noteworthy example of a 24-year-old programmer in Russia who nailed Citibank for $10 million electronically. He is now serving time in the United States.

Theft of Intellectual Property and Corporate Espionage

A more common, and often undetected, crime occurs every day at companies around the world. With so much money invested in storing important company data on computers, it's easy to see why eventually stealing it and selling it to the competition has become big business. Employees of the target company generally commit this type of computer crime. In some cases, the competition will employ shady characters to penetrate and steal vital trade secrets and other company data. Using this information, they can beat their competition and possibly make a lot of money in the process. With everyone being networked over the Internet these days, imagine how much easier this is. Because most company data is now stored in digital form, all it takes is a simple file transfer or an email, and that company's hard-earned intellectual property has been smuggled undetected to the outside world.

Software companies are particularly susceptible to this. Many software companies put millions of dollars into designing top-of-the-line software packages for other companies to buy. These packages often cost anywhere from a few hundred to several hundred thousand dollars to purchase. More often than not, however, someone inside leaks the software out to the Internet "warez" (pirated software) community, and, within a few hours, it can spread around the world. Although most of the people that pirate this software do not profit from its use or trade, it often ends up being used at companies where no legitimate license is owned. By this, the company can potentially make money using a product it never paid for, which takes money from the pockets of the software company that initially publishes it.

The Internet piracy community spans the globe. One merely has to enter "warez" in one's favorite search engine and click on some of the results. WARNING: Several of these sites contain nothing more than banner ads to pornography Web sites and other offensive material.

▶ The Internet is littered with "Warez" groups, Web sites, and pirated software. Read more about piracy and how it might affect the Internet economy at `http://www.findarticles.com/m0NEW/2000_April_6/61411395/p1/article.jhtml`.

Financial data kept by a company can also be worth the criminal act of stealing it and transferring it. Most notably, stocks information, customer databases, and other financial records can be very valuable to the right people.

Credit Card Theft and "Carding"

Most everyone now uses the Internet as a place to buy and sell goods and services of every description. Most often, the transaction is paid for with a credit card. The company selling the products or services receives this credit card information and stores it somewhere electronically in order to maintain records and fulfill the customer's order. Most Web sites offering credit card transactions do so over SSL (Secure Sockets Layer.) This only encrypts the information being transferred between the customer and the company. After the data is in the hands of the company, they can store it in any number of ways. Most often, this information is not stored securely, and is compromised by crackers or criminal employees.

There have been a lot of credit card database thefts in the news lately. In a few cases, the company that had the credit card numbers stolen was storing them unencrypted on the Web server that they used to take the orders from! All the thief had to do was break in and steal a simple text file with all this customer information. It doesn't matter who you are either. Notably, Bill Gates of Microsoft had his number pilfered on two separate occasions.

You might be wondering what good these credit card numbers are to someone other than the card owner. What many people don't understand is that credit card fraud is simple, it's easy, and it's very hard to catch the crook responsible. With the Internet, it has become a great deal easier to commit credit card fraud than without it. Most businesses that accept credit cards numbers for payment do not require any type of verification that the person using the card number is who they say they are. All the thief need do is set up some sort of drop, go shopping, and then meet the deliveries at his drop and collect the goods.

With the Internet being so open and anonymous, it's not hard to take someone's number and go shopping in relative safety. Credit card companies are struggling to catch their breath with the rampant explosion of Internet fraud cases they endure daily. Most people also have credit cards that allow money withdrawals and transfer of funds, creating even more ways for a criminal to take advantage of them. Some people also pay criminals good money for credit card numbers, making it more lucrative than ever to commit fraud.

Cracking for Knowledge

We've covered a lot of reasons someone might be motivated to break into or crack computer systems. One reason that doesn't come up often is the simple pursuit of knowledge. Many crackers are driven by the challenge of figuring out how a system works, how to break into it, and how to make it more secure. For these individuals, it is not about being destructive, or gaining notoriety—it is the thrill of the game. Breaking into a well-protected computer system is like an intense game of chess. It requires intelligence, a lot of abstract and forward thinking, and patience. Often, this type of cracker uses what he learns to be a better administrator, or a better programmer. The things he can learn will often be shared with others in the community, furthering the collective knowledge base that is so critical to those that work in the field of information security.

There are also crackers who use the knowledge they gain to proliferate more attacks on other systems, for whatever reason. The information they glean from penetrating the barriers of other networks is often shared with like-minded people over the Internet, thus propagating the problem. It is almost like a continual game, one side against the other, trying to remain one step ahead of the bad guys.

Breaking In to Break In

Right off, the phrase "breaking in to break in" might not make any sense to you at all, but it will. Many attackers crack systems for the sole purpose of having a compromised system from which to launch other attacks from. This is beneficial in many ways, especially if the cracker has several systems through which he can chain connections, one machine to the next. Think of it as stringing popcorn on fishing line. If each piece of popcorn represents a compromised system, and the line is the network connection from one machine to the next, it is easy to visualize the benefits. The farther away the attacker is from his own home base, and the more machines he's running through to achieve this, the harder it will be for anyone to ever discover his true identity. Each machine the connection is chained through adds another degree of complexity when security managers try to backtrack to find the culprit. If the machines are in different countries, if the connections cross international borders, traversing political and language barriers, it probably isn't even worth trying to track the cracker down at all. The most skilled attackers use methods such as this to keep their identity a complete secret. This helps keep them protected, and at the very least buys them some time should anyone come looking for them.

Summary

This chapter explained in what ways and to whom you might be vulnerable as it pertains to network security. Obviously there are countless variations and methods that can be used against you, but there are also technical limitations on how far and in what direction a security attack can go. This is the age of digital paranoia, and, because of that, there are many doomsayers in the world. Whether it is for attention, or money, or both, many people that don't know what they are talking about spout ridiculous rumors and myths about using computers and the Internet.

As you have read, there are plenty of ways that you can be a victim of Internet security issues. You can be targeted. You can suffer frustration, data, and financial loss. Your personal privacy can easily be violated. You are also completely capable of defending yourself. The most important thing you can do is educate yourself on the risks and the steps that are necessary to effectively combat the hackers and crackers. It is just as important to know what threats don't concern you or your personal or system security, and also when someone is trying to con you.

As with any other problem in the world, ignoring security issues will not make them go away. Using a computer now carries with it some personal responsibility. You are the only one who can take these matters into your own hands to protect yourself. This doesn't mean you need to mortgage your house to buy a top-of-the-line firewall to protect your cable modem or DSL line. By taking a proactive stance about your computer security and remaining current on the latest issues, you can stay one step ahead of those who might want to do you harm.

9

DISPELLING SOME
OF THE MYTHS

The Defender's Toolkit

IN THIS PART

Firewalls

Security is a process, not a product.

—Bruce Schneier, *Counterpane Labs*

IN THIS CHAPTER

This chapter covers firewalls, what they are, how they work, and who makes them.

Firewalls have been around for years, and now serve as pillars for the information security strategies of most organizations. Although firewalls are fundamentally very important, any organization that relies entirely upon a firewall to fulfill its security needs does so foolishly. Firewalls are not bulletproof. In fact, recently many of the most popular firewall platforms have fallen victim to some of the problems that have long plagued operating systems and applications. Buyers, beware!

Although parts of this chapter will be familiar territory to veteran administrators, some of the material presented here might be new ground. We will investigate what firewalls are, what they do, and more importantly, what they do not do. At the end of this chapter, the reader will understand the basics of firewalling, where and why it can be useful, how to do further research on the subject, and where the "We have a firewall—we are safe" philosophy falls flat on its face.

What Is a Firewall?

A *firewall* can be any device used as a network-level access control mechanism for a particular network or set of networks. In most cases, firewalls are used to prevent outsiders from accessing an internal network. However, firewalls can also be used to create more secure pockets within internal LANs for highly sensitive functions such payroll, payment processing, and R&D systems. They are not limited to perimeter use exclusively. The firewall devices themselves are typically standalone computers, routers, or firewall "appliances." Firewall appliances are usually proprietary hardware devices often running a custom or proprietary OS. The Cisco PIX series is a good example of a firewall appliance.

Firewalls are designed to serve as control points to and from your network. They evaluate connection requests as they are received. Firewalls check whether or not the network traffic should be allowed, based on a predefined set of rules or "policies." Only connection requests from authorized hosts to authorized destinations are processed; the remaining connection requests are discarded.

NOTE

As high-speed, residential Internet service continues to make its way into the world, organizations will be forced to face the growing issues surrounding the remote user. Forward-thinking security officers should begin looking at the adoption of "personal firewalls" now, to help address this growing threat. Although they are relatively new, products by Network Associates, InfoExpress, and F-Secure (and other vendors) will become more critical in defending external assets.

Most firewalls accomplish this by screening the source and destination addresses along with port numbers. For example, if you don't want folks from www.mcp.com connecting to your FTP site (via FTP), you can bar their access by blocking connection requests from 206.246.131.227 to your FTP site's address (*ftp.yoursite.example)* on port 21. On their end, the mcp.com folks see a message that reports "Connection Refused" or something similar (or they might receive no notice at all; their connection attempts might simply be blocked).

Other Features Found in Firewall Products

Firewalls can analyze incoming packets of various protocols. Based upon that analysis, a firewall can undertake various actions. Firewalls are therefore capable of performing conditional evaluations. ("If this type of packet is encountered, I will do this.")

These conditional constructs are called *rules*. Generally, when you erect a firewall, you furnish it with rules that mirror access policies in your own organization. For example, suppose you had both accounting and sales departments. Company policy demands that only the sales department should have access to your FTP site. To enforce this policy, you provide your firewall with a rule; in this case, the rule is that connection requests from accounting to your FTP site are denied.

In this respect, firewalls are to networks what user privilege schemes are to operating systems. For example, Windows NT enables you to specify which users can access a given file or directory. This is discretionary access control at the operating-system level. Similarly, firewalls enable you to apply such access control to your networked workstations and your Web site.

However, access screening is only a part of what modern firewalls can do. Over the past two years, firewall vendors have begun implementing the "kitchen sink" approach to feature development—that is, many vendors have been tossing every feature BUT the kitchen sink into their firewall offerings. Some of the added features include

- **Content filtering.** Some organizations want to stop their users from browsing particular Web sites: Web-based email sites, "underground" sites, day trading gateways, sites with pornography, and so on. Content filtering features and services can help block these sites, as well as protect against some types of ActiveX and Java-based hostile code and applets.

- **Virtual Private Networking (VPN).** VPNs are used to tunnel traffic securely from point A to point B, usually over hostile networks (such as the Internet). Although there is a wide range of dedicated VPN appliances on the market today, vendors such as Checkpoint and Cisco are happily rolling VPN services into their firewall offerings. Many firewall products now offer both client-to-enterprise VPN functionality, as well as LAN-to-LAN functionality.

10

- **Network Address Translation (NAT).** Network address translation is often used for mapping illegal or reserved address blocks (see RFC 1918) to valid ones (for example, mapping 10.0.100.3 to 206.246.131.227). Although NAT isn't necessarily a security feature, the first NAT devices to show up in corporate environments are usually firewall products.

- **Load Balancing.** More of a generic term then anything else, load balancing is the art of segmenting traffic in a distributed manner. Although firewall load balancing is one thing, some firewall products are now supporting features that will help you direct Web and FTP traffic in a distributed manner.

- **Fault Tolerance.** Some of the higher-end firewalls like the Cisco PIX and the Nokia/Checkpoint combination support some fairly intricate fail-over features. Often referred to as High-Availability (HA) functionality, advanced fault-tolerance features often allow firewalls to be run in pairs, with one device functioning as a "hot standby" should the other one fail.

- **Intrusion Detection.** The term "intrusion detection" can mean many things, but in this case, some vendors are beginning to integrate an entirely different product type with their firewall offering. While this doesn't create a problem in itself, people should be weary of the kind of work load this might impose on their firewall.

Although the thought of managing all these features from within a single box or product can be appealing, one should approach the kitchen sink mentality with a fair amount of skepticism. Firewalls have always been viewed as playing pivotal roles in organizations' security models. Borrowing from the KISS (Keep It Simple, Stupid) principle that is held so dear in the network administration world, we could suggest that going the route of feature bloat might not be the smartest thing to do when it comes to a security product. But we need not speculate on this…the latest round of firewall vulnerabilities have confirmed our suspicions for us. Read on.

Firewalls Are Not Bulletproof

Although vendors like to think their firewall products are immune to the problems that plague operating system and application developers, the fact of the matter is that they are every bit as vulnerable. Consider a sample of some of the issues that have crept up in firewall products:

- May 1998: It was discovered that Firewall-1 had several reserved keywords that, when used to represent a network object, would open a gaping security hole. (The named object would be interpreted as "undefined," and unless other changes were made, the object would be accessible to any address.) You can better understand this vulnerability (and get a list of those keywords) by downloading http://www.checkpoint.com/techsupport/config/keywords.html.

- June 1998: It was discovered that the Cisco PIX Private Link uses a small (48-bit) DES key. It's conceivable that this can be cracked. The CIAC reported the following:

  > PIX Private Link is an optional feature that can be installed in Cisco PIX firewalls. PIX Private Link creates IP virtual private networks over untrusted networks, such as the Internet, using tunnels encrypted with Data Encryption Standard (DES) in ECB ("electronic codebook") mode. An error in parsing of configuration file commands reduces the effective key length for the PIX Private Link DES encryption to 48 bits from the nominal 56 bits. If attackers know the details of the key-parsing error in the PIX Private Link software, they will know 8 bits of the key ahead of time. This reduces the effective key length from the attacker's point of view from 56 to 48 bits. This reduction of the effective key length reduces the work involved in a brute-force attack on the encryption by a factor of 256. That is, knowledgeable attackers can, on the average, find the right key 256 times faster than they would be able to find it with a true 56-bit key.

  Cisco found a fix for this problem. Check `http://www.cisco.com/warp/public/770/pixkey-pub.shtml` for details.

- July 1999: Problems were discovered in "ipchains," the firewall code found natively in Linux. Remote attackers could use the flaw to send data to supposedly blocked ports. More information can be found here: `http://www.securityfocus.com/bid/543`.

- May 2000: A buffer overflow was discovered in Network Associates Gauntlet firewall product that reportedly let intruders execute malicious code on the firewall itself—remotely. It turns out, however, that the bug wasn't part of the original firewall code. Instead, the culprit was introduced through the content filtering (Cyber Patrol) system NAI had acquired and rolled into the Gauntlet product line. Nevertheless, organizations using the newer version of Gauntlet were forced to deal with the problem. You can read the full thread here: `http://www.securityfocus.com/bid/1234`.

- June 2000: A denial of service attack using fragmented packets was discovered that could disable all Checkpoint Firewall-1 firewalls. At the time of this writing, there was a workaround available, but the fundamental problem was still not remedied. More information can be found here: `http://www.securityfocus.com/bid/1312`.

- June 2000: Another denial of service attack was discovered in CheckPoint FW-1, this one targeting Firewall-1's mail handler. Again, no patch had been released at the time of this writing. More information can be found here: `http://www.securityfocus.com/bid/1416`.

- July 2000: During the Black Hat briefings, two well-known security researchers, John McDonald and Thomas Lopatic, reported a number of vulnerabilities they found in Checkpoint's Firewall-1 product. (See it at `http://www.dataprotect.com/bh2000/blackhat-fw1.html`.) This was significant, as Checkpoint's product is one of the most widely deployed firewalls in the world.

10

FIREWALLS

By no means is this list conclusive—this is simply a taste of some of the recent problems discovered in today's firewall products. Also, consider that the some of these issues are *directly* related to non-core functionality found in firewall products that the vendors have added: content filtering and encapsulation (for VPN use).

It remains to be seen whether the firewall vendors will treat security considerations equally with that of feature additions. However, to the vendors' credit, they claim that most of their clients aren't asking for more security, but rather more features. I present the question to the reader: What do you think is more important in your firewall? Do us all a favor—let your vendor know how you feel.

A Look Under the Hood of Firewalling Products

In the esoteric sense, components of a firewall exist in the mind of the person constructing them. A firewall, at its inception, is a concept rather than a product; it's the idea surrounding the access control mechanism that enables traffic to and from your network.

In the more general sense, a firewall consists of software and hardware. The software can be proprietary, shareware, or freeware. The hardware can be any hardware that supports the software.

Firewall technologies can generally be classified into one of three categories:

- Packet-filter–based (usually routers, Cisco IOS, and so on)
- Stateful packet-filter–based (Checkpoint FW-1, PIX, and so on)
- Proxy-based (NAI Gauntlet, Axent Raptor, and so on)

Let's briefly examine each.

Packet-Filter–Based Firewalls

Packet filtering firewalls are typically routers with packet-filtering capabilities. Using a basic packet-filtering router, you can grant or deny access to your site based on several variables, including

- Source address
- Destination address
- Protocol
- Port number

Router-based firewalls are popular because they're easily implemented. (You simply plug one in, provide an access control list, and you're done.) Moreover, routers offer an integrated solution. If your network is permanently connected to the Internet, you'll need a router anyway. So, why not kill two birds with one stone?

On the other hand, router-based firewalls have several deficiencies. First, they usually aren't prepared to handle certain type of denial of service attacks. Many of the denial of service tactics used on the Internet today are based on packet mangling, SYN flooding, or forcing other TCP/IP-based anomalies. Basic routers aren't designed for handling these types of attacks. Second, most routers can't keep track of session state data. Administrators are forced then to keep all ports above 1024 open in order to handle TCP sessions and session negotiations properly. Although this is arguably not a huge security concern (because there shouldn't be any listening services running on those ports anyway), it's not generally a good practice to leave unused ports open to the outside.

Finally, using ACLs (access control lists) on high-end routers that are supporting extremely busy networks can contribute to performance degradation and higher CPU load. However, for most low-speed connections (such as T1 circuits) on lower-end routers (such as Cisco 2500 series routers), normal packet filtering will not tax the router to any significant degree.

> **NOTE**
>
> For a long time, it was believed that putting access control lists (ACLs) on routers would greatly degrade their performance. Although sticking a 100 rule ACL on a Cisco 7000 supporting a dozen ATM connections might not be the best of ideas, placing basic ACLs on routers supporting low-speed (10Mbps or lower) connections doesn't usually degrade their performance noticeably. Two members of the underground, rfp and NightAxis, published some basic findings on this subject that can be found at `http://www.wiretrip.net/rfp/`. Since then, other studies have also been performed (your mileage can vary). Remember, even the low-end Cisco 2500 series routers were based on Motorola 68030 and 68040 chip sets, and the newer ones are using even more advanced RISC-based chips. Routers are more powerful then many people give them credit for. Test it yourself—see what you find.

> **TIP**
>
> Many network administrators will use ACLs on their perimeter routers in conjunction with a more advanced firewall to create a multitier approach to network access control.

Stateful Packet-Filter–Based Firewalls

Stateful packet filtering builds on the packet filtering concept and takes it a few steps further. Firewalls built on this model keep track of sessions and connections in internal state tables, and can therefore react accordingly. Because of this, stateful packet-filtering–based products are more flexible than their pure packet-filtering counterparts. In addition, most stateful packet-filtering–based products are designed to protect against certain types of DoS attacks, and to add protection for SMTP-based mail and an assortment of other security-specific features.

Checkpoint pioneered the technique called "stateful inspection" (SI), which takes stateful packet filtering up one notch. SI enables administrators to build firewall rules to examine the actual data payload, rather then just the addresses and ports.

> **NOTE**
>
> Because stateful packet-filtering–based firewalls track session states, they can keep the ports above 1024 closed by default and only open the high ports on an as-needed basis. As simple as this might sound, this is why most administrators consider stateful packet filtering to be the minimum technology they will implement for their firewall solutions.

Proxy-Based Firewalls

Another type of firewall is the proxy-based firewall (sometimes referred to as an application gateway or application-proxy). When a remote user contacts a network running a proxy-based firewall, the firewall proxies the connection. With this technique IP packets are not forwarded directly to the internal network. Instead, a type of translation occurs, with the firewall acting as the conduit and interpreter.

How does this differ from stateful packet filtering and generic packet filtering, you ask? Good question—and one that many people ask. Both packet filters and stateful filtering processes examine incoming and outgoing packets at the network and session levels (see Chapter 4, "A Brief Primer on TCP/IP"). They examine IP source and destination addresses along with ports and status flags, compare them to their rule sets and table information, and then decide whether the packet should be forwarded. Proxy-based firewalls, on the other hand, inspect traffic at the application level in addition to lower levels. A packet comes into the firewall and is handed off to an application-specific proxy, which inspects the validity of the packet and application-level request itself. For example, if a Web request (HTTP) comes into a proxy-based firewall, the data payload containing the HTTP request will be handed to an HTTP-proxy process. An FTP request would be handed to an FTP-proxy process, Telnet to a Telnet proxy process, and so on.

This concept of a protocol-by-protocol approach is more secure then stateful and generic packet filtering because the firewall understands the application protocols themselves (HTTP, FTP, SMTP, POP, and so on). It's more difficult for intruders to sneak past something that is watching more than just the ports and IP addresses. However, notice that I used the word "concept" in reference to it being more secure. The truth of the matter is that in real-world applications, this approach has had its fair share of problems.

Proxy-based firewalls have always been slower then stateful packet-filtering–based ones. Now, for most networks (10Mbps or slower), this difference is moot. However, for heavily loaded networks (T3s at 45Mbps, multiple T3s approaching 100Mbps, and so on), this becomes a much larger issue. As technology improves, the gap might close, but for now the use of pure proxy-based technology is still a concern for high-volume networks.

> **NOTE**
>
> Network Associates is working on a cross between proxy and stateful packet filtering called "adaptive proxy technology." It remains to be seen how groundbreaking this will truly be, but you can read all about it here: `http://www.nai.com/asp_set/buy_try/try/whitepapers.asp`

In addition to the performance problem, the proxy-based solution also has some adaptability issues. Suppose, for example, that a new protocol is invented to manage your coffeemakers at home. For the sake of example, we'll call this protocol the Percolation Control System, or PCS for short. Now, let us also assume that PCS uses TCP and runs over port 666. Administrators of stateful packet-filtering–based firewalls will simply have to build a new rule into their firewall allowing traffic over TCP on port 666, and it's a done deal. Administrators of proxy-based firewalls, however, have a new problem: They don't have a proxy (yet) for PCS. It's a brand new protocol. Although some proxy-based firewalls (such as NAI's Gauntlet) have a generic proxy for such problems, now we're back to basic packet filtering, which defeats the purpose of having a proxy to begin with.

However, taking this example one step further, let's say the proxy-based firewall vendor eventually writes a PCS-proxy, and all is well in Coffeeville. Soon after, some mischievous helpdesk contractors resurrect their old copies of network DOOM, which also runs over port 666, and they attempt to start abusing an old addiction. Low-and-behold, network DOOM won't make it through the proxy-based firewall, but it will through the stateful packet-filtering–based one.

We will cover how this can be used maliciously a little later on, but suffice it to say that the proxy-based approach is a little more secure from a theoretical standpoint—but the products based on this approach can also be a big pain in the butt.

Pitfalls of Firewalling

One pitfall in the world of firewalls is that security can be configured so stringently that it can actually impair the process of networking. For example, some studies suggest that the use of a firewall is impractical in environments where users critically depend on distributed applications. Because firewalls can implement such strict security policies, these environments can become bogged down. What they gain in security, they lose in functionality. To some, this might be viewed simply as an inconvenience. However, the problem can bring about long-term effects that are far more damaging. For example, inevitably all administrators face the classic square off between user X who needs to do Y, and the security problems that surround her request. Although the dilemma touches on a number of information security principles, one of the largest being policy definition, it can also cross some organizational boundaries as well. If, for example, the technical staff loses its battle to block service Y, they then run the risk of having an organization-wide precedent set. This can lead to the security personnel getting crushed by the business people, and sooner or later something is opened up on the firewall that really shouldn't be. On the other hand, smart organizations know to examine these situations on a case-by-case basis and act accordingly. Unfortunately, we don't all work for "smart" organizations….

Firewalls can help create sticky situations. The solution is to know how to avoid these situations, and know what to do when you do lose a battle. For example, if some bone-head VP gets the approval to allow third-party access to the payroll system through the Internet, rather then lose sleep over it, consider ways of controlling the damage. Segment the payroll systems onto a separate subnet, look to implement stronger system-level audit logs, work at getting an Intrusion Detection System (IDS) implemented on the questioned segment, and so on. Many times, perceived losses can be turned into long-term victories, if you play your cards right.

> **TIP**
>
> Although users might seem more like pesky annoyances then necessary evils, it's important to remind yourself that the network is there for one reason: connectivity. Although security is an important part of an administrator's responsibility, so is basic usability. At the end of the day if the users can't do their job, we're all going to be in trouble. Good administrators know which battles to fight, and which ones to work on from another angle…

Another more serious issue is that of a perceived and false sense of security. Administrators who are content that their firewalls will protect them from all evils are setting themselves up for a rude awakening. Part of the challenge of deploying a firewall is to help build a feeling of safety without overdoing it. Fun challenge, huh? The reason that this balance is so important is that, without secondary levels of defense, you are placing all your eggs in one basket. If your firewall is broken, your internal networks can easily be destroyed. Firewalls are *part* of a security model; they shouldn't be *the* security model because they have their own set of downfalls. Remember, tiered security models are your friend.

There is hope. Five years ago, we were fighting battles with the CIOs to get firewalls in the first place. Now we're fighting battles trying to convince them that just a firewall isn't enough. Hey, at least we're making progress.

Firewall Appliances

The word *appliance* became all the rage in late 1999 as the term appeared to be universally adopted by marketing departments across the globe. The concept of an appliance is a simple and arguably quite appealing one: a turnkey, integrated hardware/software solution that comes ready to run, securely, out of the box. Traditional firewalls were typically software products that ran on an underlying (mainstream) operating system. Before installing the firewall product, you had to first build and configure the underlying OS as well as secure it. Firewall appliances, on the other hand, offered the lure of "solid-state" technology (meaning "no moving parts"), and highly optimized kernels that could support high levels of packet processing.

Or so the story went. However, it soon became obvious that appliance was not synonymous with solid state, as vendors started shipping appliances that relied on hard drives and hidden operating systems. The talks of high optimization were tainted by people shipping stock BSD kernels and basic firewalling code. Unfortunately, it is probably more accurate to say that the term *appliance* now defines the difference between something you can kick (a machine in a 2U chassis) and something you can throw (a manual and a CD-ROM).

However, that's not to say that there aren't a lot of good appliance-like firewalls out there. Nokia, for example, took the Checkpoint FW-1 code and ported it to their IPSO operating system (an OS with BSD roots that was optimized for routing) to produce their "IP" series of firewall appliances. The units are quite reliable, and perform extremely well. Cisco has since moved the PIX to a solid-state design. Both the Cisco PIX and the Nokia IP series use Intel x86 hardware under the hood. Units like the Netscreen firewalls have always been in a slimline chassis and in appliance form as well.

Should you move to a firewall appliance? It really depends on what your needs are. Some people like the ability to use standard UNIX commands on their firewalls for examining logs, parsing tables, and so on, so using an appliance might stymie them a bit. However, by using a standard OS such as Microsoft Windows NT or Sun Solaris, you do increase the risk of an oversight or misconfiguration. These problems can allow the firewall machine itself to become a vulnerable target. For some, the appliance approach is a little more bulletproof, and appliance performance figures will soon match that of most Sparc-based firewalls, if they haven't already. For others, having the mainstream OS under the hood might be an advantage.

NOTE

The term solid state originally came from the world of electrical engineering. The term was used in reference to the move from vacuum tubes to transistors. However, the term has recently been bastardized by vendors and marketing departments alike, and is now commonly used to convey the concept of "no moving parts."

10

FIREWALLS

Building Firewalls in the Real World

"Okay," you ask, "So, what's the best firewall, and what's the best way to deploy it?" Ah, if only life were so simple. The short answer is that there is no single, best solution. However, there are some good tips and guidelines that can help you come to a strong decision, and I will do my best here to get you started down the right road.

Let's begin with a few prepurchase guidelines:

1. Understand that firewall platforms change—there is no superior firewall platform. For example, VendorX might have their head in the clouds for a few revisions, and then get their act together for the next version of their product. By the same token, VendorY and VendorZ might have great products one year, and deep-six them the following year after all their lead developers die bungee-jumping in Kazakhstan. Keep up with the testing done by magazines like *Network Computing* and *InfoWorld*, talk to your peers, and, above all else, *test the products if you can*. Think of a firewall as a new car: If you don't like how it feels, you don't want to be driving it for the next few years.

2. Understand and document your requirements. Do you need your firewall to support Token Ring, or just Ethernet? Do you need your firewall to support Network Address Translation (NAT)? How many interfaces do you need? Does the firewall need to run on a particular platform? People all too often get caught up in extreme benchmarking numbers and massive feature lists. But if you don't need your firewall to manage your toasters, and you don't have 15 OC12 links coming into your DMZ, you might not need the fastest and the shiniest. Remember what your firewall is primarily going to be used for: controlling access into and out of your network.

3. Know your limitations. If you are primarily a Windows NT shop with no UNIX expertise, going out and purchasing a UNIX-based firewall that requires a lot of command-line interaction might not be the best of ideas. Keep in mind that a good portion of firewall failures are because of "pilot error"—that is, the firewall does not fail, the person administering it does. Know your limits. If you or your staff don't understand how to use it, or if the technology is way over your head, that is only going to come back to haunt you. Don't choose the firewall with the prettiest GUI, but don't pick one that takes a Ph.D. to administer, either.

4. Go with a product that has been at least ICSA certified, and preferably something that has a respectable installed base of users. Just because it says "firewall" in the product literature doesn't mean it's secure. Go with something that has been proven on the battlefield.

> **NOTE**
>
> One of my employer's clients (a Fortune 100 company) contracted our team to take a look at a new firewall "appliance" that they were thinking of migrating to. This client was looking at purchasing these units in bulk, but wanted a third-party evaluation done before they jumped ship from their main firewall vendor. Within three days of our team banging on the units, we discovered that, not only were we able to format the entire box through the Web administration interface, but the units that the vendor had shipped us had pirated copies of a popular graphics package stored on the hard drive. (Whoops.) Sometimes "too good to be true," is, well, too good to be true.

Before you buy a firewall, you should seriously research your own network, your users, and their needs. You should also generate a visual representation of the connections that will be traveling through your firewall and document those findings. Not only will this help you with your requirement gathering, it will leave a paper trail detailing why certain openings were made, and what processes and people were behind those openings. Should anything come into question years from now, you (or your successor) will have something to turn to for help.

There are five primary steps you must take when building a firewall:

1. Identify your topology, application, and protocol needs.
2. Analyze trust relationships and communication paths in your organization.
3. Evaluate and choose a firewall product.
4. Plan and deploy the firewall correctly.
5. Test your firewall policies stringently.

Identifying Topology, Application, and Protocol Needs

Your first step is to identify your topology, application, and protocol needs. This step is more difficult than it sounds, depending on the size and composition of your network. If you run one of the few homogenous networks in existence and only need to support basic protocols (SMTP, HTTP, FTP, and so on)—you are in luck. The task ahead of you is pretty easy.

But if you are like the majority of the organizations out there, you need to support a mix of platforms, protocols, and applications. Although this might appear to be easy, this can get messy really quickly. For example, your application developers might say, "We just need access to the Lotus Notes servers from the Internet." Sounds simple enough, right? Well, let's dig a bit deeper. What kind of access? "Well, we need to replicate data to our suppliers, and we need to be able to use the Lotus Notes clients remotely."

10

FIREWALLS

Whoa! That's a little more in depth then just "accessing Notes." It sounds as though we might need to support the ports related to the Notes clients (TCP port 1352). We will need to support the ports relating to the replication process, if the developers want to access anything via the Web interface. Plus, we'll need to support HTTP (usually over port 80), and what about remote management?

"Oh yeah, we'll be using PCAnywhere to manage the servers remotely."

Yuck! Okay, you see where I'm going with this: Simple requests can turn out to be more complex then they initially seem. Plan accordingly! You will need to *dig deep* into your organization, and make sure you talk to everyone who will be using/depending on this firewall.

TIP

Although it smells like a CYA (Cover Your Ass) move, when going through requirement-gathering phases, it's a good idea to be as loud and as encompassing as possible within your organization. That way, if a user or project team approaches you after the firewall deployment with some bizarre need or functionality requirement, you have some room to stand your ground on why the function wasn't built into the deployed model. "Why didn't you inform me of this during my requirement-gathering phase?" You might be surprised at how much room this tactic can give you to breathe.

Companies focused on e-commerce sometimes separate their product network from that of their internal LAN-based network services. For example, let's say that you're building a new e-commerce site selling the new integrated PCS-enabled toaster/coffeemaker combos. You'll want 24×7 Web server farms, 24×7 payment processing gateways (often called *merchant gateways*), possible email servers, and needed support systems (application servers, database servers, and so on). Now, you will most likely want to separate these mission-critical 24×7 systems from less critical day-to-day internal systems, such as the internal email SMTP gateway, the internal FTP sites, the proxy servers, and so on. This quickly becomes a topology issue: How many interfaces will your firewall need to support this configuration? Better yet, how many firewalls will you need? Do you need hot-standby functionality? Will your firewall need to support extended high-availability (HA) protocols such as HSRP and VRRP?

Better to ask these questions beforehand then to get stuck with a solution that won't scale.

Analyze Trust Relationships and Communication Paths in Your Organization

Just as it's important to understand applications and protocols heading outbound from your organization, you also need to take the time to understand internal, or "inbound" processes as well. This is important for a number of reasons. First, in the end, the applications you are supporting have to work. If you move the middle-tier (the application servers) of your three-tier e-commerce solution to your firewalled segment, and the servers become cut off from their database counterparts, you'll have a lot of angry users on your hands (and a broken application). At the same time, if a server that is "Internet exposed" has free, unrestricted access to your internal networks and infrastructure, you have a potential security nightmare on your hands if that machine is ever compromised by a hostile intruder.

Again, this is more up-front investigative work you need to perform. This might involve discussions with individual departments. Certain network segments might need to access one another's resources. To prevent total disruption of your current system, it's wise to perform a detailed analysis of these relationships first.

TIP

> Throughout this process, use considerable tact. You might encounter users or managers who insist, "We've been doing it this way for 10 years now." You have to work with these people. It's not necessary that they understand the process in full. However, if your security practices are going to heavily impact their work environment, you should explain why. This is also an area where up-front policy creation helps—if there are defined, ratified policies in place before going into potential conflicts, your chances of coming out of meetings unscarred greatly increase. Managers tend to avoid monkeying with policies that have been ratified "by above."

Evaluate and Choose a Firewall Product

Next, based on what you discover about your network and those who use it, you need to evaluate and decide on a firewall product. Before conducting purchasing research, you should generate a list of must-haves. You'll ultimately base your purchasing decision on this list. Now, the preferred way of handling the next step is to get your top firewall choices into a lab to do some testing. However, not everyone has a test lab and a few extra weeks to play with cool security products. If you do, enjoy it for those of us who don't!

The next best thing is to get a product demo, visit someone who does have a lab, or ask your vendor for suggestions on how you can see the product in a live environment. If your vendor is good, they'll most likely be able to help you out. Common criteria most people use in deciding on a firewall include

- **Capacity.** Can the firewall support the throughput that you estimate? Does it have room to scale? Typically, if you are talking speeds of T3 (45Mbps) or less, almost any firewall will work.

- **Features.** Although we talked about the problems of feature bloat earlier, features still count. Make sure your firewall can do what you need it to do. However, be realistic with what you are going to use it for. If you aren't going to manage your toaster with it, you don't really need that feature.

- **Administrative interface.** You've got to live with this thing. If you aren't comfortable with the interface, or if you don't understand the interface, chances are you might mess it up. Avoid pilot-error—go with something you like.

- **Price.** Okay, who are we kidding? This is always a factor. Although many people have traditionally opted to go the route of CheckPoint FW-1, often times even a basic deployment of FW-1 is intense on the pocketbook, costing 5 to 10 times as much as other products. Take a look at all your options; sometimes the second-best will still enable you to be just as secure for a lot cheaper.

- **Reputation.** Has the vendor typically been responsive to product vulnerabilities? What's the product's track record? Does it have a deployed user base, or is it a recent addition to the scene?

Also, consider looking at independent testing labs and respected technical, *testing-oriented* trade magazines for other sources of information.

▶ Network Computing magazine tests firewall products a few times a year, and usually does a fairly good job in their reviews. Check out `http://www.nwc.com` for more information.

Deploying and Testing Your Firewall

Finally, after you've purchased your firewall, you'll put your research to good use by implementing your firewall and its supporting rule set(s). First, make sure that the firewall itself is secured. If the unit is an appliance, chances are there is little outside of changing default passwords that you'll need to do to harden the unit. However, if it is an NT- or UNIX-based firewall, make sure that the OS on which you deploy the firewall software is properly hardened. (See Chapter 19, "Microsoft;" Chapter 20, "UNIX;" and Chapter 21, "Novell," for more information).

The next step is to put your new firewall into your production environment. If this is planned properly, and in the right environment, you might even be able to transition the firewall into the production environment by moving one server at a time behind it. However, often times it is not this easy. Expect at least a few problems, and also budget some time for network down time. (Also, be prepared to field some fairly angry users.) It is extremely unlikely that you'll get it right the first time. That is, unless your network environment is extremely simple, or you are a rule set wizard. If you get it right on the first try, congratulations—you are one of the few! Otherwise, join the ranks of the rest of us, and don't be too hard on yourself. This stuff isn't rocket science, but it's not Tinker toy construction, either.

Finally, you'll need to test your rule sets. For this, I recommend extensive test runs. There are really two phases:

- Testing the rule set from the outside
- Testing the rule set from the inside

Consider using the NMAP tool to take snapshots of your network from an internal perspective (inside the firewall), and from an external perspective (outside the firewall). Make sure the external view is in line with what you expect.

Above all else, remember—DEFAULT DENY should be your mindset. If you don't know what it is, don't allow it through your firewall. Better to struggle through learning about protocols and application dependencies than to unknowingly open huge holes into your enterprise. Think minimalist.

TIP

People often make the mistake of "firing and forgetting" with their firewalls. They deploy them, they test them, and then they forget about them. One of the top things you should look to implement after your firewall deployment is a process for reviewing your firewall logs. Not only will this help you identify potential problems and trends with your configuration, it will help you get an advanced warning of who is at your doorstep. If any potential intruders come around to rattle your doorknobs, your firewall logs will be the first place where you'll spot them. Use your logs—they are your friend.

Sample Failures of Firewall Technology

Let me first start by saying that this section is not designed to be an all-encompassing view of how firewalls can be circumvented. In fact, quite the opposite. My goal is to simply provide you with clear, simple examples of how firewalls can fail you. I would also argue that these aren't even failures of the firewalls themselves, but rather of their deployers and the expectations placed on them.

I assume you are familiar with the tool netcat.

The "Whoops, Where Did My Web Server Go?" Problem

Picture this: You have a stateful packet-filtering–based firewall that allows inbound traffic through port 80 to a single NT-based Web server. That NT Web server is behind the firewall, with most of the more trivial services shut down. (Workstation service, server service, FTP service, Gopher service—all are disabled.) Your perimeter router is secured, and let us also assume that the firewall itself is properly configured and secured.

But somehow, using this configuration, an intruder is able to get administrative shell access, via Telnet, to your protected NT Web server in under two minutes. How is this possible?

Microsoft's Internet Information Server (IIS the Web server used natively on NT) installs a number of nasty sample scripts by default. Combine this with the RDS/MDAC problem (see Chapter 19 for further explanation), and intruders can not only execute commands remotely on the NT server (via standard HTTP requests), they can build FTP scripts. Using RFP's `msadc.pl` Perl exploit script on a vulnerable Windows NT/IIS installation combined with netcat and the echo command, an intruder can

1. Create an FTP script that will retrieve a copy of netcat.
2. Execute that FTP script using `msadc.pl` and `FTP -s -a <scriptname>`.
3. Create a script to shut down the Web server, and bind netcat to port 80 using `nc -l -p 80 -e cmd.exe`.
4. Telnet into the Web server (`telnet 10.0.0.2 80`) over port 80 to connect to an active copy of netcat (see Figure 10.1).

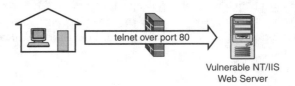

FIGURE 10.1
Firewall only allowing inbound data through port 80.

So although the configuration appears to be solid, the intruder is sitting there with an administrative shell on your NT machine. What went wrong? Firewalls are not a substitution for endnode security. Even if you deploy the tightest configuration possible on the firewall (short of disconnecting the network), a single open vulnerability on a single end-node can blow your whole model.

Now, a proxy-based firewall would have blocked the netcat shell because the Telnet traffic over port 80 would not have been viewed as valid HTTP requests. However, proxy-based firewalls would not have stopped the RDS/MSADC. It *is* valid traffic, and the attacker could have altered his or her attack accordingly. However, let's not pick on stateful packet-filtering–based firewalls exclusively.

> **NOTE**
>
> There is another point to made here: Blocking types of outbound traffic can be a good thing, although few administrators consider doing this. During one penetration test we ran into a savvy admin who had blocked outbound FTP access from his Internet-exposed Web servers. Even though we were able to execute commands on the target machines by manipulating faulty CGI scripts, we were unable to fetch our intrusion tools (such as netcat) via FTP. This slowed us down quite a bit.

Using SSH to Bypass Rule Sets

This scenario is a bit different. Let's say that our network policy prohibits the use of unencrypted POP from outside of the organization because it passes clear-text passwords. Let's assume that using our proxy-based firewall we've blocked external POP access to the organization's POP mail server, which inhibits external users from checking their mail while at home. Let us also assume that we allow the use of SSH (Secure Shell) outbound.

We discover one day that one of our more clever users is checking his mail from home, using POP remotely. Worse, we soon discover that he is doing so across the Internet via his cable-modem attachment. His POP password is now being sent across the Internet in the clear, validating our original concern. So how could this happen with us blocking inbound POP at the firewall?

There is neat little feature found in most SSH clients called "tunneling." Tunneling allows you to seamlessly transport other types of connections through established SSH sessions. In our scenario, this user would initiate an outbound SSH session from within the organization from the UNIX server running POP. He would connect to a server at his ISP, and set up a listening tunnel on the ISP's server on port 1828 that would redirect a session back to the POP server. This tunnel would then enable him to connect to the internal POP server from home, after he modified his POP client to connect on port 1828 (rather then 110) on his ISP's machine. As long as the SSH session remained active, the tunnel would work (see Figure 10.2).

Effectively, our clever user bypassed our rule set. Although the POP request comes in encrypted from the ISP's machine (because it's over the SSH session), its path to the ISP machine is still out in the open. So where did we go wrong? Well, combine the fact that proxy-based firewalls can't "peek" inside of encrypted traffic with the rather useful tunneling feature of SSH, and you have the makings of our little problem. Although naive administrators might be tempted to blame the firewall for this problem, the simple fact of the matter is that firewalls have their weaknesses—blocking SSH inbound tunnels is one of them.

These are just two examples. Trust me, there are many more.

10

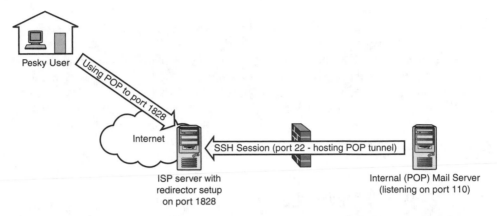

FIGURE 10.2
Firewall blocking POP (port 110) inbound.

> **NOTE**
>
> The inability to eavesdrop on encrypted tunnels applies to SSL, as well. In fact, during one of our team's engagements, we found ourselves cut off from email because of the client's restrictive proxy. This proxy, however, allowed outbound SSL. Just for fun one of our team members took putty, an open-source SSH-client, and modified it to tunnel SSH through SSL. Voil[ag]a— we had our email connection, and the firewall admin was none the wiser. Encryption will continue to be both a blessing and a curse to security administrators in years to come.

Building a Firewall with the Firewall Toolkit (FWTK)

Although a bit dated, a good exercise and perfectly feasible firewall solution is to use the TIS Firewall Toolkit (TIS FWTK). TIS was acquired by Network Associates Inc., but the original toolkit has fortunately lived on. The FWTK is based on application proxy-based technology. The package (which is free for noncommercial use) includes proxies for the following services:

- Telnet
- FTP
- Rlogin
- Sendmail
- HTTP
- X Window system

For each such proxy, you must specify rules. You must edit three files to establish your rules:

- `/etc/services`. This file is already on your system. It specifies what services your machine will support and what ports those services run on. (Here, you set the ports your proxies will run on.)

- `/etc/inetd.conf`. This file is also already on your system. It's the configuration file for inetd. The `inetd.conf` file specifies what server is activated when outsiders request a particular service. (Here, you specify your proxies, using them to replace the default servers.)

- `/usr/local/etc/netperm-table`. This is a FWTK file. In it, you specify who can use the services you provide.

You can use two schemes for permissions:

- That which is not expressly allowed is denied.

- That which is not expressly prohibited is allowed.

I recommend the first, which is far more prohibitive.

Granting or denying access with the FWTK is easy. You can apply wide-sweeping masks of addresses and hosts that are denied access. You can use asterisks to indicate an entire range of addresses:

```
http-gw:        userid          root
http-gw:        directory       /somewhere
http-gw:        timeout 90
http-gw:        default-httpd   www.myserver.net
http-gw:        hosts           199.171.0.* -log { read write ftp }
http-gw:        deny-hosts      *
(http-gw is the proxy for HTTP.)
```

As you can see, you must configure access rules for each service. This is one of the pitfalls of using application gateways. Another pitfall is that every application session must be proxied. This can be a laborious and cumbersome environment for inside users. (Inside users must also have their outbound traffic proxied. This can represent significant overhead because inbound traffic also has a resource impact on outbound traffic.)

Application gateways are more suitable if you have no outbound traffic—for example, when your site serves clients outside the firewalls with archived information. A typical example is when you have clients who pay a subscription fee to retrieve technical specifications from your server. The technical specifications are sensitive materials, and therefore, only your clients should be able to retrieve them. In this case, an application gateway is perfect.

10

Application gateways are less suitable for corporations, universities, ISPs, or other environments where more fluid communication (and more interfaces with the general public) is required. For example, in such environments, you cannot be certain that users will always connect from specific servers or networks. They might come in from a wide variety of IP addresses. If you're using an application gateway, and you need to authorize a user connection within Netcom, unless that address is static, you must allow everyone from Netcom.

If you haven't yet purchased a firewall (or if you simply want to learn about them), you should get the FWTK. By configuring it and testing your rules, you will learn much about how firewalls work.

▶ Obtain a copy of the TIS Firewall Toolkit at `ftp://ftp.tis.com/pub/firewalls/toolkit/README`.

▶ The FWTK requires a UNIX system and a C compiler. Moreover, although the FWTK is known to compile on SunOS and BSD without problems, configuration issues exist for Linux. To sort out these problems quickly, there is no better document than Creating a Linux Firewall Using the TIS Toolkit by Benjamin Ewy. That document is located online at `http://www2.linuxjournal.com/cgi-bin/frames.pl/lj-issues/issue25/1204.html`. Patches for use with the FWTK on Linux are located online at `ftp://ftp.tisl.ukans.edu/pub/security/firewalls/fwtkpatches.tgz`.

> **NOTE**
>
> Another more generic proxy-based technology is SOCKS. SOCKS has great significance because it is well established and support for it is already included in many browser packages, most notably Netscape Navigator. A good site for comprehensive coverage of SOCKS technology is `http://www.socks.nec.com`.

Commercial Firewalls

This next section provides details on firewall vendors, their products, and any special characteristics their firewall might have. I am not recommending these firewalls, but rather simply providing this list as a resource.

BorderManager

BorderManager is the premier firewall for Novell environments, but it will still protect UNIX- and NT-based systems. The product offers centralized management, strong filtering, and high-speed, real-time analysis of network traffic. Also, BorderManager offers the ability to create "mini-firewalls" within your organization to prevent internal attacks from departments or local networks.

Firewall Type: Stateful packet-filter–based

Manufacturer: Novell Inc.

Supported Platform: Novell NetWare

Further Information:

`http://www.novell.com/products/bordermanager/index.html`

FireBOX

Firewall Type: Stateful packet-filter based

Manufacturer: Watchguard

Supported Platform: UNIX

Further Information: `http://www.watchguard.com`

Firewall-1

Checkpoint's Firewall-1 is one of the most frequently deployed firewalls in the industry today. The product features packet filtering, strong content screening, integrated protection against spoofing, VPN options, real-time scanning for viruses, and a wide assortment of other features. It is one of the most feature-rich firewalls out there, but is also one of the most expensive.

Firewall Type: Stateful inspection-based

Manufacturer: Check Point Software Technologies Ltd.

Supported Platforms: Windows NT and UNIX

Further Information: `http://www.checkpoint.com/`

FireWall Server

Firewall Type: Proxy-based

Manufacturer: BorderWare

Supported Platforms: Custom (proprietary OS running on Intel hardware)

Further Information: `http://www.borderware.com`

Gauntlet Internet Firewall

Remember the TIS FWTK? It originally formed the basis for Gauntlet. The latest release of Gauntlet offers a hybrid application-proxy and packet-filtering approach, along with VPN, content filtering, and virus scanning features.

10

FIREWALLS

Firewall Type: Hybrid Proxy-based with stateful packet filters

Manufacturer: Network Associates

Supported Platforms: UNIX, Windows NT, DMS, ITSEC E3, and IRIX

Further Information: `http://www.nai.com/asp_set/products/introduction/default.asp`

GNAT Box Firewall

GNAT is a firewall appliance. You can manage the GNAT box with either a command-line or Web-based interface. GNAT filters incoming traffic based on IP source address, destination address, port, network interface, and protocol.

Firewall Type: Stateful packet-filter based

Manufacturer: Global Technology Associates

Supported Platforms: N/A (appliance)

Further Information: `http://www.gnatbox.com/`

Guardian

Guardian is an NT-based firewall.

Firewall Type: Stateful packet-filter based

Manufacturer: NetGuard Inc.

Supported Platform: Windows NT

Further Information: `http://www.netguard.com`

NetScreen

NetScreen is a firewall appliance that supports IPSEC, DES, and triple DES encryption.

Firewall Type: Stateful packet-filter–based

Manufacturer: NetScreen Technologies Inc.

Supported Platforms: N/A (Appliance)

Further Information: `http://www.netscreen.com/`

PIX Firewall

The PIX, along with Firewall-1, are the two most widely deployed firewall products today. The PIX is a firewall appliance that is devoid of any moving parts. It supports IPSEC, and can be administered through Telnet or SSH sessions, or through the Cisco Security Policy Manager (CSPM) framework product.

Firewall Type: Stateful packet-filter–based

Manufacturer: Cisco Systems Inc.

Supported Platforms: N/A (Appliance)

Further Information: `http://www.cisco.com/warp/public/751/pix/`

Raptor Firewall

Firewall Type: Proxy-based

Manufacturer: Axent

Supported Platforms: Solaris and Windows NT

Further Information: `http://www.raptor.com/products/datasheets/prodsheet.html`

SideWinder

Firewall Type: Proxy-based

Manufacturer: Secure Computing

Supported Platform: UNIX (custom build, however, ships with the product)

Further Information: `http://www.securecomputing.com`

Sonicwall

Firewall Type: Stateful packet-filter based

Manufacturer: SonicSystems

Supported Platforms: N/A (appliance)

Further Information: `http://www.sonicwall.com`

Summary

Firewalls are not bulletproof. Anyone relying on them for the majority of their security is setting themselves up for a nasty fall. However, in many cases, firewalls are quite necessary and can prove to be very useful. A firewall's success depends on the proper utilization of feature sets, proper configuration, and proper monitoring. As with any security product, testing it before purchasing it is key. If you can test them yourself, great; otherwise look to third parties and industry-recognized security sources for further information.

10

FIREWALLS

Books and Publications

Internet Firewalls and Network Security (Second Edition). Chris Hare and Karanjit Siyan. New Riders. ISBN: 1-56205-632-8. 1996.

Internet Firewalls. Scott Fuller and Kevin Pagan. Ventana Communications Group Inc. ISBN: 1-56604-506-1. 1997.

Building Internet Firewalls. D. Brent Chapman and Elizabeth D. Zwicky. O'Reilly & Associates. ISBN: 1-56592-124-0. 1995.

Firewalls and Internet Security: Repelling the Wily Hacker. William R. Cheswick and Steven M. Bellovin. Addison-Wesley Professional Computing. ISBN: 0-201-63357-4. 1994.

Actually Useful Internet Security Techniques. Larry J. Hughes, Jr. New Riders. ISBN 1-56205-508-9. 1995.

Internet Security Resource Library: Internet Firewalls and Network Security, Internet Security Techniques, Implementing Internet Security. New Riders. ISBN: 1-56205-506-2. 1995.

Network Firewalls. Steven M. Bellovin and William R. Cheswick. IEEECM, 32(9), pp. 50–57, September 1994.

Session-Layer Encryption. Matt Blaze and Steve Bellovin. Proceedings of the Usenix Security Workshop, June 1995.

IP v6 Release and Firewalls. Uwe Ellermann. 14th Worldwide Congress on Computer and Communications Security. Protection, pp. 341–354, June 1996.

Internet Resources

Firewalls FAQ. `http://www.faqs.org/faqs/firewalls-faq`

There Be Dragons. Steven M. Bellovin. Proceedings of the Third Usenix UNIX Security Symposium, Baltimore, September 1992. AT&T Bell Laboratories, Murray Hill, NJ. August 15, 1992. `http://www.zeuros.co.uk/generic/resource/firewall/papers.htm`

Keeping your site comfortably secure: An Introduction to Internet Firewalls. John P. Wack and Lisa J. Carnahan. National Institute of Standards and Technology. `http://csrc.ncsl.nist.gov/nistpubs/800-10/`

SQL*Net and Firewalls. David Sidwell and Oracle Corporation. `http://www.zeuros.co.uk/generic/resource/firewall/papers.htm`

Covert Channels in the TCP/IP Protocol Suite. Craig Rowland. Rotherwick & Psionics Software Systems Inc. `http://csrc.ncsl.nist.gov/nistpubs/800-10.ps`

A Network Perimeter with Secure External Access. Frederick M. Avolio and Marcus J. Ranum. A paper that details the implementation of a firewall purportedly at the White House. `http://www.alw.nih.gov/Security/FIRST/papers/firewall/isoc94.ps`

Packets Found on an Internet. Steven M. Bellovin. Lambda. Interesting analysis of packets appearing at the application gateway of AT&T. `ftp://ftp.research.att.com/dist/smb/packets.ps`

X Through the Firewall, and Other Application Relays. Treese/Wolman. Digital Equipment Corp. Cambridge Research Lab. `ftp://crl.dec.com/pub/DEC/CRL/tech-reports/93.10.ps.Z`

Benchmarking Methodology for Network Interconnect Devices (RFC 1944). S. Bradner and J. McQuaid. `http://archives.neohapsis.com/archives/rfcs/rfc1944.txt`

Vulnerability Assessment Tools (Scanners)

IN THIS CHAPTER

With vulnerability announcements being released at a dizzying pace, most organizations face an uphill battle when it comes to hunting down the security holes that reside on their systems. In an attempt to aid organizations in this ongoing quest, a number of commercial and open source efforts have risen to automate the process of vulnerability discovery. These vulnerability assessment tools, or *scanners,* come in many shapes and sizes, with varying degrees of accuracy. This chapter will outline some of the pros and cons of using these tools, as well as identify where their use can be helpful. We will also shed some light on what's important when selecting such a tool to aid in the never-ending war of keeping your environment secure.

The History of Vulnerability Scanners

Turn back the calendar to the early 1990s. The Internet is off the ground and running rampant in universities. CERT is up and operational. The World Wide Web is more-or-less an experiment that is creeping into Gopher's territory. Vendors are vehemently denying most security bugs, and UNIX administrators are just beginning to feel the wrath of the clever attackers. Internet security practices as we know them today are in their infancy, but the blueprints for modern day tool sets are actively being drawn up.

In 1992, a computer science student named Chris Klaus was experimenting with Internet security concepts. He created a scanning tool, Internet Security Scanner (ISS), that could be used to remotely probe UNIX systems for a set of common vulnerabilities. In Chris' words:

> ISS is a project that I started as I became interested in security. As I heard about crackers and hackers breaking into NASA and universities around the world, I wanted to find out the deep secrets of security and how these people were able to gain access to expensive machines that I would think were secure. I searched [the] Internet for relative information, such as Phrack and CERT advisories.

> Most information was vague and did not explain how intruders were able to gain access to most systems. At most the information told administrators to make password security tighter and to apply the vendor's security patches. They lacked real information on how an intruder would look at a site to try to gain access. Having talked with security experts and reading CERT advisories, I started trying to look for various security holes within my domain.

> To my surprise, I noticed that many of machines were adequately secured, but within a domain there remained enough machines with obvious holes that anyone wanted into any machine could attack the weak 'trusted' machine and from there could gain access to the rest of the domain.

> —Chris Klaus. (Found in the ISS version 1.0 readme file, 1993.)

Although the cynic in me is inclined to ask what has changed since then (many of Chris' observations still ring true today), ISS was one of the early, if not the first, remote vulnerability assessment scanners to be deployed en masse on the Internet. ISS looked for a few dozen common security holes and flagged them as issues to be resolved. Although a few people were nervous about the tool's obvious power in the wrong hands, most administrators welcomed it with open arms.

A few years later, Dan Farmer (of COPS fame) and Wietse Venema (of TCP_Wrapper fame) authored a similar tool called SATAN (Security Administrator Tool for Analyzing Networks). SATAN essentially did the same thing as ISS, but had some advancements: a more mature scanning engine, a Web-based interface, and a wider assortment of checks. Unlike ISS, however, the pending release of SATAN became a media-crazed event. So hyped was its release that in April 1995 (the month it was officially released), *TIME* magazine wrote an article on it and Dan Farmer. CERT even issued an advisory on its abilities (CA-1995-06). Many people feared that the release of SATAN would bring about total chaos on the Internet.

Obviously this was not the case, as SATAN's release did little more then cause traffic for a few days while people downloaded it.

> **NOTE**
>
> Oddly enough, although Farmer lost his job at SGI over SATAN, Klaus managed to use ISS to build a multimillion dollar security products juggernaut—Internet Security Systems (ISS).

Since then, the vulnerability assessment scene has continued to grow and mature. Today, there are more than a dozen scanners in circulation, each with its own set of strengths and weaknesses. The fundamental concepts, however, have not changed much since the early days of ISS and SATAN.

How Vulnerability Scanners Work

As you will see in both the Microsoft and UNIX chapters, vulnerabilities come in many flavors. However, there are primarily two classifications for operating system vulnerabilities: ones that are local exposure points (host-level), and ones that are remote exposure points (remote-level).

In addressing remote exposure points, there are a number of methods one can use to approach the task of automated vulnerability scanning. For example, one approach might involve using a port-scanning tool such as nmap, identifying the operating system, and then logging all the listening ports. The user would then be given a list of ports (that is, 21, 25, 53, 80, and so on) and an OS type (that is, Linux Kernel 2.2). This approach has a few problems, however, as the user is left with a ton of data (that is, port information) and no details as to what services are actually vulnerable. The user is simply given a blueprint of their system. Identifying what those listening services are, and whether they are vulnerable or not, is an exercise left to the user. For example, if my data set tells me that machine X is running the Linux 2.2 Kernel and has a service listening at port 21, I still have very little idea as to whether I am vulnerable to any of the wu-ftpd buffer-overflow bugs. In fact, I don't even know whether this particular system is running wu-ftpd—it might be running ProFTPd or glftpd, instead. So even when hunting down a single port, I still need to

a) Identify what is listening at that port

b) Identify what version that service is

c) Research whether there are any known vulnerabilities associated with that service and version number

Although this approach might be feasible for a dozen machines or so, it obviously won't scale in mid- to large-sized organizations where thousands of machines are present. The task at hand then moves from difficult to impossible.

A more practical approach would be to build on the previous model of port-scanning and OS identification, and then add some mechanism to identify the listening service types and versions. You would then have another piece of the puzzle completed. Going back to the wu-ftpd buffer overflow example, by identifying the service version, you would now know

a) That the server is Linux Kernel 2.2-based

b) That port 21 is listening

c) What the service type and version is

Let's say that your service query process informs you that you are using wu-ftpd version 2.4.2. This gets you even closer, as now you simply need to research whether wu-ftpd version 2.4.2 has any known vulnerabilities.

NOTE

You should note the difference between *port scanning* and *vulnerability scanning*. Although most vulnerability scanners do indeed scan for open TCP and UDP ports, this is only one of their many features. In contrast, although port scanners like nmap are capable of performing some interesting feats (such as OS fingerprinting), they rarely contain any sort of vulnerability database. In short, most vulnerability scanners take port scanning a few steps farther.

The last remaining component to this process is research—knowing what versions of what services are vulnerable. In many ways, this ties into what attackers do: scan, query, research, and exploit. In this case, it turns out that wu-ftpd version 2.4.2 is, indeed, vulnerable to a known attack type.

Vulnerability Assessment Tools (Scanners)

Chapter 11

219

11

VULNERABILITY
ASSESSMENT TOOLS
(SCANNERS)

Based on the sheer number of known product vulnerabilities (estimated between 2,000–3,000 to date), creating a thorough system to properly identify and track *all* these product vulnerabilities is a fairly daunting task. The mining and managing of this vulnerability data presents the biggest challenge and the biggest argument for using an automated tool.

Although implementation details vary, based on these examples, you can deduce that there are a number of common components throughout most scanning approaches:

- **The vulnerability data.** Vulnerability assessment scanners have internal databases of vulnerability information that help them to accurately identify remote system exposure points.

- **The scanning mechanism.** The technical guts of the scanner lie in its capability to properly identify services, subsystems, and vulnerabilities. Depending on how the scanner was written, it might not be efficient at scanning large ranges of machines.

- **The reporting mechanism.** Finding a problem is one thing; adequately reporting on it is something entirely different. Some products are stronger than others when it comes to clearly stating what they've discovered.

Some scanners will break this mold, but they are more often the exception than the rule.

NOTE

A more thorough—and definitely more dangerous—approach is to create a tool that looks for vulnerabilities and actually attempts to *exploit* them. SNI started going down this path with their original Ballista product. In theory, this would definitively end the problems associated with misdiagnosed vulnerabilities (also referred to as *false positives*). However, it could also bring about some serious chaos. For example, exploiting vulnerabilities such as the BIND NXT bug crashes the DNS server. If this particular exploit were implemented, all DNS servers running vulnerable versions of BIND would be disabled during every scan!

What to Look For When Choosing a Scanner

Like any product-purchasing decision, before answering the question of which product is right, you first need to decide your specific requirements. For example, if plotting vulnerability-remediation progress over time is something you want automated, then a product's capability to log and plot multiple scan sets is a feature you need to look for. If you have a large NetWare environment, you might want to make sure that the scanner has NetWare-specific checks. If you have to scan 50–100 hosts, efficiency might not be an issue. However, if you need to scan thousands at a time, you'll want to make sure the scanner can scale to that range. Again, many of these issues are specific to what you'll need your vulnerability scanner to do.

There are also some common areas of concern that all products need to address. A few of the issues that you will come into contact with in choosing a vulnerability scanner include

- **Completeness of the vulnerability checks**. I don't recommend falling into the trap of playing the numbers game when picking a scanner. However, the number of vulnerabilities a scanner looks for is still important. At a bare minimum, a scanner should look for the known critical vulnerabilities that allow for root/administrator-level compromises.

- **Accuracy of the vulnerability checks.** It's important that scanners have a good set of vulnerability checks. However, a scanner's capability to accurately identify those vulnerabilities is also important. Missing a bunch of holes is as equally undesirable as being forced to sift through a report identifying hundreds of non-existent vulnerabilities. Like intrusion detection systems, some scanning products still have problems with false positives.

- **Scope of the vulnerability checks.** It should be noted that most of the vulnerability scanners are designed to discover remote vulnerabilities, not local (host-level) ones. However, a few products like ISS and Webtrends have system-level agents that will also look for local vulnerabilities—vulnerabilities that would otherwise be undetectable by remote scans. While these system agents often address a greater range of vulnerabilities, they also require installation, making them a management nightmare for large environments.

- **Timely updates.** Although scanners will always be one step behind the vulnerability announcements, they should be updated at a fairly regular (once per month or more) interval. You'll want to look for a scanner that has a significant R&D team behind it that is consistently updating the product.

- **Reporting capabilities.** Finding vulnerabilities is important, but properly describing the problems and their subsequent fixes is also important. So is the accurate ranking of the vulnerabilities. This is of particular concern for larger organizations because they usually rely on system administrators to remediate the discovered problem.

- **Licensing and pricing issues.** Some of these products are licensed per node, some per server scanned, and some are free. Some of them have an easy licensing system (like NAI); others (like ISS) require a convoluted key-cutting system. Attempting to provide accurate prices and licensing information in this book would be an exercise in futility, as the vendors are constantly changing the terms. However, it should be noted that licensing issues should be thoroughly investigated before purchasing decisions are made, as some of these pricing schemes are just downright obnoxious. When in doubt, however, there is always Nessus, which is free.

No scanner that I know of has addressed all these issues well, but Nessus and ISS Internet Security Scanner come pretty close.

Vulnerability Assessment Tools (Scanners)

CHAPTER 11

221

11

VULNERABILITY
ASSESSMENT TOOLS
(SCANNERS)

▶ In January 2001, Neohapsis labs released a fairly comprehensive analysis of these tools for Network Computing magazine. Based on the given requirements, Nessus and ISS Internet Security Scanner came out on top of the scanner shoot-out. You can find the story here: `http://www.nwc.com/1201/1201f1b1.html`.

Fundamental Shortcomings

Just about every security tool discussed in this book has had a set of fundamental problems, and vulnerability scanners are no different. Knowing their limitations is as important as knowing their strengths.

The major shortcomings of these products can be grouped into three categories: completeness, timeliness, and accuracy. First, reviews of these products have shown that many of them catch a fairly high number of known vulnerabilities, but none of them are equipped to identify all of them. As of the fourth quarter of 2000, there were a still a number of the SANS Top Ten that went unnoticed by these products.

▶ You can view the SANS Top Ten list of common vulnerabilities here: `http://www.sans.org/ topten.htm`. While not a definitive list by a long shot, it does list some of the more common holes found on machines today.

Second, most of these products are updated once a quarter, if that often. If a vulnerability is announced in January, your scanner might not be equipped to detect that vulnerability until March. That leaves you with two months to fend for yourself when it comes to scanning. Now, your internal threat identification effort should be on top of this problem anyway, but the point is that these scanners should not be your primary method of defense when it comes to hunting down remotely exploitable exposures.

Another problem is that most modern-day scanners are simply implementing "banner-grabbing" techniques to identify service versions. This technique is arguably sufficient for most environments; however, it can create some interesting scenarios. For example, by simply telnetting to port 25 (SMTP mail) and 21 (FTP), one can identify versions of these two services.

Note that these two machines appear to be running Microsoft Exchange 5.5 and version 4.0 of the Microsoft FTP server. However, many services such as Bind, sendmail, and wu-ftpd are now allowing administrators to change these banners in their configuration files. Although this is not a security threat, changing a default wu-ftpd banner to "Fabio's favorite FTP Server version 1.0" will completely confuse most vulnerability scanning tools. The strange and disturbing moral of this story is that if you want your scanners to be effective, don't change your default banners.

Finally, these products still struggle with false positives. Frequently on large and diverse networks, vulnerability scanners will misfire and report on vulnerabilities that simply do not exist.

Although it's better to be safe then sorry, this does create some overhead as personnel then have to run around trying to hunt down phantom vulnerabilities.

Top Vulnerability Scanners

In an ideal world, technology-purchasing decisions would be backed by proper requirement gathering, proper testing, and realistic budgeting. However, I've grown to realize that people rarely have the luxury of doing things the right way. It is for this very reason that I've picked what I consider to be the top vulnerability scanners on the market today, and listed them here. This is not to say that the other products won't do a sufficient job—these are just my personal favorites based on my field experiences and testing. I still encourage the reader to perform some level of investigation when choosing a product to adopt, but the list of products in the following sections should get you started.

Axent NetRecon

Axent's NetRecon complements Axent's existing security product line of firewall and intrusion detection suites. NetRecon's strengths lie in its interface, strong reporting abilities, its moderately sized vulnerability database, and its capability to perform what is often referred to as secondary exploitation—using knowledge gained from one server to assess another. Although it's rare that I've found this final feature useful, it is something not seen in many other products.

NetRecon has traditionally not been as thorough as Nessus, Cybercop Scanner, or ISS, but it is still a fairly comprehensive scanning tool that can be quite useful. It can also report into Axent's Enterprise Security Manager (ESM), which can be used for more general risk assessment efforts.

> Vendor: Axent/Symantec
> Headquarters: Rockville, MA (USA)
> Platform: Windows
> Product: NetRecon
> URL: http://www.axent.com

ISS Internet Scanner

ISS initially built its company on Internet Scanner, and it has long been regarded as the de facto standard in the industry for vulnerability scanning. Internet Scanner has a strong reporting back-end, a comprehensive set of vulnerability checks, and a very usable GUI. ISS has obviously spent as much time polishing the product as they have on the back-end scanning engine itself. For example, the scanner provides a significant amount of background data on each vulnerability check.

Internet Scanner uses a Microsoft ODBC–based back-end to store its scan data, which can be used later for doing long-term trending. As in NetRecon's integration with ESM, Internet Scanner integrates with the ISS Decisions product. Combined with scanner data, ISS Decisions can be used in conjunction with other security products (firewalls, intrusion detection systems, and so on) to paint a more global picture of vulnerability and threat points.

Although Internet Scanner traditionally hasn't had as many problems with false positives as other products, it does still lag behind on the update front. The other negative point worth mentioning is the fact that in my experience Internet Scanner appears to have become less stable in the 6.x series of releases. I've had numerous problems with it crashing during large scans, and occasionally I'll have to clear out its internal database and start again clean before it will cooperate. It has always been recoverable, however.

It should be noted that ISS also makes two other scanning products, System Scanner and Database Scanner, although both are agent-based and incapable of scanning remote systems.

Vendor: Internet Security Systems, Inc.

Headquarters: Atlanta, GA (USA)

Platform: Windows NT Workstation version 4.0

Product: Internet Scanner

URL: `http://www.iss.net`

Network Associates Cybercop Scanner

Cybercop Scanner's roots come from NAI's (Network Associates, Inc.) acquisition of SNI (Secure Networks, Inc.) and their Ballista product. Although Cybercop Scanner has an impressive number of vulnerability checks and moderate reporting abilities, it also comes with a number of surprisingly useful tools. Two of the tools that are of particular interest are CASL, and the SMB grinder. CASL enables the GUI-based construction of IP packets, whereas the SMB grinder is similar to the password cracking capabilities of L0phtCrack.

Cybercop's primary downsides revolve around it lacking some fundamentally important vulnerability checks, and its bizarre licensing scheme. NAI usually tries to sell Cybercop on a per-node basis, as opposed to a per-number-of-servers-scanned basis. This can create some horrendously high pricing schemes, depending on the alignment of the stars and the salesperson's current commission plan.

Vendor: Network Associate, Inc.

Headquarters: Santa Clara, CA (USA)

Platform: Windows NT and UNIX

Product: Cybercop Scanner

URL: `http://www.nai.com`

The Open Source Nessus Project

Nessus was written by Renaud Deraison, an open source author living in Paris, France. Renaud discovered Linux at age 16 and has been hacking it ever since. In 1996, Renaud began attending 2600 meetings and subsequently developed a strong interest in security. This spawned a partnership between Renaud and two other programmers, and together they wrote their first auditing tool in 1997. After tackling that project, Renaud conceived Nessus in early 1998.

Nessus is quickly becoming the Linux of the vulnerability-scanning field. Driven by the open source movement, Nessus wasn't much to speak of a few years ago but is now gaining ground on—and sometimes surpassing—its commercial counterparts. Nessus employs an extensible plug-in model that enables the security community to add scanning modules at will. This gives Nessus a development edge because any check that it does not have can be created by anyone with some time and coding abilities on their hands.

Nessus uses a console-engine model, in which the console might or might not reside on the same computer as the scanning engine. This distributed architecture allows for some interesting flexibility, as you don't need to be anywhere close to the scanning engine in order to control it.

At the time of this writing, Nessus had more than 500 vulnerability checks, some of which still aren't available in the commercial scanning tools. Depending on how the development efforts continue to progress, Nessus could surpass commercial scanners in overall thoroughness in the coming year.

> Vendor: NONE (open source)
>
> Headquarters: NONE (Released out of France, however)
>
> Platform: UNIX (Windows console available)
>
> Product: Nessus
>
> URL: `http://www.nessus.org`

Whisker

Whisker was written by a hacker by the name of "rain forest puppy" (rfp), who has carved out a niche for himself in regards to discovering Web-based vulnerabilities. Whisker doesn't fit the general definition of a vulnerability scanner as it is specifically focussed on scanning for known vulnerable CGI scripts. In fact, the *only* things it looks for are vulnerable CGI scripts. However, its list of CGI checks is more comprehensive than all the commercial scanners combined. Because of this, I highly recommend you use Whisker in addition to a mainstream scanner.

> Vendor: NONE (open source—rfp labs)
>
> Headquarters: Chicago, IL (USA)
>
> Platform: Windows and UNIX

Vulnerability Assessment Tools (Scanners)

CHAPTER 11

225

11

VULNERABILITY
ASSESSMENT TOOLS
(SCANNERS)

Product: Whisker

URL: http://www.wiretrip.net/rfp/

Other Vulnerability Scanners

The following is a list of scanners that are up-and-coming (although this is not as comprehensive a list as the previous one). I do encourage the reader to continue to monitor the progress of these products, and test them whenever possible.

BindView HackerShield

Vendor: BindView

Headquarters: Houston, TX (USA)

Platform: Windows

Product: HackerShield

URL: http://www.bindview.com

Cisco NetSonar

Vendor: Cisco Systems

Headquarters: San Jose, CA (USA)

Platform: Windows

Product: NetSonar

URL: http://www.cisco.com

SAINT

Vendor: World Wide Digital Security, Inc.

Headquarters: Bethesda, MD (USA)

Platform: UNIX

Product: SAINT

URL: http://www.wwdsi.com

SARA

Vendor: NONE (Open Source)

Headquarters: NONE

Platform: UNIX

Product: SARA

URL: http://www-arc.com

Webtrends Security Analyzer

Vendor: Webtrends

Headquarters: Portland, OR (USA)

Platform: Windows and UNIX

Product: Security Analyzer

URL: `http://www.webtrends.com`

Summary

Although vulnerability scanners are by no means an all-encompassing solution to identifying vulnerabilities and locking down systems, they can still be extremely valuable tools. As with any security tool, however, one should be aware of the weaknesses these tools exhibit. They are consistently behind when it comes to vulnerability announcements, they do not always report information accurately, and they are not exhaustive when it comes to the depth of their vulnerability data. Using a scanner in conjunction with a solid vulnerability identification effort and a solid set of system lock-down procedures, however, will result in a strong strategy for combating the overall problem.

Intrusion Detection Systems (IDSs)

IN THIS CHAPTER

Intrusion detection is one of the hottest areas in the information security landscape. Although the promise of technology that automatically detects, alerts, and possibly stops hostile intruders is extremely attractive, the technology is also very young. This chapter provides the reader with a guide to intrusion detection system (IDS) products, and introduces some of the ins and outs of implementing intrusion detection system (IDS) solutions. The chapter also sheds some light on how to select the best IDS for your environment and your needs, and gives you a realistic review of what these systems can and cannot do.

An Introduction to Intrusion Detection

The term intrusion detection means many things to many people; however, for the sake of clarity we're going to define it as the act of detecting a hostile user or intruder who is attempting to gain unauthorized access. Assuming this definition, a number of popular methods are used to detect intruders—for example, inspecting system, Web, application, firewall, and router logs for hostile or unusual activity. Some system administrators will implement binary integrity checkers such as AIDE or Tripwire, in hopes of catching successful attackers when they deposit Trojan code on compromised servers. (Chapter 20, "UNIX," has further details on Tripwire.) Other administrators will simply monitor event logs looking for failed user login attempts.

Although all these methods are helpful, they become difficult, if not impossible, to perform on a daily basis. Introduce a few hundred machines, and the task becomes downright overwhelming. Enter: the intrusion detection system.

The roots of modern-day intrusion detection systems lie in the Intrusion Detection Expert System (IDES) and Distributed Intrusion Detection System (DIDS) models that were developed by the U.S. Department of Defense (DOD) back in the late '80s and early '90s. These were some of the first automated systems to be deployed. Today, most intrusion detection (ID) systems are designed with the same goal in mind: to help automate the process of looking for intruders. This can be as simple as the real-time parsing of firewall logs looking for port scans, or as complex as applying inspection routines to raw network traffic looking for buffer overflow attempts.

Traditional IDS classification schemes put most systems into two distinct camps: misuse detection models and anomaly-based detection models. This chapter focuses on two implementations of the misuse detection model: network-based intrusion detection systems (NIDS) and host-based intrusion detection systems (HIDS). Readers should note that many other intrusion detection models do exist, but are less popular. However, most modern-day IDS implementations can be grouped into one of these categories:

- **Network-based IDS.** In their current form, NIDS devices are raw packet-parsing engines—glorified sniffers on steroids. They capture network traffic and compare the traffic with a set of known attack patterns or signatures. NIDS devices compare these signatures every single packet that they see, in hopes of catching intruders in the act. NIDS devices can be deployed passively, without requiring major modifications to systems or networks.

- **Host-based IDS.** These systems vary from vendor to vendor, but they are usually system centric in their analysis. Most host-based IDSs will have components that parse system logs and watch user logins and processes. Some of the more advanced systems will even have built-in capabilities to catch Trojan code deployments. Host-based systems are agent-based—that is, they require the installation of a program on the systems they protect. This allows them to be more thorough on some levels, but also more of a headache to deploy and administer.

- **Anomaly-based IDS.** Anomaly-based systems are a bit more obscure, and are often times referred to as more of a "concept" than an actual model. The philosophy behind anomaly-based approaches is to understand the patterns of users and traffic on the network, and find deviations in those patterns. For example, a user who normally logs in Monday through Friday but is now logging in at 3 a.m. on a Sunday might be flagged as a potential problem by an anomaly IDS. In theory, an anomaly-based IDS could detect that something was wrong without knowing specifically what the source of the problem was.

The most common IDS types, both commercial and deployed, are HIDS and NIDS models. Although working models of anomaly-based IDSs exist, they are rarely deployed outside of government and academic circles.

12

INTRUSION
DETECTION
SYSTEMS (IDSs)

NOTE

Many people unfamiliar with the intrusion detection system field confuse the technology with access control devices such as firewalls. Intrusion detection systems, in their current form, do not serve as a method of access control. While a number of them can be configured to interact with firewalls, this is not their primary purpose. Beginners should think of intrusion detection systems as a type of burglar alarm, and not as a lock or door.

Who Should Be Using an IDS

Although IDS technology is certainly attractive, before sinking any time into IDS research, you should first ask whether an IDS makes sense for your organization. If, for example, an organization is lacking basic security fundamentals such as firewalls, system/OS lockdown procedures, or virus protection, an IDS deployment shouldn't take priority over those efforts. An IDS should be installed only after other facets of the information security strategy have already been initiated (see Chapter 3, "Building a Roadmap for Securing You Enterprise"), or to solve specific situations or shortcomings. For example, if a new e-commerce initiative is launched that you simply cannot secure adequately, an IDS might help you keep a sharper eye on it. In addition, some people use IDSs as a validation tool for their firewall rulesets. But if your network is a chaotic collage of vulnerabilities, an IDS will simply help you become the master of the obvious. You'll already have problems that an IDS certainly won't fix. Remember, modern-day IDSs are still, for the most part, reactive devices. They won't fix your problems.

However, if deploying an IDS is in your future, the following sections should guide you to making informed product decisions.

Network-Based IDSs

Essentially, network-based IDSs are designed to inspect network traffic and look for known attack patterns or "signatures." They perform this task by examining each and every packet that traverses the monitored network segment. This is usually accomplished by putting the network interface card (NIC) in "promiscuous" mode, and passing every frame to the running IDS process for analysis.

One of the most appealing aspects of the NIDS model is that NIDS devices are passive. In most cases, the rest of the systems don't even know they are there. Even better, deploying NIDS devices doesn't require the involvement of system administrators, a resource that becomes a stumbling point for large HIDS deployments.

Although the NIDS design is moderately effective, it brings with it a few interesting issues. For starters, the attack signatures are based on *known* attack types. This means that most attacks that the devices have not been programmed for will pass by, unnoticed. This places the users of these systems one step behind in a game that most are already losing. For example, when the BIND NXT bug hit the Internet in 1999, no NIDS product on the market was able to detect the exploitation of the hole. Why? Because it was a new vulnerability and IDS programmers hadn't built a check for it into their signature libraries yet. One by one, vendors began creating signatures for the attack, but most of these updates occurred weeks, sometimes months, after the attack was widespread.

▶ For a description of the BIND NXT vulnerability, along with other BIND vulnerabilities, see:
  http://www.isc.org/products/BIND/bind-security-19991108.html

In short, if the IDS is not updated on a constant basis, it will be unable to help identify new attacks and trends—much like vulnerability assessment (VA) scanners. (See Chapter 11, "Vulnerability Assessment Tools (Scanners).") Unfortunately, even when vendors and administrators alike work to keep NIDS devices up to date, they will still be one step behind.

Another issue that plagues the NIDS model is the widespread deployment of switched environments. Switches, by their very nature, reduce the amount of traffic that is "sniffable." NIDS devices rely on their capability to view all network traffic. If the NIDS devices can't see the traffic, they can't inspect it.

NIDS devices are also traffic-sensitive. Although some of the higher-end NIDS systems such as Enterasys Dragon and Network ICE's BlackICE are currently pushing the 100Mbps boundaries, most NIDS devices struggle in high-bandwidth environments.

Finally, IDS evasion via packet-mangling techniques and other clever tricks is a big problem. A number of papers and studies have been released detailing methods of fooling intrusion detection devices. These techniques revolve around resequencing attacks, fragmenting attacks, and performing other techniques that could be used to confuse NIDS devices. Vendors have responded to many of these issues, but evasion techniques will continue to be a problem for many NIDS solutions.

▶ Two security experts, Timothy Newsham and Thomas Ptacek published one of the more famous of the IDS evasion papers, in 1998. It continues to be referenced years later because many vendors have failed to address the problems Newsham and Ptacek pointed out. You can find the paper at `http://www.robertgraham.com/mirror/Ptacek-Newsham-Evasion-98.html`.

Host-Based ID Systems

The host-based model varies from the NIDS model on a number of fronts. First and foremost, the host model is a more intrusive one. Whereas NIDS devices are passive, host-based systems require agents to be installed on all monitored systems. This isn't usually a problem on a few dozen machines, but placing agents on a few hundred, or worse, a few thousand, machines is no small chore. The potential overhead in deploying and managing a large number of agents has led many organizations to install the host-based models on critical machines, and use NIDS devices for the rest of the enterprise.

> **NOTE**
>
> Don't assume that you are stuck with choosing between the host and network models. Most vendors agree that the ideal IDS deployment consists of an integrated approach, incorporating both host-based and network-based detection. In fact, this holistic model is quickly being adopted and is already implemented in products from Internet Security Systems, Inc. (ISS), Symantec, CyberSafe, and Enterasys.

Some of the host-based models are more full-featured than others. For example, most products will monitor system logs for basic events such as failed login attempts, the creation of new user accounts, or access violations. Some will monitor kernel messages for certain types of activity that might be interpreted as hostile. More advanced HIDS agents will watch for the installation of Trojan code and back-door programs, and even terminate rogue processes.

Although all these features sound cool, and can be quite useful, the host-based model is not without its problems. For example, HIDS agents are still limited by the same factors that plague the NIDS model: They primarily look for known problems. If a HIDS agent is programmed to spot Back Orifice (a well-known Trojan), it will most likely be successful in performing that task. When a new next-generation Trojan hits the scene, however, there is a good chance the HIDS agent will miss it until a product update/revision is released.

Another problem, albeit minor for most environments, is that of CPU load. HIDS agents are active processes, and will consume CPU cycles. On underutilized machines. This is a moot point. However, for machines that are squeezed for every single CPU cycle, a busy HIDS agent might be the straw that breaks the camel's back.

Despite these shortcomings, one of the primary benefits of deploying host-based IDSs is the fact that they will centralize and parse your system logs. This alone is a huge benefit because most organizations do not review their system logs until something goes wrong.

What to Look for When Choosing an IDS

You should note two points above all others when reading this section. First, there is no "one size fits all" IDS solution on the market today, and I highly doubt there will be one anytime soon. The IDS product landscape is a diverse one. Products like ISS RealSecure are easy to install, have a wide range of features, but often fall over in high-bandwidth environments. Enterasys Dragon performs well and is liked by most UNIX-savvy individuals, but its user interface and the learning curve associated with the product will turn away most NT-focused administrators. BlackICE's raw power and simplicity might tempt some small organizations, but when you need to manage hundreds of thousands of events, Cisco's IDS with the Cisco Secure Policy Manager (CSPM) is a much more manageable solution. In short, organizations need to understand what their parameters are, and adopt a product that best serves those requirements.

Second, the product balances change almost yearly. For example, between 1999 and 2000, Cisco went from having one of the worst user interfaces (an HP OpenView hack) in the market, to one of the best (CSPM). In three years time the product known as ID-track from the company called Internet Tools was acquired by Axent, expanded upon, relabeled as NetProwler, and later acquired by Symantec when Axent and Symantec merged. NFR Security, Inc. (NFR) was way ahead of the IDS technology curve in 1998, and is considered by most to be somewhat behind in 2001. The bottom-line is this: Consider the comments in this text, the reviews that are published in magazines, and anything else that you might find on the Internet, but be conscious of the age of the information. The issues will stay somewhat constant, but who and how they are addressed could change in as short a time as six months. Although products like firewalls are fairly mature, and are now mostly differentiated by features, speed, and price, the IDS market is anything but mature. The only thing that you can be sure of on the IDS front is that nothing will remain the same.

Common Evaluation Criteria

When choosing an intrusion detection system, understand that you are choosing two things: a) a product and b) a partner (vendor) who will be updating that product. Although the vendor (or team, in the case of open-source solutions) behind the product is always a consideration, it becomes even more critical in the intrusion detection market. Because IDSs are so time-sensitive, so dependent on product updates, a good system will become increasingly less useful if it is not attended to properly and regularly. Evaluating the vendor's track record in regard to product updates is a worthy effort.

On the product side, there are a number of issues and features that can be found in one IDS, but not in another. However, many of the "bells and whistles" of these products are just that—cute features. Make sure that you evaluate the core components first, and then examine the bonus features. The following is a list of core components that you will want to evaluate when making IDS selection decisions:

- **Depth of coverage.** One of the more important components of an intrusion detection system is its ability to detect a wide array of attacks. Although a great back-end engine, diverse customization options, and a slick management interface are all strong selling points, if the product is incapable of detecting more than a handful of attacks, it will do little good. Make sure that any NIDS solution you examine is bundled with a healthy set of attack signatures. On the HIDS front, be sure that the product does more than inspect a few log files for a handful of events, and make sure that the product supports all the platforms that you need to monitor. If, for example, the HIDS agents only support Windows NT but you have both Solaris and Linux machines, you are going to come up short in regard to overall coverage.

- **Accuracy of coverage.** This is a hard factor to determine without thorough testing, but it should be noted that not all signatures have been created equal. False positives are a big problem with most NIDS solutions, and in large environments these misfires can jeopardize the overall effectiveness of the intrusion detection effort. Products designed with the reduction of false positives in mind will become more desirable in the coming years.

- **Robust architecture.** There are multiple components to an intrusion detection solution, and it is important that both the engines and the IDS framework itself have been designed with strength in mind. On the engine/agent side, products should be able to withstand both attacks and basic evasion techniques. Although evasion has traditionally been a problem that has plagued NIDS devices, and will most likely continue to trouble them for some time, insightful vendors have continued their attempts at addressing these issues. Less insightful vendors have chosen to ignore them, which not only reduces product effectiveness, but also reduces confidence amongst security professionals.

- **Scalability.** There are multiple components that affect IDSs on the "scaling" front, but the two biggest are in the areas of high-bandwidth monitoring and data management. The bandwidth issues apply to NIDS devices in that many products have problems monitoring high-bandwidth, high-session environments. On the management front, some products struggle with monitoring, storing, and presenting large volumes of alert data. For example, if you deploy a few dozen sensors (host- or network-based) on a high-traffic/high-alert network, they will be pumping a lot of data back to the centralized databases and/or consoles. Some back-end systems will crumble under such loads, or, worse, the volume of data will make it incredibly hard for the security officers to sort through the alerts. However, it should be noted that these issues are not relevant in all environments. For example, if you are looking to place a few ID devices to watch over a few T1 connections, you aren't likely to run into bandwidth and data storage issues.

- **Management framework.** Being able to detect attacks is crucial for an IDS, but equally important is the ability to clearly and efficiently present the data related to those attacks. If security officers are unable to easily access attack and alert data, the overall usefulness of IDS will be limited. When evaluating intrusion detection systems, be sure to use the management console in a live environment. Make sure you are comfortable with a system's management framework, and make sure it allows you to access the information you want easily. In short, the management framework that is used to control and monitor the devices is almost as important as the HIDS and NIDS devices themselves.

- **Timely updates.** Much like in the vulnerability assessment (VA) product field, as new attacks continue to surface the need for timely IDS product updates becomes critical. Operating an outdated IDS is analogous to operating an airport without radar. Although updates are a bigger issue in regard to NIDS products, the issue is still relevant to all IDS models.

- **Customizability.** Some intrusion detection products allow for a diverse range of customization, whereas others are fairly static and inflexible. For some organizations, customization features will not be a big issue because they will be operating IDS solutions with out-of-the-box configurations. For others, customization is a must. However, when choosing an IDS vendor, it's wise to evaluate your needs now, as well as in the future. Although you might not require the ability to write a custom signature today, you might need that functionality in the future.

- **Skill set requirements.** Intrusion detection devices should be treated like any other component of enterprise IT—properly trained staff should be operating the solution. Unfortunately, the one thing both administrators and managers alike seem to cast aside are the issues surrounding IDS upkeep.

SNORT and Other Open Source IDS Solutions

There are a number of open source IDS solutions in the community that are worth investigating. The most popular of which is SNORT, created by Marty Roesch. SNORT is often considered to be the Linux of the intrusion detection field. It touts a very active development community, a wide set of signatures, and a large base of deployed users. SNORT uses an NIDS model, and has a fairly extensive set of plug-ins and supporting applications. For example, the Carnegie Mellon CERT team has created a front-end Web interface for SNORT called Analysis Console for Intrusion Databases (ACID). ACID allows administrators and security officers a more user-friendly view of SNORT output, which is natively quite raw. SNORT is actively being developed on UNIX, although Windows ports of the application exist.

▶ SNORT'S home page: `http://www.snort.org`

▶ ACID's home page: `http://www.cert.org/kb/acid/`

Two other popular open source IDS tools are Argus and SHADOW. Both are UNIX based. Argus is a basic traffic auditing tool, and SHADOW has long been a favorite among government and military personnel.

▶ You can find a good list of open source HIDS and NIDS tools at Security-Focus' Web site:
  `http://www.securityfocus.com/templates/tools_category.html?category=16` and
  `http://www.securityfocus.com/templates/tools_category.html?category=17`

While some components of open source IDS tools are a bit behind those of their commercial counterparts, portions of programs like SNORT are quite advanced. In the coming years, it will be interesting to see if the successes of open source initiatives like the FreeBSD and Linux projects will be shared by the open source intrusion detection community.

Intrusion Detection Product Listing

The following is a list of some of the more common intrusion detection products on the market today. I've attempted to list all the major players, but please remember that the IDS industry is still quite young, with new vendors popping up almost monthly. Use this section as a guide, but make sure you do some online research when investigating IDS solutions.

Anzen Flight Jacket

Anzen has based its NIDS product on the NFR NIDS engine. Anzen took NFR's base product and built a set of signatures around the framework NFR provides out of the box. Readers should note that all of the benefits, and many of the shortcomings, of NFR's product are also exhibited by Anzen's product. Anzen did not have a HIDS offering at the time of this writing.

Vendor: Anzen

Headquarters: Ann Arbor, MI (USA)

Platform: Appliance

Product: Anzen Flight Jacket

URL: http://www.anzen.com

Axent/Symantec NetProwler and Intruder Alert

Axent's IDS strategy integrates its host-based system (Intruder Alert) with its network-based system (NetProwler). Although the two can be tied together using a common management platform, their similarities end there. NetProwler has traditionally possessed some interesting features not found in other IDSs, but lacks some of the back-end support to handle many NIDS evasion techniques. NetProwler only runs on Windows NT. In contrast, the HIDS Intruder Alert has one of the broadest offerings on the market in terms of supported operating systems.

Vendor: Axent/Symantec

Headquarters: Rockville, MA (USA)

Platform: Windows, various UNIX versions

Product: NetProwler, Intruder Alert

URL: http://www.axent.com

Cisco Secure IDS

Cisco acquired the NetRanger NIDS with its acquisition of the Texas-based "Wheelgroup" corporation in the late '90s. NetRanger served as the foundation of what is now the Cisco Secure IDS suite. Cisco has multiple sensor offerings, ranging from their smaller x86-based appliance (the Cisco 4210) to their more industrial-strength appliance offering (the Cisco 4230), to an intrusion detection "blade" that fits into Catalyst 6500 series of switches. Although Cisco's NIDS engines are fairly strong, Cisco leap-frogged the industry when they launched IDS management capabilities within the Cisco Security Policy Manager (CSPM) framework. The new interface can handle hundreds of thousands of events, and offers large organizations a solution that is truly scalable. Cisco did not, however, have a HIDS offering at the time of this writing.

Vendor: Cisco Systems

Headquarters: San Jose, CA (USA)

Platform: Appliance

Product: Cisco Secure IDS

URL: http://www.cisc.com

CyberSafe Centrax IDS

CyberSafe offers an integrated host- and network-based IDS solution that is tightly integrated under a unified management console. Centrax is primarily Windows-based, but does have some limited support for specific UNIX platforms. Although the NIDS engine has traditionally been a little weak in terms of signature numbers and engine design, CyberSafe has one of the strongest HIDS offerings in the industry.

> Vendor: CyberSafe, Inc.
>
> Headquarters: Issaquah, WA (USA)
>
> Platform: Windows NT, UNIX (Solaris and AIX)
>
> Product: Centrax
>
> URL: http://www.cybersafe.com

Enterasys Dragon IDS

Enterasys acquired the Dragon IDS with its acquisition of Network Security Wizards in 2000. Dragon is a UNIX-based system that was built for easy monitoring of high-bandwidth environments. Dragon has traditionally been less polished than most IDS offerings, but far more robust. Organizations with UNIX expertise that require a highly customizable and extremely powerful NIDS solution will probably like Dragon a great deal. Those that have lower requirements or primarily Windows-based operations might be more comfortable with other offerings. Enterasys also offers a HIDS agent that ties into the Dragon framework, but that component is still quite young.

> Vendor: Enterasys Networks, Inc.
>
> Headquarters: Andover, MA (USA)
>
> Platform: Appliance and UNIX
>
> Product: Dragon
>
> URL: http://www.enterasys.net

ISS RealSecure

ISS was one of the first vendors to completely integrate its host-based and network-based offerings into a unified management framework. ISS RealSecure has one of the easiest management consoles to use, and its server and network sensors have matured greatly over the years. RealSecure runs on an assortment of platforms including Windows NT and many versions of UNIX, and has one of the broadest sets of attack signatures in the industry today. RealSecure is not without its downsides, however, as the NIDS engines have traditionally struggled in high-bandwidth environments, and the back-end database that drives the management platform is still based on Access MDBs. For low-bandwidth, Windows-based operations, however, RealSecure is tough to beat.

> Vendor: Internet Security Systems, Inc.
>
> Headquarters: Atlanta, GA (USA)
>
> Platform: Windows NT, Windows 2000, Solaris, HP/UX, AIX
>
> Product: RealSecure
>
> URL: http://www.iss.net

Network ICE BlackICE Sentry

Network ICE is a relative newcomer to the IDS scene, but has already left a significant mark on the market. Their NIDS offering, BlackICE Sentry, is a Windows NT–based solution that boasts a substantial signature base with an easy-to-use interface. BlackICE is also a favorite among home users because watching all the attacks that come in through cable and DSL connections can be an enjoyable pastime. BlackICE's biggest weakness has traditionally been in relation to its centralized console and management features. Running a single instance of BlackICE is easy; running a few dozen has traditionally been painful.

> Vendor: Network ICE, Inc.
>
> Headquarters: San Mateo, CA (USA)
>
> Platform: Windows NT
>
> Product: BlackICE
>
> URL: http://www.networkice.com

NFR Security Intrusion Detection System

NFR has long been acknowledged as one of the first vendors to address many of the well-known NIDS evasion techniques. NFR's Intrusion Detection System is a NIDS-based product that allows a high degree of customization through the use of "ncode," a scripting language NFR developed. NFR's product has traditionally been enjoyed by experienced IDS veterans operating in low-bandwidth environments. Although the product is capable of handling various types of packet-mangling attacks, it tends not to hold up in high-bandwidth situations.

> Vendor: NFR Security, Inc.
>
> Headquarters: Rockville, MD (USA)
>
> Platform: Appliance
>
> Product: NFR IDS
>
> URL: http://www.nfr.com

Summary

Intrusion detection technology can be a powerful ally. If organizations lack the ability to detect and respond to attacks, malicious users have a higher chance of successfully hurting these organizations. However, intrusion detection is far from a mature technology. Organizations looking to adopt IDSs should carefully gather their requirements, document their needs, and be prepared to support another operational system in moving forward. IDSs are not silver-bullet solutions, but their usefulness can be realized through intelligent deployment efforts.

Further References

The IDS Frequently Asked Question (FAQ) list. This is a great place for beginners: `http://www.ticm.com/kb/faq/idsfaq.html`. The ARACHNIDS database is an interesting open-source effort for community-driven IDS signature development: `http://www.whitehats.com/ids/index.html`

Talisker's IDS page. Talisker keeps good track of all the latest IDS products and round-ups. If it's an IDS product, he'll have it listed: `http://www.networkintrusion.co.uk/`

Two very informative mailing lists for in-depth IDS discussions are the Security Focus IDS list (Focus-IDS), and the IDS list run from the University of Australia. HTML archives of them can be found here: `http://archives.neohapsis.com/archives/sf/ids/http://archives.neohapsis.com/archives/ids/`

The Practical Intrusion Detection Handbook. Paul Proctor. Prentice Hall. ISBN: 0-13-025960-8. 2001.

This is one of the best IDS application books I've seen.

Intrusion Signatures and Analysis. Cooper, Northcutt, Fearnow, Frederick. New Riders Publishing. ISBN: 0735710635.

This is another outstanding IDS application.

Intrusion Detection. Rebecca Bace. Macmillan Technical Publishing. ISBN: 1-57870-185-6. 2000.

Bace provides some of the best insight and history of the intrusion detection scene, complete with insights into different models and theories.

12

INTRUSTION
DETECTION
SYSTEMS (IDSs)

Logging and Auditing Tools

IN THIS CHAPTER

This chapter explains why logs are important, how to create a logging strategy, and how to avoid some of the common pitfalls. We will introduce the tools and techniques that will help you get the most from your logs without losing your mind.

Why Log?

Logs are another set of double-edged swords that quietly lie behind the scenes. They can completely save your butt, or completely overwhelm you, depending on the situation. Their importance, however, is frequently underestimated.

Logs are useful for a number of things. They can help you troubleshoot problems. They can be used for tracking down network anomalies. They can help trace an intruder's steps, or help solidify your case in a court of law. However, if you don't have a logging strategy, rest assured you will eventually come to regret it.

Logs from a Cracking Perspective

If your operating system already supports logging, you might be tempted to skip using additional logging tools. Try to resist that temptation. You can't always trust your logs. In fact, altering logs to cover one's tracks is one of the first things crackers learn. The practice has become so common that there are tools that automate the process. Here are a few:

- **UTClean.** UTClean is a utility that erases any evidence of your presence in wtmp, wtmpx, utmp, utmpx, and lastlog. Check out UTClean at
  http://packetstorm.securify.com/Exploit_Code_Archive/utclean.c.

- **remove.** remove will clean utmp, wtmp, and lastlog, erasing any evidence of your presence. Check out remove at http://packetstorm.securify.com/UNIX/penetration/log-wipers/remove.c.

- **marry.** marry is a tool for editing utmp, wtmp, and lastlog entries. Check out marry at http://packetstorm.securify.com/UNIX/penetration/log-wipers/marry.c.

> **NOTE**
>
> wtmp, wtmpx, utmpx, and lastlog record and report user information, including what time this or that user accessed the system. For example, grepping for a last entry on root will produce output like this:
>
> ```
> root        console  Fri Jun 19 17:01 - down   (00:01)
> root        console  Fri Jun 12 12:26 - down   (4+02:16)
> root        console  Tue May 19 10:45 - down   (01:50)
> root        console  Fri May  1 11:23 - down   (00:02)
> ```

```
root        console  Fri Apr 24 09:56 - 09:56  (00:00)
root        console  Mon Mar 23 02:53 - down   (00:01)
root        console  Mon Mar 23 02:43 - down   (00:01)
```

When an intrusion occurs, system administrators turn to these logs to determine who accessed the machine and when.

▶ It should also be noted that "rootkits," packages designed to cover an intruder's tracks and provide back doors into the system, usually contain log cleansers as well. One of the largest collections of rootkits I've seen can be found at `http://packetstorm.securify.com/UNIX/penetration/rootkits/`.

Forming a Logging Strategy

To hedge your bets against crackers tampering with your log entries you should create a logging strategy that is difficult to circumvent. The easiest way to achieve this is to write your logs to a one-way write-once device, or to copy your logs to a secured logging server. Some administrators have their UNIX machines write their logs to a serial port that is attached to a standalone machine. Although this is certainly quite secure, the model doesn't scale very well.

One model that is a little more scalable revolves around using the syslog protocol. Syslog is a native service on almost every UNIX platform, and recently add-on products have made it available on other platforms (such as Windows NT) as well. Although there are some more secure alternatives to syslog, syslog is now common across most router and firewall products. This ubiquity gives administrators a common denominator in which to centralize all logging. For example, administrators could configure all hosts to log to a protected and centralized syslog-based logging server—giving security teams a single point in which to coordinate log data (see Figure 13.1).

When configured properly, the only traffic allowed to the syslog server is traffic destined to UDP port 514 (the syslog port). By sending system logs to a separate, secure machine, you make it a LOT more difficult for intruders to clean their tracks.

▶ Adiscon makes a great Windows NT-based utility called Event Reporter that enables you to send the Windows NT event logs to a syslog-based server. See `http://www.eventreporter.com` for more information.

▶ Last year a program called SRS (Secure Remote Streaming) came onto the scene. SRS was written to replace syslog with security at the core of its design. It's not as frequently adopted as syslog, but it is certainly worth checking out as a more secure alternative: `http://www.w00w00.org/files/SRS/`.

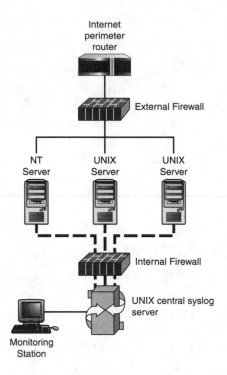

FIGURE 13.1

Centralizing logging.

In addition to centralizing your logs, you might want to consider using at least one third-party logging or parsing tool. This approach has several advantages. First, although the cracker community is familiar with operating system-based logs, few crackers have the knowledge or the means to circumvent third-party logging software. Second, good third-party software packages derive their logs independently of the operating system logs. You'll know that intruders have penetrated your system when this information is compared, and there's a discrepancy between your third-party logs and your regular logs.

This is especially true if you insulate your third-party logs. For example, suppose you use a third-party logging tool to later verify the integrity of operating system-based logs. Although expensive, writing those third-party logs to write-once media guarantees you one set of reliable logs, and reliability is everything.

NOTE

Developers have been working on methods of preventing crackers from altering logs. For example, 4.4BSD introduced *secure levels*, a system by which the kernel and system files are protected from modification by intruders. (These secure levels can be set so that even root can't alter the data.) However, in June 1998, the secure levels scheme was cracked. (The problem is by no means confined to UNIX, either. Windows NT server logs can be corrupted and flooded with errors when attacked by a utility called *coke.*)

Using third-party products is prudent in case your out-of-the-box logging utilities fail. For example, on some versions of Solaris, the tmpx file will truncate incoming hostnames, rendering any data obtained via last erroneous and incomplete.

Coming at this from a different angle, it's now a pretty common procedure for crackers to kill your logging capabilities prior to launching a real attack. If the target is running an unpatched version of Solaris 2.5.x, for instance, you can kill syslogd simply by sending it an external message from a nonexistent IP address. Similarly, if syslogd accepts remote messages, anyone can make a false entry in the log.

You should consider an alternative logging system for all these reasons. The next section briefly covers several good ones.

Network Monitoring and Data Collection

The following tools not only report data from logs, they also collect data from diverse sources. Note that some of these tools are starting to tread pretty close to the Intrusion Detection space, which we covered in detail in Chapter 12, "Intrusion Detection Systems (IDS)." It will be interesting to see whether the two types of utilities will interoperate over time.

SWATCH (The System Watcher)

The authors wrote SWATCH to supplement logging capabilities of out-of-the-box UNIX systems. SWATCH, consequently, has logging capabilities that far exceed your run-of-the-mill syslog. SWATCH provides real-time monitoring, logging, and reporting. Because SWATCH is written in Perl, it's both portable and extensible.

SWATCH has several unique features:

- A "backfinger" utility that attempts to grab finger information from an attacking host.
- Support for instant paging (so you can receive up-to-the-minute reports).
- Conditional execution of commands. (If this condition is found in a log file, do this.)

Lastly, SWATCH relies on local configuration files. Conveniently, multiple configuration files can exist on the same machine. Therefore, although originally intended only for system administrators, any local user with adequate privileges can use SWATCH.

Author: Stephen E. Hansen and E. Todd Atkins

Platform: UNIX (Perl is required)

URL: `http://packetstorm.securify.com/UNIX/IDS/swatch-3.0b4.tar.gz`

Watcher

Kenneth Ingham developed Watcher while at the University of New Mexico Computing Center. He explains that the Computing Center was being expanded at the time. As a result, the logging process they were then using was no longer adequate. Ingham was looking for a way to automate log scanning. Watcher was the result of his labors.

Watcher analyzes various logs and processes, looking for radically abnormal activity. (The author sufficiently fine-tuned this process so that Watcher can interpret the widely variable output of commands such as `ps` without setting off alarms.)

Watcher runs on UNIX systems and requires a C compiler.

Kenneth Ingham

Kenneth Ingham Consulting

1601 Rita Dr. NE

Albuquerque, NM 87106-1127

Phone: 505-262-0602

Email: `ingham@i-pi.com`

URL: `http://www.i-pi.com/watcher.html`

lsof (List Open Files)

lsof version 4 traces not simply open files (including network connections, pipes, streams, and so on), but the processes that own them. lsof runs on many UNIX systems, including but not limited to the following:

- AIX
- BSDI BSD/OS
- NetBSD 1.[23] for Intel and SPARC-based systems
- FreeBSD
- Digital UNIX (DEC OSF/1)
- HP-UX

- IRIX
- Linux
- NEXTSTEP 3.1 for NEXTSTEP architectures
- SCO UnixWare
- Solaris and SUN OS

Author: Vic Abell

Platform: UNIX

URL: `ftp://vic.cc.purdue.edu/pub/tools/unix/lsof/`

Private-I

Private-I has two primary functions. First, it serves as a back-end log archiver for Cisco IOS-based routers, PIX and Checkpoint firewalls, and RedCreek VPN devices. Second, it is capable of generating real-time alerts based on known firewall and IOS event codes. Because Private-I has been designed to process the vendor-specific event codes piped to it via syslog, it can alert administrators of problems in real-time, as well as produce informative reports.

OpenSystems.com

55 West St.

Walpole, MA 02081

USA Phone: 508-668-2460

URL: `http://www.opensystems.com`

WebSense

Though WebSense is best known for its screening capabilities, the product also has powerful logging capabilities. (These have recently been enhanced as the product has been designed to work closely with PIX firewalls from Cisco.)

WebSense, Inc.

World Headquarters

10240 Sorrento Valley Rd.

San Diego, CA 92121

Phone: 858-320-8000

Fax: 858-458-2950

Email: `info@websense.com`

URL: `http://www.websense.com/`

13

LOGGING AND
AUDITING TOOLS

Win-Log version 1

Win-Log is a very simple utility for Windows NT. It logs when, how often, and how long Windows NT is used. (You can use this utility to ascertain whether someone has been rebooting your box, even if they somehow circumvent Event Logger.)

iNFINITY Software

Email: jcross@griffin.co.uk

URL: http://www.isoft.demon.co.uk/

NOCOL/NetConsole v4

NOCOL/NetConsole v4.0 is a suite of standalone applications that perform a wide variety of monitoring tasks. This suite offers a Curses interface, which is great for running on a wide range of terminals. (It does not require X to work.) It is extensible, has support for a Perl interface, and operates on networks running AppleTalk and Novell.

NOCOL/NetConsole v4

Location: ftp://ftp.navya.com/pub/

Tools for Analyzing Log Files

The following tools examine log files, extract the data, and generate reports.

NestWatch

NetWatch can import log files from all major Web servers and several firewalls. NestWatch runs on Windows NT and can output reports in HTML and distribute these to servers of your choice.

Scandinavian Security Center

Hermodsvej 5A, 2.

DK-8230 Aabyhoej

Denmark

Phone: + 45-8744-7800

Fax: + 45-8744-7820

Email: scansec@sscnet.com

URL: http://www.sscnet.com/nestwatch.html

NetTracker

NetTracker analyzes both wall and proxy files. The product has extensive filtering and reporting, and can export data to Excel and Access file formats. (The product also can analyze general access logs and format custom reports suitable for graphing.) NetTracker runs on Windows 95/Windows NT; a 30-day evaluation is available on the Web.

> Sane Solutions, LLC
>
> 35 Belver Ave., Suite 230
>
> North Kingstown, RI 02852
>
> Phone: 401-295-4809
>
> Email: info@sane.com
>
> URL: http://www.sane.com/products/NetTracker/

LogSurfer

LogSurfer is a comprehensive log analysis tool. The program examines plain text log files and based on what it finds (and the rules you provide), it can perform various actions. These might include creating an alert, executing an external program, or even taking portions of the log data and feeding that to external commands or processes. LogSurfer requires a C compiler.

> Univ. Hamburg, Dept. of Computer Science
>
> DFN-CERT
>
> Vogt-Koelln-Strasse 30
>
> 22527 Hamburg, Germany
>
> Location: ftp://ftp.cert.dfn.de/pub/tools/audit/logsurfer/

WebTrends for Firewalls and VPNs

WebTrends for Firewalls and VPNs combines Web link, usage, and traffic analysis with log analysis for the following firewall:

- Firewall-1
- NAI/TIS Gauntlet
- Raptor
- Cisco PIX
- Lucent Managed Firewall
- IBM eNetwork Firewall
- Novell Proxy Server
- Netscape Proxy Server
- Microsoft Proxy

WebTrends can pull some very impressive statistics and writes to a wide variety of database report formats. (This product runs on Windows NT and Windows 95.)

WebTrends Corporation

851 SW 6th Ave.

Suite 1200

Portland, OR 97204

Phone: 503-294-7025

Fax: 503-294-7130

Email: sales@webtrends.com

URL: http://www.webtrends.com

Analog

Analog is probably the only truly cross-platform log file analyzer. Analog currently runs on the following operating systems:

- Macintosh
- OS/2
- Windows 95/NT
- UNIX
- VAX/VMS
- RISC/OS
- BeOS
- BS2000/OSD

Not only is Analog cross-platform, it also has built-in support for a wide variety of languages, including English, Portuguese, French, German, Swedish, Czech, Slovak, Slovene, Romanian, and Hungarian.

Analog also does reverse DNS lookups (slowly), has a built-in scripting language (similar to the shell languages), and has at least minimal support for AppleScript.

Lastly, Analog supports most of the well-known Web server log formats, including Apache, NCSA, WebStar, IIS, W3 Extended, Netscape/iPlanet, and Netpresenz.

Author: Stephen Turner

University of Cambridge Statistical Laboratory

URL: http://www.statslab.cam.ac.uk/~sret1/analog/

Specialized Logging Utilities

These utilities are included more for academic reasons then anything else. Although still useful, their utility is quickly being absorbed by that of network-based intrusion detection systems. However, readers are still encouraged to download them and try them out.

Courtney

Courtney is a Perl script designed to detect and log SATAN attacks. As described in the Courtney documentation:

> Courtney receives input from tcpdump counting the number of new services a machine originates within a certain time window. If one machine connects to numerous services within that time window, Courtney identifies that machine as a potential SATAN host.

System requirements include libpcap-0.0, tcpdump-3.0, and perl5.

Author: Marvin J. Christensen

URL: `http://packetstorm.securify.com/UNIX/audit/courtney-1.3.tar.Z`

NOTE

Tools like NMAP and STROBE (port scanners) by default open many socket connections in a short period of time. This behavior is highly unusual and is easily distinguished from legitimate user activity. Tools like Courtney rely more on the behavior of incoming hosts (and their control loop) than they do on the type of data being transmitted.

Gabriel

Gabriel serves the same purpose as Courtney—to log and warn of SATAN attacks. However, Gabriel is designed very differently and relies on one server and a series of clients to constantly distribute status reports. These status reports indicate various patterns of resource usage by remote hosts. When a host appears to be eating an inordinate number of resources (or requesting an abnormal number of connections), that host is flagged at a high priority. (Note: Gabriel relies largely on `syslog`.)

You need a generic UNIX system, a C compiler, and network include files to run Gabriel.

Los Altos Technologies, Inc.
01 First Street, Suite 790
Los Altos, CA 94022
Phone: 800.999.UNIX
Fax: 650-623-0848
Email: `info@lat.com`
URL: `http://www.lat.com/gabe.htm`

Summary

Never underestimate the importance of keeping detailed logs. Not only are logs essential when you're investigating a network intrusion, they're also a requisite for bringing charges against an attacker. Sparse logs simply won't do.

In recent years, many criminal cracking cases have ended in plea bargains. One of the primary reasons for this is because perpetrators were often kids—kids who were just "having a little fun." But, plea bargains are becoming less prevalent as real criminal elements migrate to the Net. Real criminals know that proving a case before a judge or jury is very difficult (especially if the prosecution has little Internet experience). When judges and jurors are asked to send a human being to prison, they need substantial proof. The only way you can offer substantial proof is by having several fail-safe methods of logging.

Crimes perpetrated over the Internet are unlike most other crimes. For example, in a robbery case, crooks are placed in a lineup so the victim can identify the culprit. In burglary cases, fingerprints will generally reveal the identity of the perpetrator. On the Internet, however, you have neither a physical description nor fingerprints. Therefore, without logs, making a case against a cracker is almost impossible.

Password Crackers

CHAPTER

14

IN THIS CHAPTER

This chapter examines password crackers and other programs designed to circumvent password security. Although password cracking is a core skill of most intruders, it is also important for system and network administrators to understand the INs and OUTs of password security. Comprehending where and why passwords can fail is paramount in maintaining enterprise security; many times, passwords are the first and unfortunately only lines of defense. This chapter explains how passwords are stored, how they can be stolen, how they are cracked, and what you can do to minimize the risks associated with using passwords.

An Introduction to Password Cracking

Passwords and "pass phrases" are used for everything ranging from logging into terminals to checking email accounts, from protecting Excel spreadsheets to securing the encryption keys for PKI-enabled enterprise networks. Their use in the enterprise is widespread, to say the least.

Password crackers are programs that aid in the discovery of protected passwords, usually through some method of automated guessing. Although some applications and poorly designed infrastructure equipment will encrypt or encode passwords, most modern day operating systems and devices create a *hash* of the password instead. I will go into the differences between hashing and encrypting in the next section, but for now simply note that they are two different methods of storing password information.

Although some poor encryption mechanisms can be easily reversed, modern day hashing methods are *one-way*—that is, they can not be reversed and therefore decryption is not an option. Although the use of one-way algorithms can sound like a rock-solid solution, it simply makes the task at hand a little more time consuming. To circumvent the challenges created by hashing, password crackers simply employ the same algorithm used to encrypt the original password. The tools perform comparative analysis (a process explained later in this chapter), and simply try to match their guesses with the original encrypted phrase or password hash.

Many password crackers are nothing but guessing engines, programs that try word after word, often at high speeds. These programs rely on the theory that eventually you will encounter the right word or phrase. This theory is sound because humans are lazy creatures. They rarely take the trouble to create strong passwords. However, this shortcoming is not always the user's fault:

> Users are rarely, if ever, educated as to what are wise choices for passwords. If a password is in the dictionary, it is extremely vulnerable to being cracked, and users are simply not coached as to "safe" choices for passwords. Of those users who are so educated, many think that simply because their password is not in /usr/dict/words, it is safe from detection. Many users also say that because they do not have private files online, they are

not concerned with the security of their account, little realizing that by providing an entry point to the system they allow damage to be wrought on their entire system by a malicious cracker.

—*A Survey of, and Improvements to, Password Security*. Daniel V. Klein, Software Engineering Institute, Carnegie-Mellon University, Pennsylvania. (PostScript creation date reported: February 22, 1991.)

It should be noted, however, that the raw "It's-not-in-the-dictionary" approach is now somewhat misleading as well. Password-cracking dictionaries now contain hundreds of thousands of popular names, characters, musical bands, slang, expletives, and an assortment of culturally popular terms that might or might not be in a classic dictionary. We'll explore the depth and versatility of password guessing later on, but the new rule of thumb is to avoid any kind of word all together. For example, "808state" is easily guessed by most password crackers, not only because it's based on a word (state) and a number (808), but also because it's the name of a popular band out of Manchester, England. Stronger passwords can be created by using a combination of letters, numbers, and extended characters. Acronyms work wonderfully, for example, "I'm trying to learn information security techniques quickly!" could be translated to "IT2LISTQ!". This is a MUCH harder password to guess, but is not all that difficult to remember.

The simple password problem is a persistent one despite the fact that it is easy to provide password-security education. It's puzzling how such a critical security issue (which can easily be addressed) is often overlooked. The issue goes to the very core of security:

> Exploiting ill-chosen and poorly-protected passwords is one of the most common attacks on system security used by crackers. Almost every multiuser system uses passwords to protect against unauthorized logons, but comparatively few installations use them properly. The problem is universal in nature, not system-specific; and the solutions are simple, inexpensive, and applicable to any computer, regardless of operating system or hardware. They can be understood by anyone, and it doesn't take an administrator or a systems programmer to implement them.

—"Understanding Password Security for Users On and Offline." K. Coady. *New England Telecommuting Newsletter*, 1991.

14

TIP

One additional password pitfall that is frequently overlooked is the password overload scenario. If users have a multitude of passwords to remember, there is a greater chance that they will write them down, use weaker passwords, or introduce an assortment of other insecure password practices into your environment. This is where centralized authentication systems, directory services, and single-sign on solutions can help you. Not only do they reduce operating costs and complexity, they ultimately help you with your overall security posture.

Password Cryptography 101

The etymological root of the word *cryptography* is instructive. The word *crypto* stems from the Greek word *kryptos*. *Kryptos* describes anything that is hidden, obscured, veiled, secret, or mysterious. The word *graph* is derived from *graphia*, which means *writing*. Thus, *cryptography* is the art of secret writing. Yaman Akdeniz, in his paper *Cryptography and Encryption*, gives an excellent and concise definition of cryptography:

> Cryptography, defined as "the science and study of secret writing," concerns the ways in which communications and data can be encoded to prevent disclosure of their contents through eavesdropping or message interception, using codes, ciphers, and other methods, so that only certain people can see the real message.

> —"Cryptography and Encryption." Yaman Akdeniz. Cyber-Rights & Cyber-Liberties (UK), August 1996, at `http://www.leeds.ac.uk/law/pgs/yaman/cryptog.htm`. Criminal Justice Studies of the Law Faculty of University of Leeds, Leeds LS2 9JT.

To illustrate the process of cryptography, I'll reduce it to its most fundamental parts. Imagine that you created your own code in which each letter of the alphabet corresponds to a number (see Figure 14.1).

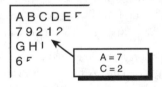

Figure 14.1

A primitive example of a code.

Figure 14.1 shows part of a *table*, or *legend*. Below each letter is a corresponding number. A = 7, B = 2, and so forth. This is a code of sorts. If you write a message using these rules, only you and the recipient will know what the message really says.

Unfortunately, such a code can be easily broken. For example, if each letter has a fixed numeric counterpart, you will only use 26 different numbers (perhaps 1 through 26, although you could choose arbitrary numbers). Lexical analysis would reveal your code within a few seconds. (Some software programs perform such analysis at high speed, searching for patterns common to your language.)

ROT-13

Another slightly more complex method is to make each letter become another letter, based on a standard incremental or decremental operation. One system that works this way is ROT-13 encoding. In ROT-13, a substitute letter is used. Moving 13 letters ahead (see Figure 14.2) in the chosen alphabet derives the substitute letter.

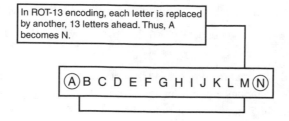

FIGURE 14.2

The ROT-13 system of letter substitution.

This, too, is an ineffective method of encoding or encrypting a message (although it worked in Roman times for Caesar, who used a shift-by-three formula). Some programs quickly identify this pattern. However, this doesn't mean that techniques such as ROT-13 are useless. I will illustrate why, and in the process, I can demonstrate the first important point about encryption:

> Any form of encryption can be useful, given particular circumstances. These circumstances might depend upon time, the sensitivity of the information, and from whom you wish to hide data.

In other words, techniques such as ROT-13 can be quite useful under the right circumstances. Here's an example: Suppose a cracker wants to post a new cracking technique to Usenet. He's found a hole and wants to publicize it while it's still exploitable. To prevent security specialists from discovering that hole as quickly as the crackers, the cracker uses ROT-13 to encode his message.

There are a number of organizations that download Usenet traffic on a wholesale basis. In this way, they gather information about the cracker community. Some organizations even use popular search engines to ferret out cracker techniques. These search engines employ *regex* (regular expression) searches (that is, they search by word or phrase). For example, the searching party enters a combination of words such as

- `crack`
- `hack`
- `vulnerability`
- `exploit`

When this combination of words is entered correctly, a wealth of information emerges. However, if the cracker uses ROT-13, search engines will miss the post. For example, the message

```
Guvf zrffntr jnf rapbqrq va EBG-13 pbqvat. Ohl, qvq vg ybbx fperjl hagvy
jr haeniryrq vg!
```

14

PASSWORD CRACKERS

is beyond the reach of the average search engine. What it really looks like is this:

```
This message was encoded in ROT-13 coding. Boy, did it look screwy until
we unraveled it!
```

Most modern mail and newsreaders support ROT-13 encoding and decoding (Free Agent by Forte is one; Netscape Communicator's Mail package is another). Again, this is a rudimentary form of encoding something, but it demonstrates the concept. Now, let's get a bit more specific.

DES and Crypt

Today, Internet information servers run many different operating systems. However, for many years, UNIX was the only game in town. The greater number of password crackers were designed to crack UNIX passwords. Let's start with UNIX, then, and work our way forward.

In UNIX, all user login IDs and passwords are centrally stored in either one of two files: the `passwd` file, usually found in the `/etc` directory, or a file called `shadow`, also located in the `/etc` directory. These files contain various fields. Of those, we are concerned with two: the login ID and the hashed password.

TIP

Using "shadow passwords" is the preferred way of storing password hashes. The `/etc/shadow` file is only accessible by the root account and system services, as opposed to `/etc/passwd`, which is readable by everyone. If you have any systems that are still storing password hashes in `/etc/passwd`, either upgrade them to shadow passwords or remove them from your environment as soon as possible.

The login ID is stored in plain text, or humanly readable English. The password is stored in encrypted form. The encryption process is performed using Crypt(3), a program based on the data encryption standard (DES).

IBM developed the earliest version of DES; today, it is used on all UNIX platforms for password encryption. DES is endorsed jointly by the National Bureau of Standards and the National Security Agency. In fact, since 1977, DES has been the generally accepted method for safeguarding sensitive data. Figure 14.3 contains a brief timeline of DES development.

DES was developed to protect certain nonclassified information that might exist in federal offices, as set forth in Federal Information Processing Standards Publication 74, *Guidelines for Implementing and Using the NBS Data Encryption Standard*:

> Because of the unavailability of general cryptographic technology outside the national security arena, and because security provisions, including encryption, were needed in unclassified applications involving Federal Government computer systems, NBS initiated

a computer security program in 1973 which included the development of a standard for computer data encryption. Because Federal standards impact on the private sector, NBS solicited the interest and cooperation of industry and user communities in this work.

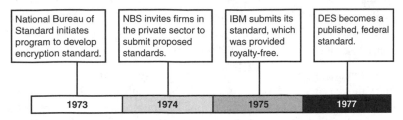

| National Bureau of Standard initiates program to develop encryption standard. | NBS invites firms in the private sector to submit proposed standards. | IBM submits its standard, which was provided royalty-free. | DES becomes a published, federal standard. |

| 1973 | 1974 | 1975 | 1977 |

Brief Timeline of the Data Encryption Standard Development

FIGURE 14.3

A brief timeline of the development of DES.

Information about the original mechanical development of DES is scarce. Reportedly, at the National Security Agency's request, IBM made certain documents classified. However, the source code for Crypt(3) (the current implementation of DES in UNIX) is widely available. This is significant because in all the years that source has been available for Crypt, no one has yet found a way to easily reverse-encode information encrypted with it.

There are several versions of Crypt, and they work slightly differently. In general, however, the process is as follows:

1. Your password is taken in plain text (or, in cryptographic jargon, *clear text*).
2. Your password is used as a key to encrypt a series of zeros (64 in all). The resulting encoded text is thereafter referred to as *cipher text*, the unreadable code that results after plain text is encrypted. This cipher text is sometimes referred to as a *hash*, as well, but the term only loosely fits in this case.

14

NOTE

One-way hash functions are frequently used as an alternative to actually encrypting passwords. By using hashing algorithms such as MD5 or SHA-1, a digital footprint can be created of the password that doesn't contain the actual password itself. This varies from the process of encryption because the output does not contain the original input in any form, and it is therefore impossible to derive the original input from the output. Many modern UNIX systems are moving towards the use of MD5 hashes instead of relying on the crypt/DES process. If you are interested in one-way hashing techniques, or cryptography in general, Bruce Schneier's *Applied Cryptography* (John Wiley & Sons, ISBN 0-471-12845-7) is a must-have.

Certain versions of Crypt, notably Crypt(3), take additional steps. For example, after going through this process, the encrypted text is again encrypted, numerous times, using the password as a key. This is a fairly strong method of encryption; it is extremely difficult to break. It is estimated, for example, that the same password can be encoded in 4,096 different ways. The average user, without any knowledge of the system, could probably spend her entire life trying to crack DES and never be successful. To get that in proper perspective, here's an estimate from the National Institute of Standards and Technology:

> The cryptographic algorithm [DES] transforms a 64-bit binary value into a unique 64-bit binary value based on a 56-bit variable. If the complete 64-bit input is used (i.e., none of the input bits should be predetermined from block to block) and if the 56-bit variable is randomly chosen, no technique other than trying all possible keys using known input and output for the DES will guarantee finding the chosen key. As there are more than 70,000,000,000,000,000 (seventy quadrillion) possible keys of 56 bits, the feasibility of deriving a particular key in this way is extremely unlikely in typical threat environments.
>
> —"Data Encryption Standard (DES)," *Federal Information Processing Standards Publication 46-2,* NIST, December 30, 1993. `http://csrc.nist.gov/fips/fips46-2.txt`.

One might think that DES is entirely infallible. It isn't. Although the information cannot be reverse-encoded, passwords encrypted via DES can be revealed through a comparative process. The process works as follows:

1. You obtain a *dictionary file*, which is really no more than a flat file (plain text) list of words (commonly referred to as *wordlists*).

2. These words are encrypted using DES.

3. Each encrypted word is compared to the target password. If a match occurs, there is a 98% chance that the password was cracked.

The process itself is both simple and brainless, yet quite effective. However, password-cracking programs made for this purpose are often times a little more clever. For example, such cracking programs often subject each word to a list of rules.

A *rule* could be anything, any manner in which a word might appear. Typical rules might include

- Alternate uppercase and lowercase lettering.
- Spell the word forward and then backward and then fuse the two results (for example, can becomes `cannac`).
- Add the number 1 to the beginning or end of each word.

Naturally, the more rules you apply, the longer the cracking process takes. However, more rules also guarantee a higher likelihood of success for a number of reasons:

- The UNIX file system is case sensitive (`WORKSTATION` is interpreted differently than `Workstation` or `workstation` is).

- Alternating letters and numbers in passwords is a common practice.

Password crackers have had a tremendous impact on Internet security, chiefly because they are so effective:

> Crypt uses the resistance of DES to known plain text attack and make [sic] it computationally unfeasible to determine the original password that produced a given encrypted password by exhaustive search. The only publicly known technique that can reveal certain passwords is password guessing: passing large wordlists through the crypt function to see whether any match the encrypted password entries in an /etc/passwd file. Our experience is that this type of attack is successful unless explicit steps are taken to thwart it. Generally we find 30 percent of the passwords on previously unsecured systems.
>
> —*UNIX Password Security—Ten Years Later*. David Feldmeier and
> Philip R. Karn. Bellcore.

Password-cracking programs are improving in their effectiveness, too. The newer programs incorporate more extensive rules and diverse wordlists. Most wordlists are plain text files with one word per line. These files range in size from 1MB to more than 20MB. Many wordlists are available on the Internet; they come in a wide variety of languages (so an English-speaking American cracker can crack an Italian machine, and vice versa).

▶ There are several popular wordlist collections. Some are simply dictionaries, and others contain hyphenated words, uppercase and lowercase, and so on. Perhaps the most definitive collection is available on the Packetstorm Web site. Its page is `http://packetstorm.securify.com/Crackers/wordlists/`.

The Password-Cracking Process

If you're new to system administration, you're probably wondering how you can benefit from password crackers. Passwords crackers can help you identify weak passwords on your network.

Ideally, you should run a password cracker once a month. If your network supports several platforms, you might need a wide range of password-cracking utilities. Although password crackers such as John the Ripper can crack both Windows NT-based password files and UNIX-based ones, most password crackers are designed to crack only a single type of password.

To crack passwords, you need the following elements:

- Sufficient hardware (A Pentium-III based machine will do nicely)

- A password cracker (such as John the Ripper, Crack, L0phtCrack, and so on)
- A password file (`/etc/shadow`, the NT SAM file, and so on)

I discuss methods of grabbing password files (like the UNIX shadow file, or the Windows NT SAM file) throughout this book, and we will examine the password-cracking programs themselves in the next section. On the hardware front, however, you need only really know one thing: More is better.

Cracking passwords is a CPU- and memory-intensive task. It can take days, weeks, months, or even years depending on the strength of the password and the algorithms used. To crack passwords effectively, you need suitable hardware. The more powerful the hardware, the faster you will be able to crack even relatively strong passwords.

For cracking common password files, like those found on UNIX and Windows NT systems, I have found that to comfortably handle large password files, you should have the following resources:

- A 400Mhz Pentium II or better
- 64MB of RAM or better

A single-processor Pentium-II based system dedicated to password cracking can chew through most NT SAM (password) files in under 48 hours. Dual-processor, Pentium-III–based systems (or higher) will work even faster.

There are techniques, however, for overcoming hardware restrictions. One is the parlor trick of *distributed cracking*. In distributed cracking, you run the cracking program simultaneously on separate processors. There are a few ways to do this. One is to break the password file into pieces and crack those pieces on separate machines. In this way, the job is distributed among a series of workstations, thus cutting resource drain and the time it takes to crack the entire file.

The problem with distributed cracking is that it makes a lot of noise. Remember the Randal Schwartz case? Mr. Schwartz probably would never have been discovered if he were not distributing the CPU load. Another system administrator noticed the heavy processor power being eaten. (He also noted that one process had been running for more than a day.) Distributed cracking really isn't viable for a cracker unless he is the administrator of a site or he has a network at home (which is not so unusual these days; I have a network at home that consists of Windows 95, Windows NT, Linux, Sun, and Novell boxes).

The Password Crackers

The remainder of this chapter is devoted to individual password crackers. Some tools are made for cracking UNIX `passwd` and `shadow` files, some are for cracking NT SAM files, and some work across applications and services you might not have ever heard of. Some of the tools here are not even password crackers; instead, they are auxiliary utilities that can be used in conjunction with existing password-related tools.

Password Crackers for Windows NT

Windows NT keeps password hashes in a protected portion of the Registry called the *SAM*. However, there are a number of ways to get these hashes. The easiest method is to use the `rdisk` command to create a backup of the SAM, and then copy that file to a password-cracking machine. `rdisk /s-` will create a compressed SAM image in the `repair` directory of the `%systemroot%` (usually `c:\winnt\repair`).

Another trick is to sniff the password hashes off of the wire. L0phtCrack, for example, has this feature built in. Regardless of how you get the NT password hashes themselves, the following utilities can be used to aid your Windows NT-based cracking efforts.

L0phtCrack

L0phtCrack is the most celebrated NT password-cracking tool to date, primarily because it uses a two-prong approach, as explained by its authors:

> Passwords are computed using 2 different methods. The first, a dictionary lookup, called dictionary-cracking, uses a user supplied dictionary file. The password hashes for all the words in the dictionary file are computed and compared against all the password hashes for the users. When there is a match the password is known. This method is extremely fast. Thousands of users can be checked with a 100,000-word dictionary file in just a few minutes on a PPro 200. The drawback to this method is that it only finds very simple passwords…. The second method is the brute-force computation. This method uses a particular character set such as A–Z or A–Z plus 0–9 and computes the hash for every possible password made up of those characters.

When L0phtCrack was released, it caused considerable debate, especially because the program's authors pointed out that Microsoft's password algorithm was "intrinsically flawed." Microsoft officials hotly disputed that claim, but their efforts were for naught. L0phtCrack works very well, and it is now an accepted fact that Windows NT's password-hashing techniques are flawed from a security standpoint.

To effectively use L0phtCrack, you need the password hashes.

L0phtCrack is located at `http://www.l0pht.com/L0phtcrack/`.

14

PASSWORD
CRACKERS

John the Ripper by Solar Designer

John the Ripper is one of the most diverse password crackers in circulation today. John runs on both DOS and Windows32 platforms (95, 98, NT, 2000, and so on) as well as on most flavors of UNIX. The binary distribution was released in December 1996, and the package has continued to be updated ever since.

John's real strength lies in its diversity. John can crack UNIX files natively and Windows NT SAM files with the use of pwdump. Modules have been created to attack other platforms such as LDAP and Kerberos as well. John can also perform true brute-forcing of password files—that is, password cracking going beyond basic dictionary-based guessing. Brute-forcing is a technique that utilizes standard or extended character sets to literally try every combination possible. It is extremely resource intensive, and has only become practical in recent years by the rapid advances in processing power.

Penetration testers and crackers alike love John because they can perform cross-platform password cracking on a single, centralized machine. John is maintained by Solar Designer, and its home page is `http://www.openwall.com/john/`.

NTCrack

NTCrack is a curious utility. As its authors explain, it isn't really intended for cracking passwords in a practical sense. However, it does demonstrate that a brute-force cracker can work against Windows NT. The program's purpose is to perform high-speed, brute-force attacks against an NT box. As reported by the folks at Somarsoft, the original maintainers of the program:

> The program below [NTCrack] does about 1000 logins per minute, when run on a client 486DX-33 with 16MB of RAM, a server 486DX2-66 with 32MB of RAM, and a 10 MBps Ethernet. This is equivalent to testing 1,152,000 passwords per day. By comparison, there are perhaps 100,000 common words in the English language.

To prevent such attacks, it is suggested that you enable account lockout, rename the Administrator account, disable network logins for Administrator, and disable SMB over TCP/IP (if appropriate). You can read more about passfilt and securing Windows NT servers in Chapter 19, "Microsoft."

You can find NTCrack at `http://www.wiretrip.net/na/NTCrack.zip`.

NT Accessories

The NT accessories listed in Table 11.1 are indispensable.

TABLE 14.1 Accessories for Use in Cracking NT Passwords

Application	Description and Location
Samdump	Samdump is a utility that automates the process of dumping NT password hashes. It dumps these values from the SAM file located either in the Registry on an emergency repair disk or off the hard disk drive. Samdump is available at `http://packetstorm.securify.com/Crackers/samdump.zip`.
Pwdump	Pwdump is similar to samdump. It dumps NT usernames and passwords. (Fortunately, pwdump requires Administrator privileges.) Pwdump is available at `http://packetstorm.securify.com/Crackers/NT/pwdump2.zip`.
NTFSDOS	NTFSDOS is a tool that allows you to mount NTFS volumes and view them as though they were FAT32. You can use this tool to extract SAM password information from a NTFS drive. NTFSDOS is available at `http://packetstorm.securify.com/NT/hack/ntfsdos.zip`.

Notes on NT Password Security

Rather than simply use the utilities described here, you might want to investigate exactly what factors led to such poor password security in NT in the first place. The following documents are excellent resources:

- **A L0phtCrack Technical Rant.** A detailed analysis (really, the gory details) of NT password weaknesses. Authored by `mudge@l0pht.com`. `http://www.l0pht.com/L0phtcrack/rant.html`

- **On NT Password Security.** Jos Visser. An excellent paper that discusses both the mechanical and theoretical problems with the NT password scheme. The author also discusses how to perform an attack against Windows NT password dumps. `http://www.osp.nl/infobase/ntpass.html#crack2`

- **NT Cryptographic Password Attacks and Defences FAQ.** Alan Ramsbottom. This document provides information on why certain Microsoft fixes didn't work, as well as perspective on the weakness in Microsoft's implementation of DES. `http://www.indigo-blue.demon.co.uk/`

UNIX Password Cracking

This next section discusses the issues surrounding UNIX password cracking. Most of these programs were designed for UNIX as the hosting platform, but some of them will run on other platforms such as DOS and Windows 95. All of them are, however, designed to crack UNIX passwords.

About UNIX Password Security

UNIX password security, when implemented correctly, is fairly reliable. The main problem is that people continue to pick weak passwords. Unfortunately, because UNIX is a multiuser system, every user with a weak password represents a risk to the remaining users. This is a problem that must be addressed:

> It is of utmost importance that all users on a system choose a password that is not easy to guess. The security of each individual user is important to the security of the whole system. Users often have no idea how a multiuser system works and don't realize that they, by choosing an easy-to-remember password, indirectly make it possible for an outsider to manipulate the entire system.
>
> —"UNIX Password Security." Walter Belgers. December 6, 1993.

▶ The paper "UNIX Password Security" gives an excellent overview of exactly how DES works into the UNIX password scheme. It includes a schematic that shows the actual process of encryption using DES. For users new to security, this paper is an excellent starting point. You can find "UNIX Password Security" at `http://packetstorm.securify.com/papers/unix/password.ps`.

What are weak passwords? Characteristically, they are anything that might occur in a dictionary. Moreover, proper names are poor choices for passwords. However, there is no need to theorize on what passwords are easily cracked. Safe to say, if the password appears in a password-cracking wordlist available on the Internet, the password is no good.

▶ Start your search for wordlists at `http://packetstorm.securify.com/Crackers/wordlists/`.

By regularly checking the strength of the passwords on your network, you can ensure that crackers cannot penetrate it (at least not through exploiting bad password choices). Such a regimen can greatly improve your system security. In fact, many ISPs and other sites now employ tools that check a user's password when it is first created. This basically implements the philosophy that

> …the best solution to the problem of having easily guessed passwords on a system is to prevent them from getting on the system in the first place. If a program such as a password cracker reacts by guessing detectable passwords already in place, then although the security hole is found, the hole existed for as long as the program took to detect it…. If however, the program which changes users' passwords…checks for the safety and guessability before that password is associated with the user's account, then the security hole is never put in place.
>
> —*Improving System Security via Proactive Password Checking*. Matthew Bishop, UC Davis, California, and Daniel Klein, LoneWolf Systems Inc. *Computers and Security* [14, pp. 233–249], 1995.

▶ The paper "Improving System Security via Proactive Password Checking" is probably one of the best case studies and treatments of easily guessable passwords. It treats the subject in depth, illustrating real-life examples of various passwords that you might think are secure but actually are not. You can find "Improving System Security via Proactive Password Checking" at `http://seclab.cs.ucdavis.edu/papers/bk95.ps`.

Crack

Crack is the de facto standard for UNIX password cracking. It was written by Alec D. E. Muffett, a UNIX software engineer in Wales. In the documentation, Muffett concisely articulated the program's purpose:

> Crack is a freely available program designed to find standard UNIX eight-character DES encrypted passwords by standard guessing techniques.... It is written to be flexible, configurable and fast, and to be able to make use of several networked hosts via the Berkeley rsh program (or similar), where possible.

Crack runs on UNIX only. It comes as a tarred, g'zipped file and is available at `http://www.users.dircon.co.uk/~crypto/`.

To get Crack up and running, set the root directory. You assign this variable (`Crack_Home`) in the configuration files. The `Crack_Home` variable tells the Crack program where Crack's resources reside. To set this variable, edit the shell script `Crack`. After you do that, you can begin.

NOTE

Most distributions of Crack are accompanied by a sample wordlist. However, that wordlist is limited. If you anticipate cracking large password files (or files in other languages), you will probably need additional dictionary files.

You begin your Crack session by starting the program and providing the name of the file to crack (as well as any command-line arguments, including specifications for using multiple workstations). A bare command line looks like this:

```
Crack my_password_file
```

What follows is difficult to describe, so I ran a sample Crack session. Crack started the process and wrote the progress of the operation to files with an out prefix. In this case, the file was called outSamsHack300. The following is an excerpt from that file:

```
1: pwc: Jan 30 19:26:49 Crack v4.1f: The Password Cracker,
➥(c) Alec D.E. Muffett, 1992
2: pwc: Jan 30 19:26:49 Loading Data, host=SamsHack pid=300
```

```
3: pwc: Jan 30 19:26:49 Loaded 2 password entries with 2 different
➥(salts: 100%
4: pwc: Jan 30 19:26:49 Loaded 240 rules from 'Scripts/dicts.rules'.
5: pwc: Jan 30 19:26:49 Loaded 74 rules from 'Scripts/gecos.rules'.
6: pwc: Jan 30 19:26:49 Starting pass 1 - password information
7: pwc: Jan 30 19:26:49 FeedBack: 0 users done, 2 users left to crack.
8: pwc: Jan 30 19:26:49 Starting pass 2 - dictionary words
9: pwc: Jan 30 19:26:49 Applying rule '!?Al' to file 'Dicts/bigdict'
10: pwc: Jan 30 19:26:50 Rejected 12492 words on loading, 89160 words
➥(left to sort
11: pwc: Jan 30 19:26:51 Sort discarded 947 words; FINAL DICTIONARY
➥(SIZE: 88213
12: pwc: Jan 30 19:27:41 Guessed ROOT PASSWORD root (/bin/bash
➥(in my_password_file) [laura] EYFu7c842Bcus
13: pwc: Jan 30 19:27:41 Closing feedback file.
```

Crack guessed the correct password for root in just under a minute. Line 1 reveals the time at which the process was initiated (Jan 30 19:26:49); line 12 reveals that the password—Laura—was cracked at 19:27:41. This session occurred on a 133MHz processor and 32MB of RAM.

Because the password file I used was small, neither time nor resources were an issue. In practice, however, if you crack a file with hundreds of entries, Crack will eat resources voraciously. This hunger is especially evident if you use multiple wordlists that are in compressed form. (Crack automatically identifies them as compressed files and decompresses them.)

As mentioned earlier, you can get around this resource drain. Crack can distribute the work to different workstations of different architectures. You can use Crack on an IBM compatible running Linux, a RS/6000 running AIX, and a Macintosh running A/UX.

Crack is extremely lightweight and one of the best password crackers available.

> **TIP**
>
> To perform a networked cracking session, you must build a `network.conf` file. This file identifies which hosts to include, their architecture, and several other key variables. You can also specify what command-line options are invoked as Crack is unleashed on each machine. In other words, each member machine can run Crack with different command-line options.

John the Ripper by Solar Designer

John was discussed in the NT section so I will only briefly touch on it here. Although John can crack both NT- and UNIX-based passwords, the one thing that is unique about John on the UNIX side of the fence is its capability to do raw brute-forcing. Performing a raw brute-force attack (trying every possible combination of characters) was impractical on hardware of a few years ago, but is a reality today. If you want to get medieval on a UNIX password file, John is the tool for you.

CrackerJack by Jackal

CrackerJack runs on the DOS platform but cracks UNIX passwords. Contrary to popular notions, CrackerJack is not a straight port of Crack. Nevertheless, CrackerJack is extremely fast and easy to use. For several years, CrackerJack has been the choice for DOS users.

Later versions were compiled using GNU C and C++. CrackerJack's author reports that, through this recompiling process, the program gained noticeable speed.

Some noticeable drawbacks to CrackerJack include

- You can only use one dictionary file at a time.
- Memory-allocation conventions prevent CrackerJack from running in Windows 95.

Despite these snags, CrackerJack is reliable and requires only limited resources. It takes sparse processor power, doesn't require a windowed environment, and can even run from a floppy.

▶ CrackerJack is widely available. Here are a few reliable sites:
```
ftp://ftp.sonic.net/pub/users/z/hacking/jack14.zip
http://packetstorm.securify.com/MSDOS/penetration/jack14.zip
```

PaceCrack95 (`pacemkr@bluemoon.net`)

PaceCrack95 runs on Windows 95 in console mode or in a shell window. Its author reports that the development of PaceCrack95 was prompted by deficiencies in other DOS-based crackers. He writes

> Well you might be wondering why I have written a program like this when there already is[sic] many out there that do the same thing. There are many reasons, I wanted to challenge myself and this was a useful way to do it. Also there was this guy (Borris) that kept bugging me to make this for him because Cracker Jack (By Jackal) doesn't run in Win95/NT because of the weird way it uses the memory. What was needed was a program that runs in Win95 and the speed of the cracking was up there with Cracker Jack.

To the author's credit, he created a program that does just that. It is fast, compact, and efficient.

You can find PaceCrack95 at `http://tms.netrom.com/~cassidy/utils/pacec.zip`.

Star Cracker by the Sorcerer

Star Cracker, which was designed to work under the DOS4GW environment, is a complete password-cracking suite. Some of its more interesting advantages are

- **A fail-safe power outage provision.** If a blackout in your city shuts down your computer, your work is not lost. Upon reboot, Star Cracker recovers all work previously done (up until the point of the power outage) and keeps right on going.
- **Time-release operation.** You can establish time windows when the program does its work. That means you could specify, "Crack this file for 11 hours. When the 11 hours is up, wait 3 hours more. After the 3 hours, start again."

Star Cracker really makes the password-cracking process painless.

You can find Star Cracker at `http://packetstorm.securify.com/Crackers/starcrak.zip`.

Merlin by Computer Incident Advisory Capability (CIAC) DOE

Merlin is not a password cracker. Rather, it is a tool for managing password crackers as well as scanners, audit tools, and other security-related utilities. In short, it is a fairly sophisticated tool for holistic management of the security process.

Merlin works on UNIX platforms only. It has reportedly been tested (with positive results) on a number of flavors, including but not limited to IRIX, Linux, SunOS, Solaris, and HP-UX.

One of the main attractions of Merlin is that, although it was specifically designed to support only five common security tools, it is highly extensible. (It is written in Perl almost exclusively.) You could conceivably incorporate any number of tools into the scheme of the program.

Merlin is a wonderful tool for integrating a handful of command-line tools into a single, easily managed package. It addresses the fact that the majority of UNIX-based security programs are based in the command-line interface. The five applications supported are

- COPS
- Tiger
- Crack
- Tripwire
- SPI (available to government contractors and agencies only)

Note that Merlin does not supply any of these utilities in the distribution. You must acquire these programs and then configure Merlin to work with them (similarly to the way one configures external viewers and helpers in Netscape's Navigator). The concept might seem lame, but the tool provides an easy, centralized point from which you can perform some fairly common (and grueling) security tasks. In other words, Merlin is more than a bogus front-end. In my opinion, it is a good contribution to the security trade.

> **TIP**
>
> Those programmers new to the UNIX platform might have to do a little hacking to get Merlin working. For example, Merlin relies on you to have correctly configured your browser to properly handle `*.pl` files. (It goes without saying that Perl is one requisite.) Also, Merlin apparently runs an internal HTTP server and looks for connections from the local host. This means you must have your system properly configured for loopback.

Merlin (and programs like it) represents an important and growing trend (a trend kicked off by Farmer and Venema). Because such programs are designed primarily in an HTML/Perl base, they are highly portable to various platforms in the UNIX community. They also tend to consume few network resources, and after the code is loaded into the interpreter, they move pretty fast. Finally, the tools are easier to use, making security less of an insurmountable task. The data is right there and easily manipulated. This trend can only help strengthen security and provide newbies with an education.

You can find Merlin at `http://packetstorm.securify.com/UNIX/audit/merlin-1.0.tar.gz`.

Cracking Cisco, Application, and Other Password Types

Although you can certainly use password crackers for devious activities, there are plenty of legitimate reasons for needing to access data that might be password protected. For example, if an employee forgets the password to a protected-access database, or if someone leaves the company without passing on the pass phrase for a zip file, an organization might have legitimate needs to get at that data.

The following section goes over some of the password crackers for less common (not OS related) applications. I encourage the reader to note the diverse assortment of password crackers listed. Hopefully this list will help dispel the myth that application-level passwords are inherently secure. The truth of the matter is that rarely do application vendors create secure password-protection mechanisms—most are easily broken.

Cracking Cisco IOS Passwords

Cisco stores encrypted login, username, and "enable" passwords in standard IOS configuration files. If these configuration files are not protected, they can be run through decryption scripts that will reveal the passwords in clear text. We will talk more about securing Cisco equipment in Chapter 22, "Cisco Routers and Switches," but, for now, know that protecting your configuration files is extremely important.

Many scripts exist for decrypting standard Cisco passwords. One such script can be found at `http://packetstorm.securify.com/new-exploits/ios7decrypt.tar`.

▶ A neat tool for auditing Cisco router configuration files can be found at `http://www.scrypt.net/~g0ne/`. Cisco administrators would be wise to check this one out.

Commercial Application Password Crackers

There are a number of companies that provide commercial password cracking services and tools. Three of the fairly well known ones are

- PWD Service, Inc. `http://www.pwdservice.com`
- Password Crackers, Inc. `http://www.pwcrack.com`
- Sumin & Co. `http://www.lostpassword.com`

Here is just a sample list of some of the applications these organizations offer password-cracking software for:

- Microsoft Word
- Microsoft Excel
- Microsoft Access
- Microsoft Outlook
- Microsoft Project
- Microsoft Backup
- Microsoft Money
- Lotus 1-2-3
- Lotus Word Pro
- Quickbooks
- ACT
- Paradox
- M.Y.O.B

- Quicken
- Peachtree Accounting
- PKZIP
- WordPerfect

It's important to note that many of these password crackers do their cracking in less then a few seconds. Although I am not a password or cryptography expert, I think it's safe to draw the conclusion that most application-based password protection schemes are little more then an annoyance for intruders. If you can crack them with a $30 piece of software in a few seconds, realize that anyone else can, too.

ZipCrack by Michael A. Quinlan

ZipCrack does just what you think it would: It is designed to brute-force crack passwords that have been applied to files with a `*.zip` extension. (In other words, it cracks the password on files generated with PKZIP.)

No documentation is included in the distribution (at least, not the few files that I have examined), but I am not sure there is any need for documentation. The program is straightforward. You simply provide the target file, and the program does the rest.

The program was written in Turbo Pascal, and the source code is included with the distribution. ZipCrack works on any IBM compatible that is a 286 or higher. The file description reports that ZipCrack cracks all the passwords generated by PKZIP 2.0. The author also warns that, although you can crack short passwords within a reasonable length of time, long passwords can take "centuries." Nevertheless, I sincerely doubt that many individuals provide passwords longer than five characters. ZipCrack is a useful utility for the average toolbox. It's one of those utilities you think you will never need, and later, at 3:00 in the morning, you swear bitterly because you don't have it.

Zipcrack can be found at `http://packetstorm.securify.com/crypt/msdos/ZIPCRACK.ZIP`.

Glide (Author Unknown)

Glide does not provide a lot of documentation. This program is used exclusively to crack PWL files, which are password files generated in Microsoft Windows for Workgroups and Windows 95. The lack of documentation, I think, is forgivable because the C source is included with the distribution. The utility will only work, however, for PWL files created by early releases of Windows 95. Microsoft changed the PWL format in such a way that releases of 95 from OSR2 onward can no longer be cracked by Glide.

Glide can be found at `http://packetstorm.securify.com/Crackers/glide.zip`.

14

PASSWORD
CRACKERS

AMI Decode (Author Unknown)

AMI Decode is designed expressly to grab the CMOS password from any machine using an American Megatrends BIOS. Before you search for this utility, however, you might use the factory default CMOS password. It is, oddly enough, AMI. In any event, the program works, and that is what counts.

AMI Decode can be found at `http://packetstorm.securify.com/Crackers/bios/amidecod.zip`.

PGPCrack by Mark Miller

Before readers who use PGP get all worked up about PGPCrack, a bit of background information is in order. Pretty Good Privacy (PGP) is probably the strongest and most reliable encryption utility available to the public sector. Its author, Phil Zimmermann, summed it up as follows:

> PGP uses public-key encryption to protect email and data files. Communicate securely with people you've never met, with no secure channels needed for prior exchange of keys. PGP is well featured and fast, with sophisticated key management, digital signatures, data compression, and good ergonomic design.

PGP can apply a series of encryption techniques. One of these, which is discussed in Chapter 15, "Sniffers," is IDEA. To hint about how difficult IDEA is to crack, here is an excerpt from the PGP Attack FAQ, authored by Route (an authority on encryption and the editor of *Phrack* magazine):

> If you had 1,000,000,000 machines that could try 1,000,000,000 keys/sec, it would still take all these machines longer than the universe as we know it has existed and then some, to find the key. IDEA, as far as present technology is concerned, is not vulnerable to brute-force attack, pure and simple.

In essence, a message encrypted using a 1,024-bit key generated with a healthy and long passphrase is, for all purposes, unbreakable. Why did Mr. Miller author this interesting tool? Passphrases can be poorly chosen, and if you are going to crack a PGP-encrypted message, the passphrase is a good place to start. Miller reports

> On a 486/66DX, I found that it takes about 7 seconds to read in a 1.2 megabyte passphrase file and try to decrypt the file using every passphrase. Considering the fact that the NSA, other government agencies, and large corporations have an incredible amount of computing power, the benefit of using a large, random passphrase is quite obvious.

Is this utility of any use? It is quite promising. Miller includes the source with the distribution as well as a file of possible passphrases. (I have found that at least one of those passphrases is one I have used.) The program is written in C and runs in DOS, UNIX, and OS/2 environments.

You can find PGPCrack at `http://packetstorm.securify.com/crypt/pgp/pgpcrack99.tgz`.

Other Resources

This section contains a list of sources for further education. Some of these documents are not available on the Internet. However, you can obtain some articles through various online services (perhaps Uncover) or at your local library through interlibrary loan or microfiche. You might have to search more aggressively for some of these papers, perhaps using the Library of Congress (locis.loc.gov) or perhaps an even more effective tool, such as WorldCat (www.oclc.org).

NOTE

Many of the files for papers have `.ps` extensions. This signifies a PostScript file. *PostScript* is a language and method of preparing documents. It was created by Adobe, the makers of Acrobat and Photoshop.

To read a PostScript file, you need a viewer. One good viewer is Ghostscript, which is shareware at `http://www.cs.wisc.edu/~ghost/`.

Another good package (and a little more lightweight) is a utility called *Rops*. Rops is available for Windows and is located at

- `http://www5.zdnet.com/` (the ZDNet software library)
- `http://oak.oakland.edu` (the Oak software repository)

Internet Resources

Observing Reusable Password Choices. Purdue Technical Report CSD-TR 92-049, Eugene H. Spafford, Department of Computer Sciences, Purdue University, July 3, 1992. Search string: `Observe.ps`

Password Security: A Case History. Robert Morris and Ken Thompson, Bell Laboratories. Date: Unknown. Search string: `pwstudy.ps`

Opus: Preventing Weak Password Choices. Purdue Technical Report CSD-TR 92-028, Eugene H. Spafford, Department of Computer Sciences, Purdue University, June 1991. Search string: `opus.PS.gz`

Federal Information Processing Standards Publication 181. Announcing the Standard for Automated Password Generator. October 5, 1993. `http://www.alw.nih.gov/Security/FIRST/papers/password/fips181.txt`

Augmented Encrypted Key Exchange: A Password-Based Protocol Secure Against Dictionary Attacks and Password File Compromise. Steven M. Bellovin and Michael Merrit, AT&T Bell Laboratories. Date: Unknown. Search string: `aeke.ps`

A High-Speed Software Implementation of DES. David C. Feldmeier, Computer Communication Research Group, Bellcore, June 1989. Search string: `des.ps`

Using Content Addressable Search Engines to Encrypt and Break DES. Peter C. Wayner, Computer Science Department, Cornell University. Date: Unknown. Search string: `desbreak.ps`

Encrypted Key Exchange: Password-Based Protocols Secure Against Dictionary Attacks. Steven M. Bellovin and Michael Merrit, AT&T Bell Laboratories. Date: Unknown. Search string: `neke.ps`

Computer Break-Ins: A Case Study. Leendert Van Doorn, Vrije Universiteit, The Netherlands, January 21, 1993. Search string: `holland_case.ps`

Security Breaches: Five Recent Incidents at Columbia University. Fuat Baran, Howard Kaye, and Margarita Suarez, Center for Computing Activities, Colombia University, June 27, 1990. Search string: `columbia_incidents.ps`

Optimal Authentication Protocols Resistant to Password Guessing Attacks. Li Gong, Stanford Research Institute, Computer Science Laboratory, Men Park, CA. Date: Unknown. Search string: `optimal-pass.dvi` or `optimal-pass.ps`

Publications and Reports

Undetectable Online Password Guessing Attacks. Yun Ding and Patrick Horster, *OSR*, 29(4), pp. 77–86. October 1995.

A Password Authentication Scheme Based on Discrete Logarithms. Tzong Chen Wu and Chin Chen Chang, *International Journal of Computational Mathematics*; Vol. 41, Number 1--2, pp. 31–37. 1991.

Differential Cryptanalysis of DES-Like Cryptosystems. Eli Biham and Adi Shamir, *Journal of Cryptology*, 4(1), pp. 3–72. 1990.

A Proposed Mode for Triple-DES Encryption. Don Coppersmith, Don B. Johnson, and Stephen M. Matyas. *IBM Journal of Research and Development*, 40(2), pp. 253–262. March 1996.

An Experiment on DES Statistical Cryptanalysis. Serve Vaudenay, Conference on Computer and Communications Security, pp. 139–147. ACM Press. March 1996

Department of Defense Password Management Guideline. If you want to gain a more historical perspective regarding password security, start with the *Department of Defense Password Management Guideline.* This document was produced by the Department of Defense Computer Security Center at Fort Meade, Maryland.

▶ You can find the *Department of Defense Password Management Guideline* at `http://www.alw.nih.gov/Security/FIRST/papers/password/dodpwman.txt`.

Summary

Password crackers provide a valuable service to system administrators by alerting them of weak passwords on the network. The problem is not that password crackers exist; the problem is that they aren't used frequently enough by the good guys. Administrators should take the time to build password cracking into their monthly routines. By doing so, they can proactively pursue any weaknesses in their enterprise that result from weak passwords. However, administrators should also take care to ensure that both the raw password files and the results of their cracking efforts be deleted after their cracking sessions. Leftover password files can create issues that are worse then bad passwords themselves.

Finally, although the days of passwords serving as a primary means of authentication might be numbered, their overall use is not. Pass phrases will be used for some time to come for protecting keys, certificates, and a varying assortment of protected data. The technology might become more complex, but the solution to the surrounding problems will not. Education is key—use it.

14

Sniffers

IN THIS CHAPTER

Sniffers are devices that capture network packets. Their legitimate purpose is to analyze network traffic and identify potential areas of concern. For example, suppose that one segment of your network is performing poorly: Packet delivery seems incredibly slow, or machines inexplicably lock up on a network boot. You can use a sniffer to determine the precise cause.

> **NOTE**
>
> The term sniffer is derived from a product, called the Sniffer, originally manufactured by Network General Corporation. As Network General dominated the market, this term became popular, and protocol analyzers have since then generally been referred to as such.

Sniffers vary greatly in functionality and design. Some analyze only one protocol, whereas others can analyze hundreds. As a general rule, most modern sniffers will analyze at least the following protocols:

- Standard Ethernet
- TCP/IP
- IPX
- DECNet

Proprietary sniffers are expensive (vendors often package them on special computers that are "optimized" for sniffing). Freeware sniffers, on the other hand, are cheap but offer no support.

In this chapter, you examine sniffers as both security risks and network administration tools.

Sniffers as Security Risks

Sniffers differ greatly from keystroke-capture programs. Here's how: Key-capture programs save, or *capture*, keystrokes entered at a terminal. Sniffers, on the other hand, capture actual network packets. Sniffers do this by placing the network interface—an Ethernet adapter, for example—into promiscuous mode. Sniffers also differ in one key aspect from other attack methods—sniffers are passive, only listening to the network traffic.

A sniffer always functions in a promiscuous mode. Normally, a system's network card will only grab packets destined for that system. In promiscuous mode, however, instead of ignoring all other packets, the system captures every packet that it sees on the network. To further understand how promiscuous mode works, you must first understand how local area networks are designed.

Local Area Networks and Data Traffic

Local area networks (LANs) are small networks connected (generally) via Ethernet. Data is transmitted from one machine to another via cable. There are different types of cable, which transmit data at different speeds. The five most common types of network cable follow:

- **10BASE-2**. (10Mbps) Coaxial Ethernet (thinwire) that, by default, transports data distances of up to 600 feet.

- **10BASE-5**. (10Mbps) Coaxial Ethernet (thickwire) that, by default, transports data distances of up to 1,500 feet.

- **10BASE-F**. (10Mbps) Fiber optic Ethernet.

- **10BASE-T**. (10Mbps) Twisted pair Ethernet that, by default, transports data distances of up to 300 feet.

- **100BASE-T**. (100Mbps) Fast Ethernet that, by default, transports data distances of up to 300 feet.

Data travels along the cable in small units called *frames*. These frames are constructed in sections, and each section carries specialized information. (For example, the first 12 bytes of an Ethernet frame carry both the destination and source address. These values tell the network where the data came from and where it's going. Other portions of an Ethernet frame carry actual user data, TCP/IP headers, IPX headers, and so forth.)

Frames are packaged for transport by special software called a *network driver*. The frames are then passed from your machine to cable via your Ethernet card. From there, they travel to their destination. At that point, the process is executed in reverse: The recipient machine's Ethernet card picks up the frames, tells the operating system that frames have arrived, and passes those frames on for processing.

Sniffers pose a security risk because of the way frames are transported and delivered. Let's briefly look at that process.

Packet Transport and Delivery

Each workstation in a LAN has its own hardware address or Media Access Control (MAC) address. This address uniquely identifies that machine from all others on the network. (This is similar to the Internet address system.) When you send a message across the LAN, your packets are sent to all connected machines.

Under normal circumstances, all machines on the network can "hear" that traffic going by, but will only respond to data addressed specifically to them. (In other words, Workstation A will not capture data intended for Workstation B. Instead, Workstation A will simply ignore that data.)

If a workstation's network interface is in promiscuous mode, however, it can capture all packets and frames on the network. A workstation configured in this way (and the software on it) is a sniffer.

What Level of Risk Do Sniffers Represent?

Sniffers represent a high level of risk. Here's why:

- Sniffers can capture account names and passwords.
- Sniffers can capture confidential or proprietary information.
- Sniffers can be used to breach security of neighboring networks, or to gain leveraged access.

In fact, the existence of an unauthorized sniffer on your network might indicate that your system is already compromised.

Has Anyone Actually Seen a Sniffer Attack?

Sniffer attacks are common, particularly on the Internet. A well-placed sniffer can capture not just a few passwords, but thousands. In 1994, for example, a massive sniffer attack was discovered, leading a naval research center to post the following advisory:

> In February 1994, an unidentified person installed a network sniffer on numerous hosts and backbone elements collecting over 100,000 valid user names and passwords via the Internet and Milnet. Any computer host allowing FTP, Telnet or remote log in to the system should be considered at risk...All networked hosts running a UNIX derivative operating system should check for the particular promiscuous device driver that allows the sniffer to be installed.
>
> —Naval Computer and Telecommunications Area Master Station LANT advisory

▸ You can access the Naval Computer and Telecommunications Area Master Station LANT advisory at http://www.chips.navy.mil/chips/archives/94_jul/file14.html.

The attack on Milnet was so serious that the issue was brought before the Subcommittee on Science, Space, and Technology at the U.S. House of Representatives. F. Lynn McNulty, Associate Director for Computer Security at the National Institute of Standards and Technology, gave this testimony:

> The recent incident involved the discovery of "password sniffer" programs on hundreds of systems throughout the Internet... The serious impact of the recent incident should be recognized; log-in information (i.e., account numbers and passwords) for potentially thousands of host system user accounts appear to have been compromised. It is clear that this incident had a negative impact on the operational missions of some Government

agencies. Moreover, this should be viewed as [an] ongoing incident, not an incident that has happened and been dealt with. Indeed, administrators of systems throughout the Internet were advised, in turn, to direct their users to change their passwords. This is, indeed, very significant, and we may be seeing its effects for some time to come. Not only is it difficult, if not impossible, to identify and notify every user whose log-in information might have been compromised, it is unlikely that everyone, even if notified, will change his or her passwords.

▶ You can access McNulty's full testimony at `http://www-swiss.ai.mit.edu/6.805/articles/mcnulty-internet-security.txt`.

That attack is regarded as one of the worst in recorded history, but it was rivaled only months later. In the second incident (the attack was based at `Rahul.net`), a sniffer ran for only 18 hours. During that time, hundreds of hosts were compromised. The following was reported by Sarah Gordon and I. Nedelchev in their article *Sniffing in the Sun: History of a Disaster*.

The list contained 268 sites, including hosts belonging to MIT, the U.S. Navy and Air Force, Sun Microsystems, IBM, NASA, CERFNet, and universities in Canada, Israel, the Netherlands, Taiwan and Belgium...

▶ You can see the Gordon/Nedelchev article at `http://www.command.co.uk/html/virus/sniffing.html`.

Institutions and private companies are naturally reluctant to admit that their networks have been compromised, so sniffer attacks aren't usually publicly announced. There are some case studies on the Internet. Here are a couple well-known victims:

- California State University at Stanislaus
- A United States Army Missile Research Laboratory, White Sands Missile Range

▶ For more information about the Stanislaus incident, visit `http://yahi.csustan.edu/studnote.html`.

For more information about the U.S. Army Missile Research Laboratory, White Sands Missile Range incident, see the GAO report at `http://www.securitymanagement.com/library/000215.html`.

The Department of Defense, in particular, has experienced numerous attacks and been the victim of sniffers on its networks. In one of the more interesting incidents, intruders installed sniffers on DoD systems, compromising numerous user accounts. This incident, which occurred in February 1998, is referred to as Solar Sunrise by DoD officials. The incident involved two teenagers from California and their mentor in Israel.

▶ Numerous discussions on this incident can be found online including `http://www.sans.org/newlook/resources/IDFAQ/solar_sunrise.htm`.

What Information Do Sniffers Capture?

Sniffers will capture all packets on the network, but in practice, an attacker has to be choosier. A sniffer attack is not as easy as it sounds. It requires some knowledge of networking. Simply setting up a sniffer and leaving it will lead to problems because even a five-station network transmits thousands of packets an hour. Within a short time, a sniffer's outfile could easily fill a hard disk drive to capacity (if you logged every packet).

To circumvent this problem, crackers generally sniff only the first 200–300 bytes of each packet. The username and password are contained within this portion, which is really all most crackers want. However, it is true that you could sniff all the packets on a given interface; if you have the storage media to handle that kind of volume, you would probably find some interesting things.

Authentication information is one of the most common targets for sniffer activity. In particular, information sent to Ports 23 (Telnet) and 21 (FTP) are valuable because authentication information (like usernames and passwords) is sent in clear text in these protocols. Port 513 (rlogin) is also useful when trust relationships don't exist. (If a trust relationship does exist, then no username or password is required, but the system becomes a potential target for spoofing.)

Where Is One Likely to Find a Sniffer?

You are likely to find a sniffer almost anywhere. However, there are some strategic points that a cracker might favor. One of those points is anywhere adjacent to a machine or network that receives many passwords. This is especially true if the targeted machine is a gateway to the outside world. If so, the cracker will want to capture authentication procedures between your network and other networks. This could exponentially expand the cracker's sphere of activity.

NOTE

I do not believe that, in practice, any sniffer can catch absolutely all traffic on a network. This is because, as the number of packets increase, the chance of lost packets is high. If you examine technical reports on sniffers, you will discover that at high speeds and in highly trafficked networks, a more than negligible amount of data can be lost. (Commercial sniffers, which tend to have better design, are far less likely to suffer packet loss.) This suggests that sniffers might be vulnerable to attacks themselves. In other words, just how many packets-per-second can a sniffer take before it fails in its fundamental mission? That is a subject worth investigating.

Security technology has evolved considerably. Some operating systems now employ encryption at the packet level and therefore, even though a sniffer attack can yield valuable data, that data is encrypted. This presents an additional obstacle likely to be passed only by those with deeper knowledge of security, encryption, and networking. An example of this is the Windows NT/2000 authentication mechanism.

Where Can I Get a Sniffer?

Sniffers come in two basic flavors: commercial and freeware. If you're just learning about networking, I recommend getting a freeware sniffer. On the other hand, if you manage a large network, your company should purchase at least one commercial sniffer. They are invaluable when you're trying to diagnose a network problem.

Commercial Sniffers

The sniffers in this section are commercial, but many of these companies offer demo versions. Prices range from $200 to $2,000.

Sniffer Portable Analysis Solutions from Network Associates

Network Associates has produced several levels of network analysis tools including Sniffer Basic (formerly NetXRay by Cinco Networks), Sniffer Pro LAN, Sniffer Pro WAN, Sniffer High-Speed, and Sniffer Packet over SONET. These sniffers decode more than 240 LAN/WAN protocols, and Sniffer Pro High-Speed works with ATM and Gigabit Ethernet.

SnifferPro is a powerful tool providing visibility into the data network. It allows the user to perform a variety of functions including capturing network traffic, diagnosing network problems, and monitoring network activity in real-time. Figure 15.1 shows an example of a SnifferPro session in progress. The Expert window displays accumulated objects, symptoms, and diagnoses in the Expert Overview pane, while the Capture gauge shows the status of the capture in progress. The Capture function of this easily used and popular sniffer stores the actual packets from a network and decodes them, providing the user with detailed information about various network transactions. The Dashboard displays a network segment's packet rate, percentage of utilization, and error rate in real-time.

SnifferPro can collect data about conversations between network nodes in real-time. Figure 15.2 shows an example of this feature. A display of the network's traffic map depicting traffic patterns between network nodes can be seen, as well as traffic count statistics for node pairs.

15

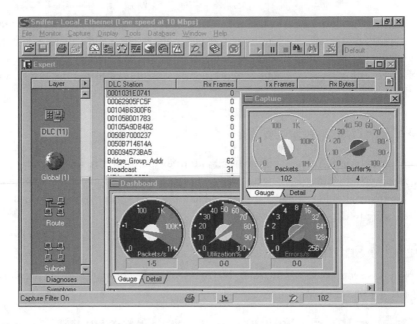

FIGURE 15.1

SnifferPro's real-time Expert and Capture gauge windows.

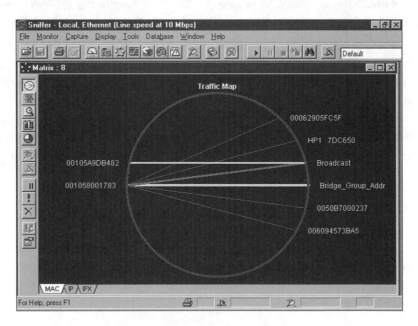

FIGURE 15.2

SnifferPro's Traffic Map Matrix display.

Network Associates also offers a sniffer rental service, from which a client can receive a portable computer with the latest sniffer software loaded. Both weekly and monthly rentals are offered.

>Network Associates, Inc.
>Sniffer Technologies
>3965 Freedom Circle
>Santa Clara, CA 95054
>Phone: 800-Sniffer
>URL: `http://www.networkassociates.com/`

Shomiti Systems Surveyor, Explorer, and Century LAN Analyzers

Shomiti Systems LAN Analyzers are heavy-duty hardware/software solutions that support 10/100Mbps and gigabit Ethernet. The systems work with both Ethernet and token ring networks and offer real-time reporting. Surveyor operates on Windows 95/98/2K or NT. Shomiti also offers a plug-in module for Surveyor, which provides Quality of Service analysis for factors important to voice-over IP applications.

>Shomiti Systems, Inc.
>1800 Bering Drive
>San Jose, CA 95112
>Phone: 408-437-3940
>Email: `info@shomiti.com`
>URL: `http://www.shomiti.com`

PacketView by Klos Technologies

PacketView is a DOS-based packet sniffer designed for use in Ethernet, token ring, ARCNET, and FDDI environments. It runs about $300. You can try before you buy by downloading a demo version located at `www.klos.com/get.pvdemo.html`.

>Klos Technologies, Inc.
>12 Jewett
>Cortland, NY 13045
>Phone: 607-753-0568
>Fax: 561-828-6397
>Email: `sales@klos.com`
>URL: `http://www.klos.com/`

15

SNIFFERS

Network Probe from Network Communications

Network Communications produces several network analyzers including the Ranger Network Probe and the 8000 Network Probe for both LANs and WANS. They can capture and analyze packets from the following protocols: AppleTalk, Banyan, DEC Net, Microsoft, IBM, NFS, Novell, SMB, Sun NFS, TCP/IP, Token Ring/LLC, X-WINDOWS, and XNS.

Network Communications Corporation

7601 Washington Avenue South

Edina, MN 55439

Phone: 952-946-8800

Fax: 952-946-8822

Email: sales@netcommcorp.com

URL: http://www.netcommcorp.com

LANWatch by Precision Guesswork

LANWatch is a software-based sniffer solution for both DOS (LANWatch 4.1) and Windows 95/98/2K/NT(LANWatch32) platforms. It will monitor packets from the following protocols: TCP, UDP, IP, IPv6, NFS, NetWare, SNA, AppleTalk, VINES, ARP, NetBIOS, and some 50 others. LANWatch monitors traffic in real-time and can display a wide range of usable statistics. A demo version is located at www.guesswork.com/demo.html.

Precision Guesswork

Five Central Street

Topsfield, MA 01983

Phone: 978-887-6570

Email: info@precision.guesswork.com

URL: http://www.guesswork.com

EtherPeek from WildPackets Inc. (formerly AG Group)

EtherPeek (4.0 is the latest version at the time of this writing) is available for both Windows and Macintosh platforms. EtherPeek supports major protocol suites including IP, IPv6, AppleTalk, NetWare, IPX/SPX, NetBIOS, DECnet, SMB, and OSI/TARP. It runs from $900 to $1,350, depending on the type of license you purchase.

WildPackets, Inc.

2540 Camino Diablo, Suite 200

Walnut Creek, CA 94596

Phone: 925-937-7900 or 800-466-2447

Email: info@wildpackets.com

URL: http://www.wildpackets.com/

NetMinder Ethernet by Neon Software

NetMinder Ethernet is a Macintosh-based protocol analyzer that can produce automatically updated HTML output reports. These reports are updated in real-time, allowing system administrators to access their latest network analysis statistics from anywhere in the world and from any platform. (Naturally, the application also provides real-time analysis in the standard GUI environment.) A demo version is available at `http://www.neon.com/demos_goodies.html`.

Neon Software

3685 Mt. Diablo Blvd., Suite 253

Lafayette, CA 94549

Phone: 800-334-NEON

Email: `info@neon.com`

URL: `http://www.neon.com`

DatagLANce Network Analyzer by IBM

DatagLANce is a network analyzer that IBM withdrew from its product line. DatagLANce was designed for both Ethernet and token ring networks, and, to my knowledge, is the only sniffer written expressly for OS/2. DatagLANce can analyze a wide range of protocols, including but not limited to NetBIOS, IBM LAN Manager, TCP/IP, NFS, IPX/SPX, DECnet, AppleTalk, and Banyan VINES. (DatagLANce can also output analysis data in many different formats.)

IBM

Product Numbers: 5622-441, 5622-442, 5622-443

LinkView Network Analyzers by Acterna

LinkView Network Analysers support token ring, Ethernet, and fast Ethernet but are designed chiefly for protocol analysis on internetworks. They therefore automatically segregate IP-reporting statistics from other protocol statistics. LinkView Classic runs on Windows 95/98, and Windows NT SP4. LinkView Classic is a software-only LAN analyzer that works with most third-party network cards. The Acterna Advanced Ethernet Adapter is a hardware extension for LinkView Classic that runs on Windows 95/98. The LinkView software is available at `http://www.tinwald.com/sc_forms/linkview_classic_software.htmllv_classic_software.html`.

Acterna, Inc.

1030 Swabia Court

Research Triangle Park, NC 27709

Phone: 800-346-6332

Email: `linkview.info@wwgsolutions.com`

URL: `http://www.linkview.com`

15

SNIFFERS

ProConvert from WildPackets, Inc. (formerly Net3 Group)

ProConvert is not a sniffer, but is instead a tool for integrating data from disparate sniffers. This allows data from different vendors' formats to be converted into a single format, allowing the user to view packets on a platform separate from the one on which the packets were captured. ProConvert decodes (and provides universal translation between) EtherPeek, Fireberd500, Internet Advisor LAN, LAN900, LANalyzer for Windows, LANWatch, Network Monitor, NetXRay, LinkView, and tcpdump formats. In other words, ProConvert is the Rosetta stone for sniffer logs. It can save you many, many hours of work.

> WildPackets, Inc.
>
> 2540 Camino Diablo, Suite 200
>
> Walnut Creek, CA 94596
>
> Phone: 925-937-7900 or 800-466-2447
>
> Email: info@wildpackets.com
>
> URL: http://www.wildpackets.com/

LANdecoder32 by Triticom

LANdecoder32 is an extremely popular sniffer for use on Windows 95/98 or Windows NT/2000. It has advanced reporting capabilities and can be used to analyze frame content. Other features include remote monitoring (requiring RMON on the remote system), ASCII filtering (filter by string), and real-time reporting. Demonstration versions can be obtained by contacting Triticom.

> Triticom
>
> P.O. Box 46427
>
> Eden Prairie, MN 55344
>
> Phone: 952-829-8019
>
> Email: info@triticom.com
>
> URL: http://www.triticom.com/

LanExplorer Protocol Analyzer from Sunrise Telecom

LanExplorer Protocol Analyzer decodes all popular protocols, including TCP/IP, 802.3, 802.5, VLAN, Apple, Novell, and Microsoft as well as VoIP protocols including H323, H225, H245, RTP, and RTCP. LanExplorer runs on Windows 95/98/2K and NT and uses existing Ethernet, Fast Ethernet, token ring, or WAN network interface cards. A trial version can be obtained from www.intellimax.com/download.htm.

> Sunrise Telecom, Inc.
>
> 22 Great Oaks Blvd
>
> San Jose, CA 95119

Phone: 408-363-8000

Email: `info@intellimax.com`

URL: `http://www.intellimax.com/`

Freely Available Sniffers

There are also many freeware and shareware sniffers available. These are perfect if you want to learn about network traffic without spending any money. Unfortunately, some are architecture-specific, and the majority are designed for UNIX.

Esniff is a standard, generic UNIX-based sniffer. It was one of the first sniffers and was originally released in *Phrack* Magazine (an online hacker zine). Esniff is a very small C program that requires a C compiler and IP include files. A modified version for Solaris 2.X called sol-sniffer.c also exists. Esniff is available at the following locations:

`http://rootshell.com/archive-j457nxiqi3gq59dv/199707/Esniff.c.html`

`http://www.chaostic.com/filez/exploites/Esniff.c`

Gobbler (Tirza van Rijn)

Gobbler was an excellent early tool for those who wanted to learn about sniffers. It was designed to work on the MS-DOS platform, but ran in Windows 95.

An example of how Gobbler has been used as a tool for diagnosing network traffic jams can be found in a case study provided with the documentation. Here's a snippet of that paper:

> A bridge was having problems in getting through its startup sequence using the `bootp` protocol. "The Gobbler" packet catcher was used to capture the packets to and from the bridge. The dump file viewer and protocol analyzer made it possible to follow the whole startup sequence and to track down the cause of the problem.
>
> T.V. Rijn and J.V. Oorschot, *The Gobbler, An Ethernet Troubleshooter/Protocol Analyzer.* November 29, 1991. Delft University of Technology, Faculty of Electrical Engineering, the Netherlands.

▶ Gobbler is no longer widely distributed or used, but it can be found at the following addresses:

`http://packetstorm.securify.com/NT/audit/`

`http://agape.trilidun.org/hack/network-sniffers/`

Ethload (Vyncke, et al.)

Ethload is a shareware packet sniffer/packet analyzer written in C for Ethernet and token ring networks. It runs well with any of the following interfaces:

• Novell ODI

- 3Com/Microsoft Protocol Manager
- PC/TCP/Clarkson/Crynwr

Further, it analyzes the following protocols:

- TCP/IP
- DECnet
- OSI
- XNS
- NetWare
- NetBEUI

Unfortunately, the source code is no longer available. The author explains:

> After being flamed on some mailing lists for having put a sniffer source code in the public domain and as I understand their fears (even if a large bunch of other Ethernet sniffers are available everywhere), I have decided that the source code is not made available.

Ethload consists of more than 65,000 lines of C code. Two versions are available: You can either register your copy by sending in $200, or you can have an unregistered copy. The registered version has additional functions: more diligent support, printouts, periodic statistics gathered into a file, more buffers, and so on.

For a free sniffer executable on a DOS/Novell platform, Ethload is excellent.

▶ Here are a few sites that offer Ethload:

```
http://www.ping.be/~pin01407/
```

```
http://www.computercraft.com/noprogs/ethld104.zip
```

```
ftp://ftp.simtel.net/pub/simtelnet/msdos/lan/ethld200.zip
```

TCPDUMP

TCPDUMP is one of the most popular tools for network diagnostics and analysis. TCPDUMP can be used to monitor and decode all IP, TCP, UDP, and ICMP headers. The user can vary the amount of the packet that is grabbed, but the default is 64 bytes. TCPDUMP was loosely based on Sun's etherfind and was designed to aid in ongoing research to improve TCP and Internet gateway performance. TCPDUMP is a UNIX-based program, but a Windows version now exists known as WINDUMP. TCPDUMP can be obtained at

```
http://www.tcpdump.org/
```

WINDUMP can be found at

```
http://netgroup-serv.polito.it/windump/
```

LinSniff

LinSniff is a password sniffer. To compile it, you need all necessary network include files (`tcp.h`, `ip.h`, `inet.h`, `if_ther.h`, and so on) on a Linux system. It is available at

`http://packetstorm.securify.com/Exploit_Code_Archive/linsniff.c`

Sunsniff

Sunsniff is also designed specifically for the SunOS platform. It consists of 513 lines of C source, coded reportedly by crackers who want to remain anonymous. It works reasonably well on Sun, and is probably not easily portable to another flavor. This program is good for experimentation and can be found at

`http://securax.org/l0t/prog/sniffers/sunsniff.c`

linux_sniffer.c

This program's name pretty much says it all. It consists of 175 lines of C code, distributed primarily at cracker sites on the Net. This program is Linux-specific. It is another utility that is great for experimentation on a nice Sunday afternoon; it's a free and easy way to learn about packet traffic. linux_sniffer.c is available at

`http://rootshell.com/archive-j457nxiqi3gq59dv/199707/linux_sniffer.c.html`

Defeating Sniffer Attacks

Now that you understand how sniffers work and the dangers they pose, you are probably wondering how to defeat sniffer attacks. Get ready for some bad news: Defeating sniffer attacks is not easy. You can take two approaches:

- Detect and eliminate sniffers
- Shield your data from sniffers

Let's briefly look at the pros and cons of each method.

Detecting and Eliminating Sniffers

Sniffers are extremely difficult to detect because they are passive programs. They don't generate an audit trail, and unless their owner is very stupid (sniffing all traffic instead of the first *X* number of bytes-per-connection), they eat meager network resources. Some operating systems provide a mechanism to determine whether a network interface has been placed in promiscuous mode, which can aid greatly in determining if a sniffer is running on a specific host.

15

On a single machine, it is theoretically feasible to find a sniffer that has been installed. For example, you could rely on the MD5 algorithm (see Chapter 18, "Trojans," for more on MD5), providing you have a decent database of original installation files (or a running database of files installed). If you intend to use MD5 and search by checksum, you should obtain md5check, an AWK script that automates the process. md5check was originally distributed by CERT and works well for SunOS. md5check is located here:

`http://wd.twbbs.org/ftp/security/md5check/`

Certainly, searching by checksum on a single box is effective enough. However, finding a sniffer on a large network is difficult. The question of detecting sniffers on diverse architecture is a bitter debate in the security community. (You can see folks arguing this issue for weeks at a time without resolution.) However, there are at least four tools that can help—if you have the right architecture:

- **Snifftest**. Written by "Beavis and Butthead," Snifftest will detect a sniffer on SunOS and Solaris. It is especially useful because it will detect a sniffer even if the network interface isn't in promiscuous mode. It works solely for SunOS, and requires a C compiler and all TCP/IP header files. It is located at `http://rootshell.com/archive-j457nxiqi3gq59dv/199707/snifftest.c.html`.

- **Nitwit**. Nitwit runs as a NIT (Network Interface Tap) and can detect sniffers, even if the network interface is not in promiscuous mode. It is similar to Snifftest in that regard. Nitwit is available at `http://www.megamine.com/utilities/unixsniffers.shtml`.

- **Promisc**. Written by `blind@xmission.com`, Promisc will detect sniffers on Linux. (There are some reports of this program working on SunOS, but these have not been verified.) Promisc is available at `http://geek-girl.com/bugtraq/1997_3/0411.html`.

- **cpm**. cpm is an old favorite that can detect promiscuous mode on SunOS 4.x. (Again, you need a C compiler and the necessary include files.) cpm is available at `ftp://ftp.cerias.purdue.edu/pub/tools/unix/sysutils/cpm/`.

Unfortunately, these tools only work on SunOS or Solaris. Detecting a sniffer in heterogeneous networks is more difficult—difficult, that is, without physically checking each machine. For example, suppose your network is made up exclusively of AIX systems. Suppose further that someone goes into an empty office, unplugs a RS/6000, and hooks up a PC laptop. They use this as a sniffer. This is difficult to detect unless you are using *network topology maps* (tools that red flag any change in topology) and check them daily. Otherwise, the network appears just as it did, with no indication of trouble. After all, the PC has the same IP as the RS/6000 did. Unless you run daily scans, you would probably never detect the PC.

A more recent tool that has been developed by the L0pht group of "grey-hat" hackers is called AntiSniff. AntiSniff gives network administrators the ability to remotely detect computers that are packet sniffing, regardless of the operating system. According to the developers, AntiSniff works by running several nonintrusive tests designed to determine whether or not a remote computer is listening in on all network communications. This tool can be obtained at

```
http://www.l0pht.com/antisniff/
```

A more complicated situation occurs when intruders attach physical devices that sniff. (For example, they can splice themselves in at points not visible to the naked eye. I've seen offices that run their coax wire overhead, in the space above the ceiling. This allows anyone in an adjacent office to snag the wire and patch themselves in.) Other than physically checking each wire lead throughout the network, there is no easy way to identify a spliced connection. (Although, again, network topology mapping tools would warn that an extra IP had been added to your subnet. Unfortunately, however, most small businesses can't afford such tools.)

At day's end, however, proactive solutions are difficult and expensive. Instead, you should take more defensive measures. There are two chief defenses against sniffers:

- Safe topology
- Encrypted sessions

Let's quickly cover both defenses.

Safe Topology

Sniffers can only capture data on the instant network segment. That means, the tighter you compartmentalize your network, the less information a sniffer can gather. Unfortunately, unless your firm is an ISP—or you have unlimited resources—this solution can get expensive. Compartmentalization requires expensive hardware. There are three network interfaces that a sniffer cannot easily cross:

- Switches
- Routers
- Bridges

You can create tighter network segments by strategically placing these devices on the network. You could possibly compartmentalize 20 workstations at a crack—this seems like a reasonable number. Once a month, then, you could physically check each segment (and, perhaps once a month, you could run MD5 checks on random segments). It should be noted that programs such as macof have been developed to flood switches in the hope that they would fail open. This would then eliminate the protection that switching might otherwise have provided.

15

SNIFFERS

Network segmentation is only practical in smaller networks. If you have more than 500 workstations split among more than 50 departments, full-scale segmentation is probably cost prohibitive. (Even if there's a budget for security, you aren't likely to convince administrative types that you need 50 hardware devices just to guard against a sniffer.) In that case, encrypted sessions are the better choice.

Encrypted Sessions

Encrypted sessions provide a different solution. Instead of worrying about data being sniffed, you simply scramble the data portion of the packet beyond recognition. The advantages to this approach are obvious: Even if an attacker sniffs data, it will be useless to him. However, the disadvantages are weighty.

There are two chief problems with encryption. One is a technical problem, and the other is a human problem.

Technical issues include whether the encryption is strong enough and whether it's supported. For example, 40-bit encryption might be insufficient, and not all applications have integrated encryption support. Furthermore, cross-platform encryption solutions are rare and typically available only in specialized applications.

Moreover, human users can resist using encryption. They might find it too troublesome. (For example, can you imagine forcing Macintosh users to use S/Key every time they logged in to the server? These folks are accustomed to ease-of-use, not generating one-time passwords for every new session.) Users might initially agree to such policies, but they rarely adhere to them.

In short, you must find a happy medium—applications that support strong, two-way encryption and also support some level of user-friendliness. That's why I like Secure Shell.

Secure Shell (SSH) provides secure communications in an application environment like Telnet. SSH binds to port 22 and connections are negotiated using RSA. All subsequent traffic is encrypted using IDEA after authentication is complete. This is strong encryption and is suitable for just about any nonsecret, nonclassified communication.

Secure Shell is a perfect example of an application that meets user and administrative standards.

Versions of SSH and OpenSSH (a free version of SSH) exist for Windows 95/98/NT/2K, Linux, and many different versions of UNIX. Check out Secure Shell at

`http://www.ssh.org/`

`http://www.openssh.com`

Summary

Sniffers represent a significant security risk, mainly because they are not easily detected. You would benefit tremendously by learning how to use a sniffer and understanding how others can employ them against you. The best defenses against sniffing are secure topology and strong encryption.

Further Reading on Sniffers

The following documents (many of them online) offer further information about sniffers and the threats they pose:

- **The Sniffer FAQ**. Christopher Klaus. `http://www.netsys.com/firewalls/ firewalls-9502/0320.html`

- **Tik-76.115 Functional Specification**. (Specification for a sniffer application used in visualization of TCP/IP traffic.) `http://mordor.cs.hut.fi/tik-76.115/ kesa-96/palautukset/Sniffers/pt/tm/FM_3.0.html`

- *Sniffers and Spoofers*. (*Internet World, December 1995*.)

- **Computer Hacker Charged with Credit Card Theft**. (Case in which cracker used a sniffer to capture credit card numbers; ZDNET.) `http://www5.zdnet.com/zdnn/ content/zdnn/0523/zdnn0012.html`

- **Privacy and Security on the Internet**. (Lawrence E. Widman, M.D., Ph.D., University of Texas Health Science Center.) `http://www.med-edu.com/internet-security.html`

Virtual Weapons of Mass Destruction

IN THIS PART

Denial of Service Attacks

IN THIS CHAPTER

In this chapter you learn about denial of service (DoS) attacks, how they work, their history, targets, and programs used to launch them.

What Is Denial of Service?

Denial of service is the category of attacks that cause a loss of service, or an inability to function. They come in many forms and strike many different targets. The results can last for minutes, hours, or days and can impact network performance, data integrity, and system operation.

The first DoS attack of significance was the Morris Worm, estimated to have taken some 5,000 machines out of commission for several hours. At the time (November 1988), it was a disaster for academic and research centers but had little impact on the rest of the world. Today, comparable DoS attacks, such as those against Yahoo!, Amazon, and other major Web sites (February 2000), have resulted in millions of dollars in lost business and revenue. The frequency of denial of service attacks is increasing at an alarming rate, due in part to the prevalence of tools written for this purpose. The complexity of the attacks is also being taken to new levels, which mandates the need for stringent security practices and the implementation of new protection mechanisms.

Many denial of service tools are written as proof-of-concept code examples to demonstrate insecurities within common operating systems, such as Windows, Linux, Solaris, and the BSD-derived UNIXes. The Morris Worm was an experiment in distributed computing, albeit a little forcefully done. Poor development practices and a failure to introduce security early into new applications and operating systems cause many of these exploitable problems to exist. The growing complexity of network design and organization pushes the limits of current technology and exacerbates new vulnerabilities. The presence of denial of service is a double-edged sword. On one hand, it is unfortunate that conditions exist to allow denial of service techniques to proliferate. On the other, its presence is part of the technology evolution that generates higher security products and applications.

The standard for security has risen greatly, and this is apparent with the reaction to denial of service attacks. Only recently are we seeing legislation that deals with this form of attack. It is no longer considered a silly prank when revenue is lost in our Internet-driven economy.

How Denial of Service Works

Denial of service attacks are generally brought on by exploiting programming flaws in software and by writing specialized programs whose purpose is to perform attacks. Denial of service attacks generally work in one of the following ways:

- Bandwidth consumption
- Resource saturation
- System and application crash

Bandwidth consumption is an attack against network resources and refers to the complete use of available network bandwidth by an attacking computer or computers. This makes network response slow or stops the server completely while the attack is ongoing and causes an inability to reach services such as Web sites, email, and files. Resource saturation targets specific computer systems that provide services such as Web, email, DNS, and FTP and causes them to slow or halt. System and application crashes result in denial of service, as the particular system or software freezes, crashes.

Bandwidth Consumption

Each network can support only a finite amount of network traffic at one time, and this amount is dependent upon a few factors: network speed, equipment types, and their performance. Common communication links from an ISP to an organization are ISDN, DSL, Broadband (using cable modems), T1, and T3. These link types also reflect different bandwidth capabilities. Common Local Area Network (LAN) topologies use 10BASE-T and 100BASE-T. For further information about network bandwidth and speeds, see `http://www.speedguide.net/Cable_modems/bandwidth.shtml`.

Denial of service by bandwidth consumption occurs when the entire capacity of the network link is used. When the network bandwidth capacity is reached, new network data cannot be sent. This means new connections to the Internet, file servers, Web servers, email servers, or any other function that requires network communication will not work. Connections that are already established will slow to a crawl, freeze, or be disconnected.

Attacks against bandwidth can occur via specialized attack programs and misconfiguration of network equipment. The programs used to cause denial of service are discussed later in the section "Recent DoS Attacks." Misconfiguration of network equipment includes any device that connects to the network, such as computer systems, routers, switches, and other devices.

Bandwidth attacks are active; the denial of service occurs only as long as the bandwidth is fully used. As soon as the attacking program stops sending data or the device is configured properly, bandwidth again becomes available. Most network functionality will return to normal, except for a few connections that might need restarting.

Common attacks include protocol-based exploits that consume network bandwidth by sending crafted network data. The access device, such as a router, can fail as it becomes inundated with more traffic than it can process. Another form of bandwidth attacks relies on the reaction of network-connected systems and devices to specific network data. Many or all of the computers on the target network can be made to respond simultaneously to network traffic such as IP broadcasts (IP packets that are sent to the broadcast address of a network instead of to a specific machine), thereby consuming all of the available bandwidth. The "Smurf" attack is one popular example of this form of attack. This and other forms are outlined in the section "Recent DoS Attacks."

Resource Saturation

Like a network, each computer system also has a finite set of resources including memory, storage, and processor capacities. *Resource saturation* is the event of using up all of one or more of these resources, which leaves none for other applications. The SYN flood is a popular example of an attack that uses all the available networking resources on a system.

Each operating system that supports TCP/IP network connectivity has limitations on the number of connections that can be maintained at one time. The SYN flood exploits the three-way handshake of a TCP connection, which is outlined in Chapter 4, "A Brief Primer on TCP/IP." The SYN flood succeeds by creating "half-open" connections on the port on the target server. Half-open connections are those in which the three-way handshake is not completed. Normally, the handshake completes, or times out, causing the connection to be deleted. Each port can only support a finite number of half-open connections and when this number is exceeded, no other new connections can be made. By sending only the first packet of the TCP handshake with invalid or spoofed source addresses, the server responds to the SYN packet with an acknowledgement. Because this acknowledgement goes to a falsified address, the response to it never arrives. This causes a backlog of half-open connections that it are waiting to complete, disallowing new connections from being accepted.

The Web server is a good sample target for a denial of service attack, although any network service can be targeted. As we have all probably experienced, a busy Web server tends to respond more slowly to our requests. A bit of knowledge about TCP/IP and the Hypertext Transfer Protocol (HTTP) is needed to understand how these attacks work. A single HTTP request and connection is made when the browser connects to the Web server. This request asks the server for a particular file; the server then sends the file, and the connection is closed. Under these circumstances, a Web server can handle a large number of requests because the requests usually take a very short time to complete, and they arrive one after another. As the server receives more simultaneous requests, the application becomes loaded as it processes all of these connections at the same time. Even with this slowdown, the Web server can still function.

In order to cause the Web server to stop functioning, the attacker needs to increase the time needed to handle these connections or to increase the processing power needed to handle each one. A SYN flood against a Web server makes the server unable to accept new connections by exceeding the maximum number of connections for the port it uses. The SYN flood is difficult to defend against. If the attacker forges packets to look as if they are coming from an unreachable system, the server has no way of knowing that they are not typical traffic. The server then responds as it would to any other connection and waits for a timeout to occur before it realizes it should close the connection. As outlined in the SYN flood description above, the denial of service occurs when the Web server receives a large number of these forged packets, so many that it cannot handle any more new connections and inevitably is stuck waiting for these falsified connections to timeout before it can continue processing. Similar attacks are the ICMP and UDP flood, which use other protocols to achieve the same effect.

Another example of resource saturation can occur with the use of external programs such as Common Gateway Interface (CGI) programs with the Web server. Programs that store data in files on the Web server can be exploited to fill the hard disk on the server. The server operating system uses files for much of its normal functionality, and, when full, it can often fail to function. Similarly, applications that allocate a lot of memory or require a lot of processing power for complex computations can be exploited to use all of those resources, preventing new processes and applications from functioning. These attacks are not exploitable only via the Web server—any access to the system might allow an attack to succeed. The email bomb discussed in the "Exploitation and Denial of Service" section is a good example of this.

System and Application Crash

System and application crashes are fast and easy approaches to denial of service, wherein a programming flaw is exploitable and causes the application or operating system to crash. A well-known example of these crashes include the "Ping of Death" attack that uses oversized ICMP echo requests. The target machine would crash due to improperly implemented handling of this network data.

These attacks are also commonly directed against network access devices such as IP routers, cable routers, managed Ethernet switches, VPNs, and other application specific devices. These devices often support some form of management interface including a Command Line Interface (CLI) and a Web management interface. Through various methods including a large number of simultaneous connections, buffer overflows in user input routines, and improper data validation, these devices have been made to crash. A denial of service attack on an access device has a wider influence than an attack on a single machine because these devices are typically gateways to multiple networks.

Many of these attacks can be prevented by safe configuration of the network device. This includes changing factory-set default passwords and configuring the device to allow management from only a select group of machines.

Exploitation and Denial of Service

This section outlines common attacks through the denial of service methods outlined in the previous section:

- Email bomb resource attacks
- Protocol attacks

Email Bomb Resource Attacks

Email bombs are insidious attack methods that make up for simplicity with their effects.

A traditional *email bomb* is simply a series of messages (perhaps thousands) sent to your mailbox. The attacker's object is to fill your mailbox with junk or to fill the hard disk or file system on which the mail server runs with junk. If mailbox quotas are used, the receiver of an email bomb cannot receive new messages until the mailbox is cleaned up. If the file system of the mail server is full, no other users can receive new messages. Email bombs lead to loss of important data, and increased bandwidth and resource usage, which can translate into higher network charges. If you use a dial-up connection, that can also translate into increased connection charges and wasted time.

Email Bomb Packages

Email bomb packages are programs that automate the process of email-bombing someone. System administrators should be aware of these packages and the filenames associated with them. (While this knowledge will not prevent your system from being attacked, it might prevent your users from attacking other systems.)

Table 16.1 lists the most popular email bomb packages and filenames associated with them. If you run a network with multiple users, you should scan your drives for those filenames.

TABLE 16.1   Common Email Bomb Packages and Associated Filenames

Bombing Package	*Filenames*
Up Yours	upyours3.zip
Kaboom	kaboom3.zip
The Unabomber	unabomb.zip
The Windows Email Bomber	bomb02b.zip
Gatemail	gatemail.c
UNIX Mailbomber	mailbomb.c
Avalanche	alanch3.zip, alanch35b.zip
Aenima	aenima17.zip, aenima20.zip
Serpent (Linux)	serpent.zip
Euthanasia	euthan15.zip
Ghost Mail	gm51.zip
HakTek	hatetuk.zip

Many of these files can be found at `http://web.searchalot.com/home/hazfresse//bomber.htm`.

Dealing with Email Bombs

Kill files, exclusionary schemes, or mail filters are all cures for an email bomb. Using these tools, you can automatically reject mail sent from the source address with these tools. There are various ways to implement such an exclusionary scheme. UNIX users can find a variety of sources online.

If you use Windows or MacOS instead, I would recommend any of the mail filter applications listed in Table 16.2. Many of these are shareware, so you can try them before you buy them.

TABLE 16.2 Popular Mail Server Filter Applications and Their Locations

Filter Package	Location
SIMS (MacOS)	http://www.stalker.com/
EIMS(MacOS)	http://www.eudora.com/
Musashi (PPC, MacOS)	http://www.sonosoft.com/musashi.html
E-Mail Chomper (Win95/98/NT)	http://www.sarum.com/echomp.html
SPAM Attack Pro (Win 95/NT)	http://www.softwiz.com/
Spam Buster (Win 95/98/NT)	http://www.contactplus.com/
SpamKiller (Win 95/98/NT/ME/2000)	http://www.spamkiller.com/

If someone starts bombing you, you can also try a human approach by contacting the attacker's postmaster. This is generally effective; the user will be counseled that this behavior is unnecessary, and that it will not be tolerated. In most cases, this proves to be a sufficient deterrent. Some providers have strong appropriate usage policies and will immediately terminate the user's account if used it is inappropriately.

Lastly, know this: Not all ISPs are responsible. Some of them might not care whether their users are email-bombing others. If you encounter this situation, you don't have many choices. The easiest cure is to disallow any traffic from their entire domain.

Email Bombs as Security Risks

In many circumstances email bombs can result in denial of service. For example, one individual bombed Monmouth University in New Jersey so aggressively that the mail server temporarily died. This resulted in an FBI investigation, and the young man was arrested.

NOTE

Most mail packages will die given the right circumstances on the right platform. For example, one of my clients found that directing a 40MB mail message to mailserv on UnixWare will kill the entire box. The freeze is unrecoverable except via reboot, and reboot is no recovery at all. There is no fix for this.

If you experience this level of attack, you should contact the authorities. This is especially so when the attacker varies his origin, thus bypassing mail filters or exclusionary schemes at the router level. Chances are, if the attack is that persistent, your only remedy is to bring in the police.

The recent trend towards email-based viruses also presents a denial of service condition. The automation and integration of newer applications allows greater flexibility and increased functionality, but also presents security risks if not used appropriately. Windows-based macro and Visual Basic Script (VBS) viruses demonstrate this clearly. The VBS.LoveLetter or "I Love You" virus and the VBS.SST worm or "Anna Kournikova" virus show the fine line between viruses and denial of service. Both viruses exploit the capabilities of Microsoft's Outlook mail client to automatically execute executable code contained in messages. The virus code replicates and sends itself to many other recipients, magnifying the problem and resulting in widespread infection and loss of service as files are deleted and mail servers cease functioning. Disabling Windows Scripting Host can help alleviate the problem of automatic execution. See `http://www.sophos.com/support/faqs/wsh.html` for further information.

List Linking

List linking attacks have similar effects to email bombs, but their appearance is more inconspicuously malignant. In *list linking*, the target subscribes you to dozens of mailing lists, which can fill your mailbox and possibly the mail server with data.

> **NOTE**
>
> Mailing lists distribute mail messages collected from various sources. These messages typically concentrate on a special-interest subject. These mail servers (sometimes called *list servers*) collect such messages and mail them to members of the list on a daily, weekly, or monthly basis. Members can subscribe to such a list in several ways, though most commonly through email.

Mail-bombing packages automate the process of list linking. For example, Kaboom and Avalanche are two well-known email bomb packages that offer point-and-click list linking. The results of such linking can be disastrous. Most mailing lists generate at least 50 mail messages daily, and some of those include binary attachments. If the attacker links you to 100 lists, you will receive 5,000 email messages per day. Furthermore, you must manually unsubscribe from each mailing list once you are linked. Moreover, attackers often choose times when you are known to be away, such as when you are on vacation. Thus, while you are absent, thousands of messages accrue in your mailbox. This can amount to a denial of service attack, particularly if your system administrator puts quotas on mailboxes.

List linking is particularly insidious because a simple mail filter doesn't really solve the problem—it just sweeps it under the rug. Here's why: The mail keeps coming until you unsubscribe from the lists. In fact, it will generally keep coming for a minimum of six months. Some mailing lists request that you renew your membership every six months or after some other specified period of time. This typically entails sending a confirmation message to the list server. In such a message, you request an additional six months of membership. Naturally, if you fail to provide such a confirmation message, you will eventually be taken off the list. However, in this scenario, your first opportunity to get off the list will not occur for six months. Therefore, no matter how irritating it might be, you should always deal with list linking immediately.

The cure for list linking is to unsubscribe from all lists you have been linked to. Doing this is more difficult than it sounds for a variety of reasons. One reason is that new lists seldom include instructions to unsubscribe. Therefore, you might be forced to trace down that information on the Web. If so, expect several hours of downtime.

> **TIP**
>
> To help fight against list linking, most mailing list administration software requires confirmation of subscriptions and also provides passwords for list members. These passwords are used to modify the user's subscription information and provide authentication. It is useful to keep copies of the initial subscription messages after signing on to a mailing list. These informational messages are invaluable and often contain the pertinent information needed to unsubscribe and maintain list membership.

Your ability to quickly and effectively unsubscribe from all lists will also depend largely on your email package. If your email client has powerful search functions that allow you to scan subject and sender headings, you can gather the list server addresses very quickly. However, if you use an email client that has no extended search functions, you are facing an uphill battle. If you are currently in this situation and have been list linked, communication with the maintainer of the list is often useful. Most mailing lists function by programs that automate most of the functionality that the list provides. Contact with a real person is vital in the event of list linking. Should all attempts to unsubscribe fail, the user can implement permanent mail filtering, or, in the worst case scenario, a new email address might be warranted.

A Word About Mail Relay

Another issue related to mail bombing and list linking, as well as the overall presence of Unsolicited Commercial Email (UCE) or "spam," is the ability of the attacker to relay mail. In order to obscure their identity, most mail bombs arrive from fictitious users. The ability to falsify attacker's identity arises from the configuration of various ISPs' mail servers. Mail relaying allows a mail server to be used to send mail to foreign networks.

As part of the transaction for sending a mail message, the software used to send mail connects to the mail server. The recipient's address and the sender's address are specified, and the message is then transmitted. Mail relaying occurs when either the sender's address or the system from which the sender connects to the server is not on the same network as the server. Mail servers that are configured to relay allow foreign users and systems to send mail to any other user. Servers that are configured to disallow relaying will not allow messages with sender addresses on unknown networks, or from systems on those networks.

In general, mail relaying is seen as a security risk and is disabled. For those systems that allow relaying, little that can be done to prevent its misuse. Filtering packages are incapable of supplying the needed security. Filtering by domain name or IP addresses might disallow legitimate email from being sent; this is not the desired outcome. For example, filtering to stop UCE from AOL will likely disallow millions of users' email from being delivered.

The issue of mail relaying is complex because messages such as mail bombs and UCE are syntactically the same as legitimate mail messages. Therefore, it is important to be aware of this issue as it relates to denial of service because it is one piece of the prevention puzzle.

Protocol Attacks

Attacks against network protocols make up a large portion of the denial of service attacks that occur. Protocol attacks result in bandwidth consumption, system crashes, and resource saturation, causing denial of service conditions. These attacks are very threatening and can stop network connectivity and system functionality for an indeterminate amount of time. Prevention of protocol attacks also requires considerably more advanced and complex procedures and countermeasures.

Protocol attacks strike at the heart of IP implementations. Hence, they can crop up on any platform. Worse still, because IP implementations are not drastically different from platform to platform, a single DoS attack might well work on several target operating systems. A well-known example of this is the LAND attack, which could incapacitate almost two dozen different operating systems, including Windows NT and a slew of UNIX flavors. Other examples include the previously mentioned SYN, UDP, and ICMP flood attacks.

Furthermore, analysis of DoS code releases shows consistently that, when a new attack is out, it will eventually work on nearly all platforms, even if it doesn't initially. New strains of DoS attacks are released about every two weeks or so. Such releases are typically written on a single build platform (Linux, for example) to attack a single target platform (Windows NT, for example). After such code is released, it is examined by the hacker and cracker communities. Within days, someone releases a modified version (a *mutation*) that can incapacitate a wider variety of operating systems.

The "Ping of Death," SYN flood, UDP flood, and fragmentation attacks should sound familiar by now. These protocol attacks rely on the continued existence and use of these common protocols. Their effects are widespread because of the prevalence of vulnerable operating systems and network equipment. New methods to prevent and defend against exploitation at this basic level have arisen. These methods are outlined in the denial of service attack index that follows.

Denial of Service Attack Index

Here is a comprehensive index of recent and old DoS attacks; each is fully documented. The fields provided and their significance are as follows:

- **Filename.** The filename provided is the one by which the attack is most well known. However, as folks distribute exploit code, different people name the file different things. There are various reasons for this, but the most common is to obscure the exploit code from system administrators. Since system administrators generally know the filenames of such tools, crackers rename them.

- **Author.** In this field, you often see aliases or email addressed, instead of real names. In the index, I have made every good faith effort to obtain the name, email address, or alias of each program's original author. If you authored one of the following programs and credit has erroneously been given to some other party, please contact Sams and let them know.

- **Location.** This is the location of the source code for the exploit. From this URL, you can download the source and test it on your own machine.

- **Background.** The Background field denotes locations where further documentation can be found. This usually points to an article or mailing list posting that details the attack's chief characteristics.

- **Build Operating System.** This field indicates either what platform the attack code was written on or which operating system will successfully run the code.

- **Target Operating System.** This field indicates what platform can be successfully attacked using the source code found at the Location.

- **Impact.** This field briefly describes the effect of an attack using the source code.

- **Fix.** This field points to URLs that hold patches or workarounds.

Recent DoS Attacks

Smurf

Filename: `smurf.c`

Author: TFreak

Location: `http://www.rootshell.com` and search for "smurf"

Background: `http://www.cert.org/advisories/CA-1998-01.html`

Build Operating System: UNIX

Target Operating System: Any system that responds to ICMP data.

Impact: Causes denial of service via spoofed ICMP echo requests to a network broadcast address.

Fix: Disable IP directed broadcasts on the router and configure operating systems not to respond to packets sent to IP broadcast addresses.

Fraggle

Filename: `fraggle.c`

Author: TFreak

Location: `http://www.rootshell.com` and search for "fraggle"

Background: Smurf with a UDP twist, see the rootshell entry.

Build Operating System: UNIX

Target Operating System: Any system that responds to UDP data.

Impact: Causes denial of service by making systems send UDP network data to a spoofed target.

Fix: Disallow unused ports on the firewall and configure network equipment and operating systems not to respond to UDP broadcasts.

The following flood attacks are general mechanisms that are still common today, although the technology has been available for quite some time.

ICMP Flood

Filename: `pingflood.c`

Author: Various

Location: `http://www.rootshell.com` and search for "pingflood"

Background:
`http://www.rycom.ca/solutions/whitepapers/toplayer/dos_attacks.htm`

Build Operating System: UNIX

Target Operating System: Various

Impact: Denial of service via network bandwidth overutiliziation.

Fix: Block ICMP traffic at the firewall and at the operating system. Monitor the network for attack signatures.

SYN Flood

Filename: `synflood.c`

Author: Various

Location: `http://www.rootshell.com` and search for "synflood"

Background:
`http://www.rycom.ca/solutions/whitepapers/toplayer/dos_attacks.htm` and
`http://www.niksula.cs.hut.fi/~dforsber/synflood/result.html`

Build Operating System: UNIX

Target Operating System: Various

Impact: Denial of service as the target system exceeds its maximum number of half-open/queued connections.

Fix: Configure the operating system to allow a higher number of open connections. Monitor the network for attack signatures.

UDP Flood

Filename: `udpflood.tgz`

Author: Various

Location: `http://www.rootshell.com` and search for "udpflood"

Background:
`http://www.rycom.ca/solutions/whitepapers/toplayer/dos_attacks.htm`

Build Operating System: UNIX

Target Operating System: Various

Impact: Denial of service as the target system receives more traffic than it is capable of handling at one time.

Fix: Disallow UDP traffic and services on the firewall and operating systems. Monitor the network for attack signatures.

Historical List of Well-Known DoS Attacks

The following attacks are early, well-known and well-documented denial of service attacks. The vulnerabilities allowing most of these attacks to succeed have been solved in newer versions of operating systems, but many organizations still have older and unpatched systems around. If you are responsible for securing a network, make sure you cover these bases. Fixes are available for all of these attacks and should be understood and implemented. Take a moment now to run through the following attacks to see if you're vulnerable. Most are easily fixed.

For more information about past and present denial of service attacks organized by operating system, software and device, see "The DoS Database," `http://www.attrition.org/security/denial/`.

Teardrop

Filename: `teardrop.c`

Author: `Route@infonexus.com`

Location: `http://www.rootshell.com` and search for "teardrop"

Background: See the source and comments.

Build Operating System: UNIX

Target Operating System: Windows 95 and Windows NT

Impact: IP fragment attack will lock up the target.

Fix: Search for "teardrop" in the knowledge base at `http://support.microsoft.com/`

Teardrop was an early denial of service attack that spawned several variants. This set the stage for many new denial of service attacks and approaches to denial of service tool creation.

Bonk, Boink Attacks

Filename: `bonk.c, boink.c`

Author: The people at ROOTSHELL.COM

Location: `http://rootshell.com/` and search for "bonk" or "boink"

Background: See source.

Build Operating System: UNIX

Target Operating System: Windows 95 and Windows NT. Patched and later versions are unaffected.

Impact: This utility will crash any Windows 95 or NT box, and it is basically a modified version of code previously written by `route@infonexus.com`. The malformed packet has a fragment offset that is greater than the header length.

Newtear Attack

Filename: `newtear.c`

Author: `Route@infonexus.com` (Michael Schiffman)

Location: `http://www.rootshell.com/` and search for "newtear"

Background: See source.

Build Operating System: Linux, BSD

Target Operating System: Windows 95 or Windows NT < SP3. Windows 2000 is not affected.

Impact: A variation of Teardrop that results in blue screen. The system crashes as a result.

Fix: Search for "modified teardrop" in the Knowledge Base at `http://support.microsoft.com/`.

INETINFO.EXE Attack

Filename: `inetinfo, inetinfo.c, inetinfo.pl`

Author: Bob Beck. Also by Chris Bayly and Evan L. Carew

Location: `http://www.rootshell.com` and search for "inetinfo"

Background: `http://support.microsoft.com/support/kb/articles/q160/5/71.asp`

Build Operating System: UNIX, others

Target Operating System: Windows NT 4.0. SP >2 and 2000 are unaffected.

Impact: Arbitrary text targeting ports 135 and 1031 will kill IIS.

Jolt

Filename: `jolt.c`

Author: Jeff W. Roberson

Location: `http://www.rootshell.com` and search for "jolt"

Background: `http://www.rootshell.com`

Build Operating System: UNIX

Target Operating System: Windows 95. 98/NT/2000 is unaffected.

Impact: Varying results; Windows 95 freeze or blue-screen.

Fix: `http://support.microsoft.com`

TIP

The patch for Jolt only works if you also install the VTCPUPD patch, which is available at `http://support.microsoft.com/`.

Jolt was reportedly derived from older DoS attacks for POSIX and SYSV systems. As a side note, its author reports that some systems will blue screen when attacked.

Jolt2

Filename: `jolt2.c`

Author: Phonix (`phonix@moocow.org`)

Location: `http://www.rootshell.com` and search for "jolt2"

Background: `http://www.rootshell.com`

Build Operating System: UNIX

Target Operating System: Windows 98/NTsp5/NTsp6/2000.

Impact: 100% CPU utilization.

Fix: `http://support.microsoft.com/`

LAND

Filename: `land.c`

Author: The people at `http://www.rootshell.com`

Location: `http://www.rootshell.com` and search for "land" Background: `http://www.cisco.com/warp/public/770/land-pub.shtml`

Build Operating System: UNIX

Target Operating System: Many networked operating systems, including older versions of BSD, Linux, Solaris, Digital UNIX, HP-UX and Windows 95, Cisco IOS.

Impact: Connects request packets specifying source and destination as the same lock up the target.

Fix: `http://support.microsoft.com/`

The LAND attack sent tremors through the Internet community, primarily because of the sheer number of systems affected. In particular, it was learned that certain network hardware was also vulnerable to the attack, including routers.

> **NOTE**
>
> Only certain hardware was vulnerable to LAND. It is known that NCD X Terminals, Catalyst LAN switches (Series 5000 and Series 2900), and Cisco IOS/700 were all vulnerable. If you fear that your router is vulnerable, I suggest compiling and using `land.c` as a test.

You should contact your vendor regarding fixes. It can take time to route out all LAND variations because so many mutations have cropped up. One version crashes Windows 95 and NT, even with Service Pack 3 installed. Windows NT is currently up to service pack 6a. If your systems are current, this attack does not pose a threat. Workarounds for Cisco hardware can be found at `http://www.securityfocus.com`. Otherwise, contact your respective vendor.

If your operating system is Windows 95, get the patch for the original LAND attack as well as several mutations. That patch can be found by searching for "land" under the Windows 95 knowledge base at `http://support.microsoft.com/`.

Pong

Filename: `pong.c`

Author: FA-Q

Location: `http://www.ludat.lth.se/~dat92jni/dat/pong/pong.c`

Background: See source code.

Build Operating System: Linux

Target Operating System: Windows 95, but can affect most other network OSes.

Impact: Targets are flooded with spoofed ICMP echo requests to the network broadcast address. Flood caused Windows 95 to crash.

Fix: Configure routers and network equipment to disallow traffic to broadcast addresses.

The Pentium Bug

Filename: `pentium_bug.c`

Author: Whiz (`whizpig@tir.com`)

Location: `http://www.rootshell.com` and search for "pentium"

Background:
`http://support.intel.com/support/processors/pentium/ppiie/descrip.htm`

Build Operating System: Any Pentium

Target Operating System: None; this is firmware bug.

Impact: The target locks up.

Fix: `http://support.intel.com/support/processors/pentium/ppiie/descrip.htm#Workaround`

This hole affects early Pentium processors up to the Pentium II. It allows malicious users with physical access to issue illegal instructions that cause the system to function improperly, often triggering a system crash. This form of attack demonstrates that denial of service is not limited to network-based attacks. Keep in mind the physical access component of computing, and be sure to be attentive to its security.

Winnuke

Filename: `winnuke.c`

Author: _eci

Location: `http://www.rootshell.com` and search for "nuke" Background: See the source code.
Build Operating System: Linux, BSDI

Target Operating System: Windows 95 and Windows NT. 98/2000 are not affected.

Impact: Windows 95 and NT failed to react properly to packets with the Out-of-band (OOB) flag set. Often caused a system panic requiring reboot.

Fix: `http://support.microsoft.com/`

Winnuke will kill any unpatched Windows 95 or Windows NT box, forcing a reboot. This attack has gone through several mutations and is available for many build operating systems. The "nukenabber" tool helps to identify the presence of this tool on a network.

Nukenabber is a small, compact port sniffer written by `puppet@earthling.net`. The program listens on ports 139, 138, 137, 129, and 53. These are all ports on which DoS attacks have been implemented in the past. Nukenabber notifies you when your machine is under Winnuke attack. The program is available here:

`http://www.dynamsol.com/puppet/nukenabber.html`

Ping of Death

Filename: `pingexploit.c`, `win95ping.c`

Author: Bill Fenner (`fenner@freebsd.org`)

Location: `http://www.rootshell.com` and search for "ping"

Background: See the source code.

Build Operating System: BSD UNIX, other ports are available.

Target Operating System: Windows 95 and Windows NT 3.51. Windows 98/NT4/2000 are not affected.

Impact: Oversized ICMP echo request packets (> 64k) were not handled appropriately, causing a system crash.

Fix: `http://support.microsoft.com/`

DNSKiller

DNSKiller will kill a Windows NT 4.0 box's DNS server. The source was written for a Linux environment. However, it can also well run on BSD-ish platforms. For more information, see `http://archives.neohapsis.com/archives/bugtraq/1997_1/0152.html`.

arnudp100.c

arnudp100.c is a program that forges UDP packets and can be used to implement a denial of service attack on UDP ports 7, 13, 19, and 37. To understand the attack, I recommend examining the following paper: *Defining Strategies to Protect Against UDP Diagnostic Port Denial of Service Attacks* by Cisco Systems. Another good source for this information is CERT Advisory CA-96.01.

▶ Cisco Systems' Defining Strategies to Protect Against UDP Diagnostic Port Denial of Service Attacks can be found online at `http://cio.cisco.com/warp/public/707/3.html`.

Distributed Denial of Service Attacks

In early 2000, the Internet community saw a new method of attack unleashed upon several popular Web sites including CNN, E*Trade, Datek, Amazon.com, Yahoo!, and Buy.com that caused them to be unreachable for several hours. These attacks were unlike normal denial of service attacks in that the flood of network traffic appeared to come from many different systems, simultaneously, Network administrators and security personnel scrambled to identify the causes and sources of the attacks, as well as to find methods to stop them and bring their crawling Web sites back into service. Rumors spread about a coordinated underground cracking community conspiring to attack simultaneously. The reality soon became known, that a new form of attack—the distributed denial of service (DDoS) attack—would become a nightmare for Web sites and businesses.

Distributed denial of service attacks, as the name implies, occur when a several systems, from a handful to thousands, simultaneously attack a specified target. Some of the well-known and analyzed attack forms are: Trinoo (or Trin00), Tribe Flood Network (TFN), TFN2k (an updated version of TFN), and Stacheldraht (German for "barbed wire").

These attacks function via a master and slave mechanism. The master is the controlling station where the attacker defines the target and method of attack. The slave stations are remote systems that have been compromised and have had the attack tool installed. The master signals the slave stations to launch the attack. The attack is also stopped by another signal from the master system.

A good general overview of distributed denial of service attacks can be found in *Distributed Denial of Service Attacks*, by Bennett Todd, at `http://www.linuxsecurity.com/resource_files/intrusion_detection/ddos-faq.html`.

This section provides an index of distributed denial of service attack tools. The background information includes full analyses of the attack methods and source code.

Trinoo (Trin00)

Filename: `trinoo.tgz`

Author: Project DoS

Location: `http://packetstorm.securify.com/distributed/`

Background: `http://staff.washington.edu/dittrich/misc/trinoo.analysis`

Build Operating System: UNIX

Target Operating System: UNIX

Impact: Denial of service until the attack is stopped.

Fix: Patch systems to prevent compromise, monitor UDP traffic for trinoo fingerprints, and run DDoS scanner tools such as RID (available at `http://packetstorm.securify.com/distributed/`) to detect the presence of the program on your network. Blocking UDP traffic on high numbered ports might stop the problem, but might also cause other network applications not to work.

Tribe Flood Network (TFN)

Filename: `tfn.tgz`

Author: Mixter

Location: `http://packetstorm.securify.com/distributed/`

Background: http://staff.washington.edu/dittrich/misc/tfn.analysis

Build Operating System: UNIX

Target Operating System: UNIX

Impact: Denial of service until the attack is stopped.

Fix: Use RID (see trinoo entry) to scan for the presence of the software on your network, block all ICMP echo traffic. (This might not be possible depending on network needs of the organization.)

TFN2k

Filename: tfn2k.tgz

Author: Mixter

Location: http://packetstorm.securify.com/distributed/

Background: http://packetstorm.securify.com/distributed/TFN2k_Analysis.htm

Build Operating System: UNIX

Target Operating System: UNIX, Windows NT/2000

Impact: Denial of service until the attack is stopped.

Fix: Disallow unnecessary TCP, UDP, and ICMP network traffic. Protect systems against compromise by frequent monitoring and updating. Use application proxies to prevent the attack.

Stachledraht

Filename: satchel.tgz

Author: Unknown

Location: http://packetstorm.securify.com/distributed/

Background: http://staff.washington.edu/dittrich/misc/stacheldraht.analysis

Build Operating System: Linux, Solaris

Target Operating System: Linux, Solaris

Impact: Denial of service until the attack is stopped.

Fix: Use RID (see link in trinoo entry) to scan for the presence of the software on your network, and block all ICMP echo traffic. (This might not be possible depending on network needs of the organization.)

Summary

Denial of service attacks represent the newest trend in hostile Internet activity and are evolving at an alarming rate. The care and diligence used to design and implement networks, software, and operating systems has a great effect on the ability of the attacker to cause denial of service. Prevention and awareness are two factors that have an immediate impact on the success of these attacks. Filtering of unnecessary services and network data, stronger authentication and access control of remote systems and users, and proactive monitoring and updating of systems and software can help protect your network against these attacks.

Other DoS Resources

Finally, you will find several useful links for further information on DoS attacks.

Strategies to Protect Against Distributed Denial of Service (DDoS) Attacks. `http://www.cisco.com/warp/public/707/newsflash.html`

CERT Advisory CA-2000-01 Denial-of-Service Developments. `http://www.cert.org/advisories/CA-2000-01.html`

Denial of Service (DoS) Attack Resources. `http://www.denialinfo.com/`

Denial of Service Attacks—DDOS, SMURF, FRAGGLE, TRINOO. `http://www.infosyssec.com/infosyssec/secdos1.htm`

Network Ingress Filtering: Defeating Denial of Service Attacks Which Employ IP Source Address Spoofing. `ftp://ftp.isi.edu/in-notes/rfc2267.txt`

Results of the Distributed-Systems Intruder Workshop. `http://www.cert.org/reports/dsit_workshop.pdf`

Consensus Roadmap for Defeating Distributed Denial of Service Attacks. `http://www.sans.org/ddos_roadmap.htm`

Viruses and Worms

Do you have a virus? No instruments, no senses can tell you if you are in the presence of the predator.

—Richard Preston, *The Hot Zone*

If doctors and pharmacists worked like anti-virus vendors, we'd all be immunized against all illnesses. Would this improve our viability as a species?

—David Harley, *Icarus*

IN THIS CHAPTER

This chapter addresses one of the best-known, most-feared and least-understood problems in information security. It explains what viruses and worms really are (and aren't), summarizes the means of limiting their impact, and, most importantly, includes some pointers to further information.

Understanding Viruses and Worms

Computer viruses are perhaps the most well known and feared security threats of all. Certainly, they're among the most misunderstood. All viruses entail a certain degree of damage, but their impact, with some very prominent exceptions, is mostly social.

Every virus does cause some (usually) limited denial of service because they all steal disk space, memory, and/or clock cycles (processor time). Some cause unintended (accidental) damage on some systems. Some do intentional damage to files and file systems, and a few can make some hardware effectively unusable by trashing firmware (CIH, for example). At this time, no known virus directly damages hardware, although the possibility of such a virus can't be discounted. However, some of the most successful viruses (in terms of survival) achieve longevity by virtue of the fact that they do nothing but replicate and therefore aren't conspicuous. Direct damage tends to be noticeable. However, some viruses cause serious damage to data by slow and insidious corruption, and others continue to survive despite their high damage profile.

It has to be said even an innocuous virus can cause problems just by being there, or even by being misdiagnosed as being there. This can result in secondary damage because of inappropriate action taken by poorly informed virus victims. It can also result in social damage. Such damage can include loss of reputation, scapegoating of the victims of a virus attack, or even legal action. A victim might be accused of failing to apply "due diligence", of being in breach of contract, or of being in contravention of data protection legislation. He might even be accused of implication in the dissemination of a virus, which is illegal in many countries (even those in which the actual creation of viruses is not in itself a crime).

Viruses that do no intentional damage are sometimes described as *benign*, in much the same way that a tumor might be defined as *malign* or *benign*. However, this usage is potentially misleading because the use of *benign* in this context does not mean *harmless*, let alone *benevolent*, as it might be understood to mean.

The meteoric expansion of Internet usage (especially email) since the early 1990s has raised the status of the virus from an occasional nuisance to everyone's problem. The vastly increased use of local networks and other means of sharing data and applications has also increased the risks by orders of magnitude. In brief, viruses can travel further and faster than was the case a few years ago. The big comeback story in the virus field is that of the computer worm. In the early 1990s, Internet usage became less specific to "big iron" mainframes and minicomputers reached via dumb terminals and terminal emulators. The first generation of worms declined in impact accordingly. Virus and anti-virus technology became focused on the individual desktop PC. In the latter part of the decade, however, virus writers began to rediscover worm mechanisms as a means of accelerating dissemination, until worms and worm/virus hybrids have now become one of the most aggravating problems faced by systems administrators.

This chapter, although it addresses worm mechanisms is some detail, isn't particularly focused on differentiating between viruses and worms. Even within the industry, the terms are often used interchangeably in the context of the hybrid viruses/worms that dominate the current virus scene.

What Is a Computer Virus?

Most anti-virus professionals would accept a working definition of the term *computer virus* like this: "a program that replicates by 'infecting' other programs so that they contain a (possibly evolved) copy of the virus." (F. Cohen: *A Short Course on Computer Viruses.*)

Note that the emphasis here is on reproduction by infection. A virus is not *per se* destructive, whereas a destructive program is not *per se* a virus. Furthermore, although most viruses do attempt to operate without the knowledge of the system user, this isn't a requirement either. The only defining characteristic is *replication*: the primary 'intent' of the infective program is to reproduce.

> **NOTE**
>
> The term *program* does not necessarily imply a program file, although, most viruses do in some way infect files. Nevertheless, we refer to infected and infective objects in this chapter unless we are specifically considering file infection, so as to include boot sector infectors and macro programs embedded in data files.

Infection is sometimes described in terms of attachment of the viral program to one or more programs on the target system. However, *attachment* is perhaps a misleading term, although it is conventionally used in this context because the word *attachment* has a rather different connotation in the context of email. It might be more useful to look at the process in terms of a chain of command. The viral code is inserted *into* the chain of command so that when the legitimate but infected program is run, the viral code is also executed (or in some instances, runs *instead* of the legitimate code).

We often describe infection in terms of the viral code becoming physically attached to the host program, but this isn't always the case. Sometimes, the environment is manipulated so that calling a given program calls the viral program. Sometimes, the viral program is activated before *any* program is run. This can effectively "infect" every executable file on the system, even though none of those files are actually physically modified. Viruses that take this approach include cluster or FAT (File Allocation Table) viruses, which redirect system pointers to infected files; companion viruses; and viruses that modify the Windows Registry so that their own code is called before legitimate executables.

Except for a few extraordinarily primitive and destructive examples that actually trash the host program on infection, all viruses work along these lines:

- A computer user calls a legitimate program.
- The virus code, having inserted itself into the chain of command, executes instead of the legitimate program.
- The virus code terminates and hands over control to the legitimate program.

Companion or spawning viruses follow the same sequence, but the virus code is contained in a separate file, which is (characteristically) renamed so that it will be executed instead of the program the victim thought he was launching. (It then normally hands over control to the legitimate program.)

The virus process is a little like the process of biological viral infection, although the analogy is overworked and can be misleading. Think of a person infected with an airborne disease. Whenever he exhales in a public place, he risks infecting others. Similarly, whenever an infected program is executed, the virus's infective routine also runs, and can infect one or more other objects "in range". Just as biological viruses infect hosts that are predisposed to infection, computer viruses target certain type of files and system areas, according to virus type.

What Is a Computer Worm?

Replication is also the defining characteristic of a worm, and some authorities (including Fred Cohen, the "father" of computer virology) regard worms as a subset of the genus virus. However, worms present particular problems of definition. One viable definition distinguishes between worms and viruses in terms of *attachment*. Whereas a virus in some sense "attaches" to a legitimate program, a worm copies itself across networks and/or systems without attachment. It can be said that the worm infects the environment (an operating system or mail system, for instance), rather than specific infectable objects, such as files.

Some observers have used the term *worm* to refer to *self-replicating malware* (MALicious softWARE) that spreads across networks. This doesn't really amount to a meaningful distinction because many viruses can travel between machines on a Local Area Network, for instance, without being "aware" that a target volume is not on the same machine. This isn't to say, of course, that viruses are never network aware.

Objects at Risk of Virus Infection

Thousands of new viruses have been reported in recent years. Viral mechanisms differ widely, and any type of file can be affected. However, viruses can only spread when code is executed, which means that only files or other objects (such as the boot sector) containing executable code can be carriers for further infections. This doesn't mean, however, that only binary executable files such as DOS/Windows .EXE and .COM files can be infected.

Some data files can also contain executable code in the form of embedded macros. At present, Microsoft Office includes two of the applications (Word and Excel) that are most vulnerable to virus attacks that take advantage of interpreted macro/scripting languages, such as Visual Basic for Applications and its siblings. Although macro viruses are possible (and exist) for non-Microsoft applications, word processors that store macro code in separate files rather than within document files are arguably less vulnerable. People are far less likely to swap macros than documents.

Shell scripts, batch files, interpretable source code, even Postscript files also contain executable code and could, in theory, be vulnerable to virus attack. The likelihood of such an attack depends on a number of factors, however, such as the popularity of the platform and the access controls native to the operating environment. The restricted write access allowed to unprivileged accounts in a multiuser environment like UNIX or NT does tend to impede the spread of viruses and Trojans in such environments. However, it would be unwise to rely exclusively on this fact for protection of such systems. Some of the earliest experiments with viruses were, in fact, made on UNIX systems.

Who Writes Viruses, and Why?

There are certain stereotypes associated with virus writing. On the whole, they're rarely useful. Most virus writers try, for obvious reasons, to preserve their anonymity, so testing the truth of these images is somewhat problematic. Some virus writers do discuss and display their craft and their angst in more-or-less public forums such as the newsgroup alt.comp.virus. These do seem to tend to be young males, and some research indicates that mostly they "age out" and leave the field as they acquire girlfriends and a life.

However, it's unsafe to assume that the "virus writers" who dominate such newsgroups are always who they say they are, let alone that they are as talented as they claim to be, or necessarily serious representatives of all virus writers. Indeed, it's possible that this group represents a constituency of wannabes rather than a group of real, competent virus writers. Certainly many successful viruses seem to have been written by focused loners with no particular affiliations, rather than by groups.

It's also noticeable that many of the most vociferous individuals quoted and feted by the media, law enforcement agencies, politicians, and others are not widely respected among their peers. Of course, the same is true of other types of computer vandals, not to mention many self-styled security and/or virus experts.

Some virus writers have responded to the very few serious attempts at research in this area. However, quantitative research is not realistically possible, and the research that has been done leans to the ethnographic. That is, rather than try to establish numerical data with large samples, researchers in this field have tended to rely on qualitative data, using interviews with very small samples (that is, just a handful of virus authors).

The acknowledged authority in this area is Sarah Gordon, who has written extensively in this area and in related ethical areas. Her papers for the Fourth and Sixth Virus Bulletin Conferences on *The Generic Virus Writer* are particularly relevant. A number of her papers, including both Generic Virus Writer papers, can be found at
`http://www.badguys.org/papers.htm`.

A second widespread stereotypical notion is that people who write anti-virus software also write viruses, in an attempt to drum up business for their products. I can't say with absolute certainty that no vendor or researcher has ever written a virus, released a virus, or even paid a bounty for samples of original viruses. However, it's hard to comprehend why any anti-virus professional would see a need to stray toward "the Dark Side" at this stage of the game. There are more than enough amateurs producing viruses. In Generic Virus Writer II, Gordon notes that older security professionals, especially systems administrators and such, make their own contribution to the virus glut through (probably well-meant) experimentation. However, despite the eagerness of virus writers to implicate "the enemy" in the problem, there is no conspiracy between systems administrators and vendors to keep vendor profits high. Or if there is, no one has offered me a percentage.

There are probably as many reasons for writing viruses as there are virus writers, although the reasons cited by virus writers (actual or wannabe) don't always stand up to closer analysis. Some appear fascinated by the concept of a self-replicating and/or self-modifying program, and are curious to see how far their creations spread. Indeed, some apologists suggest that virus writing is a legitimate means of research into artificial life forms, or even artificial intelligence. (However, the adaptive behavior displayed by even the most sophisticated viruses is usually rather restricted.)

Many virus authors seem to enjoy matching wits with the anti-virus establishment. Indeed, some viruses go straight from the creator to his favorite anti-virus company without any attempt to spread it through the general population. Others, however, are more concerned with inspiring the admiration of their peers, rather than gaining the attention of the anti-virus professionals. Others don't make a hard and fast distinction between writing viral and anti-viral software, and might write both. This isn't normally the case in the anti-virus industry, and those who've used their experience on both sides of the barbed wire to support of their search for a job in the industry have usually been sadly disappointed. In fact, development teams in the industry have practical as well as ethical reasons for preferring to employ programmers whose experience is in other areas. It saves them having to clean ill-founded technical preconceptions out of the newcomer's head.

There are, of course, many viruses that are intended to cause widespread damage, although deliberate destruction is the goal far less often than most people seem to believe. (Often, virus damage comes from thoughtlessness or sheer incompetence on the virus writer's part.) Some virus writers argue that computer users who don't have the technical savvy to protect themselves deserve everything they get. On the other hand, some virus writers also claim that they have no personal involvement in virus dissemination, and are not responsible for the use made of their code by others. In other words, the distributors are the problem, not the authors. This would be more convincing if such authors never made their creations available as source code and/or binaries on Web sites, in e-zines, and other locations. Then, viruses would be less easily available to anyone who asks, or trawls Vx (Virus eXchange) Web sites.

How Are Viruses Created?

Some people seem to believe that computer viruses appear spontaneously in the same way that biological viruses seem to do. This isn't quite as silly as it sounds. Completely new viruses don't just pop out of the primeval soup without warning. However it's not uncommon for a new variant (not necessarily a viable virus in terms of replication and the capability to infect) to be born without direct human intervention. For instance, a macro virus consisting of a fixed number of modules might mutate by losing some of its constituent macros or gaining unconnected (not necessarily viral) macros. WM/Cap, for example, mutated into many hundreds of variants of the original virus. However, someone had to write the original version.

It's not impossible that an operating environment might come into general use in which a viral program *could* be created from scratch without direct human intervention, but it doesn't seem to have happened yet.

Most virus writers (and a high percentage of the rest of the world) have an exaggerated view of the ability needed to produce a working virus. Undoubtedly, some virus writers produce technically competent code: many more don't. Furthermore, as we've seen, many viruses are

17

VIRUSES AND WORMS

one-trick ponies. They might do the replication trick well or not so well, but replication, even when done efficiently, represents a somewhat limited functionality, compared to that of a compiler or business application.

Older viruses were often written in assembly language. In fact, it's difficult to write some types of virus in a high-level language, even with the help of an inline assembler. This is an advantage, from the viewpoint of virus victims, in that it takes a certain level of programming expertise to create even a weak virus (or even to modify an existing virus so as to create a variant). Many variants are, in fact, simply existing viruses with a slight change that doesn't affect functionality (such as modification to unimportant embedded text). Such a change might require no programming at all.

Some virus writers and their admirers still regard proficiency in assembly language as the hallmark of programming excellence. (This is actually in sharp contrast to the professional programmer, whose choice of tool, given a choice, is liable to be somewhat more pragmatic.) However, the current is, by and large, flowing the other way.

As virus technology developed, some virus programmers turned their attention to creating kits to allow a wannabe virus author to "develop" other viruses without programming. That is, using *virus generators* to produce virus code. This has not, however, necessarily resulted in an increase in the total number of viruses "in the wild."

Kit viruses are often not actually viable (that is, they don't replicate), and are frequently detectable generically. A new kit virus might be identifiable as having been generated by a particular generator, simply by family resemblance. Thus, kit viruses have tended to contribute to the "glut" problem (the sheer weight in numbers), rather than to the "in-the-wild" problem (see next section).

Certainly, assembly language is not necessarily the language of choice among the current generation of virus writers. Interpreted macro languages (especially Visual Basic for Applications) are generally harder to use than kits, but much easier than assembler. Furthermore, disk space and main memory are no longer expensive, and grossly bloated files are less conspicuous in a Windows environment. Thus, it's become more practical (as well as easier) to write viruses and worms in C++ or Delphi.

What Does "In the Wild" Really Mean?

A virus is deemed to be "in the wild" when it has escaped or been released into the general population. The *general population* refers to computing environments outside the development environment where the virus was created and tested, or the collections of anti-virus vendors, researchers, and collectors. Viruses in these environments are typically (hopefully) processed under controlled circumstances, where no danger is posed to the surrounding communities. However, when a virus escapes a controlled environment, it might be said to be "in the wild" (often expressed adjectivally in the anti-virus community as In-the-Wild or ItW). Note, however, that in the anti-virus community, the fact that a virus is available on a vx (Virus eXchange) bulletin board or Web site does not make it In-the-Wild. Because access to such resources and exchange of viruses is voluntary, this counts as a controlled environment.

In his conference paper *Counting Viruses* (Virus Bulletin 1999), Paul Ducklin makes the distinction very clearly:

> "For a virus to be considered In the Wild, it must be spreading as a result of normal day-to-day operations on and between the computers of unsuspecting users. This means viruses which merely exist but are not spreading are not considered 'In the Wild'."

In fact, the definition used by the WildList Organization is far stricter. For a virus to be on the WildList, the nearest thing to an industry standard metric for "In-the-Wildness," it must be reported by two or more of the virus professionals who report to the WildList Organization. Furthermore, these reports must be accompanied by replicated samples. (Viruses that are reported by only one reporter are put into the supplementary list.) Clearly, this strictness means that the WildList can't represent all the ItW viruses at a given time, but does represent viruses that are genuinely "out there". Such data are often more useful than absolute numbers to the organizations and individuals using the WildList as a basis for testing and research. (Note that the WildList indicates a virus's presence "out there", but not the total number of virus incidents in which a single virus is implicated. Thus the list only provides a very rough guide to prevalence.)

What matters most for our purposes, however, is the disparity between the number of In-the-Wild viruses at one time (a few hundred according to the prevailing WildList) and the total number of viruses in existence. (At the time of writing between 50,000 and 60,000, depending on how you measure.)

How Do Viruses Work?

A virus is, conceptually, a simple program. In its simplest form, a *direct action virus* can be modeled in terms of an algorithm like this:

```
begin
  Look for (one or more infectable objects)
    If (none found)
    then
      exit
    else (infect object or objects).
    endif
end
```

They don't remain in memory, but execute all their code at once, and then hand over control to the host program.

Many viruses go memory resident (install themselves into memory) after the host program is executed, so that they can infect objects accessed after the infected application has been closed.

The term *hybrid* is sometimes used for viruses that stay active as long as the host program is running. It is also (perhaps with more justification) applied to viruses that are both direct action and memory resident.

In fact, all viable boot sector infectors are memory resident—they have to be. Otherwise, their code can only be executed during the boot process, which rather limits their opportunities to infect other boot sectors. We consider boot sector viruses in detail later on in this chapter.

Of course, all but the most incompetent viruses are a little better error-trapped than this, and at least check that the `infectable object` hasn't already been infected. You'll notice that I've also skated over the `infect object` subroutine. We'll come to infection mechanisms when we discuss the main virus types later in this section.

Some viruses, of course, do more than just replicate. We sometimes describe viruses as having up to three components: an infective routine, a payload, and a trigger. The previous models demonstrate an infective routine, although it could be said that finding an infectable object is the trigger for the infective routine. However, we more often think of the trigger as being the condition that has to exist before the payload (or *warhead*) can be executed. The payload can, in principle, be any operation that any other program can perform. In real life, however, it tends to be something flippant and irritating, like visual or audio effects, or else downright destructive. So now our model looks more like this:

```
begin
  (Go resident)
  if (infectable object exists)
  then
    if (object is not already infected)
    then
    (infect object)
    endif
  endif
  if (trigger condition exists)
  then
    (deliver payload)
  endif
end
```

The trigger condition might, for instance, be the execution of a file, or a particular date or time. The combination of a trigger and a malicious payload is sometimes called a *logic bomb*.

Viruses can be classified conveniently (but by no means definitively) into five main classes: Boot Sector Infectors (BSIs); file infectors; multipartite viruses; macro viruses; and scripting viruses.

> **NOTE**
>
> Memetic viruses (virus hoaxes and other chain letters) are not viruses in the same sense as the preceding classes because they infect people, not programs. They are considered here because hoax management is usually the responsibility of the person responsible for virus management.

Boot Sector Infectors (BSIs)

These PC-specific viruses infect the Master Boot Record and/or DOS Boot Record. At one time, these viruses accounted for the majority of reported incidents, but now they constitute a dwindling proportion of the total number of threats found in the wild, and new BSIs are something of a rarity. This might reflect the fact that people now increasingly use email and networks rather than floppy disks to exchange files. The fact that these are harder to write than macro viruses and scripting viruses (or even file viruses) is also relevant.

When a modern PC boots up, it goes through a process called Power On Self Test (POST). This stage of the boot process includes checking hardware components. Some of its information comes from information stored in CMOS, especially information relating to disk and memory type and configuration. If the CMOS settings don't match the actual drive geometry, the machine will not be able to find system areas and files where they should be, and will fail to finish the boot process.

The Master Boot Record (MBR), sometimes known as the Partition Sector, is found only on hard disks, where it is always the first physical sector. It contains essential information about the disk, giving the starting address of the partition(s) into which it is divided. On diskettes, which can't be partitioned and don't contain an MBR, the first physical sector is the boot record or DBR. On hard drives, the boot record is the first sector on a partition. The boot record contains a program whose job is to check that the disk is bootable and, if so, to hand over control to the operating system.

By default, if there is a bootable floppy present, most PCs will boot from drive A, the first floppy drive, rather than from drive C, the first hard drive. This is actually an unfortunate default because this is the normal entry point for a boot sector virus. If the PC attempts to boot from a floppy with an infected boot sector (even if the floppy doesn't contain the necessary files to load an operating system and therefore can't complete the boot process), the infected floppy will infect the hard drive. Characteristically (although not invariably), once the hard drive is infected, the virus will infect all write-enabled floppies.

NOTE

You might have heard that boot sector viruses can be disinfected without anti-virus software, using FDISK with a (largely) undocumented switch (/MBR), known in some quarters as FDISK/MUMBLE. The good news is that this works a lot of the time. The bad news is that, if you try it with the wrong virus, you can actually lose access to your data. Anti-virus software is a very imperfect technology, but it's almost invariably better and safer for removing viruses than general-purpose utilities that were never designed for that purpose. FDISK is *not* recommended as an anti-virus measure unless you know exactly what you're doing.

The majority of boot sector viruses also contain some provision for storing the original boot sector code elsewhere on the drive. There is a good reason for this. It isn't because the virus programmer kindly intends to eventually return the MBR to its original state, although retaining a copy of the original boot sector can make disinfecting the virus easier. Rather, it is because he has to. Typically, a virus will keep a copy of the original boot record and offer it whenever other processes request it. This not only enables the system to boot in the first place, but also makes it harder to detect the virus without anti-virus software that specifically recognizes it. However, some viruses simply replace the normal boot sector code with code of their own.

Some BSIs (Form is a particularly well-known and widespread example) only infect the boot record, even on hard disks. This creates particular problems with Windows NT and Windows 2000, and will usually prevent the system from booting at all. Thus a largely innocuous virus has suddenly become a major nuisance in some environments.

TIP

New boot sector viruses are comparatively rare. Nevertheless, even old favorites like Form still circulate among people who still exchange disks. Although reputable and up-to-date anti-virus software is still a must for detecting them, a simple precaution eliminates most of the risk of infection on most PCs, even from unknown BSIs. Most PCs, by default, will attempt to boot from drive A if there is a diskette there. If there isn't, it tries to boot from drive C. However, nearly all PCs can be reconfigured in CMOS to change this default. On most systems, this is done by modifying the boot order, so that the system always tries to boot from drive C first (or in the order CD drive, drive C, drive A). Other systems (notably some Compaq models) allow the setting of an option to disable booting from the floppy drive altogether. If the system user actually needs to boot from floppy, this simply involves resetting the option to default. Motherboard and PC system vendors use proprietary ways of setting CMOS options. Consult the documentation that came with your system. Note that "file and boot" (multipartite) viruses are less likely to be contained by this precaution.

File Viruses (Parasitic Viruses)

File viruses infect executable files. Historically, most file viruses have not been particularly successful in terms of their epidemiology (that is, at spreading). Many thousands have been written, but the number actually seen in the wild has been comparatively small compared to BSIs and, more recently, macro viruses. Nonetheless, those that have survived in the wild have often spread surprisingly well—CIH, for example. Some of the most prevalent contemporary file viruses, however, are more commonly described as worms, as considered later in this chapter.

After a virus infects an executable file by direct attachment, that file, when executed, will infect other files. *Fast infectors* go for instant gratification. Each time the infection routine is executed, it infects a whole directory, all folders on the current path, a whole volume/disk, even all currently mounted volumes. Even file infectors that infect only one or two files at a time can spread quickly across systems and networks in a modern environment, where multiple binary executables are opened and closed many times over a single session. Every time you open an application, at least one executable file is loaded. Some applications will open several files at startup, whereas others periodically open multiple files when performing a particular operation.

Sparse infectors forgo the temptation to infect as many files as possible, usually in an attempt to make themselves less conspicuous. They may not infect every time the virus is executed, but only under very specific conditions, even when an infectable object is there to infect.

17

> **Note**
>
> Binary executables are by no means restricted to .COM and .EXE files, but include DLLs (Dynamic Link Libraries), overlay files, VxDs and other classes of driver, overlay files, and even certain screensaver and font files.

Multipartite Viruses

File and boot viruses are the most common example of multipartite viruses, viruses that use more than one infection mechanism. In this case, both boot-sectors and binary executable files might be infected and used as the means of disseminating the virus. However, it's likely that there will be an increase in multipartite viruses consisting of other combinations of virus types.

Macro Viruses

Macro viruses infect macro programming environments rather than specific operating systems and hardware. Microsoft Office applications are by far the most exploited environment. These can be regarded as a special case of file virus, in that they appear to infect data files rather than binary executables. However, this way of looking at the process might actually confuse the issue. Macros are essentially a means of modifying the application environment, rather than (or as well as) the data file. Indeed, in the case of Microsoft Office applications that support macro programming languages (Visual Basic for Applications and, in earlier versions, WordBasic and AccessBasic), the macro language cannot be unbound from the application's own command infrastructure. Macro viruses usually infect the global template, and often modify commands within the application's menu system. Macro viruses are particularly successful against Microsoft applications because they allow executable code (macros) to exist in the same file as data. Applications that segregate macros and data into different files are less susceptible to this kind of attack.

Script Viruses

Script is rather an imprecise term, but in this context normally (currently) refers to VBScript and other malware that can be embedded in HTML scripts and executed by HTML-aware email clients through the Windows Scripting Host. Many of the viruses that use this entry point are often better characterized as worms, and are therefore treated under that heading later in the chapter. VBscript and Jscript are more virus friendly than JavaScript (for instance), primarily because they have many of the file I/O capabilities of other variations on the Visual Basic theme. Extant JavaScript malware usually takes advantage of an easily patched vulnerability in Internet Explorer.

This view of script viruses is rather restrictive. A broader definition might include HyperCard infectors, batch file infectors, UNIX shell script infectors, and many more. However, these are of less practical importance, currently.

Memetic Viruses

There is a further class of "viruses," which is unique, in that it comprises viruses that don't exist as computer code. The term *meme* seems to have been coined originally by Richard Dawkins, whose paper *Viruses of the Mind* draws on computer virology as well as on the natural sciences. A *meme* is a unit of cultural transmission, of replication by imitation, much as a gene is a unit of inheritance (a rather imprecise unit, perhaps). The memes we are most concerned with in this chapter are those sometimes known as *metaviruses*. A metavirus is itself a virus (what Dawkins calls a "virus of the mind, not a computer virus"), but purports to deal with other viruses (which are computer viruses). These viruses don't happen to exist. In other words, they are virus hoaxes. Virus hoaxes are not only a subclass of memes in general, but a subset of a particular type of meme, the chain letter. However, the virus hoax is particularly relevant to this chapter, because the administrator who manages virus incidents will usually also be the person who has to respond to plagues of virus hoaxes. The same might not be true of other hoaxes and chain letters.

The most commonly encountered hoaxes are derived from the infamous Good Times hoax of the mid-1990s. They conform to a pattern something like this:

> [THIS WARNING WAS CONFIRMED BY SYMANTEC AND MCAFEE THIS MORNING.] IF YOU RECEIVE EMAIL WITH THE SUBJECT <GREEN EGGS AND HAM> DO NOT OPEN IT, BUT DELETE IT IMMEDIATELY!!! IT CONTAINS A VIRUS THAT JUST BY OPENING THE MESSAGE TRASHES HARD DRIVES AND CAUSES MOUSE-MATS TO SPONTANEOUSLY COMBUST. MICROSOFT, AOL, IBM, FCC, NASA, CND, AND KKK HAVE ALL SAID THAT THIS IS A VERY DANGEROUS VIRUS !!! AND THERE IS NO REMEDY FOR IT AS YET. PLEASE FORWARD THIS TO ALL YOUR FRIENDS, RELATIVES, COLLEAGUES, AND ANYONE ELSE WHOSE EMAIL ADDRESS YOU HAVE HANDY SO THAT THIS DISASTER CAN BE AVERTED.

By the way, as far as I know there is no Green Eggs and Ham virus or hoax. I've just done what many real hoaxers have done and pulled a silly title out of thin air (or in this case my daughter's bookshelf). In fact, the infuriating aspect of this problem is that most hoaxers are abominably lazy and unoriginal, and the subject of the email which carries the supposed virus is often the only bit of the hoax that varies between two variants.

This sort of hoax only continues to work because masses of people with little technical knowledge of computers (let alone computer viruses) join the Internet community for the first time every day. Each one is at high risk of passing on such a hoax because they don't know any better. Of course, a hoax can be much more subtle than this, but I'm not here to tell you how to write a hoax that might fool even an expert.

Here are a few of the features that would alert the experienced hoax watcher to the unreliability of the Green Eggs and Ham alert:

- Uppercase is used throughout and the message carries clusters of exclamation marks for emphasis. This doesn't, of course, prove anything about the accuracy of the alert. Nevertheless, it's been observed many times that use of uppercase, liberal exclamation marks, and poor spelling, grammar and style characterize most of the common hoaxes. On no account, however, should you assume that an alert is accurate simply because it doesn't have these characteristics.

- The reference to McAfee and Symantec doesn't give contact or reference information. It's just there to add credibility to the hoax. There's no real indication of when it was written, either. There are hoaxes circulating the Internet right now, saying that IBM announced something "yesterday," that have been around for years. The "yesterday" is just there to give a false impression of urgency.

- It's true that some email viruses/worms arrive with a characteristic subject header. However, there are many others that don't, and it makes more sense to avoid executing *any* attachment than to try to remember which silly header goes with which virus. In fact, administrators trying to block particular viruses by filtering mail on subject alone and using inappropriate criteria are responsible for a whole subclass of indirect Denial of Service (DoS) attacks in and on themselves.

- It makes sense to be cautious about email, but just opening a message can only infect your system if you have certain mail programs (Outlook, primarily) set with incautious defaults. Most mailers don't execute code just by viewing the message. An alert that says that this will happen but doesn't specify any particular mailer, should be regarded with suspicion.

- It's implied that the malicious code works on any hardware. This is pretty suspicious. What's more, a payload that triggered as soon as you opened the message/attachment would be pretty ineffective at spreading. You might think the mouse-mat payload is a bit over the top. Actually, real hoaxes are often as ridiculous as this (although they often conceal their improbability behind technobabble).

- Of all the organizations listed, only IBM has any real expertise in viruses. The others are only listed to impress you.

- It's claimed that there is no "remedy" for the virus. Anti-virus vendors can usually supply fixes for new viruses in hours, even minutes. Of course, the effects of some viruses might be impossible to reverse, but data recovery firms can perform near-miracles sometimes.

- A virus that trashes your system as soon as you execute it is unlikely to travel very far. What is being described here sounds more like a destructive Trojan, and they don't generally spread well through email.

- The warning urges you to forward the mail to everyone you know. That makes it a chain letter. Reputable and knowledgeable organizations don't send alerts that way, although clueless ones sometimes do.

How Do Worms Work?

The 1988 Morris Worm (the Internet Worm) and its siblings, such as WANK and CHRISTMA EXEC, usually targeted heavy-duty mainframe and minicomputer hardware, mail, and operating systems. More recent threats have been aimed primarily at PCs, and, in one highly publicized incident (the AutoStart worm), Apple Macs. However, they might have the incidental effect of bringing down mail servers through the sheer weight of traffic they generate. Some of these have been variously classified by different researchers and vendors as viruses, as worms, as virus/worm hybrids, and occasionally as Trojan horses.

Today's worms and email viruses tend to be *fast burners*. They have the potential to spread globally before anti-virus vendors have time to analyze them and to distribute means of detection and disinfection. Some of the malware commonly referred to as worms are actually specialized viruses that infect only one file. This doesn't mean, of course, that a virus like Lehigh, which infects only COMMAND.COM, can sensibly be defined as a worm.

Universally accepted classifications of worms don't exist, but Carey Nachenberg, in a paper for the 1999 Virus Bulletin Conference, proposed a classification scheme along the following lines:

- Email Worms, unsurprisingly, spread via email.
- Arbitrary Protocol Worms spread via protocols not based on email (IRC/DCC, FTP, TCP/IP sockets).

As well as proposing classification by transport mechanism, Nachenberg also proposed classification by launching mechanism:

- Self-launching Worms such as the 1988 Internet Worm require no interaction with the computer user to spread: They exploit some vulnerability of the host environment, rather than in some way tricking the user into executing the infective code. However, KAK and the rather rarer BubbleBoy are examples of self-launching worms. By exploiting a bug in the Windows environment, they can execute without user intervention.

▶ For information on dealing with this problem by applying a patch, see `http://support. microsoft.com/support/kb/articles/Q262/1/65.ASP`.

- User-launched Worms interact with the user. They need to use social engineering techniques to persuade the victim to open/execute an attachment before the worm can subvert the environment so as to launch itself onto the next group of hosts. Many of today's VBScript worms fall into this or the Hybrid-launch category.

In fact, some of the worms we've seen to date are probably better classified as Hybrid-launch Worms (by Nachenberg's classification scheme) or multipartite (in terms of conventional virus terminology) because they use both self-launching and user-launched mechanisms.

Virus Characteristics

The following characteristics are not necessarily restricted to particular virus/worm classifications, but are of some importance if only because of the way the terms *stealth* and *polymorphism* are so often misused:

- **Stealth.** Almost all viruses include a degree of stealth, that is, they attempt to conceal their presence in order to maximize their chances of spreading. There have been viruses that asked permission before infecting, but this courtesy has not been rewarded by wide dissemination. Conspicuous payloads tend to be avoided, or are delivered fairly irregularly. Stealth viruses use any of a number of techniques to conceal the fact that an object has been infected. For example, when the operating system calls for certain information, the stealth virus responds with an image of the environment as it was before the virus infected it. In other words, when the infection first takes place, the virus records information necessary to later fool the operating system.

This also has implications for anti-virus tools that work by detecting that something has changed rather than by detecting and identifying known viruses. To be effective, such tools must use generic anti-stealth techniques. Of course, it isn't possible to guarantee that such techniques will work against a virus that has not yet been discovered. However, virus scanners that detect *known* viruses are at an advantage in this respect, because vendors will normally compensate for a new spoofing technique when they add detection for the virus that employs it. The trick employed by some BSIs of displaying an image of the original boot sector as if it was still where it belonged is a classic stealth technique. File viruses characteristically (but not invariably) increase the length of an infected file, and can spoof the operating system or a anti-virus scanner by subverting system calls so that the file's attributes before infection, are reported, including file length, time and datestamp, and CRC checksum.

- **Polymorphism.** Polymorphic viruses are adored by virus authors and feared by nearly everyone else. This is partly because of an over-estimation of the impact of the polymorphic threat. Non-polymorphic viruses usually infect by attaching a more-or-less identical copy of themselves to a new host object. Polymorphic viruses attach an evolved copy of themselves, so that the shape of the virus changes from one infection to another. Early polymorphic viruses used techniques such as changing the order of instructions, introducing noise bytes and dummy instructions, and varying the instructions used to perform a specific function. A more sophisticated approach is to use variable encryption, drastically reducing the amount of static (unchanging) code available to the anti-virus programmer to use to extract a pattern by which the virus can be identified. You might imagine (as many people do) that this makes polymorphism a formidable technology to counter. Indeed, the emergence of polymorphic viruses and plug-in mutation engines (enabling almost any virus author to include variable encryption in his own work without reinventing the wheel) contributed to the disappearance of some of earlier anti-virus packages. However, although polymorphic viruses are popular with virus authors demonstrating their skills, they have been less well represented in the field than in the collections of anti-virus researchers, certification laboratories, comparative testers, and others who need as complete a collection as possible. Anti-virus scanning technology has also moved on, and simple signature scanning for a fixed character string doesn't play a large part in the operation of a modern scanner.

The classifications of viral malware described earlier do not cover the entire range of objects detected by anti-virus software. Some vendors are quick to point out that what they sell is anti-virus software, not anti-malware software. Nonetheless, nowadays most commercial products detect some Trojan horses (see Chapter 18) and other objects that barely qualify as malware, let alone viruses. Such objects include intended (non-functioning) viruses, joke programs, DDoS programs (Distributed Denial of Service), even garbage files that are known to be present in poorly maintained virus collections likely to be used by product reviewers.

It might be noticeable that this chapter has been largely PC-centric. Certainly, there are more viruses that infect PC platforms (DOS and all flavors of Windows) than any other operating system. Native Macintosh viruses are far fewer. In fact, there are probably more native viruses on systems such as Atari and Amiga that have never had the same popularity (in corporate environments, at least). However, the fact that Apple Macintoshes share with Windows a degree of vulnerability to Microsoft Office macro viruses makes them the other main virus-friendly environment today.

It should not be assumed, however, that other platforms don't have virus problems. Access controls can be imposed on unprivileged accounts in UNIX (including Linux), NT, NetWare, and other platforms to restrict infection flow. However, they can't prevent unprivileged users from sharing files, if only by email. Nor can they prevent a privileged user inadvertently spreading infection. Even systems that don't support any known native viruses (servers or workstations) can carry infected objects between infectable hosts, a process sometimes known as *heterogeneous virus transmission*. It's as important to scan network file servers, Intranet, and other Web servers, regardless of their native operating system. In fact, an increasing number of products detect viruses associated with other operating environments. Thus some Mac products detect PC viruses, and vice versa.

Clearly, viruses do represent a risk on the Internet. That risk is higher for those running DOS, any variant of Windows, or certain macro-capable applications, especially the Microsoft Office applications suite. Mostly this is a matter of market share. Most virus writers target PCs and Windows because that's what they have access to. However, there are other factors that increase the risk: for example, PC hardware architecture, Microsoft's rosy view of the lack of need for security on single-user systems, and the dangers of having macro code and data in the same file. There are some tools to help keep systems safe from virus attacks listed later in this chapter. Be aware, though, that the only way to guarantee safety is by obeying Richards' Laws of Data Security—don't buy a computer, and, if you do buy one, don't turn it on. (A tip of the hat to Robert Slade for bringing that one to my attention.) Anti-virus software is mostly reactive: It responds to a perceived threat, and works most effectively against threats it can identify with precision (that is, known viruses). The best defense against unknown viruses is often to work in an environment that doesn't provide a host to particular classes of threat. Sadly, however, this is often not an option, particularly in some corporate environments where Microsoft products are considered obligatory.

Anti-Virus Utilities

Anti-virus software can generally be defined as generic, malware specific, or hybrid. Generic software commonly includes change detection software (integrity checkers), behavior monitors, and behavior blockers. It deduces the existence of a virus from a change in the environment or an infectable object (a file, for example), or from a process displaying behavior characteristic of malware. (Note that the term *malware* is increasingly used with particular reference to Trojan horses rather than viruses. Trojans are considered at length in Chapter 8, as is change-detection software.)

Malware-specific software checks infectable objects against a database of virus definitions. If a match is found, it alerts the computer user and might be able to remove the virus from the infected object. This is usually possible with boot sector and macro infectors. File viruses are sometimes harder (and sometimes impossible) to disinfect, and some vendors don't try, taking the view that it's always better to replace a binary executable than to risk disinfecting it unsuccessfully.

Scanners can be on-access (real-time or memory-resident) or on-demand. On-access scanners check files and other infectable objects as they are accessed (especially as they're opened for reading or writing), and can be implemented as a DOS TSR, Windows VxD, NT service, Macintosh System Extension, and so on. Most anti-virus packages include an on-access malware-specific component, but on-access change-detectors do exist. On-demand scanners are executed only when called by the user or by scheduling software. They do their job, then terminate.

Modern malware-specific scanners are better described as hybrid. Although they use more-or-less exact identification, most are also capable of a generic technique known as *heuristic analysis*, which is related to behavior blocking. Code is checked for characteristics that suggest a virus, either by passive analysis of the code, or by executing it under emulation, so that its behavior can be safely monitored.

Inclusion in the following list of anti-virus products doesn't necessarily constitute a recommendation. Products change, and what works for one PC, environment, or organization won't necessarily work well in another. However, these are all competent products. In general, URLs in this chapter have been modified since the previous edition of this book, so that only the relevant domain name is given. Experience indicates that actual pages move around a lot. For a comprehensive list of vendors, try `http://www.virusbtn.com/AVlinks/`.

AntiViral Toolkit Pro (AVP)

AVP has been licensed by a number of vendors, but its exact status is uncertain at the time of writing. However, this is a very popular product. Check the Kaspersky Labs site for information about Kaspersky Anti-Virus, at

`http://www.kaspersky.com/`

Kaspersky also provides a useful virus information site with virus encyclopedia at

```
http://www.viruslist.com/
```

Network Associates

The NAI range includes the current incarnations of McAfee and Dr. Solomon's for a wide range of workstation and server platforms, including PCs/Windows, Apple Macs, and UNIX (including Linux). The brand names McAfee and Dr. Solomon's are now usually applied to the same software, but the Dr. Solomon's brand is normally only used for the UK/European market. NAI's Web site is at

```
http://www.nai.com/
```

Norton Anti-Virus

Norton Anti-Virus is available for a wide range of workstation, server, and gateway platforms including DOS, Apple Macintosh, Windows 9x, and Windows NT/2000.

```
http://www.symantec.com/
```

eSafe

Eliashim, producer of eSafe and now part of the Aladdin empire, focuses primarily on gateway protection from viruses and other malicious software. Contact them at

```
http://www.eliashim.com/
```

PC-Cillin

PC-Cillin by Trend Micro can be found along with their InterScan gateway products at

```
http://www.antivirus.com/
```

Sophos Anti-Virus

Sophos is very focused on the corporate market. Products are available for a wide range of workstation, server, and gateway platforms, including PCs/Windows, Apple Macs, and UNIX (including Linux). Learn more at

```
http://www.sophos.com/
```

Norman Virus Control

Norman Virus Control (NVC) by Norman Data Defense Systems can be found online at

```
http://www.norman.com/
```

17

VIRUSES AND
WORMS

F-PROT Anti-Virus

A number of products have been based on the F-Prot detection engine. The original product (which is free for personal use) can be found at

`http://www.complex.is`

The product formerly sold by DataFellows as F-Prot Professional is now known as F-Secure, and is available at

`http://www.f-secure.com`

The Command Software version of F-Prot Professional is at

`http://www.commandcom.com/`

Integrity Master

Integrity Master, by Stiller Research, combines an advanced change detector with conventional known-virus scanning. The Stiller Web site is a good source of general information (hoax information, for example) and is located at

`http://www.stiller.com/stiller.htm`

There are hundreds of virus scanners and utilities. We have listed some previously because they have a good reputation, are easily available on the Internet, and are updated frequently. Viruses are found each day, all over the world. Most of them are unlikely ever to be seen In-the-Wild, but sometimes a formerly quiet virus will suddenly "get lucky" and go feral. New worms and other email-borne viruses like Melissa or LoveLetter can go from unknown to global within hours. Strange to think that only a few years ago, it was still normal for anti-virus software to be updated on a quarterly basis.

The second edition of this book included links to sources of freeware and shareware anti-virus utilities. These links have been removed. They haven't been replaced with more up-to-date links, as it would be doing the reader a disservice to imply that such utilities are still a realistic substitute for commercial software. This applies even for older machines, many of which are still supported by some vendors. In anti-virus as in real life, you generally get what you pay for, or sometimes less.

Future Trends in Viral Malware

Virus and anti-virus technologies continue to increase in complexity and sophistication. The likelihood of contracting a virus on the Internet increases as 'fast burner' virus dissemination techniques evolve, and the number of potential hosts increases with the expansion of the Internet itself. It depends on where you go. If you frequent the back alleys of the Internet, you should exercise caution in downloading any file (digitally signed or otherwise). Usenet newsgroups are places where viruses might be found, especially in those newsgroups where hot or restricted material is trafficked. Examples of such material include *warez* (pirated software) or pornography. Similarly, newsgroups that traffic in cracking utilities are suspect. However, the nature of the virus threat means that you are far likelier to receive an infection from someone you know, someone with no malicious intention, than from a known or anonymous virus author/distributor. We therefore recommend that you look through the guidelines to practicing "safe hex" for computer users and administrators summarized in the final section of this chapter.

Virus technology has been through a number of phases. The first big wave was the PC boot sector infector, mostly overshadowing even the parasitic fast-infector and the "big-iron" infecting worms. The second wave was largely the rise of the macro virus. Among these, the first email-aware macro viruses foreshadowed the coming of the next wave: Melissa, LoveLetter, and the macro and VBScript worms that dominate the scene at the time of writing. Many examples of the current wave of email viruses/worms are less sophisticated than the more complex, "traditional" viruses, relying to some extent on social engineering (psychological manipulation) as much as technical complexity. However, some recent examples (Hybris, MTX) combine technical complexity with social engineering.

It's been suggested that upcoming operating systems will be so secure that viruses will cease to be a problem. However, experience indicates that as particular loopholes are patched, others are found and exploited. Expect the unexpected.

Publications and Sites

The following is a list of articles, books, and Web pages related to the subject of computer viruses. Some are only included or alluded to because they were in the previous edition. Some outdated links and unobtainable references have been removed, and several have been added. (We don't guarantee that those listed are still available—in fact, you might have trouble getting hold of any but the most recent.) Inclusion of a resource in this section doesn't necessarily constitute recommendation (as the comments make clear). However, it's important to know and recognize the more prominent but poor resources, as well as the good ones.

Bigelow's Virus Troubleshooting Pocket Reference. Ken Dunham. McGraw-Hill. 2000. ISBN: 0-072-12627-2. Well-meaning but not very accurate, and sometimes misleading.

Robert Slade's Guide to Computer Viruses: How to Avoid Them, How to Get Rid of Them, and How to Get Help (Second Edition). Springer. 1996. ISBN: 0-387-94663-2. Four years is a long time in computing, but time has been kinder to Slade's book than most books on the subject. This was, until recently, easily the best introductory text on the subject.

Virus: Detection and Elimination. Rune Skardhamar. *AP Professional*. 1996. ISBN: 0-12-647690-X. Seriously inaccurate in places and contains (not very good) virus code. The poor man's Mark Ludwig…

The Giant Black Book of Computer Viruses. Mark A. Ludwig. *American Eagle*. 1995. ISBN 0-92940807-1. Ludwig is, or was, a virus writer. His books have far more to do with writing viruses than with protecting against them. Seriously outdated, too.

CIAC/US Department of Energy. This Web site has a database of virus information that was recommended in an earlier edition of this book (`http://ciac.llnl.gov/ciac/CIACVirusDatabase.html`). The database is no longer being updated, but is worth checking for information on older viruses. CIAC/DOE have done sterling work in recent years on publicizing the problems associated with virus hoaxes and other chain letters. The relevant pages continue to be maintained and expanded. `http://HoaxBusters.ciac.org/`

Computers Under Attack: Intruders, Worms and Viruses. Ed. Peter J. Denning. ACM Press 1990. ISBN 0-201-53067-8. Despite its age, this book is worth looking for. It contains some seminal papers.

Computer Viruses and Anti-Virus Warfare, Second Edition. Jan Hruska, Ellis Horwood. 1992. ISBN 0-13-036377-4. This book predates macro viruses, VBS and JS worms, Trojans, and so on, but is worth reading on earlier technologies, especially anti-virus tools.

Computer Virus Prevalence Survey. ICSA (formerly the National Computer Association) publishes a yearly survey of virus prevalence, has certification schemes for anti-virus and other security software, papers, discussion groups, and so on. `http://www.icsa.net/`

The Computer Virus Crisis (Second Edition). Fites, Johnson, and Kratz. Van Nostrand Reinhold Computer Publishing. 1992. ISBN: 0-442-00649-7. Not altogether accurate even at the time of publishing, and now seriously outdated.

PC Security and Virus Protection: The Ongoing War Against Information Sabotage. Pamela Kane. M&T Books. 1994. ISBN: 1-55851-390-6.In some aspects, outdated (and totally MS-DOS oriented) but includes some very useful material.

A Short Course on Computer Viruses (Second Edition). Frederick B. Cohen. Series title: Wiley Professional Computing. John Wiley & Sons. 1994. ISBN: 1-471-00769-2. Solid material from the man whose early research contributed massively to defining the virus/anti-virus field.

A Pathology of Computer Viruses. David Ferbrache. Springer-Verlag. 1992. ISBN: 0-387-19610-2; 3-540-19610-2. Obviously, this book predates recent developments and current pre-occupations, but is still a good basis for serious research.

The Virus Creation Labs: A Journey into the Underground. George Smith. American Eagle Publications. ISBN 0-929408-09-8. Smith's writings have long served as a very effective antidote to some of the self-righteous pomposity found in some corners of the security establishment. His book is an interesting, journalistic, alternative view across the virus/anti-virus divide.

European Institute for Computer Anti-Virus Research. Despite its name, EICAR is not exclusively focused on viruses, and its members include representatives of academia and business. Not all of them are European, either. http://www.eicar.org/

Future Trends in Virus Writing. Vesselin Bontchev. Virus Test Center. University of Hamburg. Crystal-ball gazing is a mug's game, and even the redoubtable Dr. Bontchev didn't get every predictive detail right. However, as a thumbnail guide to virus issues from a major authority in the field, this merits close attention. http://www.virusbtn.com/OtherPapers/Trends/

SherpaSoft Web page. FAQs including the VIRUS-L FAQ, the alt.comp.virus FAQ, the *Viruses and the Macintosh* FAQ, an email abuse FAQ, other papers, resources, and links. http://www.sherpasoft.org.uk

Network Associates. Requests for the Dr. Solomon's Virus Encyclopaedia cited in the previous edition are redirected to the NAI equivalent at http://vil.nai.com/vil/default.asp.

Survivor's Guide to Computer Viruses. Ed. Victoria Lammer. Virus Bulletin Ltd. 1993. ISBN 0-9522114-0-8. This book was intended as a supplement to the magazine, and includes some reprinted material. Contains some solid material on older viruses that are still in circulation.

A Guide to the Selection of Anti-Virus Tools and Techniques. W. T. Polk and L. E. Bassham. National Institute of Standards and Technology Computer Security Division. Friday, Mar 11; 21:26:41 EST 1994. Not a very useful guide to current anti-virus software evaluation, but a fair summary of the basic technology. http://csrc.ncsl.nist.gov/nistpubs/select/

Mac Virus. Susan Lesch's anti-virus resource for Macintosh users, now maintained by David Harley and containing his *Viruses and the Macintosh* FAQ, plus the definitive paper *Macs and Macros: the State of the Macintosh Nation.* http://www.macvirus.com/, http://www.macvirus.org.uk

Managing Malware: Mapping Technology to Function. David Harley. Conference Proceedings, EICAR 1999. A comprehensive primer on malware management in corporate environments. http://www.sherpasoft.org.uk/papers/eicar99.PDF

Virus Proof: The Ultimate Guide to Protecting Your PC. Phil Schmauder. Prima Tech. 2000. ISBN 0-7615-2747-8. Lazily written, incompetent, misleading, and virtually useless. Avoid.

Virus Bulletin. The only monthly magazine I know of entirely devoted to virus management. http://www.virusbtn.com/

17

VIRUSES AND WORMS

Viruses Revealed: Understanding and Countering Malicious Software. David Harley, Robert Slade, and Urs Gattiker. Osborne. ISBN-0-17-213090-3. (For publication, 3rd quarter 2001.) It's hardly appropriate for me to advertise my own book here. However, this one is almost unique among recent books on the subject, in that it's actually written by acknowledged experts in the field. Covers a wide range of issues (technology, history, corporate protection, social issues, ethics). Check the Web site at `http://www.viruses-revealed.org.uk`.

The Enterprise Anti-Virus Book. Robert Vibert. Segura Solutions Inc. ISBN-0-9687464-0-3. This is the other recent book on the subject written by an expert in the field. The author is a seasoned professional with years of experience in the design and implementation of enterprise anti-virus solutions, and his book focuses on these aspects. Not the book with all the answers, but something arguably more important: the book with just about all the questions. `http://www.segurasolutions.com/book.htm`.

Vmyths.com (formerly the Computer Virus Myths page at `www.kumite.com`). Robert Rosenberger's essential resource for hoax hunters and other professional skeptics—highly recommended. `http://www.vmyths.com/`

WildList Organization International. The authoritative source of information on which viruses are known to be in the wild. An essential resource for anti-virus software certification authorities, researchers, and so on. `http://www.wildlist.org/`

Most anti-virus vendors have virus information databases and other resources, as well as information specific to their products. The following sites are generally dependable (but none are infallible). Precise URLs aren't given, as such pages move about a lot.

`http://www.sophos.com/`

`http://www.nai.com/`

`http://www.symantec.com/`

`http://www.f-secure.com/`

`http://www.viruslist.com/`

Summary

This chapter can only give you an overview of the virus problem. If you have the misfortune to be a systems or network administrator responsible for protecting your customers from malicious software, you will need to do some serious research into virus and anti-virus technology, and I recommend that you take advantage of the information resources listed in this chapter. If you're an administrator or manager, you certainly can't afford to rely on vendor sales executives or consultants to make all the decisions for you. More often than not, these people are better acquainted with the interface of their product range than with its real-world application to real-world virus management problems.

For your delectation, we offer some guidelines that should make your computing life safer.

- Check all warnings and alerts with your IT department. If you are a manager or administrator, make sure that there is a known policy by which only authorized personnel can pass on alerts. This cuts down on panic, curbs dissemination of hoaxes and other misinformation, and reduces the risk of inappropriate action that might be worse than no action.

- Don't trust attachments. The sender might have no malicious intent, but he might not be keeping his anti-virus software up-to-date either.

- Remember that worm victims don't usually know that they've sent you an infected attachment. There is no such thing as a trusted account. If someone sends you an attachment, especially if there's no obvious reason they should, confirm with them that they did so knowingly.

- Use anti-virus software and keep it updated. However, don't assume that using the latest updates makes you invulnerable.

- If your environment allows it, disable the Windows Scripting Host. For a good summary of the process, across platforms, see `http://www.sophos.com/support/faqs/wsh.html`.

- If you use macro-virus-friendly applications like Word, ensure that macros are not enabled by default. Recent versions of Office allow macros in a document to be disabled as a default option. If you receive a document with macros from a trusted source, ask for verification. But don't trust this option absolutely.

- Disable default booting from diskette in CMOS.(This blocks infection from pure boot sector viruses.)

- Keep your browser, mail client, macro-friendly applications, and other vulnerable applications up-to-date with the latest patches.

- Back up, back up, back up.

17

VIRUSES AND WORMS

Trojans

"For they still prefer sheep to thinking men
Ah, but men who think like sheep are even better"

—Brian McNeill, *"No Gods and Precious Few Heroes"*

"Beware of geeks bearing gifts"

—Anonymous

IN THIS CHAPTER

This chapter examines a type of threat to system and Internet security that has been with us almost as long as the computer: Trojan horses, often simply referred to as Trojans.

What Is a Trojan?

Trojan horses present more difficulties in definition than at first appears. Whereas viruses are defined primarily by their ability to replicate, Trojans are primarily defined by their payload, or, to use a less emotive term, their function. Replication is an absolute value. Either a program replicates, or it doesn't. Damage and intent, however, are not absolutes, at least in terms of program function. The first clue to their nature lies in ancient history and classical mythology.

Origin of the Species

Around the 12th century B.C., Greece declared war on the city of Troy. The dispute arose when Paris, variously described as a shepherd boy and as prince of Troy, abducted Helen, the wife of Menelaus, king of Sparta, and reputed to be the most beautiful woman in the world. The Greeks gave chase and engaged Troy in a 10-year war, but failed to take the city. This, of course, is the central plot of Homer's *Iliad*.

Finally, the Greek army withdrew, leaving behind a huge wooden horse. Greece's finest soldiers hid silently inside. The people of Troy saw the horse and, thinking with stunning naivete that it was a gift, brought it inside their city. That night, Greek soldiers under the leadership of Odysseus emerged from the horse, and opened the gates to the rest of the Greek army, who destroyed the city. It has been suggested that the Trojan horse story is the origin of the saying "Beware of Greeks bearing gifts."

In computing terms, the term *Trojan horse* is most often applied to an apparently attractive program concealing in some way an unpleasant surprise.

Definitions

One well-known definition is included in the (now obsolete) RFC 1244, the first draft of the *Site Security Handbook* (the more recent draft doesn't include a definition):

> A Trojan horse program can be a program that does something useful, or merely something interesting. It always does something unexpected, like steal passwords or copy files without your knowledge.

This definition contains three useful ideas—not that they give us the best possible summary, but they serve as a good starting point for discussion of some implicit ambiguities. First, the definition doesn't say that the Trojan *always* does something useful or interesting, but that it *might*. This generality opens a wide range of possibilities, from programs whose only function is to do something malicious; through programs that do something desirable *and* something malicious but covert; to *accidental Trojans*, which are intended to do desirable things, but somehow do something undesirable as well (or instead).

Second, this definition includes the idea that a Trojan does something "unexpected" (unexpected to the recipient, or "victim", but not usually to the programmer). This assumption is common to nearly all definitions of Trojans.

Third, it contains the implication that the "payload" is something malicious. In fact, it's quite specific (intentionally or otherwise) about the fact that the cited example payloads (stealing passwords or copying files) involve unauthorized access rather than a breach of data integrity. For our purposes, this is less useful. It is overly specific about the type of security breach it appears to address (breach of privacy), and carries an assumption of malicious intent that is not universally accepted.

Most security professionals would accept a general definition along the lines of "A Trojan is a program that claims to perform some desirable or necessary function, and might even do so, but also performs some function or functions that the individual who runs the program would not expect and would not want."

I Didn't Mean It

Like many definitions, this one misses out on the idea of malicious intent. It therefore begs a number of questions about Easter Eggs (harmless code concealed more or less legitimately in production software by the original production team). Joke programs, installation routines that pass back information to the manufacturer and overwrite previous versions of system files, and accidental Trojans also present difficulties. However, as far as this chapter is concerned, these ambiguities are no bad thing. This chapter will refer (not necessarily in depth) to a whole range of relevant issues, rather than ignore everything that doesn't conform to a strict single definition.

A common modern usage distinguishes Trojans (and related *malware*, or MALicious softWARE) from viruses and worms, based on the Trojans' inability to self-replicate. In fact, Ian Whalley, in an article for Virus Bulletin (*Talking Trojan*. Virus Bulletin, July 1998) has suggested using the term *non-replicative malware* rather than Trojan horse, thus avoiding the popular confusion between replicating programs (viruses, worms) and static code (Trojans, for instance). This certainly has advantages, but reintroduces the assumption of malicious intent (by using the word *malware*). Clearly, while we may prefer not to admit to malicious intent as a defining characteristic, we can't avoid considering it as a possible or even likely characteristic.

Apart from the intent to deceive implicit in many Trojan definitions, malicious intent can cover a wide range of intentions and mechanisms.

Using the classic tripod model of data security, Trojans can be divided into three broad classes of intent:

- Intent to gain unauthorized access
- Intent to obstruct availability (deny service)
- Intent to modify or destroy data and systems without authorization

By extension of this idea, we can also postulate three further classes of accidental Trojan that allow unauthorized access, obstruct availability, or compromise integrity, but are not *intended* to do so.

A problem here is that, whereas automated examination and analysis of the binary content of a program can tell us a great deal about function, it can tell us little about the intent of the author.

Dr. Alan Solomon gave a definition in *All About Viruses* that neatly illustrates the problem from the other end:

> Suppose I wrote a program that could infallibly detect whether another program formatted the hard disk. Then, can it say that this program is a trojan? Obviously not if the other program was supposed to format the hard disk (like Format does, for example), then it is not a trojan. But if the user was not expecting the format, then it is a trojan. The problem is to compare what the program does with the user's expectations. You cannot determine the user's expectations for a program.

Solomon's scenario is useful because it shifts the focus away from the programmer's or distributor's intent and onto the recipient/user's expectations. Implicitly, it also indicates that social engineering is a major component of a Trojan horse because it manipulates the victim's expectations. The passage also restates a problem that we will need to consider in more detail. It is (sometimes) possible to analyze a virus automatically because the defining characteristic of viral code is replication. It is at least theoretically possible to deduce the ability to replicate by automatic or semi-automatic code analysis. (This is one of the ways in which heuristic virus scanners are meant to operate.) It is much more difficult, however, to deduce either the intentions of the programmer or the expectations of the program user by tracing what the code does.

Viruses and worms are sometimes referred to as a special case of Trojan horse. The argument is that, because the legitimate program now contains embedded malicious code, it has been *Trojanized* (or, less commonly, *Trojaned*). This is a defensible position, although it doesn't distinguish between a program written to be malicious and an "innocent" program hijacked by a malicious code. However, the main reason for disregarding this argument is that it compounds the popular confusion between Trojans and viruses.

All malicious programs are popularly described as viruses, irrespective of their replicative properties or the lack thereof. In fact, some programs and coding problems that aren't even malicious are also described as viruses (the so-called Millennium virus, for instance). The situation isn't helped by the fact that hoaxes almost invariably describe mythical "viruses" that would be more properly described as Trojans, if they were capable of existing at all. Even worse, anti-virus vendors, although fully aware of the distinction between replicative and non-replicative malware, continue to display nonsensical alert messages such as "Virus Trojan/W32/xxx detected in file xyz.exe ". For a scanner to alert not only on Trojans but also on other non-viruses such as joke programs, garbage files, and intended viruses (attempted viruses that can't replicate), is misleading and might inspire panic quite inappropriately.

Trojan Classifications

Trojan horses are usually regarded as representing either an attack on privacy (password stealing, for instance, leading to unauthorized access and possibly modification), or on integrity (destructive Trojans). This is a little over-simplified. After all, unauthorized modification is an attack on integrity. A privacy-invasive program often destroys files so as to cover its tracks, and an attacker might want to gain access for specifically destructive purposes. Furthermore, this approach presupposes malicious intent, which, as we've seen, isn't universally accepted as a defining characteristic. Consequently, some types are included here that are often not considered in this context.

The sort of payload you expect a Trojan horse (technically, I suppose it was a Greek horse) to carry might reflect your computing orientation. For many years, mainframe and minicomputer users tended to think in terms of programs that stole passwords or otherwise breached privacy, whereas microcomputer users tended to think in terms of destructive Trojans which formatted disks or trashed file systems. In real life, both destructive and privacy-invasive Trojans have been known at both ends of the Big Iron/PC spectrum for many years. However, recent years have seen more cross-fertilization.

Destructive Trojans

Trojans whose main purpose is destructive have long plagued microcomputer owners. The Dirty Dozen list, first published via FidoNet in the mid-1980s, originally focused on such programs, and at one time the list defined a Trojan in terms of purposeful damage. Of course, the list quickly outgrew the original dozen Trojans and went through a number of changes through the 1980s and 1990s. It might still be possible to find it on some Simtel mirror servers in the DOS/virus directory hierarchy, but it is really only of historical interest. Old Trojans of the type generally listed in DIRTYD*.ZIP are almost invariably short-lived.

Malicious, non-replicating programs have also been widely reported on Macintosh computers, including destructive Trojans. Virus Info purported to contain virus information but actually trashed disks. (It should not be confused with the informational [but obsolescent] HyperCard stack Virus Reference.) A PostScript hack that could effectively render certain Apple printers unusable by attacking firmware also excited much interest at one time. NVP modified the System file so that no vowels could be typed, and was originally found masquerading as New Look, which redesigned the display. More recently, destructive and privacy-invasive, compiled AppleScript Trojans have been noted. For more information, see http://www.sherpasoft.org.uk/MacSupporters/macvir.html.

However, the social impact of such Trojans is often disproportional to their impact in terms of actual incidents. Since they don't self-replicate, unlike viruses and worms, they are less likely to be spread by innocent third parties. They tend to be crudely programmed. Simple batch files using DEL, DELTREE, or FORMAT are still common, sometimes compiled into an .EXE or .COM file using a batch-file compiler such as BAT2COM. This makes them harder to identify. Trojans are usually *direct action*, that is, as soon as a Trojan is executed, it does all its damage at once This militates against their being spread by previous victims. There are, however, resident Trojans that install themselves so that they are run during every computing session. Often, these are associated with activities such as password stealing. However, any Trojan whose payload is not immediately and overtly malicious maximizes its own chances of being passed on.

The PKZip "Trojan virus" is described in the alt.comp.virus FAQ (which I have my own permission to quote and to correct slightly, since the FAQ is slightly out-of-date in the relevant section). I've included most of the section, since it makes an interesting case history.

> The threat described in recent warnings is definitely not a virus, since it doesn't replicate by infection.
>
> There have been at least two attempts to pass off Trojans as an upgrade to PKZip, the widely used file compression utility. A recent example was the files PKZ300.EXE and PKZ300B.ZIP made available for downloading on certain Internet sites.
>
> An earlier Trojan passed itself off as version 2.0. For this reason, PKWare have never released a version 2.0 of PKZip: presumably, if they ever do release another DOS version (unlikely, at this date, in my opinion), it will not be numbered version 3.0(0). [In fact, the latest version is 2.50 at time of writing.]
>
> In fact, there are hardly any known cases of someone downloading and being hit by this Trojan, which few people have seen (though most reputable virus scanners will detect it). As far as I know, this Trojan was only ever seen on warez servers (specializing in pirated software).
>
> There are recorded instances of a fake PKZIP vs. 3 found infected with a real live in-the-wild file virus, but this too is very rare. To the best of my knowledge, the latest version of PKZip is 2.04g [now 2.50], or 2.50 for Windows [now 2.60/2.70].
>
> There was a version 2.06 put together specifically for IBM internal use only (confirmed by PKWare). If you find it in circulation, avoid it. It's either illicit or a potentially damaging fake.

The recent rash of resuscitated warnings about this is at least in part a hoax. It's not a virus, it's a trojan. It doesn't (and couldn't) damage modems, V32 or otherwise, though I suppose a virus or trojan might alter the settings of a modem—if it happened to be on and connected....

It appears to delete files, not destroy disks irrevocably.

It's certainly a good idea to avoid files claiming to be PKZip vs. 3, but the real risk hardly justifies the bandwidth this alert has occupied.

Why is it an interesting case history? For one thing, the subject of the attack is a typical target for a destructive Trojan that passes itself off as something it isn't. PKZip is a popular and very useful shareware utility. Recently, it has been rather overshadowed by other utilities using the same compression format, which might explain why PKZip is a less attractive target for Trojanization nowadays. In the following, we allude to a similar utility for the Mac whose identity was also purloined to lure incautious victims into running an imposter program.

Second, it was a counterfeit program that made no effort to assume the appearance or functionality of the program whose identity it claimed. This is characteristic of direct action, destructive Trojans, but not a defining characteristic.

Third and most interestingly, a program that very few people ever saw became a major nuisance because of the number of people who received and passed on a "semi-hoaxified" warning about the Trojan. In fact, the impact of the chain letter was more serious than the Trojan itself was ever likely to be. (This is a not uncommon side effect of direct action Trojans, but it rarely displays such spectacular impact.)

By *semi-hoax*, we refer to a misleading alert based on a real virus or Trojan, but into which enough misinformation has been introduced to render it too inaccurate to be useful. We should probably distinguish here between a number of possibilities:

- An alert based on real malicious software, but too imprecise to be useful. (Many virus alerts passed on by non-experts fall into this category.)

- An alert based on real malicious software, but rendered less useful by misinformation based on imperfect understanding of the relevant technology. Even knowledgeable individuals can inadvertently introduce such an inaccuracy into an alert.

- An alert based on real, malicious software, but invalidated by the introduction of deliberately misleading material, exaggeration, or complete fabrication of attributes and potential for damage.

Isn't a warning either a hoax or not a hoax? I think not. The intent to hoax (or the lack of it) might be absolute, but the mixture of fact and fiction is commonplace in hoaxes, where fact lends circumstantial support to an essentially fictional assertion.

18

TROJANS

In late 1997, a bogus version of StuffIt Deluxe was distributed. (StuffIt is a another popular archiving tool used primarily on Macs.) During installation, the program would delete key system files. Aladdin systems, makers of StuffIt, issued widespread advisories about the Trojan at the time.

Malicious Trojans have also been known to masquerade as anti-virus software.

A very well known Trojan that combined sabotage and extortion was the PC CYBORG Trojan horse, or AIDS Trojan. In 1989, some 10,000 copies of an AIDS information diskette were distributed in Europe, Africa, Scandinavia, and Australia, many to medical establishments. After the program was installed and run, a hidden program encrypted the hard disk after a set number of reboots. The idea was that the victim would have to send a "license fee" to PC Cyborg's Panamanian address to get the decryption key. Fortunately, a virus researcher in the UK cracked the encryption.

▶ You can find the CIAC bulletin Information About the PC CYBORG (AIDS) Trojan Horse at `http://www.ciac.org/ciac/bulletins/a-10.shtml`.

Privacy-Invasive Trojans

Privacy-invasive Trojans generally perform some function that reveals to the programmer vital and privileged information about a system or otherwise compromises that system. Passwords are, for obvious reasons, a very common target.

They can also (or instead) conceal some function that either reveals to the programmer vital and privileged information about a system or compromises that system.

Some anti-virus companies have differentiated between PC-specific privacy-invasive Trojans and destructive Trojans by restricting the use of the term *Trojan* to destructive programs. They use the term *password stealers* for the most common privacy-invasive programs. In the latter half of the 1990s, password-stealing programs aimed specifically at AOL users seemed to become very common (some estimates at the number of such programs rose to many hundreds). Some anti-virus software uses an *APS* identifier for such programs, probably standing for AOL Password Stealer. However, AOL is not and never was the only vulnerable service. In their paper *Where There's Smoke, There's Mirrors,* Sarah Gordon and David Chess describe running user simulations on AOL over a seven-month period. While attempts were made to gain their dummy users' screen passwords, these attempts generally used direct social engineering techniques by correspondents masquerading as AOL staff, rather than indirectly with password stealing programs.

Back Door Trojans

Trojans have, from time to time, been planted in legitimate applications. Ken Thompson describes in *Reflections on Trusting Trust* a number of interesting (not entirely hypothetical) scenarios, the most famous being the Trojanized compiler scenario. In this case, production software offers the means of privileged access to anyone knowing of the back door or trapdoor described.

Back doors and trapdoors offering unauthorized access (and maybe modification) are not the only instances of unauthorized code introduced into legitimate programs, however. Many Mac owners who bought a certain brand of third-party keyboard with a Trojan hardcoded into ROM chip found that the text "Welcome Datacomp" was inserted into their documents at apparently random intervals. PC motherboards with a Trojanized BIOS were characterized by "Happy Birthday" played through the system loudspeaker at boot-up, apparently on the programmer's birthday.

Remote Access Tools (RATs)

Though few anti-virus vendors would claim to detect all known Trojans, most do detect at least some on the platforms for which they have products, especially those Trojans that do direct damage. Remote Access Tools (RATs) such as Netbus and Back Orifice, however, straddle a line between legitimate systems administration (similar to that carried out by programs such as PC Anywhere) and covert unauthorized access. When the system owner is persuaded to run the installation program, a server program is installed that can be accessed from a client program on a remote machine without the knowledge of the user. The server is used to manipulate the victim machine.

Functionally, there might be no difference between a RAT and a "legitimate" tool. The difference lies not in the functionality, but in the facilitation of the covert availability of that functionality to unauthorized individuals. As with sniffers and network scanners, it's not what the program does so much as the reason it's being used. Yet if RAT software is willingly installed, opening the system to an attack the user does not expect, does that make it a Trojan? Using Microsoft Word also makes the user vulnerable to attacks he might not have anticipated. It was, for instance, literally years before some computer users realized that using versions of Word and other Microsoft Office applications supporting macro languages made them vulnerable to macro viruses and Trojans. Does that make Bill Gates a Trojan author? No, because the functionality in this case is too generalized to be described as a back door. However, a RAT broadcasting its presence to a hacker, who probes a characteristic range of port numbers, can certainly be described as a back door Trojan. It promotes the intentions of the author and subverts the expectations of the victim.

This is a serious issue—not least in that the "Bad Guys" frequently allude to the shortcomings of legitimate software (especially Microsoft's) as if unforeseen bugs in Office justified their own premeditated activities.

Nonetheless, some RAT authors have exploited this ambivalence by producing "Professional" versions of such software and charging for them. This allows the authors to complain of the

18

TROJANS

anti-capitalist, anti-competitive behavior of security vendors who detect their program as a Trojan (or, all too often and inaccurately, a virus). It works, too. Several anti-virus vendors have dropped detection of the Professional version of Netbus, despite the murkiness of its antecedents and its continuing potential for misuse. Others have gone out of their way to distinguish between standard Netbus Pro installations and Trojanized installations.

Droppers

A *dropper* is a program that is not itself a virus, but is intended to install a virus. Curiously, given the popular association of Trojans and viruses, droppers are a comparatively rare entry point for viruses in the wild (see the preceding chapter on viruses). In the PC world, dropper programs are most commonly associated with transporting boot sector viruses across networks, and can be used for that purpose by both pro- and anti-virus researchers. They can be used as a covert means of introducing a virus onto a system, if the victim can be persuaded by social engineering techniques to run the dropper program.

Droppers have been used surprisingly frequently in the Mac world, though. The MacMag virus was introduced via a HyperCard stack called New Apple Products. The Tetracycle game was implicated in the original spread of MBDF. ExtensionConflict is supposed to identify conflicts between extensions (now there's a surprise), but installs the SevenDust virus. Both SevenDust and MBDF are still being reported in the field. Back in the PC world, the Red Team alert muddied the waters by attaching a virus dropper alleged to be a fix for a virus that didn't and couldn't possibly exist.

Jokes

Joke programs are almost as old as computing. One venerable example is the PDP Cookie program, which popped up and asked the victim for a cookie. PC and Mac users have both long been delighted or irritated by such programs. Confusion has arisen due to the habit of anti-virus software of alerting (using the word *virus*) not only on viruses and Trojans, but on joke programs such as CokeGift. This widely distributed program offers the victim their CD tray as a holder for their fizzy drink (or possibly white powder for nasal ingestion or carboniferous fossil fuel). Cute for some, irritating for others, but not exactly life-threatening. However, the practice of alerting on joke programs might have arisen in response to supposed joke programs that threaten to format disks, or claim to have done so, but make no such actual attempt. Indeed, there have been instances when, what one vendor has reported as a Trojan, another vendor reported as a joke.

Bombs

Logic bombs are malicious programs that execute their payload when a preprogrammed condition is met. When the trigger condition is a time or date, the term *time bomb* may be used. A *time-out* is a logic bomb sometimes used to enforce contract terms. Characteristically, the program stops running unless some action is taken to indicate (for instance) that the license fee has been paid, or the contractor who wrote the code has been paid. It's not unknown for a contractor to introduce some more drastic time bomb to be triggered if a dispute over payment arises.

The use of the word *bomb* does suggest a destructive payload, but this need not, in fact, be the case. *Mail bombs* and *subscription bombs*, which don't really belong in a chapter on Trojans, are DoS (Denial-of-Service) attacks intended to inconvenience the victim by battering his or her mailbox with a barrage of mail. Often this is done by subscribing the victim to large numbers of mailing lists. Email Trojans certainly exist, although email is more commonly an infection vector for viruses and worms.

The term *ANSI bomb* usually refers to a mail message or other text file that takes advantage of an enhancement to the MS-DOS ANSI.SYS driver. This allows keys to be redefined with an escape sequence, in this case, to echo some potentially destructive command to the console. Such programs were at one time quite frequently reported on Fidonet. However, nowadays few systems run programs that require ANSI terminal emulation, and ANSI.SYS is not normally installed in Windows 9x or later.

There are alternatives to ANSI.SYS that don't support keyboard redefinition, or allow it to be turned off.

Rootkits

A *rootkit* is an example of a set of trojanized system programs that an intruder who manages to root-compromise a system might be able to substitute for the commands' standard equivalents. Examples include modified versions of system utilities such as top and ps, allowing illegitimate processes to run unnoticed; daemons modified to compromise log entries or hide connections; utilities gimmicked to enable escalation to root privileges or to hide rootkit component files or other backdoor functionality (secret passwords to allow privileged access, for instance). Associated programs include packet sniffers and utmp/wtmp editors (used to doctor log files).

Rootkits exist for a number of flavors of UNIX, and are appearing in NT versions. However, one-off Trojanized versions of login (that is, versions not included in a suite of programs such as a rootkit) have been used, for instance, to harvest passwords since Pontius programmed in PILOT.

▶ You can find information on rootkits in the FAQ at `http://staff.washington.edu/dittrich/misc/faqs/lrk4.faq`.

Sarah Gordon's paper Publication of Vulnerabilities and Tool (Proceedings of the Twelfth World Conference on Computer Security, Audit and Control, 1995) includes a technical analysis of some rootkit components.

18

TROJANS

DDoS Agents

DDoS (Distributed Denial-of-Service) tools like Stacheldraht, TFN2K, and Trinoo are Trojans designed with a very specific purpose. They are intended to bring down Internet servers by remotely coordinating packet-flooding attacks from multiple machines. Typically, the intruder controls a number of master machines. These, in turn, control daemons on remote machines. Covertly installed, their presence is often concealed by the installation of rootkits. Daemons can be installed on many hundreds of remote machines, all directing flooding attacks at the victim system.

Detailed analysis of DDoS attacks and counter-attacks is beyond the scope of this chapter. However, the installation and presence of a DDoS attack tool can be detected by the same means as other malware. That is, recognition of a specific search string (Known Something Detection), heuristic scanning, and change detection. Virus scanners usually detect known DDoS tools. Network traffic can be monitored for characteristics such as IP packets with spoofed source addresses. Intrusion detection systems can be configured to scan for patterns characteristic of communications between master software and daemon software. A number of papers are available discussing these issues at greater length:

```
http://staff,washington.edu/dittrich/misc/stacheldraht.analysis

http://staff,washington.edu/dittrich/misc/trinoo.analysis

http://staff,washington.edu/dittrich/misc/tfn.analysis

http://www.cert.org/incident_notes/IN-99-04.html
```

Worms

In principle, this should probably be the longest subsection in this chapter. Many system administrators now apply the term Trojan to what the author of Chapter 17, "Viruses and Worms," described as worms. While I regard this usage as misleading, it is defensible, common, and can't be ignored.

It's defensible because, as discussed in Chapter 17, most present-day worms are reliant on social engineering to persuade the recipient to execute the malicious code. In other words, they conform to one of the definitions we've previously examined suggesting that Trojans are programs that purport to do one (desirable) thing while actually doing some other (less desirable) thing.

The usage is misleading because it defies the definition of Trojans as non-replicative malware. In the virus business, most people hold the view that viruses and worms replicate. Some believe that the class worm is a subset of the class virus, and many regard Trojans as non-replicative. These distinctions are not just academic. To fight malicious code effectively, we need to understand how it works, and distinctions are particularly important when we come to examine a multipartite threats such as MTX or LoveLetter. Modern mail-borne malware might include components which can be described as parasitic (a file virus), a worm (a network virus that doesn't infect other files by direct attachment), and/or a classic Trojan.

The theoretical basis of computer virology might be a little shaky as we consider the impact of such recent developments. However, there is plenty of information on such programs on Web sites maintained by anti-virus companies, such as those listed in Chapter 17.

Where Do Trojans Come From?

Usenet is a common source of Trojans (and viruses), especially newsgroups that carry binaries of any sort, and more particularly, groups that traffic in warez (illicit software) or pornographic material.

The AOLGOLD Trojan horse was distributed via Usenet and through email. The program was claimed to be an enhancement package for accessing America Online (AOL). The distribution consisted of an archived file that, when unzipped, revealed two files, INSTALL.EXE and README.TXT. Executing `INSTALL.EXE` resulted in expanding 18 files to the hard disk. One of the new files, called INSTALL.BAT, attempted to delete several directories on drive C, as well as running a program called DOOMDAY.EXE (which failed to execute because of a bug in the batch file).

▶ You can find the security advisory titled Information on the AOLGOLD Trojan Program at `http://www.emergency.com/aolgold.htm` or `http://ciac.llnl.gov/ciac/bulletins/g-03.shtml`.

Trojans frequently masquerade as games, joke programs, screensavers, and other programs frequently exchanged by email, especially when strict system policies or security policies are not enforced. If software contains a privacy-invasive Trojan or a destructive Trojan with a delayed payload (a time bomb or other form of logic bomb, for example), the Trojan might be distributed by a victim who is not yet aware that the program is malicious.

AOL users are frequently targeted by privacy-invasive Trojans, as we've already seen, but also by destructive Trojans.

In April 1997, someone developed a trojan called AOL4FREE.COM (not be to be confused with the AOL4FREE virus hoax that surfaced that same year—of course such confusion was part of the point of the hoax). The Trojan—claimed to be a tool to gain unauthorized access to AOL—destroyed hard disk drives on affected machines. To learn more about it, check out the CIAC advisory at `http://ciac.llnl.gov/ciac/bulletins/h-47a.shtml`.

In fact, attacks on AOL users are symptomatic of a mindset regularly encountered among computer vandals of all types. Like Usenet newbies and unwary IRC users, they are seen as a

18

TROJANS

group of "lamers" lacking low-level knowledge of the systems they use. This is seen in itself as some twisted justification, not only for jokes and hoaxes, but for intentionally destructive programs.

Direct intrusion allows installation of rootkit components and other trojanized files, especially if the intruder is able to gain root/administrator privileges.

How Often Are Trojans Really Discovered?

Trojans are frequently discovered in communities such as AOL. AOL presents an Internet service for computer users who don't want or need to be computer geeks. Many newcomers to the Internet have no interest in the finer points of networking protocols and the mysteries of Gopher, Telnet, and Archie, and AOL emphasizes user-friendliness rather than 1970s' geek cliques. Trojans in AOL usually target the least computer-literate members (new users, children) of those communities, already seen by technosnobs to be among the least computer-literate groups. This is significant because there are Black Hats (bad guys), who regard the technical ignorance of everyday users as justification of vandalism. They reason, "If lame AOLers can't learn to protect their systems, they deserve everything they get."

In the corporate arena, Trojans are a major security concern on multiuser systems. They can be insidious, too, because even after they're discovered, their footprints may remain in dark corners of the directory system or Windows Registry. Trojans are often hidden within compiled binaries. The Trojan code is therefore not in human-readable form or machine language. Without using a debugging utility, you can learn little about binary files. Using a text editor to view a binary file, for example, is futile. The only recognizable text strings will be copyright messages, error messages, or other data that prints to STDOUT at various points in the program's execution—stub loader messages, for example. In a graphical environment, recognizable strings will be even less frequent or useful. However, reverse-assembling serious quantities of potentially damaging code is not a task for the fainthearted or under-resourced. As we've already noted, such code is not always susceptible to automated analysis.

NOTE

Compiled binaries are not the only places you'll find Trojans. Batch files and other shell scripts, Perl programs, and perhaps even code written in JavaScript, VBScript, or Tcl can carry a Trojan. Scripting languages have been described as unsuitable for the creation of Trojans if the code remains humanly readable. This increases the victim's chances of discovering the offending code. In real life, though, victims often seem quite happy to run unchecked code, even when it's humanly readable. The LoveLetter virus was executed by countless recipients, even though the cleartext code clearly included a subroutine whose very name indicated that it was intended to infect files.

Nesting a Trojan within such code is, however, more feasible if the file is part of a much larger package—for example, if the entire package extracts to many subdirectories. In such cases, the complexity of the package can reduce the likelihood that a human being, using normal methods of investigation, would uncover the Trojan, especially if it's an easily overlooked short sequence like `DELTREE C:\` or `rm -rf`.

Trojans don't usually announce their intent. Worse still, many Trojans masquerade as legitimate, known utilities that you'd expect to find running on the system. Thus, you cannot rely on detecting a Trojan by listing current processes.

In detecting a Trojan by eye, much depends on the user's experience. Users who know little about their operating systems are less likely to venture deep into directory structures, looking for suspicious files. More proficient users are unlikely to have time to examine the complex system structures of modern operating systems, especially on server-class machines. Even experienced programmers can have difficulty identifying a Trojan, even when the code is available for their examination. Identification of malicious code by reverse-engineering can be more difficult and time-consuming by orders of magnitude.

What Level of Risk Do Trojans Represent?

Trojans can represent a moderate-to-serious level of risk, mainly for reasons already discussed:

- New Trojans are difficult to detect using heuristic detection. (Unless you use the somewhat sweeping heuristic that a change in a file detected automatically is likely to indicate a Trojan substituted for a legitimate file.) There is no absolute test for code to determine whether it is (or is not) a Trojan because author intent and user expectations are not generally susceptible to automated analysis.

- In most cases, Trojans are found in binaries, which remain largely in non-human–readable form. However, the fact that the code is largely static does make Trojans at least as susceptible to "known-something" detection as viruses. In other words, when a known malicious program is identified, it can be detected by software updated with an appropriate search string. Remember that, by most definitions, replication is not a characteristic of the Trojan breed. Trojans spread through the action of being copied by an attacker or a victim socially engineered into carrying out the attacker's wishes, not by self-copying. Thus it is not usually feasible for an attacker to utilize techniques such as polymorphism to reduce the chance of detection. Since the copying of the program is not a function of the program itself, the program has no means of evolving into a nonidentical copy (a morph) of itself.

18

TROJANS

Nevertheless, undetected Trojans can lead to total system compromise. A Trojan can be in place for weeks or even months before it's discovered. In that time, a cracker with root privileges could alter the entire system to suit his or her needs. Even when the Trojan is discovered, many hidden loopholes might be left behind when it is removed.

How Do I Detect a Trojan?

Detecting Trojans is easy, if you have a static search pattern to scan for. Anti-virus software routinely detects (some) Trojans using much the same pattern-searching techniques used for detecting viruses. However, identification of a known Trojan isn't always the best defense. Detection of previously unknown Trojans is also (conceptually) simple, provided you have always maintained the best security practices (literally always, at least as far as the protected system is concerned).

Most detection methods on traditional multiuser systems derive from a principle sometimes called *object reconciliation*. Object reconciliation is a fancy way of asking, "Are things still just the way I left them?" Here's how it works: *Objects* are system areas, such as files or directories. *Reconciliation* is the process of comparing those objects against a snapshot record of the same objects taken at some previous date when the protected object was known to be in a trustworthy, "clean" state.

> **NOTE**
>
> Strictly speaking, there is no such "clean state" time. Even a "day zero" installation of system software onto a virgin system assumes a program suite with no substitutions and back doors. Can you place unlimited trust in a system you didn't build totally from scratch yourself? "No amount of source-level verification or scrutiny will protect you from using untrusted code," says Ken Thompson in his Reflections on Trusting Trust. Does this mean we should give up on this approach? Of course not, but we should bear in mind that, even if we build an application from scrutinized source code, we might not be able to trust the compiler or every snippet of hardware microcode on the system motherboard.

More commonly, the process described as *object reconciliation* is known as change detection, integrity checking, or integrity management. However, these terms are not strictly synonymous.

Change detection simply describes any technique that alerts the user to the fact that an object has been changed in some respect.

Integrity checking has the same core meaning, but is often taken to imply a more sophisticated approach, not only to detecting change in spite of attempts to conceal it, but to ensuring that the reporting software itself is not subverted.

Integrity management is a more general term. It can include not only the detection of unauthorized changes, but other methods of maintaining system integrity. Such methods can include some or all of the following, in no particular order:

- Maintaining trusted backups
- Blocking unknown intrusions at entry (for instance, by running system files from read-only media or refreshing system files from trusted read-only media)
- Maintenance of strict access control
- Careful application of manufacturer patches to block newly discovered loopholes
- A finely engineered change-management system, using only signed (trusted) code.

A simple method of testing file integrity, is based on reports of changes in file state information. Different file integrity tests vary in sophistication. For example, you can crudely test a file's integrity using any of the following indexes:

- Date last modified
- File creation date
- File size

Unfortunately, none of these three methods constitute a really adequate defense against more than the crudest attack. Each time a file is altered, its values change. For example, each time the file is opened, altered, and saved, a new last-modified date emerges. However, this date can be easily manipulated. Consider manipulating this file timestamp. How difficult is it? Change the system time, apply the desired edits, archive the file, and re-set the system time. Better still, get and save the date/time information using standard C library functions (for instance), modify or replace the object, and restore the file modification date. On a single-user system (like MS-DOS) with minimal or no access controls, the coding involved is trivial. For this reason, checking time of modification is an unreliable way to detect change. Also, the last date of modification reveals nothing if the file was unaltered (for example, if it was only copied, viewed, or mailed). On the other hand, if there is a disparity between the modification date returned by the system and the date of modification recorded by a system monitoring utility, there is a distinct possibility of malicious action.

Another way to check the integrity of a file is by examining its size. However, this value can be very easily manipulated, either by trimming or padding the file itself, or by altering the value reported by the operating system.

There are other indexes. For example, basic checksums could be used. However, although checksums are more reliable than time and date stamping, they can be altered, too. If you rely on a basic checksum system (or use change detection software, which relies on simple check-summing), it is particularly important that you keep your checksum list in a trusted environment. This might mean on a separate server or even a separate medium, accessible only by root or other trusted users. Checksums work efficiently and appropriately for checking the integrity of a file transferred, for example, from point A to point B, but are not suitable for high security applications. They simply aren't designed to guard against a malicious attempt to subvert them to return false information.

NOTE

If you've ever performed file transfers using communication packages such as Qmodem, you might remember that these programs perform cyclical redundancy checksum (CRC) verification as the transfers occur. This reduces the likelihood that the file will be damaged in transit. When dealing with sophisticated attacks against file integrity, however, this technique is insufficient. Tutorials about defeating checksum systems are scattered across the Internet. Most are related to the development of viruses. (Some older virus-checking utilities used checksum analysis to detect possible infection by new viruses: that is, viruses not yet known to the compilers of virus-specific scanner databases.) You can learn more about CRC32 (and other algorithms) at `http://info.internet.isi.edu/in-notes/rfc/files/rfc1510.txt`.

A less easily subverted technique involves calculating a more sophisticated *digital fingerprint* for each file using various algorithms. A family of algorithms called the *MD series* can be used for this purpose. One of the most popular implementations is a system called *MD5*.

MD5

MD5 belongs to a family of one-way hash functions called *message digest algorithms*. The MD5 system is defined in RFC 1321 as follows:

> The algorithm takes as input a message of arbitrary length and produces as output a 128-bit "fingerprint" or "message digest" of the input. It is conjectured that it is computationally infeasible to produce two messages having the same message digest, or to produce any message having a given prespecified target message digest. The MD5 algorithm is intended for digital signature applications, where a large file must be "compressed" in a secure manner before being encrypted with a private (secret) key under a public-key cryptosystem such as RSA.

▶ RFC 1321 is located at `http://info.internet.isi.edu:80/in-notes/rfc/files/1321.txt`.

When you run a file through MD5, the fingerprint emerges as a 32-character value. It looks like this:

```
2d50b2bffb537cc4e637dd1f07a187f4
```

Many sites that distribute UNIX software use MD5 to generate digital fingerprints for their distributions. As you browse their directories, you can examine the original digital fingerprint of each file. A typical directory listing might look like this:

```
MD5 (wn-1.17.8.tar.gz) = 2f52aadd1defeda5bad91da8efc0f980
MD5 (wn-1.17.7.tar.gz) = b92916d83f377b143360f068df6d8116
MD5 (wn-1.17.6.tar.gz) = 18d02b9f24a49dee239a78ecfaf9c6fa
MD5 (wn-1.17.5.tar.gz) = 0cf8f8d0145bb7678abcc518f0cb39e9
MD5 (wn-1.17.4.tar.gz) = 4afe7c522ebe0377269da0c7f26ef6b8
MD5 (wn-1.17.3.tar.gz) = aaf3c2b1c4eaa3ebb37e8227e3327856
MD5 (wn-1.17.2.tar.gz) = 9b29eaa366d4f4dc6de6489e1e844fb9
MD5 (wn-1.17.1.tar.gz) = 91759da54792f1cab743a034542107d0
MD5 (wn-1.17.0.tar.gz) = 32f6eb7f69b4bdc64a163bf744923b41
```

If you download a file from such a server and find that the digital fingerprint of the downloaded file is different, there is a good chance that something is amiss.

With or without MD5, integrity management is a complex process. Various utilities have been designed to assist with integrity management on complex and distributed systems. The following utilities were originally UNIX-based, but similar programs are available for Microsoft operating systems.

Tripwire

Tripwire (written in 1992) is a comprehensive file integrity tool. Tripwire is well designed, easily understood, and easily implemented.

The original values (digital fingerprints) for files to be monitored are kept within a database file. That database file in simple ASCII format is accessed whenever a signature needs to be calculated or verified.

Ideally, a tool such as Tripwire would be used immediately after a fresh (day zero) installation. This gives you 100% assurance of file system integrity as a starting point (or nearly 100%—remember the Ken Thompson article). Once you generate the complete database for your file system, you can introduce other users (who will immediately fill your system with junk that, optionally, may also be fingerprinted and verified on subsequent checks). Here are some of its more useful features:

- Tripwire can perform its task over network connections. Therefore, it's possible to generate a database of digital fingerprints for some entire networks at installation time.

- Tripwire was written in C with a mind toward portability. It will compile for many platforms without alteration.

- Tripwire comes with a macro-processing language, so that your tasks can be automated.

Tripwire is a popular and effective tool, but there are some security issues common to most or all integrity management tools. One such issue relates to the database of values that is generated and maintained. From the beginning, Tripwire's authors were well aware of this:

> The database used by the integrity checker should be protected from unauthorized modifications; an intruder who can change the database can subvert the entire integrity checking scheme.

▶ Tripwire is discussed at length by its original authors in The Design and Implementation of Tripwire: A File System Integrity Checker by Gene H. Kim and Eugene H. Spafford. It is located at `ftp://coast.cs.purdue.edu/pub/Purdue/papers/spafford`.

One method of protecting the database is to store it on read-only media. This eliminates any likelihood of tampering. Kim and Spafford suggest that the database be protected in this manner, although they point out that this could present some practical, procedural problems. Much depends upon how often the database will be updated, and its size. Certainly, if you are implementing Tripwire or a similar utility on a wide scale (and using its most stringent settings), the maintenance of a read-only database could be formidable. As usual, this breaks down to a trade-off between the level of risk and the inconvenience of setting and maintaining paranoid defaults.

You can find Tripwire (and papers on usage and design) at `ftp://coast.cs.purdue.edu/pub/tools/unix/Tripwire/`. In its commercial incarnation, more information (and an unsupported but downloadable version of the original software) is available from `http://www.tripwiresecurity.com/`.

TAMU

The TAMU Tiger suite (from Texas A&M University) is a collection of tools that greatly enhance the security of a UNIX box. These tools were created in-house, in response to an extensive attack from a coordinated group of Internet crackers. The package has been upgraded and renamed TARA (Tiger Analytical Research Assistant). It incorporates a number of scripts used to scan UNIX systems for problems. More information from `http://www.securityfocus.com/tools/481`. TARA-PRO is available from `http://www-arc.com/tara/index.html`.

Hobgoblin

Hobgoblin is an interesting implementation of file- and system-integrity checking. It is both a language and an interpreter. The language, according to the authors, describes the properties of a set of files, and the interpreter checks whether the description matches the actual files, and flags any exceptions.

▶ Hobgoblin and its source are located at `ftp://ftp.su.se/pub/security/tools/admin/hobgoblin/hobgoblin.shar.gz`. You might want to check the link at `http://www.securityfocus.com/tools/132` for more information.

On Other Platforms

File integrity checkers exist for Windows, (in fact there is an implementation of Tripwire for Windows NT). Integrity checkers are not necessarily expressly designed to check multiple machines and file systems over networks. Some older DOS and Windows tools use simple CRC checksumming as an index and therefore might be easier to subvert than tools that employ MD5 and related algorithms. The majority are intended for use as a supplement to virus scanners (since detectable changes to an infectable object might indicate virus infection). This doesn't invalidate the potential usefulness of integrity checkers as a means of detecting possible substitutions of compromised code for system files.

However, change detection is less convenient on Windows platforms in that system files accessed by multiple applications can be replaced by legitimate installations and upgrades. There is often a sharper delineation on other platforms between files belonging to the system and files that belong to an application.

Furthermore, change detection only works well with certain types of binary executables, even in the context of virus detection. Many viruses and Trojans infect files whose main purpose is to contain data (spreadsheets, word-processing files, and so on). However, such files are usually intended to be modified, as are the log files used on many multiuser systems to track possible malicious action. Clearly, change detection based on the presumption that files remain static isn't going to work in these instances. In some instances, it's possible to specify changes that might signify a breach (the addition of macro code to a Word file, for instance). This approach requires that the inspecting software "know" more about the internals of the file, rather than just its digital fingerprint. That would entail serious administrative difficulties, so the approach is not well favored at present.

The safest defense, though, is to block unauthorized modification of system files proactively by code signing, read-only media, and other pre-emptive measures.

Resources

Reflections on Trusting Trust. Ken Thompson. Reprinted in *Computers Under Attack: Intruders, Worms and Viruses*. Ed. Peter J. Denning. ACM Press, 1990. ISBN: 0-13-185794-0.

18

TROJANS

Where There's Smoke, There's Mirrors: The Truth About Trojan Horses on the Internet. Sarah Gordon and David M. Chess. Virus Bulletin Conference Proceedings, 1998. `http://www.research.ibm.com/antivirus/SciPapers/Smoke/smoke.html`

Testing Times for Trojans. Ian Whalley. Virus Bulletin Conference Proceedings, 1999.

Practical Unix and Internet Security. Simson Garfinkel and Gene Spafford. O'Reilly & Associates 1996. ISBN 1-56592-148-8.

Security in Computing. Charles P. Pfleeger. Prentice-Hall International, Inc. 1997. ISBN 0-13-185794-0.

MDx-MAC and Building Fast MACs from Hash Functions. Bart Preneel and Paul C. van Oorschot. Crypto 95. `ftp.esat.kuleuven.ac.be/pub/COSIC/preneel/mdxmac_crypto95.ps`

Message Authentication with One-Way Hash Functions. Gene Tsudik. 1992. IEEE Infocom 1992. `http://www.zurich.ibm.com/Technology/Security/publications/1992/t92.ps.Z`

RFC 1446—1.5.1. Message Digest Algorithm. `http://info.internet.isi.edu:80/in-notes/rfc/files/rfc1446.txt`

RFC 1510—6. Encryption and Checksum Specifications. Connected: An Internet Encyclopedia. `http://www.freesoft.org/CIE/RFC/1510/69.html`

RFC 1510—6.4.5. RSA MD5 Cryptographic Checksum Using DES (rsa-md5des. `http://info.internet.isi.edu:80/in-notes/rfc/files/rfc1510.txt`

A Digital Signature Based on a Conventional Encryption Function. Ralph C. Merkle. Crypto 87, LNCS, pp. 369–378, SV, August 1987.

An Efficient Identification Scheme Based on Permuted Kernels. Adi Shamir. Crypto 89, LNCS, pp. 606–609, SV, August 1989.

Trusted Distribution of Software over the Internet. Aviel D. Rubin. (Bellcore's Trusted Software Integrity (Betsi) System). 1994. `ftp://ftp.cert.dfn.de/pub/docs/betsi/`

International Conference on the Theory and Applications of Cryptology. 1994 Wollongong, N.S.W. *Advances in Cryptology,* ASIACRYPT November 28–December 1, 1994. (Proceedings) Berlin & New York. Springer, 1995.

Managing Data Protection, Second Edition. Dr. Chris Pounder and Freddy Kosten. Butterworth-Heineman Limited, 1992.

Summary

Trojans are a significant security risk to any network, server, or workstation. While Windows and UNIX-hosted anti-virus software usually detects known Trojans, there are strong arguments for using integrity management tools, especially on server-class machines, to reduce the possibility of system compromise from Trojans masquerading as system utilities. This approach is viable on workstations, too, although it may be harder to implement effectively. A combination of targeted integrity management, efficiently backing up data but restoring systems from a standard day zero image rather than from backup tapes, and sound user management controlling the installation and execution of unauthorized software, is more effective than any single strategy in any server or workstation environment.

Platforms and Security

IN THIS PART

Microsoft

IN THIS CHAPTER

In earlier years, Microsoft products earned a reputation for poor security. Windows NT introduced a breakthrough in security for the Microsoft platform. Microsoft has made great strides toward securing its platform with the introduction of Windows 2000, which Microsoft released in 2000. Windows 2000 ushers in even greater security with services such as Active Directory, Public Key Infrastructure (PKI), and Kerberos. Because the Windows 2000 operating system does offer the benefits of greater security, it would be in the best interest of your company to select Windows 2000 as your standard operating system. Microsoft officials have made their message clear: They have no intention of rewriting the security controls on Microsoft Windows for Workgroups, 95, 98, or Me.

Knowing this, I only briefly discuss DOS or earlier versions of the Windows operating system. (I needed the space to cover Windows NT and Windows 2000 more thoroughly.) To that end, this chapter begins with the minimum information necessary to break a non-Windows NT box.

DOS

Microsoft Disk Operating System (DOS) is the most popular personal computer operating system in history. It is lightweight, requires little memory, and has few commands. In fact, DOS 6.22 has approximately one-sixteenth the number of commands offered by full-fledged UNIX.

Though the popularity of DOS has waned in recent years, many people still use it. (I often see the DOS/Windows for Workgroups mix on networked computers—despite the fact that the DOS/Windows combination is inherently insecure.) In the following sections, I briefly address the vulnerabilities of such systems.

IBM Compatibles in General

DOS runs only on IBM-compatible hardware. IBM-compatible architecture was not designed for security. Thus, any DOS-based system is vulnerable to attack. That attack begins with the BIOS password.

The BIOS Password

BIOS passwords (which date back to the 286) can be disabled by anyone with physical access to the box.

NOTE

BIOS passwords are used to protect the workstation from unauthorized users at the console. The BIOS password forces a password prompt at boot time. Indeed, the boot is actually arrested until the user supplies the correct password.

To disable BIOS password protection in older machines, you remove, short out, or otherwise disable the CMOS battery on the main board. Most new machines have jumpers on their motherboards that can be set to disable the BIOS password. After the BIOS password is erased, a cracker can gain access to the system. Intruders can easily compromise network workstations in this manner. However, it is not always necessary for the attacker to take apart the machine. Instead, the attacker can employ a BIOS *password-capturing utility*, which allows anyone to read the BIOS password while the machine is on. A number of BIOS password-capturing utilities exist. The most popular utilities are as follows:

- **Amidecod.** This small utility is very reliable. It will retrieve the password last used on a motherboard with an American Megatrends BIOS.

  `http://www.system7.org/archive/Passwd-Cracking/Bios-Crackers/`

- **Aw.com.** This utility will retrieve (or recover) the password used on any board with an Award BIOS. Download Award.zip at this site:

  `http://www.system7.org/archive/Passwd-Cracking/Bios-Crackers/`

After the cracker has gotten inside, he will want to gain further, or *leveraged*, access. To gain leveraged access on a networked DOS box, the cracker must obtain IDs and passwords. To do that, he will probably use a key-capture utility.

Key-Capture Utilities

Key-capture utilities capture keystrokes that occur after a specified event. (The most common trigger event is a login.) These keystrokes are recorded in a hidden file.

The directory that keystrokes are captured to can also be hidden. The most popular way of creating a hidden directory is to use the space key character as the directory's name. In Windows, the directory name appears as an underscore, which is easy to miss. Kids use this technique to hide games and racy photographs on their home and school machines.

TIP

Hidden files are generally created using the `attrib` command, or by using the key-capture utility itself; in other words, the programmer has included this feature in the software.

A number of key-capture utilities are available for DOS. Table 19.1 lists the most popular ones and their filenames. You can find each of these utilities at `http://www.system7.org/archive/Keyloggers/`.

TABLE 19.1   Popular Keystroke-Capture Utilities

Utility	Filename	Characteristics
Keycopy	keycopy.zip	Captures 200 keystrokes at a time in WordPerfect, MultiMate, Norton Editor, and a standard command-line environment.
Playback	PB19C.zip	Records and plays back keystrokes in precisely the same sequence and time as they were issued. Good for simulating logins.
Phantom2	phantom2.zip	Captures keystrokes in any environment. This utility has many amenities, including time-based playback.
Keytrap	keytrap3.zip	Powerful keystroke capture that can be performed at a specific time of day. Versions 1 through 3 can be found at this site.

In general, however, a cracker doesn't need a keystroke-capture utility. DOS does not have mandatory or even discretionary access control. Therefore, if a cracker can get a prompt, the game is over. The only way to prevent this is to load third-party security software.

Access Control Software for DOS

The following sections introduce several good packages for adding access control to DOS.

Dir Secure 2.0

Secure 2.0 prevents any unauthorized user from accessing a given directory. However, Secure 2.0 does not obscure the directory's existence; it merely prevents unauthorized access to it. The unregistered version allows one directory to be restricted. Download Sd_v2.zip at the following URL:

http://www.simtel.net/simtel.net/msdos/dirutl-pre.html/

Secure File System

Secure File System (SFS) is an excellent DOS security application suite. The suite offers high-level encryption for DOS volumes (as many as five disk volumes at one time), enhanced stealth features, and good documentation. Moreover, the SFS package conforms to the Federal Information Processing Standard (FIPS). Its compatibility with a host of disk-caching and memory-management programs makes the program quite versatile. Download version 1.17 from the University of Hamburg at the following URL:

http://www.cs.auckland.ac.nz/~pgut001/sfs/

Sentry

Sentry 6.1 is quite complete for a shareware product, even allowing you to secure individual files. It also offers password aging and some support for Windows. Download Sentry61.zip at this site:

```
http://www.simtel.net/simtel.net/msdos/security-pre.html
```

Encrypt-It

Encrypt-It offers high-level Data Encryption Standard (DES) encryption for DOS, and such encryption can be applied to a single file or to a series of files. The program also allows you to automate your encryption through macros of up to 1,000 keystrokes. The package comes with a benchmarking tool through which you can determine how well a particular file is encrypted. Check it out at this site:

```
http://www.maedae.com/encrdos.html
```

LCK100

LCK100 locks the terminal while you are away. It is impervious to a warm reboot or interrupt keystrokes (Ctrl+Alt+Delete as well as Ctrl+Break). This might be useful in environments where users are strictly forbidden to restart machines. Download Lck100.zip at this site:

```
http://www.simtel.net/simtel.net/msdos/security-pre.html
```

Gateway2

Gateway 2.05 intercepts Ctrl+Alt+Delete reboots and F5 and F8 function key calls. (Holding down the F5 or F8 key will halt the boot process and bypass configuration files such as AUTOEXEC.BAT and CONFIG.SYS. These keystrokes are one way to obtain access to a prompt.) Gateway2 also has other advantages, including password-protection support for up to 30 users on a single box. Download Gteway2.zip at the following URL:

```
http://www.simtel.net/simtel.net/msdos/security-pre.html
```

Sites That House DOS Security Tools

The following sections name several sites from which you can acquire security tools for the DOS environment.

The Simtel DOS Security Index

The Simtel DOS Security Index page offers material about password protection, access restriction, and boot protection. It is located at this site:

```
http://www.simtel.net/simtel.net/msdos/security-pre.html
```

19

MICROSOFT

The CIAC DOS Security Tools Page

The Computer Incident Advisory Capability (CIAC) page contains serious information about access restriction and includes one program that protects specific cylinders on a disk.

```
http://ciac.llnl.gov/ciac/ToolsDOSSystem.html
```

Windows for Workgroups, Windows 9x, and Windows Me

Windows for Workgroups, Windows 9x, and Windows Me have only slightly more security than DOS. All rely on the PWL password file scheme. PWL files are generated when you create your password. By default, PWL files are housed in the directory C:\WINDOWS. However, you might want to check the SYSTEM.INI file for other locations. (SYSTEM.INI is where the PWL path is specified.)

The Password List (PWL) Password Scheme

The PWL password scheme is not secure and can be defeated simply by deleting the files.

NOTE
If the cracker wants to avoid leaving evidence of his intrusion, he probably won't delete the PWL files. Instead, he will reboot, interrupt the load to Windows (by pressing F5 or F8), and edit the SYSTEM.INI file. There, he will change the pointer from the default location (C:\WINDOWS) to a temporary directory. In that temporary directory, he will insert another PWL file to which he already knows the password. He will then reboot again and log in. After he has done his work, he will re-edit the SYSTEM.INI, putting things back to normal.

In more complex cracking schemes, the attacker might actually need the password (for example, when the cracker is using a local Windows 95 box to authenticate to and crack a remote Windows NT 4.0 server). In such environments, the cracker has two choices: He can either crack the 95 PWL password file or he can flush the password out of cached memory while the target is still logged in. Both techniques are briefly discussed here.

Cracking PWL Files

Cracking standard PWL files generated on the average Windows 95 box is easy. For this, you need a utility called Glide.

Glide

Glide cracks PWL files. It comes with source code for those interested in examining it. To use Glide, enter the filename (PWL) and the username associated with it. Glide is quite effective and can be found online at the following location:

```
http://morehouse.org/hin/blckcrwl/hack/glide.zip
```

> **NOTE**
>
> To make your PWL passwords secure, you should install third-party access control software. However, if you are forced to rely on PWL password protection, you can still better your chances. Glide will not crack PWL password files that were generated on any box with Windows 95 Service Pack 1 or later installed. You should install, at a minimum, the latest service packs.

Flushing the Password out of Cached Memory

Two different functions are used in the PWL system: one to encrypt and store the password and another to retrieve it. Those routines are as follows:

- `WNetCachePassword()`
- `WNetGetCachedPassword()`

The password remains cached. You can write a routine in Visual C++ or Visual Basic (VB) that will get another user's password. The only restriction is that the targeted user must be logged in when the program is executed (so the password can be trapped). The password can then be cached out to another area of memory. Having accomplished this, you can bypass the password security scheme by using that cached version of the password. (This technique is called *cache flushing*. It relies on the same principle as using a debugger to expose authentication schemes in client software.)

You can also force the cached password into the swap file. However, this is a cumbersome and wasteful method; there are other, easier ways to do it.

> **TIP**
>
> One method is to hammer the password database with multiple entries at high speed. You can use a utility like Claymore for this, which you can download at `http://www.system7.org/archive/Passwd-Cracking/windows.html`. You fill the available password space by using this technique. This causes an overflow, and the routine then discards older passwords. However, this technique leaves ample evidence behind.

19

MICROSOFT

Either way, the PWL system is inherently flawed and provides very little protection against intrusion. If you are using Windows 9x or Windows Me, you need to install third-party access control. This chapter provides a list of such products and their manufacturers in the "Access Control Software" section later in this chapter. Not all products have a version for Windows Me. Check with the manufacturers for availability.

Summary on DOS, Windows for Workgroups, Windows 9x, and Windows Me

DOS, Windows for Workgroups, Windows 9x, and Windows Me are all excellent systems. However, none of them are secure. If your firm uses these operating systems at all, the boxes that run them should be hidden behind a firewall. This is especially so with Windows Me because it has received little scrutiny. It might contain many vulnerabilities that have yet to be revealed.

With that settled, let's examine Windows NT security.

Windows NT

Microsoft might be traditionally known for poor security, but not when it comes to Windows NT 4.0. Out of the box, Windows NT 4.0 has security measures as good as most other server platforms. The catch is that you must keep up with recent developments. If you have a connection to the Internet, you should consider subscribing to Windows Update so that it will automatically notify you about new service packs/updates.

Before you read any further, ask yourself this: Have I installed Windows NT 4.0 using NT File System (NTFS) and installed the service packs in their proper order? If not, your Windows NT 4.0 system is not secure and the rest of this chapter cannot help you. If you have not installed your system in this manner, go back, reinstall the service packs, and install with NTFS enabled.

NOTE

One would think that the order in which service packs is installed doesn't matter. Unfortunately, that is simply not true. There have been documented instances of users installing service packs in disparate order only to later encounter trouble. I recommend keeping a running record of when the packs were installed and any problems that you encounter during installation.

General Windows NT Security Vulnerabilities

Windows NT, like most operating systems, has vulnerabilities. Please note that the list of vulnerabilities discussed here is not exhaustive. Other vulnerabilities of lesser severity exist.

The Netmon Protocol Parsing Vulnerability

Windows NT Version: All versions

Impact: An attacker can gain control of your server.

Class: Critical

Fix for Windows NT 4.0 Server and NT 4.0 Server, Enterprise Edition can be found at `http://www.microsoft.com/Downloads/Release.asp?ReleaseID=25487`.

As of this writing, no fix exists for Windows NT 4.0 Server, Terminal Server Edition.

Additional Information:
`http://www.microsoft.com/technet/security/bulletin/MS00-083.asp`. The fix for this vulnerability will be included in Service Pack 7.

Credit: COVERT Labs at PGP Security, Inc., and the ISS X-force

> **NOTE**
>
> According to `http://www.microsoft.com/ntserver/terminalserver/default.asp`, Microsoft discontinued NT Terminal Server Edition in August 2000, so there is little hope that this problem will be resolved for this platform.

Several protocol parsers in Netmon have unchecked buffers. When an attacker sends a malformed frame to a server that is monitoring network traffic, and if the administrator happens to be using a protocol parser with unchecked buffers, the malformed frame would either cause Netmon to fail or cause code of the attacker's choice to run on the server. If you are running Netmon under a local administrator's account, the attacker can gain complete control over the server, but not over the domain. However, if you are running Netmon under a domain administrator's account, the attacker might be able to gain control over the domain as well.

The Predictable LPC Message Identifier Vulnerability

Windows NT Version: All versions

Impact: A local intruder can impersonate your privileges, eavesdrop on your session, or cause your server or workstation to fail.

Class: Critical—Denial of Service

Fix: `http://www.microsoft.com/ntserver/nts/downloads/critical/q266433/default.asp`. The fix for this vulnerability will be included in Service Pack 7.

19

MICROSOFT

Additional Info: `http://www.microsoft.com/technet/security/bulletin/`
`ms00-070.asp`

Credit: BindView's Razor Team

An intruder can only exploit this vulnerability locally. The intruder causes a denial of service attack on either a client or server box by sending large packets of random data to them. If the intruder identifies a system process that has an existing Link Control Protocol (LCP) connection with a privileged thread, he can then spoof the client and make requests that he wouldn't ordinarily be able to perform. The amount of damage he can perform depends on what processes are running in the thread and what they permit him to do. The intruder can also eavesdrop on your session and potentially gather privileged information.

The Registry Permissions Vulnerability

Windows NT Version: All versions

Impact: Default permissions on certain Registry values can allow an attacker to gain additional privileges on a box.

Class: Moderate to Severe

Fix: `http://www.microsoft.com/Downloads/Release.asp?ReleaseID=24501`
The Terminal Server Edition doesn't have a fix at the time of this writing.

Additional Information: `http://www.microsoft.com/technet/security/bulletin/`
`MS00-095.asp`

Credit: Chris Anley, Milan Dadok, and Glenn Larsson

The SNMP Parameters key, the RAS Administration key, and the MTS Package Administration key all have inappropriately loose default permissions. This vulnerability could enable an attacker to manage or configure devices on the network, such as misconfiguring routers and firewalls, and starting or stopping services on a machine.

The Remote Registry Access Authentication Vulnerability

Windows NT Version: All versions

Impact: Remote users can cause a Windows NT 4.0 box to fail.

Class: Critical—Denial of Service

Fix for Windows NT 4.0 Workstation, Server, and Enterprise Server Edition:
`http://www.microsoft.com/Downloads/Release.asp?ReleaseID=23077` At the time of this writing, there is no fix available for the Terminal Server Edition.

Additional Info: `http://www.microsoft.com/technet/security/bulletin/`
`ms00-040.asp`

Credit: Renaud Deraison

When an attacker sends a malformed request for remote Registry access, the request can cause the Winlogon process to fail, which in turn can cause the entire system to fail.

The Winsock Mutex Vulnerability

Windows NT Version: All versions

Impact: Local user can cause a box to stop responding to network traffic.

Class: Moderate—Denial of Service

Fix for Windows NT 4.0: `http://www.microsoft.com/Downloads/Release.asp?ReleaseID=27272`

Fix for Windows NT 4.0 Terminal Server: `http://www.microsoft.com/Downloads/Release.asp?ReleaseID=27291`

Additional Information: `http://www.microsoft.com/technet/security/bulletin/MS01-003.asp`

Credit: Arne Vidstrom

Inappropriate permissions assigned to a networking mutex can permit an intruder to run code to gain control of the mutex and then deny access to it. Doing this prevents other processes from being able to perform network operations with the machine.

Other Important Vulnerabilities of Lesser Significance

Windows NT is also vulnerable to a wide range of other things, which might not be absolutely critical but are serious nonetheless. Table 19.2 lists these problems in Table 19.2, along with URLs where you can learn more.

TABLE 19.2   Other Important Windows NT Vulnerabilities

Vulnerability	Facts and URL
Out of Band	Out-of-band (OOB) attacks are denial of service attacks with a vengeance. Many platforms are susceptible to OOB attacks, including Windows NT 3.51 and Windows NT 4.0. The fix for Microsoft is available at the following site: `ftp://ftp.microsoft.com/bussys/winnt/winntpublic/fixes/usa/NT351/hotfixes-postSP5/oob-fix/`.
Port 1031	If a cracker telnets to port 1031 of your server and issues garbage, this will blow your server off the Net. This exploits a vulnerability in the file INET-INFO.EXE. Check with Microsoft for recent patches.
NTCrash	A powerful denial of service utility called NTCrash will bring a Windows NT server to its knees. Source code is available on the Net here: `http://www3.ncr.com/support/nt/tools/ntcrash.zip`. Test it and see what happens.

19

Internal Windows NT Security

The majority of this chapter focuses on *remote security*, in which the attackers are on foreign networks. Unfortunately, foreign networks are not always the source of the attack. Sometimes, your very own users attack your server. That is what the next section is all about.

Internal Security in General

In general, Windows NT has only fair-to-good local security. This is in contrast to its external security, which I believe is very good (providing you stay up on the latest patches). At a bare minimum, you must use NTFS. If you don't, there is no point in even hoping to secure your boxes. Here's why: There are just too many things that local users can do, and too many files and services they can use.

Some system administrators argue that they don't need NTFS. Instead, they argue that between policy and careful administration and control of who accesses their machines, they can maintain a more or less tight ship. They are dreaming.

The RDISK Hole

A perfect example is the RDISK hole. RDISK is a Windows NT utility that allows you to create emergency repair disks. This is a valuable utility for a system administrator. However, when accessible to the wrong person, RDISK is an enormous security hole. Here's why: A user can instruct RDISK to dump all security information (including passwords and Registry information) into the directory C:\WINNT\REPAIR. From there, an attacker can load a password cracker. Within hours, the box will be completely compromised. This is just another reason you should not walk away from your computer and leave it logged on. Would you like to try it yourself? Issue this command at a prompt: rdisk /s.

Then go to the directory C:\WINNT\REPAIR. You will find the necessary information you need to crack the box.

Achieving Good Internal Security

Achieving good internal security is not an end. There is no list of tools that you can install that will permanently secure your box. New holes always crop up. Also, although Microsoft has done wonders to improve the security of Windows NT, pervading user-friendliness in their products continues to hamper efforts at serious security.

An amusing example of this was described by Vacuum from Rhino9 (a prominent hacker group), who made the observation that restricting user access to the Control Panel was a fruitless effort. He wrote

If you do not have access to the Control Panel from Start/Settings/Control Panel or from the My Computer Icon, click Start/Help/Index. All of the normally displayed icons appear as help topics. If you click on "Network," for example, a Windows NT Help Screen appears with a nice little shortcut to the Control Panel Network Settings.

The problem sounds simple and not very threatening. However, the rule holds true for most system resources and even administrative tools. (Microsoft probably won't change it, either. Their defense would probably be this: It enhances user-friendliness to provide a link to any program discussed in Help.)

At a bare minimum, you should install logging utilities and a sniffer. I also recommend making a comprehensive list of all applications or resources that have no logging. If these applications and resources have no native logging (and also cannot be logged using other applications), I recommend deleting them, placing access restrictions on them, or at a minimum, removing them from their default locations.

A Tip on Setting Up a Secure Windows NT Server from Scratch

To effectively erect a secure Windows NT server, you must start at installation time. To ascertain whether you should reinstall, you should measure your original installation procedure against typical preparations for a C2 system. To do that, I recommend downloading the *Secure Windows NT Installation and Configuration Guide*, which was authored by the Department of the Navy Space and Naval Warfare Systems Command Naval Information Systems Security Office. That document contains the most comprehensive secure installation procedure currently available in print. It is located at this site:

```
https://infosec.navy.mil/TEXT/COMPUSEC/ntsecure.html
```

NOTE

C2 is an evaluation level in the US Government's Trusted Computer Security Evaluation Criteria (TCSEC) program. TCSEC provides a standard set of criteria for judging the security that computer products provide. TCSEC has also come to be known as the "Orange Book" because the base set of criteria specified by TCSEC is provided in a book with an orange cover.

The Navy guide takes you through configuration of the file system, audit policy, the Registry, the User Manager, user account policy, user rights, trust relationships, system policy, and Control Panel. It also has a blow-by-blow guide that explains the rationale for each step taken.

This is invaluable because you can learn Windows NT security on-the-fly. Even though it spans only 185 pages, the Navy guide is worth 10 or even 100 books like this one. By using that guide, you can guarantee yourself a head start on establishing a reasonably secure server.

Summary of Windows NT

Windows NT 4.0 was the first step Microsoft took toward securing your network. Although Windows NT 4.0 and third-party software vendors provide you with many features to secure your Windows NT 4.0 network, Windows 2000 possesses even greater security. If you haven't yet taken the plunge to upgrade to Windows 2000, you should seriously consider doing so.

Let's move on now to examine Windows 2000 security.

Windows 2000

As with Windows NT 4.0, it is very important to install Windows 2000 using NTFS. If you don't install NTFS on your Windows 2000 domain controller, you will not have a secure installation. The focus of this section on Windows 2000 will be on improvements to security and on general Windows 2000 security vulnerabilities.

Improvements to Security

Microsoft has paid more attention to security this time around, and has fully integrated security with the new Active Directory directory service structure. Microsoft has also designed the Windows 2000 platform to be more reliable than previous versions of Windows.

Some of the security features that are new to Windows 2000 are briefly discussed in the following list:

- First and foremost is the introduction of Active Directory. It is the core of the flexibility of the Windows 2000 security model and provides information about all objects on the network. It is the basis for Windows 2000 distributed networking and facilitates the use of centralized management techniques, such as Group Policy and remote operating system operations. Active Directory replaces the security accounts manager (SAM) database area of the Registry on domain controllers storing security information such as user accounts, passwords, and group. Consequently, Active Directory becomes a trusted component of the Local Security Authority (LSA). Active Directory stores both access control information to support authorization to access system resources, and user credentials to support authentication within the domain. Windows 2000 Professional and member servers still retain the local SAM database for locally defined users and groups.

Active Directory provides a single point of management for Windows clients, servers, applications, and user accounts. With Active Directory, you can delegate specific administrative tasks and privileges to individual users and groups, thus enabling the distribution of system administration tasks to either localized or centralized administration. For example, you can assign a specific management task, such as resetting a user's password, to office administrators in specific departments of your organization so that you can free up your time for more complex tasks.

Active Directory includes built-in support for secure Internet-standard protocols such as Public Key Infrastructure (PKI), Kerberos, and Lightweight Directory Access Protocol (LDAP). Learn more about Active Directory at `http://www.microsoft.com/windows2000/guide/server/features/directory.asp`.

- Public Key Infrastructure (PKI) also lies at the core of many of the security features in Windows 2000. PKI makes use of Microsoft Certificate Services, allowing the deployment of enterprise certificate authorities (CA) in your enterprise and is integrated into Active Directory. Active Directory uses the directory service to publish information about certificate services, which includes the location of user certificates and certificate revocation lists. When your organization begins to manage digital certificates, a range of enhanced security features becomes available to you in order to secure such technologies as Digitally Signed Software, the Encrypted File System (EFS), e-mail, IP Security, and Smart Card Security.

- The EFS presents your users with the option to encrypt sensitive data on their hard disks, thus ensuring confidentiality should an intruder compromise or steal the disk.

- Kerberos is the default authentication protocol on Windows 2000, replacing Windows NT Challenge Response (NTLM) authentication. Kerberos has been around for a number of years, having been developed at the Massachusetts Institute of Technology during the 1980s.

- Internet Protocol Security Protocol (IPSec) provides advanced network security for you and your enterprise users.

Windows 2000 Distributed Security Overview

The Windows 2000 distributed security services include the following key business requirements:

- Strong user authorization and authentication
- Users log on once to access all enterprise resources
- Secure communications between external and internal resources
- Automated security auditing
- Interoperability with other operating systems

Microsoft bases Windows 2000 security on a simple model of authentication and authorization. After Windows 2000 identifies the user through authentication with a domain controller, the user is granted access to specific network resources based on permissions. This security model enables authorized users to work on a secure, extended network. The Windows 2000 distributed security model is based on delegation of trust between services, trusted domain controller authentication, and object-based access control.

Learn more about Microsoft Windows 2000 distributed security at `http://microsoft.com/windows2000/library/unzippeddocs/SecTech.doc`. Now that we've briefly examined some of the new security features in Windows 2000, let's move on to some potentially harmful vulnerabilities.

General Windows 2000 Security Vulnerabilities

Windows 2000, like most operating systems, has vulnerabilities. Please note that the list of vulnerabilities discussed here is not exhaustive. Other vulnerabilities of lesser severity exist.

The Windows 2000 Directory Service Restore Mode Password Vulnerability

Microsoft Windows Version: Windows 2000 Server and Advanced Server

Impact: A malicious user can install malicious code onto a domain server.

Class: Moderate to Severe

Fix: `http://www.microsoft.com/Downloads/Release.asp?ReleaseID=27500`. The fix for this vulnerability will be included in Windows 2000 Service Pack 2.

Additional Info: `http://www.microsoft.com/technet/security/bulletin/MS01-006.asp`

Credit: John Sherriff of the Wool Research Organization

A malicious user with physical access to and administrative logon privileges on your domain server can install malicious code if the server was promoted to a domain server using the "Configure Your Server" tool. The only domain server in the forest that can be affected by this vulnerability is the one that was installed first.

The Netmon Protocol Parsing Vulnerability

Microsoft Windows Version: Windows 2000 Server and Advanced Server

Impact: An attacker can gain control of your server.

Class: Critical

Fix: `http://www.microsoft.com/Downloads/Release.asp?ReleaseID=25485`. The fix for this vulnerability will be included in Windows 2000 Service Pack 2.

Additional Information: `http://www.microsoft.com/technet/security/bulletin/MS00-083.asp`

Credit: COVERT Labs at PGP Security, Inc., and the ISS X-force

Refer to the NT vulnerabilities section for an explanation of this vulnerability. This vulnerability affects both.

The Network DDE Agent Request Vulnerability

Microsoft Windows Version: All Windows 2000 versions

Impact: An attacker can gain complete control over your box.

Class: Severe

Fix: `http://www.microsoft.com/Downloads/Release.asp?ReleaseID=27526`. The fix for this vulnerability will be included in Windows 2000 Service Pack 3.

Additional Info: `http://www.microsoft.com/technet/security/bulletin/MS01-007.asp`

Credit: Dildog of @Stake

This is privilege elevation vulnerability. An attacker would be able to exploit this vulnerability to take any action he wanted to on your box because it enables him to run commands and programs with the privileges of the operation system itself.

The Phone Book Service Buffer Overflow Vulnerability

Microsoft Windows Version: Windows 2000 Server and Advanced Server

Impact: An attacker can execute hostile code on a remote server that is running the Phone Book Service.

Class: Critical

Fix: `http://www.microsoft.com/Downloads/Release.asp?ReleaseID=25531`. The fix for this vulnerability will be included in Windows 2000 Service Pack 2.

Additional Info: `http://www.microsoft.com/technet/security/bulletin/MS00-094.asp`

Credit: CORE-SDI and @Stake

The Phone Book Service is used with Dial-Up Networking clients to provide a prepopulated list of Dial-Up Networking servers to the client. This service has an unchecked buffer in a portion of the code that does the processing of requests for phone book updates. When an attacker sends a malformed request, it can result in overrunning the buffer. This enables the attacker to execute any code that a user logged into the server can run. In other words, the attacker can install and run code of his choice; add, delete or change Web pages; reformat the hard drive; or do any number of other tasks.

The Telnet Client NTLM Authentication Vulnerability

Microsoft Windows Version: All Windows 2000 versions

Impact: An attacker could obtain another user's NTLM authentication credentials without the user's knowledge.

19

MICROSOFT

Class: Moderate to Critical

Fix: `http://www.microsoft.com/Downloads/Release.asp?ReleaseID=24399`. The fix for this vulnerability will be included in Windows 2000 Service Pack 2.

Additional Info: `http://www.microsoft.com/technet/security/bulletin/MS00-067.asp`

Credit: DilDog of @Stake Inc.

If a malicious Webmaster operated a Telnet server and you initiate a session with that server, the Webmaster could collect your NTLM responses and then use them to possibly authenticate to your box. This is possible because, as part of the session, your box might pass your cryptographically protected NTLM authentication credentials to his server. After he has obtained these credentials, he could then use an offline brute-force attack to gain your plaintext password.

The Telnet Server Flooding Vulnerability

Microsoft Windows Version: All Windows 2000 versions

Impact: A remote user can prevent your box from providing Telnet services.

Class: Moderate to Severe—Denial of Service

Fix: `http://www.microsoft.com/Downloads/Release.asp?ReleaseID=22753`

Additional Info: `http://www.microsoft.com/technet/security/bulletin/MS00-050.asp`

Credit: Unknown

This is a remote denial of service vulnerability. A malicious remote user can send a malformed input string from his box, which would then cause the Telnet server to fail, causing the loss of any work in progress.

Summary of Windows 2000

Even though security for Windows has improved greatly with the introduction of Windows 2000, new security violations occur all the time. Hence, it is important that you keep up with new advisories related to security holes in Windows 2000.

Modern Vulnerabilities in Microsoft Applications

In this section, I enumerate security weaknesses in some very commonly used Microsoft applications. Microsoft Internet Explorer (Microsoft's Web browser, also known as MSIE), Microsoft Exchange Server (a mail administration package), and Internet Information Server (IIS) are three key networking applications.

Microsoft Internet Explorer

Microsoft Internet Explorer has several serious vulnerabilities; some of them are covered briefly here. Those vulnerabilities that are classified as either critical or severe can result in system compromise, and are therefore of great interest to system administrators.

The Active Setup Download Vulnerability

Microsoft Internet Explorer Version: 4.x, 5.x

Impact: Malicious Webmasters can download a .CAB file to any disk on your box.

Class: Severe

Fix for MSIE 4.x and 5.01: `http://www.microsoft.com/windows/ie/download/critical/patch8.htm`

Fix for MSIE 5.5:
`http://www.microsoft.com/windows/ie/download/critical/patch11.htm`

Additional Info: `http://www.microsoft.com/technet/security/bulletin/ms00-042.asp`

Credit: Unknown

A malicious Web site can download a .CAB file to any disk on your box and then use the .CAB file to overwrite files, including system files. This could render your machine inoperable and create a denial of service on your box.

The Cached Web Credentials Vulnerability

Microsoft Internet Explorer Version: 4.x and 5.x prior to version 5.5

Impact: Malicious intruders can obtain your user ID and password to a Web site.

Class: Moderate to Severe

Fix: `http://www.microsoft.com/windows/ie/download/critical/q273868.htm`

Additional Info: `http://www.microsoft.com/technet/security/bulletin/ms00-076.asp`

Credit: ACROS Security

When you use Basic authentication to authenticate to a secured Web page, MSIE caches your user ID and password. MSIE does this to minimize the number of times you must authenticate to the same site. Although MSIE should only pass your cached credentials to secured pages on the site, it will also send them to the site's nonsecured pages. If an attacker has control of your box's network communications when you log on to a secured site, the attacker can spoof a request for a nonsecured page and then collect your credentials.

The IE Script Vulnerability

Microsoft Internet Explorer Version: 4.01 SP2 and higher, when Microsoft Access 97 or Microsoft Access 2000 is present on the machine

Impact: Permits an attacker to run code of his choice on your box, potentially allowing the attacker to take full control of it.

Class: Extremely Severe

Fix: `http://www.microsoft.com/windows/ie/download/critical/patch11.htm` or set an Administrator password for Microsoft Access

Additional Info: `http://www.microsoft.com/technet/security/bulletin/ms00-049.asp`

Credit: Georgi Guninski

This vulnerability enables an attacker to embed malicious VB code into Microsoft Access via Internet Explorer. Simply visiting a malicious Web site or previewing an e-mail that contains malicious code can compromise your box.

The Microsoft Internet Explorer `GetObject()` File Disclosure Vulnerability

Microsoft Internet Explorer Version: 5.x

Impact: If you visit a malicious Web site or read a mail message with Active Scripting enabled, MSIE might disclose files on your box.

Class: Moderate to Severe

Fix: Until Microsoft releases a patch to fix this problem, you should disable Active Scripting in Internet Explorer in any zone with untrusted hosts. If you run any other products that respect Internet Explorer security zones, you should configure them to run VBScript in trusted zones only. In addition, Microsoft recommends configuring Outlook using the guidelines found at: `http://www.microsoft.com/office/outlook/downloads/security.htm`

Additional Info: `http://www.kb.cert.org/vuls/id/800893`

Credit: Georgi Guninski

Microsoft designed IE to prevent programs on Web sites from reading files on your box without authorization. Microsoft also designed Outlook and Outlook Express to prevent programs embedded in mail messages from reading files on your box without authorization. Unfortunately, a flaw in the behavior of the `GetObject` call in VBScript permits access to files despite the fact that VBScript doesn't include file I/O or direct access to the underlying operating system. This flaw can cause a malicious VBScript to forward the contents of a document through electronic mail or back to the Web site.

The Office HTML Script Vulnerability

Microsoft Internet Explorer Version: 4.01 SP2 or higher when Microsoft Excel 2000, Microsoft Powerpoint 2000, or Microsoft PowerPoint 97 are present on the machine

Impact: Permits an attacker to run code of his or her choice on a victims's box, potentially allowing the attacker to take full control of that box.

Class: Extremely Severe

Fix for Microsoft Excel 2000 and PowerPoint 2000:
http://officeupdate.microsoft.com/2000/downloaddetails/Addinsec.htm

Fix for Microsoft PowerPoint 97: http://officeupdate.microsoft.com/downloaddetails/PPt97sec.htm

Additional Info: http://www.microsoft.com/technet/security/bulletin/ms00-049.asp

Credit: Unknown

This vulnerability enables a script that is stored either on a malicious Web operator's site or in an HTML e-mail message to save an Excel 2000, Powerpoint 2000, or Powerpoint 97 file to a victim's box. The attacker can code this file to launch automatically. If this file successfully launches, it could cause a macro or Visual Basic for Applications (VBA) code to run that will potentially allow the attacker to take full control of that box.

The SSL Certificate Validation Vulnerability

Microsoft Internet Explorer Version: 4.x, 5.0, and 5.01

Note: MSIE 5.01 Service Pack 1 and MSIE 5.5 are not affected.

Impact: Two flaws exist in MSIE that can allow a malicious Web site to pose as a legitimate Web site. The attacker can trick users into disclosing information (such credit card numbers or personal data) intended for a legitimate Web site.

Class: Moderate

Fix: http://www.microsoft.com/windows/ie/download/critical/patch11.htm or upgrade to MSIE 5.5.

Additional Info: http://www.microsoft.com/technet/security/bulletin/ms00-039.asp

Credit: ACROS Penetration Team, Slovenia

When a connection to a secure server is made through either a frame or an image on a Web site, MSIE only verifies that the server's Secure Sockets Layer (SSL) certificate was issued by a trusted root, and does not verify either the server name or the expiration date of the certificate. When you make a secure connection via any other means, MSIE performs the expected validation. If a user establishes a new SSL session with the same server during the same MSIE session, MSIE does not revalidate the certificate.

19

MICROSOFT

The Unauthorized Cookie Access Vulnerability

Microsoft Internet Explorer Version: 4.x, 5.0, and 5.01

Note: MSIE 5.01 Service Pack 1 and MSIE 5.5 are not affected.

Impact: This vulnerability can allow a malicious Webmaster to obtain personal information from a user's box.

Class: Moderate

Fix: `http://www.microsoft.com/windows/ie/download/critical/patch11.htm`

Additional Info: `http://www.microsoft.com/technet/security/bulletin/FQ00-033.asp#B`

Credit: Unknown

A malicious Web site operator could entice a user to click a link on the operator's site that would allow the operator to read, change, or add a cookie to that user's box.

Microsoft Exchange Server

The following sections list important vulnerabilities in Microsoft Exchange Server 2000 and Exchange Server 5.x.

Microsoft Exchange Encapsulated SMTP Address Vulnerability

Microsoft Exchange Server Version: 5.5

Impact: Intruder can perform mail relaying.

Class: Moderate—Denial of Service

Fix: `ftp://ftp.microsoft.com/bussys/exchange/exchange-public/fixes/Eng/Exchg5.5/PostSP2/imc-fix/`

Additional Info: `http://www.microsoft.com/technet/security/bulletin/fq99-027.asp`

Credit: Laurent Frinking of Quark Deutschland GmbH

This vulnerability could enable an intruder to get around the antirelaying features of an Internet-connected Exchange server. Because encapsulated Simple Mail Transfer Protocol (SMTP) addresses are not subject to the same antirelaying protections as nonencapsulated SMTP addresses, an intruder can cause a server to forward an encapsulated SMTP address from the attacker to any e-mail address he or she wants—as though the server were the sender of the e-mail.

Microsoft Exchange Malformed Bind Request Vulnerability

Microsoft Exchange Server Version: 5.5

Impact: An intruder can cause denial of service attacks or can run code on the server.

Class: Severe—Denial of Service

Fix for X86-based Exchange: `ftp://ftp.microsoft.com/bussys/exchange/exchange-public/fixes/Eng/Exchg5.5/PostSP2/DIR-fix/PSP2DIRI.EXE`

Fix for Alpha-based Exchange: `ftp://ftp.microsoft.com/bussys/exchange/exchange-public/fixes/Eng/Exchg5.5/PostSP2/DIR-fix/PSP2DIRA.EXE`

Additional Info: `http://www.microsoft.com/technet/security/bulletin/ms99-009.asp`

Credit: ISS X-Force

The Bind function has an unchecked buffer that can pose two threats to operation: An attacker could send a malformed Bind request, causing the Exchange Directory service to crash. A carefully constructed Bind request can be sent by an attacker whose purpose is to cause arbitrary code to execute on the server using a classic buffer overrun technique.

Microsoft Exchange Malformed MIME Header Vulnerability

Microsoft Exchange Server Version: 5.5

Impact: A malicious user can cause an Exchange Server to fail.

Class: Severe—Denial of Service

Fix: `http://www.microsoft.com/Downloads/Release.asp?ReleaseID=25443` or Exchange 5.5 SP4

Additional Info: `http://www.microsoft.com/technet/security/bulletin/MS00-082.asp`

Credit: Art Savelev

The Exchange Server normally checks for invalid values in the MIME header fields. However, the Exchange service will fail if a particular type of invalid value is present in certain MIME header fields. You can restore normal operations by restarting the Exchange Server and then deleting the offending mail. The offending mail will be at the front end of the queue after you restart the Exchange service.

Microsoft Exchange NNTP Denial-of-Service Vulnerability

Microsoft Exchange Server Versions: 5.0 and 5.5

Impact: An attacker can cause the Server Information Store to choke.

Class: Medium—Denial of Service

Fix: `ftp://ftp.microsoft.com/bussys/exchange/exchange-public/fixes/Eng/Exchg5.0/Post-SP2-STORE/` or install SP1 or later

Additional Info: `http://www.microsoft.com/technet/security/bulletin/ms98-007.asp`

Credit: Internet Security Systems, Inc.'s X-Force team

When an attacker issues a series of incorrect data, an application error can result in the Server Information Store failing. It also causes users to fail in their attempt to connect to their folders on the Exchange Server.

Microsoft Exchange SMTP Denial of Service Vulnerability

Microsoft Exchange Server Versions: 5.0 and 5.5

Impact: An attacker can cause the Internet Mail Service to choke.

Class: Medium—Denial of Service

Fix: `ftp://ftp.microsoft.com/bussys/exchange/exchange-public/fixes/Eng/Exchg5.0/post-sp2-ims/` or install SP1 or later

Additional Info: `http://www.microsoft.com/technet/security/bulletin/ms98-007.asp`

Credit: Internet Security Systems, Inc.'s X-Force team

When an attacker issues a series of incorrect data, an application error can result in the Internet Mail Service failing.

Microsoft Exchange Error Message Vulnerability

Microsoft Exchange Server Versions: 5.0 and 5.5

Impact: An intruder might be able to recover encrypted data from your network.

Class: Moderate to Severe

Fix: Download the latest version of Schannel.dll. Check out this URL for information on where to obtain the latest version `http://support.microsoft.com/support/kb/articles/q148/4/27.asp`

Additional Info: `http://www.microsoft.com/technet/security/bulletin/ms98-002.asp`

Credit: Daniel Bleichenbacher

An intruder, running a sniffer on your network, might be able to observe an SSL-encrypted session, interrogate the server involved in that session, recover the session key used in that session, and then recover the encrypted data from that session.

Microsoft Exchange User Account Vulnerability

Microsoft Exchange Server Version: 2000

Impact: An intruder can remotely log on to an Exchange 2000 Server and possibly onto other servers in the affected Exchange Server's network.

Class: Moderate to Severe

Fix: `http://www.microsoft.com/Downloads/Release.asp?ReleaseID=25866`

Additional Info: `http://www.microsoft.com/technet/security/bulletin/MS00-088.asp`

Credit: Unknown

A malicious user can log on to Exchange by using an account with a known username (EUSR_EXSTOREEVENT) and a password that Exchange creates during the setup process. Normally this account has only local user rights, meaning that the account is neither a privileged account nor can it gain access to Exchange 2000 data. However, when you install Exchange 2000 on a domain controller, the system automatically gives Domain User privileges to the account, and so it can gain access to other resources on the affected domain. Microsoft recommends that you disable or delete this account after the setup process has completed.

IIS (Internet Information Server)

IIS is a very popular Internet server package and like most server packages, it has vulnerabilities. IIS is covered here in detail. However, please note that the list of vulnerabilities discussed is not exhaustive. Other vulnerabilities of lesser severity exist.

The IIS Cross-Site Scripting Vulnerabilities

IIS Version: 4.0 and 5.0

Impact: An attacker can run code on your machine masquerading as a third-party Web site.

Class: Severe

Fix for IIS 4.0: `http://www.microsoft.com/Downloads/Release.asp?ReleaseID=25534`

Fix for IIS 5.0: `http://www.microsoft.com/Downloads/Release.asp?ReleaseID=25533`

Additional Info: `http://www.microsoft.com/technet/security/bulletin/MS00-060.asp`

Credit: Peter Grundl of Defcom

When a malicious user runs code masquerading as a third-party Web site, that code can take any action on your box that the third-party Web site is permitted to take. If you designate that Web site as a trusted site, the attacker's code could take advantage of the increased privileges. The attacker can make the code persistent, so that if you return to that Web site in the future, the code will begin to run again.

The IIS Malformed Web Form Submission Vulnerability

IIS Version: 4.0 and 5.0

Impact: An attacker can prevent a Web server from providing service.

Class: Severe—Denial of Service

Fix for IIS 4.0: `http://www.microsoft.com/Downloads/Release.asp?ReleaseID=26704`

Fix for IIS 5.0: `http://www.microsoft.com/Downloads/Release.asp?ReleaseID=26277`

Additional Info: `http://www.microsoft.com/technet/security/bulletin/MS00-100.asp`

Credit: eEye Digital Security

19

MICROSOFT

FrontPage Server Extensions ship with IIS 4.0 and IIS 5.0 and provide browse-time support functions. A vulnerability exists in some of these functions that allows an attacker to levy a malformed form submission to an IIS server that would cause the IIS service to fail. In IIS 4.0, you have to restart the service manually. In IIS 5.0, the IIS service will restart by itself.

The IIS New Variant of File Fragment Reading via .HTR Vulnerability

IIS Version: 4.0 and 5.0

Impact: An attacker can read fragments of files from a Web server.

Class: Moderate

Fix for IIS 4.0: `http://www.microsoft.com/Downloads/Release.asp?ReleaseID=27492`

Fix for IIS 5.0: `http://www.microsoft.com/Downloads/Release.asp?ReleaseID=27491`

Additional Info: `http://www.microsoft.com/technet/security/bulletin/MS01-004.asp`

Credit: Unknown

An attacker can cause a requested file to be processed by the .HTR ISAPI extension in such a way as to cause fragments of server-side files, such as .ASP files, to be sent to the attacker.

The IIS Session ID Cookie Marking Vulnerability

IIS Version: 4.0 and 5.0

Impact: A malicious user can hijack another user's secure Web session.

Class: Critical

Fix for IIS 4.0 x86 platforms: `http://www.microsoft.com/ntserver/nts/downloads/critical/q274149`

Fix for IIS 4.0 Alpha platforms: Available from Microsoft Product Support Services

Fix for IIS 5.0: `http://www.microsoft.com/Windows2000/downloads/critical/q274149`

Additional Info: `http://www.microsoft.com/technet/security/bulletin/MS00-080.asp`

Credit: ACROS Security and Ron Sires and C. Conrad Cady of Healinx

IIS uses the same Session ID for both secure and nonsecure pages on the same Web site. What this means to you is that when you initiate a session with a secure Web page, the Session ID cookie is protected by SSL. If you subsequently visit a nonsecure page on the same site, that same Session ID cookie is exchanged, only this time in plaintext. If a malicious user has control over the communications channel of your box, she could then read the plaintext Session ID cookie and use it to take any action on the secure page that you can.

The IIS Web Server File Request Parsing Vulnerability

IIS Version: 4.0 and 5.0

Impact: Remote users can run operating system commands on a Web server.

Class: Critical

Fix for IIS 4.0: `http://www.microsoft.com/ntserver/nts/downloads/critical/q277873`

Fix for IIS 5.0: `http://www.microsoft.com/Downloads/Release.asp?ReleaseID=25547`

Additional Info: `http://www.microsoft.com/technet/security/bulletin/MS00-086.asp`

Credit: NSFocus

An attacker can execute operating system commands that would enable her to take any action that any interactively logged-on user could take. This would enable her to add, delete, or change files on the server; modify Web pages; reformat the hard drive; run existing code on the server; or upload code onto the server and then run it.

The Invalid URL Vulnerability

IIS Version: 4.0

Impact: Attacker can cause IIS service to fail.

Class: Severe—Denial of Service

Fix for NT 4.0 Workstation, Server and Server Enterprise Editions:
`http://www.microsoft.com/Downloads/Release.asp?ReleaseID=24403`

Credit: Peter Grundl of VIGILANTe

An attacker can send an invalid URL to the server which, through a sequence of events, could result in an invalid memory request that would cause the IIS service to fail. Microsoft engineers believe that the underlying problem actually exists within Windows NT 4.0 itself.

The Myriad Escaped Characters Vulnerability

IIS Version: 4.0 and 5.0

Impact: An attacker can slow an IIS server's response or prevent it from providing service.

Class: Medium to Severe—Denial of Service

Fix for IIS 4.0: `http://www.microsoft.com/Downloads/Release.asp?ReleaseID=20292`

Fix for IIS 5.0: `http://www.microsoft.com/Downloads/Release.asp?ReleaseID=20286`

Credit: Vanja Hrustic of the Relay Group

By sending a malformed URL with an extremely large number of escape characters, an attacker can consume large quantities of CPU time and thus slow down or prevent the IIS server from providing service for a period of time.

The Web Server Folder Traversal Vulnerability

IIS Version: 4.0 and 5.0

Impact: An attacker can take destructive actions against a Web server.

Class: Critical

Fix: http://www.microsoft.com/windows2000/downloads/critical/q269862/default.asp

Additional Info: http://www.microsoft.com/technet/security/bulletin/MS00-078.asp

Credit: Rain Forest Puppy

An attacker can change or delete files or Web pages, run existing code on the Web server, upload new code and run it, format the hard disk, or take any number of other destructive actions.

Tools

After you establish your Windows NT 4.0 or Windows 2000 server, you can obtain several indispensable tools that will help you keep it secure. No Windows NT 4.0 or Windows 2000 administrator should be caught without these tools.

Administrator Assistant Tool Kit

Administrator Assistant Tool Kit is an application suite that contains utilities to streamline system administration on Windows NT boxes.

Aelita Software

3978 North Hampton Drive

Powell, OH 43065

800-263-0036

Windows Version: Windows NT 4.0 or Windows NT 3.51

Email: Services@aelita.com

URL: http://www.aelita.net/products/AdminAssist.htm

Administrator's Pak

The Administrator's Pak includes a variety of tools for recovering crashed Windows 2000 and Windows NT 4.0 systems. This bundle includes the NT Locksmith, NTRecover, Remote Recover, and NTFSDOS Pro tools, just to name a few. The Administrator's Pak bundle is a great value for tools that will help with recovering your Windows 2000 and Windows NT boxes.

Winternals Software LP

3101 Bee Caves Road, Suite 150

Austin, TX 78746

512-330-9130

Windows Version: Windows 2000 or Windows NT 4.0

Email: info@winternals.com

URL: http://www.winternals.com/

AntiSniff 1.021

AntiSniff 1.021 is a proactive security monitoring tool that searches for computers that are in promiscuous mode. This product help administrators and security teams detect who is watching traffic at their site.

Security Software Technologies, Inc.

Windows Version: Windows NT 4.0 or Windows 9x. SST expects to release the Windows 2000 version soon.

Email: sst@securitysoftwaretech.com

URL: http://www.securitysoftwaretech.com/antisniff/index.html/

FileAdmin

FileAdmin is an advanced tool for manipulating file permissions on large Windows NT-based networks. This utility can save you many hours of work.

Aelita Software

3978 North Hampton Drive

Powell, OH 43065

800-263-0036

Windows Version: Windows NT 4.0 or Windows NT 3.51

Email: Services@aelita.com

URL: http://www.aelita.net/products/FileAdmin.htm

Kane Security Analyst 5.0

Kane Security Analyst provides real-time intrusion detection for Windows NT 4.0 and Windows 2000. This utility monitors and reports security violations and is very configurable. It assesses six critical security areas: access control, data confidentiality, data integrity, password strength, system monitoring, and user account restrictions.

Intrusion.com, Inc.—USA

1101 East Arapaho Rd, Suite 100

Richardson, TX 75081

888-637-7770

Windows Version: Windows 2000, Windows NT, or Windows 9x

Email: info@intrusion.com

URL: http://www.intrusion.com/Products/analystnt.shtml

L0phtCrack 3.0

L0phtCrack is a tool that audits Windows 2000 and Windows NT passwords. L0phtCrack is a powerful tool that really needs to be part of every administrator's toolkit. You can display various information about the password tests, including how long it took to crack each password, the cracked passwords, and encrypted password hashes.

Security Software Technologies, Inc.

Windows Version: Windows 2000 or Windows NT 4.0

Email: sst@securitysoftwaretech.com

URL: http://www.securitysoftwaretech.com/l0phtcrack/

LANguard Internet Access Control

Internet Access Control not only enables you to monitor and control Internet usage on your network, it also monitors network traffic to detect break-ins from outside your network. With Internet Access Control, you use keywords to block access to unwanted sites (such as IRC). You can also use keywords to block searches for objectionable material at search engine sites without blocking the entire search engine. With the network monitor, you can watch for suspicious incoming traffic to a specific server that shouldn't be accessible to outside traffic.

GFI Fax & Voice USA

105 Towerview Court

Cary, NC 27513

888-2GFIFAX

Windows Version: Windows 2000 or Windows NT 4.0

Email: sales@gfi.com

URL: http://www.gfi.com/

LANguard Security Reporter

Security Reporter collects data about your Windows NT 4.0 or Windows 2000 network, such as user rights, users having administrative rights, and resource permissions, among others. This information is stored in a central database. You use the information in this database to generate reports that help you to identify and fix potential security problems.

GFI Fax & Voice USA

105 Towerview Court

Cary, NC 27513

888-2GFIFAX

Windows Version: Windows 2000 or Windows NT 4.0

Email: sales@gfi.com

URL: http://www.gfi.com/

NT Crack

NT Crack is a tool that audits Windows NT passwords. This is the functional equivalent of Crack for UNIX.

Secure Networks, Inc.

Suite 330 1201 5th Street S.W.

Calgary, Alberta Canada T2R-0Y6

Windows Version: Windows NT (all versions)

URL: `http://www.system7.org/archive/Nt-Hacking/windows.html`

NT Locksmith

NT Locksmith will access a Windows NT box without a password. It is a recovery utility that allows you to set a new admin password.

Winternals Software LP

3101 Bee Caves Road, Suite 150

Austin, TX 78746

512-330-9130

Windows Version: Windows 2000 or Windows NT 4.0

Email: `info@winternals.com`

URL: `http://www.winternals.com/`

NTFSDOS Pro

NTFSDOS Pro allows you to copy and rename permissions on Windows 2000 and Windows NT 4.0 from a DOS diskette. This is a great tool to keep around for emergencies (for example, when you lose that Administrator password).

Winternals Software LP

3101 Bee Caves Road, Suite 150

Austin, TX 78746

512-330-9130

Windows Version: Windows 2000 or Windows NT 4.0

Email: `info@winternals.com`

URL: `http://www.winternals.com/`

NTHandle

NTHandle identifies open processes in Windows NT and thus allows you to keep an eye on your users.

NT Internals—Mark Russinovich

Windows Version: Windows 9x/Me, Windows NT 4.0, Windows 2000, or Whistler Beta 1

Email: mark@sysinternals.com

URL: http://www.sysinternals.com

NTRecover

NTRecover is a salvage program. It allows you to access dead Windows NT drives via serial lines—now is that cool or what? NTRecover uses a serial cable to access files and volumes on a dead NT box. You use the serial cable connection to make the disks on the dead box seem as though they are mounted on your own system.

Winternals Software LP

3101 Bee Caves Road, Suite 150

Austin, TX 78746

512-330-9130

Windows Version: Windows 2000 or Windows NT 4.0

Email: info@winternals.com

URL: http://www.winternals.com/

PC Firewall ASaP

PC Firewall ASaP is a bi-directional packet filter suite for Windows 9x/Me and Windows NT 4.0 clients.

myCIO.com (Network Associates, Inc.)

3965 Freedom Circle

Santa Clara, CA 95054

877-796-9246

Windows Version: Windows 9x/Me or Windows NT 4.0

Email: support@mycio.com

URL: http://www.mycio.com/

RedButton

RedButton is a tool for testing remote vulnerabilities of a publicly accessible Registry. Download Rbutton.zip.

Midwestern Commerce, Inc.

1601 West Fifth Avenue, Suite 207

Columbus, OH 43212

Windows Version: Windows NT (all versions)

URL: http://www.system7.org/archive/Nt-Hacking/windows.html

RegAdmin

RegAdmin is an advanced tool for manipulating Registry entries on large networks, which is a big timesaver.

Aelita Software

3978 North Hampton Drive

Powell, OH 43065

800-263-0036

Windows Version: Windows NT 4.0 or Windows NT 3.51

Email: Services@box.omna.com

URL: http://www.aelita.net/products/RegAdmin.htm

Remote Recover

Remote Recover acts in the same way as NTRecover. The difference is that it treats remote drives as though they were locally installed. It allows you to access and modify drives on unbootable or new boxes using the network and a bootable floppy.

Winternals Software LP

3101 Bee Caves Road, Suite 150

Austin, TX 78746

512-330-9130

Windows Version: Windows 2000 or Windows NT 4.0

Email: info@winternals.com

URL: http://www.winternals.com/

ScanNT Plus

ScanNT Plus is a dictionary password attack utility. Test your NT passwords.

Midwestern Commerce, Inc. (Ntsecurity.com)

1601 West Fifth Avenue Suite 207

Columbus, OH 43212

Windows Version: Windows NT 4.0

Email: Services@box.omna.com

URL: http://hotfiles.zdnet.com/cgi-bin/texis/swlib/hotfiles/info.html?b=pcm&fcode=000H36

Sniffer Basic

Sniffer Basic (formerly named NetXRay Analyzer) is a powerful protocol analyzer (sniffer) and network monitoring tool for Windows NT. It is probably the most comprehensive NT sniffer available.

> Sniffer Technologies
>
> 3965 Freedom Circle
>
> Santa Clara, CA 95054
>
> 800-SNIFFER
>
> Windows Version: Windows NT (all versions) or Windows 98
>
> **Note:** Sniffer Technologies released Sniffer Pro 4.5 for laptop platforms in January, 2001. This version includes support for Windows 2000.
>
> Email: `bcahillane@nai.com`
>
> URL: `http://www.sniffer.com/products/sniffer-basic/default.asp?A=2`

Somarsoft DumpSec

Somarsoft DumpSec dumps permissions for the Windows NT file system in the Registry, including shares and printers. It offers a bird's-eye view of permissions, which are normally hard to gather on large networks.

> SystemTools LLP
>
> P.O. Box 1209
>
> La Vernia, TX 78121
>
> 877-797-8665
>
> Windows Version: Windows NT (all versions)
>
> Email: `sales@systemtools.com`
>
> URL: `http://www.somarsoft.com/`

Somarsoft DumpEvt

Somarsoft DumpEvt dumps Event Log information for importation into a database for analysis.

> SystemTools LLP
>
> P.O. Box 1209
>
> La Vernia, TX 78121
>
> 877-797-8665
>
> Windows Version: Windows 2000 or Windows NT (all versions)
>
> Email: `sales@systemtools.com`
>
> URL: `http://www.somarsoft.com/`

Somarsoft DumpReg

Somarsoft DumpReg dumps Registry information for analysis. It also allows incisive searching and matching of keys.

> SystemTools LLP
>
> P.O. Box 1209
>
> La Vernia, TX 78121
>
> 877-797-8665
>
> Windows Version: Windows NT (all versions) or Windows 98
>
> Email: info@somarsoft.com
>
> URL: http://www.somarsoft.com/

Virtuosity

Virtuosity is a wide-scale management and Windows NT rollouts tool. (Good for heavy-duty rollouts.)

> Raxco, Ltd.
>
> Orchard House
>
> Narborough Wood Park
>
> Enderby, Leicester, UK LE9 5XT
>
> +44 (0)116 239-5888
>
> Windows Version: Windows NT 4.0 or Windows NT 3.51
>
> URL: http://www.domainmigration.com/fp_virtuosity.html

Access Control Software

The following section introduces several good packages for adding access control to Windows 2000, Windows NT, and Windows 9x/Me.

Cetus StormWindow

> Cetus Software, Inc.
>
> P.O. Box 1450
>
> Marshfield, MA 02050
>
> 781-834-4411
>
> Windows Version: Windows 2000, Windows NT 4.0 or Windows 9x/Me
>
> Email: cetussoft@aol.com
>
> URL: http://www.cetussoft.com/

19

MICROSOFT

Cetus StormWindow allows you to incisively hide and protect almost anything within the system environment, including the following:

- Links and folders
- Drives and directories
- Networked devices and printers

In all, Cetus StormWindow offers very comprehensive access control. (This product will also intercept most alternate boot requests, such as warm boots, Ctrl+Alt+Delete, and function keys.)

Clasp2000

Clasp2000

4 Grand Banks Circle

Marlton, NJ 08053

FAX: 810-821-6250

Windows Version: Windows 2000 or Windows 9x

Email: service@claspnow.com

URL: http://www.cyberenet.net/~ryan/

Clasp2000 offers strong password protection, disables access to Windows 95 and Windows 98, and intercepts warm boot Ctrl+Alt+Delete sequences.

ConfigSafe Complete Recovery v4 by imagine LAN, Inc.

imagine LAN, Inc.

74 Northeastern Blvd. Suite 12

Nashua, NH 03062

800-372-9776

Windows Version: Windows 2000, Windows 4.0 or Windows 9x/Me

Email: feedback@imagelan.com

URL: http://www.configsafe.com

ConfigSafe Complete Recovery v4 records changes and updates made to the Registry, system files, drivers, directory structures, DLL files, and system hardware. You can instantly restore a system to a previously working configuration with ConfigSafe.

DECROS Security Card by DECROS, Ltd.

DECROS, Ltd.

J. S. Baara 40

370 01 Ceske Budejovice Czech Republic

420-38-731 2808

Windows Version: Windows 2000, Windows NT 4.0 or Windows 9x/Me

Email: `info@decros.cz`

URL: `http://www.decros.com/security_division/p_list_hw.htm`

DECROS Security Card provides C2-level access control using physical security in the form of a card key. Without that card, no one will gain access to the system.

Desktop Surveillance Enterprise and Personal Editions

Omniquad, Ltd.

Hanovia House

28/29 Eastman Road

London W3 7YG, UK

+44 (0) 181 743 8093

Windows Version: Windows NT 4.0 or Windows 9x

Email: `support@omniquad.com`

URL: `http://www.omniquad.com/`

Desktop Surveillance is a full-fledged investigation and access control utility. (This product has strong logging and audit capabilities.)

HDD-Protect 2.5c

Gottfried Siehs

Tiergartenstrasse 99

A-6020 Innsbruck, Austria / Europe

Windows Version: Windows 98 or Windows 95

Email: `g.siehs@tirol.com`

URL: `http://www.geocities.com/SiliconValley/Lakes/8753/`

HDD-Protect has hardware-level access control and actually restricts access to the hard disk drive.

Omniquad Detective 2.1

Hanovia House

28/29 Eastman Road

London W3 7YG, UK

+44 (0) 181 743 8093

Windows Version: Windows NT 4.0 or Windows 9x

Email: `support@omniquad.com`

URL: `http://www.omniquad.com/`

The Detective is a simple but powerful tool for monitoring system processes. Omniquad Detective enables you to monitor computer usage, reconstruct activities that have occurred on a workstation or server, identify intruders who try to cover their tracks, perform content analysis, and define user search patterns. In all, this very comprehensive tool is tailor-made to catch someone in the act, and is probably suitable for investigating computer-assisted crime in the workplace.

Secure4U 5.0

Sandbox Security AG

Lilienthalstr. 1

82178 Puchheim

Germany

+49 (0) 89 800 70 0

Windows Version: Windows 2000, Windows NT 4.0 or Windows 9x/Me

Email: sales@SandboxSecurity.com

URL: http://www.sandboxsecurity.com/main.htm

Secure4U provides powerful filtering and access control. It specifically targets ActiveX, Java, and other embedded-text plug-ins and languages from flowing into your network.

StopLock Suite by Conclusive Logic, Inc.

Conclusive Logic, Inc.

800 W. El Camino Real

Suite 180

Mountain View, CA 94040 USA

650-943-2359

Windows Version: Windows 2000, Windows 4.0 or Windows 9x

Email: info@conclusive.com

URL: http://www.conclusive.com/

StopLock provides access control. The package also includes boot control, auditing functionality, and logging tools.

TrueFace

eTrue, Inc.

144 Turnpike Rd.

Suite 100

Southboro, MA 01772

508-303-9901

Windows Version: Windows 32-bit platforms

URL: `http://www.miros.com/solutions/face.htm`

TrueFace is a face recognition program. The software recognizes only those faces that are registered in its face database. The machine actually looks at you to determine whether you are an authorized user. The company claims that the technology on which TrueFace is based is neural net technology.

Windows Task-Lock by Posum LLC

Posum LLC

P.O. Box 21015

Huntsville, AL 35824

256-895-9857

Windows Version: Windows 2000, Windows 4.0, or Windows 9x/Me

Email: `support@posum.com`

URL: `http://posum.com/`

Windows Task-Lock 6.0 provides a simple, inexpensive, and effective way to password-protect specified applications no matter how you (or someone else) execute them. It is easy to configure and requires little to no modifications to your current system configuration. Optional Sound events, stealth mode, and password timeout are also included.

WP WinSafe

PBNSoft

Windows Version: Windows NT or Windows 9x

Email: `info@pnbsoft.com`

URL: `http://www.pbnsoft.com/`

WinSafe, a promising utility, allows you to encrypt your files using strong cryptography algorithms such as Blowfish and CAST. With WinSafe you can choose from among 28 different algorithms. Other tools included with this package are File Wiping and Merge Files. File Wiping will rewrite deleted files with random trash for the number of times that you specify. Merge Files enables you to merge two files so that you can hide one file into another.

19

MICROSOFT

CAUTION

The documentation suggests that using the Windows Policy editor to set the real-mode DOS settings could potentially conflict with WinSafe.

SafeGuard Easy

Utimaco Safeware, Inc.

2 Chestnut Place

Suite 310

22 Elm Street

Worcester, MA 01608 USA

508-799-4333

Windows Version: Windows 2000, Windows NT 4.0, Windows 9x, or MS-DOS

Email: info.us@utimaco.de

URL: http://www.utimaco.de/newpage/indexmain.html

SafeGuard Easy offers hard disk drive encryption, protection against booting from a floppy, password aging, and password authentication for Windows operating systems. SafeGuard supports several strong encryption algorithms, including both DES and International Data Encryption Algorithm (IDEA). The SafeGuard line of products includes SafeGuard VPN, SafeGuard LAN Crypt, and SafeGuard Personal FireWall. Of special interest is that these products can be installed over a network (thereby obviating the need to make separate installations).

Secure Shell

F-Secure, Inc.

5007 Lincoln Avenue, Suite 310

Lisle, IL 60532 USA

630-810-8901

Windows Version: Windows 2000, Windows NT 4.0, Windows 9x, or Windows 3x

Email: Chicago@F-secure.com

URL: http://www.f-secure.com/products/network_security/

Secure Shell (SSH) provides safe, encrypted communication over the Internet or other untrusted networks. SSH is an excellent replacement for Telnet or rlogin. SSH uses IDEA and Rivest-Shamir-Adelman (RSA) encryption and is therefore extremely secure. It is reported that the keys are discarded and new keys are made once an hour. SSH completely eliminates the possibility of third parties capturing your communication (for example, passwords that might otherwise be passed in clear text). SSH sessions cannot be overtaken or hijacked, nor can they be sniffed. The only real drawback is that for you to use SSH, the other end must also be using it. Although you might think such encrypted communication would be dreadfully slow, it isn't.

Good Online Sources of Information

This section contains many good Windows resource links. Most are dynamic and house material that is routinely updated.

The Windows NT Security FAQ

If you are new to Windows NT security, the Windows NT Security Frequently Asked Questions document is an absolute must. I would wager that better than half of the questions you have about NT security are answered in this document.

```
http://www.it.kth.se/~rom/ntsec.html
```

NTBugTraq

NTBugTraq is an excellent resource provided by Russ Cooper of RC Consulting. The site includes a database of Windows NT vulnerabilities, plus the archived and searchable versions of the NTBugTraq mailing list.

```
http://www.ntbugtraq.com
```

NTSECURITY.COM for Windows 2000 and Windows NT

This site is hosted by Aelita Software Group division of Midwestern Commerce, Inc., a well-known development firm that designs security applications for Windows 2000 and Windows NT, among other things.

```
http://www.ntsecurity.com/default.htm
```

Expert Answers for Windows 2000, Windows NT, and Windows 9x/Me

This is a forum in which advanced Windows 2000, Windows NT, and Windows 9x/Me issues are discussed. It is a good place to find possible solutions to very obscure and configuration-specific problems. Regulars post clear, concise questions and answers along the lines of "I have a PPRO II w/ NT 4.0 and IIS 3 running MS Exchange 5.0, with SP3 for NT and SP1 for Exchange. So, why is my mail server dying?"

```
http://community.zdnet.com/cgi-bin/podium/show?ROOT=331&MSG=331&T=index
```

Windows IT Security (Formerly NTSecurity.net)

The Windows IT Security site, hosted by *Windows 2000 Magazine*, is full of information about the latest in security. You can subscribe to discussion lists about advanced vulnerabilities in the Windows 2000 and Windows NT operating systems. You can find it at the following URL:

```
http://www.ntsecurity.net/
```

19

MICROSOFT

"An Introduction to the Windows 2000 Public Key Infrastructure"

"An Introduction to the Windows 2000 Public Key Infrastructure" is an article written by Microsoft Press. It presents and introduction to one of Windows 2000 new security features, PKI.

```
http://www.microsoft.com/WINDOWS2000/library/howitworks/security/pkiintro.asp
```

Windows 2000 Magazine Online

I know what you're thinking—that commercial magazines are probably not very good sources for security information. I am happy to report that this site is an exception. Some very valuable articles and editorials about Windows NT 2000 and Windows NT 4.0 appear here.

```
http://www.winntmag.com/
```

Securing Windows NT Installation

Securing Windows NT Installation is an incredibly detailed document from Microsoft on establishing a secure Windows NT server. You can find it at this site:

```
http://www.microsoft.com/ntserver/security/exec/overview/Secure_NTInstall.asp
```

Checklist for Upgrading to Windows 2000 Server

Microsoft lists the steps necessary to upgrade to Windows 2000. They include how to check whether your hardware and software is compatible with Windows 2000 and how to choose a file system. You can find it here:

```
http://www.microsoft.com/TechNet/win2000/srvchk.asp
```

The University of Texas at Austin Computation Center NT Archive

This site contains a wide (and sometimes eclectic) range of tools and fixes for Windows NT. (A good example is a fully-functional Curses library for use on NT.)

```
ftp://microlib.cc.utexas.edu:/microlib/nt/
```

Books on Windows 2000 and Windows NT Security

The following titles are assorted treatments on Windows 2000 and NT security.

Securing Windows NT/2000 Servers for the Internet. Stefan Norberg, Deborah Russell. O'Reilly & Associates. ISBN: 1-56592-768-0. 2000.

Windows 2000 Security. Roberta Bragg. New Riders Publishing. ISBN: 0-73570-991-2. 2000.

Windows 2000 Security: Little Black Book. Ian McLean. The Coriolis Group. ISBN: 1-57610-387-0. 2000.

Configuring Windows 2000 Server Security. Thomas W. Shinder and D. Lynn White. Syngress Media, Inc. ISBN: 1-92899-402-4. 1999.

Microsoft Windows 2000 Security Technical Reference. Internet Security Systems, Inc. Microsoft Press. ISBN: 0-73560-858-X. 2000.

Microsoft Windows 2000 Security Handbook. Jeff Schmidt. Que. ISBN: 0-78971-999-1. 2000.

Microsoft Windows NT 4.0 Security, Audit, and Control (Microsoft Technical Reference). James G. Jumes. Microsoft Press. ISBN: 1-57231-818-X. 1998.

NT 4 Network Security. Matthew Strebe. Sybex. ISBN: 0-78212-425-9. 1999.

Windows NT/2000 Network Security (Circle Series). E. Eugene Schultz. New Riders Publishing. ISBN: 1-57870-253-4. 2000.

Windows 2000 Security Handbook. Phillip Cox. McGraw-Hill Professional Publishing. ISBN: 0-07212-433-4. 2000.

Windows NT Server Security Guide (Prentice Hall Series on Microsoft Technologies). Marcus Goncalves. Prentice Hall Computer Books. ISBN: 0-13679-903-5. 1998.

Windows NT Security Handbook. Thomas Sheldon. Osborne McGraw-Hill. ISBN: 0-07882-240-8. 1996.

Summary

Microsoft offers a number of excellent applications, and Windows 2000 and Windows NT 4.0 are excellent server platforms. However, like their counterparts, they are not secure out of the box. To run secure Microsoft applications and servers, you must do three things:

- Patch the vulnerabilities discussed in this chapter.
- Apply general security techniques discussed in other chapters.
- Constantly keep up with advisories.

If you cover these bases, you should be fine.

19

MICROSOFT

UNIX

IN THIS CHAPTER

This chapter examines the UNIX operating system from a security perspective. We'll start with a whistle-stop tour of UNIX history, followed by an in-depth look at the issues faced when selecting a UNIX distribution. We'll then consider the security risks and countermeasures—along with some thoughts about the decisions you'll face.

We'll cover the hard core UNIX security territory and some useful follow-up material written by respected security practitioners—that way, you can dip in and out as your interest takes you.

This chapter isn't a UNIX security manual though, nor is it a step-by-step set of instructions for securing a particular UNIX distribution (see the "Host-Hardening Resources" section for pointers to checklists). You also won't find a list of the most "leet" UNIX exploits here. There are a thousand hacker sites out there waiting for you, if that is all you seek.

My primary goal is to get you thinking about UNIX security in the context of *your* environment. The way in which your organization deploys UNIX has a fundamental bearing on what you can and should be doing to secure it. Sure, there are some common issues that face the majority of us, such as OS security bugs—but computer systems don't exist in a vacuum. They are used by people to get a job done—whether it is to serve your home page to an unsuspecting world or to process credit card transactions through a major bank. Failure to grasp the local issues can lead to terminally flawed security "solutions" that simply don't fit your context. These are the "soft issues."

Also, understand that we're talking about a security process—not just an initial effort.

On a number of occasions, I'll reference specific programs or filenames. The names and locations of these programs might differ on your system—if you don't already know the differences, check your online man pages (man -k *search-clue*).

A Whistle-Stop Tour of UNIX History

The seeds of UNIX were sown in 1965 when Bell Labs, General Electric Company, and Massachusetts Institute of Technology designed an operating system called Multics. From the outset, this was designed to be a multiuser system supporting multiple concurrent users, data storage, and data sharing.

By 1969, with the project failing, Bell Labs quit the project. Ken Thompson, a Bell Labs engineer began "rolling his own"—soon to be called UNIX (a pun on Multics). The next year, Dennis Ritchie wrote the first C compiler (inventing the C language in the process), and, in 1973, Thompson rewrote the kernel in C.

UNIX was getting to be portable and, by 1975, was distributed to universities. The attraction of UNIX was its portability and low-end hardware requirements. For the time, it could run on relatively inexpensive workstations. Consequently, UNIX developed a strong following within academic circles.

This popularity coupled with the availability of a C compiler lead to the development of core utilities and programs still included in our distributions today. Many utilities have quite a rich or comical history—I recommend you check the history books. With businesses recognizing that they could save on expensive hardware and training costs, it was only a matter of time before a number of vendors packaged their own distributions. From there, the UNIX family tree explodes—splintering off into very different directions based on the motivation and financing of the maintainers.

▶ For a comprehensive history lesson, visit `http://perso.wanadoo.fr/levenez/unix/`. There is also a graphical family tree of UNIX where you can trace the origins of your favorite distribution.

▶ Matt Bishop maintains a fascinating archive of papers that record the findings of early UNIX security reviews at `http://seclab.cs.ucdavis.edu/projects/history/index.html`. Matt is probably best known though for his research into secure programming techniques. Check out his research papers and presentations.

Vendors ported UNIX to new hardware platforms and incorporated "value-added" items such as printed documentation, additional device drivers, enhanced file systems, window managers, and HA (High Availability) technologies. Source code was no longer shipped in favor of "binary-only distributions" as vendors sought to protect their intellectual property rights.

To stand a chance of securing government contracts, vendors implemented security extensions as specified in the Rainbow Series of Books, by the U.S. Department of Defense. Each book defined a set of design, implementation, and documentation criteria that an operating system needed to fulfill to be certified at a particular security level. Probably the best known level is C2, which we'll look at later.

Getting "accredited" was no mean feat. It required a significant amount of time and money. This tended to favor the big players who could afford to play the long game.

As it turns out, the security interfaces across different distributions are pretty incompatible. On top of this, the code running the C2 subsystems tended to be immature, buggy, and slow. The administrative tools were awful (and often still are) as was the support. Ask a UNIX administrator about C2 auditing, and she'll either look at you blankly or laugh.

These developments were happening against a backdrop of low technical security awareness—even lower than today. The IBM mainframe stored all the corporate secrets and was considered a well-known commodity. As for UNIX, it gained a reputation for being something of an unruly beast. The combination of its hippie culture, unorthodox parentage, and its almighty superuser (root) proved something of a nightmare for some auditors.

Consequently, the advice given to administrators was very general in nature and seemed to focus solely on who had access to root and what version of sendmail was running (because of

20

UNIX

its long history of security problems). These things are clearly important, but the fact that their shiny new systems were running a slew of overtrusting network services and buggy, privileged programs just wasn't on their radar. (And we haven't even mentioned the application programs!) Crackers were well aware of the shortcomings in popular distributions and were running rings around the less capable administrators.

However, at the other end of the spectrum was a loose community of "security pioneers"—programmers cum administrators, who developed some of the most pervasive security tools ever written. We'll cover the best ones in due course. The authors openly shared their source code with the wider community via Usenet—way before the WWW (World Wide Web) had been invented.

Recent years have seen a significant rise in the popularity and business acceptance of open source UNIX (`http://www.opensource.org/osd.html`). Traditionally, commercial support for open source distributions was limited to small specialist outfits that tended to have limited geographical presence. The recent explosion of business interest in GNU/Linux has vendors lining up to earn support dollars. Times have really changed in the UNIX world. In the world of commerce, proprietary UNIX systems once ruled the roost. Now, everyone is talking open source. What does open source bring to the party? We'll cover that shortly.

Classifying UNIX Distributions

UNIX distributions offer very different levels of security out of the box. Today, there are hundreds of distributions, although only about a dozen are in very widespread use.

From a security perspective, we can group these into the following categories.

Immature

Immature UNIX distributions include experimental, unsupported, and poorly supported distributions. These distributions ship with programs that have security vulnerabilities that are either well known, or easy to identify and exploit. You'll generally want to leave these well alone, except for maybe shooting practice in the lab.

Mainstream

Mainstream UNIX distributions are characterized by a large installed user-base, commercial support services, and, up until recently, binary-only distribution.

The best selling closed source, commercial off-the-shelf (COTS) distributions as of this writing are

- SUN Solaris
- Hewlett-Packard HP-UX

- IBM AIX

- Compaq Tru64 UNIX

Each and every one of these has suffered serious security problems. But we are not talking about isolated incidents. Every month, significant security flaws are discovered. In other words, people are finding all kinds of ways of cracking these popular systems.

The vendors started with the same common code. Serious security holes are found from time to time, but their occurrence is infrequent enough to consider the code reasonably mature from a security perspective.

The weak area tends to be the vendor enhancements. Writing secure software places certain demands on the programmer. There is little evidence to show that operating system vendors can produce secure code in a sustainable manner. It's not that the entire programming industry is stupid—that would be an injustice to some very talented code cutters. It's evidence that writing secure software, under commercial time pressures, is a "hard problem." This should not come as a startling revelation to the software industry.

▶ In case you have a hard time believing that the commercial operating system you run has a security history comparable to Swiss cheese, look up your OS in the SecurityFocus vulnerability database at `http://www.securityfocus.com/vdb/`. You might be surprised by the results.

Certainly mainstream vendors generally agree that security is important. However, the focus is on tangible security features like encryption, rather than security of design and implementation. It's a lot easier to sell features than it is assurance. Insecure software is invisible—that is, until someone decides to break in.

Many IT decision-makers implicitly trust mainstream vendors to produce a secure operating system. However, comprehensive security testing is nontrivial. It requires significant expertise to do comprehensively and takes time—both of which come at a cost. Some vendors aren't even trying though. This is evidenced by the frequency of posts to Bugtraq from independent security researchers reporting basic security flaws in COTS software. I am not aware of any COTS vendor publicly pledging that it is pro-actively auditing its distributions for security vulnerabilities as a matter of course.

This situation is exacerbated by a commonly held belief that exploiting security vulnerabilities is rocket science. That's a myth perpetuated by the news media and a section of the security industry—the truth is that anyone with even a modicum of IT skills can break into a computer system installed straight off the CD-ROM. Exploit scripts are widely available and simple to use.

This might lead you to think about legal liability issues. Surely, the law must protect the consumer? The truth is on the shrink-wrap clinging to your OS media. Read the big, fat disclaimer (known as the license agreement). Before you accuse me of being flippant, go on—read that agreement—every last word of it. Here is a snippet from a product disclaimer most likely installed on your workstation:

DISCLAIMER OF WARRANTIES: YOU AGREE THAT XYZ HAS MADE NO EXPRESS WARRANTIES TO YOU REGARDING THE SOFTWARE AND THAT THE SOFTWARE IS BEING PROVIDED TO YOU "AS IS" WITHOUT WARRANTY OF ANY KIND. XYZ DISCLAIMS ALL WARRANTIES WITH REGARD TO THE SOFTWARE, EXPRESS OR IMPLIED, INCLUDING, WITHOUT LIMITATION, ANY IMPLIED WARRANTIES OF FITNESS FOR A PARTICULAR PURPOSE, MERCHANTABILITY, MERCHANTABLE QUALITY OR NONINFRINGEMENT OF THIRD PARTY RIGHTS. Some states or jurisdictions do not allow the exclusion of implied warranties so the above limitations may not apply to you.

LIMIT OF LIABILITY: IN NO EVENT WILL XYZ BE LIABLE TO YOU FOR ANY LOSS OF USE, INTERRUPTION OF BUSINESS, OR ANY DIRECT, INDIRECT, SPECIAL, INCIDENTAL, OR CONSEQUENTIAL DAMAGES OF ANY KIND (INCLUDING LOST PROFITS) REGARDLESS OF THE FORM OF ACTION WHETHER IN CONTRACT, TORT (INCLUDING NEGLIGENCE), STRICT PRODUCT LIABILITY OR OTHERWISE, EVEN IF XYZ HAS BEEN ADVISED OF THE POSSIBILITY OF SUCH DAMAGES.

Now ask yourself, what recourse do you have if someone drives a juggernaut through your systems security via a security hole in this software? The truth is, none—zero.

Until the customer wakes up and demands security, vendors will spend more time trying to out-feature their competitors rather than auditing and fixing their existing codebase. Sexy features sell boxes.

Personally, I don't see any convincing reason that the "features versus security" status quo will change any time soon. Consequently you need to adopt some healthy skepticism. After all, outright cynicism can get a tad grating after a while.

How Secure Is Open Source?

Because I have painted a pretty dismal picture of closed source OS security, you might ask, "Is there any tangible security benefit to going open source?" My view is yes and no.

NOTE

The open source development model contrasts sharply with that of the traditional closed source one. To find out more, see Eric Raymond's classic paper at `http://www.tuxedo.org/~esr/writings/cathedral-bazaar`.

Open source proponents argue that a transparent development process, with the benefit of "many eyes" debugging and reviewing code, adds security in itself. They cite the development process of new cryptographic algorithms/protocols as an example of the need for an open code development model.

Developing secure cryptography is a "hard problem"—as is developing secure and reliable program code. At their own cost, less experienced cryptographers have often learned that a closed development model results in seemingly hard-to-break algorithms. Under the glare of an experienced cryptanalyst, however, they are soon broken.

Others feel that developing secure program code doesn't work out that way in practice. They point to the lack of experienced code auditors, the sheer volume of code to audit, and the general lack of interest. This point is worth considering. How many people do you know who actually review the source code they download? How many people do you know who have sufficient experience to actually find most, if not all, of the security holes? We all assume, "Someone else is doing it."

In reality, open source code does get reviewed—just don't expect every line of every program you download to have been reviewed by elite security researchers. In reality, software that is high profile or security related tends to grab the lion's share of attention. Even then, the sheer size and the codebase's complexity can make reviewing a formidable challenge—even for highly skilled reviewers (as evidenced by code errors that slipped by reviewers of ISC BIND V4 and SSH version 2).

It is more efficient and effective to review open source programs for security problems than it is to review closed source programs.

Reviewing closed source software relies on either black box testing (threat testing) or reverse-engineering. Both can be very time-consuming and require a great deal of patience and sound methodology on the part of the reviewers. Reverse-engineering can be incredibly tedious and exhausting—it can also be illegal (refer to your license agreement again). The current trend in lawmaking might soon outlaw reverse-engineering altogether. Our lawmakers run the risk of outlawing one of the few methods available for finding security holes in closed source software. Open source eliminates that problem.

▶ To learn more about software assurance testing (such as white box testing), check out the Cigital (formerly Reliable Software Technologies) Web site at `http://www.cigital.com/resources/`.

The view you take on open/closed source programs will strongly influence your selection of an operating system and the security tools available to you.

Some organizations can be particularly sensitive about using open source software—particularly those subject to regulatory or legal demands. The issues tend to revolve around trustworthiness (that is, no Trojan code), integrity concerns, and formal support.

The extent of the concerns will often relate to the role the software will play and who else is using it (the sheep theory). Back doors are pretty much unheard of in popular open source software. They are more likely to occur on the download site itself (after an attacker has compromised a site). This is exactly what happened to the primary TCPWrappers download site in January 1999.

CERT released an advisory (http://www.cert.org/advisories/CA-1999-01.html) reporting that the site had been compromised and a Trojan had been inserted into the TCPWrappers source. The changes were spotted pretty quickly as the modified archive files were not PGP signed by the author. However, this kind of incident is extremely rare and easy to detect.

Rather than blindly trust download sites, I recommend that you follow a policy of downloading software from multiple, well-known, separately managed sites (for example, CERT, COAST, and SecurityFocus.com). Also use cryptographic integrity software (such as MD5, PGP, or GnuPG) to verify the integrity of the archive against a known good signature (again, use unrelated sites for the comparison).

▶ For tips on using MD5, see
  http://www.cert.org/security-improvement/implementations/i002.01.html

▶ For a Win32 version of MD5, visit
  http://www.weihenstephan.de/~syring/win32/UnxUtils.html

Formal support is a separate (mostly commercial) issue that I don't plan to cover here.

But, what about using an entire operating system that is open source, such as GNU/Linux? Some people perceive that open source systems suffer more security problems than other platforms. They point to the number of security patches released and the volume of vulnerabilities reported on lists such as Bugtraq.

My view is that the kernel itself doesn't appear to suffer from any more security problems than any other UNIX kernel. It's widely regarded as more stable and better analyzed from a security perspective than any mainstream closed source UNIX.

However, a Linux distribution consists of more than just a kernel. In fact, SuSE has grown so large, it ships on seven CDs! Thousands of applications are available for Linux, many of which have not been written with security in mind. As a result, the distributors who package all this code are regularly sending out security advisories and patches. This can lead to the incorrect conclusion that all patches issued are relevant. The message: Don't install everything off the CD—be a little selective—install what you need. More on that later.

▶ For more on the open versus closed source code debate, check out these links:
  Michael H. Warfield: *Musings on open source security models.*
  http://www.linuxworld.com/linuxworld/lw-1998-11/lw-11-ramparts.html

  Simson Garfinkel: *Security Through Obscurity.*
  http://www.wideopen.com/story/101.html

  John Viega: *The myth of open source security.*
  http://www.earthweb.com/dlink.resource-jhtml.72.1101.|repository||itmanagement|
  content|article|2000|07|19|EMviegaopen|EMviegaopen~xml.0.jhtml?cda=true

The Fuzz Challenge

In 1990 and 1995, the University of Wisconsin staged the Fuzz Test—a study of how 80 popular operating system programs on 9 different platforms behaved when they were subjected to random input data streams. Clearly, a correctly written program should handle anything thrown at it—otherwise, an attacker might be able to influence a privileged program to gain unauthorized access.

The findings make interesting reading. Open source proponents argue that the results of the Fuzz Test provide empirical evidence to support their view that open source–created programs are more reliable and secure than the closed source equivalents. Needless to say, in the test the closed source programs suffered from fundamental problems not present in their open source equivalents. Check out the full report here: `ftp://grilled.cs.wisc.edu/ technical_papers/fuzz-revisited.pdf`. For the NT crowd, check out theFuzz Test's August 2000 report—testers managed to blow up 100% of NT applications.

For me, the biggest win with open source software is that, if you know what you are doing (or know someone who does), then you can change the system yourself by implementing additional defenses. We'll cover some of the more popular options later. There really is nothing to beat the sense of empowerment you get when you realize that you have complete control over the way your system operates.

Hardened Operating Systems

In this category I'm including distributions that meet one or more of the following criteria:

- The distribution shipped with "secure by default" configuration settings.
- It was programmed defensively. The programmer assumes any user could be an attacker).
- The distribution maintainers subject their existing source code to a security audit whenever a new class of security vulnerability is discovered.
- The distribution has been compiled in such a way as to contain a common class of security exploit, the buffer overflow.

OpenBSD

Probably the best known example of a free, open source, hardened UNIX distribution is OpenBSD (`http://www.openbsd.org/`). In fact, OpenBSD is one of the only distributions in general circulation to meet the first three criteria (OpenBSD's developers would probably reasonably argue that they don't need to do point 4 because they do points 2 and 3!).

Their publicly stated goal is to be "Number one in the industry for security." They achieve this by attracting security-conscious programmers and adopting a tireless approach to weeding out both possible and not-so-possible security exposures.

20

UNIX

Security benefits of OpenBSD include the following:

- Has secure "out-of-the-box" system configuration; that is, no time-consuming hardening is required.
- Ships with strong cryptography ready for use. OpenBSD includes OpenSSH for secure network terminal access, IPSEC, strong PRNG (Pseudo Random Number Generator), secure hashing, and wide support for cryptographic hardware. See `http://www.openbsd.org/crypto.html` for more details.
- Suffers fewer security vulnerabilities than any other UNIX I am aware of. Equally important though is the turnaround of fixes—typically within a day or two.
- Provides source code for independent scrutiny.
- Includes simplified installation and management in recent releases.

OpenBSD has been ported to 11 hardware platforms.

At the time of this writing, OpenBSD has no SMP (Symmetric Multiprocessing) support—this is a major drawback confining OpenBSD to single CPU use. A project to rectify this is under way but is dependent on hardware donations and developer time.

Immunix

The Immunix team has taken a very different, albeit limited, approach from that of OpenBSD. Instead of attempting to fix bad code through code auditing, they use a specially modified compiler, StackGuard, to generate object code that can detect a buffer overflow attack in progress and halt program execution. The most common type of buffer overflow is "smashing the stack."

> *"Smash the stack"* [C programming] n. On many C implementations it is possible to corrupt the execution stack by writing past the end of an array declared auto in a routine. Code that does this is said to smash the stack, and can cause return from the routine to jump to a random address. This can produce some of the most insidious data-dependent bugs known to mankind. Variants include trash the stack, scribble the stack, mangle the stack; the term mung the stack is not used, as this is never done intentionally.
>
> Extract from Aleph One's all-time classic paper *Smashing The Stack For Fun And Profit* available from `http://www.securityfocus.com/data/library/P49-14.txt`

StackGuard technology does not protect against the many other classes of attack (or even every type of buffer overflow attack)—but it does limit the damage of a buffer overflow attack to a denial of service rather than a system compromise.

▶ For a full explanation of the StackGuard approach, check out Crispin Cowans's original research work at `http://www.immunix.org/StackGuard/usenixsc98.pdf`.

As a practical demonstration of StackGuard in action, the Immunix team created ImmunixOS—a complete distribution of Red Hat Linux compiled using their StackGuard technology (the kernel itself is not StackGuarded, however).

▶ A free CD image of ImmunixOS and other goodies can be downloaded from `http://www.immunix.org`.

To gain maximum benefit from compiler-based stack protection technology, you will need to recompile all your applications. If you don't have access to source code, you will not be able to StackGuard them.

Wrappers

You can develop wrappers to sanity-check program arguments and environment variables whether you use StackGuard or not. This technique is useful for protecting a privileged (set-uid/set-gid) program that you suspect, or know, is vulnerable to a buffer overflow attack.

Sanity-checking involves creating a small C program that replaces the suspect program. The wrapper is programmed to inspect command-line arguments and environment variables for suspicious input *before* calling the real program. Attempted attacks are logged to the system log via syslog, and the vulnerable program never gets called. Arguments that satisfy your checks are passed to the real program for program execution per normal.

The wrapper will need to be installed with the same permissions as the real program. This will mean making it set-uid/set-gid. You'd better be sure your replacement code doesn't have any security weaknesses! The real program needs to be relocated to a directory only accessible by the owner of the wrapper—otherwise, users could bypass your wrapper and call the suspect program directly.

The ultimate wrapper approach is to wrap every privileged program on the system—if you have the time. Be on the alert for patches and upgrades that overwrite your wrappers with updated binaries. You'll also need to update your wrappers as new features are added to the protected programs. As you can see there is some cost in doing this on a permanent basis.

Fortunately, someone else (AUSCERT) has done the hard work of creating a wrapper for us. Source code and instructions for use are available here:

```
ftp://ftp.auscert.org.au/pub/auscert/tools/overflow_wrapper/overflow_
wrapper.c
```

The next time you learn of a suspected security problem in a closed source set-uid/set-gid program, you can create a custom wrapper while you wait on the vendor fix.

While I'm on the subject of defending against buffer overflow attacks, it would be remiss of me if I didn't mention Solar Designer's Linux kernel patch. For those wishing to delve deeper into stack attack and protection, check out the links in the following sections. They only go to prove that security is often a game of cat and mouse.

Linux Kernel Patch

Author: Solar Designer

Platform: Linux (but principles apply to other distributions).

URLs: `http://www.openwall.com/linux/` and
`http://www.insecure.org/sploits/non-executable.stack.problems.html` (In fact, explore the entire site.)

The patch provides the following features detailed in the README:

- Nonexecutable user stack area
- Restricted links in /tmp
- Restricted FIFOs in /tmp
- Restricted access to /proc
- Special handling of fd 0, 1, and 2
- Enforced RLIMIT_NPROC on execve(2)
- The destruction of shared memory segments when they are no longer in use
- Privileged IP aliases (Linux 2.0 only)

Multilevel Trusted Systems

The final category of UNIX distributions is trusted systems.

▶ Trusted operating systems (TOSs) provide the basic security mechanisms and services that enable a computer system to protect, distinguish, and separate classified data. Trusted operating systems have been developed since the early 1980s and began to receive National Security Agency (NSA) evaluation in 1984.

`http://www.sei.cmu.edu/str/descriptions/trusted_body.html`

Under the traditional UNIX privilege model, the root user has full run of the system. Root can do anything—root is god-like.

Trusted systems, however, totally change the privilege paradigm. The root user becomes a mere mortal—subject to the laws of the trusted UNIX universe.

Trusted systems provide a fine-grained mechanism for controlling what actions a user can take.

For example, as any regular reader of `news:alt.security.unix` will tell you, a frequently asked question (FAQ) is "How do I prevent my UNIX users from accessing other network systems via Telnet/rlogin from my server?"

On a standard UNIX system, your options are limited and ineffectual. You could revoke access to the Telnet binary or delete it all together—but a user can simply upload another copy and set the permissions they desire (most likely with a innocent-looking filename to avoid detection). They could use a totally different program or even develop another one.

The solution is to stop trying to control user activity from userland—it's futile. Instead of trying to prevent the user from running a command through file permissions, take a different approach—identify which system resources the command needs in order to actually function.

So, to communicate with a remote system, the Telnet program must initiate a TCP network connection to the system specified by the user (for example, Telnet *yourhost*). To do this, it needs a communication endpoint on the local system called a *socket*. Only after it has been given a socket can it connect to the destination system. After initiating a connection, the receiving Telnet daemon can accept or deny the connection based on its access control policy.

Userland programs can't just create sockets out of thin air. They need to ask the kernel. Subsequently, the Telnet program must ask the kernel to create a socket for TCP communications. This is your control point. You could choose to wait until the call to connect, but why allow the program to allocate a finite system resource (that is, a socket) in the first place if you don't want it to connect? To implement this control, you need to modify the kernel. If you're running a closed source UNIX, for most of you, the ride ends here. Modifying system call code without source is hairy. (It is possible—it's just totally unsupported.) However, admins of open source distributions win out in this situation.

▶ Thomas H. Ptacek has documented the complete process for a BSD kernel—see `http://skoda.sockpuppet.org/tqbf/sysctlpriv.html`. Repeat that exercise for every other system call supported by your kernel, and you have one part of a basic trusted operating system.

Note

A user program (often referred to as a *userland program*) cannot modify the kernel in an arbitrary way. If it could, it would be a breeze to gain root access. You could simply overwrite the memory location storing the owner ID of your current process ID with the number 0, that is, root. The next time your process was subject to an access check, the kernel would look up your process owner ID in the process table and see the number 0—you would pass any access check!

However, userland programs need a way to ask the kernel to carry out actions on their behalf. This is because the kernel is solely in charge of access to system devices—for example, the display, hard drives, memory, network interfaces, and so on. Programs make requests of the kernel via system calls. A *system call* is a discrete action such as "Open this file." The system calls supported by your system are listed in /usr/include/sys.h. Inside the kernel is a syscall table listing the system call number and a pointer to the code that the kernel calls to do the work. The kernel returns control to the userland program when the code implementing the system call returns.

20

Trusted operating systems implement the following concepts/principles:

- **The principle of least privilege.** This says that each subject (user) is granted the most restrictive set of privileges needed for the performance of authorized tasks. The application of this principle limits the damage that can result from accident, error, or unauthorized use.

- **Mandatory Access Controls (MAC), as defined by the TCSEC (Trusted Computer System Evaluation Criteria).** "A means of restricting access to objects based on the sensitivity (as represented by a label) of the information contained in the objects and the formal authorization (that is, clearance) of subject to access information of such sensitivity."

- **Privilege bracketing.** The principle of enabling and disabling privilege around the smallest section of code that requires it.

- **A trusted computing base.** The totality of protection mechanisms within a computer system including hardware, software, and firmware, the combination of which is responsible for enforcing a security policy. *Note:* The capability of a trusted computing base to correctly enforce a unified security policy depends on the correctness of the mechanisms within the trusted computing base, the protection of those mechanisms to ensure their correctness, and the correct input of parameters related to the security policy.

Until recently, the predominant consumers of TOS technology were military and government agencies. With the explosion of e-business, this has changed. This attention to Internet-facing system is a little ironic, given that survey after survey of IT security incidents conclude that 50%–80% of attacks originate from within the organization. Not only that, but internal attacks actually cost the most because insiders can cause the most damage.

At the time of writing, there are two major commercial suppliers of UNIX TOS products: HP and Argus Systems.

Hewlett-Packard Praesidium VirtualVault

The HP TOS VirtualVault only runs on Hewlett-Packard hardware. The operating system is a hardened version of HP-UX. Focused on Web-based e-business applications, VirtualVault ships with Netscape Enterprise Server and a Trusted Gateway Agent.

VirtualVault replaces the all-powerful root user with 50 distinct privileges, granting each application only the minimum operating system privileges it requires to run properly. It incorporates many of the B-level Department of Defense Trusted Computer System (TCSEC) features. See `http://www.hp.com/security/products/virtualvault/papers/` for more information.

▶ Even VirtualVault hasn't escaped the security bugfest unscathed. Check out `http://www.securityfocus.com/vdb/middle.html?vendor=HP&title=VirtualVault&version=any`.

Argus Systems PitBull

The other main player in the Trusted OS space is Argus Systems (`http://www.argus-systems.com`). Its PitBull product is available for Solaris and Windows. As of this writing, the development of ports to IBM AIX and GNU/Linux is well underway.

PitBull installs over the top of the existing operating system, replacing the guts of the mainstream OS with trusted substitutes.

▶ To encourage discussion, development, and uptake of TOS technology, the founders of Argus Systems created the online Argus Revolution site at `http://www.argusrevolution.com/`.

You can even download a free-for-noncommercial-use copy of PitBull with accompanying documentation from `http://www.argusrevolution.com/pitbullsupport.html`.

If you want to study TOS technology in any further detail, I highly recommend that you try the download.

Both of the previously mentioned products are closed source. The noncommercial, open source options include a BSD project and an offering from the NSA.

Trusted BSD

TrustedBSD (`http://www.trustedbsd.org/`) lets you peek at the code.

Currently under development, TrustedBSD is a set of security extensions to the FreeBSD UNIX operating system. The developers hope TrustedBSD will take FreeBSD into environments that have higher security requirements. The extensions are being integrated into core FreeBSD (`http://www.freebsd.org`).

NSA

The highly secretive U.S. National Security Agency (NSA) in conjunction with Network Associates, Mitre, and Secure Computing has published an open source security extension for GNU/Linux. This includes a "strong, flexible mandatory access control architecture based on Type Enforcement." According to the online documentation, the NSA developed the Flask security architecture and prototyped it in the Mach and Fluke research operating systems. By integrating the Flask architecture into the Linux operating system, they hope to substantially broaden the audience of the technology. For more details, check out `http://www.nsa.gov/selinux/index.html`.

Realities of Running TOS

The substantial security improvement provided by a TOS does come at a cost, particularly:

- The need for specialized administration skills. The administrator(s) must be well versed in both TOS concepts and real-world administration. Hiring experienced TOS administrators is not easy (they are few and far between). Also consider that internal support structures will need to change with the role-based administration inherent in TOS.

- The need to understand your application's security requirements **in depth.** Installing a TOS brings immediate benefits—your OS has suddenly become resilient against the majority of attackers. Now though, you need to tell the TOS about your applications—that is, what OS resources your applications need to access. This can be tricky for two reasons. First, application documentation rarely includes anything like the kind of detailed information you'll need to do this. Second, applications are a moving target. Testing before upgrades becomes ultracritical—a subtle, undocumented change in a rarely used application function could lead to access problems if the TOS application profile hasn't been updated. For commercial customers deploying popular corporate products (for example, ORACLE RDBMS), this will be less of a hurdle because commercial providers of TOS technologies tend to have application security profiles for common enterprise applications. Unusual closed source applications will require significant testing and observation by administrators well versed in troubleshooting TOS compatibility issues.

- Loss of flexibility. To fully realize the potential of using a TOS, you will want to lock down the privileges of applications and administrative accounts. By definition, this costs you flexibility—you will no longer be able to make major configuration changes to security-sensitive parts of the OS on-the-fly! If you value ultimate flexibility over hardcore security, then you probably don't want to run a TOS. It's a case of using the right tool for the right job. But, don't forget: Flexibility benefits the attacker, too!

- TOS systems can still be hacked if they are not configured carefully or contain security bugs. Areas to defend are detailed here: `http://www.argusrevolution.com/downloads/DefCon.ppt`.

The decision to deploy a trusted UNIX system will hinge on your analysis of risk: the value of the information you are trying to protect, the perceived threats, and the probability of attack. Security controls are an insurance policy of sorts. Your spending on security (both initial and ongoing costs) should reflect this.

Security Considerations in Choosing a Distribution

Consider the following key security factors when selecting a UNIX distribution:

- Understand the intended use of the system. What threats must the system defend against? Consider physical, human, and technological threats.

- Gauge the technical security competence and awareness of the primary administrator(s). Distributions that are a significant departure from local technical security expertise should be considered a higher risk (unless technical security training will be provided). Vendor-provided security training classes tend to be weak. The SANS Institute run good introductory courses.

▶ In 1997, the CERT coordination center produced a "Report to the President's Commission on Critical Infrastructure Protection." Security awareness and user/administrator security training were key points.

- Learn about the vendor's approach to handling reported security vulnerabilities. Do they even acknowledge that vulnerabilities occur in their distribution? Do they have a clearly documented process for handling reports from outside? Do they watch Bugtraq for reports of security problems in their software? Do they provide e-mail addresses for reporting new security problems?

- Assess the vendor's response time when fixing security vulnerabilities. The SecurityFocus vulnerability database is useful for comparing the public announcement date and vendor fix dates.

- Consider the maturity and stability of built-in security tools and interface. Weak areas tend to be C2 audit log management and analysis, mixed coverage of daemon logging to syslog, and clunky security interfaces that can result in mistakes being made in security settings.

- Do a gap analysis, comparing the native security features against your UNIX security policy. Consider the availability, cost, and installation overhead of third- party/open source tools required to plug the gap.

- Estimate the time it will take to lock down a virgin install of the distribution to comply with your policy. Calculate the cost of the administrator's time and possible delays on projects. This is the cost of buying distributions that are not secure by default. Ask the vendor to provide you with smart ways to lower this cost.

- Visit the vendor support site. How long does it take to find the security alerts/bulletins and security patches? Read a couple of security bulletins. Do they make sense? Do they tell you enough about the problem to figure out whether you would need the patch? Compare a security bulletin with the original announcement made on Bugtraq (search the archives at http://archives.neohapsis.com/search/). Does the vendor's assessment of the problem tally with the original report?

- Assess the ease of security patching. Are stable tools available to easily identify missing patches? Are these kept up to date? Can patch installation be reliably automated for server farms? Are MD5 hashes available to validate patch integrity? Bear in mind the SANS finding that failing to update systems when security holes are found is the third major security mistake.

- Check the release versions of any bundled third-party software (for example, sendmail, bind, or wu-ftpd). Make sure they are current or that the vendor has backported fixes for security problems.

20

UNIX

UNIX Security Risks

You've chosen your UNIX distribution (or someone else did it for you), and you need to know where the risks are. All operating systems have security problems—no matter what anyone might tell you to the contrary. Anything with some complexity, written by humans and managed by humans, inherits the wonderful flaws of the authors along the way.

The main risk areas on a typical, modern day UNIX system tend to be

- **Misconfigured/buggy network daemons.** These leave your system open to attack from anyone who can "see" your server across the network. The attacker doesn't need an account on your system to exploit these security holes. These are classified as *remote vulnerabilities*.

- **Poorly chosen user passwords.** Bottom line: Passwords are an inconvenience for most users. Systems configured to enforce fascist password rules only encourage users to write down their passwords. A middle ground is required—this is a people issue, rather than a technical one.

- **Buggy privileged programs (set-uid/set-gid).** What happens when an attacker subverts a program that executes with special privileges? Well, it depends on the specific vulnerability. All too often, though, system security is breached, and the attacker can take control over the operating system. These problems are classified as *local vulnerabilities*, as the attacker requires a user account to exploit them (which might or might not be obtained legitimately).

- **Filesystem nightmares.** Badly set file permissions, sloppy handling of temporary files, race conditions, and insecure defaults are all culprits. Exploiting these can lead to leakage of sensitive information, introduction of Trojan code, and destruction of data. Bottom line: An insecure filesystem affects the integrity of the entire system.

- **Insecure applications.** Näive designs and sloppy programming practices combine to produce a giant sore on your system—exposed to anyone who tries to exploit the myriad of possible weaknesses. Bolting down your UNIX server is not enough, if someone can drive a tank through your application security.

The common trait of these risk areas is insecurely written code.

We'll cover each category in more detail in the following sections.

Buzzt!

Actually, some people use these weaknesses to study attackers. Lance Spitzner used to get his kicks from blowing up things in his tanks. Today, he enjoys observing attacks launched against his honey pot system:

```
http://project.honeypot.org/
```

A sacrificial host is built—running a default Red Hat Linux install with no security patches—and connected to the Internet (typically outside a firewall or within a DMZ). A series of logging mechanisms are activated to record probes and attacks. After a compromise, Lance is able to reconstruct all the attackers' activity via the captured packet trace.

This kind of exercise provides an insight into the way attackers compromise a victim machine and, more importantly, what they do when they have.

A number of organizations run honey pots to identify new attacks "in the wild." By coordinating their efforts, they are able to track new trends and issue alerts to the wider community.

Be warned though: Having drawn attackers to your site, you had better be sure they won't compromise your real network or discover you monitoring their activity. Sophisticated attackers can identify a honey pot very quickly.

User Accounts

If you haven't read Chapter 14, "Password Crackers," I recommend that you do so now.

Users, bless 'em, can give up your system's security no matter what lockdown procedures you have implemented.

The age-old problem of poorly chosen passwords continues to plague any operating system or device that requires them.

One security practitioner I know describes passwords as "past their sell-by date." The problem doesn't seem to go away, and there is no reason to believe that it is going to. Therefore, a change of tack might be necessary, and you should give serious consideration to either moving to other forms of authentication such as one-time passwords (OTP), biometrics, or smartcards. No authentication system is perfect—many appear impressive until you start analyzing their issues. However, it doesn't take a giant leap to improve upon passwords.

Assuming you're stuck with UNIX passwords, here's what can you can do to improve things:

- Limit access to the root account on a need-to-have basis. Root is all powerful, and you'll want to avoid giving this level of access to anyone who doesn't have a legitimate need for it.

20

UNIX

- Don't give root access to anyone who can't demonstrate adequate technical expertise AND judgment. You get to define "adequate." Mistakes will happen from time to time, but allowing untrained newbies access to root is asking for trouble. At the same time though, don't make a big thing about the root account to those you refuse—it might cause resentment that could lead to other security problems!

- Set a strong password on the root account. Stick to a minimum of eight characters and include special characters.

- Disable root logins across the network. Have admins make use of su, or, better yet, deploy sudo.

NOTE

Sudo is an incredibly useful utility. It allows the administrator to permit users to run commands for which they do not usually have the privilege. For example, you have a helpdesk that needs to be able to change passwords for everybody except the administrators. This is easy with sudo. You define a sudo rule to permit anyone in the helpdesk group (or using the helpdesk user id, if you are not allergic to shared accounts) to run the `passwd` command as root—with a twist. You also define what arguments can or cannot be passed to the command. So, in this case, you would specify the administrator user ids as invalid arguments (by using the exclamation mark to signify negation). Sudo can be found here: `http://www.courtesan.com/sudo/`.

- Store the root password offline in an envelope (signed across the join) in a secure place. In large environments, make sure that a log of access is kept.

- Don't use the same passwords across all machines. The compromise of a single password should not result in a complete giveaway. Categorize your systems in virtual groups, by either risk or data sensitivity. Assign a unique root password to each virtual group. In practice, these groups can be test, development, and production. However, if you're storing the same data on all those systems, you either need to revisit your data security policy or think of another way to group your systems.

- Ban access to remote access servers that don't support encryption. Telnet and FTP send passwords in cleartext across the network. At a minimum, make sure your privileged users use `ssh` and `scp`.

- Implement password construction checks on the server. Set minimum values for password length, the number of alphanumerics, and, where supported, special characters.

- Implement real-time password dictionary checks. Use software like npasswd (`http://www.utexas.edu/cc/unix/software/npasswd/`)as a replacement for the stock password program. This type of software does require some configuration on the part of the administrator but goes a long way toward solving the problem of easy-to-guess passwords being used.

- Instigate a password-cracking policy. Every month or quarter, attempt to crack all passwords (administrator accounts included). Track the percentage cracked and set targets. Use a decent-sized cracking dictionary and add words that relate to your environment (for example, project names, team names, supplier names, nicknames, and so on).

- Create a password policy that states the required length and composition of passwords. Make sure all system users have seen it.

- Educate your users on strategies for choosing good passwords. For example, have them think of a line from a favorite song or quote and select the first letter of each word to make up a password—for example, "I Left My Heart in San Francisco" would be `IlmhiSF`. Then mutate the password by adding in special characters—for example, `!lmhi$F_`. That would take a while to crack. This can make hard passwords easy to remember.

- Don't think that by replacing letters with numbers in passwords you are going to outsmart a cracker. Password cracking programs do this automatically, too.

- Give serious consideration to enforcing account lockout after three or five failed logins. This can lead to a denial of service attack if you are in a hostile environment—a malicious user could lock out all the accounts on purpose simply by typing gibberish for users' passwords. (However, DoS is generally a low risk in an internal network.)

- Make sure that your helpdesk doesn't just re-enable locked accounts (or create new ones) for anyone who calls the desk with a friendly voice. It's a well-known fact that social engineering of over-obliging support staff is easier than bypassing a well-configured firewall.

- Don't let your support staff fall into the trap of using the same password when resetting locked accounts. Invest in some software that generates passwords that are phonetically easy to pronounce. (This won't work for multilingual support desks.) Mail the author if you find a good product.

- If a user calls to have his password reset, use a callback scheme on a prearranged number or, failing that, leave the new password on the user's voicemail. Don't tell the user the password there and then unless you know the person's voice well enough to spot an impersonator. This might sound a little too paranoid. However, consider what someone might gain by doing this and how stupid you'd look if you simply gave the password to them on a plate!

20

UNIX

- Go on walkabout every now and then to check whether users are writing passwords down. For example, are passwords written on sticky notes on monitors? If they are, have a quiet word with the user. Persistent offenders might find remembering different passwords to different machines hard. Consider using software like Counterpane's Password Safe (`http://www.counterpane.com/passsafe.html`). This installs on the client machine and can securely store passwords—unlocked via a single password. Just make sure this one is strong and not written down! This software is particularly useful for administrators.

- Make sure that your systems are using shadow passwords. It used to be that UNIX stored passwords in the /etc/passwd file. However, as CPU technology forged ahead, it wasn't long before these passwords were being cracked. Check to make sure that your passwords are being stored in a file readable only by root.

- Avoid hard-coding passwords in scripts if at all possible. If you have to, then make sure file permissions are set to user access only.

- Avoid badly written client software that stores UNIX server passwords on the client in an easy to decrypt/decipher form. XOR'd in the NT registry does this, for example.

Filesystem Security

This section reviews fundamental filesystem and privilege concepts.

When it comes to input and output, UNIX treats everything as a file. In fact, the term *file* has multiple meanings in UNIX—it can be a

- **Regular file.** A sequence of data bytes collectively regarded by the operating system as a file.

- **Directory file.** A list of filenames and pointers to file meta information (that's a fancy way for saying "information about a file"). If you have read access to a directory, it means you can read the contents of the directory—in other words, get a directory listing (a la `ls(1)`). However, only the UNIX kernel has the capability to modify the contents of this file (for example, insert a new entry).

- **Symbolic link.** Contains the name of another file. When a symbolic link is accessed, the kernel recognizes the file as such by examining its file-type. It then reads the file contents. The kernel opens the file with the name stored in the symbolic link. System administrators frequently use symbolic links to relocate data to another filesystem while maintaining the path of the parent directory. Attackers, on the other hand, use symbolic links for more nefarious purposes, as we'll cover later.

- **Character special.** Represents a byte-oriented device. It is the UNIX interface to devices that operate on a byte-by-byte basis, like a terminal device.

- **Block special.** Functions like a character special file, but for block-oriented devices such as disk drives.

- **Socket.** Allows one process to communicate with another process—whether on the local system (via Inter Process Communication) or a remote machine. Programs such as Telnet, rlogin, and FTP all use sockets.

- **Named pipe.** Supports local Inter Process Communication (IPC). Because of the type of queuing used it is sometimes referred to as a FIFO (First In First Out).

Each of these objects is stored in the filesystem. Protecting the filesystem from abuse is critical to the ongoing integrity of your operating system, application programs, and data.

File Attributes

The UNIX filesystem supports a standard set of file attributes or properties. These attributes are stored in a data structure called the *inode* (*index node*)—every file has an inode. On Solaris, the inode data structure for the traditional UNIX FileSystem (UFS) is defined in /usr/include/sys/fs/ufs_inode.h.

From a security perspective, the most important attributes include

- **The owner id.** The numeric user id that owns the file.
- **The group id.** The numeric group id that owns the file.
- **Permissions.** Combined with the owner id and group id, these determine the access controls on the file.
- **Size.** Measured in bytes.
- **Time of last access.** The time the file was last accessed, in seconds since 1970.
- **Time of last modification.** The time the file was last modified, in seconds since 1970.
- **Time of last inode change.** The time the file was created, in seconds since 1970.
- **Number of hard links.** The number of files that "point" at this file.

The permissions attribute defines the access rights of the file owner, the group owner, and all other users on the system. The root user and file owner can control access to a file by setting permissions on the file and on the parent directories.

In the standard implementation of UNIX, the root user is not subject to permission checking— root can read, write, or execute any file. Note that, in UNIX, write access is equivalent to delete—by definition, if you can write to the file, you can erase the contents of the file.

Readers unfamiliar with filesystem permissions are encouraged to read the chmod man page. For further reading, I highly recommend *Advanced Programming in the UNIX Environment*, Addison-Wesley, 1992, ISBN 0-201-56317-7.

20

UNIX

Permissions in Practice

To access a file by name, a user must have execute privilege in every directory contained in the file path, as well as appropriate access to the file itself. In the case of files in the current directory, a user needs execute privilege for the current directory.

To be able to create a file in a directory, a user must have execute permission on every directory in the path, as well as write permission in the target directory.

When it comes to deleting a file, it isn't actually necessary to be the file owner or have write permission on the file. By having write and execute permissions on the parent directory, you can delete files. This can be a "gotcha" if you're not careful.

In order to understand how the various permissions are checked when a user attempts to open a file, you need to understand how process privileges work.

Put simply, when you execute a program, a process is created. Associated with a process are at least six IDs:

- **Real User ID.** The numeric user id of your login account
- **Real Group ID.** The numeric group ID of your primary group (the group defined in your /etc/passwd entry)
- **Effective User ID.** The numeric user id used during file access permission checks
- **Effective Group ID.** The numeric group ID used during file access permission checks
- **Saved Set User ID.** A copy of the numeric user id saved by the exec function when you execute a program
- **Saved Set Group ID.** A copy of the numeric group ID saved by the exec function when you execute a program

In addition, if you are a member of more than one UNIX group, a corresponding number of supplementary group IDs will be set.

At first glance this might seem overcomplicated. To appreciate why so many IDs are required, we have to talk about a key security mechanism of UNIX, the set-uid/set-gid privilege.

The Set-uid/Set-gid Privilege

Normally, when you execute a program, a process is created that runs with the privileges associated with your user id. This makes sense; you shouldn't be able to interfere with files or processes belonging to another user. However, some programs need to carry out privileged operations. They can't do this if they execute under the user id of an unprivileged caller. To make a program privileged, the program owner (or root) can assign the set-uid or set-gid bit to the program via the chmod command.

Unlike ordinary programs, a set-uid program executes with the privileges of the program owner—not the caller. By making a program set-uid, you allow it to take actions with the authority of the program owner, on your behalf.

Set-gid works the same way but, not surprisingly, for groups. A set-gid program runs with the privileges of the owning group rather than with the privileges associated with the group of the user id who called the program.

Set-gid can also be set on a directory. Files subsequently created within a set-gid directory will have their group ownership set the same as that of the set-gid directory. Usually the group owner would be set to the users' primary group. This way, a group of users can share data despite being in different primary groups.

An example of a set-uid program is the passwd program. When you change your password, the system needs a way to modify your password entry in /etc/shadow. This file is only accessible by root because it stores passwords; however, this prevents you from legitimately changing your password. By making the passwd program set-uid, you allow a nonprivileged user id to update its password. Without the set-uid bit, users would have to ring up the administrator to have the passwords changed. Eventually, the administrator's temper is bound to fray—see the BOFH series at `http://members.iinet.net.au/~bofh/` for enlightenment.

In our example, the security of the shadow file is at the mercy of the passwd program. If the user running the password program can somehow influence the program in a way the programmer didn't consider, she might be able to directly modify the shadow file!

Therefore, set-uid programs must be programmed defensively to avoid their being subverted by an attacker to gain extra privileges. In the case of a set-uid root program, the stakes are very high—one exploitable bug will mean game over—the attacker gets root privileges.

The Umask

Our review of file permissions would be incomplete without studying the umask. The umask determines the set of permissions that will apply to a newly created file if no permissions are explicitly specified at creation time. In other words, it's the default file permission.

The umask is represented as the inverse of the file permissions. For example, if our default umask is 022, any files we create in which we don't explicitly set the file permissions will be created with 755 permissions; that is, user id has read, write, and execute permissions, whereas group ID and Other have read and execute permissions. Just remember that the umask should be set to a value opposite of the permissions you want.

A common default umask value is 022. This is usually set in a system-wide login script such as /etc/profile. This can be overridden by a user who specifies a different (usually more restrictive) value in his local login script (for example, ~user/.profile). The umask command is a built-in shell command; it can be run at the shell prompt, for example, as umask 022.

Every process on a UNIX system has a umask setting—it doesn't just affect the users who log in interactively. When the system boots and executes the system start-up scripts, a number of network daemons (services) are started. They inherit the umask value of their parent process init—usually 022. Any files they subsequently create will be given permissions set by the umask unless the programmer explicitly set permissions.

The umask setting is therefore incredibly important—if it is set too loosely, other users might be able to read, or in some cases, write over your files. Despite its importance, it is commonly overlooked by programmers.

Filesystem Risks

With the theory out of the way, let's examine the risks. The primary risks are

- **Data disclosure.** I don't want to belabor an obvious point, but this is so incredibly common that it deserves some attention. Users and programs create files in /tmp—it's a digital scrap yard. If the user doesn't specify file permissions, the umask value applies. Commonly, the default umask of 022 is set, and the file is given world readable permissions—any user on the system can read the file.

  On a typical multiuser system, it is not unusual to find copies of scripts containing database passwords, confidential business data, sensitive log information, and core files containing encrypted passwords in /tmp. The same goes for user home directories and shared areas that have not been locked down to prevent access by Other. Why break in if you can read your way to root?

- **Unauthorized data modification/deletion.** This happens in two common ways. First, through lax user practices—someone sets world writable permissions on a file. The second way is via world writable directories. If I create a file in a directory that is world writable, any local user can subsequently delete/modify it.

  This is also true for filesystems shared via NFS.

  The only exception to this is directories that have the sticky bit set (such as /tmp). If the file permissions are locked down, only the owner can write to the file. This is not always obvious, because the world writable directory might be the parentof the parent of the current directory, or the parent of the parent's parent. In an extreme case, if the / directory is world writable, an attacker can replace any file on the system—for example, by moving /usr/sbin out of the way and creating a replacement /usr/sbin, filled with Trojan programs of their choosing. This can easily lead to a total system compromise.

  The bottom line is that it's not just the parent directory that counts—but every directory along the way up to slash (/)! This problem is surprisingly common on system and application directories.

- **Resource consumption.** Each filesystem is built with a finite number of inodes. When all inodes are consumed, no more files can be written to the filesystem, regardless of available free space. This can cause system daemons to crash or hang when /tmp is involved. Unless file giveaways have been disabled in the kernel, the culprit can cast the blame on another user simply by changing the ownership of the files she has created to the victim via the `chown` command. Consuming all free space is another approach.

- **Temporary files with predictable filenames.** Programs can be subverted to overwrite or remove arbitrary files if they create temporary files with predictable filenames in directories writable by Other (commonly /tmp). Other users can guess a filename in advance and create a symbolic link to a system file. When the program runs, it writes data to the system file resulting in data corruption. If that's the passwd file, you have a denial of service attack on your hands. This is incredibly common—especially in application code and administrators' shell scripts.

- **Named pipes that trip up the `find` command.** By default, most UNIX systems ship with root crontab entries to run the `find` command. In addition, root users often run `find` to search for particular files. A user can create a named pipe that will cause `find` to hang when it reaches the pipe. The `find` command will open the pipe for reading and block (that is, hang) waiting for data. Because no EOF (End of File) will be sent, `find` will hang until it is killed. An attacker can use this method to prevent the administrator from finding the attacker's unauthorized set-uid programs. A further attack on some versions of `find` is to embed commands in the filename. If `find` passes the file to an `exec` command switch, the shell will interpret any shell meta characters (in this case `";"`) and execute the embedded commands.

▶ Privileged shell scripts that read filenames from the filesystem and blindly pass them to another program can be subverted. SNI (Secure Networks Inc.) posted an advisory way back in 1996 about this problem; it is archived here: `http://lists.insecure.org/bugtraq/1996/Dec/0133.html`. This weakness is still present in some commercial distributions today.

- **World readable/writable named pipes.** One method for processes to communicate with one another is through the file system—using a named pipe. If the pipe has been created with weak permissions, an attacker can read and write to the named pipe subverting/crashing the process at the other end of the pipe or reading privileged data.

- **Race conditions.** Matt Bishop coined the acronym TOCTTOU (Time Of Check To Time Of Use) for a common race condition—namely, when a program checks for a particular characteristic of an object and takes some action based on the assumption that the characteristic still holds true. However, if a program is subject to race conditions, an attacker can swap the object between the time the check is made and the subsequent use of the object. This tricks the program, which will then operate on the wrong object. You can see Chapter 29, "Secure Application Development, Languages, and Extensions," for more on race conditions.

20

Filesystem Countermeasures

Here are some things you can do to minimize your filesystem exposures.

- Give clear direction in your security policy about the need to protect the organization's data. Classify information by sensitivity and define what access controls are required. Give examples.

- Set the TMPDIR environment variable to a private, per-user temporary directory. Well-behaved programs check TMPDIR before using /tmp.

- Audit your shell scripts and change all references to publicly writable directories to your own tmp directory. For bonus points, create unique filenames without relying on the time, date, or process ID (or a weak pseudo-random number generator).

- Educate users about file permissions and the effect of the umask. In sensitive environments, have your users sign a usage policy that includes good stewardship of information.

- Ask users about their information-sharing needs. Create additional UNIX groups as necessary and enroll users as appropriate to support data sharing at a more granular level. The group's mechanism can be used very creatively—think long term and design a flexible group access model.

- Make sure that the system-wide umask is set to 027 in the system shell start-up files as a minimum.

- Modify system startup files to set the umask to 027.

- Create a cron job to check user start-up scripts for inappropriate umask settings.

- Audit /tmp and other shared directories on your servers now. Perform spot checks on /tmp. Persistent offenders should be warned that they are in breach of policy. If the warnings are not heeded and the information is sensitive, consider e-mailing a summary of interesting finds to management.

- Disable core file creation (not to be confused with kernel crash dumps) via the `ulimit` command. Modern UNIX kernels will refuse to dump core when a set-uid program crashes because this might reveal sensitive information. However, privileged system daemons and application processes might dump core resulting in chunks of sensitive system files being written to world readable core file. Validate your fix by sending a `QUIT` signal to a expendable network service and check that it doesn't produce a core dump in its current working directory. (/proc or lsof can help find that out.)

- Monitor /tmp for predictable filenames using a tool such as L0pht's tmpwatch available here: `http://www.atstake.com/research/tools/l0pht-watch.tar.gz`.

- Make sure named pipes are included in your file permission checks! These are used for Inter Process Communication (IPC), so that lax permissions will allow an attacker to interact with processes in ways you don't want.

- Prevent file giveaways by setting `CHOWN_RESTRICTED` to true in the kernel configuration file.

- Consider using extended ACLs (where supported) via the `getfacl` and `setfacl` commands (Solaris). These extend the access information stored in the inode. They can be used to give a user access to a file or directory even if that user is not in the owning group or is not the file owner, and the file permissions deny access by "Other." But ACLs can be a real pain to administrate. Personally, I recommend that you design a good group model and only use extended ACLs when you really need to.

The Set-uid Problem

Programming mistakes in set-uid programs have been a real source of security headaches. A single security hole in just one set-uid root program can be all that is needed for an attacker to gain root access.

The problem is widespread. We're not talking about one or two isolated instances—more like a graveyard of broken set-uid programs. Again, check the SecurityFocus.com vulnerability database for set-uid problems—there have been hundreds (thousands?)! The problem isn't going away, either—especially in third-party programs. New set-uid vulnerabilities are being reported to Bugtraq on a weekly basis.

▶ Writing secure set-uid programs can be difficult. Just because you can program C doesn't make you a security god. Heck, even the security gods get it wrong sometimes. Take, for example, the L0pht (`http://www.safermag.com/html/safer25/alerts/33.html`)—a group that knows its subject inside out.

The C language is pretty unforgiving to the developer of set-uid programs—C makes it too easy to screw up and open the barn door. Specifically, the lack of bounds checking in C has allowed many developers to write programs with buffer overflows.

However, it would be pretty lame for us to blame a language for set-uid problems. After all the security pitfalls of C are well documented—it's hardly a new language. Alas, the biggest source of security vulnerabilities is the näive programmers slapping together code they think is secure.

A typical UNIX distribution ships with a large number of set-uid root files—averaging between 70 and 100. Now, not every line of code necessarily runs with root privilege—the privilege has to be invoked by the program via a call to set-uid. But, even if the privileged lines of code are written super securely, a wily attacker can exploit a hole in the nonprivileged section of code (that is, before the call to set-uid) with devastating consequences. If the attacker exploits a buffer overflow and can force the program to make a call to set-uid—boom, game over. Any code the attacker can supply for the program to execute will run with root privileges.

20

UNIX

Security-savvy programmers throw away the set-uid privilege as early as possible in the program.

So, given the number of privileged programs, the administrator is left to ponder: "Where will the next vulnerability be found?" The answer is, we simply don't know. Hence the stock advice of any security textbook is to remove the set-uid bit from unnecessary privileged programs. This is much easier said than done. How do you know what is unnecessary? Sure, you know programs like passwd need to be set-uid, but what about all those others? Removing the set-uid bit has to be done with a great deal of care—unless you want to have a lot of free time on your hands.

A classic example of irrelevant set-uid code (at least for most people) is the KCMS (Kodak Color Management System) suite of programs. These are installed during a full install of Solaris and set-uid root. The CERT advisory CA-1996-15 describes KCMS as

> ...a set of Openwindows compliant API's and libraries to create and manage profiles that can describe and control the color performance of monitors, scanners, printers and film recorders.

So, if you are a Solaris admin, have you ever used those? The only time I have used them was to demonstrate to system administrators how easily root could be compromised.

Another more common example is the ping program. Ping sends an ICMP ECHO REQUEST packet to a remote system and waits for a response (ICMP ECHO REPLY) to check whether the remote system is alive (although not necessarily functioning). The standard implementation of ping requires a raw socket to be able to build the ICMP ECHO REQUEST packet. This is a privileged action because having access to a raw socket means you can create custom packets—very dangerous in the wrong hands. So the `ping` command is set-uid root.

Unfortunately, allowing mischievous users access to seemingly innocuous programs like ping can result in a security nightmare. Remember the Ping of Death? The `ping` command has an option whereby the user can control the size of the ICMP packet sent. It turns out that some implementations of `ping` allow users to send out very large ping packets that have caused remote systems to crash. Was anyone expecting that? Of course not. Hence the need to follow the least privilege principle. Only allow users to run what they need to run in order to do their job. Does every user on every system really need to be able to run network diagnostic tools?

Then there are those set-uid programs that don't even need to be set-uid—typically, system administration commands. The set-uid bit is redundant if only root is running it.

I am not aware of any vendors that provide any guidance, or sufficient technical program documentation to help an administrator easily identify nonessential set-uid programs.

Fortunately for Solaris and Linux users, there is some good information out there on locking down your set-uid programs.

Truly paranoid Solaris users should check out this e-mail on the YASSP (Yet Another Solaris Security Package) mailing list from a Sun employee discussing how the company locks down Internet-facing systems:

```
http://www.theorygroup.com/Archive/YASSP/2000/msg00548.html
```

Solaris 2.6 set-uid lockdown information is here:

```
http://www.ist.uwaterloo.ca/security/howto/2000-08-22.html
```

and here:

```
http://www.vetmed.auburn.edu/~whitej4/secureSolaris2.6.html#2.0
```

For Solaris 2.7 information, go here:

```
http://ist.uwaterloo.ca/security/howto/Solaris7_set-uid.html
```

So, how do you minimize your system's exposure to set-uid holes that are waiting in the wings?

1. Try to avoid installing the full distribution—install only what you need. This is a security best practice. If the code isn't on your hard drive, then no one can use it against you. But this can be hard to fulfill in a pressure-filled environment where the focus is on getting things live. Just remember the costs of post-live lockdown.

2. List all the set-uid/set-gid programs on the system. You can do this with the following commands:

   ```
   find / -perm -u+s -print
   find / -perm -g+s -print
   ```

3. Find out the stated purpose of each program. You're likely to find that some of them are totally unnecessary—neither you nor your users would ever need to run them. As long as these programs are not required for system operation, they can have the set-uid bit removed, or, alternatively, all access by Other can be removed (that is, chmod o-rwx file).

4. Identify the set-uid root programs that only root needs to run and remove the set-uid bit—they don't need to be set-uid because you'll be running them as root. There's no point in leaving potential time bombs lying around for someone to play with. Remove the set-uid bit or access by Other (either is good). This can eliminate a large number of programs.

5. Identify set-uid programs that leak sensitive system information and thereby make an attacker's life easy—for example, ps, top, and netstat. Ps and top display process information, including command-line arguments—these can contain application usernames and passwords. They also help an attacker identify usage patterns, which assists timing of attacks. Similarly, netstat reveals information about your network topology (via the -R switch) and current network connections (that is, who is talking to your system).

20

UNIX

This kind of privacy disclosure can lead to client systems being attacked. Client systems are soft targets, the "low hanging fruit" of the network. They can be used as remote password sniffers (to compromise accounts on more systems), proxies to misdirect attack investigations, and conduits to other network segments that are unreachable directly (that is, they are behind a firewall or not directly attached). It's not hard to imagine the consequences if the client victim happens to belong to the system administrator level.

So limit access to "leaky" set-uid programs on a strictly need-to-have basis. The side message is to secure your clients machines—they can be used against you!

6. Identify the set-uid root programs that only a trusted group of users need to run (for example, network operations). Create a dedicated UNIX group and enroll the trusted users in this group. Next, change the group ownership of the set-uid programs to this group (don't change the owner though because that would make the set-uid call fail). Finally, and very importantly, remove all points of access by Other (that is, `chmod o-rwx file`). These include print queue management programs, network utilities, and application management interfaces.

7. Identify the set-uid root programs you think no one will ever need. Before you remove a set-uid bit, you need to be totally convinced you won't break something. In cases like these you need to profile the programs' uses—that is, to log program invocation. One approach is to install an AUSCERT wrapper like the one discussed earlier. But, here, we're not going to use the wrapper for its intended purpose (although there is nothing stopping you from doing so). Instead, we're going to modify the wrapper to make a call to the `logger` command before the real program is called. This is unnecessary if you have C2 auditing configured and are logging calls to `exec()`. Review your logs after a month, and, if no relevant activity has been logged, then you probably have sufficient basis to remove the set-uid bit. You might want to leave your pager on for a while, though.

8. You should now be left with a handful of set-uid root programs that you consider essential. Modify the AUSCERT wrapper for those programs to make sure overly long arguments or environment variables cannot be specified. This won't protect you against all attacks but will protect you against some the common ones.

Pat yourself on the back—you've made it a lot harder for an attacker to succeed against your system.

Maintenance wise, you will find that vendor patches assume a vanilla install, and, therefore, patches and upgrades clobber your changes. Always run a file integrity checker after applying updates to identify changes—that way, you avoid your efforts being undermined by dumb scripts.

Make sure you keep an eye on Bugtraq to keep up with new set-uid exposures, and subscribe to your vendor's security alert mailing list to ensure that you hear about patches quickly.

If you have only a few trusted users on the system, you might be tempted to skip the whole set-uid removal process. Before you do, consider this: You are unwittingly making life easier for a remote attacker. If an attacker gains shell access to your machine through some 0-day (new) exploit, she will use any vulnerability she can find to elevate her privileges to root. Set-uid root programs will be at the top of her list. If you fail to bolt down your set-uid programs, an attacker will not hesitate in leveraging this against you.

Understand, though, that gaining root is not always the attackers' endgame—it depends on what they are trying to achieve. For example, you can store all your sensitive company data in a relational database that is owned by a user called "datamart." Clearly, the attacker only needs to target the data owner account (or privileged application accounts) to get full access to the database. This can be through password guessing, social engineering, or exploiting security bugs in set-uid application programs. Don't focus on root to the exclusion of your primary application accounts.

Application software often ships with set-uid/set-gid programs. In my experience these tend to be rife with problems—ignore them at your peril. It is rare to find security savvy application programmers.

Breaking Set-uid Programs for Fun and Profit

(URLs and brief descriptions of tools mentioned in the following section can be found immediately after this list.)

You're faced with a piece of software that smells of security problems. What can you do about it? Some homebrew security testing! You won't become an "Uber-hacker" overnight, but the following techniques are a good place to start:

- Search the Web for information about previous product vulnerabilities. Include any other third-party code shipped as part of the product in your search (for example, library routines).

- Install a copy of the software on a test system and observe the installation routine closely. Check the contents of any logs or temporary files created during the install. They might contain passwords or other insightful information. Check the file permissions. Could an attacker read them? Also study the default configuration. What are the weaknesses?

- Identify programs that are installed set-uid/set-gid and search available documentation for program information. (It might be sparse, though.)

- Run strings and grep on the binaries to identify weaknesses such as back doors, hard-coded calls to other programs without explicit paths, predictable temporary filenames, application-specific environment variables (which you might be able to overflow), and so on. Check for any hidden command-line arguments or back doors.

20

UNIX

- If you can identify the actual developers of the code (through the RCS (Revision Control System) strings), search the Web for other code they have developed. If you can find any open source programs, check their coding style and observe any security errors. The odds are on your side that they've repeated the same mistakes in the code you're bashing away at.

- Observe how your target interacts with the kernel. As root, run the software via a program that can trace system calls (for example, `strace` or `truss`). If these tools aren't on your system, check your distribution media. Identify how the program works. Try to identify when it makes calls to the set-id family of system calls. Focus on the sections of code that execute with set-uid/set-gid privilege.

- Now watch the program's use of library files. Run the program under a call-tracing program such as ltrace or sotruss. Check for function calls that have known weaknesses (see `http://www.whitefang.com/sup/secure-faq.html` for a list). Keep rerunning it until you know which files it accesses. Examine those files, remove them, put spurious data in them, and so on.

- Play with the command-line arguments—feed the program data it doesn't expect. If the command takes a user-specified file as an argument, try and have the program read a file that you don't have access to (such as a database file or private configuration file). Some applications are so dumb they don't even check the original owner of the supplied file, and you could be staring at your own /etc/shadow file.

- Set crazy values for the standard and application-specific environment variables. Run the application to see whether it breaks. If it does, can you exploit it in some way? Does it dump core and leak sensitive information in the core file? (Use `strings` or `gdb` to check this.)

- Deprive the program of resources it expects and see how it reacts. For example, consume all available inodes on application-related (and /tmp) filesystems. Programs that haven't been coded with extreme situations in mind can behave unpredictably—use this to help you.

- If the application ships with a network server component, use Telnet (in the case of a TCP-based server) or, better still, grab a copy of `netcat` (described in the following section) and connect to the network port(s) used by the application. Do you receive any output upon connecting? Try and stimulate a response by pressing Return or other various keys or by typing **help**. Try sending a large amount of nonsense data. Does it crash because of an overflow? If you can find specs for the protocol (or, in the case of proprietary protocols, if youcan reverse-engineer it), try overflowing specific protocol fields (for example, in the case of Web servers, the HTTP Referer field). Granted, this is not rocket science, but just try stuff. You might be surprised how effective this crude approach can be at unearthing security bugs (or just general flakiness). Remember—you might be the first person scrutinizing it this way—you never know what you might find.

- Use a network sniffer like `tcpdump` or `Ethereal` and observe the communications between the client program and network server. Look for plaintext passwords flying across the network or other information leaks. Advanced testers will attempt to replay the network traffic to see if they can reauthenticate using the captured packet data. Play "Man-in-the-Middle" (MITM) and intelligently modify the data in transit using a program like netsed.

- Check for inadequate settings on shared memory segments. Use the `ipcs` command to identify application-specific shared segments—check their permissions. Are they locked down enough? If not, read them as a non-root user. Try and decipher what you've read—check for information leaks such as weak passwords, encryption keys, fragments of database files, and so on. If you have write access, try and alter important values to affect what gets written to the user or application store.

Useful Tools for the Explorer

Tcpdump
Author: Network Research Group (NRG) at Lawrence Berkeley National Laboratory (LBNL)

URL: `http://ee.lbl.gov/` or `http://www.tcpdump.org/`

Tcpdump is the de facto UNIX network sniffer. The version shipped with your distribution is likely out-of-date. Go get the latest one.

Ethereal
Author: Gerald Combs

URL: `http://www.ethereal.com/`

Ethereal is a GPL equivalent to commercial grade network sniffers. Featuring both a GUI display and a console-only version (tethereal), it can decode an incredible number of protocols. It also supports the capability to read capture files written by many other sniffers.

Netcat
Author: Hobbit (ported to NT by Weld Pond)

URL: `http://www.l0pht.com/~weld/netcat/`

Nicknamed the "Swiss Army Knife" of networking tools, netcat allows you to make outbound or inbound TCP connections to or from any port you choose. It can optionally hex dump traffic sent and received. Netcat can be used to bypass weakly configured packet filters as well as to throw test data at a network service (useful when checking for basic overflows). Because it can run as a listening network service, you can play all kinds of interesting network tricks with it. See the README for some ideas. If you're bound to a MS desktop, you'll be glad to hear about the NT/95 port.

20

UNIX

Ltrace

Author: Juan Cespedes

URL: `http://packages.debian.org/unstable/utils/ltrace.html`

Ltrace is a Linux-only program to show runtime library call information for dynamically linked libraries. This enables you to trace function calls whether they end up calling systems calls or not. If the program you are interested in is statically linked, this program won't help. Non-Debian GNU/Linux users should be able to find packages available from their favorite package mirror.

Netsed

Author: Michal Zalewski

URL: `http://packetstorm.securify.com/UNIX/misc/netsed.tgz`

Michal is a very talented programmer, who is active in security research. While he was black-boxing a Lotus product, he wrote netsed—a small GNU/Linux–based network utility that brings the functionality of sed (stream editor) to the network. Netsed lets you change network packets on-the-fly as they pass your machine by specifying one or more search strings and a corresponding replacement. This automates an otherwise very tedious and repetitive process: Capture a data stream to a file, modify the capture file, and send downstream, for every client/server communication.

Subterfugue

Author: Mike Coleman

URL: `http://www.subterfugue.org/`

The author describes Subterfugue as a "framework for observing and playing with the reality of software." In a nutshell, you can mess with the program big time! The user creates "tricks" that affect the way the program operates (either directly or through throttling I/O). By manipulating the world that the application executes within, you can profoundly influence and analyze its actions.

Test Limitations

The previously described attacks can turn up surprising results for very little effort. It can be quite depressing though—you've locked down your UNIX server only to find that the application gives up the goods to anyone who knows the magic incantation. DIY (Do It Yourself) testing is certainly valuable and is the only option for most people. However, it is not a proper substitute for a thorough security audit by a seasoned security bug finder.

Perhaps the biggest problem with this approach is that there is really no way to know when you're done. All you can do is keep testing until you have exhausted all the tests you can throw at a program or until frustration gets the better of you. It's often a case of diminishing returns—you find some interesting weaknesses, try to exploit them, and see what happens. Eventually, boredom sets in, and you find something more interesting to do.

If you do discover weaknesses, you can report them to the vendor. Depending on your point of view, you might have mixed feelings about doing so. Vendors have a spotted history when it comes to handling security problems. Some fix promptly and notify their users; others try to sweep problems under the carpet (worse still, some threaten the messenger).

If you are concerned about revealing your identify to a vendor, you can either use an anonymous remailer or ask the folks at SecurityFocus (`http://www.securityfocus.com`) to help you. They offer a free community service to help bug finders draft an advisory. With their experience in moderating Bugtraq, they are also a good sounding board if you do have concerns.

▶ People have different views on the subject of full disclosure—it is a classic "religious" debate. Rain.Forest.Puppy (rfp), an active security researcher, developed a disclosure policy in light of his experience reporting vulnerabilities to software maintainers. You can read it here: `http://www.wiretrip.net/rfp/policy.html`.

Rootkits and Defenses

Our contemplation of filesystem security isn't complete without a mention of rootkits.

After a successful root compromise, attackers might upload and install a *rootkit*, which is a collection of replacement system programs that enable attackers to hide their tracks and easily reconnect to the system at a later time. It is not unusual for an attacker to patch the hole that enabled him to gain access, to avoid losing the system to another attacker.

Rootkits typically include replacements for the following commands:

- **ps.** Shows process information. The rootkit version hides processes run by the attacker— they simply don't show up in the output.

- **netstat.** Shows network connections, routing information, and statistics. Attackers certainly don't want you discovering them connected to your systems. So they install a modified netstat binary that effectively cloaks connections on specific ports or specific client addresses.

- **ifconfig.** The attacker might want to sniff the network to pick off authentication credentials (among other things). To do this, the network interface card must be put into promiscuous mode. A very observant administrator might notice the `"P"` flag in the output of the `ifconfig` command. The modified netstat doesn't print the `"P"`.

- **df.** Shows filesystem free space and inode usage. The attackers' toolkit and sniffer logs consume diskspace that might be noticed on a quiet system. The rootkit df ignores files stored in a particular directory or owned by a particular user id.

20

UNIX

- **ls.** Lists files. Similar to the modified `df`, the rootkit `ls` behaves just like the standard `ls` but does not report files contained in a hidden directory or owned by a particular user id.

- **sum.** Calculates checksum and block counts. Should the administrator become suspicious and attempt to checksum the files against known good files (on a "clean" system), the rootkit `sum` program will produce faked checksum values that match the original binaries. Never ever rely on `sum` for security. It is possible for an astute attacker to create modified programs that still output the same sum value as the originals. (Instead, use cryptographic routines like MD5.)

Rootkits are readily available across a range of operating systems and architectures regardless of public availability of source. Patching binaries to include rogue code is not rocket science. It involves an understanding of binary file formats (for example, ELF) and some file manipulation—so don't assume you're invincible just because you are running a closed source OS.

Rootkit Countermeasures

The primary method to detect the presence of a rootkit is to use integrity assessment software. These programs take a digital snapshot of the system and alert you to changes to important system files.

When you first install integrity assessment software, a baseline database is created. This contains a unique signature for every file that is to be watched. Then, on a basis set by the administrator, new signatures are generated and compared with those stored in the integrity database. A mismatch means a file has been modified in some way—possibly indicating your system has been compromised. Alternatively, it could just mean you've applied an OS patch!

It used to be that system administrators would use a program like `sum` to generate file signatures of important system files. However, as they were to learn, these signatures can be faked. Attackers were able to cash in on the weaknesses of these checksum generators (or simply replace the program), thereby fooling the administrator.

In 1992, Gene Kim and Gene Spafford developed the Tripwire tool. Tripwire made use of digital hashing algorithms such as MD5, to create file signatures that were impractical to forge. Even the slightest change to a file, or to the file's inode information, resulted in an unmistakably different hash. The software filled a real gap in the security toolkit and proved incredibly popular. It was ported to numerous platforms and became the de facto integrity assessment software, referenced in just about every security book you'll ever come across.

This software is today known as Tripwire ASR (Academic Source Release) version 1.3.1.

For all its good points, this software has a major limitation—the database must be stored on read-only media like a write-protected floppy disk or tape. Not surprisingly, this is an inconvenience and doesn't scale well. It may be the most common reason why sites give up using

Tripwire. Storing the database on a read-only filesystem doesn't cut it either—an attacker can simply remount it read-write.

Realizing there was something of a market for this kind of tool, and that there was some mileage to be had in a major update, the authors set up a company, Tripwire Inc. This breathed life back into a popular tool. A number of new features were added, and the product was fully commercialized.

Possibly the most useful feature added is that you are no longer forced to store the integrity database on write-protected media—the database itself is signed using a 1,024-bit El Gamal encryption algorithm—you can store the integrity database on the system itself. That's not to say storing it on write-protected hardware is not a sensible idea. But, if that is not sustainable in your environment, then this may be for you.

Tripwire uses a policy language to define what to monitor. Check out the included documentation for a useful tutorial. The commercial version is somewhat easier to configure (no compiler required and the policy language seems friendlier) and ships with some reasonable defaults. Whatever version you use, though, don't forget to add in your application files and create the baseline database as soon after OS installation as possible.

For a stealthy way of running Tripwire, consider this. Create a cron job on a separate (hardened) system to remotely copy across the binary and database files and invoke the comparison. Don't forget to erase the files after the check. (The output can be stored on the invoking system ready for checking/filtering.)

While the commercial version does offer some worthwhile benefits, don't feel you have to pay out to get the core benefit—many sites still run the ASR version without a hitch.

The commercial version is now available for Windows NT. Those running larger sites might be interested in the Tripwire HQ Manager product to centralize management of all V2+ UNIX/NT Tripwire agents.

Good news if you're a Linux user, though—the Linux port of the commercial version was made open source and can be downloaded free.

Binary and source copies are available from `http://www.tripwire.org`.

The commercially supported product is available here: `http://www.tripwire.com`

The original ASR release is available here: `http://www.tripwire.com/downloads/index.cfml?dl=asr&cfid=265337&cftoken=18379700`.

Tutorials for installing Tripwire ASR can be found here:

`http://www.securityportal.com/topnews/tripwire20000711.html`

`http://netweb.usc.edu/danzig/cs558/Manual/lab25.html`

20

UNIX

Solaris users should take a look at this CERT security improvement module at
`http://www.cert.org/security-improvement/implementations/i002.02.html`.

Kernel Rootkits

We've covered userland rootkits—with which an attacker compromises the system and replaces important system files, and now we examine the ultimate form of deception—the kernel rootkit.

To appreciate the stealth provided by a kernel rootkit, it is vital to understand the role played by the kernel. The kernel is the huge C program that runs the show—it operates at a low level interfacing directly with system hardware. An attacker who reprograms the kernel can change the behavior of the system in any way he chooses. Consequently, if an attacker modifies the kernel, he can literally change your world. Unless the attacker leaves the digital equivalent of muddy feet on the carpet, you'll probably never even know about the attack.

The means to introduce a kernel rootkit is a root level compromise (just as for a standard rootkit). The usual purpose is to hide cracker activity and provide a convenient way for crackers to reconnect later on.

A kernel rootkit really is the most devious form of back door—it is the ultimate cloaking device. All bets are off when the kernel has been subverted.

Kernel rootkits typically modify the kernel call table to redirect system calls to rogue code introduced by the attacker. The rogue code performs whatever actions the cracker intends and then calls the original OS code to let the call complete. The user is kept blissfully unaware of this.

A typical kernel rootkit

- Hides processes. No matter what tool the administrator uses, the attackers' processes are hidden—the kernel lies. This overcomes the limitations of backdooring.
- Modifies system logging routines (process accounting, C2 kernel audit, utmp, and so on).
- Hides network connections.
- Modifies NIC (Network Interface Card) status to hide sniffer activity.
- Reports false file modification times.
- Hides the presence of the module (in the case of an LKM).
- Does anything else the attacker can think of.

▶ The technical reference bible for Linux Kernel hacking can be found here: `http://packetstorm.securify.com/groups/thc/LKM_HACKING.html`

Three main methods exist to introduce rogue code into the kernel:

- Modifying kernel memory on a live system via /dev/[kmem|mem]
- Patching the kernel binary on disk
- Loading a kernel module

Traditionally, kernels were monolithic—a big slab of code did everything. Modern UNIX systems support Loadable Kernel Modules (LKM), which enable the administrator to introduce new kernel code into the operating system whilst the system is running. This could be done to provide support for additional filesystem types, network drivers, or custom security routines. Check out your man pages for the following insertion commands: `insmod`, `lsmod`, and `rmmod`.

Whatever insertion method is used, kernel integrity is paramount—if the new code doesn't behave and tramples over key kernel structures, then the system is likely to crash. This isn't too subtle. Developers of kernel code know this all too well.

The act of patching a live kernel is actually less scary than it sounds (as long as you do it correctly). This technique is sometimes used to tweak kernel parameters where no "userland" utility exists. (It is generally unsupported, however.) Inserting new kernel code involves locating and overwriting unused areas of kernel space with your code and repatching the system call table to divert callers to your code.

Kernel patching on disk involves writing your changes directly to the kernel image using a binary patcher. You seek through the binary to specific locations and overwrite with your own code. File headers are likely to need modifying, so a basic understanding of object file formats is required.

All other previously mentioned methods are possible if root access has been gained.

LKMs, however, provide the most convenient method for backdooring the kernel. Consequently, LKMs appear to be the most common delivery mechanism for rogue kernel code in the wild. Inversely, LKMs provide the good guys with a way to enhance existing security, too.

At this point you might be thinking that closed source operating systems should be safe from this kind of thing. Again, as with standard rootkits, access to source is not a major factor. (Besides, source code for some closed source operating systems circulates within the underground community.) Kernel hacking requires a familiarity with kernel structures (documented in /usr/include), some skills with a kernel debugger, and an appreciation of kernel issues (for example, how to allocate memory correctly).

For example, in December 1999, mail was sent to Bugtraq announcing the availability of a Solaris Loadable Kernel Module back door. The note was from Plasmoid, a member of The Hackers Choice (THC)—a Germany-based group with some very talented individuals. The paper is available from here: `http://www.thehackerschoice.com/papers/slkm-1.0.html`. Check out their other projects, too.

As with any program, it only takes one person to codify a kernel rootkit with a friendly user-land interface. Then anyone can install and use it on a compromised system.

▶ Rootkits come and go in popularity. A collection of current rootkits (both kernel and userland) can be found at the Packetstorm archive: `http://packetstorm.securify.com/UNIX/ penetration/rootkits/`

Even if you can't find a rootkit for your system, it is probably prudent to assume a kernel rootkit exists, and, therefore, you should implement countermeasures. This might sound like unnecessary paranoia—perhaps it is. On the other hand, bear in mind that the cracker community is very effective at sharing tools. Crackers don't tend to advertise their tools with big neon signs, though.

Protecting Against Kernel Attacks

Safeguarding against kernel attacks can be summed up in one word: prevention. You need to prevent attackers from writing to kernel memory (directly or indirectly through LKMs) or the on-disk kernel. This is easier said than done because, if they have root, they can modify the kernel. To prevent this, you need to get in there first and change the rules. But, to do this, you need to modify the kernel itself—and, if your OS doesn't have LKM support, you're on your own.

▶ The standard advice until recently has been "Disable LKM support." This is now a waste of time—Silvio Cesare has created a program to re-enable LKM support. You can download Kinsmod.c from his site, `http://www.big.net.au/~silvio/`.

If you're wondering why Tripwire isn't mentioned as a countermeasure here, you should probably re-read the introduction to this section. Tripwire is a userland tool. It doesn't run in the kernel—it makes calls to the kernel and bases its decisions on values returned by the kernel. Knowing this, an attacker can re-route calls made by Tripwire, to custom code that generates false checksums that match Tripwire's expectations. This is usually implemented by a rootkit in order to hide the presence of the rootkit on disk.

Rootkit Detection

If you can't prevent, then detect. This is a sound security principle that can be applied to many security-related situations.

Currently, there is no generalized method to identify whether a given kernel on an arbitrary system has been subject to a rootkit attack. However, there are specific detect points for a number of published back doors.

Authors of kernel rootkits might include a routine to identify that the kernel rootkit is actually inserted. For example, the Adore LKM back door written by Stealth (`http://spider. scorpions.net/~stealth/`) can be detected by making a call to setuid with a magic number.

If you supply the right number, the kernel module announces its presence. Of course, you are relying on defaults here. If your attackers used any sense at all, they would have modified the magic number or even the particular call used, and this crude detection scheme would fail.

A program that implements a number of checks for common back door modules on Linux is rkscan. Using the technique outlined previously, rkscan can identify multiple versions of popular rootkits, Adore and Knark (written by Creed). Rkscan is available from `http://www.hsc.fr/ressources/outils/rkscan/index.html.en`.

Host Network Security

This section focuses on network security at the host. This section does not discuss firewalls, network intrusion detection, and router network security issues. It deals solely with the services provided by a UNIX server to its network clients.

Network Services: General Purpose Versus "Fit for Purpose"

Is your system having an identity crisis? It probably is if you've decided it's a Web server, but it's actually running all kinds of other network services, ranging from file-sharing services (NFS, Samba, and so on) to remote printing services.

What Are Network Services?

If you are familiar with the concept and implementation of network services, skip to the next section—otherwise, read on.

A *network service* is a process (daemon) that provides a service to clients. Apart from some internal housekeeping functions, its job is to process client's requests. It's called a *daemon process* because it is detached from its controlling terminal and runs in its own session group (of which, it is the session leader). By doing this, the process can survive when the user who executed the program logs out of the system.

In order to respond to clients, network daemons bind to and listen on a TCP (Transport Control Protocol) or UDP (User Datagram Protocol) port. The program uses a network socket to send and receive data. A bound socket can be associated with a single IP address or all IP addresses on the system. This is determined by the parameters given to the bind() call. The port number selected by the programmer is based on a (voluntary) convention. For example; a Web server will listen on TCP port 80. A list of ports and their corresponding service names for your system is normally found in file /etc/services. However, vendor-supplied services files are often incomplete.

For the official IANA (Internet Assigned Numbers Authority) port listing, visit `http://www.isi.edu/in-notes/iana/assignments/port-numbers`.

The IANA listing does not include a large number of ports in use today. Unless a software developer registers the port with IANA it will not make it into IANA's list. But, that doesn't mean it can't be used—just that it might clash with an existing or future entry in their list. For an unofficial but comprehensive list, check out `http://dhp.com/~whisper/mason/nmap-services`.

The decision to use the TCP or UDP transport protocol will depend on the communication requirements of the application.

TCP is a connection-based protocol: One system (the TCP client) makes a *connect* call to establish a connection with another system (the TCP server). The kernels of both machines maintain state data about the connection. This includes the IP address of the remote system, the remote port number, sequencing data (to support reliability and reordering of out-of-order packets), and a number of other parameters. The kernel examines the header of incoming TCP/IP packets to determine which socket should receive the payload of the packet. A connection is identified by the unique tuple of source IP, source port, destination IP, and destination port.

UDP is connectionless. Put simply, one system can send one or more packets to another system (or systems, in the case of multicasting/broadcasting). The remote system will not respond (that is, it's connectionless), and reliability therefore is not guaranteed. The application program is responsible for reliability. For further details about TCP/IP, refer to Chapter 4.

The Risks of Running Network Services

Standard UNIX distributions ship with a raft of network services. That should come as no surprise—after all, they are sold as general-purpose operating systems. Unfortunately, all distributions—barring OpenBSD—ship with nonessential network services enabled. They are "on" by default.

Network services provide useful functionality to clients. Remote users can download mail, log in to the system, share data remotely, use printers attached to the server—in fact, this and much more. Most significantly though, they also enable remote attackers to break into the system, grab sensitive data, snoop the network, install Trojan programs, spy on end users, crash the system, or wipe the disks.

If you're new to IT security, you might find that last statement bewildering. Wouldn't they need to log in first? Why on earth would vendors ship software like that? Well, obviously the problems that enable attacks to happen are not part of their intended functionality. As history demonstrates, however, security bugs in network daemons are very common—so common, in fact, that, when you're done installing your operating system, the chances are extremely high that your machine is vulnerable to remote attack.

Some administrators realize this and head straight for the vendor's support site to download and install the latest security patches. With that out of the way, they make the system available on the network, knowing that the system is "secure"—at least from a remote attacker. Right? Depends on the network. In general, this isn't enough. Even after applying every security patch available from the vendor, the system is still vulnerable to network attacks for four reasons:

- Insecure network daemon settings
- Insecure network kernel settings
- Insecure network protocols
- Unpublished security bugs in network daemons

Need convincing? Well, limiting ourselves to a subset of network daemons and a subset of their default insecure settings only (and that's quite a limitation), your system is probably vulnerable to some of the following problems post-install.

Your system is most likely configured to run the X Window System (whether you knew it or not). On some default installations, a remote attacker can grab screen shots and kill users' X programs—and that's just for starters. What about capturing every key the administrator types (think passwords) or remapping the administrators' keys to carry out additional commands when they hit a particular key?

Your system is most likely running an SNMP agent. SNMP agents enable remote Network Monitoring Stations (NMS) to collect system information. In its default configuration, remote attackers can also collect, and in some cases modify your system settings. More on that later.

Your system gives away the names of user ids on the system. Traditionally, the finger service was the culprit—vendors shipped the finger server enabled by default, and remote users could query finger and gain a list of usernames ready for attempting brute-force logins. After pressure from customers, the majority of vendors now ship this service disabled. But this isn't a comprehensive solution. In its default state, sendmail enables remote users to query user ids and will report whether they exist or not. Automating this check and building a dictionary of common usernames to check for is hardly rocket science.

In addition to the categories of problems previously mentioned, your system is also vulnerable to published security bugs in network services that the vendor hasn't even fixed yet. That's right—your system could be vulnerable to problems reported in public forums, and yet your vendor doesn't have a fix ready (yet). Again, this might sound crazy. Even worse—it might take six months for a vendor to fix a nasty security hole.

Your system is also vulnerable to so-called *0-day exploits*. These are exploits for unpublished vulnerabilities typically sent between friends with the accompanying message of "Do not distribute." Ironically, they often spread like wildfire. In fact, this has lead to a number of security groups having to (somewhat embarrassingly) formally announce security problems they discovered simply because the information "leaked" from the group. The whole 0-day thing seems to generate a lot of excitement within certain sections of the security community (if script kiddies are actually considered to be part of the security community).

A group that argues against full-disclosure and releasing of 0-day exploits is the AntiSecurity movement. Check our their views at `http://anti.security.is/`. The discussion board has attracted some hardcore security people.

As someone with responsibility for securing a computer system, it's important for you to realize that thousands of people are trying to "break" (meaning "compromise") systems every day. Whether they are working for a security organization, a government agency, or an operating system vendor, or as a private individual, all around the globe people are in labs attempting to find security holes.

When security flaws are discovered, the finder has a number of options. Some people inform the vendor; some publish their findings to full disclosure mailing lists. Some tell their friends, and some tell nobody. (In fact, they might do some or all of these things at different times.)

Securing Network Services

Are you depressed yet? You might be feeling that all the "evil forces" of the world are against you. Fortunately, there are steps you can take to either eliminate or reduce your system's exposure to many of these network-borne threats.

- Disable network services you don't need.
- Use available security features of the services you do need.
- If an existing network server can't be secured as-is, find a replacement that has a proven track record.
- Assume holes. Log relevant activity, analyze intelligently, and notify vendors and others.
- Keep on top of those patches or develop workarounds.

Disabling Network Services

Do you know what network services are enabled on your systems? Many administrators simply don't know. They've never bothered to question it—they never thought it was a problem. Hopefully by now you realize that not every program your system runs is necessarily healthy for it (or you) from a security point of view.

By turning off the services you don't need, you simply eliminate the risk inherent in running them.

Before turning off unused services, you need to audit what is enabled. Specifically, you need to figure out what services are currently active or will become active if requested by a client.

Network daemons are either standalone or started by a master (or super) daemon when the system enters multiuser mode. By examining each start-up script, you can identify each daemon that is started and the command-line options it is invoked with.

Possibly the most famous master daemon is inetd. Inetd reads a configuration file (often /etc/inetd.conf) to find out which services to listen for. Upon receiving a packet, inetd *forks* (creates a copy of itself) and executes (`exec`) the program specified in inetd.conf, handing over the new client connection in the process. Inetd continues listening in the background.

Make yourself familiar with the inetd configuration file. Use the man pages to learn about services you don't recognize.

The start-up (and shutdown) scripts are normally located in the /etc/rc* directories (rc means run command). Each rc directory represents a different system run-level. The start-up scripts are easy to identify—they start with a capital "S" (the shutdown scripts start with a "K" for "kill") and are executed in numerical order (for example, S01, S02, S03, and so on). In fact, they are executed in the order generated by the filename shell wildcard character (just like `ls *`). The convention to use two-digit numbers avoids S3 executing after S24, for example.

We're interested in run-level 3—multiuser mode.

Read the start-up scripts on your system and make a list of services that are started. If you're not sure which program name represents a network daemon and which doesn't, here are some things to check for.

Check the man pages. If you are looking for a program called "nuked" and typing `man nuked` doesn't get you anywhere, try searching the man pages using the `man -k nuked` command. Man pages that describe the program as serving network clients or listening for connections are clearly good indicators of a network server.

20

UNIX

Run the `ps` command (`ps aux` or `ps -ef`). If the program is listed, run `lsof -I` and `grep` for the program name. If it appears, you can be sure it's a network daemon. The `-I` switch to `lsof` says, "list processes using a TCP/IP socket."

Check whether the name of the program (minus the `d` if there is one) is listed in /etc/services. `grep` is your friend here.

Last of all, if the program name ends in "d" (daemon)—it's probably a daemon. Okay, now we're starting to clutch at straws.

The man page for the program talks about RFC compliance. An *RFC (Request for Comments)* defines how a protocol works and what must be implemented for an implementor of the protocol to call a program RFC compliant. To gain a deep understanding of TCP/IP and application protocols (for example, FTP or HTTP), you'll find RFCs an invaluable source of information. You can find a hyperlinked archive of RFCs at `http://www.landfield.com/rfcs/`.

A Word About Privileged Ports

Programs written to listen on a port number lower than 1024 must be executed with root privilege (that is, UID 0). This rule protects sensitive system services because these run on ports lower in number than 1024 (that is, the reserved ports). The UNIX kernel enforces this restriction to prevent non-privileged users from launching fake network server processes on idle ports. Without this rule, a local user (that is, a user with an account on the system) could

- Start a fake Telnet server to capture user ids and passwords of unsuspecting Telnet clients logging in to the system. If implemented properly, the victims would never realize their accounts had been compromised.

- Start a fake domain name server (DNS) and supply false IP addressing information to DNS clients. For example, a client system attempting to visit `http://www.pottedmeatfoodproducts.com/` could be redirected to an exact clone of the site created by the attacker. Sensitive information could then fall into the wrong hands.

- Start a malicious FTP server. Every time a user connects to the FTP service, the rogue FTP program spits back specially crafted data that exploits a bug in a client FTP program. By exploiting a security weakness in the client side program, the attacker is now able to run code on the user's workstation with the privileges of the remote user!

- …and many, many more malicious acts.

On the other hand, non-privileged processes are allowed to bind and listen on port numbers higher than 1024. Network-aware application programs make use of these non-privileged ports. The advantage of using ports higher than 1024 is that programs do not need to be executed with root privilege just to bind and listen for client requests.

Unfortunately, this doesn't stop impersonation attacks. We noted earlier that, when a program makes a call to `bind()`, it has the option of specifying a single IP address or a wildcard. The wildcard tells the kernel, "Bind to all available interfaces,"—or, in other words—"Listen on every IP address on the system." You can tell which network daemons do this by using the `netstat` command. A very useful command to learn, `netstat` shows networking statistics. On most UNIX systems, `netstat -a` shows all ports that are active or in the LISTEN state. The entries marked LISTEN either have a wildcard (*) source address or a specific IP address.

If a caller to `bind()` specifies a wildcard address, a subsequent caller (that is, another program) can still impersonate the server by binding "in front" of the original server. This wouldn't be possible if the original call had been made with a specific IP address. For example, a database listener binds to port 1999 and specifies the wildcard IP address. The kernel services the request. A local attacker notices the weak binding (via the `netstat` command) and runs a rogue database listener (that is, one she made earlier). This `bind()`s to the primary IP address of the machine, allowing her to perform Man In the Middle Attacks (MITM) or just to snoop on application usernames and passwords.

Some kernels prevent this kind of attack, but, unfortunately, it is still possible on many popular distributions.

A further point to be aware of is the Strong versus Weak End System model, as defined in RFC 1122, "Requirements for Internet Hosts—Communication Layers." If your distribution follows the Weak model, remote attackers might be able to communicate with network services in ways you don't expect. Specifically, a multi-homed system can allow packets coming in on one interface to communicate with network services running on another (including a loopback) interface. So, binding network services to specific IP addresses might not gain you anything at all. See this Bugtraq thread for full details: `http://archives.neohapsis.com/archives/bugtraq/2001-03/0009.html`

Protecting Against Service Hijacking Attacks

Either fix the kernel to prevent the `bind()`-related problems, or have network applications bind to specific ports. If you have source code for the kernel, you could, of course, modify the `bind()` call to check a list of unauthorized ports before binding. But, there is a wider question: Should end-users have the capability to start up network services? Consider the other possible risks and the likelihood of these things happening in your scenario:

- A user runs a program such as netcat (renamed, of course) to listen on a high numbered port and execute a shell when a client connects. The next time the user wants to log in to the system, he just telnets to the port running netcat, and, voilà, he has a shell waiting—no authentication, no logging in, no security! It won't take long for a curious person with a port scanner to find the port. (It takes about 10 minutes on a typical LAN to port scan all 65,535 TCP ports.) Hiding network services on unusual ports does not buy you real security.

- A programmer writes a network application program but fails to write it securely. A malicious client probes the service and attempts to blackbox her way to root.

Additionally, your usage policy should state that end-users should not run unauthorized programs that listen for incoming network connections.

Detecting Fake Servers

As applies to preventing rootkit attacks, if you can't prevent attacks through fake servers, then try to detect these fakes. Fortunately, in this case, detection is trivial. The key is noticing when an unauthorized program listens on a given port. You could write a custom program to do this or use the following countermeasures:

- Run `lsof` on a regular basis and compare the results to an authorized baseline. `lsof` fills the gap that `netstat` leaves. `netstat` won't show you which process is listening on which ports—duh! Thankfully, `lsof` does. Create a list of authorized program names and their mapping to ports/IP addresses. Write a script to filter the output of `lsof` and compare the results to your baseline. Run via `cron` and have differences reported to the administrator for investigation.

- Run a port scanner and compare the results to an authorized baseline. This will tell you when an additional service is running (that is, a port is listening), but not what it is. This approach can be performed remotely without shell access to the system. The only requirement is that you be authorized by the system owner to perform port scanning and that you have network visibility of the system (that is, can send TCP and UDP packets to the server and receive replies).

- If you have kernel source code but are wary about modifying the `bind` call to limit listening services, try logging instead. Implement a simple logging routine each time `bind` is successfully called. Check the results against a baseline via a userland program, and report differences to the administrator for investigation.

At this point it's time to look at specific UNIX services. What follows is not a comprehensive list—these are the mainstay of UNIX network services.

Telnet

> **NOTE**
>
> As with many network services, the name Telnet may refer to the client program, to the protocol, and, if you add the word *daemon,* to the server-side program. In our discussion of Telnet, we will be referring to the server program. To limit confusion, references to the TEL-NET protocol will use uppercase letters.

The Telnet server provides a network virtual terminal emulation service to clients. The server portion normally listens on TCP port 23. Check out RFC 854 for the technical specification.

Essentially this means users can log in (authenticate) to the machine, perform some work on a text-based virtual terminal, and then disconnect. The TELNET protocol is defined in RFC 854. The Telnet daemon runs with root privileges.

TELNET is slowly being phased out. I say "slowly" because, although secure alternatives have been available for some time, a number of major vendors still insist on shipping distributions with TELNET enabled and no secure alternative installed.

TELNET Protocol Risks

The major security weakness of TELNET is that all communications between the Telnet client and server are passed in plaintext (that is, unencrypted) across the network. That means usernames, passwords, sensitive system data, and other possibly confidential information is visible to anyone running a network sniffer located between the client and server. Worst of all, because of the way a routed IP network functions, machines on other parts of the network might also gain visibility of the data.

This makes TELNET unsuitable for use in environments where the security of the underlying network or every host en route cannot be completely trusted. To put it another way, as a UNIX administrator, you probably have no control over security outside of your system—your options are confined to host-based network controls only.

Other attacks include insertion or replay attacks in which a Man In The Middle (MITM) changes the data on-the-fly or plays back an earlier data capture. Imagine finding yourself adding a user to the system with no hands!

Vendors can ship systems with default user ids and passwords. Unless you change default passwords or lock the accounts, a remote attacker can gain access by using Telnet.

Information Leakage

By default, vendors tend to ship the Telnet daemon with a default login prompt that greets users with the name of the operating system, the version, and sometimes the system architecture. This kind of information helps attackers. With it, they can whip out their nastiest exploits geared specifically to your platform. Why give this information away so easily to an attacker? The reality is that removing this information won't stop your operating system from being identified remotely. (To find out why, read on.) However, I would argue that announcing your system details to anyone who makes a connection to your machine is making things a little too easy! Remove product/version info from your login banner. Some sites replace the vendor greeting with a legal "No unauthorized access" message. Check with your legal department for specific wording.

20

UNIX

The TELNET daemon leaks information about your operating system in a less obvious way, too. The TELNET protocol defines a number of Telnet options. When a Telnet client connects to a Telnet server, either end can transmit Telnet options. These enable one side to express its capabilities and requested functionality to the other—for example, its terminal type. A remote attacker, able to connect to the TELNET daemon, can use this to her advantage.

There is no standard TELNET daemon implementation. Different vendors implemented different Telnet options. By examining the Telnet options and the sequence in which they are received, an attacker can fingerprint your operating system.

▶ The TESO group has developed a tool that can identify a wide range of UNIX flavors by using Telnet options. You can download it here: `http://teso.scene.at/releases/Telnetfp_0.1.2.tar.gz`

I Spy with My Little Eye

Before launching an attack on a site, an attacker will perform remote reconnaissance. They will want to find out the type and version of operating system and the services you are running. Network daemons commonly announce their software version upon a client connection. This can help when you are remote troubleshooting because network administrators can easily identify software version incompatibilities. In the same way though, it assists the attacker. Armed with this information, she can search vulnerability databases for known weaknesses or, in preparation for an attack, re-create an identical system in her lab for penetration testing.

A common reaction to this problem is to remove product/version information from system banners. This might mean

- Recompiling open source network daemons with this information stripped
- Overwriting the banner strings in closed source binaries
- Modifying configuration files (for example, /etc/issue on Solaris)

This will thwart banner grabbing.

However, even if you did this to all your network daemons, the version of your operating system and all its network software can still be identified remotely through the process of behavioral analysis.

Remote Determination of Network Service Versions

Software versions change because of bug fixes, additional software features, performance hacks, and so on. The attacker can probe for feature or bug differences between versions, thereby determining the specific version in use. This is not the long and complicated task it might sound. The attacker can make the reasonable assumption that a site is running a relatively recent version and work back. In fact, this kind of functionality is built in to some commercial vulnerability scanners.

Remote Operating System Identification

Vendors' TCP/IP stacks respond differently to a given set of packets. By remotely fingerprinting the TCP/IP stack, it is often possible to identify the operating system in use and its version. You've already learned a bit about this in Chapter 5, "Hackers and Crackers." The attacker sends a sequence of packets with specific attributes. The response packets sent by the victim server contain unique elements that, when considered together, uniquely identify a vendor's TCP/IP implementation. The queso tool originally used this approach. This strategy was then adopted and expanded by Fyodor in his nmap tool available from `http://www.insecure.org/nmap`.

Vendors TCP/IP stacks also exhibit distinguishing timing characteristics in their handling of packets. When a system receives a packet, the network interface hardware generates an interrupt. The kernel processes the packet based on information contained in the packet header. The time taken for a given platform to process the packet will vary depending on the code path taken (that is, if it's x, then do y; if it's x and z, do j). By sending multiple packets of varying complexity, it is theoretically possible to measure response times and compare them to known baselines to identify systems. This has been discussed in public forums, although no tool has been published as of yet.

Modifying network kernel parameters can defeat TCP/IP stack fingerprinting. These change the way that the TCP/IP stack behaves and will thwart known fingerprinting techniques.

This might leave you wondering whether it is worth removing system details from banners at all. There's certainly room for debate, but my personal view is that, for Internet-exposed hosts, it *is* worth the effort, as long as you understand it doesn't buy you any real security. What you're actually getting is security by obscurity. But, it might just be a reprieve from the less advanced attacker who relies on banner-grabbing–style scanning to identify potential victims. When the next remotely exploitable vulnerability gets announced, your banner-less system is unlikely to appear on the script kiddies' radar. Sure, you'll need to apply patches—but at least you might avoid the embarrassment of being nailed by an amateur!

Securing Telnet

One option is to use router- or VPN-based encryption. This is a partial solution; it does not result in end-to-end encryption. This can still leave the TELNET data stream open to MITM attacks near either end of the connection.

The superior solution and stock replacement for TELNET is Secure Shell (SSH). SSH is deployed at thousands of sites worldwide and has become the standard way of remotely accessing a UNIX server across potentially hostile networks.

SSH is a TCP-based service that, by default, listens on port 22.

An Essential Tool: Secure Shell

According to the "What is Secure Shell" FAQ at
`http://www.employees.org/~satch/ssh/faq/`:

> Secure Shell (SSH) is a program to log into another computer over a network, to execute commands in a remote machine, and to move files from one machine to another. It provides strong authentication and secure communications over insecure channels. It is intended as a replacement for Telnet, rlogin, rsh, and rcp. For SSH2, there is a replacement for FTP: sftp.
>
> Additionally, SSH provides secure X connections and secure forwarding of arbitrary TCP connections. You can also use SSH as a tool for things like [`http://rsync.samba.org`] rsync and secure network backups.
>
> The traditional BSD 'r' commands (rsh, rlogin, rcp) are vulnerable to different kinds of attacks. Somebody, who has root access to machines on the network, or physical access to the wire, can gain unauthorized access to systems in a variety of ways. It is also possible for such a person to log all the traffic to and from your system, including passwords (which ssh never sends in the clear).
>
> The X Window System also has a number of severe vulnerabilities. With ssh, you can create secure remote X sessions which are transparent to the user. As a side effect, using remote X clients with ssh is more convenient for users.

> **NOTE**
>
> Historically, U.S. vendors have not shipped Secure Shell (SSH) in their UNIX distributions. However, with the expiration of the RSA patent, recent (long overdue) changes in U.S. export legislation, and the release of public domain SSH implementation, this situation could be set to change.

As with many things in the UNIX world, SSH is the name of the protocol and an implementation.

The SSH Protocols

Two major versions of the SSH protocol exist. They are quite different and as a result incompatible.

Version 1 is defined in an IETF (Internet Engineering Task Force) draft at `http://www.tigerlair.com/ssh/faq/ssh1-draft.txt`. SSH1 is being phased out in favor of SSH2.

Copies of current Internet drafts for SSH version 2 can be found on the IETF Web site `http://search.ietf.org/ids.by.wg/secsh.html`. The specification is broken into four parts: architecture, connection protocol, authentication protocol, and transport layer protocol. If you want to know the SSH specification inside out, these are the documents to read.

SSH1 proved very popular—according to the SSH Scanner project (`http://ssh-research-scanner.ucs.ualberta.ca/ssh-stats.html`), SSH V1.5 (the last version) is still the most widely deployed. This is due, at least in part, to the lack of a free version 2 implementation—that is, until recently.

SSH Servers

Commercial SSH server software is available from SSH Communications and Data Fellows. Noncommercial SSH1 versions can be downloaded from `www.ssh.org`. The last free version is 1.2.27.

Frustrated at the lack of a truly free, up-to-date SSH, the OpenBSD team started the OpenSSH project. The stated goal of the project is to have Secure Shell technology shipped with every operating system. To avoid restrictive licensing, the team went back and reused the version 1.2.2 code, written by Tatu Ylönen. The code was developed outside of the United States to avoid restrictions on the exportation of cryptography and is available under a BSD license. This means anyone can use it, for any purpose.

The first major release, supporting SSH protocol version 1, was shipped in December 1999 with OpenBSD 2.6. As of this writing, OpenSSH 2.5.1 has been released. This is a major milestone because it provides support for the SSH2 protocol in addition to 1.3 and 1.5.

The OpenSSH Project is great news for all UNIX users—especially when you consider it has been written and reviewed to the same security principles as the OpenBSD project was. The source code has been significantly simplified to ease code review, and all code has been subjected to an extensive security review. The same statements cannot necessarily be made about the commercial alternatives.

Unsurprisingly, a number of groups have integrated OpenSSH into their base operating systems. These include Debian Linux, FreeBSD, SuSE Linux, Red Hat Linux, Mandrake Linux, BSDi BSD/OS, NetBSD, Apple Mac OS-X/Darwin, Computone, Conectiva Linux, and Slackware Linux.

Don't worry if your favorite UNIX isn't on that list. OpenSSH can be downloaded from `http://www.openssh.org/` and installed as a separate utility. Official ports exist for SUN Solaris, IBM AIX, Hewlett-Packard HP-UX, Digital UNIX/Tru64/OSF, Irix, NeXT, SCO, and SNI/Reliant UNIX. See `http://www.openssh.com/portable.html` for an up-to-date list.

Compiler-shy Solaris users can grab a compiled version in Solaris package format from `http://www.sunfreeware.com`. For Solaris users who want to install from scratch, check out this useful installation guide written CERT: `http://www.cert.org/security-improvement/implementations/i062_01.html`. (Although the guide is described as Solaris specific, it does include useful generic information.)

OpenSSH relies on two underlying packages:

- zlib available from `ftp://ftp.freesoftware.com/pub/infozip/zlib/`
- OpenSSL available from `http://www.openssl.org/`

In my opinion, OpenSSH is the way forward.

SSH Clients

Just like TELNET, SSH is a client/server protocol. To access a SSH server, the client must be running SSH clients.

UNIX users can use the OpenSSH client that ships the OpenSSH server.

My favorite Win32 client is called Putty. It's written by Simon Tatham, is free for both commercial and noncommercial use, and is open source.

Putty supports both SSH protocols and runs on Windows 95, 98, Me, NT, and 2000. It's a slick piece of code, weighing in at less than 300Kb—so you can take it on a floppy to your favorite Internet café. (Check out the Putty FAQ at `http://www.chiark.greenend.org.uk/~sgtatham/putty/faq.html` to understand the risks involved should actually you want to do this.)

Putty can be downloaded from `http://www.chiark.greenend.org.uk/~sgtatham/putty/download.html`.

Simon has also created pscp, a Win32 port of the Secure Copy program (scp on UNIX systems). Unsurprisingly, this can be used to transfer files across an SSH connection. Use this instead of FTP. A nifty GUI front-end for scp, written by Lars Gunnarsson, is available from `http://www.i-tree.org/`.

Commercial clients supporting features over and above Putty are available from Data Fellows, SSH Communications, and Van Dyke. A full list of SSH clients can be found at `http://www.ece.nwu.edu/~mack23/ssh-clients.html` and `http://www.freessh.org/`.

SSH Resources

An excellent resource to learn more about SSH, written by Sèan Boran, can be found at `http://www.boran.com/security/sp/ssh-part1.html`. I consider this a must-read for anyone looking at using SSH in a serious way. Sèan has integrated a substantial amount of previously fragmented information with his own experiences (4-plus years) in implementing SSH. He covers the configuration options and describes some of the more advanced uses of SSH such as

- SSH VPNs.
- Rdist over SSH for secure remote filesystem synchronization.
- Using SecurID with SSH.
- Tunneling VNC (Virtual Network Computing), a remote control program, over SSH (for NT administrators, he covers PC Anywhere as well). See `http://www.uk.research.att.com/vnc/sshvnc.html` for more details.

As with any complex piece of software, SSH has had security problems. For a comprehensive rundown of known security holes, check out the OpenSSH security page at `http://www.openssh.com/security.html`. If you are using a commercial version, I recommend that you check with your vendor to ensure your systems are not vulnerable.

FTP

FTP is the File Transfer Protocol. An FTP client makes a TCP/IP connection to an FTP server (TCP port 21), and authenticates (or in the case of an anonymous server, supplies an e-mail address). The client can list, put, or retrieve files.

Most client/server protocols use just one server port, whereas FTP uses two—one is a control connection for handling commands (port 21), and the other is a data connection (port 20) for transferring data. The data connection can be active or passive. The server initiates an active connection based on a port number specified by the client, whereas the client initiates a passive connection based on a port number specified by the FTP server. This has implications for your ability to successfully firewall FTP as the firewall must dynamically allow data connections based on information transferred via the command connection. This requires the firewall to be able to decode FTP command connections properly and track FTP protocol state transitions. The data connection takes place over an ephemeral port (that is, a port greater than 1024). Standard routers don't normally offer this level of sophistication, which means that network administrators have to implement very relaxed ACLs.

FTP Risks

The FTP protocol design is tricky to secure. The base FTP specification can be found in RFC 959—however, there are many extensions (see `http://war.jgaa.com/ftp/?cmd=rfc` for a comprehensive list). Firewall vendors hate it, warez peddlers love it, and security practitioners try to avoid it.

20

Some of the risks of running FTP are

- As with TELNET, there is no encryption so the MITM attacks apply.

- As with Telnet, many FTP daemons announce system/daemon version information when a client connects. This is an information leak.

- RFC-compliant FTP daemons permit port-bouncing attacks. *Port bouncing* is a technique whereby an attacker instructs a remote FTP server to port scan an unrelated system through judicious use of the `FTP PORT` command. The victim machine sees connections from the FTP server, hence the attacker doesn't get the blame. Bounce attacks can also be used to bypass basic packet-filtering devices and export restrictions on software downloads.

  This is an old problem, and some vendors eventually broke with RFC compliance to prevent this. Other vendors still ship FTP daemons susceptible to this "feature." Hobbit is credited with discovering this weakness. His paper can be viewed online here: `http://www.insecure.org/nmap/hobbit.ftpbounce.txt`.

- The FTP protocol is hard to firewall properly. To set up the data connection, TCP/IP addressing information is passed down the control connection. To figure out the correct address/port pair to allow through, the firewall must carefully monitor the control connection. Basic packet-filtering devices don't have the application layer protocol intelligence to do this, and, therefore, large holes have to be punched in network ACLs just to support FTP. A second, more serious problem is the difficulty firewalls seem to have correctly understanding the application dialogue between client and server. This can be exploited to attack other network services running on the same system with the FTP server.

NOTE

Originally reported by Mikael Olsson, the same problem was independently discovered by John McDonald (also known as Horizon) and Thomas Lopatic. This was against Checkpoint FW1 and a Solaris FTP server, but the principle applies to any other combination where the firewall incorrectly parses the FTP control stream. A technical paper demonstrating the successful exploitation of a buggy Solaris ToolTalk daemon via an FTP data channel can be found here: `http://packetstorm.securify.com/0002-exploits/fw1-ftp.txt`.

- FTP servers that ship with proprietary distributions typically provide very little access control capability.

- Access control can be confusing and prone to procedural failure. Some FTP daemons consult a file called ftpusers, which contains a list of users who may *not* use FTP. This tends to confuse novice administrators and, even in experienced hands, leads to new users not being included; that is, when a new user is added to the system, he gets FTP access by default. If your site policy is based on the least-privilege principle, this is not helpful.

- Writable, anonymous FTP servers are incredibly hard to secure. Allowing anyone to write to your filesystem is hard to do securely.

- The default umask setting on many FTP daemons results in newly created files accessible to everyone. This is commonly a result of inheriting an weak umask from inetd (the daemon that spawns the FTP deamon).

- By default, many proprietary FTP daemons do not log client connections.

Securing FTP

If you want to offer anonymous FTP services to untrusted clients, give serious consideration to using a dedicated, standalone system (on its own DMZ off the firewall). This isolates any break-in to the FTP service only. And, as the old saying goes, "A chain is only as strong as its weakest link."

▶ For an illuminating read on the pitfalls of running a misconfigured FTP and Web server on the same system, check out the following article: `http://www.dataloss.net/papers/how.defaced.apache.org.txt`

The server should be stripped down. Only the FTP service should be accessible to the untrusted clients (for example, the Internet).

A popular alternative to running a proprietary FTP daemon is the Washington University FTP daemon available from `http://www.wu-ftpd.org/`. This enhanced FTP server provides additional functionality useful for minimizing abuse. However, it has a spotted history security wise. If you choose to run it, be prepared to upgrade in a hurry when the next major hole is discovered, and every script kiddy is trawling the Internet looking for vulnerable wu-ftpd installations.

Alternatively, evaluate the benefits of running a cut-down FTP daemon. Dan Bernstein has written a drop-in FTP replacement called Publicfile, designed and written with security as its primary goal. It is ideal for anonymous FTP. The download page is `http://cr.yp.to/public-file.html`. Publicfile can also serve as a very basic Web server—serving static content only.

If at all possible, avoid running an anonymous writable FTP server altogether. You're likely to end up acting as a mirror for pirated software hidden in surreptitiously named directories. Not only that but write access to the filesystem aids an attacker who can leverage even a minor

20

UNIX

misconfiguration on your part. For a pretty comprehensive list of anonymous FTP abuses, check out `http://www.uga.edu/ucns/wsg/security/FTP/anonymous_ftp_abuses.html`.

Various schemes have been proposed to date, but none seem to be bulletproof. However, that said, you could do worse than follow CERT's advice given here: `http://www.bris.ac.uk/is/services/networks/anonftp/anonftp.html`

Finally, activate FTP daemon logging and make sure that syslog is configured to log LOG_DAEMON messages. (Check your ftpd man page for the specific logging facility used.)

The r Services

rlogind and rshd are the remote login and remote shell daemon. These so-called *r services* use TCP ports 513 and 514, respectively. The RLOGIN protocol is described in RFC 1282 and RSH in RFC.

The r services were developed at Berkeley to provide seamless ("Look, Ma—no password") authentication between trusted hosts and/or users.

Authentication between client and server is based on the client IP address, TCP port, and client username. The client IP address and username must match an entry in either the system-wide trusted hosts file (/etc/hosts.equiv), or a user trust file (~/.rhosts). An additional so-called safeguard is that the client connection must originate on a reserved TCP port—as only programs running with root privilege can do.

The r services are very popular with end-users and administrators, as manual entry of the password is not required (unlike with TELNET). Unfortunately, they are terminally insecure.

r Services Risks

Security of the r services is based on an extremely weak authentication model.

Authentication is based on weak credentials, the source IP and TCP port. The source IP and TCP port can be forged. The original designers assumed a trusted network. Even the UNIX man page for these commands recognizes this fact.

Combined with predictable sequence numbers, crackers had a field day with these services. Steve Bellovin describes address-based authentication as "a disaster waiting to happen." Check out his brief at `ftp://ftp.research.att.com/dist/internet_security/seqattack.txt`.

The following post gives a line-by-line account of a real hack where the weakness of rsh was exploited: `http://www.cs.berkeley.edu/~daw/security/shimo-post.txt`

Countermeasures

Avoid the r-services totally—switch to SSH. This protocol is just plain broken from a security perspective. Expend your security efforts on bigger rocks (for example, host hardening and security patching).

REXEC

REXEC is often confused with the other r services. However, it bears no relationship to them. REXEC runs on TCP port 512.

UNIX distributions often ship without an REXEC client program—for some, this makes the service all the more mysterious.

The REXEC protocol is predominately used by application programmers to remotely connect to a UNIX system, run a command, and exit. They do this via the REXECREXEC library call. REXEC uses standard username and password authentication. All communications are sent in clear text between client and server.

REXECREXEC Risks

- Brute-force login attempts might go unnoticed as the REXEC daemon performs pitiful logging.
- Communications are unencrypted so that all the MITM is active, and passive attacks apply.
- There is no access-control built in to REXEC. Beyond disabling the service or using third-party software, you cannot define which users can use the service. Therefore a user who normally logs in via a secure protocol could end up inadvertently sending his password (and more) across the network in plaintext, simply by using a client application which relies on REXEC.
- Some REXEC daemons produce a different error message to a client, depending on whether the username or password was incorrect. This behavioral difference permits attackers to ascertain valid usernames. Again, your system is disclosing information.

Securing REXEC

- Disable REXEC. If client applications rely upon it, figure out a migration path away and then disable it.
- If disabling is not an option, consider using SSH to tunnel the protocol. SSH provides remote terminal access.

20

UNIX

SMTP

SMTP is the Simple Mail Transfer Protocol (defined in RFC 821). Among other tasks, its job is to receive mail by accepting connections on TCP port 25 from remote mail servers. By default, UNIX comes with the sendmail program, an age-old program that implements the SMTP protocol (and more).

SMTP Risks

Sendmail is one of those programs every administrator seems to have heard of. Its history of security problems is well known. It could be the most maligned UNIX software ever written. With that reputation, it should be clear that something is fundamentally wrong with sendmail— and that something is its monolithic design.

However, the security of sendmail has improved significantly in recent years because of the efforts of its author, Eric Allman, in response to the many security problems it suffered. It's debatable though whether sendmail is totally "out of the woods," or ever will be, because of its design.

Rather than repeat a history of security flaws here (I don't think there's space), these are some generic problems that a default installation of sendmail presents:

- Sendmail is "Yet Another Daemon" that runs as root. Therefore, an exploitable vulnerability in sendmail can mean giving away root to an attacker. Even though a root-run program might temporarily drop privileges, an attacker who is able run shellcode (through a buffer overflow or string format exploit) can simply make a call to seteuid() to re-establish those privileges and have her shell code running as root.

- Sendmail is incredibly complex—its configuration file uses m4—the GNU implementation of the UNIX macro processor. Few people truly understand m4, and fewer still understand sendmail configuration. As a result, it's easy to make blunders and hard to lock it down without help from outside.

- Sendmail can be used to elicit usernames. By connecting to port 25 and issuing VRFY and EXPN commands, sendmail will confirm valid usernames. This is the first step in taking over an account. Attackers can then use remote login services and attempt to guess passwords. This guessing attack can be automated and use a large dictionary of common usernames to increase the chances of finding a valid username.

- Older versions of sendmail allow spammers to relay mail through your system. Apart from using your resources, this can make you very unpopular and result in your site being listed on RBL (Realtime Blackhole List at http://mail-abuse.org/rbl/). This is bad news for you as any mail servers your site attempts to connect to will drop the connection if they follow the RBL list.

- If incorrectly configured, sendmail leaks internal address information to the outside. Attackers can send probe e-mails to a company mail-server. By sending a malformed message, they can elicit a bounce message possibly including internal IP addresses. This assists an attacker in mapping the internal network.

- The sendmail daemon outputs its version number upon client connection. This information helps the attacker select a relevant exploit.

Securing SMTP

In my experience, few machines on an organization's network actually need to be listening for mail—they just happen to be because sendmail is active by default. To put it simply, don't run mail transfer unless you need it. Turning off your mail transfer agent does not affect your systems ability to actually send mails (such as for the output of cron jobs).

- Consider using Qmail instead of sendmail. It has been designed and coded following sound security principles and has an impressive security track record—zero security holes. Visit `http://www.qmail.org/` for more details. Recent versions of Qmail go further in easing the migration from sendmail. Qmail is available on a wide range of platforms.

- Postfix (formally Vmailer), written by Wietse Venema, is a popular sendmail-compatible alternative written to be fast, easy to install and secure. Full details are at `http://www.postfix.org/`. If you can't face Qmail, check out Postfix.

- If you must run sendmail, don't run it as root—build a `chroot` environment and run it as a non-privileged user. Russell Coker has detailed how he does this at `http://www.coker.com.au/~russell/sendmail.html`.

- A common misconception amongst administrators is that sendmail needs to be listening to the network in order to send mail from the local machine. While this is the default on many systems, it's not required. Sendmail can be invoked via cron with the `"-q"` flag to service the queue of outgoing messages on a regular basis. If all you want is the ability to send mail, then disable the sendmail startup script—you don't need sendmail listening on port 25.

▶ Carole Fennelly has written a series of useful articles about installing, configuring, and running sendmail on a firewall; look for them at `http://www.unixinsider.com/swol-04-1999/swol-04-security.html`. Carole is a regular writer of UNIX security related articles. Find out more here: `http://www.wkeys.com/media/CF/writing.html`

20

UNIX

> **NOTE**
>
> The authors of Qmail and Postfix have publicly locked horns a number of times on security-related mailing lists. There is clearly no love lost between them as they try and find security bugs in each other's software. Although this might not be a pleasant sight to the uninitiated, it does give a valuable insight into the security issues facing designers of Mail Transfer Agents (MTA), such as where the weaknesses are and how to avoid them. The bottom line is, if you want secure mail servers, use dedicated, hardened systems with shell access given to trusted users only.

DNS

DNS is the Domain Name System. It's a UDP- and TCP-based protocol that listens on port 53. TCP connections are commonly used for zone transfers.

The DNS matches IP addresses to hostnames (and hostnames to IP addresses). A DNS server is responsible, or *authoritative*, for a given part of the domain name system (for example, mybitofthenet.com).

Clients make requests of the DNS servers when they want to communicate with systems for which they have only the fully qualified hostname (for example, myserver.mybitofthenet.com).

The DNS is a critical part of the network infrastructure. Its failure—whether through administrative incompetence or denial of service—can have major consequences.

DNS Risks

The DNS protocol has security problems. A detailed description of DNS and its protocol weaknesses can be found at `http://www.geocities.com/compsec101/papers/dnssec/dnssec.html`. DNS is defined in a number of RFCs—see `http://www.dns.net/dnsrd/rfc/` for full details.

As far as UNIX host security goes, the most widely used DNS server software is BIND (Berkeley Internet Name Daemon), developed by the Internet Software Consortium (ISC). By default, the BIND daemon "named" runs with root privileges and—this is important—it doesn't permanently throw them away after binding to port 53. Therefore, vulnerabilities in BIND can result in a complete system compromise.

Let's look at the track record of BIND.

Release 8.2.3 was released in January 2001 to fix four security vulnerabilities discovered by COVERT Labs (PGP security) and Claudio Musmarra. Two buffer overflows allow remote attackers to run any code of their choosing. An input validation error enables attackers to run any code, and an information leakage allows data in the stack to be viewed by an attacker. This last one might not seem so bad. After all, it's not a direct root compromise in-waiting, but it actually assists the development of exploits against a particular site. The stack holds local variables, environment variables, and important process addresses. By gaining access to these, a buffer overflow can be written without trial and error. This is significant because buffer overflows are often a one-shot attack—if you get it even slightly wrong, you are likely to crash a service by scribbling all over stack data subsequently relied upon by the program.

BIND has had 12 security advisories from CERT in just four years—hardly an endorsement of BIND security!

A major factor is the complexity of the BIND code. Experienced C programmers comment that the BIND code is incredibly difficult to understand. When accomplished programmers struggle to comprehend what's going on, you can be sure of security problems. Complex code is hard to audit—modular designs work best, in which small, discrete programs (that are easier to audit) perform privileged operations. Of course, the ISC developers didn't set out to write something that even they would find hard to maintain—the difficulty is a result of feature bloat. Perhaps that's one of the reason's ISC recently rewrote major parts of BIND.

In January 2001, ISC announced the release of a major new version of BIND—version 9.1.0. This version includes support for DNSSEC—a protocol extension that overcomes some of the security design weakness in the stock DNS protocol (DNSSEC is defined in RFC 2535.) Notably, the code was not modularized, so now we have new code that is still hard to audit. Many sites are likely to continue running BIND 8, at least in the short term.

It turns out attackers like breaking into BIND servers, so much so that SANS rates unpatched BIND servers as the number one security problem on the Internet. Exploits for BIND abound. DNS servers are tasty targets because so much of the Internet relies upon then. With control of a BIND server, you can do truly nasty things, for example:

- Deprive a site of traffic by changing the IP/name mappings to a nonexistent address. Worse still, you can redirect traffic to a pornographic or competitor site. Lost revenue and bad press don't help a company's stock price.

- Clone an e-business site, modify the site's DNS server to map your imposter site, and collect credit card details, user account, and password details.

- Exploit trust relationships between systems by mapping an IP from one side of the trust relationship to your machine.

- Compromise one of the root nameservers.

20

UNIX

That last one is particularly worrying. The root nameservers are the starting point for addressing on the Internet. There are only 13 root nameservers in total (because of protocol limitations). Take over the root nameservers, and you can have the Internet in your hand. As an aside, the choice of platform and operating systems for these machines follows the principle of security through diversity. To quote from a Y2K statement on ICANN's (The Internet Corporation for Assigned Names and Numbers) site:

> The root servers themselves all use some variant of the UNIX operating system, however both the hardware base and the vendors' UNIX variants are relatively diverse: of the 13 root servers, there are 7 different hardware platforms running 8 different operating system versions from 5 different vendors.

This is a sound idea—used in nature by Mother Nature herself. Of course, it breaks down if you don't have sufficiently diverse administrators on hand to securely manage eight different operating systems.

Aside from security flaws, misconfiguration is common. When sizing up your site, attackers will request zone transfers from your DNS server. This is basically a dump of all the information pertaining to a particular DNS zone. This is as good as a network map! You don't want this.

Another configuration is version numbers (again). To discover the version of BIND you are running, a client can query your DNS server, and your server will tell them. This isn't so good.

The other major risk facing the DNS protocol and the BIND implementation are denial of service attacks. Numerous DoS vulnerabilities have been found in BIND. Disabling DNS servers prevents DNS queries from being resolved, thereby stopping clients relying on the DNS resolution services (that is, almost everyone) in their tracks.

Securing DNS

The obvious countermeasure is to find an alternative to running BIND. Here your choices are limited—we live in a BIND monoculture. You could switch to Microsoft's DNS implementation (that's not a recommendation), or look for a DNS server where security of implementation was a primary goal.

The only viable alternative I am aware of is the djbdns package by Daniel Bernstein. This has had sufficient production usage to be a serious contender to BIND. It was designed and written with security in mind by a programmer experienced in writing secure code. You can find out more here: `http://cr.yp.to/djbdns.html`.

If you stick with BIND, there are some things you can do. A useful summary of the issues and countermeasures is available from `http://www.acmebw.com/papers/securing.pdf`. You should at least give serious thought to the following

- Don't run BIND as root. Instead, create a new user and group. Specify these as command-line options when you execute BIND.

- Use the `chroot` command to run BIND so that it has restricted access to the filesystem. The `chroot` program enables you to specify the directory that a process will treat as its root directory (enforced by the kernel). To do this though, you need to create a mini duplicate of your operating system because BIND will no longer be able to see important system libraries and configuration files. Full instructions can be found here: `http://www.etherboy.com/dns/chrootdns.html`. See the section on `chroot` later in the chapter for some important caveats.

- The version number is hard-coded in the BIND code, so if you have source code, you can simply remove it or replace it with a fake version or silly message (have fun). Otherwise, you'll have to binary patch the executable—good luck! Recent versions of BIND can be configured to enable version requests from specific addresses only.

- Configure BIND to disallow zone transfer except to authorized servers (such as DNS slaves).

Finger

Finger has been around for years. Its problems have been discussed numerous times and are well documented—even vendors today ship it disabled. You can refer back to Chapter 8, "Hiding One's Identity," for more about finger as well.

Don't enable finger unless you don't mind your systems leaking sensitive system information like usernames, home directories, and login patterns.

Finger can be used as an early warning system that someone is checking out your site. Use TCPWrappers to wrap the finger service and enable logging. Some administrators configure TCPWrappers to return bogus finger information, feeding a less savvy attacker false usernames that they subsequently fail to log in with.

SNMP

SNMP is a protocol to support network monitoring and management. Its use is widespread, and most network monitoring products rely upon it. It runs on UDP ports 161 and 162 (for snmp traps).

For the technical details behind SNMP v1, consult RFC 1157. RFC 1441 introduces the various RFCs that make up SNMP v2.

SNMP Risks

An SNMP client authenticates to an SNMP agent via a string known as a *community name*. This community name works very much like a password. UNIX hosts often ship with an

SNMP agent enabled by default—so your system could be exposed to SNMP flaws already. Problems with default SNMP installations include

- The default read-only community name is `"public"`, and the default read/write community is often `"private"`. Hard coded "passwords" like these have blighted IT security for as long as I can remember. A full list of common passwords including SNMP community names is at `http://www.securityparadigm.com/defaultpw.htm`.

- If the read-only community can be guessed, serious information disclosure issues can crop up. The extent of the data disclosure is dependent on the MIB (Management Information Base). MIBs vary between vendors, but they usually contain the following types of information: network interface settings, network services, current network connections, administrative contacts, and server location. This assists attackers in mapping your network topology (think multihomed hosts), in performing traffic analysis (that is, who is talking to whom), and maybe even in getting some social engineering info.

- If the read/write community name can be guessed, you have the problems previously mentioned, but also, now, the attacker can modify the status of network interfaces and even reboot systems. Vendor-enhanced MIBs can allow even more devastating operations.

- Access to SNMP agents is not logged by default. You won't notice authentication failures.

- Some SNMP implementations, notably Solaris, actually run other SNMP daemons on high-numbered ports. Blocking access on a firewall to UDP port 161 might not be sufficient. Solaris users should check out `http://www.ist.uwaterloo.ca/security/howto/2000-10-04.html`.

Securing SNMP

- Decide whether you need SNMP. If your network operations team isn't monitoring servers via SNMP and you're not running any special software that relies on SNMP (some clustering implementations do), then disable it.

- Modify the default community strings to be hard-to-guess, random-looking strings. Make them long (at least 10 characters), and, whatever you do, don't use the name of your network supplier! (I've seen this too many times.)

- Configure SNMP authentication traps. If someone is trying to guess your SNMP community string, you want to know earlier rather than later. By configuring authentication traps, you can have the agent inform the SNMP master (normally the network management console) when an authentication failure happens. You might think it improbable that someone could guess a long SNMP community string. The savvy attacker will use a tool like ADMsnmp, written by the highly respected outfit ADM. Check out this post to Bugtraq for more info: `http://archives.neohapsis.com/archives/bugtraq/1999_1/0759.html`.

Network File System

The Network File System (NFS) protocol defines a way for co-operating systems to share filesystems. Today, everyone seems to refer to NFS mounts as shares.

NFS is based on the RPC (Remote Procedure Call), a protocol that defines how machines can make calls to procedures on remote machines as if they were local.

NFS implementations consist of more than just a single NFS server process. In fact, they require mountd, statd, and lockd. These daemons have had a plethora of problems—especially statd.

NFS is an insecure protocol that you don't want to run. Trust me.

Full details of NFS v2 can be found in RFC 1094. NFS v3 is defined in RFC 1813.

NFS Risks

- If you're running an unsupported or unpatched version of NFS, you're dead in the water if someone takes a shot.
- Misconfigurations are common with NFS. Sharing system-related filesystems is asking for trouble.
- Weak authentication is used. The requests can be spoofed or sometimes proxied through the local portmapper.
- No encryption is used, so your darkest secrets go across the network in plaintext.
- NFS-related daemons commonly run as root. An exploitable security hole can leave you with a root compromise on your hands.
- Watch your defaults! The file /etc/exports (or /etc/dfs/dfstab) controls which filesystems you share and with whom. Unless you specify otherwise, your implementation might default to using insecure options or giving write access by default.

Securing NFS

Don't run it! Solve security headaches in one fail swoop—turn if off! OK, so you want this functionality? Read on...

- Is NFS the right file-sharing mechanism for what you want? Given its security problems, examine your file-sharing requirements. For example, if you want a mirror of some files, you could just buy another disk (they are cheap these days) and use rdist over SSH to make replicas to other systems. If you can find a way around using NFS, then do so.
- Avoid using NFS for sensitive information and never run Internet-facing NFS servers.
- Firewall NFS to limit your exposure on the wider network.

20

UNIX

- Stay up to date with vendor security patches! NFS-related patches seem to come out thick and fast. If your vendor isn't supplying patches, this could be "a Bad Thing." They might simply not be patching known holes.

- Share filesystems on a need-to-have basis. Restrict this to read-only sharing wherever possible. Always specify nosuid as an option, to ensure that the set-id bit is not honored on files created on exported filesystems.

- Remove any references to localhost in your exports file.

- Do not self-reference an NFS server in its own export file.

- Limit export lists to 256 characters (including expanded aliases if aliases are in use).

- Consider using a replacement portmapper that won't forward, or proxy, mount requests. Check Wietse Venema's modified portmapper at `http://www.ja.net/CERT/Software/portmapper/`.

- Where read-only sharing is possible, consider mounting a locally exported filesystem as read-only (that is, in /etc/vfstab or similar).

Samuel Sheinin has written an excellent article on the risks of NFS and how to remediate them; find it at `http://www.sans.org/infosecFAQ/unix/nfs_security.htm`. If you are running NFS, consider installing the tools nfswatch.

NFS version 4 is the next generation of NFS. Production ready implementations are not readily available as yet. See `http://www.nfsv4.org` for more information.

Alternatives to NFS include AFS (`http://www.contrib.andrew.cmu.edu/~shadow/afs.html`) and CODA (`http://www.coda.cs.cmu.edu/`).

The Caveats of chroot

A common countermeasure aimed at security network services is to run them in a chroot environment. chroot changes the process's idea of its root directory. The idea is to prevent the process from having access to any files outside of the chroot directory. Therefore, if the network service is compromised, the rest of the system is protected. However, it's not as simple as that.

The most common mistake is to think that chroot is like a virtual computer—a totally distinct environment. It isn't. It's a filesystem abstraction; there are escape routes from chroot environments. Here are some details:

- If the process can run as root, your security is hosed. After compromising a chroot'ed network service running as root, the attacker can create device files to access RAM directly via the mknod command. The attacker can then modify the process's idea of the root directory and have unrestricted access to the system.

- Some distributions suffer from a bug in their `chroot` call. An attacker who has compromised the `chroot` environment can force a second `chroot` and then `cd` out of the restricted area. For more details, see `http://www.bpfh.net/simes/computing/chroot-break.html`. To prevent this requires a kernel change. See `http://archives.neohapsis.com/archives/nfr-wizards/1997/11/0091.html` for more details.

Better the Daemon You Know...

Take a multilayered approach to securing network services—that way, if one layer of defense fails, you haven't given up the farm.

- Disable the services you don't need.

- Add firewall services you do need. (This could be an expensive market-leading product or a hardening UNIX system with packet forwarding enabled and kernel-based IP filtering in effect.)

- In addition to a network firewall, consider the use of kernel-based access controls to protect your network services from internal systems (which themselves might have been breached or are simply in the hands of a malicious employee). Today, many UNIX systems ship with kernel-based IP filtering. Learn how to use this feature.

- Consider the use of TCPWrappers. This software protects TCP-based network services that are launched by inetd. Normally, when inetd receives a connection from a client, it consults inetd.conf and launches the program that corresponds to the port on which the connection was received. With TCPWrappers installed, inetd calls tcpd, which consults the hosts.allow and hosts.deny files. These files control client access to services based on IP address. For example, you might want to limit SSH access to a range of addresses where you know your shell users are located. Or, you might allow only cluster members to access cluster-based daemons. For extra bonus points, you can set up fake daemons to pick up on suspicious activity. For example, create a fake finger daemon that outputs nonsense data or an HTTP daemon that sends out redirects to the attacker's machine. Parse the logs using a tool like swatch (covered in Chapter 13, "Logging and Auditing Tools").

- Read the man page for the network service you want to protect and identify command-line options that can be used to control access, improve logging, or limit dubious functionality. For example, on many systems, syslogd listens to the network for syslog messages. Therefore, an attacker can send spurious messages to either mislead you or fill up the disk. By specifying a command-line switch, you can disable this function.

- If you have a source, consider compiling with StackGuard. This will eliminate common types of buffer overflow.

- Make sure the service is launched with a sane umask value. Umask is inherited from the parent process, so this could be inetd or init. Limit this value to no access by Other as a minimum. Check it out on your system.

20

UNIX

- Verify that network server programs and configuration files cannot be overwritten by a nonprivileged user. Check for weak permissions on the files themselves and their parent directories.

- A common sign of intrusion is a second inetd appearing in the process list. Intruders start another copy of inetd with their own configuration file to install a back door—such as a password-protected shell when they connect on a specific port. Consider moving the real inetd to an alternative location and replacing it with a fake inetd that notifies you when it is executed. (You'll need to update your startup files to reflect the path change.) Of course, this is an attack-based countermeasure specific to only one kind of attack, albeit a popular one.

- Install a lightweight intrusion detection system such as snort (`http://www.snort.org`), with a signature set that reflects the services you are offering. Integrate this into a centralized monitoring scheme, such as a central syslog server and swatch (see Chapter 12, "Intrusion Detection Systems," and Chapter 13, "Logging and Auditing Tools").

A good example of a patch tool is the Solaris *patchdiag* tool officially available to SUN customers who have a support contract. As with any patch tool, it had its fair share of teething troubles when it was first released. However, by now the tool has matured. *Patchdiag* allows you to download a daily updated patch meta file containing an up-to-date list of patches available for each Solaris package. Upon execution, *patchdiag* compares the installed patches with those available from SUN.

Even better still is the Red Hat Update Agent (`http://www.redhat.com/support/manuals/RHL-6.2-Manual/ref-guide/ch-up2date.html`), which automatically identifies missing patches. You can either manually select which patches to download and install or let the Agent do it all for you. Unregistered users can use the (much slower) public download site.

Unless you run a trusted UNIX distribution, vendor security extensions or third-party software will be required. A popular option is *sudo*—we'll cover this and alternatives later. Mainstream vendors have started picking up the ball—SUN has introduced the Role Based Access Control (RBAC) System in Solaris 8.

Assessing Your UNIX Systems for Vulnerabilities

A common strategy to assess your system for vulnerabilities is to do this in a number of phases:

1. Use a network-based vulnerability scanner to identify remotely exploitable security holes. Attackers can exploit these vulnerabilities from across the network—they don't need a UNIX account on the victim machine. Fixing these tends to be priority #1 in most shops.

2. Eliminate false positives by manually double-checking the results. For a number of reasons, scanners sometimes report false positives. Log on and check for them. There is probably nothing worse than a security newbie running a vulnerability scanner, taking the results as gospel, and dumping the output on the system administrator's desk. (A number of large, respected accounting firms gained a reputation for doing this.) Know the weaknesses as well as the strengths of your tools or look a fool in front of a knowledgeable system administrator.

3. Prioritize the findings based on your understanding of the vulnerabilities and the risk they pose in the context of your site. The scan reports generally include background information on specific vulnerabilities to help you do this. Hopefully this book will serve to sharpen your understanding of the issues.

4. Draw up a plan for fixing the problems. Identify what needs to be done and who is going to "own" the change. Test the changes on a nonproduction system and ensure applications are fully tested. Start fixing—one major change at a time.

5. Use a host-based vulnerability scanner to identify locally exploitable security holes. Host-based scanners should produce few false positives because they run on the machine itself. Manual checking should be minimal if the product is even remotely decent. At a minimum, your host-based scanner should be able to identify missing security patches, insecure network services, user account problems, and common filesystem insecurities. Don't just take the tool vendor's word for it either—always evaluate before you buy against a system build that you are familiar with.

6. Identify the biggest risks. Given your knowledge of the local user base, state these risks in the fix plan and start fixing.

▶ Commercial and freeware network vulnerability scanners have been around for some time. Personally, I like the Nessus network vulnerability scanner. It's reliable and extensible—new checks are relatively easy to add via the NASL scripting language. The wide and enthusiastic user base and scripting language result in a fast turnaround for new tests. Often, NASL scripts are available within a day of vulnerability being announced. This is significantly faster than other scanners I've used—even expensive commercial products. Another useful feature is automated updates of new checks, ensuring that you keep current.

▶ If you're assessing vulnerability scanners, take a look at `http://www.networkcomputing.com/` `1201/1201f1b1.html` for some interesting insights into the effectiveness of popular scanners.

As with any vulnerability scanner, you can get false positives. The comprehensiveness of the NASL scripts varies, so I recommend that you manually check the results to save embarrassment. However, unlike with the commercial scanners, you can at least review the source and improve it if you have better ideas.

20

UNIX

The freeware site is at `http://www.nessus.org/`.

For those who want formal support, the creators of Nessus will happily sell you a support contract.

▶ Host-based scanners are specific to a particular UNIX flavor, so your options will be tied to the popularity of your platform. A comprehensive list of commercial scanners is available here:

`http://website.lineone.net/~offthecuff/h_scan.htm`

Just remember that the market leader is not necessarily the best—it might just have the nicest GUI. If the guts aren't up to the task, no GUI will make up for that. The host-based scanner market is relatively immature compared with network vulnerability scanners—be sure to validate vendor claims before you buy (and watch out for ancient checks being touted as "state of the art").

One thing I can promise you though—as you go through the dragged-out process of locking down a fully operational production system, you'll soon realize that applying your security standard to a virgin system is a walk in the park.

The Cost of Belated Security Hardening

The next time someone (your manager, the project manager, the marketing manager) asks you to release a system to your user community before you've had a chance to harden it (for example, because of late delivery of hardware), ask him to sign a purchase order. Tell him that this is to cover the costs of making the system compliant post–go-live. When they laugh, point out that making security changes to operational systems increases risk—however well researched, things might just break. To reduce the risk of a bad change hitting during peak activity, many organizations have change policies that only allow changes to be made off-peak. Personally, I don't know any CIOs that allow changes to be made to systems without application people running some tests—the costs start to skyrocket. It's also a bad practice to make a whole slew of changes in one shot because backing out the change becomes non-trivial. This results in a string of late nights that further amplifies the cost of post-live hardening. Factor in "just-in-case" data backups, and you're talking serious money.

The rush to save a day before the hardening activity can easily cost an organization thousands of dollars in overtime to put things right later, as well as leaving a drawn-out window of exposure. The decision-makers in your organization should be made aware of this problem before you hit it. With their buy-in, this kind of situation can be avoided. As well as the overtime savings, the other selling point is avoiding low staff morale. Unless someone is shooting for overtime cash, I don't know of anyone who wants to arrive back in the office at midnight to make a change. If the change goes wrong, they could be left with a night's restore activity. Losing key personnel the following day is also not a "good thing."

Host Lockdown

Host lockdown is the process of making a system compliant with your UNIX security policy. In other words, it is configuring the system to be significantly more resistant to attack.

There are three common approaches:

- **Manually make the changes required by your policy.** This is certainly useful the first couple of times you do it because you get to see what you are changing. After that, making changes manually is a boring waste of time, which can easily lead to things being missed or mistakes being made.

- **Write some scripts to automate the changes.** This requires some scripting capability, a test machine, and some time (well, in fact, quite a lot of testing time if you want to cover everything). This time is probably best spent on site-specifics (like in-house application hardening) because writing operating system–hardening scripts is a bit like reinventing the wheel (see the following section).

- **Identify a hardening tool that can best match your security standard.** Recent years have seen the development of some excellent hardening scripts for the most popular platforms. In the following section, we cover the primary ones. The key here is to understand what the tool does and doesn't do and how to configure it for your site policy. You can fill in the gaps through homegrown scripts.

Host-Hardening Resources

These tools are distribution specific because of the differing UNIX security interfaces and platform-specific risks. This shouldn't be treated as a definitive list though—for example, Linux has many, many hardening projects. I've been a little selective and picked out the one's which are sufficiently well developed to be usable in a production environment. As per usual though, test any such tools on a nonproduction system first.

For some distributions, I don't know of a specific tool—so I've listed well-regarded hardening documents. So with that disclaimer in place, let's look at the options.

SUN Solaris

Solaris users are spoilt for choice these days. The obvious question is, "Which hardening tool should I go for?" To help you decide, check out this SANS-sponsored report that compares the most popular Solaris hardening tools: `http://www.sans.org/sol11c.pdf`.

YAASP (Yet Another Solaris Security Package)

YASSP (Yet Another Solaris Security Package)

Primary Author: Jean Chouanard

URL: `http://www.yassp.org/`

YASSP supports Solaris versions 2.6, 2.7, and 8 on both Sparc and Intel. YASSP looks set to become the de facto tool for hardening Solaris. The SANS Institute has stated that it will promote YASSP's use globally.

YASSP ships as a tar ball containing packages in Solaris package format, some shell scripts, and a set of security tools to replace or supplement stock Solaris programs.

The following packages will be installed by default:

- SECclean: The core package, securing your Solaris installation
- GNUgzip: gzip 1.2.4a [GNU]
- PARCdaily: Some daily scripts, logs rotation, backup, and RCS for systems files
- WVtcpd: tcp_wrappers 7.6 and rpcbind 2.1 [Wietse Venema]
- PRFtripw: Tripwire 1.2 [Purdue Research Foundation of Purdue University]
- OPENssh: OpenSSH 2.3.0p1 [OpenSSH.com]

From a general Solaris-hardening perspective, by default, YASSP does the following:

- Turns off ALL network services in /etc/inetd.conf (configurable) and disables nonessential services started from /etc/init.d.
- Turns off rhosts authentication, disables unused system accounts, disables FTP access to system users, and sets minimum password length to eight.
- Disables stack-smashing attempts (commonly caused by buffer overflows) and activates logging at the kernel level by a parameter change in /etc/system. (Note that this doesn't prevent data segment buffer overflows.) This can actually break your applications, so testing, as ever, is essential.
- Runs Casper Diks "fix-modes" script to lock down filesystem permissions. It also disables honoring of set-uid bit on newly mounted filesystems.
- Modifies behavior of the TCP/IP stack to both improve security and increase resilience to denial of service (DoS) attacks. (This is helpful, but it will not defeat the problem).

Don't be alarmed by that thorough approach—the default packages and installation settings are certainly appropriate for an Internet-exposed or highly sensitive internal server. However, for internal multiuser systems, you'll definitely want to investigate the configuration options available in yassp.conf. You could easily end up breaking application functionality if you don't modify the defaults.

For those installing Solaris from scratch, primary YASSP author Jean Chouanard has helpfully documented that process (starting with the Solaris CD in hand) at http://www.yassp.org/os. html.

YASSP is a no-brainer to install. After you've downloaded the YASSP tar ball, you install as follows:

```
# uncompress yassp.tar.Z
# tar xvf yassp.tar
# cd yassp
# ./install.sh
... check and modify all the configuration files ...
# reboot
```

The post-install steps require you to edit a small number of configuration files and create the Tripwire integrity database, as follows:

- Edit and configure /etc/yassp.conf.
- Edit and configure /etc/hosts.deny /etc/hosts.allow.
- Edit and configure /etc/sshd_config /etc/ssh_config.
- Read `http://www.yassp.org/after.html` and the papers linked under `http://www.yassp.org/ref.html`.
- Make any additional changes and install any additional software.
- Create the Tripwire database and save it to read-only media.

Personally, I think YASSP is the future of Solaris hardening (at least for virgin systems). It's been well tested, can be deinstalled as easily as it is installed, and seems to have attracted some talented individuals to keep it updated.

TITAN (Toolkit for Interactively Toughening Advanced Networks and Systems)

TITAN
Primary Author: Brad Powell
URL: `http://www.fish.com/titan/`

TITAN predates YASSP and takes a different approach. It is based on the KISS approach (Keep It Simple, Stupid).

Rather than create a mammoth script that attempts to do everything, TITAN's authors wrote a set of Bourne shell scripts (referred to as *modules*) invoked by the TITAN program itself. Each module targets a specific aspect of operating system security. Modules can be included (or excluded) via the use of a configuration file specified at runtime. This enables you to create different configuration files to reflect the different security postures required by individual systems (for example, firewall, mail server, workstation, and so on).

A TITAN module consists of two primary functions: fix and check. As you'd expect, the fix function does the actual work—it makes the changes—whereas the check function looks to see if the fix has already been applied. You tell TITAN in which mode to run a particular script through the configuration file.

20

This makes it easy to check that a system has been configured to your security policy. For me, this is the real strength of TITAN.

To install TITAN, copy the TITAN archive to a target server, run the install program, and customize the configuration file. You're all set to invoke the main TITAN shell script (supplying the name of your configuration as an argument). If you're having problems with a module, you can run TITAN in debug mode.

Run TITAN periodically via `cron` in check mode, and you have an extensible, host-based scanner.

TITAN version 3.7 supports Solaris only; however, version 4 (in Alpha as of writing) promises scripts for Linux, FreeBSD, and True 64.

The tool itself is structured to accommodate any operating systems but until now few modules actually existed for any other distribution.

Another great thing about TITAN is that you don't need to be a programming genius to add extra modules—nor do you have to jump through hoops. (Remember KISS?) Assuming you are competent at Bourne shell scripting, there is no new programming language to learn—just some conventions to follow (just copy and customize the supplied template file).

Note that, unlike YASSP, TITAN doesn't install any security tools. (It does include Casper Dik's fix-modes script, but that's a one-shot tool, so I'm not counting that.) I recommend that you run YASSP first to harden and install the tools and then monitor with TITAN on an ongoing basis. For huge server farms, TITAN output can get overwhelming—consolidate the output using Perl.

When I first started using TITAN, it had an annoying habit of changing things even when you asked it to only check. The principle of a passive check mode hadn't been implemented consistently throughout all the modules. A quick check through the most recent set of scripts suggests the authors have rectified this problem (although I couldn't find a reference to it in the change log).

This is a handy reminder: Always understand what actions a hardening script will take *before* you run it.

> **NOTE**
>
> The authors comment that TITAN doesn't actually stand for anything. They just came up with the name, and it stuck.

GNU/Linux

There are a host of projects seeking to protect the world's favorite penguin (in case you've been living under a rock, a penguin is the Linux mascot). Here's a select few:

Bastille Linux

> Bastille Linux (v1.1)
>
> Primary Author: Jay Beale
>
> URL: `http://www.bastille-linux.org/`

The Bastille Hardening System is an open source, community-run project suitable for Red Hat and Mandrake systems. (The authors have declared it should be portable to any Linux distribution.)

The stated mission of the project is to provide the most secure, yet usable, system possible. The authors have drawn on a wide range of security sources, including the SANS Linux hardening guide, Kurt Seifried's Linux administrators' security guide, and more. The creators, Jon Lasser and Jay Beale, rank administrator education as a key goal.

Bastille focuses on four key lockdown areas:

- It implements network packet filtering in the kernel (using ipchains). This limits your visibility on the network. (This doesn't "hide" your system—rather it sets up access controls to your systems' network services.)

- It downloads and installs the latest security patches (not many tools do that). The caveat here is that it doesn't check the digital signatures on the downloaded files. (You can do this manually using PGP or the open source GnuPG software from `http://www.gnupg.org/`.)

- It increases the system's resistance to many types of local attacks by removing the privilege bit from a number of set-uid programs.

- It disables nonessential network services.

As a tool, Bastille's notable features include the following:

- Bastille can be run on living systems (that is, not just new installs).

- Bastille is self-aware. This has more to do with multiple runs on the same machine. Bastille knows what it did the last time it was run, so it won't repeat itself. Note that Bastille does *not* detect your initial security settings during its first run. (It will prompt you to turn off things that you might already have disabled.)

- Bastille has a primitive, but handy, Undo feature. Essentially, it takes a backup of files before modifying them. It replicates the directory structure and permissions under the Undo directory. There is no automagic back out—if you need to undo an action, you do it by hand.

20

UNIX

- Bastille has a so-called *impotent mode* (also known as *shooting blanks mode*). This is definitely recommended for first-time users. Bastille will tell you what it would have done, given your answers, without actually doing it. This might save you having to undo things later

The Interactive-Bastille.pl Perl script is written with the novice in mind. The user is prompted to answer yes or no for each hardening question. Each question is supplemented by explanatory text to help someone unfamiliar with Linux security. At the end of the Q&A session, the user runs BackEnd.pl, and the changes are made.

To make those exact same changes across a number of machines, just copy the Bastille-input-log—generated during the first run—and feed the log results as input to the BackEnd Bastille script on the target servers. This technique is fully explained in the Bastille documentation (docs/readme.automate). A slicker automation procedure is apparently in the works, but the current approach, although basic, does work.

A Linux novice will have a steep learning curve with whatever tool they end up using. Bastille makes a lot of effort to ease this burden and, to some extent, does achieve this. (I know of nothing better.)

Hewlett-Packard HP-UX

I am not aware of any publicly available hardening scripts for HP-UX. If you have some time, I recommend you port TITAN and donate your changes back to the TITAN crew.

However, Kevin Steves from HP has created a very useful hardening guide.

The paper for HP-UX 10 can be found here: `http://people.hp.se/stevesk/bastion.html`.

The HP-UX 11 paper is here: `http://people.hp.se/stevesk/bastion11.html`.

Kevin has written a very readable guide starting from the installation of HP-UX through securing the host and creating a recovery tape.

IBM AIX

Again, I am not aware of any publicly available hardening scripts for AIX.

A basic guide for securing AIX has been developed by IBM. It is available here: `http://www.redbooks.ibm.com/redbooks/SG245971.html`.

FreeBSD

FreeBSD users should check out the Security HOWTO available at `http://people.freebsd.org/~jkb/howto.html`.

The FreeBSD ports collection (security tools ported to FreeBSD) is available at `http://www.freebsd.org/ports/security.html`.

What do you do if you're unable to find a hardening tool for your operating system's specific distribution or version? Unfortunately, vendors have a poor track record of creating credible hardening tools. Check with your user group (if it exists) and the Usenet newsgroup for your distribution. You might wind up having to rewrite the scripts from one of the tools previously mentioned. If you're an HP-UX or AIX admin interested in security, here is the perfect opportunity to make a name for yourself!

Summary

A single chapter on UNIX security never can do the subject justice. Rather than attempt to cover all aspects of UNIX security, I've hopefully got you thinking about the issues. Specific technology problems come and go (well, they don't always go), but the thought processes and security principles tend to remain static. If I've got you thinking about your environment in a new way, then I've met my goal. The great thing about UNIX is the open community that supports her. Although there are many problems, there are many more solutions. Good luck keeping her safe!

Novell

A little neglect may breed mischief... for want of a nail, the shoe was lost; for want of a shoe, the horse was lost; and for want of a horse, the rider was lost.

—Benjamin Franklin, *Poor Richard's Almanack,* 1758

IN THIS CHAPTER

A venerable operating system still in use in many shops, NetWare isn't as dead as pundits would have you believe. Here we discuss pointers and practices, tools and tips for locking down this operating system—which is still frequently found at the heart of an enterprise's authentication infrastructure.

The OS Facts of Life

Let's cut to the chase here: What I *don't* find interesting are exploits or practices that cover older, unpatched versions of the operating system. These are cases of simple neglect—about as interesting as listening to your father's apocryphal college stories or last year's stock reports.

We've said it in earlier chapters and will say it again: Running an unpatched OS is begging for trouble. Your first rule of thumb with *any* OS has got to be *"stay current."*

With this in mind, here I'll rudely ignore anything before NetWare 4, and talk about NetWare 4 and NetWare 5. Novell hasn't supported NetWare 3.11 in years, and they recently announced that they'd stop supporting NetWare 3.2 as well. Your initial reaction might be, *"So what? Why should I care whether it's supported, as long as the current config is working okay?"*

However, because the frequent discovery of operating system security problems is a fact of life, to stay secure, you need some way to fix these problems. Specifically, you either need source code to the operating system (plus the requisite know-how) to fix a given problem, or you need vendor support.

Source code isn't available for NetWare—so you *have* to have Novell's support to address newly discovered OS problems.

Conclusion: Using a version of NetWare with no support is not exactly a smart or secure thing to do. If you use NetWare 3, or (egads!) NetWare 2.86, you're *on your own*. Not too fun. Stop reading here, and go do something about it. After you've upgraded, come back; we'll talk more.

Still here? Okay, so you're using NetWare 4 or NetWare 5—go out and get the latest patches. There is a *huge* number of security patches available. For reference, in this chapter, I discuss NetWare 4 SP 8A, and NetWare 5.1 SP 1. These *minimum patch levels* are surely different now, so go download the latest ones.

NOTE

Novell's Minimum Patch List for all its products can be found at `http://support.novell.com/misc/patlst.htm`.

Finally, if you are a true-red Novell shop, it's likely that you are using Novell's BorderManager as a software firewall, and that you're using GroupWise as your email system. Although the following does apply to the host operating system that these products live on, it's not a guide to securing these specific products. See Chapter 10, "Firewalls," for firewall information; see Part VII, "Bringing It All Together," for more guidelines on securing network applications.

Watching the Big Three

After you patch, life with NetWare consists of being careful about three environments that substantially affect your security:

- Server environment—Server console and configuration
- Client environment—Workstations, client software and configuration
- NDS (Novell Directory Services) environment

In what can be a hugely complex system, it's useful to distill all your NetWare security concerns into these three groups. Not every individual is responsible for each group, but every individual suffers the consequences if these categories are not tended to. (If you're "lucky" enough to be the only person in your shop who tends to all three of these, pat yourself on the back and demand a raise.)

Accordingly, you'll want to figure out who's responsible for what in your organization—it doesn't do any good for only one of these subsystems to be locked down.

Server Environment

It's an understatement to say that, when an intruder is able to access your server console, the battle is lost. If you're new to NetWare, here's a basic, horrible fact about the OS:

> There *is* no explicit login to the console. The default access when you boot up amounts to "The dude who's driving is large and in charge."

Huh? This sounds awfully weird, if you're used to UNIX or (properly configured) NT. Why would the console offer supervisor privileges to just anybody?

The answer is, it doesn't *explicitly* offer these privileges. Many of NetWare's NLM (NetWare Loadable Module) tools require authentication before they allow you to perform privileged operations.

But, because NetWare in its default configuration allows anybody who is driving the keyboard to load an NLM, it implicitly allows the driver to perform *any* privileged operation that is coded into that NLM.

For example, simply by loading an NLM (and without causing undue suspicion—you don't have to reboot to do these things), you can

- Set the administrative password (which would alert the real administrator that something's awry)
- Add an additional administrative user to the system with a password of your choice (which would not alert the administrator)
- Snag the entire NDS database (if you're driving a server with a replica on it) for offline decryption with publicly available tools
- Commit other mayhem at will

Sound bad? It is. Again, merely by inserting the right floppy diskette in the drive—or by loading an NLM from a user's directory on the server—you can, as an untrusted user, be treated as a trusted user at the console.

Novell offers a partial solution, the SECURE CONSOLE command.

It's a hard call: On the one hand, SECURE CONSOLE protects your servers from a keyboard interloper who wants to

- Load NLMs from anywhere but SYS:\SYSTEM or C:\NWSERVER
- Gain access to the NetWare debugger (right-shift+Alt+left shift+ESC), and possibly hand-enter malicious code
- Change the time to try to break security

On the other hand, SECURE CONSOLE can be a real pain when you have to do maintenance. Even a legitimate user (you) can't change the time to correct for clock drift, you can't add a search path, and you cannot load NLMs from anywhere but the two system locations. It would be a wonderful thing if you didn't have to *reboot* the system to disable it.

Unfortunately, using SECURE CONSOLE is a must if your physical security is at all in question—if there's even a possibility of an unauthorized person sitting down at your server keyboard even for a moment.

Physical Security

Here's the obvious: Keep your consoles (*and backup tapes!*) behind locked doors. But as with other operating systems/routers/pieces of key infrastructure, there is usually some point when your space gets shared, be it with the cleaning people, outside consultants, or your own folks.

NOTE

I was once in an IT shop where an application consultant was invited to set up his office in the computer room—there wasn't any extra office space. That's Huge Problem #1. Then, the consultant started doing ad hoc training for users of his application—right in the data center.

Huge Problem #2? He gave out the passcode to the data center door, and the user was sitting at an NT console merrily playing Solitaire when the consultant arrived. ("Oh, was that a server?") Notwithstanding how trusted the consultant was, the user could have been anybody. All of the data center's physical security was compromised the instant the consultant was trusted in the data center.

A corollary: Any server that is *not* physically secure *must not* be part of your production NDS tree. Any machine that isn't physically secure can't be considered trusted, and any untrusted console can wreak havoc on your tree. This means new servers that are being set up on an unsecured workbench; lab machines; test machines, and so on.

Naturally, any switches or hubs that your servers—or administrative workstations—are connected to also need to be behind locked doors, particularly in light of how easily NetWare's default remote control encryption is defeated. (See the section "RCONSOLE," later in the chapter.)

Physical security can be a pretty large and ongoing task (for more on physical security you can refer to Chapter 26, "Policies, Procedures, and Enforcement)." After you've set up physical security for your production servers, you need policies, procedures, and regular checkups to make sure that your secured areas *stay* secure.

Securing an Insecure Console

The best thing to do with an idle console is to use a utility to lock down the keyboard, and only unlock it if someone authenticates. NetWare 5 has just such a utility, scrsaver.nlm. It's pretty easy to use; just type

```
scrsaver help
```

at the console prompt for on-the-fly directions.

I like to set up the screensaver to kick in and lock down after four minutes of idle time. (You can see what this looks like in Figure 21.1) The screensaver is *not a default action;* you must load and configure the screensaver each time. You can do this by putting the following line in your AUTOEXEC.NCF:

```
scrsaver enable; delay=240
```

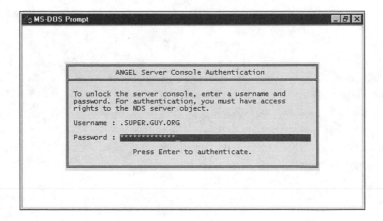

FIGURE 21.1
It's a good idea to load scrsaver.nlm upon server startup, so that it locks down the keyboard when the console has been idle.

Some folks also like to start the screensaver up as the last action of the AUTOEXEC.NCF. This way, even if someone does get access to one of the servers right after boot time, they need to authenticate.

In this case, the last line of your AUTOEXEC.NCF should look like this:

```
scrsaver enable; delay=360; activate
```

> **NOTE**
>
> Activating the screensaver at boot time is not a sure-fire way of keeping someone out of your console; an intruder could, at first-stage boot time, avoid execution of the AUTOEXEC.NCF by typing **server -na** from the DOS prompt.

NetWare 4 Console Lock

NetWare 4 doesn't have a cool password-protected screensaver. Novell's considering making one available, and it might be by the time you read this. Check out the status of this enhancement request at

`http://support.novell.com/cgi-bin/search/tidfinder.cgi?2952871`

In the meantime, you can always use the MONITOR.NLM to manually lock your console down when you're not using it (see Figure 21.2), or get a third-party tool (check the end of this chapter for product listings).

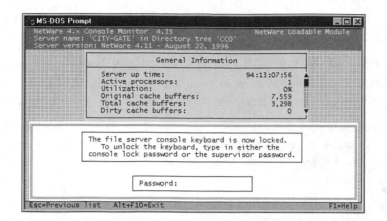

FIGURE 21.2
Although NetWare 4's MONITOR.NLM has a lock function, it requires an administrator to explicitly lock the server, rather than doing so after a timeout.

RCONSOLE

RCONSOLE, the remote-control tool for NetWare servers, can be a NetWare administrator's best friend. Unfortunately, it's not exactly a very secure friend.

The first problem with RCONSOLE is that, by default, its password is stored in plain text. If you're an old-style CNE (Certified NetWare Engineer), your AUTOEXEC.NCF might have a line like

```
LOAD REMOTE MYPASSWORD
```

in it. (If you use INETCFG.NLM to configure remote access, the password is stored in plain text in SYS:ETC.)

Obviously, this is a Bad Thing. You don't want someone printing out your AUTOEXEC.NCF for troubleshooting purposes, and then accidentally leaving it around for the entire world to see. Furthermore, because RCONSOLE sends screens over the network "in the clear," someone with a sniffer could watch you scroll through or edit your configuration file and read your password.

What to do? NetWare has a method of "encrypting" the REMOTE password (REMOTE ENCRYPT at the server console), but it is worthless in terms of secure encryption. In less than a second, you can use a DOS-based, publicly available tool, REMOTE.EXE, to break even the largest passwords encrypted this way. Don't use REMOTE ENCRYPT; it will do nothing but give you a false sense of security.

In short, using RCONSOLE over potentially untrusted networks is a really bad idea. If you really must use it, make sure that

- Your data link and network infrastructure is secured from eavesdropping.
- The two server-possible directories in which the password might be stored are unreadable by anybody but Admin-equivalents (directories such as SYS:SYSTEM and SYS:ETC).

RCONJ, the "pure Java" version of RCONSOLE, has similar problems, and should be treated with similar care. If you are serious about secure remote control of the console—and you should be, if you are responsible for an enterprise's security—see the end of this chapter for third-party tools that are much more secure.

Network Computing's October 16, 2000, issue has a detailed workshop by Kevin Novak that discusses RCONSOLE and RCONJ, available at http://www.networkcomputing.com/1120/1120ws1.html.

UNIX-Compatibility Utilities

Speaking of plain-text remote control utilities, XCONSOLE, the Telnet server for NetWare, is no safer than RCONSOLE. It uses plain-text Telnet for the authentication, and either Telnet or the X protocol—both non-encrypted protocols—for the session data. You should avoid XCONSOLE as well, unless you're absolutely sure that your infrastructure is un-tappable.

The same goes for FTP. Although FTP is arguably less of a risk than RCONSOLE if non-administrative users are ftping, FTP is just as grave a risk as RCONSOLE if administrative users ftp in to the server. All passwords for FTP are sent in the clear. Avoid, avoid, avoid.

As with any service, if you have no pressing business reason for using the service, you should probably use UNICON.NLM to deconfigure both of these tools(see Figure 21.3).

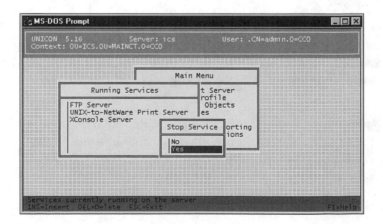

FIGURE 21.3
Use UNICON, NetWare's UNIX Services Configuration tool, to stop unwanted UNIX-compatibility services from running.

NOVELL

WWW Services

In the past, NetWare 4.1 and IntranetWare shipped with the NetWare Web Server—not the Netscape Enterprise Server. The Web server included a PERL.NLM, that allowed arbitrary execution of code on the server—a very bad thing indeed.

Although this hole has long been plugged in newer versions of the Web server, we mention this because the Web server is *not* part of the NetWare 4 core OS and thus not part of the OS's service pack. You need to go out and separately update it (or, upgrade to NetWare 5).

Finally, as with any Web server, you'll want to search-and-destroy any sample scripts. Leaving them there is simply asking for trouble.

NETBASIC.NLM

Get rid of NETBASIC.NLM unless you have a pressing need for it. There are several attacks involving NETBASIC. This is particularly true of NetWare 4, which doesn't have NetWare 5's SCRSAVER.NLM. *Even if you've used the* SECURE CONSOLE *command*, NETBASIC.NLM allows someone who accesses the console to

- Drop to a NETBASIC shell
- Copy untrusted NLMs into the SYS:SYSTEM directory
- Copy the NDS files from the hidden SYS:SYSTEM_NETWARE directory to arbitrary locations on the file server
- Perform trusted file operations that could potentially make your life miserable

Again, if you've got NetWare 5 and SCRSAVER.NLM (or NetWare 4 and a third-party utility), this isn't *as* hot an issue, but it is still due diligence to remove this tool from the server unless you need it.

TOOLBOX.NLM

Toolbox is one of the most useful administrator tools available for NetWare. It even attempts to keep its operations secure—you must authenticate to the tree before it will obey your commands. However, Toolbox is frequently used in batch files, and administrators tend to save authentication information to the Toolbox database. (For example, many administrators use Toolbox to reboot the server, purge limbo blocks from volumes, and so on.)

In a nutshell, an intruder who's familiar with Toolbox will likely type

```
AUTH LOAD
```

at the console. If an administrator has previously done an AUTH SAVE, then the intruder can use Toolbox's functions without logging in.

Basically, if you're doing AUTH SAVEs, the same rules apply to Toolbox as were previously described for NETBASIC. If a screensaver is unavailable, the potential amount of damage is huge. If a screensaver is in use, AUTH SAVE has a more acceptable level of risk.

Server Environment Parameters

There are publicly available tools that can spoof NCP (NetWare Core Protocol) packets—thus making hijacking a session a real possibility. To prevent this from happening to your users, you'll want to set your server's NCP parameters to include packet signature, packet length, and packet component checks.

For example, to get the highest level of NCP security, you'd type

```
SET NCP Packet Signature Option = 3

SET Reject NCP Packets with bad components = ON

SET Reject NCP Packets with bad lengths = ON
```

at the server console. (NetWare 4 users have to put these in the AUTOEXEC.NCF as well.)

> **NOTE**
>
> You will definitely want to do tests in your environment before you enable a packet signature level of 3. Level 3 means, "Don't communicate with ANYBODY if they don't sign their packets." This might be a bad thing if you haven't enabled your clients' packet signature options. (Although, Novell's latest client defaults to "will-do," as discussed later in the chapter.)
>
> Furthermore, you will want to test your servers to see how they'll hold up under the load with a signature level of 3. The amount of processing dedicated to cryptographically signing packets is non-trivial.

Bindery Context

A bindery context is *only* necessary on a server if its third-party software doesn't understand how to communicate via NDS. Unfortunately, there are still NetWare utilities that don't. Upgrade them, if you can, to utilities that are NDS savvy because there are publicly available tools that attack based on bindery contexts. (See the "Guest and Other No-Password Users" section for an example of this.)

NetWare servers default to having a bindery context; get rid of it by typing

```
set bindery context=
```

(That's right, there's nothing to the right of the equal sign). The system will warn you that bindery services have been disabled. If you don't need 'em, this is a good thing.

Client Environment

You'll want to stay native with your NetWare client—that is, use Novell's client, *not* Microsoft's. Microsoft's client doesn't support packet signing—neither advisory (Level 2) nor mandatory (Level 3).

The NetWare client defaults to the same thing that the server does—Level 1: "Perform packet signatures only if the other side requires it." So, if you're using the latest version of the NetWare client, you won't have a problem setting the server to a mandatory packet-signature level. Still, if you're serious about requiring packet signing, you'll want to set your clients to Level 3.

Again, *make sure to test* any parameter changes in your environment before rolling them out. As advisories come out, you might find yourself changing a large number of client workstations at a time. ZenWorks or other desktop management can make this easier and quicker.

Windows: The Weakest Link

Without getting into operating system holy wars here, let's just say that you need to pay special attention to Windows workstations where administrative users log in. The PWL files (in Windows 9x) and the SAM (of Windows NT/2K workstations) are very easily cracked.

This is fine if you only log in at workstations that have tight physical security. But what about when administrators need to log in from the field? If you must do this, consider using some sort of encrypted remote control, rather than using the desktop of the workstation that you are working on (for example, Citrix, PCAnywhere, and so on). The last thing you want to do is leave your administrative NDS password—and username—as a dropping on the user's highly insecure workstation.

Also, check out Chapter 18, "Trojans," for information on protecting your workstations from programs that can hijack login information. Because it's likely that you're in a NetWare environment, you might want to use ZENWorks to assign policies that lock down your client workstations.

Finally, if you have public terminals, or a Citrix remote login system, you will definitely want to disable the "Advanced" function of the client. The browse functions of the Advanced tab provide more information to an intruder than you want to disseminate. (If you do this, you'll want to enable "context-less" login, unless you want your users typing `.myname.mydepartment.mylocation.myorg` as their username.)

Novell Directory Services (NDS) Environment

Any directory service (DS) needs to be maintained from birth and throughout its life. Neglect and oversight are the main reasons a DS fails—whether in the security space, or simply from the functionality perspective.

A Good Start: Intruder Detection

Intruder detection is a way of making NDS count the number of failed login attempts within a certain time frame—and lock the account for a certain amount of time if the number of failed logins exceeds a certain limit.

Let's look at an example. An intruder writes a program to do a dictionary or brute-force attack on a given user's login, say, user name "JOE," using the authentication calls that are available via the NetWare API. If there is no intruder detection, the intruder can cycle through thousands of possible passwords in a relatively short time.

If the admin has enabled Detect intruders, as shown in Figure 21.4, the following happens: Because the intruder is trying more than seven passwords in a 30-minute period, the account is locked for 15 minutes. All of a sudden, rather than being able to cycle through thousands of passwords, the intruder can only cycle through seven before the account gets locked. This is an extremely good protection against systematic, online, real-time password cracking.

The bad news is intruder detection is not enabled by default. You'll need to go into NWAdmin and enable it per OU (organizational Unit) as part of your "new tree SOP (Standard Operating Procedure)."

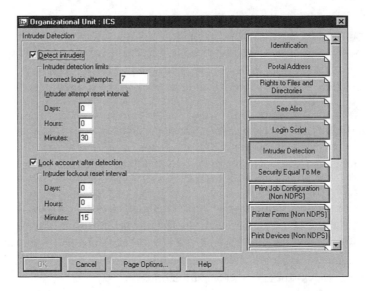

FIGURE 21.4
You'll want to use NWAdmin to enable intruder detection on each organizational unit in your tree.

User Names: Admin

Admin is the first user created in a new NDS tree. The first thing a lot of folks do after installing a new NDS tree is to rename the Admin user to something nonobvious and put Admin into a nonobvious container (like `.GSmith.abc.myorg.`) This container should be stored separately from that of regular users.

This is a good measure, as far as attacks from outside your organization go, but it's not foolproof. As we've discussed elsewhere, lots of security problems come from the inside.

A temp worker—intern, air conditioning repair person, or receptionist—might see an administrative user log in (like, um, YOU while you log in to solve a problem for this person)—and thus gain information about an administrative user's login name. Perhaps it's not THE Admin user, but it's *an* Admin user—which is all potential crackers are looking for. So, move the Admin user if you want, but know that this is not a cure-all.

Naturally, you'll want to make sure that *all* administrative users have *very good* passwords. Use NWAdmin to make sure that administrative users have policies in place to require a password of sufficient length.

Guest and Other No-Password Users

Unless you have a need for a Guest account—and most organizations do not—delete the Guest user. (NetWare 5, happily, does not supply a Guest user by default when you install a new NDS tree.)

If you're administrating an existing NDS tree, you will want to check for users with no passwords on a fairly regular basis (or, use NDS auditing software, discussed later in the chapter). Even if these accounts have NO special privileges, they will allow an attacker to browse the tree and gather an intruder's best friend, more information. If they belong to a container that's been given special authority (a bad idea—see the section "Unintended Consequences of Container Rights"), suddenly you've got a problem on your hands.

How do these no-password accounts "show up?" There are tools (for example, backup, anti-virus, print servers) that generate accounts so that the program can log in to the tree without operator intervention. You'll want to make sure that these accounts do NOT allow an interactive login—at least, not without requiring a password. Try it; if the tool account allows you to log in, restrict the account to certain network addresses only—the network addresses of the station that runs the program, such as the anti-virus console, the print server, and so on. (Some of these types of tools don't allow you to specify a password, so changing the password won't fly.)

You—and an intruder—can find accounts with no passwords, if you have a bindery context set (see why a bindery context isn't a good thing?), with the freely-available CHKNULL program. A good NDS auditing tool will also find these.

> **NOTE**
>
> There is literature out there that implies that you can also use NLIST to find null password information. This is not the case. NLIST will show you what the policies are for users—that is, if a null password is allowed, and what the minimum password length is. These are useful things to know (because you don't want a user to have too short of a password, or to be allowed to blank it), but be aware of the difference.

Enforcing User Authentication Policies

NetWare has a bunch of good password management built into NDS. Each site is different, but typically, enabling the password management can greatly increase your security. Using NWAdmin, you can set

- Whether a user can change his password
- Whether a password is required
- The minimum password length
- Whether periodic password changes are required, and how many days are required between changes
- The number of times the user can procrastinate a required periodic password change before getting locked out (called *grace logins*)
- Whether unique passwords are required

These policies are delegated *per user*, not as part of a group. You'll want to use NWAdmin's Details on Multiple Users feature (see Figure 21.5) if you want to change the policies of many users at once.

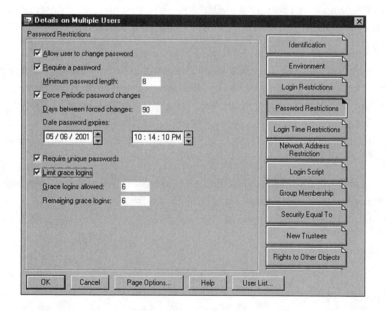

FIGURE 21.5

If you are changing the password policies of a bunch of users at one time, use NWAdmin's Details on Multiple Users options.

If your organization believes that passwords are too easily compromised (by users writing them down, sharing them, and so on), you can investigate alternative login methods, such as biometrics. The Novell Modular Authentication System (NMAS) supports third-party authentication such as fingerprinting, SecurID, and so on. You can read more about NMAS at

`http://www.novell.com/products/nmas/details.html`

Understanding and Applying NDS "Best Practices"

The Novell Directory Service is the heart of your NetWare network. Servers, accounts, file systems, certificates—everything—relies on NDS being configured correctly. If you or your system administrators don't fully grok NDS, or take short cuts, you are likely to make mistakes that will leave you vulnerable to attack.

> **NOTE**
>
> There is a huge body of work about NDS—most of it, naturally, written by Novell. If you are shaky on your NDS understanding, or want to make sure you fully understand it, a good place to start is the Novell Research AppNote, "Learning and Applying the Rules of NDS Security," found at `http://developer.novell.com/research/appnotes/1997/august/02/index.htm`.

Unintended Consequences of Container Rights

Container rights are one of the most convenient NDS features—you apply rights to an organizational unit (OU), and the rights flow down so that children containers and their objects inherit these rights. Convenient—yet dangerous.

With many objects and subcontainers in a tree, it can be difficult to visualize just what the consequences of inherited rights can be.

One common—and bad—practice that some IT shops have is to link administrative rights to an OU, for example, the "SysAdmins" OU. They figure, "Anybody in this OU is an administrator, so what's the harm?" The answer is, "It can be plenty of harm."

For example, a recently discovered problem (`http://Feldman.org/zen`) with the ZenWorks workstation manager allowed *any* workstation object to assume the rights of its container—without a user being logged on. This made it easy for an untrusted user to get sneaky and run programs with those rights. In the case of a container that was assigned Admin rights, the *workstation* assumed the Admin rights—because it was part of the container. All of a sudden, the intruder had admin rights, too.

If the container had *not* been given special rights, the damage of this exploit would have been minimized. Lesson: Don't assign sensitive rights to a container, ever.

What are *sensitive rights*? Some of them include

- Security equivalencies to administrative users
- Any rights to the root of any volume
- Any rights to SYS:\etc
- Any rights to SYS:\system

Use groups instead of containers to assign these types of rights. This is a good administrative practice. Because a group is a central point of administration, the potential for admin error is decreased.

There's nothing inherently wrong with grouping; the problem only has to do with *inheritance*—and thus, containers. Although Novell (and other literature) will tell you that problems with inheritance can be handled with an IRF (Inherited Rights Filter), consider the previous problem. Would an IRF block rights to *workstation objects* in the *same* OU as the administrative users? No! An IRF "flows down" through the tree. Objects in the *same* container get the same rights as the user in the container.

In a nutshell, inheritance can be a tricky beast. Be careful.

NDS Auditing Tools

NDS can be a big and complex beast—the fact of the matter is that any good directory service is. Your best bet if you are serious about keeping an eye on NDS is to invest in third-party auditing software. NWAdmin enables you to do searches on various NDS attributes (for example, the "Security Equivalent to Me" search shown in Figure 21.6, which reveals all the users that other users are equivalent to). However, search on every single property from NWAdmin can be cumbersome and/or impossible. I do not recommend Novell's AUDITCON for anything but a very small organization.

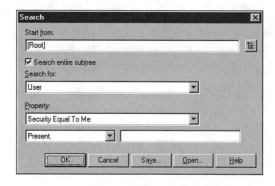

Figure 21.6

NWAdmin will enable you to do basic property searches, but isn't sufficient for hardcore auditing.

It's beyond the scope of this chapter to review every auditing tool available, but the following are a sampling of what's available.

AuditTrack
Manufacturer: WebTrends

URL: `http://www.webtrends.com/products/adttrk/intro.htm`

AuditTrack allows auditing and reporting of server access and file manipulation activity.

Includes predefined audit rule sets; additional audit instruction sets that define who and what to monitor can also be defined. Options allow for the auditing of files, workstations, users, or user groups. Alarms can be configured to notify the administrator if suspicious file activity is taking place, or if a security breach occurs. AuditTrack also has a custom reporting and graphing facility.

AuditWare for NDS
Manufacturer: Computer Associates

URL: `http://www.computerassociate.com/products/auditware_nds.htm`

A Windows-based advanced NDS reporting and security analysis tool. Generates comparison, analysis, security, and documentation reports.

Can locate potentially hazardous stealth users that cannot be seen because the Browse privilege has been filtered out. Can also locate "dangerous" users—those who have supervisor privileges but do not meet minimum password requirements.

bv-Control for NDS
Manufacturer: BindView

URL: `http://bindview.com/products/bv-Control/NDS/index.html`

A tool to automate the analysis and documentation of server and NDS configuration; it looks for improperly configured servers and out-of-date or conflicting executables (including EXEs, NLMs, services, and device drivers) that can cause your servers to perform poorly and crash.

JRButils
URL: `http://www.jrbsoftware.com`

Command-line–based utilities for the rugged individualist who lives for the CLI. Users can use these utilities to perform operations on objects selected via wild cards, container, membership of a group, or via a list in a file. When displaying information, filters can be applied. Can be used for automation of operations such as mass user creation, customization, deletion and for performing security checks.

Kane Security Analyst

Manufacturer: Intrusion.com

URL: `http://www.intrusion.com/Products/analystnt.shtml`

An assessment tool that claims to provide centralized audit data of key Windows NT and Novell NetWare security features. It evaluates password strength, access control, user account restrictions, as well as having a data monitoring facility. Provides report card summaries and more verbose reports.

LT Auditor+

Manufacturer: Blue Lance

URL: `http://www.bluelance.com/ltauditor/default.html`

A Windows-based intrusion detection/audit trail security software solution. LT Auditor+ supports NT and/or Novell networks. Alerts can be configured to respond to specific events either system-wide or at particular workstations; it also provides off-site paging and email alerts via an SNMP console.

Commercial Secure Remote Control Products

SecureConsole for NetWare

Manufacturer: Protocom Development Systems

URL: `http://www.serversystems.com/frames/sc_cs.htm`

A native Win32 application, which provides single sign-on to a NetWare console. It does this by checking a user's current NDS credentials and looking them up in the SecureConsole database. Standard NDS security features such as secure password authentication, single sign-on and intruder lock out are supported. Generates SNMP alerts to one or more network management consoles when it detects attempted unauthorized access or other abnormal server conditions.

Secure Remote Console

Manufacturer: AdRem Software

URL: `http://www.adremsoft.com/arcon3/index.htm`

Offers 128-bit encrypted remote console operations. Access control is available that allows users and groups of users to be permitted specific console commands and server screens.

Useful Freeware

Most of the following is available from `http://www.netwarefiles.com`, a repository of a bunch of free or shareware utilities.

BURGLAR.NLM

A venerable tool, Bart Mellink's BURGLAR.NLM creates a supervisory user of your choice. You need access to the server console and about five free nanoseconds to do this—reason #9,285 to secure your server consoles from unauthorized personnel.

HOBJLOC.NLM

Novell Consulting's answer to crackers who create "hidden" users, that is, users invisible even to administrative users. Finds them so that you can root them out. (Commercial auditing tools do this too, but this is free.)

Pandora

"The Leatherman" of NetWare cracking tools, written by Simple Nomad and friends. Runs under Linux as well as Win32. Includes offline NDS cracking tools—so that you can audit your NDS passwords—as well as online denial of service tools. You can find both Pandora and enough NetWare-related documentation to feed a family of four for a month at `http://www.nmrc.org`. As of this writing, the NMRC is probably your best bet for up-to-date information and code from the underground.

REMOTE.EXE

Written by TheRuiner, *Instantly* cracks even the longest of "encrypted" remote console passwords. Want to see some fun? Type "remote encrypt" at the server console, and enter the longest password you can. Then take the remotely encrypted string, and feed it to REMOTE.EXE.

```
985FF510136420112F1D366A207616903FBEEDEBCDCDDCCCCDCCBDB4CCBCCDCD4BCDBB03
```

is instantly decrypted to

```
THEREISNOREMOTEPASSWORDSECURITY
```

It's a small and useful demo tool that turns even the most doubting of Thomases into a true believer in REMOTE's lack of real encryption.

SETPWD.NLM

Developed at the University of Salford in the U.K., P.R. Lees' SETPWD.NLM allows you to set anybody's password from the server console. Is this reason #9,286?

Further Reading

Mastering Netware 5.1. James E. Gaskin. Sybex Publications, July 2000. ISBN: 078212772X

The Complete Guide to Novell Directory Services. David Kearns, Brian Iverson. Sybex, March 1998. ISBN: 0782118232

Special Edition Using Netware 5.0. Peter Kuo, John Pence, Sally Specker. Que, August 1999. ISBN: 0789720566

Novell's Guide to NetWare 5 Networks. Jeffrey F. Hughes, Blair W. Thomas. IDG, 1999. ISBN: 0764545442

Novell's Guide to Integrating NetWare 5 and NT. J. D. Marymee, Sandy Stevens, Gary Hein. IDG, October 1999. ISBN: 0764545809

Novell's Guide to NetWare 5 and TCP/IP. Drew Heywood. IDG, March 1999. ISBN: 0764545647

Novell's Guide to LAN/WAN Analysis. Laura A. Chappell. IDG, March 1998. ISBN: 0764545086

Novell's Four Principles of NDS. Jeff Hughes. IDG Books Worldwide, 1996. ISBN: 0-76454-522-1

NetWare Web Development. Peter Kuo. Sams Publishing. 1996. ISBN: 1575211866

Summary

As with other operating systems, keeping NetWare secure is a matter of being diligent about staying current with OS levels, patches, and best practices. Some NetWare tools and/or services are security liabilities; as with any other OS, your rule should be "If I don't need it, I won't run it." Some of NetWare's more insecure tools have third-party replacements that are more secure.

Understanding NDS rights is vital to making sure that you don't cause unintended security consequences. And NDS-specific auditing tools can help make sure that your secured network stays secure.

Cisco Routers and Switches

IN THIS CHAPTER

Administrators and security professionals alike often spend a significant amount of time configuring and securing the various firewalls, Web servers, and surrounding systems that make up their enterprise environments. Unfortunately, infrastructure devices such as routers and switches are frequently neglected in this effort. This neglect can often lead to sniffed sessions, route changes, and some overall really Bad Things.

In this chapter, I will be focussing on the steps necessary to configure, deploy, and help keep your infrastructure equipment safe from hostile attackers. I have chosen to focus on Cisco products simply because they are by far the most predominant in use. However, users of products from Extreme, Juniper, or other routing and switching vendors might still find this chapter useful, as many of these techniques apply to non-Cisco equipment as well.

Please note that this chapter assumes basic familiarity with Cisco routing equipment.

The Problems with Infrastructure Equipment

Although it is safe to assume that most hacking targets are end-node systems—such as Web, application, or database servers—many people foolishly ignore the security issues surrounding their infrastructure equipment. This can, unfortunately, be a colossal blunder. The truth of the matter is that not only can routers and switches be compromised, they can be used as stepping stones for further attack, as well as become incredibly useful information gathering devices for attackers.

Cisco routers and switches have their own OS, otherwise known as Cisco IOS (Internetwork Operating System). Although Cisco's track record with security is fairly good, it is by no means flawless. Cisco has had some security problems in the past, and as with any OS, if those problems are not patched or addressed, you leave yourself open to further troubles.

Of particular concern is the fact that routers and switches can be used to not only map target networks, but also to mask one's identity, help create sniffing stations, and create some overall widespread chaos. For example, most Cisco switches have the capability to create a *monitor port* that can mirror or *port span* any other port on the switch. This effectively allows an administrator, or an intruder, to duplicate any traffic that the switch sees, and dump it down a specified switch port. So, although administrators might take comfort in their switched environment's apparent immunity to sniffer-based eavesdropping problems that HUBed environments face, all bets are off if the intruder has access to configuring the switch.

Other shenanigans can include static route entries and ICMP (Internet Control Message Protocol) redirect messages, conveniently disabled Access Control Lists (ACLs), or even bizarre network address translation (NAT) rules. Rest assured that, if an experienced intruder gets into your routing and switching architecture, you will have a *very difficult* time permanently locking him out of your systems and network.

NOTE

The authors of the book @Large wrote about a cracker who had stolen thousands of passwords by compromising Internet backbones routers and setting up customized sniffers. Although it is true that sniffing was easier back then (because many of the routers in the earlier days of the Internet were based on UNIX OSs such as IBM's AIX), source code for Cisco's IOS has been seen circulating through some underground channels. Although I know of no documented cases of Trojaned IOS code, it is certainly possible. People taking comfort in IOS being more "specialized" and subsequently more obscure, do so foolishly.

22

NOTE

Most of the examples in this chapter will be demonstrated on the "router" versions of IOS. Although the versions of IOS found on switches are similar, for simplicity's sake, we will only be showing examples from the router version of IOS.

Keeping Up with IOS Revisions

Keeping "current" with IOS changes is pivotal. Much as this point was driven home in the Microsoft, Novell, and UNIX chapters of this book, the same holds true with Cisco IOS. However, Cisco actually does a better job with OS revisions, version control, and release strategies than most other software vendors. When Cisco says that a version of their software "is stable," it might actually, in fact, be stable.

The first thing you should do while analyzing the state of your infrastructure equipment is to investigate the various versions of IOS running on your systems. This can be accomplished by using the Show Version command). Should you discover that you are running older versions of IOS, consider the phrase "If it isn't broken, don't fix it" before moving towards massive upgrade efforts. More important than the age of the IOS version is where that version is in its release life cycle. Cisco has designated three stages that a particular IOS version resides in during its release cycle:

- **Early Deployment (ED).** This is usually a version of IOS with new features that might still have some bugs in it.
- **Limited Deployment (LD).** These IOS builds are usually considered "interim" builds. They are usually released with fixes to specific problems found in ED builds.
- **General Deployment (GD).** General deployment builds are focussed on stability, and are usually fairly "bug free."

▶ Cisco's full release strategy is actually a fair bit more complex then what we've outlined previously—we are simply going over the basics here. A great document that details numbering, life cycles, and other versioning tidbits can be found on Cisco's site here: `http://www.cisco.com/warp/public/cc/pd/iosw/iore/prodlit/537_pp.htm`

Although you might be tempted to use the "latest and greatest" version of IOS, I caution you to only use what you need, and to stick to GD builds whenever possible. GD builds tend to have the majority of the bugs worked out of them, and are usually quite solid. The only exception to this rule of thumb is in relation to security problems—if an IOS version contains a known security vulnerability, you really have no choice but to upgrade.

▶ If you maintain Cisco equipment, it would be wise to subscribe to Cisco's mailing list that announces the security field notices. You can find subscription information for the list at `http://www.cisco.com/warp/public/707/sec_incident_response.shtml`.

Securing and Configuring Cisco Routers

Cisco routers are easier to protect, at a host-level, than many UNIX systems are, simply because they have fewer services that can be accessed remotely. Sure, they perform some complex routing calculations and play pivotal roles on the Internet, but they don't have services running on them such as BIND, IMAP, POP, or sendmail—services that have proven to be points of entry on UNIX-based platforms again and again.

However, despite the fact that routers tend to be generally less accessible, a number of configuration tasks should be performed to limit a router's accessibility even further.

Securing Login Points

Unfortunately, the majority of Cisco routers today are still managed over Telnet, which does not employ any type of encryption. Telnet passes all traffic in the clear, so it is quite easy to pick up login passwords if you have sniffers in place. Although Cisco IOS version 12.1 brought SSH version 1 to most router platforms, Cisco has yet to work out some of the bugs in their SSH implementation.

▶ SSH is a secure replacement for Telnet (among other things). You can find out more about SSH at `http://www.tigerlair.com/ssh/faq/ssh-faq.html`.

Until Cisco decides to get serious about using SSH (and hopefully they will adopt SSH version 2 sometime soon), we are stuck using Telnet. Fortunately, we can do a number of things to help restrict access to Cisco routers, and help limit the chances of unauthorized users accessing our routers.

You can log in to a Cisco router four ways:

- Via the physical *console* port
- Via the physical *auxiliary* port
- Via other physical serial ports (only on models equipped with such ports, or *lines*)
- Via telnetting into one of the unit's IP addresses

Three of these methods require physical access, which makes our life a little easier. We will discuss the fourth method, logging in using Telnet, first.

Cisco routers have five *virtual terminals*, or *vtys*, that you can telnet to. There are two things you need to worry about with Telnet logins. First, you want to make sure that all the vtys have passwords enabled. You can do this by issuing the following commands from the configuration mode:

```
Router1(config)#line vty 0 4

Router1(config-line)#password fabi0!
```

This sets the vty password to "fabi0!". Next, you will want to add a level of defense to help prevent attackers from telnetting into the router and remaining idle, which can tie up all five vtys. The following commands will not solve the problem entirely, but will definitely help:

```
Router1(config)#line vty 0 4

Router1(config-line)#exec-timeout 1

Router1(config-line)#exit

Router1(config)#service tcp-keepalives-in
```

These commands set the vty time-out value to one minute, and force the use of TCP keep-alives to help combat orphaned sessions. In addition to these commands, you can use a standard access list to limit the number of workstations that can telnet into the router itself. For example, assuming your management segment (where you will be telnetting from) is 10.1.1.0, the following will limit inbound Telnet sessions to this range:

```
Router1(config)#access-list 1 permit 10.1.1.0 0.0.0.255

Router1(config)#access-list 1 deny any

Router1(config)#line vty 0 4

Router1(config-line)#access-class 1 in
```

When it comes to physical access concerns, there are two things we want to watch out for: the console port and the auxiliary port. The auxiliary port is often used for "out of band" management via devices such as modems, so it is extremely important that this port be protected as well. You can protect both ports using passwords by issuing the following commands:

```
Router1(config)#line aux 0

Router1(config-line)#password fabi0!

Router1(config)#line console 0

Router1(config-line)#password fabi0!
```

NOTE

There is one other method of helping combat the problems surrounding Telnet—don't use it. Some administrators resort to recycling their terminal server and dial-up equipment, and attaching it to the Cisco router AUX or CONSOLE ports. They can then SSH or dial into the terminal server, and then hop onto the router from there. Also, directly connected dial-up access to routers is actually quite feasible because bandwidth is not an issue during text-based configurations. Just make sure that you require authentication.

Keeping Administrators Accountable

Finally, in the interest of good auditing/accounting practices, it's a good idea to remove the use of "shared" accounts. A shared account is one that is used by multiple people, with no method of clarifying true ownership. By default, Cisco devices have two levels of access: User mode and the privileged Enable mode. You can think of Enable mode as the equivalent of root in UNIX, or Administrator in Windows NT.

By default, users are authenticated based solely on passwords—no usernames are required. This is true for both the regular Login mode, as well as Enable mode. Unfortunately, most organizations never move away from this model and, therefore, have multiple people sharing the router passwords. By implementing AAA (Authentication, Authorization, and Accounting) services in conjunction with RADIUS or TACACS, administrators can tie their Cisco infrastructure to a centralized username repository such as NDS (Novell Directory Services), AD (Active Directory), or any other centralized password store. By implementing such an authentication model, administrators will be forced to log in to routers using their username and password credentials, leading to the possibility of clean audit trails.

▶ AAA configuration is beyond the scope of this chapter, but a good start to learning more on the subject (including sample configurations) can be found at http://www.cisco.com/univercd/cc/td/doc/product/software/ios120/12cgcr/secur_c/scprt1/scathen.htm.

Disabling Unnecessary Services

The next step in securing your Cisco equipment is to disable unnecessary services. Sound familiar? It should—this is the standard technique that should be employed across all OS platforms.

First, disable the small servers. These services are rarely used, and are not needed in most environments:

```
Router1(config)#no service udp-small-servers
```

```
Router1(config)#no service tcp-small-servers
```

Next, disable the finger service:

```
Router1(config)#no ip finger
```

Although the finger service doesn't pose any threat by itself, it can be used as a reconnaissance tool by hackers to scope out further information. After disabling finger, make sure that the HTTP (Web) server is not running. Although it is disabled by default, it's better to be safe then sorry by using this command:

```
Router1(config)#no ip http server
```

Cisco devices have a Cisco-proprietary protocol called CDP, or Cisco Discovery Protocol. Like finger, CDP is not a threat in and of itself, but can be used to gain information that an intruder shouldn't have access to. You can disable CDP on a per-interface basis with these commands:

```
Router1(config)#int eth0/0
```

```
Router1(config-if)#no cdp enable
```

Or you can choose to disable it entirely by issuing this:

```
Router1(config)#no cdp run
```

Finally, although I recommend using the Network Time Protocol (NTP) to synchronize time across your infrastructure (see the next section for NTP implementation issues), if you do not plan on deploying NTP you should make sure it is disabled by issuing this:

```
Router1(config)#no ntp
```

22

CISCO ROUTERS
AND SWITCHES

> **NOTE**
>
> It never hurts to double-check your work. Consider periodically running nmap against your routers to check for running services. It's a good habit to form, and it might save your butt some day.

Network Management Considerations

Locking down terminal access and disabling unnecessary services are important steps in securing your infrastructure. However, the task does not end with a few configuration settings. There are a number of procedural and management aspects of infrastructure security that should be taken into consideration as well.

Do you keep backups of your router and switch configurations? If not, why not?

If so, where are those configuration files stored? Are they secure?

Are the passwords in those configuration files secure?

Do you track when people log in to your routers, change configurations, or bring WAN links down?

Have you centralized your logging efforts for coordination purposes?

Can you monitor and manage your infrastructure securely?

Fortunately, it's not too hard to address most of these issues. With a little planning, a few service additions, and some configuration changes, even shaky situations can be drastically improved.

Centralizing Logging

Security gurus will explain that syslog is not the most secure protocol out there because it passes its information in the clear over UDP. Unfortunately, right now, there are few alternatives. Assuming you have a syslog server set up, you can use the following commands to pipe your output to that server:

```
Router1(config)#logging trap notifications
```

```
Router1(config)#logging facility local6
```

```
Router1(config)#logging 10.1.1.2
```

These commands will instruct the router to output all notifications (trap notification) to the logging host (10.1.1.2), using the `facility local6`.

NOTE

Syslog uses facilities to help designate between log entry types: auth, auth-priv, cron, daemon, kern, lpr, mail, mark, syslog, user, uucp, and local0 through local7. You can think of these as simply categories of message types. Although you can configure your router or switch to report using any of these, most administrators pick one of the "local" settings for their infrastructure equipment. See the UNIX man pages for syslogd and syslog.conf for more information.

Password Storage Considerations

Many people store their router configuration files and images on FTP or TFTP servers. Although keeping backup copies of both images and configuration files is a great practice, it is *crucial* that these files be protected. Make sure that the server they are hosted on is secure, and that the file permissions on those configuration files limit their accessibility.

> **NOTE**
>
> Frequently during penetration tests, you will come across the systems that store the router configuration files. Although the routers themselves can be quite difficult to break into, after stumbling across unprotected configuration files you can usually decrypt the passwords and subsequently access the routers fairly easily. In these scenarios, the configuration files—not the routers themselves—become the weak link in the chain. You can read more about Cisco password storage at `http://www.cisco.com/warp/public/701/64.html`.

Next, consider implementing two precautionary measures on the password front. First, use Cisco's "secret" password convention as opposed to the normal "enable" password. The storage of the enable secret password uses an MD5 hash that is not reversible, but the regular "enable" password can be trivially decrypted. You can make the switch to using "enable secret" by using the following commands:

```
Router1(config)#no enable password
Router1(config)#enable secret #fabi0!
```

This code removes the regular enable password, and replaces it with the secret of #fabi0!. Another precautionary measure is to use the password encryption service available on most Cisco devices. This service applies to usernames and first-level login passwords only. Although the password encryption service still implements an incredibly weak encryption mechanism, it will at least allow you to avoid storing your user and login passwords in clear text. You can enable the password encryption service by using the following:

```
Router1(config)#service password-encryption
```

Time Synchronization

The network time protocol (NTP) was designed to synchronize the clocks of systems and network devices to some sort of time reference. NTP is an industry-standard Internet protocol, whose foundation was defined in RFC 1059. NTP is considered to be highly accurate, and quite transportable—there are implementations of it on Windows-based operating systems, UNIX systems, and a myriad of routing and switching devices.

> **NOTE**
>
> Although something as seemingly trivial as time might not seem critical in the area of security, this couldn't be farther from the truth. Time plays a critical role in basic auditing, accounting, and event correlation. I personally learned this the hard way when I was once asked by a client to track an internal user's illegal activity on the Internet. The trail lead me to the proxy server logs, which were slightly out of sync with the log data I was given. I didn't think this was a big deal until I realized that the proxy servers were servicing requests at the rate of 60-per-second! That minute's worth of discrepancy sent me sifting through thousands of requests.

If you can successfully deploy NTP in your environment, you might be thanking yourself later. Assuming you have some NTP servers to poll from, the following commands will configure your router to synchronize with an NTP-enabled time source (in this case, an NTP server at 10.1.1.9):

```
Router1(config)#ntp server 10.1.1.9
```

▶ The official NTP home page, which contains links to FAQs, RFCs, and code, can be found at `http://www.eecis.udel.edu/~ntp/`.

▶ You can also find a brief primer on NTP at `http://www.nwc.com/1002/1002ws1.html`.

SNMP Considerations

Some organizations use SNMP heavily. Others do not, but leave the protocol enabled in hopes that some day their horrendously expensive network management "framework" product will do something useful. Regardless of what role SNMP plays in your environment, here are two bits of advice:

- If you aren't going to be using SNMP, disable it.
- If you are going to use it, configure it properly.

Disabling `snmp` is pretty simple—simply find all your `snmp` statements and negate them with the `no` command, like this:

```
Router1(config)#no snmp-server community fabio RW
Router1(config)#no snmp-server packetsize 2048
Router1(config)#no snmp-server engineID local 00000009020000107BCDE841
```

However, if you are using SNMP and cannot disable it, you can do a number of things to further secure its use. First, SNMP has essentially two modes: a READ-ONLY (RO) mode, and a READ-WRITE (RW) mode. If at all possible, use the READ-ONLY mode. By restricting the use of SNMP to READ-ONLY, even in the event that the community string is discovered attackers will be limited to using SNMP for reconnaissance purposes. They will be unable to use it to modify configurations. If you must use the READ-WRITE mode of SNMP, make sure that your READ-WRITE and READ-ONLY community strings are different. Finally, you can use Access Control Lists (ACLs) to restrict SNMP usage to only the workstations or management machines that need it. For example, if your network management segment is 10.1.1.0, the following ACLs will block SNMP from everything but that segment:

```
Router1(config)#ip access-list standard 1
Router1(config-std-nacl)#permit 10.1.1.0 0.0.0.255
Router1(config-std-nacl)#deny all
Router1(config)#snmp-server community fabio RO 1
```

Remember, it is a good strategy to keep necessary services exposed to as few machines as possible.

Preventing Spoofing and Other Packet Games

You might be tempted to skip this section. Don't. If there is one thing you do with your infrastructure, I beg of you to implement these recommendations. So important is the following material that, had the majority of network administrators implemented these suggestions, the massive distributed denial of service (DDoS) attacks that occurred in February 2000 might not have been possible.

Although certain types of DDoS starvation attacks will continue to be virtually impossible to stop, some preventative measure can be taken. Many of the denial of service attacks that occur on the Internet originate with forged, or *spoofed*, source addresses. This makes it incredibly hard for a victim to trace an attack back to its origin, much less stop it. The following precautionary measures will not only protect your network from some types of potentially hostile traffic, they will also help protect the Internet community as a whole from your network. Should any of your machines fall prey to malicious intruders, you can use your border routers to help shield your fellow net-citizens from your misfortune. If your infrastructure is designed and protected properly, should any attackers beat your system administrators to the implementation of a patch, your routers might still be able to help stop hostile activity.

In short, implementing the following recommendations is not only a good idea for your own safety, but for the safety of the Internet community as a whole.

Egress Filtering

Frequently, network administrators keep a sharp eye on what enters their network, but never watch for what exits it. Filtering the traffic that leaves a network, or *egress filtering*, will help lower the risk of your environment being used as a DDoS platform, as well as make it less attractive to intruders.

22

CISCO ROUTERS
AND SWITCHES

The primary method used to stop outbound spoofing is the implementation of ACLs on the perimeter routers. It is generally considered a good practice to configure and apply these lists to the interface through which the packets come into a network, rather then the interface through which they leave. This not only makes the lists easier to read, but it also protects the router itself from spoofing attacks.

▶ The ICSA released a tool called NetLitmus that can be used for testing egress filtering. You can read more about it at `http://www.icsa.net/html/communities/ddos/alliance/checker/index.shtml`.

For this example, assume that the local network uses the address block of 172.16.1.0 (mask 255.255.255.0—a class C). Also assume that the local area network is attached to the first Ethernet port, Ethernet 0/0.

With this configuration, you would want to make sure that all IP packets leaving the network have a source address falling in the 172.16.1.0 range. Anything not having a source address in that range is obviously spoofed. There are two steps to enforcing this policy. The first is the creation of the ACL itself:

```
Router1(config)#access-list 100 permit ip 172.16.1.0 0.0.0.255 any
```

The second is the implementation of the ACL on the proper interface, in this case, Ethernet 0/0:

```
Router1(config)#int eth0/0
Router1(config-if)#ip access-group 100 in
```

▶ Chris Brenton wrote a brief but good paper on egress filtering for SANS. It's worth a quick read, and you can find it at `http://www.sans.org/y2k/egress.htm`.

▶ Curious readers might also want to check out RFC 2267, "Network Ingress Filtering." The RFC discusses another method of helping defeat denial of service tools. RFC 2267 can found in a number of places, one them being `http://archives.neohapsis.com/archives/rfcs/rfc2267.txt`.

Stopping Silly Packet Games

There are a number of tricks and miscellaneous packet nonsense that attackers might attempt when attacking your network. Although the likelihood of their success using solely these techniques is rather limited, you still don't want this type of traffic bouncing around on your network.

First, you'll want to disable IP source routing. IP source routing allows for the specification of a predefined path that a packet should take, and is often used in spoofing-based attacks. Packets being source routed rarely have a legitimate origin. It is therefore safe to disable this feature on at least your Internet-facing routers, with this command:

```
Router1(config)#no ip source-route
```

Another common attack uses directed broadcasts in an effort to flood a victim's network with ICMP echo replies. This attack, otherwise known as *smurfing*, can be used to channel a number of networks to mistakenly respond to ICMP echo requests that were forged en masse. Unless you know of a specific application in your environment that might rely on directed broadcasts, you should disable this feature on every active interface of every active router:

```
Router1(config)#int ethernet 0/0
Router1(config-if)#no ip directed-broadcast
```

It is a good idea to disable `proxy-arp` on interfaces that don't require it:

```
Router1(config)#int ethernet 0/0
Router1(config-if)#no ip proxy-arp
```

Finally, there are a number of ICMP services that you might want to disable. However, because a number of ICMP services are quite useful, and sometimes even required for proper functionality, our recommendation is to start by disabling ICMP redirects, and move on from there if necessary. The easiest way to disable ICMP redirects is the following:

```
Router1(config)#int ethernet 0/0
Router1(config-if)#no ip redirects
```

However, if you want to gain more granular control over ICMP, you might want to look into using ACLs.

Summary

Securing infrastructure equipment is critical for two reasons:

1. If an attacker gains access to your infrastructure equipment, she can do an incredible amount of damage.
2. If security is executed properly, not only will you protect your own network, you will help protect the Internet as a whole.

The steps we've outlined are fairly simple to implement, but can still be very effective. Finally, as in dealing with any vendor, make sure that someone in your organization is monitoring Cisco security advisories. Timeliness counts with routers and switches, too.

Further Reading and Reference

The following are *highly* recommended for further reading on the subjects of Cisco security features, and infrastructure security in general.

Cisco IOS Password Encryption Facts.

http://www.cisco.com/warp/public/701/64.html

Cisco Product Security Incident Response.

http://www.cisco.com/warp/public/707/sec_incident_response.shtml

Essential IOS Features Every ISP Should Consider.

http://www.cisco.com/warp/public/707/EssentialIOSfeatures_pdf.zip

Improving Security on Cisco Routers.

http://www.cisco.com/warp/public/707/21.html

Mastering Cisco Routers.

Chris Brenton. Sybex. ISBN: 0-782-12643X

Phrack 55: Building Bastion Routers Using Cisco IOS.

http://www.phrack.com/

Macintosh

IN THIS CHAPTER

Thousands of hacking programs exist for the Macintosh, yet many people still believe that security on the Macintosh platform isn't an issue! In the past, Macintosh news sites were such advocates for the Mac OS that they did not want any negative press for Apple. Now times have changed—security is being recognized by everyone, and posting a hacking-related story does not mean you are supporting the hackers.

Sites like mSec (`www.msec.net`), SecureMac.com and Freaks Macintosh Archives (`http://freaky.staticusers.net/`, a Mac hacker site) have reported on hacking vulnerabilities since they opened. Macinstein.com was one of the first sites to cover Macintosh security issues openly.

In the rest of this chapter, I will cover Macintosh security topics from internal desktop security to Internet security. For now, I want to cover some of the servers available.

Establishing the Macintosh as a Server

Today, it is common to have Macintosh computers in every environment and it is becoming more common to see them used as servers. There are many server software packages available, including IRC, FTP, Hotline, Mail, and Web.

Establishing a Macintosh Internet information server was once a pretty daunting task. Not any more. Today, there are many server suites available that will have you up and running in minutes. I list a few in Table 23.1.

TABLE 23.1 Popular Macintosh Server Suites and Their Locations

Server	Location
AppleShare IP	`http://www.apple.com/appleshareip/`
CL-HTTP	`http://www.ai.mit.edu/projects/iiip/doc/cl-http/`
Hotline	`http://www.bigredh.com/`
HomeDoor	`http://www.opendoor.com/homedoor/`
MacHTTP	`http://www.starnine.com/machttp/machttp.html`
Quid Pro Quo	`http://www.socialeng.com/`
WebSTAR	`http://www.starnine.com/webstar/webstar.html`
WebTen 3.0	`http://www.tenon.com/products/webten/`

Of the server suites listed, I will only go into detail on two of them, WebSTAR and Hotline.

Of the servers mentioned in Table 23.1, the one that has received the most publicity is WebSTAR. WebSTAR has had substantial publicity about its security features. The first mainstream media attention the software package received occurred when a cash reward was offered for anyone who could penetrate the Web server. Most recently, the U.S. Army decided to switch its Web server platform to the Mac OS and run WebSTAR. Before discussing specific vulnerabilities on the Macintosh platform, I want to briefly cover that story.

WebSTAR Server Suite Recruited by U.S. Army

On September 14, 1999, StarNine (now known as 4D Inc.) announced that the U.S. Army's main Web site, `www.army.mil`, was being served by WebSTAR Server Suite software on the Mac OS. A Windows NT–based server had previously been serving the Army site when it was hacked in late June 1999 by a 19-year old Wisconsin man.

▶ For more information you can refer to `http://www.webstar.com/press/press_releases/pr091499.html`.

This sudden switchover caught the attention of everyone. WebSTAR's press release was plastered all over news, and Apple ran commercials showing Army tanks surrounding the G3 Macintosh.

Hotline for Sharing Ideas and Files

Hotline is not a Web server or email server; you do not use a Web browser to access it. Hotline is its own server and its own client. Out of all the Macintosh communities, Hotline seems to be the fastest growing network, with hundreds of servers going up monthly. Anyone can host a server, run the application, and become an administrator who can share his files with the world. Anything you want to download you can find somewhere on Hotline. Hotline was first made for the Macintosh and demand called for a Windows-compatible version, which is now also available. Let's go through some of the details.

Hotline Communications has made two products: a server that enables users to connect and a client application that enables users to chat, send messages to each other, download files, stream media, and post news.

Anyone with an Internet connection can host a server. The software is free, and with the tracker system, anyone can find a server to fit his needs. The tracker is a list of servers that are online. You can search the servers' descriptions or names to find a server that will fit your needs. Any type of file imaginable is on Hotline.

To list all the uncensored servers, open the server window and click the button Add Tracker. Enter **tracked.group.org** for the name and address. Refresh the list, and now you have access to anything you desire.

▶ For a Macintosh Hacking server where you can find all the hackintosh files, get the Hotline client and connect to the server Freaks Macintosh Archives. The address is `fma.dhs.org:1234` or search for `FMA` on the tracker. From there you can talk to Macintosh hackers, programmers, and power users whose ideas exceed most Mac users. Plus you can talk to some of the original Macintosh hackers like The Weasel, who started the e-zine HackAddict.

Vulnerabilities on the Macintosh Platform

I will now go over some different software vulnerability issues for the Mac OS. I don't believe that you can understand security fully without understanding what the hacker uses and knows.

AtEase Access Bug

Application: AtEase 5.0

Impact: This opens documents with other programs.

Class: Not critical

Fix: Disable the programs that allow this access.

Credit: charlie chuckles

I spoke with charlie chuckles a while ago (in October 2000). He had noticed that no papers had been written on the unusual way of accessing files with AtEase, so he wrote the following:

This is a [problem] for AtEase 5.X... When I say the phrase "AtEase," it usually implies some sort of inferiority to everything else. But AtEase isn't really the problem here. It's the applications and some of their round about ways of opening files and the system administrator's not noticing. So I guess it sort of IS an AtEase problem by not covering every single [strange] way that programs ask for files. That was pretty deep.

The first thing I want to cover in here are the older tricks that have been on the market for a while. Everyone knows about the web browser trick (type "file:///drive name/" and read all the files on the drive). That is commonly accessible because all users are given access to some browser in their user folder. There was another trick that I'd seen using Apple Works, but I could never get it to work. I think it's because the person who wrote it was a failure with a wooden leg and real feet.

Now forward! to read/write! Let's pretend you are in a biosphere. Now let's pretend your user has access to MS Word. In version 8 (and the equivalent Excel release and probably the rest of Office) there is a find file function. Here's how to use it:

Launch MS something. File>open. Click the Find button. On the Find Window select the drive you want to search and what you want to search for. If you want all the files list leave the search field empty. It will take a while if there are a lot of files on the drive to be searched (4 minutes for 30,000 on beige g3s). The files will list and you can select what to open with read/write privileges.

I'm pretty sure this works because the method of opening the files was not covered in AtEase. There are other examples of this. In a graphic converter, you can go to file>browse folder and look at the drives with read/write access. Same with Netscape (read only). These are all very [strange] methods of opening and browsing the files. I'm sure there are many other applications that are like them. Keep your peepers on the screen, squire.

AtEase PowerBook 3400 Bug

Application: AtEase 4.0

Impact: Disk drives can be corrupted.

Class: Critical

Fix: Upgrade; the fix is out.

Credit: Unknown

If you have a PowerBook 3400 and you are thinking about installing At Ease 4.0, do not enable the floppy disk boot security feature. If you do, your disk volume will become permanently corrupted, and you will be unable to access the disk by any conventional means (including boot floppy, SCSI drives, CD-ROMs, or other methods).

Denial of Service by Port Overflow

Mac OS Versions: 7.1, 7.8

Impact: Attackers can down the machine by port scanning.

Class: Moderate

Fix: Get OpenTransport 1.2.

Credit: VallaH

Mac OS machines running TCP/IP and System 7.1 or System 7.8 are vulnerable to a denial of service (DoS) attack. When these machines are the target of heavy port scanning, they die (7.1 crashes, and 7.8 runs the CPU to 100% utilization). Reportedly, this was repaired in OpenTransport 1.2.

23

DiskGuard Bug

Application: DiskGuard

Impact: DiskGuard 1.5.3 can deny even authorized users access to their disk drives.

Class: Serious

Fix: Upgrade

Credit: Unknown

Sometimes, even security applications create security problems. Such is the case of DiskGuard, an extremely popular security program that restricts access to folders, files, and disk drives. It was quite a surprise, then, when users installed version 1.5.2 and discovered that their disk drives were no longer accessible. *Macworld* took DiskGuard's manufacturer, ASD Software, Inc., to task in an article that discussed the problem. The author, Suzanne Courteau, wrote the following:

> Security software is supposed to keep the bad guys out, but let you in. In some cases, version 1.5.3 of ASD software's DiskGuard was preventing even a system's owner from

accessing their machine. This week the company posted a patch for its security software application; version 1.5.4 fixes several compatibility problems—including locked and inaccessible hard drives—between DiskGuard 1.5.3 and several Mac systems. If you use DiskGuard on a PowerMac 7200, 7500, 8500, or a PowerBook 5300/5300c, ASD's technical support recommends you upgrade. The patch is available directly from ASD Software (909/624-2594) or from the ASD forum on CompuServe (Go ASD).

More solutions to regain access can be found at `http://www.asdsoft.com/Support/Emergency.ssi`.

ASD Software, Inc. can also be contacted at the following:

ASD Software, Inc.

4650 Arrow Highway, Ste. E-6

Montclair, CA 91763

Email: `info@asdsoft.com`

URL: `http://www.asdsoft.com/`

FWB Hard Disk Toolkit 2.5 Vulnerability

Application: FWB Hard Disk Toolkit 2.5

Impact: Removes drivers for protection to access hard drive.

Class: Serious

Fix: Upgrade

Credit: Space Rouge

In an advisory, Space Rouge explains the problem, the exploit, and the fix. In short, replace the driver for the drive. The hard disks locking functionality isn't fully working any more, and the data can be accessed.

▶ The full advisory written by Space Rouge back in 1998 is at `http://www.l0pht.com/advisories/fwb.txt`.

MacDNS Bug

Application: MacDNS

Impact: MacDNS is vulnerable to DoS attacks.

Class: Moderate

Fix: None

Credit: Matt Leo

MacDNS provides Domain Name Service lookup for networks and runs on Macintosh Internet servers. Unfortunately, MacDNS will die when bombarded with requests at high speed. (The problem was initially discovered when a firewall tried to resolve forwards on each and every URL requested. This flooded the MacDNS server with thousands of requests.) This has now been confirmed as a bona fide DoS attack that can be reproduced by remote attackers. Leo suggests packet filtering. Otherwise, contact Apple for further information.

> **NOTE**
>
> Apple has released more documentation on configuration of MacDNS to allow more connections. Full documentation can be found at Apple's Web site, `http://til.info.apple.com/techinfo.nsf/artnum/n22035?OpenDocument&software`.

Network Assistant

Application: Network Assistant

Impact: Remote users can access your drives and network.

Class: Serious

Fix: Change the default password.

The default password for Network Assistant is "ZYZZY". Do us all a favor; change the password so it is not the default.

Password Security on Mac OS 8.0 Upgrades

System: Mac OS 8.0 with PowerBooks 2400 and 3400

Impact: Password protection will not work.

Class: Serious

Fix: Find patch at `http://til.info.apple.com/techinfo.nsf/artnum/n26056`.

Credit: Apple

If you install 8.0 over earlier versions, the Password Control Panel is disabled, and password protection will not work. To remedy this, either install the patch or install 8.0 clean and keep an earlier version with which to boot. Whenever you want to adjust the password settings, boot with the earlier version.

Sequence of Death and WebStar

Application: WebStar and NetCloak combined (not WebStar alone)

Impact: WebStar servers with NetCloak can crash after receiving the Sequence of Death.

Class: Serious

Fix: Remove NetCloak or order an upgrade.

Credit: Jeff Gold

This is a garden-variety DoS vulnerability in early WebStar releases, and has nothing to do with Apple. (In fact, this hole can only be reproduced on a server that is also running NetCloak.) Gold found that if you append certain strings to an URL, the WebStar server will crash. *Macworld* ran a story on this hole, and the folks at that magazine did some testing themselves:

> …for Mac Webmaster Jeff Gold, frustration turned to alarm when he realized that a mere typo caused his entire Mac-served site to crash. Gold's crash occurred while he was using StarNine's WebStar Web server software and the plug-in version of Maxum Development's NetCloak 2.1, a popular WebStar add-on. Adding certain characters to the end of an URL crashes NetCloak, bringing down the server. To protect the thousands of sites using NetCloak, neither Gold nor *Macworld* will publicly reveal the character sequence, but it's one that wouldn't be too difficult to enter. After further investigation, *Macworld* discovered that the problem surfaces only when a server runs the plug-in version of NetCloak. When we removed the plug-in and used the NetCloak CGI instead, the Sequence of Death yielded only a benign error message.

▶ The previous paragraph is excerpted from an article by Jim Heid, titled Mac Web-Server Security Crisis: Specific Character Sequence Crashes Servers. It can be found online at `http://macworld.zdnet.com/daily/daily.973.html`.

NetCloak is manufactured by Maxum Development. You can contact Maxum for upgrade information:

Maxum Development Corporation
P.O. Box 315
Crystal Lake, IL 60039
Phone: 815-444-0100
Fax: 815-444-0301
Email: `info@maxum.com`
URL: `http://www.maxum.com/`

About File Sharing and Security

File sharing is yet another security problem in Mac OS. The degree of the problem depends on what disks and resources are shared out. The Macintosh file sharing system is no less extensive (nor much more secure) than that employed by Microsoft Windows 98.

Sharing can be complex. Your choices will depend on the trust relationships in your organization. Making poor choices can be costly over time. For example, one of my clients runs a telephone solicitation room. In his business, advertising leads are everything. And, because people routinely defect from one company to another, he wanted to take every possible step to secure his databases.

Unfortunately, his network (which included many Macintoshes) was poorly organized. Salespeople had the same level of database access that the copy department did. This allowed salespeople to walk off with valuable ad leads. (And, within several weeks of a defection, his advertisers would be hammered with calls from rival telephone solicitors.)

The programmer who originally set up the network wrote custom client applications for the sales department, which was okay, but he shared out the central file server to everyone. (In other words, clients sent their queries to the file server, and all requests were processed there.) People had been using the system that way for years, and no one wanted to change. My client was in a jam. Ultimately, we solved the program by building him an intranet. The database was moved to a Web server, and I had my co-workers replicate the client interface in HTML.

To prevent disasters like that, you should carefully plot out sharing privileges at the time of installation. (And, naturally, if you don't need file sharing, turn it off. Later in this chapter, I examine programs that can block unauthorized access to folders and control panels, so you can ensure that sharing stays off.) However, perhaps the most important step you can take to keep a Macintosh network secure is this: Educate your users.

Macintosh users are not security fanatics, but that's no crime. Still, a lot of UNIX and Windows NT users ridicule Macintosh users, claiming that they know little about their architecture or operating system. With Apple's release of Mac OSX in 2001, which is based on the BSD platform, that will change. However, we are sure to find new holes and will include OSX as one of many vulnerable platforms. The operating system wars crop up endlessly on Usenet. However, I'll tell you a secret: It's not what operating system you use, but the productivity you demonstrate when using it. The same people who criticize Macintosh users often spend hours (or even days) trying to get their 800MHz machines (and 24meg video cards) to work. They struggle with Plug and Play (which doesn't) and can usually be found with the hood off their box, their hands pressed deep into an endless mess of cables and cards. In contrast, I have only twice seen any of my Macintosh clients with the tops down on their rigs. So, if you use a Macintosh, more power to you.

However, Macintosh users are not very security conscious, and that's a fact. So, anything you can do to change that is wonderful. At the very least, each user should establish a strong password for himself as the owner of the machine. (Macintosh passwords are subject to attack the same as any other password on other platforms.) Finally, (and perhaps most importantly), guest access privileges should be set to inactive.

Mac OS 9 File Security

Mac OS 9 offers many more security features. One of the more notable features is the ability to encrypt and decrypt files using the 56-bit key.

You can encrypt your files on-the-fly. To do so, open the Apple File Security program located in the security folder within the Application folder on the hard disk.

Server Management and Security

Establishing a Web server is a formidable task, but it's nothing compared to maintaining one. This is especially so if the Web server is only a small portion of your network, or if you have to dole out different security privileges to different departments or clients.

There are two paths you can take:

- Hire out for custom programming
- Rely on third-party applications

Custom programming is expensive and time-consuming. If you want to throw up a few Web servers and manage them remotely, I recommend using prefabricated tools for this task. And, if your environment is predominantly Macintosh, the applications that follow are indispensable.

EtherPeek by WildPackets, Inc.

WildPackets, Inc.

2540 Camino Diablo, Suite 200

Walnut Creek, CA 94596

Phone: 800-466-2447

Email: info@wildpackets.com

URL: http://www.wildpackets.com/

WildPackets, Inc., formerly known as AG Group, has the most outstanding network utility around. EtherPeek is a protocol analyzer for Macintosh that supports a wide range of protocols, including but not limited to the following:

- IP
- AppleTalk
- Netware
- IPX/SPX
- NetBEUI
- NetBIOS
- DECnet
- SMB
- OSI TARP

EtherPeek is not your run-of-the-mill protocol analyzer but a well designed commercial sniffer. It includes automatic IP-to-MAC translation, multicasts, real-time statistics, and real-time monitoring. EtherPeek also includes integrated support for handling the LAND denial of service attack that recently took down so many servers. If you are in a corporate environment, this would be a wise purchase.

InterMapper 3.0 by Dartmouth Software Development

Dartmouth Software Development

Dartmouth College

6028 Kiewit Computer Center

Hanover, NH 03755-3523

Phone: 603-646-1999

Email: `Intermapper@dartmouth.edu`

URL: `http://www.dartmouth.edu/netsoftware/intermapper/`

InterMapper (developed by Bill Fisher and Rich Brown) is an excellent tool that can save Macintosh system administrators many hours of work. The application monitors your network for possible changes in topology or failures in service. (Network management is achieved using the Simple Network Management Protocol.)

One especially interesting feature is InterMapper's capability to grab a network snapshot. This is a graphical representation of your network topology. (Network topology is more or less automatically detected, which saves a lot of time.) InterMapper even enables you to distribute snapshots across several monitors for a widened view.

The network snapshot is extremely detailed, enabling you to quickly identify routers that are down or having problems. (You can actually specify how many errors are permissible at the router level. When a particular router exceeds that limit, it is flagged in a different color.) Clicking any element (whether machine or router) will bring up information boxes that report the element's IP address, the traffic it's had, how many errors it's had, and so forth. If there has been trouble at a particular node, you will be paged immediately. In all, InterMapper is a very complete network analysis and management suite.

InterMapper provides simultaneous support for both AppleTalk and IP. Check out the demo version at `http://www.dartmouth.edu/netsoftware/intermapper/demoForm.html`.

MacPork 3.0

MacPork is a small program that enables you to scan a server for tracking holes and exploiting them. MacPork scans more than 271 vulnerabilities and retrieves passwords and information in 175 different manners. MacPork has been designed to find 177 Trojans installed on different servers. MacPork includes an intelligent search engine that can find eventually exploitable servers in two seconds. MacPork knows 66 ways to overflow a system and 86 holes in UNIX protocols (FTP, SMTP, NetBIOS, Finger, Rservices, and RPC). If you are lazy, you can launch

30 simultaneous scans and go to bed. A few hours later, you will have a detailed log. MacPork runs in the background, so that you can do everything else during a scan. An exclamation point icon ("!") in a little window will alert you if MacPork finds something.

Notice that this application is no longer in development; watch the Web site http://freaky.staticusers.net/ for new information.

MacRadius by Cyno

Cyno Technologies, Inc.

1082 Glen Echo Avenue

San Jose, CA 95125

Phone: 408-297-7766

Email: CynoTek@cyno.com

URL: http://www.cyno.com/

RADIUS technology is imperative if you run an ISP or any system that takes dial-in connections. Management of user dial-in services can be difficult, confusing, and time consuming. That's where RADIUS comes in. Authors of the RADIUS specification describe the problem and solution as follows:

> Since modem pools are by definition a link to the outside world, they require careful attention to security, authorization and accounting. This can be best achieved by managing a single "database" of users, which allows for authentication (verifying user name and password) as well as configuration information detailing the type of service to deliver to the user (for example, SLIP, PPP, telnet, rlogin). RADIUS servers are responsible for receiving user connection requests, authenticating the user, and then returning all configuration information necessary for the client to deliver service to the user.

▶ To learn more about RADIUS, you should obtain RFC 2058, which is located at http://info.internet.isi.edu:80/in-notes/rfc/files/rfc2058.txt.

In short, RADIUS offers easy management of a centralized database from which all dial-in users are authenticated. RADIUS implementations also support several different file formats, including native UNIX passed files. Lastly, RADIUS implementations offer baseline logging, enabling you to determine who logged in, when, and for how long.

If you've ever dreamed of having RADIUS functionality for Mac OS, MacRadius is for you. It is a very refined application, offering you the ability to build complex group structures. In this way, adding new users (and having those new users automatically inherit the attributes of other users) is a simple task. And, of course, all of this is packaged in an easy-to-use, graphical environment characteristic of Macintosh applications.

Network Security Guard

MR Mac Software

P.O. Box 910091

San Diego, CA 92191-0091

Download: `http://freaky.staticusers.net/network/NetworkSecurityGuard.sit.hqx`

Have you ever dreamt about SATAN for Mac OS? What about a program that would automatically scan your Mac OS hosts for security vulnerabilities? If so, you need to get Network Security Guard.

Network Security Guard operates over AppleTalk and checks for the following:

- Default passwords
- Accounts without passwords
- File sharing
- File permissions

But wait. There's more. Network Security Guard has a brute force password cracking utility so you can test the strength of network passwords. And your reports can be formatted in several ways and forwarded to you over the network. Lastly, you can schedule timed security assessments. All these features make Network Security Guard a great choice. It can save you many hours of work. (Sorry, this application is a commercial one, not shareware. However, it's well worth the cost.) No official Web site for this product has been found. I'm sure MR Mac is still willing to accept money for the commercial product via U.S. Postal Service.

Oyabun Tools

Team2600.com

Email: `sixtime@team2600.com`

URL: `http://www.team2600.com/`

Oyabun Tools released by Team2600 is an application you can use to send remote commands to control your Mac. For example, if you notice your Macintosh server is slowing down and you are not at the office to reboot it, you can use the Oyabun Send to restart the machine. This program does not require any installation—just double-click! Oyabun Tools consists of two products:

Oyabun Send lets you send shutdown/restart/sleep commands over the Internet to other Macs that already have Oyabun Tools Pro installed.

Oyabun Tools Pro lets you send shutdown/restart/sleep commands to other Macs over the Internet. It also lets you set up Macs to receive these commands. This package has everything that comes in the Oyabun Send package.

Silo 1.0.4

Silo, created by Logik, a Macintosh security guru, is a remote system analysis tool designed for security and administrative evaluation purposes. It features full documentation; remote concept password and file structure generation; network mapping; OS fingerprinting; and remote system, client, administrative, domain, protocol, and network analysis and monitoring.

▶ Logik's home page can be found at `http://logik.accesscard.org/`. Download Silo from `http://freaky.staticusers.net/update.shtml`.

Timbuktu Pro 2000

> Netopia, Inc.
> 2470 Mariner Square Loop
> Alameda, CA 94501
> Email: `pfrankl@netopia.com`
> URL: `http://www.netopia.com/`

Timbuktu Pro 2000 for Mac OS is a powerful and versatile remote computing application. Although not specifically a security program, Timbuktu Pro is a valuable tool for any Web administrator. Timbuktu Pro currently supports TCP/IP, AppleTalk, IPX, and Open Transport. Through these protocols, you can remotely manage any box (or series of them).

Internal Security

Internal security is one of the most important parts of security. Even if your computer is secure from others on the Internet, if someone sits down at your computer for 10 minutes while you are out, your computer is at risk. All your data can be stolen, or your computer can be compromised.

BootLogger

BootLogger is one of the more simple security applications. It basically reads the boot sequence and records startups and shutdowns. It is not a resource-consuming utility. I suggest using this utility first. If evidence of tampering or unauthorized access appears, then I would switch to Super Save.

▶ BootLogger is available at `http://freaky.staticusers.net/security/BootLogger.sit.hqx`.

DiskLocker

DiskLocker is a utility that write-protects your local hard disk drive. Disks are managed through a password-protected mechanism. (In other words, you can only unlock the instant disk if you have the password. Be careful not to lock a disk and later lose your password.) The program is shareware (written by Olivier Lebra in Nice, France) and has a licensing fee of $10.

▶ DiskLocker is available for download from `ftp://ftp.amug.org/`.

Empower by Magna

Magna

1999 S. Bascom, Ste. 700

Campbell, CA 95008

Phone: 408-879-7900

Fax: 408-879-7979

Email: `mailto:sales@magna1.com`

URL: `http://www.magna1.com/`

Empower offers powerful access control for the Macintosh platform, including the ability to restrict access to both applications and folders.

Ferret

Ferret is a small application that quickly gathers all important information (logins/passwords) from a system by descrambling all passwords into plaintext. It is meant to be used with a startup disk, or when you only have a few seconds of access to the machine. You can also drag and drop preferences onto it to get the information you want from a particular file (for example, when you are only able to access a preference file, and cannot directly access the machine).

Ferret can gather important information from preference files on any mounted volume, including AppleShare mounted hard drives. Ferret can discover logins and passwords stored in any of the following applications: FreePPP, MacSLIP, OT/PPP (ARA), Internet Control Panel (Internet Config), Netscape Communicator, Eudora, AIM, ICQ, Gerry's ICQ, Apple File Sharing Registry (Users & Groups), Carracho Bookmarks/Server Data Files, and Hotline Bookmarks/Server Data Files.

▶ Ferret can be downloaded from `http://freaky.staticusers.net/hacking-misc/Ferretv0.0.1b4.sit`.

Filelock

Filelock is a little more incisive than DiskLocker. This utility will actually write-protect individual files or groups of files or folders. It supports complete drag-and-drop functionality and will work on both 68KB and PPC architectures. It's a very handy utility, especially if you share your machine with others in your home or office. It was written by Rocco Moliterno of Italy.

▶ Filelock is available from `http://hyperarchive.lcs.mit.edu/HyperArchive/Archive/disk/filelock-132.hqx`.

FullBack

Highwinds Trading Company, LLC

Telephone: 302-761-9824

Email: support@highwinds.com

URL: http://www.highwinds.com/

Highwinds has been creating security/encryption products since 1999. FullBack is a secure, easy-to-use archiving and backup program. The deluxe version provides 512-bit randomly generated encryption keys. Product information is available at http://www.highwinds.com/ BackupSystem.html.

Invisible Oasis

Invisible Oasis is a keystroke logger. This application records everything typed into a daily log. The extension installed is invisible, as is the folder where the logs are kept. To see whether you have this extension installed, use a program such as Apple ResEdit and go to Get Info. Go into your preference folder, which is in your system folder. Get info on the hidden folder and unhide. You can open the logs with any text-editing program.

▶ Invisible Oasis is available for download at http://freaky.staticusers.net/security/ keyloggers/InvisibleOasis_Installer.sit.

ResEdit can be found by searching for it on http://www.VersionTracker.com

KeysOff and KeysOff Enterprise

Blue Globe Software

P.O. Box 8171

Victoria, British Columbia

V8W 3R8, Canada

Email: cliffmcc@blueglobe.com

URL: http://www.blueglobe.com/~cliffmcc/products.html

KeysOff enables you to lock out certain keys, preventing malicious users from accessing the menu bar, mouse clicks, the power key, and command-key shortcuts. (The program also prevents unauthorized users from loading disks.) This is one of the most simple, cost-effective, and useful security programs available.

LockOut

Maui Software

Email: development@mauisoftware.com

URL: http://www.mauisoftware.com/#LockOut

LockOut is an easy-to-use application. It does not offer full security but is cost effective.

MacPassword

The industry standard for full password protection on Mac OS, MacPassword is a fully developed commercial application. It not only provides multiple levels of password protection (for both disk and screen), but it also incorporates virus scanning technology. It's definitely worth the money. However, you can always check it out free. The demo version is available at many locations across the Internet. MacPassword is available from ftp://rever.nmsu.edu/pub/macfaq/MacPasswordDemo.sit.bin.

OnGuard Emergency Passwords

Several security programs use emergency passwords. These are passwords generated by the program in case the admin forgets his password. They usually give the user complete access to a computer.

In theory, you'll need all sorts of software registration information for the software vendor to give away the emergency password. In reality, you only need to find the algorithm used to be able to generate the emergency password.

nOGuard is a program that generates emergency passwords for PowerOn Software's OnGuard 3.1 and 3.3. It was created by Prozaq of mSec.

▶ The most up-to-date version is available for download at http://freaky.staticusers.net/security/onguard/nOGuard2.sit.

Password Key

CP3 Software

P.O. Box 4722

Huntsville, AL 35815-4722

Email: carl@cp3.com

URL: http://www.cp3.com/

Password Key logs unauthorized access attempts, locks applications, and temporarily suspends all system operations until a correct password is supplied.

23

MACINTOSH

Password Security Control Panel Emergency Password

PowerBook users can use the Password Security Control Panel to protect their computers. Displaying a dialog box that requests a password every time the hard drive is mounted, Password Security provides a convenient security measure.

As pointed out by a previous advisory, Password Security generates an emergency password every time it displays the password dialog box. This emergency password gives the same access level to the laptop as the owner's password does.

This is, of course, a huge security breach, allowing anyone who can figure out the emergency password to access the computer and even to change the owner's password. The program PassSecGen (created by Prozaq, a member of the Macintosh security group mSec) generates the emergency passwords for the PowerBook security control panel.

▶ The most up-to-date version of the Password Security Generator is available for download at `http://freaky.staticusers.net/security/powerbook/PassSecGen1.0.sit`.

Secure-It Locks

Secure-It, Inc.

18 Maple Court

East Longmeadow, MA 01028

Phone: (800) 451-7592 or 413-525-7039

Email: `secure-it@secure-it.com`

URL: `http://secure-it.com/`

Secure-It, Inc., provides physical security products for the Macintosh, including disk drive locks. These prevent anyone from loading unauthorized code onto your machine while you're away from your console. (They make them for PowerBooks, too.)

Super Save 2.02

For the ultimate paranoiac, Super Save will record every single keystroke forwarded to the console. However, in a thoughtful move, the author chose to include an option with which you can disable this feature whenever passwords are being typed in, thus preventing the possibility of someone else later accessing your logs (through whatever means) and getting that data. Although not expressly designed for security's sake (more for data crash and recovery), this utility provides the ultimate in logging.

▶ Super Save is available at `ftp://ftp.amug.org/pub/amug/bbs-in-a-box/files/recent/supersave-2.02.sit.hqx`.

Password Crackers and Related Utilities

The following utilities are popular password crackers or related utilities for use on Macintosh. Some are made specifically to attack Macintosh-oriented files. Others are designed to crack UNIX password files. This is not an exhaustive list, but rather is a sample of the more interesting tools freely available on the Internet.

> **NOTE**
>
> Many of the applications that crack FileMaker Pro files are version specific. There has not been a crack for recent versions of FileMaker Pro in years. If you find a old FMP file on disk and it is protected, the FMP-cracking applications in this section would be useful.

FirstClass Thrash!

This is an interesting collection of utilities, primarily designed for the purpose of conducting warfare over (or against) a FirstClass BBS. It has features that could be easily likened to Maohell. These include mailbombing tools, denial of service tools, and other assorted scripts useful in harassing one's enemies. It's primarily used in warfare.

▶ FirstClass Thrash! is located at `http://freaky.staticusers.net/attack/FCThrash.sit`.

FMP Password Viewer Gold 2.0

FMP Password Viewer Gold 2.0 is another utility for cracking FileMaker Pro files. It offers slightly more functionality (and is certainly newer) than FMProPeeker 1.1.

▶ FMP Password Viewer Gold 2.0 is available at `http://freaky.staticusers.net/cracking/FMP3.0ViewerGold2.0.sit.hqx`.

FMProPeeker 1.1

This utility cracks FileMaker Pro files. FileMaker Pro is a database solution from Claris (`http://www.claris.com`). Although more commonly associated with the Macintosh platform, FileMaker Pro now runs on a variety of systems. It is available for shared database access on Windows NT networks, for example. In any event, FMProPeeker subverts the security of FileMaker Pro files.

▶ FMProPeeker is available at `http://freaky.staticusers.net/cracking/FMProPeeker.sit.hqx`.

Killer Cracker

Killer Cracker is a Macintosh port of Killer Cracker, a password cracker formerly run only on DOS- and UNIX-based machines.

MacKrack

MacKrack is a port of Muffet's famous Crack 4.1. It is designed to crack UNIX passwords. It rarely comes with dictionary files, but still works quite well and makes cracking UNIX `/etc/passwd` files a cinch. (It has support for both 68KB and PPC.)

▶ MacKrack is located at `http://freaky.staticusers.net/cracking/MasterKrack1.0b14.sit`.

MagicKey 3.2.3a

Made by System Cowboy of the hacker group Digital-Rebels.org, MagicKey is a password-auditing tool for AppleTalk. The application audits an AppleTalk user's file for weak passwords or no passwords with the brute-force method.

▶ MagicKey3.2.3a can be downloaded from `http://freaky.staticusers.net/security/auditing/MK3.2.3a.sit`.

MasterKeyII

MasterKeyII is yet another FileMaker Pro–cracking utility.

▶ MasterKeyII is available at the following site in Las Vegas: `http://freaky.staticusers.net/cracking/MasterKeyII1.0b2.sit.hqx`.

McAuthority

McAuthority is a password-security application that uses brute force to attack a server to gain access to the password-protected areas. This application was made by nulle, one of the greatest Mac hack programmers. His Web site went down, and I have not been able to get in contact with him.

▶ McAuthority can be downloaded from `http://freaky.staticusers.net/jp/McAuth1.0d6-FAT.sit`.

Meltino

Meltino is a sleekly designed UNIX password cracker by the Japanese programmer nulle. This is one of the most popular Macintosh UNIX password crackers. This application supports MD5 encryption as well as DES encryption. Meltino also supports the UltraFastCrypt (UFC) algorithm.

▶ Meltino 2.0.1 can be downloaded at `http://freaky.staticusers.net/cracking/Meltino/Meltino2.01_PPC.sit.bin`.

PassFinder

PassFinder is a password-cracking utility used to crack the administrator password on older FirstClass systems. This is an important utility as many FirstClass Bulletin Board Systems (BBS) are still running older versions of the software because of the cost of upgrades. The program suite FirstClass is a gateway system, commonly used for serving email, UUCP, and even news (NNTP). In essence, FirstClass (which can be found at `http://www.softarc.com/`) is a total solution for mail, news, and many other types of TCP/IP–based communication systems. It is a popular system on the Mac OS platform. (It even has support for Gopher servers and FTP and can be used to operate a full-fledged BBS.) Because FirstClass servers exist not only on outbound Internet networks, but also on intranets, PassFinder is a critical tool. By cracking the administrator password, a user can seize control of the system's incoming and outgoing electronic communications. (However, this must be done on the local machine. That is, the user must have access to the console of the instant machine. This is not a remote cracking utility.)

▶ PassFinder is available at `http://www.neverness.net/archives/hacking/applications/PassFinder.sit`.

> **TIP**
>
> Apparently, FirstClass 2.7 does not provide a facility for recording or logging IP addresses. (Reportedly, this simple hole exists in earlier versions.) Therefore, an attack on such a server can be performed in a fairly liberal fashion.

Password Killer

Password Killer is designed to circumvent the majority of PowerBook security programs.

▶ Password Killer (also referred to as PowerBook Password Killer) can be found online at `http://freaky.staticusers.net/cracking/Passwordkiller.sit.hqx`.

Anonymous Email and Mailbombing

Sometimes you have to send anonymous email. There are things you don't want people seeing and knowing it came from you. Caem lets you send mail anonymously.

▶ Logik, the programmer of Caem, takes his work seriously and updates the program often. You can find updates and news at `http://freaky.staticusers.net/reviews/caem3.html`.

Mailbombing is the act of sending a lot of email to a person to flood his mailbox. One of the newest, more effective mailbombers is entitled Bomba. I do not suggest sending a mailbomb to anyone. Try sending it to yourself to see how it works. If you have ever received a mailbomb, you understand.

Bomba is available for download at `http://www.team2600.con` or at `http://freaky.staticusers.net/attack/mailbombing/bomba.sit`.

Macintosh OSX

With the release of Mac OSX, we will be seeing a lot of new security vulnerabilities. Sites like SecureMac.com will be sure to cover them.

There are a few security applications already out for the new OS like Brian Hill's firewall configuration utility BrickHouse. With the OS X interface, you can edit the settings to the firewall to allow/deny specific ports and IP addresses. For a review, go to `http://www.securemac.com/brickhouse.cfm`.

I suggest reading the document by Peter Heins titled *Secure Installation of OSX* at `http://www.securemac.com/osxsecurity.cfm`.

Apple has also prepared a article on making OSX a bit more secure. It is located at `http://til.info.apple.com/techinfo.nsf/artnum/n60112`.

Apple's OSX is sure to open new opportunities for hackers since the OS is based on the BSD (UNIX) platform. Sites like `www.securityfocus.com` will list security issues that affect Mac OSX because of the structure of BSD platform.

Tools Designed Specifically for America Online

I remember back in the days when AOL was well known for its rooms like MacFilez, MacWarez, and Zelifcam. All those were warez chat rooms on AOL where users and groups such as NEO would freely trade illegally registered files also known as *warez*. After the Internet was integrated into AOL 3.0 and crackdowns happened, everyone moved off of AOL to Hotline and IRC. All the tools and scripts that were used are at one location: `http://freaky.staticusers.net/aol/`. I don't suggest using these programs. Your AOL account might be terminated because, in using these programs, you might violate their terms of service agreement.

Summary

In general the Mac OS is more secure than other operating systems because the main security focus in recent years has been on other platforms.

But be careful in thinking that your Macintosh is secure! For every hack that exists for the PC, there is an equivalent hack for the Mac OS. Don't believe me? Take a look at the Mac Hacking CD-ROM Freaks Macintosh Archives Hackintosh v1. It's packed with hacking and security tools, as well as with their exploits, and textfiles to learn more. The CD-ROM even has the Macintosh Security speech from Defcon 7 (a yearly hacking conference held in Las Vegas) in mp3 and Real Video. And with the release of Mac OS X, we are bound to find many more security holes.

Resources

The following list of resources contains important links related to Macintosh security. You'll find a variety of resources, including books, articles, and Web sites.

Books and Reports

Secure Installation of OSX. This article written by `mpetey@securemac.com` is a good paper to have on hand when installing OSX. Security will become more of an issue as the hackers get to play around with OSX. The article is available at `http://www.securemac.com/osxsecurity.cfm`.

The $10,000 Macintosh World Wide Web Security Challenge: A Summary of the Network and the Attacks. Chris Kilbourn. digital.forest. (Formatting provided by Jon Wiederspan.) Available at `http://www.forest.net/news/challenge.html.`*mpetey@securemac.com*`http://www.securemac.com/osxsecurity.cfm`

Macintosh Security Auditing. This article explains different tools that can be used to audit your network for security problems. One of the main points of the article is that commercial auditing programs do not exist for the Macintosh, so you can use the efficient, free tools that were made by hackers. The article is at `http://www.securemac.com/secauditing.cfm`.

Macintosh Security Internet Basics. Sans.org published this excellent white paper. Written by Patrick Harris, this document covers the basics of Macintosh security. It can be viewed at `http://www.sans.org/infosecFAQ/mac_sec.htm`.

Macs & CableModems. Everyone has heard about the security issues of cable modems and that cable modem networks are easy targets to be scanned. If you use a cable modem at home or at work, read up on this issue at `http://www.securemac.com/secauditing.cfm`.

Make Your Mac Hacker-Proof. An excellent article to motivate users to use firewall software to protect their Macintoshes. Also includes some safety strategies for configuration of the firewall. See it at `http://macworld.zdnet.com/2000/07/features/online_security_sb2.html`

Connections and Protections—Cable and DSL Connections and Security Measures. Peter N. Heins (`mpetey@securemac.com`) describes the difference between DSL and cable and covers security aspects of what the snoopers can see and how. `http://www.securemac.com/dslcable.cfm`

Apple has set up a developer area devoted to implementation of security on its Web site, `http://devworld.apple.com/Mac OS/security.html`.

Many firewall documents for the Mac OS can be found at the Firewall Guide Mac OS section, `http://www.firewallguide.com/macintosh.htm`.

How Macs Work. John Rizzo and K. Daniel Clark. Ziff-Davis Press. ISBN: 1-56276-146-3.

Voodoo Mac. Kay Yarborough Nelson. Ventana Press. ISBN: 1-56604-028-0.

Sad Macs, Bombs, and Other Disasters. Ted Landau. Addison-Wesley Publishing Company. ISBN: 0-201-62207-6.

The Whole Mac Solutions for the Creative Professional. Daniel Giordan, et al. Hayden Books. ISBN: 1-56830-298-3. 1996.

Building and Maintaining an Intranet with the Macintosh. Tobin Anthony. Hayden Books. ISBN: 1-56830-279-7. 1996.

Sites with Tools and Munitions

Freaks Macintosh Archives. Warez, security, cracking, hacking. `http://freaky.staticusers.net/`

CIAC U.S. Department of Energy. `http://ciac.llnl.gov/ciac/ToolsMacVirus.html`

SecureMac.com security site. `http://www.securemac.com/`

Macman's Mac site. `http://www.macman.net/`

Neverness.net. hacking, phreaking, crypto. `http://www.neverness.net/`

AOL Specific Tools. Hacking and cracking utilities for use on America Online. `http://freaky.staticusers.net/aol/`

Hacking Mac's Heaven! Hacking and cracking tools and links from the Netherlands. `http://macheaven.terrashare.com/`

E-Zines

Macinstein. The ultimate Macintosh resource site on the Net. Search engine, Daily Mac News, Sherlock plug-in, press releases, top sites, message boards, polls, contests and more! *Macinstein* now has free Web pages for Mac enthusiasts. `http://www.macinstein.com/`

MacCentral. Extensive and very well presented online periodical about Macintosh. `http://www.maccentral.com/`

Macintosh Networking Guide. Good About.com Networking guide for the Mac OS. Try setting up your own small network with the help of this article! `http://machardware.about.com/compute/machardware/msubnetworkguides.htm`

MacHome Journal Online. Good, solid Internet magazine on Macintosh issues. `http://www.machome.com/`

SecureMac.com. Macintosh security news and advisories. `http://www.securemac.com/`

MacAssistant Tips and Tutorial Newsletter and User Group. A very cool, useful, and, perhaps most importantly, brief newsletter that gives tips and tricks for Mac users. Commercial, but I think it is well worth it. A lot of traditional hacking tips on hardware, software, and special, not-often-seen problems. These are collected from all over the world. $12 per year. `http://www.macassistant.com/`

MacFixIt.com. Troubleshooting solutions for the Macintosh. If there's a issue with anything Macintosh related, you'll find it here. This site has very active responsive message boards for good technical interaction. `http://www.macfixit.com/`

MacDirectory. This full-color magazine with daily e-news featuring press releases, news, product info, and much more is a must for all true Mac peepz. It frequently covers security issues dealing with firewalls and networking.

MacSlash. MacSlash is a well-organized Macintosh-specific site. This site utilizes the Slashcode, which is the same code used by Slashdot.org. Well worth a daily visit! `http://www.macslash.com/`

MacTech. Well-presented and important industry and development news. You will likely catch the latest dope on new security releases here first. Also, some very cool technical information. `http://www.mactech.com/`

Happle. The Macintosh underground e-zine dedicated to Macintosh hacking, warez, and much more—11 issues of jam-packed Happle! This publication was started by a Macintosh hacker named hackmak, and then soon after taken over by Jambo. Jambo is the only machacker I know who wears a skirt. Seriously though, Jambo is from Scotland, and he plays a bagpipe. To this day, his e-zine *Happle* is the most downloaded Mac hack zine around. Each issue is filled with articles ranging from coding, phreaking, and cellphones tohacking, cheats, and warez. If you're interested in Macintosh hacking, this would be a good site to read. `http://freaky.staticusers.net/textfiles/zines/Happle/` or `http://jambo.accesscard.org/`

23

MACINTOSH

VAX/VMS

IN THIS CHAPTER

Although the world of VMS is a bit dated, VAX/VMS machines are by no means extinct. This chapter goes over some of the security features for VMS, and includes a short catch-up course for those unfamiliar with the platform. Even if you do not administer or maintain VAX/VMS systems, you might find this chapter somewhat useful, if for no other reason than the VAX's relevance in computing history.

The History of the VAX

To begin the lesson, I will start with a brief overview of the rise of Digital Equipment Corporation (DEC), the company that manufactured the once-popular product, the VAX (virtual address extension).

In one way or another, DEC has always been there at critical moments in computer history. (You might recall that Ken Thompson was first hacking UNIX on a DEC PDP-10.)

▶ To appreciate just how long DEC has been delivering computer products to the industry, take a moment to catch this link: `http://www.crowl.org/Lawrence/history/`.

This link will take you to Lawrence Crowl's wonderful computer history page, which shows photographs of machines that mark milestones in our computer culture (starting with the very first computer ever constructed by Charles Babbage, circa 1823). The first DEC PDP-1 appears on that page.

To get a full-screen view of that machine, catch this link:
`http://www.cs.orst.edu/~crowl/history/dec_pdp1_2.full.jpg`.

The machine looks, quite frankly, like a prop in some terrible B movie from the 1950s—something you would expect to see in a mad scientist's laboratory. DEC quickly moved on to produce a wide range of products, including the very first minicomputer—the DEC PDP-8.

▶ You can see this machine on Mr. Crowl's page as well, located full size at
`http://www.crowl.org/Lawrence/history/dec_pdp8.full.jpg`.

In 1978, DEC created the first VAX, the Digital VAX 11/780. This machine offered 32-bit architecture and 1MIPS performance. By standards of the day, the 11/780 was powerful and fast. (It was also backward compatible with the PDP line that preceded it.) The price tag? A mere $200,000.

NOTE

MIPS stands for so many million instructions per second.

Curiously, the 11/780 became so popular that it would establish itself as the benchmark machine for the MIPS index. In other words, it became the yardstick by which to measure performance of all workstations that followed. (This occurred despite the fact that the IBM 370/158 was reportedly comparable in terms of speed and processing power. The IBM 370/158 never reached the popularity status of the 11/780.)

To reiterate, the 11/780 was a $200,000 machine that could carry out roughly 1 million instructions per second. Fantastic. Today, if you were to advertise this machine for sale on the Internet, you would have to pay the buyer to haul it away. It is considered by today's standards either junk or, perhaps more charitably, a collector's item. However, one thing made the 11/780 a special innovation and still singles it out from other machines in computer history: The 11/780 could support two operating systems. One was a system—UNIX—that was known reasonably well at the time. The other system was something a little different. It was called VMS (Virtual Memory System). We will be examining VMS in just a moment. First, however, I want to give you an idea of what the VAX is all about.

The VAX is a multiuser system. Many readers might not be old enough to remember the VAXstations, so I'll offer a little description. The MicroVAX stands nearly three feet tall. On the right side of the machine is a panel that, when opened, reveals the cards. These cards are quite large, although not nearly as large as the panels of, say, a SPARCstation 4/330 VME deskside computer (but certainly larger than most modern motherboards for personal computers).

The terminal is a VT220, with a viewing screen of approximately 8½ inches. At the back of the terminal are various connectors. These include a data lead connection, a printer connection, and a serial port. The serial port can be set to an amazing 19200 baud and terminal emulations available included VT220 and VT100. If you connect a modem to the terminal, you have to set modem commands by hand. (In other words, you would have to send raw modem commands from a blank screen that sports a blinking cursor. As an example, you would typically dial by issuing the command `ATDT5551212`.)

Firmware is contained within the terminal. This is software hard-coded into the board itself. (PC users should think of firmware in exactly the same way as the CMOS. It is a small software module that performs a limited number of tasks, including setting the machine's parameters.) Unfortunately, there is no facility by which to capture a figure of the screen, so I must describe it. When the terminal boots, you are presented with a copyright screen and then a blank screen with a blinking cursor. The terminal is then ready to accept commands. To manipulate the settings in the firmware, you choose the F3 (function 3 or Setup) key. This brings up a menu at the bottom of the screen where you can review and change various settings. These include not only the way that communications are conducted, but also how the screen is laid out and behaves. For example, you have a choice of either an amber background and a black foreground or the reverse. You can specify a typewriter keyboard or data mode, which is more commonly used when interfacing directly with the VAX. You can also manipulate the number of characters per line and lines per screen. (Additionally, the firmware has short help messages embedded within it. These generally appear at the bottom of the screen, in the status area, as do the setting values for each facet of your environment. These can indicate which printer you are using, whether you want local echo, whether you want type-ahead mode, and so forth.) No mouse, hard disk drive, floppy drive, or other components are either present or required.

You have a wide range of choices regarding communication. For example, you can change the bits (typically 7 or 8) and also the parity of these (none, odd, or even). This makes the VT220 terminal valuable not only to interface with VAXen (slang for VAX machines), but also a wide variety of UNIX machines. For example, you can use a VT220 terminal as a "head" for a workstation that otherwise has no monitor. Plugging the terminal into the first serial port of the workstation will generally do this. (For most versions of UNIX, you generally need to strip the eighth bit.)

TIP

For Linux hackers: You can also "add" an Internet node to your box using such a terminal. To do so, you plug the terminal into either COM1 or COM2. You then edit `inittab` to respawn another instance of `getty` on that port. For this to work, you need to ensure that the cable used is a null modem cable. You also should set the emulation to VT100. When the Linux box reboots, a login prompt will appear on the VT220. From there, log in as any valid user, and you are ready. This is significantly valuable, especially if you are trying to train someone in programming or navigation of the Net via a CLI (command line interface). It is important to note that, if you are using the same COM port that normally supports your mouse, you need to kill `gpm` (general purpose mouse) support.

These terminals, although intended for use with the VAX, can also be used as the most inexpensive method ever of accessing the Internet. Naturally, you need an old-style dial-up connection to do so (perhaps via Delphi), but there is no comparison to the price. Such terminals can now be purchased for $20. Add to this the price of a 19200 baud modem, and you are done. They are also great for connecting to local BBSs.

TIP

Such a terminal does not have environment variables per se and therefore reports none. All the environment variables are obtained from whatever shell you happen to acquire on the remote machine.

These terminals are used to connect to the VAX. (Note, too, that I have described only very early implementations of VT terminals. Much later models support various types of colors and graphics not available to the early VT100 and VT220 terminals. These newer models are extremely functional but can run as high as several hundred dollars. Good examples are the VT330 and VT340.)

Finally, you can connect to a VAX without such a terminal. Typically, this is done using PC software that supports VT100 terminal emulation. (Kermit is another popular and compatible emulation.)

VMS

The VMS operating system is unique, but bears similarities to several others. Logging in works much as it does on a UNIX system. You are presented with a login prompt (`Username:`) and a password prompt. If you enter the correct information, you are dropped to a prompt represented by a dollar sign (`$`). You are also given a series of values when you log in, including your username, your process ID, and so forth.

Some common VMS commands are listed in Table 24.1.

TABLE 24.1   Common VMS Commands

Command	Purpose
HELP [args]	If issued alone (without arguments), this command will bring up the prompt Topic. The HELP command is generally followed by whatever command you want to learn about.
COPY [arg1 arg2]	Will copy an existing file or files to another file or directory.
DIRECTORY	Works very much like the DOS command dir, giving the contents of a directory and the attributes associated with the files therein.
MAIL	Invokes the email program interface for VAX. This works (roughly) like standard mail in UNIX. When preparing to compose a message, you are prompted for recipient and subject.
LOOK	The VAX equivalent to the UNIX command ps, LOOK shows you your current processes.

24

VAX/VMS

TIP

There is a nice table of command translations from VAX to UNIX. The table has been around for a while and basically offers UNIX users and others a brief reference. It is located at `http://www.geek-girl.com/Unixhelp/VMStoUNIX.html`. You might want to take a brief look at Table 24.1 because you will see some of these commands throughout the chapter.

VMS has many of the amenities of other operating systems. The commands might be just slightly different. For example, the C shell in UNIX has a facility that will recall commands previously typed at the prompt. This facility is called `history`. (DOS has a similar command module, usually loaded at boot time, called `DOSkey`.) In VMS, you can recall commands recently typed by holding down Ctrl+B. There are other control key combinations that will stop a process, list all processes, resume a process, report current user statistics, and edit the current command line.

There are still many VAX servers on the Internet, and VMS is still very much alive. The newest version, called OpenVMS, is available for both VAX and Alpha machines. Alphas are extremely fast workstations (now at speeds exceeding 1000Mhz) that can run OpenVMS, Linux, or Tru64/Digital UNIX.

The majority of VAX servers on the Net are older. Many are machines located at university libraries. These provide users with facilities for searching electronic card catalogs. In all likelihood, most older VAX machines are at least as secure as their UNIX workstation counterparts. One contributing factor to this trend is the fact that the people who administer it generally understand the VMS platform. If there is a hole in a VMS system it is most likely because the system administrator was either lazy and left it unpatched, or botched a configuration option.

Security in VMS

Security in VMS is well supported. For example, there is a strong model for access control. (Whether the system administrator properly implements that access control is another matter.) Access control on VMS is at least as comprehensive as that on the Novell NetWare platform. Here are some of the values that can be controlled:

- **Time.** You can control both the days of the week and the hours of the day at which a user can access a given area of the system. (The default setting enables the user access at any time, 24 hours a day, 7 days a week.) The time access feature works similarly to a firewall: That which is not expressly permitted is denied.

- **Mode.** This is an interesting feature. You can specify the mode in which a user can connect and interact with the system. Therefore, you can restrict remote network logins to certain times or eliminate them completely. Because this can be done incisively by user, this feature makes remote security much stronger than on many other platforms. You can hardly begin to crack if you are restricted from even logging in. (Next, we'll discuss some utilities that also force callback verification on remote dial-up users.)

- **Resources.** You can control the resources available to the user at login. This is useful for setting directories beyond which the user might not be able to travel.

This is really just scratching the surface of the access control available in VMS. In fact, there are multiple levels of privileges, and these can be applied to groups. Groups can be restricted to certain resources, and so on. In other words, access control is a complex issue with VMS. There are many, many options. It is for this reason that crackers have a halfway decent chance of finding a hole. Sometimes, complexity can be a security risk in itself. Crackers are well aware of this:

> The greatest advantage of VMS is its flexibility. The system manager can choose to implement or ignore a wide range of security features, fortunately for the [cracker], they all seem to ignore the important ones. It is possible to protect all, any or none of the files created. It is also possible to provide general or restricted passwords, or no passwords at all. Access codes can be global or limited. The use log can be ignored, used only for record keeping, or be employed as a security control tool.

▶ The previous paragraph is excerpted from Lex Luthor's Advanced Hacking VAX's VMS (Legion of Doom. June 1, 1985). It can be found online at `http://www.linealtap.8m.com/vax-lod.html`.

NOTE

It should be noted that the use of groups differs between UNIX and VMS. ACLs, in combination with VMS groups, allow for more granular control over files, directories, volumes, and so on.

Advanced Hacking VAX's VMS is one of the definitive texts on cracking the VMS system. It was authored by Lex Luthor (an alias, of course), who in 1984 established a bulletin board called the Legion of Doom. From this (and through other means), Luthor gathered together a loosely knit cracker group that went by the same name. Legion of Doom pulled off some of the most extraordinary cracks ever done. LoD published many electronic journals on the Internet that simplified the art of cracking, including the LoD Technical Journal. The federal government waged a fleetingly successful war against members of the group. The infamous group is long gone, and today, the activities of the former LoD members are a little piece of Internet folklore.

▶ Perhaps one of the best documents available on the Internet for information on how to secure a VMS box was written by neither a cracker nor a hacker. It is A Practical Exercise in Securing an OpenVMS System, written by Rob McMillan of Prentice Centre, the University Of Queensland. It can be found at `ftp://ftp.sunet.se/pub/security/csir/auscert/papers/Practical.Exercise.Securing.OpenVMS.txt`.

Attacking a VAX (or any VMS-based system) is quite different from attacking a UNIX system. First, the concept of the password file is different and so is its structure. UNIX systems maintain `/etc/passwd`, which defines the username, password, login shell, and group. In contrast, the VMS system uses a file that defines many other variables, not simply these values, as described in the following:

> Every DEC running VMS holds the user profiles in a file called SYSUAF (System User Authorization File). For every user on the system, including the System Manager, there is a record which tells the computer when and how a user can log onto the system. It also gives details of password aging, password lengths and all the facilities that a user has when they are logged on.
>
> *The Five Minute Guide to VMS Security: Product Review PC-DEC-AUDIT*. AudIT Magazine. 1994.

This comprehensive approach to the password file has its pitfalls. If a cracker gains access to the file and cracks it (using the utilities described later in this chapter), the whole system is subject to breach, then and there. However, the likelihood of that happening is poor.

The user, by the way, is identified through the use of a user identification code (UIC). This is very similar in ways to the UID in UNIX. It identifies the user and what groups that user might belong to. As you might have guessed, the UIC comes from the centralized database:

> When you log in to a system, the operating system copies your UIC from your user authorization (UAF) record in the system user authorization file (SYSUAF.DAT) and assigns it to your process. It serves as an identification for the life of the process.

▶ The previous paragraph is excerpted from OpenVMS Guide to System Security: Contents of a User's Security Profile. 4.1.1.3 How Your Process Acquires a UIC, which can be found online at `http://wawona.ethz.ch/OpenVMS_docu/721final/6346/6346pro_005.html #index_x_453`.

In 1993, a version of VMS called SEVMS was approved as meeting the criteria for a Class B1 secure operating system. Although the version approved (v6.2) is nowhere close to the latest version of VMS, nor do many organizations outside of the government adhere to this rating system, it's worth mentioning because few operating systems meet this criteria.

▶ You can read more about SEVMS at `http://www.openvms.digital.com/openvms/Security.html`.

Some Old Vulnerabilities

A discussion of some common vulnerabilities, or *holes*, follows.

The `mount d` Hole

If two successive `mount -d -s` commands are sent within seconds of one another (and before another host has issued such a request), the request will be honored. This was originally reported by CERT in March 1994 and applies to VAX machines running any variant of Digital UNIX.

The Monitor Utility Hole

In VMS there is a utility called Monitor, which monitors classes of systemwide performance data (either from a process already running or from a previously compiled monitor file). The following vulnerability was not a critical one, but did bear some concern:

> Unauthorized privileges may be expanded to authorized users of a system under certain conditions, via the Monitor utility. Should a system be compromised through unauthorized access, there is a risk of potential damage to a system environment. This problem will not permit unauthorized access entry, as individuals attempting to gain unauthorized access will continue to be denied through the standard VMS security mechanisms.

▶ The above paragraph is excerpted from a CERT advisory titled VMS Monitor Vulnerability. It can be found online at `http://www.cert.org/advisories/CA-92.18.VMS.Monitor.vulnerability.update.html`.

The monitor problem was a local problem and not a particularly critical one. For specific information on that hole (and the fix), obtain the Defense Data Network Advisory concerning it at DDN Security Bulletin 9223, `http://csrc.nist.gov/secalert/ddn/1992/sec-9223.txt`.

Historical Problems: The Wank Worm Incident

Sometime in the fall of 1989, a worm that compromised machines on DecNet was released. On infected machines, the program would print to the terminal a message that the machine had been "Wanked." The message purported to come from Worms Against Nuclear Killers, or WANK. It was reported in the CERT advisory about the Wank Worm:

> This worm affects only DEC VMS systems and is propagated via DecNet protocols, not TCP/IP protocols [as at the time DEC didn't support TCP/IP natively]. If a VMS system had other network connections, the worm was not programmed to take advantage of those connections. The worm is very similar to last year's HI.COM (or Father Christmas) worm.

▶ The previous paragraph is paraphrased from a CERT advisory titled "WANK" Worm On SPAN Network. It can be found online at `http://www.cert.org/advisories/CA-89.04.decnet.wank.worm.html`.

In that advisory, an analysis of the worm was provided by R. Kevin Oberman of the Engineering Department of Lawrence Livermore National Laboratory. Oberman's report was apparently generated on-the-fly and in haste, but it was quite complete notwithstanding. He reported that the worm was not incredibly complex but could be dangerous if it compromised a privileged account. The worm would enter a system, check to see whether it was already infected, and, if not, perform some or all of these procedures:

- Disable mail to certain accounts

- Change system passwords, using a random-number generator, and, in doing so, lock out the system operator
- Use the instant system as a launching pad to attack new ones

Within his analysis, Oberman included a quickly hacked program that would halt the march of the Wank Worm. The source of that program can still be examined online in the original advisories at http://www.cert.org/advisories/CA-89.04.decnet.wank.worm.html.

What's really interesting is the degree of seriousness in the tone of the advisory. Think about it for a moment: It was just less than one year before that the Morris Worm incident sent a ripple through the Net. The mere mention of a worm during those months could cause a panic. Oddly, though, because of the curious name of this particular worm, some administrators initially took the warnings for a joke.

In addition, the Wank Worm was irrelevant to a large portion of the Internet. Because the worm only affected those running DEC protocols (and not TCP/IP), only a limited number of potential victims existed. However, although that number was relatively small in proportion to the entire Internet, there were a great many sites using DecNet.

An interesting treatment of the event can be found in *Approaching Zero: The Extraordinary Underworld of Hackers, Phreakers, Virus Writers, and Keyboard Criminals*:

> The arrival of the worm coincided with reports of protesters in Florida attempting to disrupt the launch of a nuclear-powered shuttle payload. It is assumed that the worm was also a protest against the launch. The WANK Worm spread itself at a more leisurely rate than the Internet Worm, sending out fewer alarms and creating less hysteria....A method for combating the worm was developed by Bernard Perrot of the Institut de Physique Nucleaire at Orsay, France. Perrot's scheme was to create a booby-trapped file of the type that the worm could be expected to attack. If the worm tried to use information from the file, it would itself come under attack and be blown up and killed.

▶ The previous excerpt is from an article by Paul Mungo and Bryan Glough. It can be found online at http://www.ut.ee/ri98/villem/approaching_zero.html.

Auditing and Monitoring

Auditing capabilities in the VMS environment are advanced. There are different ways to implement auditing—implementation is usually dependent on the applications and the system administrator's personal preferences. However, by default, VMS will log all logins, failures to login, changes in system privileges, and so forth. The default configuration provides a minimum of logging.

That minimum, however, can be quickly surpassed if need be. The system operator can apply special access controls on individual files and directories, a user account, or processes. When undesirable or suspicious activity occurs in relation to these access control policies, an alarm is generated. The system operator defines what form the alarm will take. (For example, it is common for system operators to redirect alarm information to a specific console so that such messages visibly appear and can be quickly perused at any time.) Of course, severe paranoia in this type of environment can add up to sacrificing a fair amount of disk space.

For example, a system operator can configure the system to generate alarms on a mere attempt to access a file for which the user has no privileges. Users attempting to access the protected file could generate a significant amount of log data. It would be analogous to the issuing of an alarm for each time that a shell user attempted to access a root-owned file or directory on a UNIX system. Interestingly, the alarm can be generated in response to a violation of policies set against the user, as opposed to global restrictions placed on the file. I am not sure which model is actually more secure, but I would guess it would be the VMS model.

The logging capabilities of VMS are quite granular. You can monitor a wide range of events, ranging from users accessing a file to users starting a protocol-based process. (You can even log users attempting to change the time.) In addition to this native monitoring, there are several utilities (some of which I mention later in this chapter) that can trap terminal sessions and monitor them for inactivity and perhaps other undesirable behavior.

Various utilities make it easier to crack the VMS platform or, having cracked it, to avoid detection. As with any other system, these utilities are sometimes of significant advantage to both the root operator and the cracker. The following sections describe some popular cracking utilities.

watchdog.com

▶ A hacker with the handle Bagpuss wrote watchdog.com. The purpose of watchdog.com is simple: It keeps tabs on users logging in and out of the machine. It is an early warning system that can alert you to when the system operator (or other similarly privileged user) logs on. The source code and full explanation of watchdog.com are located at `http://www.wordserf.co.uk/mh/vaxhackpro.html`

Stealth

▶ Bagpuss also wrote Stealth. The purpose of this utility is to evade detection in the event that someone (the system operator, perhaps) issues the `SHOW USER` command. This command is much like combining the `W`, `WHO`, and `PS` commands in UNIX. It identifies the users currently logged in to the machine and their status. Stealth prevents the user from being visible on such a query. The source code for Stealth is at `http://www.wordserf.co.uk/mh/vaxhackpro.html`

GUESS_PASSWORD

▶ GUESS_PASSWORD is designed to crack the password file of the VMS system. The program works quite well, but you have to wonder about its actual value. These days, it is unlikely that a system administrator would leave the `SYSUAF.DAT` file unprotected (where the passwords are actually located). However, if a cracker could find such an unprotected password file, this utility would assist in cracking it. GUESS_PASSWORD (with source) is available at `http://www.uniud.it/ftp/vms/uaf.zip`

WATCHER

▶ WATCHER is a snooping utility, most commonly used by system administrators. Its purpose is to watch terminal sessions. WATCHER is a good resource from a security point of view. It will monitor how long a terminal has been idle. The system administrator (or the user) can set the time period after which idle sessions can be automatically killed. (Idle terminal sessions are in themselves a security risk. Crackers watch accounts that remain idle for long periods of time. These accounts are deemed good targets.) WATCHER is available at `ftp://ftp.wku.edu/madgoat/WATCHER.zip`

Checkpass

▶ Checkpass is a tool that examines the relative strength or weakness of a given password in the `SYSUAF.DAT` file. It's good for versions 5.4 and later. Checkpass is available at `http://www.decus.org`

Crypt

▶ As you might guess, Crypt is a DES encryption module for the VMS operating system. Interestingly, it also provides support for UNIX and DOS. M. Edward Nieland, who wrote these tools primarily in C and FORTRAN, developed it (along with the previous utility). The CRYPT utility is located at `http://www.decus.org`

DIAL

A secure dialback module, DIAL is designed to prevent unauthorized remote users from gaining access to your system. It is explained in the DIAL users guide:

> Only pre-authorized users and their work location telephone numbers can gain access to the system through DIAL. After access is granted the user is disconnected from the incoming call and dialed back at the authorized telephone number. This provides the user with free access to his accounts over public telephone lines.

▶ The system works through the maintenance of a file that lists all valid users and their telephone numbers. (Read: This could be one method of circumventing this security. Reach that file, and you reach DIAL.) Roger Talkov at Emulex wrote it in C. DIAL is available at `http://www.decus.org`

CALLBACK.EXE

▶ Written by Robert Eden of Texas Utilities, CALLBACK.EXE performs essentially the same functions as DIAL. It was written in FORTRAN. CALLBACK.EXE is available at `http://www.openvms.compaq.com/freeware/CALLBACK/`

TCPFILTER (G. Gerard)

TCPFILTER is a utility that restricts outgoing connect requests. As described in the documentation, the utility does the following:

> (It) allows the filtering of outgoing UCX TCP/IP calls. Each attempt to open an outgoing call is verified with a table of addresses, and the call is either allowed or forbidden. The validation of the call can be done with two different mechanisms: with ACL, or with image names. The use of ACL allows controlling each user by the means of an identifier.

▶ The previous paragraph is excerpted from a file titled TCPFILTER.DOC ENGLISH by G. Gerard. It can be found online at `http://www.openvms.compaq.com/freeware/TCPFILTER/TCPFILTER.DOC`. The program TCPFILTER itself is available at `http://www.openvms.compaq.com/freeware/TCPFILTER/`.

I should point out that the term *call* means an outgoing TCP/IP connect request. That is, you can restrict connect requests to specific IP addresses, based on user information in the Access Control List.

Changing Times

The VAX/VMS combination was once a very popular one, and as I have already related, OpenVMS is alive and well. However, changes in the computer industry and in public demand have altered the Internet's climate with regard to VMS. In addition, Compaq acquired DEC in early 1998, bringing OpenVMS under the same umbrella as Tru64, along with a market-dominating line of Intel x86-based machines.

While the platform is still supported, with Compaq pushing Windows 2000, NetWare, Linux, and Tru64, VMS is likely to take a backseat. This is especially so with regard to Tru64 because it is a 64-bit system. Imagine for a moment a 64-bit system running at gigahertz speeds on the RISC-based Alpha platform. In my opinion, this configuration is the most powerful currently available to the average user. Such a machine (loaded with at least 512MB of RAM) is vastly superior in my opinion to Pentium-based machines. The days of the old VAX/VMS are probably over.

Today's cracker probably knows little about VMS systems. More concentration has been allotted to UNIX and as of late, Windows NT. If I were going to contract someone to crack a VAX,

I would look for someone in his mid-30s or older. Certainly, the advent of the PC has contributed to the lack of VMS security knowledge. Young people today work mostly with PC- or Macintosh-based machines. It is therefore rare to come in contact with a VAX anymore, except at larger libraries or universities.

At day's end, VMS is an interesting, durable, and relatively secure platform. However, DEC was always exceptionally close-mouthed about the security weaknesses of VAX/VMS. If you retrieve all the known advisories on VAX/VMS, you will see that DEC has routinely declined to include information that could potentially be used by crackers. (Most often, DEC would advise VAX users to contact their local DEC representative.) Some might view this as a smart move and one that might have contributed to it traditionally being difficult to crack VAX servers. Others will point at this being more along then lines of "security by obscurity." Regardless, if the system administrator of a VAX has been on his toes and the system kept up to date with patching after a cracker has tried all the default passwords, there is little left to do but turn to social engineering.

▶ Stay on top of security and OpenVMS by watching the OpenVMS home page, `http://www.openvms.compaq.com`, and keeping an eye on the patch site, `ftp://ftp.service.digital.com/patches/public/vms/`.

Summary

The VAX/VMS system is an antiquated one at this stage of the game. However, it is not out of the scene yet. If you are considering a career in Internet security, you might want to take some brief courses in VMS. If you are like me and prefer the more direct approach, buy a used VAX and set yourself to the task of cracking it. These can often be acquired for practically nothing today in the usenet `misc.forsale.computers.workstation` group. Many sellers even have the original installation media.

In closing, it is my opinion that the security of the VAX is advanced and even somewhat elegant. However, as with all OSs, the name of the game is staying on top of security configurations and prompt patching. In this respect, it's just another OS that needs proper attention to remain secure.

Resources

VAX Security: Protecting the System and the Data. Sandler and Badgett. John Wiley & Sons. ISBN: 0-471-51507-8.

A Retrospective on the VAX VMM Security Kernel. Paul A. Karger, Mary E. Zurko, Douglas W. Bonin, Andrew H. Mason, and Clifford E. Kahn. *IEEE Transactions on Software Engineering*, 17(11):1147-1163. November 1991.

Database Security. S. Castano, M. G. Fugini, G. Martella, and P. Samarati. Addison-Wesley Publishing Company. 1995. (Good chapter on VAX/VMS.) ISBN: 0-201-59375-0.

Security Guidance for VAX/VMS Systems. Debra L. Banning. Sparta, Inc. 14th National Computer Security Conference, Washington, D.C. October 1991.

A Practical Exercise in Securing an OpenVMS System. Rob McMillan. Prentice Centre, The University Of Queensland. `ftp.sunet.se/pub/security/csir/auscert/papers/Practical.Exercise.Securing.OpenVMS.txt`

How VMS Keeps Out Intruders. Tanya Candia. *Computers & Security*, 9(6):499-502. October 1990.

ESNET/DECNET Security Policy Procedures and Guidelines. D. T. Caruso and C. E. Bemis, Jr. *ESnet/DecNet Security Revised Draft*. December 1989. `http://www.es.net/pub/esnet-doc/esnet-decnet-security.txt`

Approaching Zero. The Extraordinary Underworld of Hackers, Phreakers, Virus Writers, and Keyboard Criminals. Paul Mungo and Bryan Glough. `http://www.ut.ee/ri98/villem/approaching_zero.html`

VMS Monitor Vulnerability. CERT advisory. CA-92:16. September 22, 1992. `http://www.cert.org/advisories/CA-92.18.VMS.Monitor.vulnerability.update.html`

24

VAX/VMS

Bringing It All Together

IN THIS PART

Mining the Data Monster

IN THIS CHAPTER

Computer security is a process, not a product. The process is constant, and not following it can prove disastrous. Generally speaking, the security process goes something like this:

1. After configuring your system as securely as possible with help from resources discussed in this chapter, you, or some other party, discover a vulnerability.

2. An exploit for that vulnerability becomes public knowledge.

3. Your system's vendor responds, typically with a patch or upgrade.

4. By staying on top of alerts posted by vendors and security organizations, you learn of the exploit, assess its potential impact on your organization, and, if appropriate, you download the fix, test it, and install it.

With luck, the fix works, without negative effects, and the process begins anew as you await the discovery of the next vulnerability. The key is this is an iterative process, and an important part of the process is staying on top of the information available, without suffering information overload.

Information Overload

This chapter offers a laundry list of mailing lists, Web sites, and FTP archives that house security information. That's great. However, if you subscribe to any security mailing list, you'll immediately discover that list members are only slightly more courteous than Usenet users. These folks argue like school children, and they'll do it on your time.

This dissension is a major problem. Your mailbox will be filled with, say, 100 messages daily when only 12 of them have valuable information. The rest will consist of arguments, "me-too"s, and, sadly, spam.

> **NOTE**
>
> Nothing is worse than an argument between competing vendors. These arguments sometimes continue for days with participants making allegations of slander, libel, and so on. In 99% of cases, such saber rattling ends with a whimper (instead of a bang). Meanwhile, list members are bombarded with nonsense. What makes things even worse is that participants often change the subject line or vary their posting addresses, making it difficult for you to filter out the noise.

This might not seem like a serious problem, but it is. If you run a heterogeneous network, you need to subscribe to several lists. Because the average list generates about 30 messages a day, you might end up receiving between 150 and 300 messages daily.

Here are some suggestions to help you out:

- Compartmentalize. Before joining a slew of mailing lists, prepare your system to compartmentalize the output. Set up an old box expressly for receiving mail. Allot one email address for each mailing list you join. For example, create accounts ntsec, sunsec, and hpuxsec to receive mail related to NT security, Sun security, and HP-UX security. This will at least separate the material by operating system or subject. (If you don't have a permanent network connection, you can still do this by establishing Web-based mailing addresses. Many companies provide free email accounts to the public. The downside with that, of course, is that many mailing lists will block domains such as `hotmail.com`, `altavista.net`, and `dejanews.com` because these domains are often used for spamming).

- Subscribe to digests or moderated groups only. Most mailing lists offer a digested or moderated version of their list. These versions generally have a lesser noise-to-signal ratio. In other words, irrelevant posts and messages are edited out prior to distribution. You therefore receive more relevant and pertinent information.

It might be worth your time to automate at least the cursory analysis of advisories and mailing list messages. For example, if you maintain a network that runs three or four platforms, the amount of security mail you receive each day will be more than you can humanly read. With the use of Perl scripts, you can develop a primitive but effective method of mining data automatically. It works like this:

1. As suggested previously, structure your directory to reflect the names of various operating systems (`/aix`, `/linux`, and so on) and various security issues (such as `/denial_of_service`).

2. When a mail message arrives, it's examined by subject line and the first six lines of the body. If an operating system name appears in those lines, the mail is redirected to the appropriate directory.

3. Once a day, a Perl script traverses those directories, scanning for original posts. (In other words, all "Re:" posts are discarded from the list.)

4. The resulting messages are printed.

This process ensures that we see every original advisory. The obvious problem with this approach, however, is that often, meaningful discussion appears in follow-up posts. Most moderated mailing lists enable you to search for a particular "thread" of interest. This way, your time is focused on the few items of importance to you, rather than on several issues that do not affect you.

25

MINING THE DATA MONSTER

How Much Security Do You Need?

Do you really need all that information from all those lists? Probably. Most vendors wait until strategically favorable moments to distribute patches on hard media. Therefore, by the time you get a CD-ROM with patches, your system can be 30–100 patches behind. In the interim, your system isn't safe.

Additionally, if you don't keep up with developments on at least a weekly basis, bringing your network up to date might prove to be an overwhelming task.

> **NOTE**
>
> Another irritating factor is that some vendors aren't in any hurry to publicly acknowledge flaws in their software. Microsoft is sometimes guilty of this, denying problems until proof becomes so widespread that they no longer have plausible deniability. Even then, the information often only becomes available in knowledge base articles and such.

Just as a car manufacturer cannot be held responsible if the owner has not maintained brakes and tires, a computer vendor cannot be responsible for a system that is not configured securely with up-to-date patches. The bottom line is that it's your responsibility to chase down security information. If your network gets cracked, it's you (and not your vendor) who shoulders the blame. You must keep yourself informed on recent developments.

The remainder of this chapter identifies key sources of up-to-date security information. I strongly suggest that you assign someone in your organization to track such information.

General Sources

The following sources have both up-to-the-minute information and legacy information.

The Computer Emergency Response Team (CERT)

Computer Emergency Response Team (CERT) Coordination Center
Software Engineering Institute
Carnegie-Mellon University
Pittsburgh, PA 15213-3890
URL: http://www.cert.org

The Computer Emergency Response Team (CERT) was established in 1988, following the Morris Worm incident. Since then, CERT has issued hundreds of security advisories and has responded to more than 200,000 reports of Internet break-ins.

CERT not only issues advisories whenever a new security vulnerability surfaces, but it also

- Remains on call 24 hours a day to provide vital technical advice to those who have suffered a break in
- Uses its Web site to provide valuable security information, both new and old (including papers from the early 1980s)
- Publishes an annual report that can give you great insight into security statistics

There was a time when CERT did not publish information on a hole (a vulnerability) until after a fix has been developed. Opinion on this stance varied. Some felt it was counterproductive to advertise an exploit until it was fixed. On the other side of the fence were those who believed that, by the time the "white hat" community became aware of a vulnerability, the "black hat" cracking community was well aware of it and probably had been circulating information about it through their channels for some time. By not publishing the information right away, CERT was keeping the ethical hacking community unaware and vulnerable. In October 2000, CERT compromised by adopting a policy whereby it will issue an alert 45 days (in most cases) after its initial report, regardless of vendor action. Complete details on CERT's disclosure policy can be found on its Web site at `http://www.cert.org/faq/vuldisclosurepolicy.html`. CERT advisories generally contain location URLs for patches and vendor-initiated information. From these sites, you can download code or other tools that will help proof your system against the vulnerability.

CERT is also a good starting place to check for older vulnerabilities. The database goes back to 1988.

NOTE

A bit of trivia: The first CERT advisory was issued in December 1988. It concerned a weakness in FTPD.

There are several sources where you can obtain CERT advisories, including

- **The CERT mailing list.** The CERT mailing list distributes CERT advisories and bulletins to members. To subscribe, send email to `majordomo@cert.org` and include `"subscribe cert-advisory"` in the body of the message. For more details about signing up, see `http://www.cert.org/contact_cert/certmaillist.html`.

- **The CERT Web site.** If you don't want to clog your email directory with advisories, you can still obtain them from the CERT Web site. To do so, point your browser to `http://www.cert.org/nav/alerts.html`.

- **The CERT FTP site.** If you don't have access to a browser, you can retrieve CERT advisories via FTP at `ftp://ftp.cert.org/pub/`.

The U.S. Department of Energy Computer Incident Advisory Capability

Computer Incident Advisory Capability (CIAC)

Computer Security Technology Center

Lawrence Livermore National Laboratory

7000 East Ave

P.O. Box 808

Livermore, CA 94550

URL: `http://www.ciac.org/ciac`

Computer Incident Advisory Capability (CIAC) was established in 1989. CIAC maintains a database of security-related material intended primarily for the U.S. Department of Energy. However, most information (and most tools) housed at CIAC is available to the public.

The CIAC site is an excellent information source. Here are some CIAC resources available to you:

- **CIAC virus database.** This database contains specifications and descriptions for thousands of viruses. Listings include the virus filenames, aliases, types, features, disk locations, and effects. Often, additional information is available, including identifying information, checksums, and methods of detection and elimination.

- **CIAC security bulletins.** CIAC bulletins are very much like CERT advisories. They describe particular vulnerabilities and possible solutions. CIAC has a search engine, as well, so you can rake through past bulletins, looking for interesting information.

- **CIAC security documents.** CIAC has an interesting and ever-growing collection of security documents. Some are how-to in nature (for example, how to secure X Window), whereas others are informational (such as lists of security information links). Most are available in both plain text and PDF formats.

- **CIAC tools.** CIAC has links to excellent security tools, most of which are free. There are tools that support DOS/Windows 9x, NT/2000, UNIX, and Macintosh. Some are free only to government agencies and their contractors.

CIAC has a searchable archive of advisories and bulletins at `http://www.ciac.org/cgi-bin/index/bulletins`.

Important information provided by CIAC to the public includes the following:

- Defense Data Network advisories
- CERT advisories
- NASA advisories
- A computer security journal by Chris McDonald

The National Institute of Standards and Technology Computer Security Resource Clearinghouse

Computer Security Resource Clearinghouse (CSRC)

National Institute of Standards and Technology (NIST)

Gaithersburg, MD 20899-0001

URL: `http://csrc.nist.gov/`

The NIST CSRC Web site offers a sizable list of publications, tools, pointers, organizations, and support services. In particular, the following resources are extremely helpful:

- **NIST Information Technology Laboratory (ITL) computer security bulletins.** Bulletins from ITL cover various topics of current interest. Although ITL documents seldom deal with specific vulnerabilities, they do apprise readers of the latest developments in security technology.

- **CSRC drafts.** CSRC drafts record important security research being conducted at NIST and elsewhere. These documents can help you define security plans and policy. (A sample title is *User Guide for Developing and Evaluating Security Plans for Unclassified Federal Automated Information Systems*. This document explains ways to develop and evaluate security plans.) In particular, CSRC has a multitude of documents that deal with security policy.

- **The CSRC search engine.** CRSC provides a search engine that links information from a wide range of agencies and resources.

The CSRC advisory page has links to other valuable references including the Federal Computer Incident Response Capability (FedCIRC), CERT, the National Infrastructure Protection Center (NIPC),and the Forum of Incident Response and Security Teams (FIRST). These sources provide up-to-the-minute warnings about various vulnerabilities.

You can retrieve FedCIRC advisories (without visiting CSRC) by pointing your browser to `http://www2.fedcirc.gov/alerts/advisories_2001.html`.

The BUGTRAQ Archives

The BUGTRAQ archives contain all messages sent to the BUGTRAQ mailing list. The majority of these messages describe holes in the UNIX operating system. The site is of particular interest because it features a search mechanism that enables you to search based on platform (Sun, Linux, Microsoft) viruses, IDSs, advisories, and other topics.

The BUGTRAQ list is an excellent resource because it isn't inundated with irrelevant information. The majority of posts are short and informative. Chris Chasin, the founder of BUGTRAQ, describes the list as follows:

> This list is for *detailed* discussion of UNIX security holes: what they are, how to exploit, and what to do to fix them. This list is not intended to be about cracking systems or exploiting their vulnerabilities. It is about defining, recognizing, and preventing use of security holes and risks.

BUGTRAQ is probably the Internet's most valuable resource for online reporting of UNIX-based vulnerabilities. There are more than 20 different mailing lists that focus on specific platforms and security issues including forensics, security basics, VPN's, mobile code, and others. Visit it at `http://www.securityfocus.com`.

The Forum of Incident Response and Security Teams (FIRST)

FIRST is a coalition of many organizations, both public and private, that work to circulate Internet security information. Some FIRST members are

- DoE Computer Incident Advisory Capability (CIAC)
- NASA Automated Systems Incident Response Capability
- Purdue University Computer Emergency Response Team
- Stanford University Security Team
- IBM Emergency Response Service
- Australian Computer Emergency Response Team

FIRST exercises no centralized control. All members of the organization share information, but no one exercises control over any of the other components. FIRST maintains a list of links to all FIRST member teams with Web servers. Check out FIRST at `http://www.first.org/team-info/`.

Mailing Lists

Table 25.1 identifies key security mailing lists. The majority of these lists issue up-to-the-minute advisories.

TABLE 25.1   Mailing Lists for Holes and Vulnerabilities

List	Description
`majordomo@iss.net`	The alert list at Internet Security Systems. Alerts, product announcements, and company information from Internet Security Systems. To subscribe to this and other ISS lists, complete the form at `http://iss.net/vd/maillist.html`. Or to subscribe via email to the iss' alert mailing list, send an email to `majordomo@iss.net` and put `"subscribe alert"` in the message body.
Securityfocus mailing lists	BUGTRAQ as well as several other mailing list are available at `http://www.securityfocus.com`. To subscribe, go to `http://www.securityfocus.com/about/feedback/subscribe.html` and complete the form. There are check boxes for you to pick which mailing lists you want to join. As of this writing, there are 20 lists to choose from. Their Mailing Lists pull-down menu has an Other Lists link with pointers to even more mailing lists hosted by other sites.
`firewall-wizards-request@nfr.com`	The Firewall Wizards mailing list. Maintained by Marcus Ranum, this list is a moderated forum for advanced firewall administrators. To subscribe, go to: `http://www.nfr.com/mailman/listinfo/firewall-wizards`.
`mailman-owner@redhat.com`	Get information regarding Red Hat mailing lists. For a full listing of all the mailing lists managed by Red Hat, see `https://listman.redhat.com/mailman/listinfo/`.
`majordomo@lists.us.checkpoint.com`	The Firewall-1 security list. This list focuses on issues related to CheckPoint's Firewall-1 product. To subscribe, see `http://www.checkpoint.com/services/mailing.html`.
`majordomo@lists.gnac.net`	The Firewalls mailing list. This list focuses on firewall security (previously `firewalls@greatcircle.com`). To subscribe, send an email message with the command `subscribe firewalls` in the body.
`majordomo@toad.com`	The Cyberpunks mailing list. Members discuss issues of personal privacy and cryptography. (If a major cryptographic API is broken, you'll probably hear it here first.) To subscribe, send a message with the command `SUBSCRIBE` in the body.
`majordomo@uow.edu.au`	The Intrusion Detection Systems list. Members of this list discuss real-time intrusion detection techniques, agents, neural-net development, and so forth. To subscribe, send a message with the command `subscribe ids` in the body.

25

MINING THE DATA MONSTER

TABLE 25.1   Continued

List	Description
`risks-request@csl.sri.com`	The Risks forum. Members of this list discuss a wide variety of risks that we are exposed to in an information-based society. Examples are invasion of personal privacy, credit card theft, cracking attacks, and so on. To subscribe, send a message with the command SUBSCRIBE in the body.
`ssl-talk-request@netscape.com`	The Secure Sockets Layer mailing list. Members of this list discuss developments in SSL and potential security issues. To subscribe, send a message with the command SUBSCRIBE in the body.

For a thorough compilation of mailing lists, you can also go to `http://www.securityfocus.com`. Select mailing lists from their main page. You will see about 20 lists. To see even more, click, "other lists" or go directly to it by going to `http://www.securityfocus.com/focus/home/menu.html?fm=8,23,0&action=unfold` and explore the lists available by category.

Usenet Newsgroups

You can also occasionally collect interesting information that doesn't appear elsewhere from Usenet security groups. Table 25.2 outlines some newsgroups that discuss security holes. Some newsgroups such as alt.2600 are included so that the reader can get an idea of how the hacker community shares, debates, and brags. The newsgroups are not all intended for everyday reading, but are interesting to visit once in a while. One final note: Newsgroups come and go, and activity might decrease over time. Make use of a newsgroup search engine such as DejaNews to find newsgroups that are active and relevant to you.

TABLE 25.2   Security Newsgroups

Newsgroup	Topics Discussed
`alt.2600.crackz`	Hacking, cracking. This group focuses mainly on cracks. This is a distribution point for cracks and warez.
`alt.2600.hackerz`	Hacking, cracking. This group is similar to `alt.2600`.
`alt.computer.security`	General computer security. Roughly equivalent to `comp.security.misc`, described later.
`alt.hackers.malicious`	DoS, cracking, viruses. These folks focus on causing damage to their targets.

TABLE 25.2   Continued

Newsgroup	Topics Discussed
`alt.security`	Very general security issues. Occasionally, there is some interesting information here. However, this group also carries personal security information, such as discussions about alarms, pepper spray, and personal security.
`alt.security.pgp`	Pretty good privacy. This group spawns interesting (and occasionally exhaustive) debates on cryptography.
`comp.lang.java.security`	The Java programming language. This group has interesting information. Certainly, whenever some major defect is found in Java security, the information will appear here first.
`comp.security.firewalls`	Firewalls. This group is a slightly more risqué environment than the Firewalls mailing list. The discussion here is definitely noteworthy and worthwhile.
`comp.security.misc`	General security.
`comp.security.unix`	UNIX security. This group often has worthwhile discussions and up-to-date information. Probably the best overall UNIX newsgroup.
`comp.os.linux.security`	Good Linux security. It contains a broad range of security-related topics including firewalls (ipchains), networking, and system administration.

Vendor Security Mailing Lists, Patch Depositories, and Resources

Finally, this section identifies vendor sites, patch archives, and lists that house important security information.

Silicon Graphics Security Headquarters

Silicon Graphics, Inc.

2011 N. Shoreline Blvd.

Mountain View, CA 94043

URL: `http://www.sgi.com/support/security/`

The Silicon Graphics Security Headquarters provides the following services to the public:

- **SGI security advisories.** SGI advisories provide up-to-the-minute information on vulnerabilities in the IRIX operating system. These advisories are available at `http://www.sgi.com/support/security/advisories.html`.

- **SGI security patches.** SGI provides a patch archive. This is a good place to find solutions to older vulnerabilities. SGI patches are located at `http://www.sgi.com/support/security/patches.html`.

- **Q's toolbox of programs.** This is a collection of security-related programs that can help shore up your SGI system's security. (These include scanning tools, logging utilities, and even access control list tools.) Get those programs at `http://www.sgi.com/support/security/toolbox.html`.

- A site with several FAQs, which would be of interest not only to security managers but also to administrators and developers, is `http://www-viz.tamu.edu/~sgi-faq/faq/html-1/`. A sample tip that can be found here is what to do when you've forgotten the root password.

The Sun Security Bulletin Archive

Sun Microsystems, Inc.

901 San Antonio Road

Palo Alto, CA 94303 USA

Sun Microsystems provides up-to-date security bulletins about many of its products. These bulletins are available on the SunSolve server at `http://sunsolve.sun.com/pub-cgi/show.pl?target=security/sec`.

The Xforce Vulnerability Database

This site, `http://xforce.iss.net`, maintains an excellent vulnerability database. It is searchable by the name of the vulnerability, or by system platform. The site also has a Security Library with links to dozens of other sites, presentations, and PDF documents for ISS products.

The National Institutes of Health

The Computer Security Information page at the National Institutes of Health (NIH) is a link page. It has pointers to online magazines, advisories, associations, organizations, and other Web pages of interest in security. Check out the NIH page at `http://www.alw.nih.gov/Security/security.html`. This is a big site. You might do better examining the expanded index as opposed to the front page. That index is located at `http://www.alw.nih.gov/Security/tcontents.html`.

Eugene Spafford's Security Hotlist

Eugene Spafford's site can be summed up in five words: the ultimate security resource page. Of the hundreds of pages devoted to security, this is the most comprehensive collection of links available. In contrast to many link pages whose links expire, these links remain current. Check it out online at `http://www.cerias.purdue.edu/coast/hotlist/`.

SANS Institute

The SANS Institute offers free subscriptions to newsletters that do a lot of the data mining for you. SANS pulls news of critical security news from several of the sources mentioned previously (CERT, NIPC, bugtraq, and so on) as well as vendor sources that were not mentioned. SANS also puts together three digests:

- Security Alert Consensus (SAC)—weekly
- SANS NewsBites—weekly
- SANS Windows Security Newsletter—monthly.

One that is particularly noteworthy is the SAC. When subscribing from the SANS Web site, you can specify which platforms you are interested in. This enables you to "personalize" your newsletter and limit the "noise" you might otherwise have to sift through. Currently, SANS collects news from 72 sources so you only need to read one. Sign up at `http://www.sans.org/sansnews`.

Summary

Your key to success is timely access to relevant information. Too much information, and you might not pay enough attention to an important issue that gets lost in the noise. So, before you go and subscribe to every list you find, keep in mind that there is a fair bit of redundancy and overlap in what many of them cover. Look through the lists' archives and see which lists suit you—which go into the level of detail you are comfortable with, and pay attention to issues that are relevant to your situation. This will be time well spent because the window between vulnerability announcements is becoming shorter and shorter.

Policies, Procedures, and Enforcement

IN THIS CHAPTER

This chapter discusses the creation and enforcement of security policies for an organization.

The Importance of Security Policies

The computing and network environment within an organization is often the component that draws the line between success and failure of the company. The reliance on computers and the Internet in our daily work requires security considerations in many areas. The security of the network, servers, and desktop computers is understood to be a complex and serious undertaking, but not the only factor that brings security to a company. The work done to bolster the security of the network and computer systems can be rendered useless if users do not work in a secure manner. It can also become a wasted effort if administrators do not maintain it. Security also decreases if it does not adapt to the changing work environment. Security is the responsibility of every person within an organization. All computer administrators, computer users, and even those employees who do not use computers in their daily practice share the responsibility for the overall security of a company.

The goal of this chapter is to provide a basis by which security policies can be created and enforced. The examples used are drawn from real security policies but organized as a sample security policy for Company Z, a hypothetical high-technology firm.

This chapter organizes the discussion of security policies around the following themes:

- Site and infrastructure policies
- Administrative security policies
- User or employee security policies

The issues of physical access, acceptable use, authentication, and incident response are common to each of these subjects and important to the creation of a security policy. This chapter uses sample Company Z policies to demonstrate these important components.

Site and Infrastructure Security Policy

A site and infrastructure security policy outlines security in regards to the office, building, or buildings in which the company functions, and the computing and network infrastructure it uses. The business site provides the first physical perimeter for the organization, as well as the first focus for security. The computing infrastructure includes desktop systems, servers, network equipment such as routers and firewalls, and other computing resources used within the organization. The procedures and methods applied to these systems, the environment in which they exist, and their use constitute the site and infrastructure security policy.

Facilities and Physical Security Considerations

In this inter-networked age, many people often associate security with the more virtual aspects—network, operating system and application security, the underground, crackers, and all of the media-hyped fear, uncertainty, and doubt that surrounds these aspects. Prior to this time, the term *security* conjured images of armed guards or large, burly men posted by each door. Physical security is a large component of any security policy, and rightfully so. The front door is the most easily utilized point of attack.

The site and infrastructure security policy should outline the methods used to provide and control physical access to the building and the conditions under which access is granted. Important elements are

- Methods of physical access
- Procedures by which access is granted, modified, or denied
- Access restrictions based on employee status
- Hours of operation
- Points of contact for access
- Procedures for incident handling and escalation levels

Physical access methods describe the actual means of accessing the facility, offices, labs, or other areas. These are often a lock and key, proximity cards, or biometric methods. Consideration should also be given to guidelines for the appropriate use and handling of the keys. The procedures used to obtain keys/cards and by which access is granted or modified should be outlined clearly, as it is often a point of confusion for both new and long-time employees. Equally important is a list of the people and departments to whom an employee must go to gain access to the business site—filling out forms or asking approval becomes futile if the person to whom these request should be addressed is unknown.

Many organizations distinguish between full-time, part-time, and contract employees and limit facility access based on these categories. Along with the hours of operation, the site security policy should specify any restrictions for special employees during and outside of regular working hours. Related to the segmentation of employees, the segmentation of the facility is also common. Labs, offices, and storage areas often merit access restrictions in order to prevent unauthorized entry.

Should an incident occur, the procedures for incident handling are vital to the security of an organization, as well as the safety of the employees. Incidents vary in nature, from unauthorized visitors and broken access methods to the removal of employees. Many organizations have security personnel to assist in these matters and suggested methods to react to specific situations. Defined escalation levels help an employee understand incident seriousness and to decide when is the appropriate time to notify external support, such as local law enforcement and legal counsel.

Company Z has installed and uses proximity-based card readers at all external entrances, lab doors, storage closets, and key financial offices for access control.

The administration has defined the following security policy that regulates access into the facility:

- During weekday business hours—between 8 a.m. and 6 p.m.—card access is not required for full-time and part-time employees.
- Contract employees are required to sign in with the receptionist.
- All external doors are locked outside of normal business hours, and card access is required for full-time and part-time employees.
- Contract employees are restricted from access outside of normal business hours unless specialized access forms are filled out and approved by the hiring manager.
- Access to restricted labs, storage areas, and financial offices is gained via specialized access forms and management approval.
- Access cards are obtained at the security office after the hiring manager approves access forms.
- Misplaced or stolen access cards must be reported immediately to security.
- Access cards should be kept on the person at all times; cards should not be loaned to anyone or left unsecured.

The following security policy for incident response is also provided to employees:

In order to ensure safety and security within the Company Z facility, employees should read and understand the following guidelines for dealing with incidents:

- In the event of an unauthorized visitor, the employee should immediately notify the security department and request assistance for removal of the visitor.
- Should the visitor be witnessed committing an act of larceny, attack, or destruction of property, notify the security department, and they will then contact the appropriate authorities.
- All witnesses should provide the security department with an affidavit indicating their presence and the details of the incident, and should be available for further questioning by security and the appropriate authorities.
- All doors, locks, and access methods that are non-functional should be reported to the security department. Security will coordinate with maintenance to fix the broken equipment.
- Managers should be notified when an employee is involved with a breach of security.
- Employees should not handle these situations alone, but instead should notify security and allow the security staff to control the situation.

This example demonstrates important aspects of a site and infrastructure security policy. Constraints on physical access are defined, including the actual methods that employees use to enter the facility and the differentiation between employee types. The processes and procedures used to control access and to acquire the appropriate privileges are outlined, including the identification of the responsible individuals. The response guidelines for any incidents are clearly outlined with the safety of the employee in mind. Individuals trained to handle incidents of this nature are identified and involved in each response method.

Infrastructure and Computing Environment

The following aspects of security are commonly considered when creating a security policy for the infrastructure and computing environment:

- Physical access to computer systems and facilities
- Security considerations for laptop computers and PDAs
- Voice and data network security
- Remote network access to computer systems and resources
- Security monitoring and auditing
- Authentication and access control

Physical Access to Computer Systems and Facilities

The computer systems used throughout an organization can be categorized into the following classes:

- Public terminals
- Desktop systems
- Server systems

Each of these classes of systems can be addressed individually within the site and infrastructure security policy.

Public Terminals

As with the building and facilities, control of physical access to the computing environment is an important component to its security. Once someone is inside a building, finding an unoccupied terminal or computer system is often easily accomplished. Without a policy for protecting these systems, unauthorized users can gain access to important and private resources, information, and files. Computer terminals in publicly accessible areas should be controlled carefully by limiting access to network facilities and resources, and establishing usage policies for employees and guests.

Returning to the hypothetical case, Company Z has an open atrium area that contains several terminals accessible to employees and visitors. The following security policy, which provides regulations for the use of these public terminals, is posted in plain view:

Rules and Restrictions for Public Terminal Usage

- Visitors must see reception in order to receive a guest account.
- Guest accounts are capable of accessing the Internet only.
- No Internal systems or resources are available via guest logins.
- Guest accounts are automatically logged out after 15 minutes of idle time.
- Employees should log out before leaving the terminal.
- Please report all malfunctioning systems to the IT department.

Administrative Policies for Public Terminals

- Public terminals are secured to the desktops via anti-theft alarm devices and cable locks.
- All systems configured for public use are on a restricted-access network.
- Systems are configured with guest accounts that have no access to company resources or systems.
- Guest accounts are automatically logged out after a specified amount of idle time.
- Guest accounts should be set to expire when no longer needed, based on the requirements of the guest.
- Publicly accessible systems should allow no access to internal systems or resources.
- Publicly accessible UNIX systems should be configured with a minimal set of utilities, have no network services running, and provide a restricted and inescapable shell to guests; the account should be removed when the visitor leaves the premises.
- Publicly accessible Windows systems should not be domain members and guest accounts should have only the local user-group privileges.
- Menus and commands should also be configured to allow access only to the appropriate Web browser program on the system and no other applications.

Public terminals are often presented to accommodate the network needs of visiting employees, vendors, and business partners. These terminals require special consideration for security and posted regulations for their use in order to protect the computing infrastructure. The Company Z policy distinguishes between visitors and employees who use the terminals and presents significantly more restrictions to the visitors. The administrators of these systems also have a security policy that outlines the measures used to configure the systems. This ensures that all publicly accessible systems are configured alike and helps ensure a known level of security.

Desktop and Server Systems

Public terminals are not the only systems that require guidelines. Desktop systems often have the most lax security because individual employees often administer their own machines or have special privilege and access to their respective system. It is often infeasible for the Information Technology staff to administer all desktop workstations, therefore the development of a security policy that governs their creation and use is very important. The site and infrastructure security policy for desktop systems establishes the standards used to create them, including operating systems, applications, and utilities. The security constraints generally consist of configuration information by which administrators can replicate the desktop system at a known level of security. The policies also present the guidelines for the desktop system's interaction with servers and the network.

The security policy for desktop users is discussed later in the chapter.

Given the understanding that desktop systems are likely to be uncontrolled by the IT staff, effective infrastructure policies attempt to minimize the amount of data, applications, and other information that remains on the desktop system. This enhances both the security and availability of information within the organization. Many companies centralize storage of user data and applications to a single server or set of servers. In the event of a failure of a desktop, the effort required to make it functional again is minimized—all of the essential and important data is on the server and does not become lost or require significant time and effort to restore.

Server systems become a focal point as they have the responsibility to reliably store and provide access to shared data, private user information, applications, and services for the organization.

A server security policy should encompass the following components:

- Service configuration
- Shared data permissions and access control
- User private data permissions and access control
- Backup and restoration procedures
- Incident response

The service configuration entails the initial method used to secure the server. Most operating systems provide a vast array of potential services and capabilities, not all of which are needed or desired by the organization. Each of these services has its own security ramifications, which should be considered when enabling or disabling it. The decision to allow a service is often an issue of cost versus risk analysis. If the service provides a required function that has inherent security risks, the administrators should determine if there are suitable replacements for the service. If any substitutes are available, the cost and effort required to implement them should be weighed against the security risks and cost of the original. It is important to document within the security policy the foundation for decisions and to identify the known security risks accepted by the organization. Also related is the maintenance of the software and operating systems running on the servers—security measures should be updated frequently, as new vulnerabilities are discovered. Updates should be applied and monitored. The people writing the security policy probably will not always be employed at the organization, therefore knowing the background of a decision is important to the future maintainers of the security policy.

Company Z's Server Security Policy is as follows:

- Servers should be configured to support only the required services and to disable unnecessary software and services in order to minimize security risks.

- Server systems should be physically secured, allowing only administrative access.

- Server operating systems and software should be updated when new vulnerabilities and subsequent patches are released.

- In the event of incidents such as hardware failure, system compromise, or other attacks, the server should be removed from the network and left in its current state in order to allow effective forensics work.

- A contingency plan should be created and followed to recover from disasters. For in-depth information on their content and creation, see the Disaster Recovery Journal sample recovery plans at `http://www.drj.com/new2dr/samples.htm`.

To focus on security policies instead of system configuration, the Company Z Server Security Policy leaves out most of the technical details related to the secure lockdown of servers and operating systems. The standards of configuration, access, and maintenance are important components that should be incorporated into the policy. Incident response for servers is reasonably complex; in order to avoid damaging potential evidence after an attack is discovered, the system should be left intact for security analysis and forensics work.

Shared data is often the primary purpose of a server, allowing employees to access common files, applications, and other data. Server operating systems generally support multiple methods to provide multiuser access to data. When establishing the infrastructure security policy, the technical details surrounding shared data should be clearly outlined.

The Site and Infrastructure Security Policy for Company Z establishes the following criteria for shared data on servers:

- No data sharing should be initialized via the "Everyone" group on Windows servers or "World" read/write access on UNIX systems.

- Access by the "Everyone" group and "World" read/write permissions should be removed or disabled from the shared data.

- Global or common access to all employees should be controlled via membership in the specially created "Employees" group on the servers.

Policies, Procedures, and Enforcement
CHAPTER 26

603

26

POLICIES,
PROCEDURES, AND
ENFORCEMENT

- When needed, smaller privilege groups should be created and shared data coordinated with those groups to meet the access control requirements for a user.

Company Z's policy emphasizes a strict level of security for shared data. It identifies and distinguishes between unconditionally shared data and the true need for shared data. Data is shared only between employees, and security control is exercised to ensure that only authorized individuals have access to it. In this model, access control is achieved via membership in various user groups, and permission is adjusted accordingly.

User private data includes a user's respective "home" directories or the areas in which his personal files are stored. Because these files are also often kept on the server, it is important to outline the level of security the user can expect, as well as the method by which it is provided.

Company Z details this security policy for user home directories and private storage areas:

- Server-based user home directories are provided for the storage of private and personal data.

- On Windows servers, the permissions should be set to allow the respective user full read and write permissions for a directory, and also to allow the system backup process to access the data when backing up the storage system.

- No other users should have access to any home directory aside from their own.

- Users are encouraged to use their server-based directories for data storage in order to provide security and to facilitate the simple recovery of data in the event of an incident.

Employees often store personal and sensitive information on their systems as work and personal life cannot be completely segregated. In order to provide data security and to avoid data loss in the event of a desktop system, users at Company Z are encouraged to store their data on the servers and are provided a high degree of protection from prying eyes.

Backup and restoration procedures serve many functions in an organization. These include protection of data in the event of a catastrophic incident, restoration of accidentally removed files, and provision of general infrastructure reliability. Backup data is often used in the forensics of security incidents to assess the reliability of data—data altered by an attacker can often be detected by a comparison between it and the version that is on the backup media. The physical storage of the media on which the backups are done is also important to security. Many organizations use special offsite storage organizations to assure that the backups are securely stored.

Company Z's security considerations for system backups include

- All backups are to be stored in a locked storage area prior to offsite storage.

- Weekly backups are moved into offsite storage via a storage company representative at a scheduled pickup time.

- Backups consist of one full system backup, per system, per week with nightly incremental backups of all modified data.

- Use of backup and restoration applications should be restricted to authorized administrators only.

- In the event of a disaster, hardware failure, or other event that results in the loss of data, the employee should notify the IT staff.

- Information will be restored from the last full archive with the incremental changes layered over, up to the time of the event.

Backups provide a level of reliability and security to the information stored and used within the organization. The security policy specifies the method for backups, recovery during incidents, and privileges required to access the information. The physical security of the backup data is also emphasized in order to create a comprehensive policy that effectively protects the organization.

Incident response takes on several meanings, but can be summarized as the best course of action in the event of anomalous circumstances. For the purposes of this discussion, the actual circumstances are not as important as the reaction to them. Security policies provide key benefits in the area of incident response by identifying and organizing information vital to a safe reaction. Security policies should include the suggested methods to react to incidents and pertinent contact information. The primary goal of incident-response guidelines is to avoid the knee-jerk, emotionally motivated responses that often happen quickly and without careful analysis. By having a step-by-step approach to handling incidents already in hand—including the proper steps to identify, control, and resolve issues—those involved can react safely.

Physical Security Considerations for Laptop Computers and PDAs

As technology advances, we see the creation of new, smaller, and more powerful computing devices. In light of the prevalence of telecommuters and remote offices, and the frequency of business travel, these small computing devices such as laptops and PDAs require special security considerations. The theft and misuse of these devices present a high risk to the infrastructure of an organization, as they often function with the same level of access as their larger and less portable cousins. Many of these portable computers have special security methods that allow the user to protect the device and the information they store on it. The company policies that govern the use of laptops and PDAs should require putting these capabilities to use.

Company Z has established a set of Security Policy Considerations for Laptops and PDAs. These physical and configuration considerations include

- Laptops and PDAs should be configured to support power-on passwords if possible, in order to protect against unauthorized use if stolen.

- Users should log out and power off the system when not in use, instead of putting the system into standby mode. This prevents unauthorized users from impersonating you, should they gain access to the system.

- Private and sensitive data should be protected via encryption and passwords, if possible.

- Users should use different passwords on all of their portable and non-portable systems to defend against compromise of multiple systems via a stolen password.

- When temporarily leaving your workspace, care should be taken to either lock the system via a password-protected screensaver or log out completely.

- Laptops and PDAs should be physically secured by a locked cable, tether, or other security device at all times.

- If no security method is available, the system should be locked in a cabinet drawer or other secured storage area when not in use.

Voice and Data Network Security

The network is the lifeline for the computing infrastructure. The phone system that provides voice communications forms a network of interconnected phones. Desktops connect to servers and the greater Internet via the local area network. Customers, partners, and employees contact the company via the network. The majority of internal communication likely occurs via the voice and data networks. Security policies should attend to the security of network communication. By addressing the risks and defenses against them, the networks can function more securely.

The phone system within an organization often crosses the boundaries of voice and data communications. The desktop computer can interact with modern phone systems to retrieve voice mail, leave messages for others, and administer the system. As with the previous areas of concern, physical access should controlled. The operational constraints—such as Personal Identification Numbers (PIN) for users—and standard configurations should provide a more secure environment. An often forgotten security aspect of the phone system is the provision of remote dial-in capabilities that support both phone system administration and network access.

Several concerns for the phone system are outlined in this Company Z security policy:

- Physical access to the phone system hardware and system configuration terminals is restricted to phone administrators and phone company personnel.

- The phone system hardware should exist in a secured area that requires specialized access methods via keys or electronic cards.

- Default PINs for new users should be randomly chosen.

- When establishing a voice mail account, avoid using PINs that can be easily guessed, such as an extension number, the surname of the user, or other identifiable information.

- Dial-in modems used for administration of the phone system should be protected with passwords.

- Network access via dial-in modems should be authenticated and logged via a centralized authentication and reporting system.

- Modems meant for dial-in should be programmed to prevent dial-out capabilities.

- Installation of new modems should be coordinated through the phone and IT group in order to provide the necessary security and network infrastructure to maintain security.

- Phone line audits should occur regularly to verify the functionality of existing modems and to identify unauthorized modems.

This security policy addresses the phone system rather extensively. A comprehensive security policy takes into consideration all aspects of an organization and does not focus only on the computing environment. All aspects of security in an organization are related; a breakdown in the security of one area provides access despite the security measures of another. A weakness in the phone system security policy might allow an unauthorized intruder to access system and network resources even if other system and network security measures are in place.

The data network should be extended the same security features as the voice network. Network and telecommunications hardware such as routers, switches, and network lines (ISDN, DSL, T1, and so on) should be physically secured to avoid accidental or intentional disruption of network services. Beyond the physical aspects, the network requires a high degree of security and diligence to maintain that level. The first tier of protection is generally a firewall at the Internet access point (as you learned in Chapter 10, "Firewalls"). The specific firewall rules and filters should be defined based on the network access needs of the organization. A reasonably safe, but somewhat restrictive, guideline is the exception method. This dictates a global rule to deny access to everything first, and then makes exceptions for those network services deemed necessary.

After the firewall, network architecture and organization should also be considered to protect and isolate information as it travels on the network wire. The network hardware must be protected from network attacks and unauthorized configuration attempts.

Company Z has a diverse network that separates servers from the normal desktop computing network. The Internet access point is protected by a firewall. The data network portion of its security policy reads as follows:

- Firewalls are used to protect the internal networks in a restrictive fashion.

- Filtering and rules on the firewall support outgoing connections from employees so as not to restrict their ability to use the Internet.

- Filtering and rules on the firewall allow only incoming connections to the company Web server, mail servers, and name servers (DNS).

- The customer support network exists on a different network number and interface than the administrative and corporate network, and with fewer restrictions in order to support the required services of that organization.

- All access to network equipment, where supported, shall be protected via non-default passwords.

- Managed network equipment, including firewalls, routers, switches, modems, and other communication devices, are configured to allow administrative access from only a small number of administrative systems, in order to protect them from unauthorized configuration changes.

- All configuration changes to network equipment must be logged for reference.

- In the event of network attacks, the network administrators should notify the corporate security department, in case legal intervention is required.

- Network equipment should be configured to enable only those protocols in use by the organization, disabling all other features.

- Response to incidents should occur in the following manner:

  1. Attempt to identify the cause.

  2. In the event of network disruption and loss of service from attack, network administrators should attempt to identify the source of the attack. Firewall rules should be modified to control the effects, if possible.

  3. Restore service to the company as quickly as possible while attempting to preserve evidence of the issue.

  4. Upon resolution of an incident, incident forms should be filled out and submitted to the manager of the network group.

  5. Analysis of the incident should be discussed in a group meeting to identify weaknesses in the organization and help prevent future issues.

- To protect against equipment failure, spare network hardware should be available.

- To facilitate ease of replacement and security of the configuration of network equipment, the configuration information should be maintained on the administrative servers.

- Where possible, network equipment should be configured to boot and download its configuration from the administrative servers, in order to preserve the integrity and reliability of the configuration.

- Network equipment that is not managed via SNMP should have that protocol disabled. The SNMP (Simple Network Management Protocol) allows administrators to see and modify the settings and configuration for a device with little or no authentication and access control.

- If using SNMP for management of the device, SNMP access should be restricted to administrative servers.

Network equipment presents a complex set of security requirements that should be outlined in the security policy. This allows for a safe installation and a maintained degree of security. The security policy incorporates physical orientation and configuration to defend against unauthorized access and management of the device. Authentication and access restrictions are implemented, as well as reliability in the configuration methods. The services provided by the equipment are tailored to the needs of the organization, allowing a known set of security concerns to be identified and resolved.

Remote Network Access

Remote network access is a convenience that allows employees to do their daily work, regardless of their location. This functionality requires an extension of the network security policy discussed above, focused on the methods and use of remote access. Remote access can be provided via Virtual Private Networks and the previously mentioned dial-in modems. The provision of these capabilities often conflicts with the security policy for the network because the policy generally seeks to keep outsiders from accessing internal information and resources.

Here is Company Z's Remote Access Security Policy:

- The company provides remote access capabilities via a Virtual Private Network solution that supports remote dial-in Internet service providers and broadband cable-modem users.
- Configuration of the VPN hardware and software follows the security policy set forth for other network equipment.
- Users requiring remote access capabilities must receive approval from their manager and the IT department and fill out the required forms before remote access is provided.
- Remote access is authenticated via passwords, security tokens, or single-use passwords.
- Remote access passwords should follow the security policy guidelines for authentication.
- Remote access software, configuration, and account information is to be used only by the employee for whom it is intended.
- If access by multiple remote machines is required, this should be indicated on the Remote Access Form.
- Remote access should be used only when required and not left unattended by the employee.
- Acceptable use of this resource is outlined in the User Security Policy.

Remote access is a subfunction that inherits security policy guidelines from several areas. The administration and configuration of the VPN falls under the Company Z's Network Devices Policy, whereas the authentication and use of the VPN by employees is governed by the Authentication and User policies, discussed later in the chapter.

As you can see, a comprehensive security policy is very easily scaled to meet new requirements and functionality within an organization. The effort expended in the early development stages of the security policy or policies simplifies its extension greatly.

Security Monitoring and Auditing

Central to a comprehensive security policy, and the components that unify procedures and response, is the discussion of monitoring and auditing. *Security monitoring* verifies the configuration guidelines and technical requirements outlined in the security policies. *Security auditing* entails a consistent set of practices that enforce the security policies set forth for the organization.

Monitoring is the policy action that becomes part of the ongoing standard security process in the company. The installation of a firewall is one element of the security monitoring system—it focuses on the network access points. Other aspects of monitoring are the use of security cameras, anti-virus software, server disk quotas, intrusion detection devices, and network management software. The monitoring component of a security policy enhances the security in an organization by validating the other elements in the policy, ensuring their existence and correctness.

Monitoring capabilities also affect the safety and effectiveness of incident responses. It provides evidence for legal issues and an informative basis for post-mortem analysis of incidents. This analysis is very useful to assist in prevention and understanding of problems.

Finally, security monitoring provides the capability for the organization to recover from incidents by providing in-depth information about it. Network attacks can be monitored and defended against, spurious hardware failures can be traced and rectified and the actions of unauthorized intruders can be watched and recorded.

The monitoring methods for a server, network, or other computer equipment are often those that gather and analyze statistics. The statistics gathered provide the reference point for normal operation and for that which is abnormal. This information is often gathered by hand, or eye, in the case of security cameras and monitoring. The level to which the monitoring is automated increases its effectiveness. To allay the fears that this task is incredibly difficult, it is important to note that many operating systems and software have the capabilities to perform a large portion of the monitoring and auditing functionality—the features simply need to be enabled. Authentication policies including the identification of password criteria, the use of password aging, and keeping a password history to avoid repetition are enforced by common features in most operating systems. Access control methods and auditing capabilities are inherent parts of server operating systems. Network management protocols allow for special alerts and notices to be sent under special conditions. An example is SNMP, which can be configured to notify administrators when special events occur. SNMP has weak security and should be investigated prior to its implementation, and is mentioned here due to its wide use. An alarm company, monitors the alarm system, and the proper authorities are notified automatically when it is set off.

Company Z's Security Monitoring Policy reads

- Closed-circuit television cameras are installed throughout the organization and at entry/exit points.
- This video information is recorded and monitored by the security group.
- Network equipment management and monitoring occurs via automated management software that notifies administrators via pager in the event of anomalous issues.
- Anti-virus software monitors all programs, documents, and email messages for viruses and automatically cleans discovered viruses.
- Users and administrators are automatically notified via email when a virus is discovered.
- All servers are monitored via monitoring programs and built-in functionality that complies with the established security policy.

Auditing ensures that the security policy is in place and followed. The measures used to audit include the services of contract security firms to analyze the an organization's networks, systems, and policies—often unbeknownst to the employees. Other forms of auditing include random and frequent verification of the policies by administrators or special internal teams designed for such tasks. The reference to auditing in the security policies of an organization also has a psychological affect that helps foster greater security awareness and action. Employees are less likely to adhere to security policies if they feel there is no enforcement. By outlining the presence of auditing methods, without necessarily clarifying the exact procedures, frequency, or schedule, an organization makes its employees more aware of security issues. A greater emphasis on secure thought and use is the natural result. Consider Company Z's Security Policy for Enforcement and Auditing:

- Periodic and random security audits will be performed on servers and network equipment to ensure proper configuration, diligent updates and application of patches, and compliance with other security policy regulations.
- These audits may be performed by internal staff or external agencies with or without the knowledge of the administrators and users of the systems. (For some useful information about audits and pitfalls to avoid, see the article "Audits from Hell" by Carole Fennelly at http://www.sunworld.com/swol-02-1999/swol-02-security.html.)
- Desktop systems and users will be audited for compliance with the Site and Infrastructure Policy, with regard to configuration, up-to-date software, and network services.
- Audits of users for compliance with the Acceptable Use Policy will also be conducted to assure the safety and security of the computing environment.

Notification to employees of the audit policy enforces compliance of security policies and also forewarns them of repercussions for compliance failures. Administrators have the largest responsibility and expend the most effort to enforce adherence to security policies. Audits might seem forceful, but an environment with so many security components requires dedication and diligence to maintain security.

Authentication and Access Control

Authentication and access control are two aspects of security in which administrators and users must participate equally for any level of effectiveness to exist. Security policies need to present the regulations and requirements clearly and should help employees understand the seriousness of compliance. Authentication policies establish the best practices and exact implementations used to provide access to desktop systems, servers, and local network resources, and from remote sites. There are well-known methods to provide authentication and several guidelines that create a more highly secure environment. The authentication issues addressed by the security policy are important to most other areas covered within the policy. Access control is related to authentication and is often used simultaneously because the authentication of a user instantiates group membership and provides access to resources.

Not surprisingly, authentication security involves the implementation and use of various forms of authentication. Commonly used means are passwords, Personal Identification Numbers (PINs), single-use passwords, public-key encryption, proximity cards, smart cards, other code-generation tokens, and biometric agents. The most commonly used authentication method is the username/password combination. In comparison to other authentication methods, this is also the most easily compromised—theft of passwords comes in many different forms, often due to the individual's choice of password. People tend to gravitate towards easily remembered words or phrases when selecting passwords, such as names of family members, pets, hobbies, or other interests. Unfortunately, attackers often easily guess these passwords. In the quest to balance ease of use with high security, authentication security policies help users create stronger passwords that might not be so easily discerned. The policies also provide guidelines by which users can increase the security of their daily work. The enforcement of these guidelines often occurs as a feature of the operating system or programs doing the authentication.

Authentication security policy also differentiates between where and how authentication methods are used. Security requirements for access to different systems, networks, or facilities often mandate the need for each user to maintain several authentication methods. This is especially true for computer and network administrators. Users are not the only group governed by authentication policies. Administrators need to be even more concerned with authentication security because they have and control access to highly privileged accounts, systems, and resources. There are several guidelines for the handling and use of passwords, also. These guidelines help to keep users continually thinking of security in everything they do.

Company Z's Authentication Security Policy for users and administrators includes these guidelines:

- On systems where credentials are the username/password pair, passwords should meet the following criteria:
  - Password should be at least eight characters.
  - They should be a combination of letters, numbers, and extended or special characters.
  - The company will maintain a history of a user's last five passwords to prevent repetition.
  - Passwords should be sufficiently different from any password in the history to prevent patterns of easily obtained passwords.
  - Common dictionary words are not allowed.
  - Passwords will expire every 12 weeks, requiring the user to create a new one.
  - Passwords should be chosen carefully by avoiding family or pet names, personal interests, or other information that can be linked and easily identified.
- Administrators must abide by the criteria set forth for users, with the addition that their passwords will expire more frequently, at six weeks.
- Passwords for privileged accounts will change every four weeks to provide higher safety because these accounts are shared amongst several administrators.
- Remote access will be granted using single-use passwords and code-generating security tokens to prevent theft of user credentials.
- All user accounts will have a password. Any user account without a password will be disabled or have a random password generated for it.
- Newly created accounts will have randomly generated passwords that expire upon first login, requiring the user to set a new password.
- Passwords should never be written down or stored on a recoverable medium such as paper, sticky notes, or white-boards.
- Users should never tell anyone their passwords.
- Administrators will never ask users for their passwords. In the event that someone does ask for the password, please report it immediately to IT and the security group.
- When automating tasks that require authentication, avoid storing passwords clearly in data files. If possible, encrypt or hash the password prior to storing it, in order to prevent the theft of the passwords.

- When using smart cards, proximity cards, or other hardware token-based authentication methods, keep the device on your person at all times, and do not let others borrow it.

- When using public-key encryption methods for authentication, private key information should be protected via file access restrictions or storage on external devices such as smart cards.

- When using encryption, private and secret keys can be escrowed by the administration to protect the data from loss and to ensure that access is attainable when required.

- All authentications, whether successful or failures, are logged by the system being accessed.

- Systems should be configured to allow three failed login attempts before account lock-out occurs.

- In the event of login failure and account lock-out, internal accounts should be configured to allow logins again after 30 minutes. The use of permanent lock-outs are also supported by many operating systems. These require an administrator to intervene and reopen the account. A permanent lock-out can result in a denial of service condition if an attacker attacks multiple accounts.

- Remote access accounts should be disabled after three failed login attempts, requiring administrative intervention for the reuse of the account.

- Administrators should implement login notices that are displayed prior to login prompts. These notices should warn unauthorized users that their actions are monitored and attempts to enter the system are prohibited. Legal ramifications might result from continued use by unauthorized personnel.

- In the event of lost or stolen passwords and authentication devices, IT should be notified immediately in order to disable access for that account and to begin the creation of new access credentials.

- Administrators should confirm the identity of users before issuing new passwords. This can be done in person with the presentation of a badge or photo ID, the use of a special recovery password, a personal identification number, social security number, or other method that is normally known only by the user and administrator.

As you can see, the use of authentication is serious business. Users and administrators need to be made aware of the negative effects of authentication misuse. To summarize, the important components of authentication are

- Teaching users and administrators to use authentication methods securely through strong password creation, as well as to keep passwords secure.

- Authentication logging and monitoring.

- Different authentication methods should be defined and used for different applications to provide the highest level of security, instead of standardizing on a single authentication method. For example, remote access often merits a stronger authentication mechanism than internal server access does.

- The importance of strict authentication security policies, such as password expiration and selection criteria, to make attack and compromise difficult.

Access control is the next related component to authentication. Access control exists at several levels—network access, data file access, and resource access. Network access is determined by protocols, port numbers, source and destination systems, and networks. Network access control is most likely maintained by the firewall, and these policies were discussed earlier in the chapter. Data file and system resource access control is accomplished via operating system functionality, such as file permissions linked to user and group memberships. An access control security policy presents the user with a set of best practices for utilizing this functionality. Consider Company Z's Access Control Policy:

- Network access control occurs via the firewall, which is configured to allow Internet access for employees. If a required service is blocked by the firewall, contact the IT or network administration group to discuss possible solutions.

- Employees are granted access to global company computing resources via their desktop login procedure.

- Common file shares are automatically initialized at login time. The user has rights to add to common areas, but not to remove files or folders unless the user created them.

- UNIX user accounts should be created with membership in the Global users groups or equivalent (operating system dependent).

- UNIX user accounts should have their own private group as the default group membership, which allows them to set permissions safely on their files and directories.

- Windows accounts should be members of the Domain Users group.

- Home directories should be created to allow access only by the owner of the directory.

- The UNIX umask setting allows users to specify a default permission level for newly created files. This should be set to create files that disallow everyone else to modify or execute them. (The default umask is generally 022, which creates files with read and write permissions for the owner and read permissions for the group and world.)

- The UNIX SetUID/GID settings should be avoided unless absolutely necessary.

- The permissions of user resource settings including `.login`, `.profile`, and `.rhosts` should be secured against unauthorized modification.

- Users should contact the IT department if any uncertainty exists when setting access control methods.

- If unauthorized access to files, folders ,or other data is suspected, notify the IT department for an investigation.

- Automatic scans will execute on a regular basis to search for unsafe access control settings on user files, folders, and applications.

- The Windows NT and 2000 operating systems provide access to everybody (via the special "Everybody" group) by default. This group access should be removed and replaced with the Domain Users group, if access to all employees is to be granted.

> **NOTE**
>
> The Windows NT and 2000 operating systems support a slightly different access control mechanism than UNIX. The Windows mechanism has the standard read, write and execute permissions like UNIX, but also has several special attributes such as full-access and modify. The full-access permission allows the individual to modify all of the permissions, including change the permissions for others. This is often not the desired effect, so in cases where the user requires only read, write, and execute access, full-access should not be enabled. The `modify` attribute allows a user to make changes to a file already in existence, but not to create new files or folders.

Access control policies can present useful technical information to the users and promote security awareness. Noting the technical details of access control mechanisms for the operating systems in use is beneficial because the casual user is often unaware of their existence or their use. The identification of contacts and procedures for access control issues is used to help the user learn and utilize secure settings.

Acceptable Use

Acceptable use is a general set of guidelines for administrators and users that emphasizes best practices and security awareness in daily work. Administrators and users share most responsibilities for security, but the privilege and access levels of administrators mandate several strict rules to prevent the misuse of their power.

Administrative Security Policies

The administrator's job is to adhere to the site and infrastructure policies as well as to work in a secure manner outlined by his own "acceptable use" policies. Given the nature of administrator privileges and access, certain rules are required to govern their use and prevent the abuse of those privileges. Because of these higher privileges, the administrator also needs to be extremely diligent in his security awareness and action.

None of the policy issues presented here are exclusive or independent of the others. This is also the case for administrative and user security policies. The administrative security portion of the security policy outlines acceptable use and procedures for administrators to consider and abide by when following the entire security policy. Administrative policies define rules and accepted processes by which the computing infrastructure is established and maintained. They also outline a hierarchy of responsibility, escalation matrices, and procedures for everyday security awareness and implementation, as you can see in Company Z's Administrator Acceptable Use and Procedures Policy:

- Unauthorized access to user files and information is prohibited unless the administrator is actively resolving an issue with the user.

- Administrators monitoring user data and voice communications, including authentication, email, Web traffic, and phone conversations, is acceptable only when working to solve problems or during security audits. The practice of automated monitoring via intrusion detection systems and other equipment should be identified and outlined separately.

- When troubleshooting problems, administrators should ask permission and make the user aware that access to these forms of information will occur.

- Administrative adherence to this policy and the remaining security policies outlined in these documents will be randomly and periodically audited for compliance.

- Noncompliance with the security policies results in notification to management and a documented warning. Further noncompliance or abuse may affect the employment status of the administrator.

- Purposefully executed events that result in loss of service, compromise of a system, or altered functionality will be investigated, and the appropriate actions will be taken against the administrator.

Acceptable use policies should be clear and concise when presenting the rules and regulations. Serious security and confidentiality issues can arise when acceptable use is not well defined. The policy should discuss acceptable use with regards to administrative interaction with users, their data, and private information. Earlier in the general security policy, it is recommended that users store their personal files in protected home directories on centralized servers. Users are unlikely to do so if the administrators who maintains those servers do not have her own rules regarding access to these files. Computer and network administrators often have complete access to every action and keystroke of users. This is a very powerful position that can easily be abused if strict policy and enforcement is not in effect. It is not sufficient to simply state the rules; the results of failure to follow the rules should also be clarified.

Acceptable Use Policies for Users

This section outlines the rules for acceptable use that apply to the users in an organization. The previously outlined security policies should also be adhered to and practiced as a normal part of daily operation.

Company Z's User Acceptable Use Policy reads

- Use of computer, network, and company resources is granted under the proviso that users read, understand, and comply with the security policy in full and indicate so by signing and returning the policy to the IT department.

- Users should adhere to the authentication policy and treat all passwords as private, personal property.

- Users agree not to abuse the computer, network, or other company resources to create loss of service, system compromise, or to weaken existing security measures. Failure to comply might result in punitive action by the company and affect the user's employment status.

- Users agree to participate in random periodic audits of their processes and procedures for compliance with the outlined security policy or policies.

- All incidents including hardware failures, computer attacks, and unauthorized entry or access should be reported to the appropriate security or IT departments.

- Employees should request identification from unknown visitors seeking entrance to the facilities and direct them to reception or security for access.

- Employees should not allow unknown individuals or non-employees to access computer and network resources.

- The management of an organization should support employees and the policy when access is denied to individuals; the policy is weakened when exceptions are made for people known to the manager, but unknown to the employee who previously denied them access.

- Laptops, PDAs, and other portable devices should not be left unattended.(Also refer to the security considerations for these devices outlined earlier in the policy.)

- Users should lock their terminals prior to leaving the work area.

- Users agree to follow the site and infrastructure security guidelines with respect to the security of desktop computer systems, their use, and the services provided by them.

Acceptable use encompasses more general guidelines that relate to the technical implementation details provided by the security policy. These regulations emphasize the importance of security to their daily work habits by summarizing some of the important components of the overall security policy. Authentication, physical security, and proper contact and response are important elements with which the user is frequently involved.

Enforcement of Policy

A set of regulations and guidelines is only useful when it is followed. This section summarizes the methods of enforcement presented throughout the chapter and discusses the need for enforcement measures. Without enforcement, security policy is likely to be followed for a short time after implementation, but generally falls into a state of disuse. The goals of the security policy at a global level are to instantiate a set of processes and methods that enhance the security of an organization, and to create a state of security awareness in the minds of all employees. The processes and procedures provide the means to implement security, and security awareness allows it to be sustained in the organization.

The first aspect of the security policy that enforces compliance is the binding nature of a written contract. The employee should read and agree to the security policy by signing it. The policy should then be securely stored. The legalities of a signed contract should be discussed with the legal counsel for the organization. The psychological affects are also beneficial to security policy enforcement. People have a heightened awareness when they feel bound, legally or otherwise, to a particular set of rules.

Auditing of the environment and its users for compliance with the security policies is a common method of enforcement. There are generally two types of audits—notified or scheduled audits and blind audits. Scheduled audits are announced to the employees and help establish compliance where it is otherwise lacking. As in a military inspection, users have an established period of time to ensure their practices are inline with the documented security policies. These audits are useful to bring the security of an organization up to an acceptable level, as the employees scramble to comply. Inspections of this nature often involve several stages. The first occurs at the technical level, wherein the systems, network, and facilities are analyzed for their security components, to assure they meet the requirements of the security policy. The practices of users are then assessed to determine if there are improper habits or actions that negate security. A final stage is the analysis of the auditing methods to ensure they gather the appropriate information and meet the goals of the audit.

Blind audits—audits that are random and periodically scheduled without any notification to those being audited—are useful to establish the constant security awareness needed to maintain security as the organization flourishes. Blind audits come in the form of simulated attacks or planned scenarios to exemplify a particular security practice. Blind network and computer system analysis often appears as a real attack, and the results are generally surprising even in organizations with strict security policies. Social engineering is a particularly important aspect of these audits because it demonstrates the level of security awareness present among the employees. This aspect of the audit might include attempts to enter the facility, acquisition of passwords or access keys, and attempts to gather private information about the organization. The response of the employee and the ability of the auditor to garner this information demonstrates

Policies, Procedures, and Enforcement
CHAPTER 26

619

26

**POLICIES,
PROCEDURES, AND
ENFORCEMENT**

the level of awareness and the level of compliance with current security policies. The knowledge that an audit could occur at any time, without notification, forces employees to incorporate security awareness and practices into their daily routines. This enhances the security of an organization over the long run.

Summary

Security policies are dynamic and complex procedures, processes, and methods used to enhance the security within an organization. It is important to remember that the creation of security policy is not a one-time event. Policies must be flexible and scalable to meet the ever-growing and changing demands of the organization. Enforcement of the policies also helps to assure the validity of a security policy. Portions of the policy might no longer be applicable, and, as new technologies become available, the emphasis and individual requirements to maintain security can change. Enforcement involves a constant analysis of the results of the audits and the policy. Policies are not bipolar; non-compliance in some instances does not necessarily indicate an incorrect practice. Failures common to large groups of employees or common across related practices should be analyzed to determine if the mandate is valid and applicable. An organization should also avoid establishing unchanging practices. New security methods and practices should be researched continuously in order to enhance the security of an organization through more efficient, easier-to-use technology.

Documented security policies provide a consistently high degree of security to an organization through their comprehensiveness, consistency, and simplicity of use. They educate users and administrators in secure practices, set an appropriate level of security as needed by the environment, and provide recourse for the effects of misuse. When creating security policies for your organization, consider the sample guidelines presented here, their focus, and principles—use this knowledge to determine the best and most appropriate policies applicable to your organization.

For more information on some of the topics discussed here, see the following documents.

Password Security

The Memorability and Security of Passwords—Some Empirical Results. Ross Anderson , Alan Blackwell , Alasdair Grant and Jianxin Yan. `http://www.securityfocus.com/data/library/tr500.pdf`

Audits and Analysis

Improving the Security of Your Site by Breaking into It. Dan Farmer. `http://www.alw.nih.gov/Security/Docs/admin-guide-to-cracking.101.html`

There Be Dragons. Steven Bellovin. `http://www.securityfocus.com/data/library/dragons.ps`

Site Security Policies

Site Security Handbook. RFC #1244. `http://www.ietf.org/rfc/rfc1244.txt?number=1244`

Site Security Handbook. RFC #2196. `http://www.ietf.org/rfc/rfc2196.txt?number=2196`

Incident Handling

An Introduction to Incident Handling. Chad L. Cook. `http://www.securityfocus.com/focus/basics/articles/inchan.html`

System Configuration

Analysis of the Security of Windows NT. Stefan Axelsson and Jonsson Erland. `http://www.ce.chalmers.se/staff/jonsson/nt-part2.pdf`

Practical UNIX & Internet Security, Second Edition. Simson Garfinkel and Eugene Spafford. O'Reilly & Associates. ISBN: 1565921488, 1996.

Firewall Information

Firewalls For Beginners. Sunil Hazari. `http://www.securityfocus.com/focus/basics/articles/fwbeg.html`

Internal Security

The most peaceable way for you, if you do take a thief, is, to let him show himself what he is and steal out of your company.

—William Shakespeare, *Much Ado About Nothing*

IN THIS CHAPTER

This chapter focuses on securing your network from the inside, with the assumption that all your external security efforts are in vain if inside security is a pushover. Secondly, because "inside jobs" are rarely pretty or welcome, this chapter details some practices that avoid—in the best case—and detect—in the worst case—an intruder in your midst.

Internal Security: The Red-Headed Stepchild

It's probably a good bet that your network perimeter is incredibly more secure than the inside of your network; most networks are "crunchy on the outside, chewy on the inside." You can probably blame the "Firewalls-fix-everything" mentality of the last several years for this. This means that your *internal* vulnerabilities might very well be the cause of your worst security nightmare.

In fact, although the Computer Security Institute's most recent *Computer Crime and Security Survey* says that 90% of respondents detected security breaches, the report goes on to say that only 25% of the respondents detected breaches from the *outside*. Do the math.

NOTE

You can see the executive summary of the Computer Security Institute's 2000 Computer Crime and Security Survey at `http://www.gocsi.com/prelea_000321.htm`

(See the "Resources" section at the end of the chapter for more surveys, articles, and so on.)

The survey goes on to state that 71% of respondents detected unauthorized access by insiders. Clearly, internal security is a *huge* problem. The ICSA (International Computer Security Association) agrees, believing that insiders cause 80% of security problems.

NOTE

Stressing that firewalls are not a security panacea, the ICSA outlines some internal security problems in its Firewall Buyers Guide at `http://www.icsa.net/html/communities/firewalls/buyers_guide/chap_2.shtml`

Internal Risks: Types of Harm and Vectors

Fine. So breaches of internal security are common. But what's the worst thing that could happen? What are the risks? But more to the point, what can you do about these risks?

Many times, assessing an organization's internal risks can point directly to the necessity of implementing particular policies. It's useful to break these risks down into *types of harm* and *vectors*.

Some of the common types of harm that you'll want to consider are

- Server compromise
- Network infrastructure compromise
- Application level compromise
- Workstation compromise (trojans)
- Loss or theft of proprietary data
- Transmission of inappropriate or harmful data to business partners
- Denial of service

When we talk about *vectors*, we're really talking about the human factor—any type of human action that can introduce harm into your network. The human factor is rather complex; it's useful to further break down this factor into *organizational roles* and *type of intent*.

Some types of intent typically are

- **Well-meaning/Unwitting.** A person accidentally introduces harm into the network,
- **Scofflaw.** A person knowingly bypasses security checkpoints.
- **Disgruntled/Malicious/Opportunistic.**

The types of organizational roles are

- **Members of the public.** That is, users of a kiosk, or simply folks who are wandering your building and stumble across an unlocked wire closet.
- **Temporary employees.**
- **Departmental users.** Each department should really be considered separately because each can present a different level of privilege and/or risk.
- **Infrastructure, server, or application administrators.**

To visualize the way that these two factors interact to generate a level of risk, it's useful to set them into a chart where the upper left represents the least amount of risk, and the lower right represents the most risk.

TABLE 27.1   Human Vectors: Degree of Risk

Human Vectors: Degree of Risk	*Well-meaning/ Unwitting*	*Scofflaw*	*Disgruntled/ Malicious/ Opportunistic*
Members of public (kiosk, unlocked wire closet)	Least risk		
Temporary employees		↖	
Departmental users (each considered separately)		↘	
Infrastructure, server, or application administrators			Most risk

Obviously, a malicious administrator is your organization's worst nightmare, but gone are the days when "only" IT professionals could rock the network boat. Today's high-profile security problems coupled with "script kiddie" exploits and a permissive workstation policy means that any jerk with an attitude, an IQ of more than 80, and a PC can take advantage of your untended network. To fight back, enact a strong Acceptable Use Policy (AUP); check up on it with auditing and IDS tools; and enforce it. (See Chapter 26, "Policies, Procedures, and Enforcement," for more info on building an AUP.)

Scofflaw Employees

Scofflaw employees—that is, employees who want to bypass your normal security measures for their own convenience—can also be a huge problem.

The classic example of a scofflaw employee is one who ignores policy, bypasses the organization's remote access mechanism, and decides to install a modem and PCAnywhere on her PC—many times without a reasonably good password. All of a sudden, there is an open door from the outside to your internal network, not a good thing.

Other examples include VIP users who do not want their Internet access to be monitored by IT; they therefore bypass corporate firewalls and dial into their own ISPs, which don't necessarily have the same type of security policies that the organization does.

> **NOTE**
>
> I knew one VIP user in particular who bypassed his organization's email system—a system that scanned inbound and outbound email for viruses. He decided to use a dial-up account with a local vendor, which did not have virus protection on the mail gateway.
>
> To make a long story short, his workstation hadn't received the most recent virus pattern update yet; and one of his cronies sent him a virus that messed up his workstation, necessitating an "emergency" call to the help desk. Scofflaws oftentimes shoot themselves in the foot while they're putting the organization at risk.

As workstation-based trojans become more common, bypassing a site's security checkpoints becomes worse and worse. Consider AOL's recent problem with a workstation-based trojan; hundreds of member accounts were compromised when employees executed an interesting-looking program that arrived by email.

> America Online Inc. acknowledged last week that 200 member accounts were compromised when targeted AOL employees opened infected e-mail attachments. The attachments unleashed a Trojan horse program that created a connection to the employees' machines, allowing intruders to access password and credit-card information.
>
> *AOL Investigates Theft of Account Data, Computerworld*, Ann Harrison, June 26, 2000

These AOL employees were scofflaws in that they ignored an AOL policy: They opened executable content from untrusted sources because it looked less boring than the work that they were doing. Scofflaw users *will* become more and more of a threat as these types of Trojans proliferate. (See Chapter 18, "Trojans," for more information.)

You can mitigate this risk somewhat by using desktop management tools to "lock down" the desktop—and in some organizations this can in fact be appropriate—but in the end, it's a policy problem, not a technology problem. Desktop management is only effective if the politics of an organization allow it to be.

Bottom line: Top-level management wouldn't allow a VIP to erect a ladder on the side of the building to bypass corporate security's checkpoints; it also should not allow *anyone* to bypass network security's checkpoints. If top-level management truly understands the parallel, you have a powerful ally in the battle against scofflaws.

IT Employees

Of course, just because "everybody" is now a potential problem doesn't mean that disgruntled IT workers and coders aren't of concern. More potential privileges mean more potential problems, naturally. Case in point is the oft-cited "logic bomb."

Although the identification of the first software bomb is not certain, a classic example occurred in 1988 when a Texas firm called IRA suffered the deletion of some 168,000 payroll records from a database. This was shown to have been caused by a logic bomb planted by an employee named Burleson which was triggered 6 months after he left the firm.

Computer Crime: An Historical Survey, Richard E. Overill, Defence Systems International 98. `http://www.kcl.ac.uk/orgs/icsa/Staff/overill.htm`

System administrators and network infrastructure administrators can also be part of the problem—but they can also be part of the solution. If you have more than one hand in every pot, it's a *lot* harder for one person to leave back doors, plant subversive code, and so on. That is, collaborative practices mean that systems and code are always subject to someone else's review (see the next section, "Risk Mitigation Policies")—which means that you can nip problems in the bud. (See also Chapter 13, "Logging and Auditing Tools.")

Risk Mitigation Policies

You'll want to establish clear, written policies in partnership with your organization's management team. This partnership can't be emphasized enough—a policy without teeth might as well never have been written. You'll want to

- Establish good physical security for all infrastructure—no matter how "insignificant" a piece of infrastructure might seem.

- Get management to build some level of concern for network security into the hiring process.

- Explicitly forbid bypassing security checkpoints (such as firewalls, remote access servers, and so on) in your AUP.

- Establish desktop management policies as they relate to virus/trojan protection and levels of workstation lockdown.

- Encourage *small* teams of administrators to collaborate. If there's more than one administrator watching the henhouse, it's less attractive to act the fox.

- Employ intrusion-detection systems (see Chapter 12, "Intrusion Detection Systems (IDS)"), being careful to employ those that can handle high-bandwidth internal networks.

- Audit your systems and procedures periodically. (See Chapter 11, "Vulnerability Assessment Tools (Scanners)," and Chapter 13, "Logging and Auditing Tools.")

- Maintain current levels of OSes and applications. (Vendors usually patch script kiddie exploits rather quickly.) (See Part VI, "Platforms and Security," for more information on maintaining current levels.)

Physical Security

It's actually pretty easy to practice due diligence with physical security. You've just got to be meticulous and consistent, and take it seriously. Pretend that someone could burglarize you personally if you're not careful. It might help to pretend that you live in New York.

In all seriousness, physical security is where the battle can easily be lost—although it can't be totally won with just physical safeguards. Little things like the ability to reboot a server from a floppy, or finding an unused username on a printout—or even finding a tape with a copy of a security database on it—make an intruder's job easier. Let's make it *hard*.

Here are some "DOs" and "DON'Ts" that will make your job a little easier, an intruder's life a little harder, and your data a little more secure:

DOs

- **DO** lock every wiring closet—and keep them locked.
- **DO** use switches rather than hubs, *especially* for LAN segments that have administrative users on them. (They still must be physically secure to ensure that someone can't access the switch and packet sniff via port mirroring.)
- **DO** change locks or door passcodes immediately when employees leave.
- **DO** erase hard drives, flash, and so on, when you take them out of service. Nobody's going to remember to do it before the surplus auction, and all sorts of passwords and/or sensitive data might be on them.
- **DO** erase old backup tapes before disposing of them.
- **DO** write nonsense data to magnetic media when you are erasing it. Dropping a partition table is NOT good enough. (Degaussing is okay, though.)
- **DO** use a paper shredder. Don't laugh. Dumpster diving is more common than you think.
- **DO** lock your server cabinets when you're not using them.
- **DO** restrict or forbid the use of modems on desktops; they are the number one method of bypassing your organization's security checkpoints.
- **DO** make sure that any "road" laptop or PDA has appropriate data protection software and hardware installed before deployment.
- **DO** consider whether user access to floppy disks or other removable media make sense for your environment; they constitute a possible bypass of your security checkpoints.
- **DO** consider the use of smart cards/token-based security devices rather than passwords for administrative users or sensitive systems. Many operating systems now support token-based authentication in addition to passwords.
- **DO** remember that your phone PBXs also must be secured.

DON'Ts

- **DON'T** send off-site backups to unsecured locations.
- **DON'T** give keys to vendors. Let them in to do their work, and then politely wave bye-bye when they leave.
- **DON'T** allow anyone other than key personnel ad hoc access to the data center.
- **DON'T** share wire closets with user-oriented peripherals such as printers.
- **DON'T** put servers into unsecured areas.
- **DON'T** leave server keys attached to the back of a server. Believe it or not, other people will think of this, too.
- **DON'T** let cleaning people—or other untrusted service people—into secured areas without an escort.
- **DON'T** store any sensitive data on user hard drives—if you must, think about hard drive encryption products.
- **DON'T** discuss passwords or other sensitive information over unsecured channels such as cell phones, 800Mhz radios, or instant messaging.
- **DON'T** put consoles, keypads, or administrative workstations near windows.

The Hiring Process

Naturally, J. Random Hacker isn't going to show up and reveal his otherworldly activities at a job interview. And even doing background checks can turn into nothing more than lip service, depending upon who's doing the checks—and whether the individual has been caught in the past.

Still, there are things you can do to minimize your risks during the employment process. Start out by doing a "due diligence" background check—particularly for employees that will be involved in any level of IT. Do your homework and use a reputable agency to do your background checks—as with anything else in computing, "Garbage in, garbage out." If you are using an internal HR check or some other check that you don't get invoiced for, communication is the key. Don't *assume* that silence from your background check folks means "Everything is OK." Lack of "NACK" (*N*egative *ACK*nowledgement) does *not* mean "ACK." It might simply mean that your request form got thrown out with lunch's pizza box. See http://www.nwc.com/1201/1201colfeldman.html for more discussion of the hiring process.

After you've worked with management to establish an Acceptable Use Policy, your next step is to work with HR to integrate it as part of the employment process for *any* employee. You want it integrated for two reasons: First, because it sends a message, and might dissuade an employee from snooping or fiddling where he or she doesn't belong. Second, if termination or disciplinary action is necessary because of AUP violation, it's definitely a *lot* easier to do if you have an "I-have-read-and-understood-this" AUP to back you up.

Establishing Desktop Lockdown

Lockdown, in the desktop management context, means that you've managed to apply the straps to your users in such a way that they can't hurt themselves—or your network. In the best case, this is done in such a way that the users don't feel constricted or stifled. Having a heart-to-heart with management about the level of lockdown can be only a good thing. Users get extremely irrational about losing *any* amount of autonomy, and you will *definitely* want management to buy into any lockdown that you need to enact.

It should be pointed out that desktop management—*any* desktop management—that resides on a local workstation can be bypassed by a clever user unless there is serious physical security in place (no floppies, an "unpickable" case lock, and so forth). This, of course, is the type of security that you *must* have if you have public information terminals, kiosks, and so on. The point is that any workstation that isn't physically secured can usually be booted from alternative media, and then the local OS can be modified to a malicious user's heart's content.

Still, desktop management and lockdown for nonpublic users are important due-diligence measures, and definitely should not be skipped. The important thing here is to prevent either well-meaning or scofflaw users from hurting themselves and others. Defeating a truly noncasual and malicious user isn't the primary purpose of desktop management.

▶ As far as manual procedures go, you can see some sample system lockdown checklists at
  `http://www.nswc.navy.mil/ISSEC/Form/index.html`.

Virus protection, of course, is a mandatory component to desktop management. Virus protection is (or should be) such second nature to today's IT staff that we mention it here simply to ask one question: Can the user turn off virus protection?

Some virus protection suites let the user do this; others password-protect the entire control panel. You should certainly password-protect the control panel if possible, but you should also enact desktop management policies that check and reinstall virus protection if the workstation's otherwise permissive operating system allows its removal.

Good desktop management tools enable you to not only "force" certain applications, but they can also

- Force applications to be configured in a certain way (notably browsers)
- Restrict users from running anything but a certain set of applications
- Restrict use of removable media
- Prevent users from modifying system configuration

Restricting Content

It used to be that IT managers were only worried about what users were able to download; that is, folks were concerned about employee abuse of the Internet. At the time, there wasn't technology to check *what* the actual downloaded content was—so managers contented themselves with blocking sites based upon *where* the user tried to surf. Certain software manufacturers also became service organizations (notably Cyber Patrol; see "Products: Content Management,") that maintained a list of URLs in certain categories: adult-oriented, comedy, shopping, news, and so on. As a manager, you could then block various categories with a perimeter device that had access to these lists.

This strategy, however, wasn't complete in and of itself. Objectionable sites surface overnight, and the list didn't always reflect reality. And, filtering outbound URLS does nothing to fight questionable content that *leaves* your site.

Because one of the risks to your organization is the unauthorized disclosure of content (customer lists, intellectual property, and so on), one of the hottest topics in corporate security today is that of *content management* (also called *content filtering*, *content services*, and *content restriction*). Content management works in conjunction with your perimeter security devices. The software can perform lexical analysis, pattern matching—even image recognition. (Yes, *those* images.)

Another risk faced by your organization is the transmission of inappropriate content (pornographic, libelous, or otherwise offensive data) or dangerous content (such as Trojans and viruses) to business partners. You'd have to be nuts to think that *any* tool could totally eliminate the possibility of inappropriate content making it through your checkpoints. But content management tools can limit the possibility. Virus gateway protection software is one example of specialized content management.

Some vendors label their products as content filters, when in fact they are *site filters* or *URL filters*. Again, rather than checking the *data stream* for objectionable content, they check the *Web address* against a categorized list of known Web sites. Site filtering has merit. It can definitely decrease the amount of daytrading/time-wasting/non–work-related surfing at your organization—but it's not *content* filtering. It is only as effective as the folks who update the lists are. And, site management doesn't do anything for your intranet.

That said, content management tools fall into two categories: those that offer generic content-checking services to the network, and those that operate solely on a specific application.

Those that offer generic content services tend to do it via CheckPoint Software's CVP (Content Vectoring Protocol). CVP accepts a connection from a client, proxies the request to the server, scans the content, and either modifies or denies the request when content does not pass muster.

There is not yet an RFC-based content restriction protocol that has been widely implemented. If you're not using Firewall-1 or another firewall that supports CVP, you might have to purchase individual products that separately monitor Web content (HTTP), email (SMTP), news (NNTP), and FTP.

You'll also probably have to put up with some degree of false positives—yet another thing to administrate. For example, content filters commonly block Network Computing's "Centerfold," a showcase of innovative companies' networks.

Still, content filters can be worthwhile, if you target and configure them correctly. See the section "Products," later in the chapter for a sampling of content-filtering tools. Look for content management to change and grow in the next couple of years; hit the Web or magazines like Network Computing for the latest scoop.

Administrative Collaboration

At first, administrative collaboration doesn't seem like much of a security practice. How can teamwork make your internal network a safer place?

First, consider that any illegal or unethical action involving partners automatically means that there are witnesses and possible leads to an investigation. As Benjamin Franklin said, "Three can keep a secret if two of them are dead."

Secondly, take the case where there is no explicit partnership during a questionable activity. The fact that there is another administrator who has responsibility for the system involved means that the system itself is under scrutiny. The fact that there is third-party scrutiny of the system might discourage the perpetrator in the best case, or at least lead to discovery of the questionable activity.

You should be careful, however, to avoid assigning too many hands to any given pot. Not only can this lead to system chaos, but it also can make unethical activity harder to trace either during an incident or an audit. You definitely want a limited pool of individuals accountable for a given system.

Products

Products change all of the time—you'll want to check the latest industry magazines and Web sites to make sure that you've got the latest options in front of you. The following sections list sample products in various categories so that you can get off on the right foot.

Desktop Management

Product: LANDesk

Company: Intel

URL: `http://www.intel.com/network/products/landesk_mgmtsuite_v6.htm`

Description: Platform agnostic desktop management; works with Win9x, WinNT/Win2K, Netware, and Linux.

Product: Systems Management Server (SMS)

Company: Microsoft

URL: `http://www.microsoft.com/smsmgmt/exec/default.asp`

Description: Certainly the easiest way to manage the desktops of a Windows network. Works with Win9x and NT with ZAK (Zero Administration Kit) and Win2000's Group Policies.

Product: ZENWorks for Desktops

Company: Novell

URL: `http://www.novell.com/products/zenworks/desktops/`

Description: Desktop management using NDS (Novell Directory Services) as the configuration data store. Scales extremely well.

Laptop/PDA Security

When a portable device walks away, it's not pretty; the loss of the device is nothing compared to the potential loss of sensitive information. Although "password-at-power-up" is popular, it is not a good solution after someone has stolen your device; use real data encryption instead. There are a huge number of options, and it's not our intention here to offer a complete buyer's guide. Rather, this is a starting point. When you're looking to buy portable device security solutions, consider whether

- **Physical tokens are available.** If the device will be used in a public place, there is always the risk of someone "keystroke watching" during password entry, and later stealing the device.

- **What type of encryption is used.** Some vendors use a proprietary algorithm that hasn't been publicly examined for flaws. Stay well away from these, as well those algorithms that use "obscuring" tactics like XOR (bit-complement), which are *not* secure.

PDA Security

Product: MemoSafe

Company: DeepThought

URL: `http://home.golden.net/~deepnet/memosafe.html`

Description: MemoSafe uses the public domain SAFER-SK cipher to encrypt your MemoPad memos.

Product: ReadThis!

Company: PixIL

URL: `http://members.nbci.com/PixIL/Software/ReadThis/`

Description: A module that requires HackMaster, and encrypts arbitrary Palm records; beware, as the default method is "XOR"—as stated previously, *not* a secure method. Fortunately, an externally available IDEA encryption module is available. Source is only available for the external module.

Product: Safe

Company: Palmgadget.com

URL: `http://www.palmgadget.com/palmsafe.html`

Description: Triple-DES memo pad encryptor; the source code is available for inspection, which is a real plus.

Laptop Security

Product: Invincible Disk

Company: Invincible Data Systems, Inc.

URL: `http://www.incrypt.com/idisk01.html`

Description: Encrypts an entire hard drive using the Blowfish encryption algorithm. Supports physical tokens.

Product: SafeHouse for Windows

Company: PC Dynamics

URL: `http://www.pcdynamics.com/SafeHouse/`

Description: Offers several different encryption options, including Blowfish, and triple DES; but also includes the not-so-secure DES algorithm, as well as a proprietary algorithm that has not been publicly scrutinized.

> **NOTE**
>
> If you use UNIX or Linux on laptops, see the section "Resources" later in the chapter for a paper describing encrypted file systems such as cfs, sfs, cryptfs, and so on.

Physical Security

Product: Barracuda Anti Theft Devices

Company: Barracuda Security Devices International

URL: `http://www.barracudasecurity.com`

Description: Barracuda's flagship product is a PC card that is inserted into an expansion slot; it monitors all computer components. You are paged when any component is tampered with or removed. A terribly shrill alarm goes off as well.

Product: Modem Security Enforcer

Company: IC Engineering, Inc.

URL: `http://www.bcpl.lib.md.us/~n3ic/mse/mseinfo.html`

Description: Modem Security Enforcer includes callback authentication, password protection, firmware password storage (inaccessible to internal users), nonvolatile memory storage settings, and a completely configurable interface. There is a 9600bps version and a 19,200bps version.

Product: ModemLock for SmartCard Modems

Company: Intertex Data AB

URL: `http://www.intertex.se/html/modemlock.html`

Description: Software that restricts incoming or outgoing modem use. Unfortunately, it requires that you use Intertex's brand of smart card modems.

Content Management

Product: eSafe Gateway

Company: Aladdin Knowledge Systems

URL: `http://www.ealaddin.com/esafe/gateway/index.asp`

Description: Filters Web traffic for hostile applets, viruses; can do URL filtering; inspects MIME encoded mail.

Product: MIMESweeper product family: MAILSweeper; PORNSweeper; WEBSweeper; SECRETSweeper

Company: Content Technologies

URL: `http://www.contenttechnologies.com/products/default.asp`

Description: The kitchen sink, oven, stove, and dust-buster of content management. Filters everything from MIME-encoded email to porn-bearing-GIFs.

Product: SuperScout, CyberPatrol, SurfControl

Company: SurfControl

URL: http://www.surfcontrol.com/

Description: All products use the same CyberNOT subscription list, and perform varying degrees of site filtering. SuperScout in particular can deny/allow sites based on file types.

Product: Various

Company: CheckPoint

URL: http://www.checkpoint.com/opsec/security.html#Content_Security

Description: List of companies and products that have partnered with CheckPoint, and use CVP (Content Vectoring Protocol) as a central service for content scrutiny.

Resources

Computer Security Institute's 2000 Computer Crime and Security Survey.
http://www.gocsi.com/prelea_000321.htm

Computer Crime & Security Survey 1999.
http://www.deloitte.com.au/downloads/Computer_Crime99.pdf

Computer crime—an historical survey. Richard E. Overill.
http://www.kcl.ac.uk/orgs/icsa/Publications/crime.html

Risk Assessment Strategies. Workshop about risk management.
http://www.nwc.com/1121/1121f3.html

How to Fire A System Administrator. M. Ringel and T. Limoncelli. http://www.bell-labs.com/user/tal/papers/LISA1999/adverse.html

A Contextual Love Letter for You. http://www.nwc.com/1117/1117colfeldman.html

Zero Administration Kit for Windows (Win9x and WinNT desktop management).
http://www.microsoft.com/windows/zak/

Using Group Policy Scenarios (Win2000 desktop management).
http://www.microsoft.com/technet/win2000/win2ksrv/technote/gpscena.asp

Palm Security: Encryption Tools.
http://palmtops.about.com/gadgets/palmtops/library/weekly/aa06182000a.htm

Encrypting Your Disks With Linux. Covers technologies that work on Linux and other UNIX derivatives. http://drt.ailis.de/crypto/linux-disk.html

Using Win2000's Foolproof Encryption. Uses Win2000's native file encryption technology.
http://www.nwc.com/1121/1121ws1.html

Summary

Good internal security amounts to doing the same things you do for external security, and practicing due diligence as regards self-auditing and policy enforcement. There are tools that can help, such as auditing tools/security scanners, content filtering tools, desktop management, and IDS, but in the final analysis, no tool can replace meticulous and sharp-eyed individuals.

Network Architecture Considerations

IN THIS CHAPTER

This chapter discusses considerations for network architecture that enhance the security of the computing and network environment.

Network Architecture

The Internet is known as the network of networks. Each network plays an important part in the greater security of the Internet. By emphasizing security when designing and implementing your network, you can make your little corner of the Internet a safer place to be. The creation of a network environment for an organization should be thought out well in advance, rather than simply plugging equipment together. The goal of this chapter is to present you with important considerations for your network design that will enhance the security of your organization and those with which it interoperates.

The term "network architecture" collectively describes the requirements, organization, methods, and equipment used to create a network including its physical components and security awareness. A secure network architecture is arrived at by considering all of these elements, their use and their relationship to each other. Before you can make a network architecture secure, it is important to know the components used to create the network and the threats against them. Once the organization of the components and their threats is understood, a valid architecture can be designed.

Network Components

Without network components, there is no network, and without consideration for these components, there is no security! The first step toward a secure network topology is to examine the devices and systems used to implement it. The following considerations and types of equipment are common to an organization:

- Access devices
- Security devices
- Servers and systems
- Organization and layout

Access Devices

The access device is the piece of network equipment that provides Internet access and intercommunication between networks and is the first element required for an Internet-accessible organization. Organizations may not need an access device, but if they want to communicate with other networks or to provide access from the outside to employees or Internet users, an access device is needed. Access devices come in many forms; the most common are modems and routers.

There are generally two (or more) interfaces on an access device. The interfaces to which the network of the organization connects are considered the internal interface of the router (or other equipment). The interfaces that connect to the Internet service provider (ISP) are the external interfaces. The internal network comprises those systems and equipment on the internal side of the router. The network or networks accessible from the Internet form the external network.

The use of the access device has a direct effect on the security of a network topology because it helps define the Internet access model used in the organization and is the first point where defense is needed. There are many access models that designers can use, including highly restrictive exception-based access, open, and a combination in between. Exception-based access models apply a default restriction that disallows all access, followed by exceptions for needed services and connectivity. This is a commonly used method of protection where the firewall is configured to block traffic to all but a few specified protocols and services on specific systems. An example of exception-based access is to disallow all traffic to the Web server except for TCP traffic to port 80 (the IP protocol and service port (HTTP) that the Web server uses). Exception-based access models are useful in simple network environments where there is little network diversity or need for complex filtering rules.

An open model allows access to everyone unless otherwise explicitly prohibited. This model focuses on only the services provided by a network and its systems. It uses firewall rules to allow or disallow access from specific networks and systems to explicit services such as a Web server or email and provides granular access control. This model takes no action on the remainder of the ports and protocols that are not in use, however, which can present a security risk in some network environments.

The following examples demonstrate the usefulness and dangers of an open access model.

In a simple network environment, where the Web server is connected directly to the Internet, an open model might create unnecessary security risks. In this case, the firewall allows access to the Web server from specific friendly networks and systems, but does not affect any other traffic to or from the Web server, including hostile traffic from the Internet. This presents a danger if an attacker compromises the Web server. The attacker can then set up a new and unauthorized service on that system, which runs unaffected by the firewall. An exception-based model would protect against this.

Open models are useful to provide granular access control and protect against unauthorized traffic to specific services, as is often used with domain name servers and email servers. Domain name servers and email servers often have secondary relays that provide service to Internet systems and protect the primary system from exposure to the Internet. The primary systems can be configured with an open access model that allows network traffic to the domain name and email services only from the relay servers. This example also assumes that the network topology protects the primary servers from external attack.

28

NETWORK ARCHITECTURE CONSIDERATIONS

There are several schools of thought when determining which model of access should be used. The exception-based model is more restrictive and places the brunt of the security responsibilities on the firewall's strengths. The open model relies more on the systems in use to assure that they are configured securely and provide minimal possibility for compromise and modification.

Security Devices

Firewalls, Virtual Private Network (VPN) servers, and intrusion detection systems (IDS) are commonly used examples of security devices. Firewalls are used to protect the internal network from external threats by allowing or disallowing certain types of network traffic and data. Firewalls are not meant only for the edge of the network, but anywhere that traffic restrictions are required or recommended. VPN devices are used to provide secure remote access from the Internet to users by creating an encrypted tunnel through which the remote computer accesses the internal network of an organization. Intrusion detection systems provide active monitoring and notification of known attacks on systems and networks by watching network data. These devices provide the first and most obvious level of security and are vital to any network topology.

Servers and Systems

Servers and systems are all of the computers used within the organization. These systems include Web, mail, login, file and print servers, desktop computers, and network management systems. The requirements for these systems influence the network architecture and include the network services offered, and they also dictate to whom access is provided. Each service provided affects the security of the network and the system on which it runs. Consideration given to these effects results in a network architecture that minimizes the risks and effects of a security breach.

As you have learned throughout this book, attackers will often scan for servers that provide services to both the Internet and internal networks; the compromise of these systems allows the attacker a doorway into the organization. Servers that run multiple services also present security risks because each service provides a potential doorway into that particular system. It is particularly important to examine the history of an application or service for security vulnerabilities. Email, Web, DNS, and FTP servers have a long history of vulnerabilities, and their simultaneous use on a single system provides several access points for an attacker.

Organization and Layout

The organization and layout of the network takes into consideration the implementation of these components. This includes the physical placement and organization of the network equipment and wiring, as well as the method by which Internet access is provided. Identifying network service requirements and the relationship of users to these services is important to the security of a network architecture.

Many operating systems and servers arrive configured by default to provide every service it supports, despite the fact that an organization rarely needs or uses all of them. If an organization needs file sharing, printing, Web, and email capabilities, the servers that provide these services should have all their other services disabled. If these services are provided to different groups within the organization or if a clear need for these services to share information is not established, they should be run on different systems and networks that reflect the users' access needs.

Threats

The threats to a network should be known in advance of the design. The threats outlined here are organized into three categories:

- External attacks
- Internal attacks
- Physical attacks

Understanding the threats posed to a network connected to the Internet has several key benefits. This knowledge allows the network designers to protect against attack and compromise of systems, limit the effects of vulnerabilities, and isolate their interactions. The secure network architecture affects the ability of an organization to react quickly to an incident and to recover safely without loss while also adding to reliability and performance. The threats to a network and its systems are partially mitigated with a secure network architecture. Other factors that help alleviate risk are good security maintenance and diligence with regard to analysis of new and better security technologies.

External Attacks

External attacks are those that originate either from the Internet or from systems beyond the access device and target internal or external systems. External attacks are the most publicized and the most well-known form of attack. Stories of Web page defacements, viruses, Trojan programs, and denial of service by malicious system crackers and cyber-terrorists are common. Although invasive, reconnaissance probes and scans are not attacks. They are often precursors to an attack, however, because they provide vulnerability information to the attacker. The network components and their organization can minimize the risk associated with these attacks. External attacks occur against accessible services, systems, and networks; protection against external attacks includes the use of firewalls, network monitoring devices, distribution of services across multiple networks, and the establishment of bandwidth restrictions by protocol and service.

To protect against external attacks, it is useful to run services such as domain name servers, Web servers, and mail servers on separate systems and to restrict network access to them with a firewall. It is also beneficial to isolate these systems so they are unable to access any other system.

These methods protect the systems from compromise by establishing only one point of access to each system. Multiple services on a single system might present higher risk for denial of service and system compromise because there are several points to attack and the compromise of one service can provide access to the data for all other services on that system. The example of a single system that acts as a mail, Web, and domain name server establishes three targets for attack. Denial of service against any of these targets results in a loss of service to all of them, and compromise of any one service provides the attacker with access to the data of the remaining two.

Internal Attacks

As the name implies, internal attacks originate from inside the organization. Despite the media attention given to external attacks, internal attacks are more widespread and frequent than those committed by outsiders. Disgruntled employees, curious users, or accidental misuse all contribute to the frequency of internal attacks. Defense against these attacks is more complex because designers attempt to provide high security without restricting the needed functionality of the network. Users should only be given enough access and privileges to accomplish their work and to protect against internal threats. Examining network data paths and splitting services across multiple networks and systems help provide higher security and minimize the effects of attack.

Users should not, for example, be given full network access to all systems, servers, and network equipment. Most organizations do not want all users to have access to financial systems, or for all users to have access to sensitive project materials. The use of multiple networks and servers to differentiate between groups and departments allows enforcement of these restrictions.

Physical Attacks

Physical access is the final threat category. The ability to walk up to a system or piece of network equipment is the most dangerous of the risks. Simple actions such as unplugging equipment, rearranging cables, or physically damaging components can render the network unusable for long periods of time and at a high expense for repair. The location and access to the equipment that provides network service should be organized and secured. Aside from physical damage to network equipment, another aspect of physical attacks is the ability for a user to see and analyze network traffic that travels over the same network wires of the user's desktop computer. If the network is not physically laid out safely, the user can use a packet sniffer to intercept and read the passwords and private information of other users. This can be prevented by physically isolating network traffic, based on the needs of a particular system.

Approach to Network Architecture

The approach to network architecture and its design is the philosophy and model used to outline the network requirements and components for an organization. Although there are several schools of thought on this subject, the approach used here reflects a compromise between the idealistic and the realistic implementations. The ideal implementation provides complete and guaranteed security. The realistic model recognizes the need for services that have a higher potential for vulnerabilities. These services provide important aspects of service to the organization and to its customers and partners. In an ideal networked world, there are no vulnerabilities, and no services that are risky are used, which provides complete security.

As you know, there is no such concept as guaranteed or total security. The reality of the environment presses the network designer toward a high degree of security across the infrastructure. The level of security required in an organization should also be determined based on its needs rather than on following a generic recipe. Despite the creation of a secure network architecture, security is still a continuous process that requires constant vigilance. Unfortunately, few organizations have dedicated teams to security development, implementation, and maintenance, though a greater focus and presence of security-specific staff is now developing. Due to the lack of dedicated personnel, organizations tend to focus security efforts on those areas deemed most vulnerable—the "squeaky wheel" approach to security. This often precludes the maintenance and upkeep of security for the internal network and systems because they are considered protected by firewalls and other security mechanisms. Although lax internal security is not ideal, it emphasizes the need for a strong network architecture and infrastructure at its earliest stages of design. The higher the initial level of security, the easier it will be to develop and follow standards and procedures to maintain that level.

You can measure the security of a network architecture by its capability to manage risk and mitigate the effects of attack. The organization of functionality into levels of security relative to network access is a reasonable method to begin the design. When the threats to a network are understood, network designers should carefully consider the requirements, components, and features that are used in the network and their relationships with each other. The requirements establish the purpose for the network such as supporting the ability of its users to share data, communicate among each other, and interact with external sources. The components of a network include the actual hardware used to create the network and the organization and layout of the topology. The features are those capabilities and requirements outside of the initial needs that conform to a set of best practices and ancillary functionality. Finally, it is important to understand the relationships of all of these components because security is only as strong as the weakest link in the chain.

Security Zones

Several zones of security are common to networks, and the consideration designers give to them affects the network architecture used. These zones outline security in relation to network access and provide the initial sections of the network architecture. The security zones are organized into the external, the internal, and the intermediary tier.

The Great Beyond

The external network is, generally and in practice, the most open of the tiers and consists of everything from the access device outward to the Internet. The organization has little or no control over the information, systems, and equipment that exist in this domain. The security of the ISP and all of the external organizations to which it connects should not be assumed. It is useful to investigate the security practices and features that an ISP provides including the control and management of the access device and the filtering and network topology of the ISP. Many ISPs manage the access device and secure it to prevent access and tampering by anyone other than the ISP; others require the organization to manage it. Many ISPs perform some level of packet filtering and firewalling on their own to detect and block improper data and attacks before they have a chance to reach the ISPs' customers. The network topology of the ISP also plays a role in the security for an organization. The physical relation between the individual customers of an ISP and the data paths established should be identified. Ideally, the amount of data from different organizations that travels across the same network wires should be minimized. This limits the effects on multiple customer networks in the event that the ISP falls victim to attack. The use of a common gateway by the ISP leads to a potential performance bottleneck and security risk as a single point of failure. ISPs with diversified networks and multiple points of access can provide higher security and reliability against attacks.

These considerations are beneficial to the organization, but finding a provider that implements many security measures may be difficult and expensive. An important philosophy to keep in mind when creating a secure network architecture is to secure the elements controlled by the organization as strongly as possible. Many organizations rely on the security provided by the ISP or any intermediary networks and fail to implement any internal security measures. Therefore, the consideration of ISP security is important, but the emphasis should be placed on the creation of a secure network architecture for the organization. Solutions that mitigate weak ISP security include the creation of a Public Key Infrastructure and the use of encrypted network communications with applications such as Secure Shell (SSH), SSL-enabled Web servers, and Virtual Private Networks (VPNs).

Internal Networks

The second zone is the internal network, where the vital computing assets should be safely protected. This area often has the most restrictive security measures and is where the majority of users operate on a daily basis. The internal network is generally the least open and has multiple layers of protection for the servers, desktops, and other computer systems and equipment used in the organization. The use of firewalls, multiple networks, and constraints on network data paths provides a higher level of security. The discussion on internal networks continues in greater depth in the section "Protecting the Castle."

Intermediate Networks

The third zone is a compromise between the previous two zones and consists of the networks that provide services to both the internal and external networks. In general, it is considered very dangerous to make a single server or device exist simultaneously on an internal and an external network. A system configured in this manner is called a multihomed system and should be avoided. Secure network architectures begin to differentiate between those systems and services to which the Internet has access and those to which it does not.

Two intermediate networks are common in organizations. The first is a place for publicly accessible services such as the mail server, Web server, and Domain Name servers to internal users and those on the Internet. The second is a semiprivate network used by the organization, its business partners, and customers; this network requires specialized access only to those parties. This first area is often referred to as the "service network," or the De-Militarized Zone (DMZ), and is seen as a less protected area of the entire network infrastructure because it provides network services to the Internet.

A service network generally exists between the router to the ISP and the internal network. It can be created by adding another interface to the firewall, or by placing systems on the same network as the firewall. It is useful and more secure to create and protect the service network through another firewall interface in order to provide more restrictions of network access to the service network. Using this method, the organization can then restrict access to those services to authorized networks and systems, and prevent known hostile sites and competitors from accessing the Web site. The service network also benefits from a redundant or extra network link. With a single network connection to the ISP, a denial of service attack that utilizes all of the network bandwidth by attacking a system in the service network also denies service to the corporate network.

Although expensive and more complex, incorporating multiple network access points and connections to provide different network paths for a single or multiple service networks and the internal network helps provide a higher degree of security and reliability. Should an attacker attempt a denial of service attack, the access point under attack can be temporarily shut down, while the network remains operational through the secondary access point. People often consider the service network as less secure and internal networks as more secure, but this is inaccurate. The internal network has a more restrictive protection method that severely limits access from the Internet. The service network has different requirements in that it needs to allow access from the Internet to certain services. Systems in the service network often have a higher degree of individual system security with a less restrictive protection method. More care is often given to systems on the service network due to their increased exposure. In order to prevent compromise, an organization should maintain and patch the server software and operating system, protect them with strong filtering and access control policies, and monitor network traffic. In the ideal world, the same security considerations are given to all machines, regardless of their locations, but in practice, most organizations become more lax with the security of internal systems because of the other, broader security protection methods defined by the network architecture. The firewall used to protect the internal network is seen as the foolproof defense mechanism. Equal focus should be placed on firewall policies such as access control and service restrictions, as well as system configuration and maintenance that keep the systems at their highest possible security levels.

The service network is a protective buffer zone for the company and is not the only intermediary network that may be needed by an organization. Many organizations partner with various other companies, provide support to customers, and share information between them. This function creates the need for an extranet in order to restrict access to sensitive information and resources from external users. The extranet is a semiprivate network that shares data between the organization and its partners and customers. The information accessible on this network is often a subset of the information available on the corporate intranet, and requires explicit security measures to secure it. An extranet can be created by dedicating a piece of the network to these semiprivate servers and protecting them with a firewall. The access granted by the firewall should reflect the organizations that need it. Restricting access only to the networks and systems of the partner organizations instead of the entire Internet increases the security of the extranet.

Protecting the Castle

In this section, the discussion focuses on the architecture of the internal network. The security considerations for network design are applicable to all areas of network architecture, however.

Isolation and Separation

The idea of isolation and separation might seem contradictory to the concept of a network, where all things are connected, but the secure network architecture considers the relationship of each component and function to determine whether it needs to interact with the others. Separation of networks is the use of multiple physical and virtual networks to establish boundaries between unrelated network functions where no intercommunication is needed. It can also come in the form of physically disconnected networks, or virtually separate, wherein the devices do not allow network data to pass between them.

There are two levels to consider when dealing with isolation and separation. The organization of the packet or the low-level network data that travels electronically across the wire is the first level, and the organization of the systems that comprise the network is the second.

The relationships between users, groups of users, departments, and multiple locations within an organization require the network designer to consider the use of distinct networks in their network architecture. Some users may require access to the Internet without any other internal access, whereas others may need access to vital corporate information. The security of the network infrastructure becomes weak if these requirements are not assessed and if no distinction is made.

An organization often has several different and unrelated functions. A security risk is presented if these different groups are provided access to the networks and systems of the other. Publicly accessible terminals, for example, should not be on the same network as file, authentication, and email servers for the organization because that allows unauthorized individuals to access these systems.

Network Data

Network architecture does not focus only on the orientation of computer systems and their locations relative to each other, but also on the organization of network data. Security and performance are enhanced if consideration is given to the paths taken by packets. The topics discussed here are:

- Networking concepts
- Segments
- Switches and hubs
- Routers
- Network numbers
- Physical considerations

Each of these topics has an important role in the security of a network architecture and should be examined prior to its design.

Networking Concepts

Before delving too far into the technical aspects of network data, it is important to further clarify the levels of networking that are discussed here. The term network refers to several facets of intercommunication between systems. The highest level of networking concerns the orientation of systems in relation to each other. The external and internal networks, service networks, extranets, and firewalls refer to the relationship of networked systems to each other.

Wading deeper into the technical details of networking, the next level is that of the protocol. Networks communicate via a number of different protocols. These protocols are independent of each other but often exist simultaneously. The most prominent of the protocols is the Internet Protocol (IP). Every system that interacts with the Internet uses IP. Each IP network is defined by a set of numbers that establish a range of values that can be assigned to systems. Routers are used to transfer information from one IP network to another. Although this discussion focuses on IP networks, other commonly recognized protocols include IPX/SPX, Systems Network Architecture (SNA), and AppleTalk.

An organization often has several different IP networks in use to isolate functional areas. The differentiation of IP networks has already been introduced with discussion of the service network and internal network. The internal network of an organization often consists of several networks including a corporate network for all of the users, management networks for network management of systems and devices, test networks to isolate laboratory systems, server networks, and even individual department networks. The need for all of these different functions requires consideration when designing the network. The decision to establish multiple networks in an organization is made by examining the function and organization of systems, the relationships they have with other systems in the organization, and determining which data sharing is acceptable.

The next area of networking discussed here is at the physical and electrical level. The wires and equipment used to create the network, their layout, and the factors used to determine the layout present a third area for consideration. The design of a secure network architecture examines all of these components and determines the requirements and appropriate methods for their implementation.

Segments

Think of a segment as a single piece of wire, onto which several computers can attach for network access. Each computer that attaches to a single segment can see all of the network traffic on that segment and shares the total bandwidth available for that segment. In the case of a 100Mb/s network with several computers attached via a hub, they all share the bandwidth available. In the event that one of the machines is performing a network-intensive task, the availability of bandwidth for the other systems is diminished. Should a malicious person attack one of the systems on this segment and utilize the entire network bandwidth, denial of service occurs for every system on that segment. If a single system is compromised by an attacker, it is possible for that individual to watch all of the network traffic that is on that segment, identify the other systems, and proceed to compromise them. This includes communication between individual machines on that segment and any communication between one of these machines and other segments, networks, or the Internet.

Network segmentation is an important consideration when determining the relation and proximity of various systems. When designing a network architecture, it is important to understand the types of network data that will be traveling on the network. Web, file, and printer data are the commonly known information types that are first recognized. Information such as user credentials, including usernames, passwords, encryption keys, and other private or sensitive information, such as financial data and company private information, also passes along the network segment and poses even greater security threats. An attacker can view and steal sensitive information when care is not taken to define secure network segments. In the highest security environment, careful concern is given to the segmentation of systems. In the best-case scenario, user credentials and other sensitive information is not observable from any other system and the electrical path taken by the data forms a direct line to the destination system.

Switches and Hubs

Network segmentation is affected by the network equipment chosen to provide service. Ethernet switches and hubs are two of the most common pieces of network equipment used in an organization. Along with Ethernet, many organizations use Asynchronous Transfer Mode (ATM) or Token Ring for their network interface type. Switches and hubs allow multiple systems to be connected to the same network. The difference is in the electrical methods by which this sharing occurs. All of the systems connected to a hub share the same segment. When data arrives on one port, the hub multiplexes the data to all of the other ports on that hub. Network switches provide a higher level of security. Every port on a switch forms a separate segment from all other ports on that switch. When data arrives on one port, the switching technology determines to which port it needs to go, and switches it to that port instead of multiplexing it to all of its ports. The only time a switch will multiplex data occurs when it receives a broadcast packet.

Broadcasts are special transmissions that have no particular machine as a destination. All systems see broadcasts and respond depending on their relation to the message. Broadcast storms occur under circumstances where one system sends an incorrect packet that causes all other systems to respond simultaneously, causing every system to again respond to those incorrect packets. This creates an endless cycle of broadcasts that saturates the network and causes a loss of service to the broadcast domain. Broadcast domains describe a single LAN, or network, wherein broadcast traffic propagates, and the desire to keep network traffic from permeating certain areas of the network or reaching particular machines should be examined.

Collisions are related to broadcasts. Whereas broadcasts occur at the IP layer of networking, collisions occur at the Ethernet layer. Collisions occur when two systems transmit network data simultaneously. All network transmissions occur as a series of electrical signals over the network wire. When two systems transmit data simultaneously, these signals collide, and the resulting signal and packet are corrupt. Collision domains are those areas wherein collisions are propagated, similarly to IP broadcasts. Hubs propagate collisions, but switches do not. Collisions also affect the performance of a network, so the use of Ethernet switches provides higher reliability.

By connecting a single system to each port on a switch, no system on the switch can view network traffic from another, unless they are communicating directly with each other. Careful thought during network architecture design allows for the creation of a well-organized and secure network. Using a switched network, it is feasible to ensure that each system has a direct electrical path to servers and important systems, thereby protecting it from eavesdropping. The benefit of a switched Ethernet is also weakened when a hub is connected to a switch because it causes network traffic to be available to multiple systems. When attaching hubs to a switch in order to provide network access to more systems, the types of network traffic and the sensitivity of the information should be considered.

28

NETWORK
ARCHITECTURE
CONSIDERATIONS

Routers

The use of routers at the network access point has been mentioned earlier in the discussion, but routers are not only useful at the edge of the network; they are used to create the separate networks and broadcast domains within an organization to form several internal networks isolated by function, data, or department. The equipment and management cost associated with routers versus network switches is higher, but in some cases a routed network makes more sense for the preferred architecture. Broadcast messages are transmitted across switches but not across routers. The use of routers is important to an organization for network isolation, as well as to add reliability. Routers allow the simultaneous use of multiple paths to a given destination and are capable of changing between them automatically in the event of failure. Routers often incorporate security measures akin to firewalls that allow restriction of network data types to and from its networks. Diversification, redundancy, and security of internal networks can be achieved at a higher degree with routers, at some expense to simplicity and ease of management and higher cost.

The configuration of the router is pivotal to the security of the network because an attacker can modify the path of network traffic via changes to the router. Detailed information on secure router configuration for Cisco routers (the most commonly used router products) can be found at "Improving Security on Cisco Routers," `http://www.cisco.com/warp/public/707/21.html`. You can also refer to Chapter 22.

Network Numbers

IP network numbers can be organized in many different ways, with various sizes. Consideration for the security of a network architecture when creating an IP network is useful to protect against rogue systems. A network is defined by a set of four numbers and an associated network mask. The network mask defines a network by carving out a range of numbers that are considered one network. All of the systems on a single network are configured with the same network mask, thereby ensuring that they can all communicate with each other. Subnetting is the method of dividing networks into small, arbitrarily sized chunks. In the early days of the Internet, networks were divided into several classes—A, B, C, and the special D/E classes of networks. These classes can accommodate different numbers of hosts:

- Class A—~16 million hosts
- Class B—~65 thousand hosts
- Class C—254 hosts

Network classes D and E were specialized ranges of network addresses, reserved for multicast and experimental use. As the use of the Internet grew rapidly, these network ranges became impractical for organizations. Few organizations could utilize a complete class A network, but may have had slightly more than could be accommodated in a class B network; a similar effect occurs between class B and class C networks. The use of Variable Length Subnet Masking

(VLSM) and Classless Inter-Domain Routing (CIDR) resolves the problem by allowing for the creation of small-sized networks and allowing for dynamic routing of data between them. This is now the standard method by which ranges of IP addresses are given to companies by their ISP and traffic routed to and from those networks.

These concepts are useful to an organization when creating a security-conscious network architecture. The temptation to implement large network classes is present because of their ease of use, but this is often not the best solution for security. The relationship between the network numbering and the organization of equipment needed to sustain it has an effect on the security of the network architecture. Large, flat networks where all machines in an organization are on one network create several security risks. The effects of denial of service attacks via network data storms are widespread, affecting all of the systems on the network. The network equipment required to maintain a flat network of this nature often results in many shared segments that can leave systems vulnerable to compromise. An attacker can easily add another machine to a flat network of this kind because the ability to monitor and maintain a large network becomes difficult and unwieldy. This system can then be used to attack other systems or steal information as it travels over the network. Establishing a smaller-sized network is useful when determining which systems should be members of a single broadcast domain. You should take care to ensure that the network is not defined so small as to limit its scalability. As noted, the definition of network ranges should consider the ability of users and intruders to incorporate foreign network equipment into the environment.

The introduction of foreign computers and network equipment into the environment can adversely affect the network. Common cases of this occur when users initialize new systems and mistakenly configure them with an IP address that is already in use, or incorrectly configure the network address for the system. Two systems attempting to utilize the same IP address will attempt to fight for that address; this causes network confusion in the network equipment and loss of service or unreliable service for those machines. This is especially dangerous if the system attempts to use the IP address of an important system, such as the gateway or server, because all systems on the network will then flood the badly configured system and will lose connectivity to the intended server or network. Attackers can use this tactic to assume the identity of a specific system such as an email server or authentication server. Spoofing these servers by assuming their addresses and identities causes other systems to unwittingly transmit information to the falsified computer. The attacker can then gather information that allows her to compromise other systems.

A badly configured network address also causes an inability to communicate with other systems on the network and results in abnormal network performance. Tightly controlled network addresses and subnet definitions help defend against these negative effects. The security of a network architecture is enhanced by defining and organizing networks based on relationship and function to each other. Desktop computers often exist on the same IP network, using different physical segments to communicate with servers and gateways. This minimizes the ability of an attacker to compromise the servers and limits the zone of vulnerability to desktop computers with limited privilege. Servers can be placed on different networks with higher bandwidth capacities in order to serve multiple clients without performance degradation. This is also useful to serve multiple networks that do not need to or should not communicate with each other, such as customer and internal networks. The separation by function also limits the effects of misuse and malfunction. The previous example of a user system misconfigured as the gateway would not affect the entire organization in a diversified network environment.

Other technologies that have increased the flexibility and security of internal networks are Network Address Translation (NAT) and proxy servers. This functionality allows greater control and restriction of network traffic and the protection of internal systems. With NAT, the network addresses of the internal network to remain hidden while still providing access to external resources. The router or firewall that performs NAT translates all of the network traffic that passes outward so it appears to originate from that firewall or router. This is a useful capability because it obscures the layout of the internal network, as the external systems see network data arriving from the firewall only. Attacks directed toward internal servers are then made more difficult because NAT also protects the internal network. Unless configured explicitly to redirect incoming network data to a system on the internal network, a NAT device will only allow the return traffic for an internal system to pass. NAT also has the added benefit of allowing for the creation of new networks without acquiring new IP address ranges from the ISP.

A common example of Network Address Translation use for security occurs when an internal network is configured with a "reserved" set of IP addresses. The so-called RFC Networks are specified as private and internal networks that can be used by any organization simultaneously because they are not routed. See RFC #1597, "Address Allocation for Private Internets," http://www.ietf.org/rfc/rfc1597.txt?number=1597 for more information.

In this case, the internal network is a private network, and NAT is used to make all traffic appear to come from the NAT device—the firewall or router. The attacker can only scan and probe the NAT device, and has little or no information about the topology of the internal network and its systems. Consequently, the attacker cannot target specific systems, making compromise more difficult. The potential for denial of service does exist, though, because an attacker can target the NAT device if it is the single ingress and egress point for the network.

Proxy servers provide a similar functionality to NAT, but without any packet data modification. They obscure the internal network and system topology and allow restrictive filtering rules to be applied. A proxy establishes a single system, or set of systems, that acts as the point of contact for a particular service. For example, a Web proxy server is the contact point for all internal Web-surfing users. The users' Web browser software is configured to point at the proxy server. Instead of contacting the remote Web server for a particular site, the Web browser sends the request to the proxy server, which then retrieves the appropriate Web content and passes it back to the requesting browser. The use of proxy servers allows a more restricted and controlled set of filter rules to be established on the firewall because all Web traffic to and from the Internet focuses on a single machine, the proxy server, instead of many different user systems. It also affords internal systems some protection against malicious content because it can be filtered and analyzed by the proxy server before transmission to the requesting system.

Physical Considerations

The physical wiring used to create the network also requires consideration for security. As with most technology, there are several ways of obtaining a single result. Networking is no different, and the selection of cable types and implementation affects the security, reliability, and performance of a network. Twisted-pair telephone-style cable is the most commonly used in the networks of today. The use of twisted-pair cable forces a star topology for the network. A star has a center point with several tines protruding from it. Each individual cable forms a separate network segment that can be combined into a larger segment only via a hub. When connected to an Ethernet switch, the connection between the computer and the switch forms a single, private segment. Only one computer at a time is connected to the switch via twisted-pair cables. Other, older cable types are still in use today, including coaxial cable, often called thin-net. Coaxial cable allows for a less expensive network, but also a network with less bandwidth. This network cable is shared by several or many systems at one time and forms a single segment on which each computer can see the traffic of the others.

When evaluating the cable type used for an organization, most designers will standardize on twisted-pair cabling. It is important to understand the benefit to security that is gained from the physical wiring, and to know that its inherent security benefits can be nullified with a poor network architecture. The privacy provided by a single segment can be done away with by the use of hubs that multiplex network traffic. In turn, the use of Ethernet switches does not guarantee privacy of the data if their use is not consistent and well-organized throughout the organization.

Along with the cable type, the location and organization of equipment also plays an important role in the security of a network architecture. As outlined in the discussion of threats to a network, physical disruption produces more difficult, expensive, and widespread effects on network service. Organizations need to consider the placement of vital network equipment and systems, including routers, access devices, firewalls, and servers. These important components should be physically secured from access by unauthorized individuals. Networking closets are often used for cable termination points and are also securely locked. A malicious user or unauthorized intruder should be prevented from modifying the network topology and adding a system to the network for the purposes of eavesdropping. Organizations that have large networks and multiple locations also build distributed redundancy into their network architecture. The ability to secure the network and systems is the basic need for a secure network architecture. The flexibility and resilience of a network in the face of incidents provides the high level of security that separates adequate functionality from the robustness of a strong network.

28

NETWORK
ARCHITECTURE
CONSIDERATIONS

Network Separation

Separation of networks often comes in the form of specialized network functionality such as network management, monitoring, and remote access. Access to these functions may merit separation from the remainder of the network infrastructure. Different broadcast domains and network numbers communicate among each other via routers and by adding extra network interfaces to servers and network equipment.

Network Management

Network management refers to the control, configuration and maintenance of the network hardware used throughout an organization. Many of these devices provide network, terminal, and Web browser-based access to administer and configure them. It is advisable to disallow the ability to manage these devices from the Internet and other in-band networks. In-band network management occurs when the administrators connect to the device over one of the networks that the device services. In-band management of a router, for example, occurs when the administrator connects to it from the Internet over the external interface or from the internal network over the internal interface. Remote management of a router that ties the Internet to a service network or internal network should not be allowed from the Internet. Although outsiders cannot access the router directly from the Internet, they can access it from an Internet-accessible system in the service network. Compromise of a service network-based system provides the attacker with access to the network equipment. If possible, it is best to establish a management network on a third network interface and to restrict management access to the router from only that special network.

A management network is often a separate physical connection to the devices and on which there are only a handful of dedicated management stations. No other network should have connectivity to the management network, unless controlled through a single, high-security system; access otherwise occurs by physical presence at one of the management stations. The use of a management network severely limits the ability of an attacker to access important systems and equipment, which decreases the risk of compromise.

Monitoring

Network monitoring is a useful function that aids in the security of a network by debugging problems and maintaining performance. The separation of network data may hinder the ability to monitor sections of the network. Therefore, it is important to consider what monitoring should be used and where and to incorporate the required changes or equipment into the network architecture.

Several methods of network monitoring should be considered, as well as their placement in the design of the network. Intrusion detection is a relatively new innovation that is proving useful in the network. These intrusion detection systems (IDS) are placed throughout the network and actively monitor for known signs of attack. The placement of an IDS is often useful at network access points, including the service network, near the inside and outside of firewalls, remote access devices including VPNs and dial-in servers, and near key systems. Firewalls also act as a form of monitoring for a network. Their role is more active in that they manipulate network traffic by allowing or disallowing information to pass through. The effects of many attacks can be limited by regular and frequent analysis of these monitoring methods, including log analysis and configuration of the equipment to notify administrators in the event of an attack condition.

Other considerations for monitoring include the ability for administrators to monitor network traffic and analyze it for insecurities as part of the regular maintenance. The network and its implementation affect the ability to monitor traffic in this way. Network equipment often supports monitoring with SNMP and RMON, two standardized protocols used for this purpose. A final method of network monitoring is via complex network management software suites. These packages use a number of different protocols and methods to acquire and analyze information and provide fast alert and responses to anomalous conditions. These tools often utilize special agents that run in conjunction with the systems and equipment being monitored; these packages are not affected by the physical orientation of the network, however.

Remote Access

If remote access methods are needed in the organization, the methods to provide it should be considered during the creation of the network architecture. Two methods are commonly used: VPN solutions and dial-in modem access. VPN solutions come in two forms—the hardware device and software application. The hardware VPN device provides several benefits; it is a specialized device that often provides a high level of performance and incorporates its own security methods. The software VPN solution runs as an application or service on existing server systems and often relies on the security mechanisms of its respective operating system.

The effects on the network architecture required to support a VPN are similar for each solution. VPN devices can be more easily integrated in a secure manner into the network environment because the access to and control of the device are more easily dictated. The software service requires more attention. To achieve the highest security, the VPN software should run on a dedicated server and be treated as a device with no other services present. The operating system should be configured in a secure manner and no other internally used services should be run on the system in order to prevent access to the internal network. Software VPN solutions are affected by the vulnerabilities of the operating system as well as any insecurities in the software.

Dial-in support via modems and access servers provides a direct connection to the internal network. The considerations for dial-in methods include the use of a management network to control the device to protect it from unauthorized configuration changes. The dial-in server often relies on other servers on the network to provide authentication of its users. The network path used for authentication should also be private. Finally, dial-in servers should disallow remote networks to route traffic across their dial-in lines. Attackers will often use "war-dialing" software to scan phone numbers for dial-in servers. While the scanning cannot be prevented, the proper organization and configuration of dial-in equipment will limit the risk of compromise.

There are several considerations given to the placement of VPN and dial-in systems in order to protect the internal network. When defining the network architecture, the designers should identify the functionality supported and provided by the remote access. VPNs can provide transparent access to all of the resources of a network, allowing the remote system to appear and function as it would if it were physically located at the organization. Dial-in access, unless combined with a VPN solution, is often used to provide more limited services such as email and Web access. Despite the differences in methods, both supply the same basic functionality—access from remote, distrusted networks and locations. Therefore, it is advisable to place remote access servers on a separate network and to control access to the facilities which it uses. The previously mentioned management network should also be used to control and configure these systems.

The placement of remote access equipment follows the same logic used for other network equipment: the limitation of the effects should an attack occur. Attackers will attempt to find the targets that provide them with the most access to other systems and equipment. Remote access devices are easily identifiable targets and should be protected adequately.

Network Isolation

Network isolation is a slightly different concept than separation. Isolation of networks affects the flow of network data, which services run on particular systems, and where they are located. It does not affect any of the internal or external network data from traveling across those same paths. Isolation is often used to enhance the security and efficiency of the network by isolating certain network traffic to certain physical wires and networks. Network isolation is achieved with the use of multiple physical and virtual networks within a single organization to separate functionality. Network designers can enhance security by organizing the network into its functional areas and considering the impact that each of these functions has on security.

One example of network isolation is to design the network so that the credentials of remote access users do not travel across any network wires or circuits that are exposed to users or other systems. The simplest method to provide this security is to connect the remote access server directly to the authentication server with a single cable. Another method is to use a switched network topology, keeping the authentication server and remote access device on their own private segments. The data sent from one to the other will then travel between only the two systems and their segments, where no other system can view it.

Isolation is discussed in the following contexts:

- Service differentiation
- VLANS
- Firewalls

The first and most obvious concept is the isolation of external from internal network traffic. Service differentiation is the identification and categorization of network services. The network services provided by an organization can be categorized as external-only, internal-only, or bridge services. As the name implies, external- and internal-only services provide functionality to either the external or internal network, but not both. Bridge services provide functionality to both the internal network and the external network. External services should be isolated in a service network, or hosted by the ISP for the organization. Also, the management of these services should occur via the previously mentioned management network. Internal services should be protected from external Internet or service network access.

It is considered dangerous to attach systems and equipment directly to the Internet without some form of protection, so be sure to protect service networks with protection mechanisms such as a firewall.

The simplest network topology takes a router and connects one interface to the ISP and the other to a multiplexing device such as a hub. All of the internal systems are then connected to the hub. Without getting into the detail of network numbering, this is effective to provide Internet access to all of the internal systems in the organization, but it also allows all systems on the Internet to communicate directly with each system on the internal network. Each system is susceptible to attack, and the entire computing infrastructure could be compromised.

The requirement for Internet access should be categorized into outgoing and incoming access. Outgoing access refers to the most common concept of Internet access—the ability to communicate with Web servers, send email, and download files. Most systems require outbound Internet access, but typically need securing from arbitrary inbound Internet traffic. All network communication and protocol detail aside, the ability to perform these actions does not require internal systems to provide access to those on the Internet. When defining a network architecture, it is important to identify the services and systems that do require access initiated by Internet-based systems. The security considerations for the network architecture now take a basic shape as three organizational classes of network—the external, the intermediary, and the internal network.

Services Differentiation

The computing services provided by an organization form the basis of the network. Aside from the configuration and security methods used to protect the individual servers and operating systems, isolation of the network services is an important security tactic because it protects from

28

NETWORK ARCHITECTURE CONSIDERATIONS

attack and restricts the effects of an attack. The services are those features that the users require and are provided by computers and network equipment. Common services include:

- Domain Name System (DNS)
- Email
- Web serving
- File sharing
- Printing
- Network login

DNS

The Domain Name System servers in an organization often serve the internal users as well as the external Internet. The application that provides DNS services has a history of vulnerabilities (as you learned in Chapter 20, "UNIX") that have allowed attackers to compromise the system on which it runs and to corrupt its records. Given this history, careful attention to security is required. If the organization maintains their own DNS server, it is often best suited for the service network in order to protect the internal network from adverse effects of attack. As part of the network architecture, security is also bolstered by redundancy. The use of multiple DNS servers provides a level of reliability in the event of failure or attack on one, and the placement of these merits consideration in the network architecture. Multiple DNS servers should not be placed on the same network; the purpose of redundancy is to provide a high level of reliability in the event of the failure of one network. If both DNS servers are located on the same network or on a single service network, they can both be taken out of service by a single attack. The ideal solution is to locate redundant DNS servers on separate networks that have differing paths to them. This prevents attackers from disabling all domain name services without a complex attack method. DNS servers should be protected by a firewall, and primary servers should be configured with access control restrictions that disallow arbitrary queries and DNS zone transfers to unknown servers.

The separation of DNS usage also requires consideration. Many organizations use a single DNS server, with or without redundancy, to answer both internal and external queries. This means that the Internet-based systems have access to the name server, as well as the internal systems. This bridging of the internal and external networks may present a high security risk if the name server is compromised. Another security risk when using a common name server is the revelation of information. The common DNS server stores all of the name and network information for both internally and externally accessible systems. An attacker can glean this information from the server, arrive at a reasonable idea of the internal network architecture, and identify potential target systems.

One solution to these problems is a split-DNS topology, which creates two distinct name servers—one for systems on the internal network and one for those on the Internet to use. The records in each are then updated independently, and external systems have no access to information about internally networked systems. The attacker no longer has a potential bridge between the internal and external networks, and the effects of the attack are limited.

▶ For further information about securing specific DNS servers, see *Securing Domain Name Service* at `http://www.securityportal.com/cover/coverstory19990621.html`.

Email

Email is one of the most important network services to an organization, and the establishment of email services in the network architecture requires careful planning. It is inadvisable to support email with a single mail server. Mail servers often store the contents of users' mailboxes, including company private and confidential information. A single point of failure is present when using only one server. It is equally dangerous to provide access to the primary mail server from the Internet because an attacker may expose or have access to its private information. One solution is to establish mail relays at different locations on the network and then allow access to the primary mail server only from those relay systems. The mail relays are often located on the service network and further away at the ISP to provide several levels of redundancy in the event of attack or connectivity issues with the organization.

If an attacker can succeed in compromising the primary mail server, the attacker can then access many other sensitive resources of the organization. The use of a mail relay defends the primary mail server and limits the effects of the attack. The mail relay can and should be protected with strong filtering rules on the firewall, and the primary mail server should also be strictly access-controlled to allow inbound mail only from the relay servers.

▶ Specific information regarding the configuration and security of email server software can be found at `http://www.securityportal.com/lasg/servers/email/`. See also *Securing corporate email* at `http://www.zdnet.co.uk/itweek/brief/1999/41/network/`.

Web Serving

Many companies have a corporate Web site that provides the virtual storefront to the Internet and an intranet, or internally located Web site that contains private company information. The corporate and internal Web sites should be hosted on separate machines in order to isolate the information accessible by Internet users from employees. The network location of corporate Web sites should be determined based on how much traffic the site sees. An extremely popular Web site located on the service network with other network services such as mail relays and DNS servers may put those servers at risk in the event of a denial of service attack. The entire bandwidth can be consumed, rendering the other services unusable. The careful placement of redundant and distributed Web servers helps minimize the risks associated with this service.

Web sites can be located on remote servers hosted by the ISP, or Web traffic can be load-balanced among several servers placed in close proximity to each other or even in remote areas.

▶ Further useful information to secure your Web server can be found in *Securing Public Web Servers* at http://www.cert.org/security-improvement/modules/m11.html.

File and Printer Sharing

File sharing is a staple of network life that is utilized at a majority of organizations. It is also one of the more common insecurities found on a network. The network architecture that supports security and services that hold potential risks does so by carefully controlling the network access to the file servers. When sharing filesystems among multiple systems on the internal networks, access should not be available to the extranets, service network, or Internet. File sharing should never be allowed from unknown or external systems.

▶ A useful article on the topic of securing multiple network server types can be found in *Securing Network Servers* at http://www.cert.org/security-improvement/modules/m07.html.

Network Login

Network logins are the methods used by users to authenticate to a remote or local system. This includes interactive access to UNIX accounts, Windows Domain authentication, authentication to Web sites, and any other service that requires user credentials for access. There are many methods for network login, many of which are very insecure. The insecurities of network logins come from the use of cleartext authentication methods wherein the user credentials are transmitted over the network without any encryption or other data obfuscation.

Security considerations for a network design include the isolation of traffic that carries credentials to minimize the opportunity for eavesdropping and the use of VPN systems to provide encrypted communication that protects the credentials during transit. Other protection mechanisms include firewall rules to disallow the protocols that are known to function insecurely from passing the boundary of the internal networks.

Telnet, remote shells, and FTP are commonly used services whose traffic should not be allowed outside of the internal network, if used at all. These services transmit user credentials without any form of encryption, allowing an attacker to eavesdrop and intercept the information.

VLANS

The use of Virtual Local Area Networks (VLANs) is a relatively new approach to network topology that arose with the development of new network equipment. VLANs provide an alternative to the normal routed and switched network topology by simplifying diverse networks through more intelligent hardware. The VLAN allows groups of systems on different physical networks and segments to communicate seamlessly without the need for a router. One of the drawbacks of routed and switched networks is that the physical location of systems often dictates their presence on a particular network. For example, putting two systems that are physically in the same room onto two different networks requires that the network cables terminate at two different places, one at each network access point. If the network equipment is not physically located in the same area, this becomes quite unmanageable. VLANs allow for this capability and do so transparently.

The use of VLAN technology also has security considerations that may encourage their use. The nature of virtual and dynamically specified networks allows for fine-grained tuning of network traffic. The ability to shape the flow of network traffic is the ability to control it, which provides very flexible security capabilities that make it more difficult for network eavesdropping and provide for more easily thwarted denial of service attempts. It is important to note that part of the benefit of VLAN technology comes from its manageability. Administrators can more easily monitor network information, gather statistical information, and notice and resolve anomalous conditions.

Firewalls

The use of firewalls in a network architecture is generally seen as a requirement for any organization that has Internet access. As you learned in Chapter 10, firewalls are useful tools, and their use in the network architecture provides greater security. As mentioned earlier, firewalls are often used to protect internal networks from access by unauthorized Internet-based systems. They can also be used to protect service networks and extranets. The use of firewalls is not a guaranteed preventative method, however. When designing a network, it is important to determine the restrictions needed for the organization and where the firewall is most beneficial. Multiple firewalls are often utilized to protect network access points, and specialized networks throughout the infrastructure.

Firewalls come in several different forms including dedicated firewall appliances, software-based firewall suites, and as built-in functionality of network equipment. When considering security for a network architecture, it is often useful to utilize more than one of these methods. Routers are useful for the application of generic filtering rules such as disallowing access to particular port numbers or services. Hardware and software firewalls can then work in conjunction with the routers to perform more fine-grained filtering based on more granular details such as protocol flags and options.

Summary

The key to establishing a strong and secure network architecture is to identify the features and functionality needed by the organization, to understand the relative security risks, and to make decisions about their implementation based on this knowledge. When designing the network, identify the parties who use it, their purposes for using it, and their requirements for effective work and functionality. Create a balance between security and functionality in order to arrive at a network architecture that is both secure and usable. When these aspects of network design are considered, along with the technical details presented here, a network architecture that is secure, strong, and flexible is more easily created.

Secure Application Development, Languages, and Extensions

IN THIS CHAPTER

This chapter covers secure application development including the design and implementation of Internet applications, systems, and the languages used to create them.

Security And Software

This chapter explores the importance of security to software development efforts including Internet systems, applications and the languages used to create them. Although software development encompasses a large variety of possible efforts, the need for security is common across them all. Strong security is a continuous process, not a feature, that arises from comprehensive and well-thought-out design and development methods and a continuous analysis throughout the life of the application. While there is no such concept as guaranteed security, the goal is to create software with security in mind and establish a high degree of protection that makes attack and exploitation difficult or unfeasible.

This chapter presents several guidelines that assist in evaluating and bolstering the security of an application or product through the phases of a development cycle. The approach used here differs from common practice. Many sources of information on secure application development focus on the technicalities of the code and implementation, while ignoring other elements in the process. This discussion outlines a complete process that introduces security to the entire development cycle.

Security in an application comes not only from the code used to create it. It begins with the initial idea for an application and carries through the design and implementation phases to form a cycle of security analysis. Each of these phases depends on the others to provide the highest level of application security needed and possible. This cycle continues throughout the application's lifespan and should be considered with each of its incarnations, enhancements, or modifications. The information presented here is important for both technical and non-technical readers. Managers and non-technical staff who work in a software development environment need to understand the role of security within their application, the procedures and methods by which security is created, and the issues they might face as a result of weak or strong security. Software developers and engineers need to understand methods to design and write code with security in mind, as well as the security issues that might arise from their efforts.

Application development includes a wide array of software development efforts. Although this chapter focuses primarily on Internet-related applications, the concepts presented are applicable and important to all forms of software development. The discussion covers software applications that run on the desktop computer or server, Web-based applications, operating system issues, and Internet appliances. A thought process that is mindful of security can be developed by considering the material presented in this chapter; this is large step toward the creation of highly secure applications. As a result of high security, the reliability of an application is also enhanced.

Developers achieve security awareness and thoughtfulness through careful implementation and an aversion to pitfalls. Development managers should emphasize development processes and procedures that enforce security requirements. At the end of this discussion developers and development managers should be able to establish a procedure for secure application development that includes the creation of a security architecture and the ability to examine the design and implementation for relevant security issues.

What Is a Secure Application?

The concept of a secure application might conjure analogies to a battle-hardened, armored tank, ready to respond to all natures of attack and impervious to all but the strongest bombs. While such tight security might be the goal in some applications, it is likely the exception rather than the rule. Security should be applied and integrated as is appropriate for the specific task or function at hand. An application cannot be made secure by following a checklist of safeguards that, when put together, spits out an armored application. A secure application emphasizes thoughtful analysis, diligent design, and a focused implementation. Its developers consider the security issues of similar applications and analyze innovations for new risk areas while balancing the level of security required by the users of the application. In order to make all of this happen, it is useful to know the effects of insecurity on an application.

NOTE

The term *application* often refers primarily to one particular program or set of programs. The guidelines presented here are useful and applicable to many forms of software development including Internet and system applications and embedded Internet Appliances. The term *application* should therefore be understood to refer to any of these development efforts, as the concepts are applied to them.

The Enemy Within (Your Code)

Common and well-known attacks such as denial of service, buffer overflows, and race conditions can plague applications with poor methods of input validation and data protection. This section provides a brief overview of common vulnerabilities that need consideration when first developing an application.

TIP

Be sure to consider the relevance and effects of the attacks described here when examining an application under development. Also look at similar applications and those with which the new application competes.

Configuration Issues

Security problems with the configuration of an application and the environment in which it runs are very common. Applications often store configuration information in a file or database, write runtime information to other files, and provide multiple services simultaneously. Default configurations—a computer system's operational settings upon installation and without any user modification—can be very dangerous. These out-of-the-box configurations exist to help users run the application with the least amount of effort, but can unwittingly leave them open to attack.

The default configuration often enables every option available in the software, to demonstrate its rich feature set. There is a disadvantage to having every option enabled—the user might not understand or even be aware of the enabled options provided. If a vulnerability is discovered, the user is unknowingly at risk. It is not possible to force a user to read and understand documentation about all configuration options, therefore a responsible developer thinks carefully about which options are enabled for regular operation and which should remain disabled.

Two well-known examples illustrate the dangers of insecure default configurations. The first example is inetd, the UNIX Internet Server daemon.

Inetd enables users to access a UNIX system via protocols such as Telnet, FTP, and remote shell. (Many other services are available through inetd; see the manual page for inetd for more information.) Typical early versions of inetd had a standard configuration that enabled all of its services. Various security holes were found in many of these services, making many systems vulnerable to attack, often without the knowledge of administrators.

Another example of insecure default configurations can be found in Web server software.

Apache on UNIX and the Internet Information Server (IIS) from Microsoft are two of the most popular Web server applications in use on the Internet. These Web servers come with sample applications that demonstrate various pieces of functionality. In early versions of Apache and Microsoft Internet Information Server (IIS), these samples had numerous vulnerabilities and were installed by default, allowing attackers to compromise the systems. Many users and administrators were not even aware of the existence of these applications, or that they were present on their Web servers. These common holes are still present today and part of the many Web server security analyses.

TIP

Take care to document features when creating them and provide information about them in any configuration files.

Race Conditions

As the name indicates, a *race condition* is a window of opportunity in a running application that allows another process or application to exploit the privilege or functionality of the first. Race conditions can occur when complex or multistep procedures run, when an application interacts with other processes or resources, or when a functionality is poorly organized.

Figure 29.1 shows a simple example of a race condition. An application normally runs with the privileges of its user. The application then enters a section of code that increases the normal privileges and modifies a system setting. Upon completion of the modification, the privileges return to normal. Through a weakness in the implementation, a *rogue application* attempts to "win the race" by exploiting the higher privileges. If the program uses Inter-Process Communication (IPC) or temporary files, or takes a long time to perform the operation and does not protect these methods, the rogue application can insert its own commands, which are executed by the application.

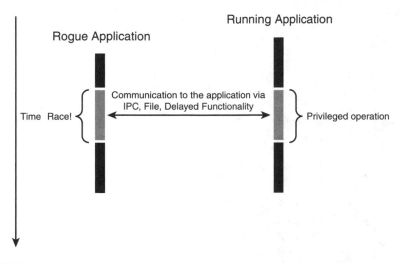

FIGURE 29.1

A race condition: the window of opportunity.

NOTE

An operating system typically supports several methods by which different processes or applications can communicate. These methods are known as *Inter-Process Communication (IPC)* methods; they include the use of sockets-based communication, semaphores, pipes, and shared memory.

Figure 29.2 demonstrates a race condition with temporary files. In the course of normal execution, the running application makes changes to system settings by creating a temporary file with new settings and then copying that file to the appropriate location. When finished, the running application then deletes the temporary file and continues running. If a window of opportunity exists, during which an attacker can insert his own configuration information into the file after it is created and just prior to its being copied, a race condition is present. This can occur as a result of poorly organized functions, wherein related steps are not grouped logically within the code, or if the temporary file is not properly protected.

The access points of IPC methods such as sockets or shared memory should be initialized with the proper protections, or a rogue application can interact with the application. Good and logically organized code and functionality minimizes the window in which a race condition can occur. This can be done by grouping areas of privileged functionality where the code would otherwise repeat multiple privilege increment and decrement calls. Related functionality should also be organized and executed efficiently.

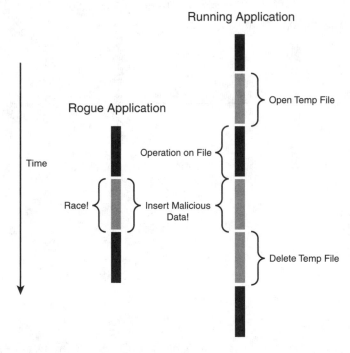

FIGURE 29.2

A temporary file race condition.

Buffer Overflows

Buffer overflows are perhaps the most notorious and widely publicized attacks. These are complex attacks that exploit the fundamental hardware and software capabilities of a system.

For those who are not software developers, a few concepts need explanation. First, it is useful to understand what a *buffer* is. The computer system has a pool of Random Access Memory (RAM) organized into small chunks by the operating system that runs applications. In order to share this memory among the operating system's many processes and applications, a special memory manager coordinates which chunks of the RAM pool are in use and which are available to run an application. When an application is first run, memory is allocated for the application and all of its functions and variables.

As the application runs, more memory can be allocated for new variables and de-allocated when no longer in use. A *buffer* is a chunk (or several chunks) of memory used to store a variable. Different buffers can and often do exist side-by-side in memory. A buffer that holds a variable can exist next to a piece of memory that holds a function or another application. For example, when you enter your username at a prompt or window, the program has declared a buffer, in which the characters of the name are stored. Figure 29.3 shows a buffer that is used for the username "NAME."

29

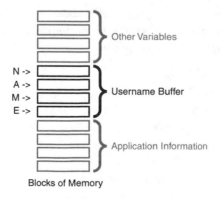

Blocks of Memory

FIGURE 29.3

A buffer that holds the value "NAME".

A buffer overflow occurs when a buffer is too small to accommodate the amount of data provided. The data that does not fit into the buffer will overwrite the next chunks of memory. Herein lies the danger of buffer overflows. The memory that is overwritten with the extra data can be another variable in the running application, a variable for another application, or the application's stack. The *stack* contains application-specific information, such as the physical locations of the application's functions and variables.

This alters the path that the application would normally follow, causing it to use bad data, crash, or execute new functionality. The execution of new functionality is usually the goal of a buffer overflow exploit—whether to provide access to the system or to modify its settings.

When its owner accesses the overwritten memory next, the new data might be invalid, and the application can crash or function improperly. Buffer overflows are exploited by crafting the overflow data into something useful that the machine can understand. This could mean executing another program, causing harm to the system or stealing information.

To better demonstrate this concept, consider the postal machine that scans letters for their destination city. Assume envelope A is destined for New York, NY, and envelope B is destined for Boston, MA. The ZIP code of envelope B has special wet ink that "overflows," overwriting the ZIP code of New York on envelope A with that of Boston when the envelopes are automatically stacked at the postal facility. The postal machine scans envelope A and reads the overwritten ZIP code. The letter is then routed to Boston.

Buffer overflows are often more malicious than mere accidents, so let us assume that a valuable sum of cash is destined for a postal box in New York. The thief, or attacker, knows the exact location of the letter and creates an envelope with runny ink that overwrites the ZIP code on the envelope with the ZIP code for Boston when they are stacked. The attacker rents the Boston postal box with the same number as the original destination in New York and proceeds to steal the money.

A postal machine is only capable of recognizing ZIP codes, no matter from where they come. A computer is capable of executing instructions, no matter from where they come. Therefore, a buffer overflow attack that overwrites the original instructions of an application with new instructions can cause the computer to execute anything an attacker wishes.

The exploitation of a buffer overflow in an application is an extremely dangerous problem. Figure 29.4 demonstrates the memory layout of a typical buffer overflow. The application developer declares a buffer that will hold an 8-character username. An attacker tests for an overflow by entering a 10-character name, "myusername" at the prompt. The program then starts to copy that name to the previously declared buffer, but the name is 10 letters; the last 2 letters overflow the buffer and crash the program. After confirming that a buffer overflow exists, the attacker crafts a special set of input made of valid machine instructions that executes a malicious program to steal passwords on a system. The attacker then uses this special input set as the input to the username prompt of the affected program, again causing a buffer overflow. Now, the memory is corrupted with these new instructions in such a way that they are executed, causing the malicious program to run and cause harm.

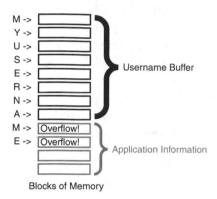

FIGURE 29.4
The memory layout of a buffer overflow.

TIP

For in-depth technical detail on buffer overflows, the following articles are useful resources:

Compromised—Buffer—Overflows, from Intel to SPARC Version 8 by Mudge, a gifted hacker and VP of @Stake, a top security consulting firm.

`http://www.l0pht.com/advisories/bufitos.pdf`

The Tao of Windows Buffer Overflow by DilDog, another gifted hacker of @Stake.

`http://www.cultdeadcow.com/cDc_files/cDc-351/`

Smashing the Stack for Fun and Profit by Aleph1 of SecurityFocus.com, originally issue 49 of the *Phrack* online magazine.

`http://www.securityfocus.com/data/library/P49-14.txt`

Data Protection

The scope of data protection is broad—it extends from the internal methods of an application out to the operating system and all of the systems to which it connects. This description focuses on data protection within an application and the operating system in which it runs. These concepts can then be extended to interconnected systems.

29

SECURE APPLICATION DEVELOPMENT, LANGUAGES, AND EXTENSIONS

Applications seldom function completely independently of the underlying operating system and other applications. There are many ways for an application to interact with its operating system. Information is often shared via the previously mentioned IPC mechanisms and files are a common method by which information is stored, manipulated, or moved within a system.

It is important to remember that, in most cases, the application and its operating system are using the same physical processor and memory—while this might seem obvious, the security ramifications are often forgotten. A developer cannot assume that the memory used by an application is accessible only by that application. The underlying operating system controls access to memory, and therefore has access to all memory available—whether used or unused. If an application is using and manipulating information that should be considered secret, it is vital to protect internal data. Important and secret information such as passwords and encryption keys require special handling. Without the proper protection and initialization, this information can be accessed by exploiting operating system functionality. Establishing authentication and access control methods can protect data. These mechanisms validate the sender of a message within the system and determine which processes, applications, and systems can access a particular resource.

Temporary Storage

Temporary storage in files is not itself a vulnerability, but it merits discussion because it exacerbates the problems of data protection and race conditions. Temporary storage is used when manipulating information such as application or system configuration files and when updating other data stored in files. When temporary files are initialized with weak security, an application becomes vulnerable to attacks that allow unexpected information to be inserted into the files. Weak security in temporary files is defined by the permissions that allow or disallow an outsider to access the contents of the file, and the predictability of the filename. An attacker that knows the name of the temporary file prior to its creation already has a jump on the race condition. At the moment when the file is created and initialized an attacker can attempt to modify it. The race then begins to insert data before the function finishes and removes the file. The results of an exploit vary depending on the use of the temporary storage; typical examples are modification of a system configuration and the alteration of user information and application data.

TIP

When using temporary files, check for their existence during initialization of the routine and set permissions to restrict access only to the application.

Denial of Service

Denial of service is a common form of attack and can be initiated from the network or on a local system. These attacks exploit a design's failure to address the negative events in an application. Applications should be developed with an understanding of the functionality they provide and the functionality they do not provide. This allows the developer to build safeguards into the application that protect it from denial of service. These attacks come in several flavors—network bandwidth saturation, system resource utilization, and application flaws.

Network bandwidth saturation results when the entire capacity of a network link is filled with data, preventing new communications from proceeding and slowing down those already in progress. This occurs when the network hardware, which is a specialized computer, is unable to process new network data quickly enough. Therefore, the network hardware is overcome, causing delays in new network traffic or even its complete cessation.

System resource utilization is similar to network bandwidth saturation, except the saturation occurs on the individual system instead of the network wire to which it attaches. System resources—memory, disk storage, processor utilization, and operating system–specific features such as processes and files all have limits; physical limitations of the hardware naturally reflect on the limitations within the operating system. Examples of physical limitations to a system are the amount of memory and disk storage available, and how fast a processor can execute instructions. Examples of operating system–specific limitations that are dependent upon the hardware configuration are the number of files and processes that can exist and the number of users who can work simultaneously.

System-based denial of service exploits the confines of these limitations by using all of the available resources of the target. These attacks come in many forms. Many operating systems stop functioning properly when all of the disk storage space or memory is used. Users can be denied access if the maximum number of users is exceeded. A processor can be completely utilized by endless complex functions, causing all other functions to slow or halt. An application that creates multiple processes can cease to function if the process limits of the system are met.

Developers can be misled into believing that these network and system limits make it impossible to avoid or prevent denial of service attacks, but this is not the case. Strong design and implementation of an application can overcome and protect against denial of service and many other forms of attack. There are caveats, however—the nature of the Internet creates situations wherein factors beyond the control of the developer are present. It is impossible to completely eliminate all possibilities for attack because of the Internet's dependencies on external environments. The goal then becomes to establish an environment that makes it difficult for an attack to succeed. Forethought and analysis in the design and development of an application limit the situations in which an attack succeeds.

To help safeguard against denial of service in networked applications, it can be useful to set high-watermarks within the application that limit and detect abnormally frequent connection attempts, such as 20 connections-per-second for a given service. These abnormalities might be signs of denial of service if an attacker is attempting to starve the resources of the system. Other protections include resource monitoring and limitation that give the application complete control of its execution.

TIP

To protect against denial of service attacks, begin to consider where potential vulnerabilities exist in an application. Start early in the design phase and continue the analysis through the completion of the application.

Input and Output Methods

User-supplied or external input is the most obvious and prevalent point of entry for attacking an application. Whether data is coming from a network, from a keyboard connected to the system, or from a user environment, the security of the input method demands careful consideration. These functions are the doorways to the application for many of the aforementioned attacks; they allow the user to alter the path of the running application by providing different inputs. Application design and implementation must have a defined set of criteria for input. This includes the explicit data types and values that are and are not acceptable, the reaction to unacceptable data, and the path of that data through the application.

Application output can also pose a risk when users blindly write data to files, terminals, or devices. It is equally important to validate output before actually committing the data. The conditions that allow for successful output should be defined and documented, in order to provide a level of assurance within the application that any outbound information has been checked. Application output often uses external functionality provided by the operating system or another application; therefore, it is extremely important to provide some protection methods before setting the data out into the wild where it could react poorly with the external elements.

TIP

Criteria for user-supplied input should be defined, and associated functionality should be developed to support its validation. These criteria should outline what is and is not acceptable. Anytime that externally defined data crosses the boundary of an application or module, it should be validated.

A Security Architecture

A security architecture for an application outlines a comprehensive method for the development of highly reliable and secure applications. It establishes a process and a framework by which the security needs of an application are analyzed, defined, and implemented. This section explores in detail several components that constitute a security architecture.

Components of a Security Architecture

A comprehensive security architecture is best achieved through an increasingly granular approach that begins from an external viewpoint and progresses through the details of the implementation. The following components organize the information needed for the creation of an application's security architecture:

- Risk assessment and response
- Security requirements
- Design phase security
- Implementation phase security

Set the Stage for Security

Risk assessment is an important process in the development of any product or application. The creation of an application begins with the spark of an idea. It is likely that this application idea solves a problem, or provides new usefulness or innovation that was previously done ineffectively or inefficiently, or not done at all, by existing applications. While analysis is done to determine the shortcomings in function of the older applications, security considerations are often forgotten. The tendency to focus strictly on the functionality an application provides and the benefits to the explicit dilemma it solves increases the potential for security risk. It is extremely important to solve the security problems of an application, as well as the functional problems.

Therefore, the first stage in the creation of an application's security architecture is to document the risks inherent in existing applications that are to be replaced by the new creation. Developers should also note risks related to an application with which the new program will interact. The new application often faces all of the security issues that similar applications face, as well as new issues that arise from innovation.

Assessing the security risks of an application requires some diligence on the part of the application designers; if the designers have any level of security experience, the effort to assess risks quickly becomes smaller. The most basic research that identifies the security issues with related applications involves a search through the archives of vendor-specific support issues. The Web sites of these organizations generally have special areas and forums that announce the availability of patches to security problems in their applications. This research gives a sense of the common issues faced by the new application and the functionality it provides. Further research in security-specific forums provides more technical detail regarding the natures of the problems, as well as a broader sense of the security issues related to a specific application area.

As vulnerabilities in the pertinent technical areas are researched, it is important to document them. Creating a list of security risks and vulnerabilities helps establish a scope for the application under development, by determining which issues are likely to affect the new development.

The known vulnerabilities of an existing application can provide hints toward the presence or lack of a security architecture in its design. The vulnerabilities can often be categorized as implementation flaws, design flaws, and functional flaws. *Implementation flaws* relate to the actual code used to make the application; they provide only a small amount of insight to the security architecture. Implementation security is discussed in detail later in the chapter. *Design and functional flaws* reflect the thought and effort put into the design of the application. An application with a security architecture highlights and strengthens the functionality by making security awareness an inherent part of it. Shortcomings in design and function leave holes in the thoroughness of functionality, often creating security risks.

Consider the Functionality *Not* Provided

Strong designs recognize the functionality provided, as well as that which is not provided. The most basic level of functionality possible is defining what an application does. This is done under a completely positive view because it outlines only what an application does under the most pristine circumstances. It naively assumes that the world is perfect and that nothing bad will ever happen when the application is running. This means that all inputs will be completely understandable and fit the expected input "mold"—for example, "All usernames will be alphanumeric values of a determined length and no user will, accidentally or otherwise, enter a character that is not either a number or letter." This view also assumes that all network connections would be from known clients, and that these clients would all communicate with the proper protocol—for example, "All clients connecting to the application will adhere to the known messaging sequence required to perform the defined communication." Finally, it assumes that all interaction with the operating system occurs in a sterile environment that the application expects—for example, "Each and every file that is modified always exists and is correctly formatted." Obviously, this is not necessarily the case and cannot be expected. Unfortunately, many applications rarely make it beyond this level of design. A comprehensive design takes into consideration the imperfections in the real world. A design of this nature recognizes that establishing rules and schemes provides reliability.

Considering both positive and negative scenarios for an application's operation is vital when creating an application. The negative view defines the reaction to unknown input, invalid syntax and communications, and anomalous conditions that might occur. The application needs to respond properly to events that are not expected or defined. Table 29.1 compares a basic design versus a more comprehensive design and the effects each has on user input, file access, and client connections.

TABLE 29.1   Effects of Basic Versus More Comprehensive Security Design on Application Functions

Effected Application Function	*With Basic Design*	*With Comprehensive Design*
User Input	Application receives invalid input and crashes because the non-alphanumeric value is misunderstood.	Application examines the input for invalid values and responds with an error message, indicating a non-alphanumeric value was found.
File Access	Application expects to find a database file in the proper format, ready and waiting for access. Instead, an ill-formatted file or a link to another file by that name is opened, data becomes corrupted, and the application crashes.	Application checks for the existence of a named file that is of the appropriate type, as well as the internal format of the file.
Client Connections	Application expects a client to connect with the first message being "hello." If a client connects and transmits any other value, the application waits indefinitely, disallowing any other client from connecting, and is no longer functioning.	Application validates the transmission and responds with a warning indicating that the received message was an unexpected value.

The degree to which designers and developers formulate answers to negative results plays a significant factor in the reliability and security of an application. While it is often difficult and infeasible to explicitly handle every known exception, general rules can easily be created to handle undesired events. These three examples present extremely simple scenarios that might seem unrealistic, but all have occurred more than once in many applications.

Come Here for Guaranteed Security

This discussion would be incomplete without mention of third-party organizations, whether commercial or public domain, that provide security software, development kits, and hardware to enhance the security of applications. Many of these commercial organizations present their products as providing "guaranteed" security.

However, there is no hardware or software substitute for a well-thought-out design. Often, managers, designers, and developers are led to believe that the addition of some complex and expensive security components offered by a commercial security organization provides "guaranteed" security. This is simply untrue; "guaranteed" security is a fallacy. This concept preys on victims who understand security as a feature or component that can be plugged in for immediate security satisfaction. If only one bit of information is gleaned from these pages, let it be the fact that *security is a continuous process*!

Few applications are devoid of security components, but it is not sufficient to simply incorporate the most commonly known components in order to render a design or implementation secure. The inclusion of security components without consideration for their use does not enhance the security of an application and can, in fact, hinder it. The products offered by security companies are very valuable and useful when used properly, but they cannot guarantee the security of an application. The inclusion of third-party security technologies should be examined for usefulness and value, given the security requirements that are established for the application.

Security Requirements

In conjunction with identifying related security risks known to a specific application or application genre, developers must assess the security requirements for their application. This analysis should arrive at a balanced measurement of the level of security required for an application. It does not have to ponder the extremes of the security spectrum. Given the understanding that true and guaranteed security is nonexistent, protecting against known risks and minimizing the number of successful attacks and their effects is generally an acceptable level of security. Those involved with the development cycle of the application should determine their own "acceptable" security level, by examining the known risks, the goals of the application, and the methods used to implement the desired security level.

To arrive at security requirements, managers and developers can find it useful to concentrate on the following, commonly known risk areas:

- User authentication and access control
- Data storage of confidential information
- Security in external network communications
- Security of entry points for external applications and the operating system

From these four general areas application designers and developers can identify a minimal set of important features to analyze. Depending on the functionality of the application, some risk areas are more pertinent than others.

To Secure or Not to Secure

The addition of security to an application affects an application in several ways. It immediately becomes more complex, as the code path takes a new turn to accommodate the security methods. The performance of an application might be hindered, especially with the addition of encryption operations. These operations are CPU intensive due to the complex algorithms involved. The efficiency of an application can also be sacrificed if security is applied in areas where it provides few benefits. This can occur if security methods are blindly applied to all components of an application without thought as to their requirements. The following sections provide a reasonable starting point to determine a basic level of security requirements.

> **TIP**
>
> It is a good practice to consider the security required for each module or component within an application. Resist the urge to apply blanket security methods across multiple modules or components. Instead, determine the most suitable level of security for each.

Assessing Authentication and Access Control Requirements

User authentication is often handled by the operating system on which the application runs, but several classes of application might need to deal with authentication on its own. Embedded applications, applications that function independently of the operating system, and distributed Web applications often need to accommodate some level of user authentication and access control. Common examples of applications that require these security methods are Internet commerce (e-commerce) applications, wherein users make purchases via a Web site, or customer database access. In both cases, the possibility for many different users or groups of users to use the system requires stringent control of accessible data. The applications need methods to allow separate users to access the systems via a login method; they also need restrictions regarding the individual users' respective financial data.

To determine the authentication and access control requirements, designers should examine the interactions within the application and with the world that surrounds it. This includes the methods by which users access the application—sitting directly at a terminal or accessing from the network are two methods that might require different authentication schemes. An application that is accessed only while sitting at the desktop can effectively be secured via the authentication methods of the operating system on which it runs. Network applications that are accessed by multiple users simultaneously, or through which users access data from common databases, provide strong impetus for access control and authentication. The level of granularity and flexibility of the access control and authentication capabilities provided by the operating system help determine if proprietary methods should be developed. Standalone or embedded applications are often developed from scratch and therefore require their own specialized methods.

Requirements for Data Storage

Data storage reflects the method used to store private and sensitive information. This includes the correct use of the file protection methods of the underlying operating system (such as restricted file permissions) and stronger methods of protecting individual data elements (such as encryption). In many cases, the use of operating system permission methods is sufficient to provide the required degree of security. Encryption can be used to protect extremely sensitive data, such as user credentials and credit information.

The level to which the application needs to store data, and the nature of that data drive the requirements for data storage security. The storage of sensitive information is often the gating factor in determining if high security encryption is needed. User credentials, such as passwords, addresses, phone numbers, and financial data, should be considered sensitive and also treated with high security. Configuration information can often be secured sufficiently with standard file permission methods.

When forming the requirements for data storage, designers might be tempted to standardize on one level of security. For instance, if a password is stored in a configuration file along with other non-sensitive information, the temptation might be strong to use encryption on the entire file as a blanket security method. To determine data storage requirements, examine the needs of all components involved. In this example, applying encryption to nonsensitive data might be considered inefficient due to the computational expense of the encryption operations, as well as the lack of granular control of the other information in the file. A single element cannot be accessed easily if the entire file is encrypted. The complexity involved to access other elements is then increased dramatically.

Network and Entry Point Security Requirements

Applications communicate to users, the operating system, and other applications through entry points. These might be on the same machine as the application or across a network; often, they are on both. The methods for providing entry points to the application and support for network communication are often one and the same; therefore, they are grouped together here.

Security of network communications is best addressed by examining the content of the messages being sent. Applications that utilize network communication for informational messaging or passing static data might not require any stronger reliability than the protocol supports. Again, as in the case of Internet commerce, an application that sends and receives sensitive user information likely warrants the addition of a higher security method. Entry points also determine security requirements for applications that communicate in a networked environment.

The entry points to an application require a high level of analysis because they encompass and provide the network communication functionality. Others also interact with the application through the entry points. These functional areas can be protected via a combination of available operating system methods and the defined access control and authentication schemes used within the application. Analysis of the interactions that an application has with the outside world allows the designers to determine the most suitable level of security needed. These interactions and subsequent entry points are categorized as

- Network interaction
- Interaction with other applications
- Interaction with its respective operating system

These categories are well-known functional areas, and designers probably already know if their application interacts in any of these manners. The next step is to consider each area's security.

Network, Application, and System Interactions

The popularity of the Internet gives rise to many new applications that interact with other components within local systems and with remote systems. Applications that function independently of other applications and interact only with themselves obviously do not require networking risk analysis. The majority of the applications targeted by this chapter do perform some level of external communication, though.

Network interaction can be present at several levels. An application can be completely client/server–oriented, for use on remote systems spread across the Internet. The need for security in these applications becomes considerably more complex than it is in standalone applications.

Several dependencies should be discerned. The level to which the developers wish to provide security mechanisms in the application should be considered. The designers might decide not to provide any internal security mechanisms. The security of the networked application then relies on the security of the networks on which it runs and communicates; the network topology and firewall determine the maximum level of security that an application can experience. The designer might choose to eschew dependencies and provide the highest degree of security possible within the application. These are the two extremes—most applications fall somewhere in the middle.

Applications can also use network facilities for localized communication that is not destined to go beyond the confines of the system on which it runs. Consideration should be given to the nature of this communication in order to determine if the implementation creates unnecessary risk.

The need for interaction between applications or with the operating system does not imply a requirement for network communication. Designers should investigate the implementation methods that provide the required functionality. Applications often use sockets-based communication methods to provide these entry points because they are fast and easily implemented. The use of sockets can provide more functionality than is needed, however. Applications that need to communicate only with other applications on the local system or with their own operating systems have many communication methods at their disposal, such as non-Internet sockets and IPC mechanisms.

29

SECURE APPLICATION DEVELOPMENT, LANGUAGES, AND EXTENSIONS

Commonly, UNIX systems use socket communications because of their ease of use and plethora of documentation. UNIX supports several flavors of sockets-based communication, two of which are the popular IP socket and UNIX domain sockets.

IP sockets, as the name implies, use the IP protocol for communication, and support remote network communication, which allows local and remote processes to communicate with the application. Many applications that communicate only with processes on a local system and that do not require network communication capabilities use IP sockets as a standard interface. IP sockets are not ideal in this situation because they automatically provide access to local and remote clients.

Domain sockets use an internal UNIX protocol for communication and do not support network communication; they do provide a connection-oriented communications channel. Domain sockets have their share of risks if used improperly. UNIX domain sockets support the passing of file descriptors as well as informational data. This means that pointers or handles to other parts of the system can be passed from one application to another. This functionality is available only in UNIX domain sockets. If this capability is not desired or warranted, diversion from sockets-based communication to another IPC mechanism might be a better choice.

Considering the kind of information sent to and from the application helps define the requirements for its communication method. Designers should evaluate the interaction capabilities of the application before incorporating a standard function. In this example, the application using IP sockets is at risk because it allows remote systems to connect to the application when they should not be allowed. A better design documents the requirement for interaction with only local applications. This comprehensive requirement leads the developer to use something other than IP sockets.

NOTE

For in-depth information about programming with sockets and Inter-Process Communication, see the following well-known books on the subject:

UNIX Network Programming, Volume 1: Networking APIs—Sockets and XTI by W. Richard Stevens. Prentice Hall. ISBN: 013490012X.

UNIX Network Programming, Volume 2: Interprocess Communications by W. Richard Stevens. Prentice Hall. ISBN: 0130810819.

Operating System Interactions

Interaction with the operating system often creates another level of security issues. Many levels of interaction can occur with an operating system—network interaction, Inter-Process Communication, and the manipulation of files have already been mentioned. Two other types of interaction also require attention: The execution of external programs and the use of system and other externally defined calls are common sources of exploitation. Important issues such as permissions, authentication, access control, and input validation should be considered in conjunction with operating system interactions.

System calls and external applications present a high degree of risk when used improperly because of their natures. These functions often exist in libraries that are used by many applications simultaneously and that often provide direct access to operating system components and resources. Exploitation of a single application through these functions can affect several applications and the system.

System calls provide access to many general-purpose and system-specific functionalities. They allow an application to interact with specific hardware components as well as kernel-level functionality. The safety of the operating system and components needs to be considered when using system calls. If an application ties together user or network data with the operating system via system calls, designers must minimize exposure to dangerous, unexpected, and improper data.

The execution of external applications is another common, unsecured interaction. Developers often design an application to call upon other applications by various methods. There are several reasons a developer might want to do this, such as to differentiate between functions or to establish environmental control. Calling other applications also allows developers to use existing functionality and to expedite the application's implementation.

There is an inherent danger in calling another program from within an application—the external program can rarely be trusted. The application exists in a dynamic environment where it is possible to modify or replace any program. The problem lies in the methods used to call the application. UNIX-based systems often support functions called `system()` and `exec()`, which pass the supplied parameters as a string to the execution of the standard UNIX shell and subprocess, respectively. The `system()` call returns to the calling program when complete, but `exec()` terminates the running program and replaces it with the called program. Windows-based systems have the `exec()` call that allows the execution of other programs. Unlike UNIX, the Windows version of `exec()` runs the specified program in a subprocess, and the calling function does not terminate. Without input validation, attackers can put shell meta-characters into the input stream, forcing the shell to run possibly harmful commands and parameters. The use of these functions is generally frowned upon, and effort should be made to avoid their use because they allow the execution of untrusted and uncontrolled applications. Alternatively, designers can incorporate the required functionality directly into an application. The use of freely available, open-source software greatly decreases the effort needed to do so.

Many operating systems also allow functionality to run at different privilege levels. UNIX has its "root" privileges, Windows has "Administrator" and "SYSTEM" privileges. These special

29

SECURE APPLICATION
DEVELOPMENT,
LANGUAGES, AND
EXTENSIONS

accounts can perform administrative tasks and have more interaction with the operating system and its services than other accounts do. Programs can be written to elevate privilege levels when specialized functionality is needed. An application and the operating system on which it runs can be compromised if privileges are not carefully controlled.

The model of least privilege suggests that an application should run with the minimum set of privileges needed to perform most functions. Functionality that requires higher privileges should be isolated into its own module, however that is defined—as a process, a class, an application, or even another system. Even then, that set of functionality should also run at the least privileged level until those elevated privileges are required. At that time, higher privileges should be obtained and, upon completion of the functionality, privileges should be returned to the minimum level.

> **NOTE**
>
> *Meta-characters* are characters that take on special meaning in a given context. For example, within the standard UNIX shell, the semicolon (;) is a command separator, that is, many commands can be put on a single line when a semicolon is between them. The pipe (|) character sends terminal output to whatever follows the pipe, allowing the output from one program to be fed into another.

Throw Away That Security Blanket

Some application developers choose to forget or ignore security within their applications and put themselves at the mercy of the customer's network or operating system and its security features. Using this blanket security model shuns the responsibility to provide secure applications to the public. The security philosophy advocated in this chapter purports a strong and comprehensive security ideology that assumes nothing about the security of components external to the application. An application should always be as secure as it can be with respect to itself and the external components with which it interacts. The level of follow-through is left to the discretion of the designer or developer, however.

Identification of the Risk Areas

As stated, a good process for application development includes the definition of a strong security architecture. This provides a new level of comprehensiveness that fosters analysis and provides a documented overview of potential security problems, as well as the methods for resolving them. When creating a security architecture for an application, possible attacks can be classified in the following categories:

- Subversion of the application
- Subversion of the system and external applications
- Cessation of functionality

Often, an attacker's goal is to gain access to resources or assume control of an application or the system on which it runs. Short of this, an application can simply be forced to crash, which can also cause the entire system to crash.

Subversion of the application occurs when the attacker causes the application to do something it was not intended to do, or to execute some level of unintended functionality. These vulnerabilities are broad in nature and effect. Exploitation of buffer overflows, race conditions, and data input are examples. The effects are limited to the running application.

Subversion of the system and external applications occurs when the exploit affects other running applications or system resources. This can include execution of other applications, such as a shell in UNIX, or utilization of a connection to another application using the vulnerabilities outlined here. The effects of the attack are not limited to the running application, and that application is often used as a conduit to other systems, applications and the operating system.

An application can completely cease to function and crash due to attacks. This is a form of denial of service that targets the limitations of the application, rather than the network or operating system. Applications that are well designed and securely coded provide a high level of security and reliability that protects against denial of service.

Security Response

Once the risks and requirements are identified, the response to these issues is the logical next step. Identification of potential security issues is not very useful without a known path to protect against those risks. The defense methods become a natural part of the design in this phase of the development cycle.

Knowledge of the various vulnerabilities, interactions, and areas of analysis discussed previously form the basis of a security response. Knowing the relationship of existing vulnerabilities in the target environment and in similar applications establishes the minimum level of security required. Ideally, the new application provides more security than its predecessors and competitors, by addressing all of the known vulnerabilities and analyzing for new issues. The next steps involve a careful look at all of the interactions within and around the application. It's useful to start at the external view and progress inward through the application. To define areas that need higher security, analyze all methods by which the application communicates and interacts with the network, operating system, and other applications. Analysis of the information passed across these channels further clarifies the security requirements.

Security-Aware Designs

The security of an application depends on the comprehensiveness of thought and analysis done during the application's design phase and prior to its actual implementation. The design phase ties together all the requirements and considerations outlined during the early gestational phases of the application idea, and provides an explicit implementation path. The concept of security in software development is often ignored during the initial stages and sometimes throughout the life span of a development effort or is viewed as a feature that can simply be added at a later point. Security is not a feature, but an integral part of all phases of a software development cycle. Good security arises from a combination of good processes, good practices, and continuous analysis. The earlier an organization introduces security analysis to the development cycle, the stronger the application will be. This section suggests a process by which the elements of secure application development can be implemented and enforced.

Design Phase Analysis

A comprehensive design provides solutions to the problem addressed by the product, and also takes into consideration the effects of the innovation. The security of an application is also created and enhanced by a comprehensive design.

Once an organization discards the idea of security as a feature, it becomes apparent that security needs consideration early. While each organization might have different methods of designing a product or application, the following approach is useful to assure a high level of security in a design. The design phase analyzed from three viewpoints:

- Global
- Organizational
- Component

The *global viewpoint* is the highest view of the system; it identifies the needs addressed by the application and its feature set. The *organizational viewpoint* highlights the individual components that make up the application. The *component viewpoint* goes to the next level of granularity, by examining the explicit details of each component and its implementation. The incremental approach used here allows for a deeper and more comprehensive analysis that also provides an easily understood process flow. This helps managers and developers put the appropriate procedures into place to ensure the consideration of security in their application.

The Global Viewpoint

Many applications arise from an unfulfilled need or the inadequacy of current solutions. A good design identifies the following security concerns:

- Security issues related to existing solutions to the problem or the need being solved
- The application's response to those security issues
- The potential security vulnerabilities that exist in the innovations being made

A global analysis provides information that an attacker would otherwise find after the application is released. At this phase, a security architecture should be defined for the application. This architecture formalizes the level of security needed in an application. It helps establish the application's security scope by identifying the relationship of the application to its surroundings and the level of security provided by them. A security architecture also highlights the need for, and amount of, independent security that an application must provide, as well as the features required.

A global analysis and establishment of a security architecture are done via the incremental categorization of the modules, components, interfaces and methods used in the application. Their location and relationship to each other and their exposure to external applications, users and interfaces are important points.

The global viewpoint of an application initially presents the proverbial "black box"—the only details known are those seen by outsiders. These external features and functional requirements are then separated into *modules* for security analysis.

Searching vendor advisories, newsgroups, mailing lists, and online forums for disclosed vulnerabilities in competing or similar applications is a good way to learn about some of the major security issues related to the application. It also helps point out ineffective solutions to vulnerabilities found in similar applications.

Case Study, Phase I

This hypothetical example is a case study for the development of an Internet commerce application. It will be used throughout the remainder of the chapter to exemplify the guidelines and information presented here. This service allows users to connect from their browsers to make online purchases.

The first level in the design of this application is the definition of its capabilities, independent of the implementation methods used. These features might include the following:

- The selection of an appropriate operating system to host the applications
- Database access for storage of private and public information
- Web serving
- Connectivity of these parts using custom-developed applications
- Connectivity to financial institutions for the transactions

From the global viewpoint, a designer discerns the security features required for each component of these functions.

The database stores private information on many different users, including passwords, credit card numbers, and contact information. In order to protect this information, the database should have security components that support restrictions to objects and perhaps their encryption.

The Web server should support secure communications with the Secure Sockets Layer (SSL) protocol, and some method of interfacing with external applications and the database. This could be via Java servlets and applets, or CGI programs.

Network communications are an inherent part of this system. The Web server and database server software probably run on separate machines, hence a means to secure the network communication between them is required.

The last component to be considered is the actual connection to the organization that authorizes the transactions. This could be a bank or credit card company that authorizes the expenditures by users. Connections are likely accomplished with a modem or other piece of telecommunications equipment that interacts with the financial organization and performs the validation. These connections require high security, in order to avoid access by unauthorized users.

These insights are gleaned from knowledge of the field, analysis of competing products, and familiarity with customer requirements. At this point, diligent research needs to be done to document past and current security vulnerabilities in related products. The resulting list should identify the risk areas that need addressing. Security features missing from the initial requirements list are often identified through this analysis, another of its benefits.

In our Internet commerce example, researchers found the following vulnerabilities in comparable products:

- Databases had no protection schemes, resulting in the exposure of private customer information.
- The Web server had holes that allowed the execution of arbitrary code on the system. The server's default configuration also allowed directory traversal, which allows external users to access many private files and directories on the system.
- The CGI applications used to communicate with the database had vulnerabilities that allowed remote attackers to impersonate other customers.

The research also indicates that data protection, buffer overflows, default configuration, and input validation issues need to be avoided because these vulnerabilities occurred frequently with similar applications. It also showed that vendors have added security features and patches that will protect against these problems. This makes authentication and access control important requirements, along with network security.

At this point, the designer knows of vulnerabilities associated with the application, the methods by which other organizations respond to them, and a set of important security features that form the basis of a security architecture. The security architecture develops further in the next phase of design.

The Organizational Viewpoint

Security is not an exact science; its needs are specific to each application and environment. Therefore, it is not sufficient to look at security from only the global view. Although an otherwise well-designed application might exist independently of all other applications on the system, the interaction of all components in that application might pose security threats. The organizational viewpoint identifies the individual elements or groups of elements that form the entire application, their functions, and their relationships with each other. An element could be a function, a class, a process, or a set of these elements that are grouped by their relationship to the application.

An application is typically made of several functional modules, such as the user interface, networking or communication components, or data storage and retrieval tools.

While a module might seem reasonably secure, its relationship with the other components might be executed insecurely. Similar to the analysis of the interactions of the application, organizational level analysis takes the functional requirements and determines the architecture used. The functional requirements allow the designer to identify a set of components and methods that provide the functionality; an analysis of the security between them as they interact yields the safest choices for inclusion with the application.

The incremental identification, organization, and categorization of each component in the application continues in this phase. A logical place to begin—and particularly suspect in terms of security—are the edges of a module. The *edges* are the entry or exit points where data crosses the boundaries between modules. For example, data crosses boundaries between modules during these functions:

- Passing of data as parameters
- Setting global variables
- Manipulating shared memory
- Writing data to files
- Sending data across a communication channel such as the network
- Receiving user input

Case Study, Phase II

In the organizational phase of designing the sample Internet commerce application, each application component—the Web server, the database server and the associated applications—is categorized into its functional module for further analysis.

The database server has a storage component, an authentication and access control component, and a communication component. The Web server has the Web serving component, an external programming model, and secure client communication and secure database communication components. Interactions between these components form a definable path, with several points where security must be strong. Following an interaction between the Web server and the customer, a client Web browser transmits sensitive data to the Web server. This data is

then passed to the custom application that interacts with the database and the financial institution. Following the data path through the application, a developer can observe points of vulnerability in the client communication, the Web server application interaction, the
communication from the Web server to the database, and the interaction between them.

The security requirements begin to take shape. The application must address these risk areas
and provide security in these forms:

- Secure communication to the client Web browser in the form of encrypted network com-
  munication, authentication of users, and access control mechanisms on their information.
- Safe interaction between the Web browser and the e-commerce application to ensure the
  safety of the system
- Application integrity of the commerce program
- Secure communications with the database
- Security of database objects

From these requirements, an architecture begins to take shape. The use of SSL on the Web
server protects the server-to-browser communications. The application will have its own
authentication mechanism that allows clients to sign in safely. Data validation and protection
mechanisms will also be implemented in an organized fashion that uses only the minimum
required privilege to operate. Functionality will be incorporated into the application for object
protection and encryption on the database server. The actual implementation details will be
developed in the final component phase.

Pertinent security methods will rise to the surface when the following questions are asked in
the organizational phase:

- How will we protect information passed?
- What are the effects if one module passes spurious data to another?
- Have the constraints of the data been defined?
- Is there a preferred method of passing data that lends itself to increased security?
- Which components, applications, and users need access to the data? What kind of access
  is required—read-only or both read and write capabilities?

The Component Viewpoint

The final viewpoint from which design analysis occurs is the dissection of the individual components within an application. The smallest design and implementation details can introduce
obvious and obscure security problems that are difficult to find post-release. Poor implementation can also undo the effort put into the security of a design.

Some of the precautions suggested here fall into what are considered good coding practices and are not necessarily security specific, but they do have an effect on the security of an application.

The security architecture that is defined for an application will mandate that there be a series of checks and balances to which the application must conform. These checks and balances will provide a high degree of assurance that an application acts in a uniform manner in the event of unexpected data or information.

The component view examines each piece that forms a module. (Modules, in turn, form the application.) These components should be analyzed for their individual security features and the interactions with other components within that module. Starting points when examining programmatic issues within a module are

- Return values
- Precedence and prerequisites
- Data validation
- Identified response and recovery
- Permissions and privilege

Return values are indicators of success or failure within a function. Components of an individual module are made of functions, which interoperate and have established relationships that allow the program to perform properly. Developers should also understand what it means when a function fails, and should react appropriately to that failure. A complete understanding of these relationships allows a developer to understand the dependencies between functionalities. Based on these dependencies, components within a module can be organized to enhance reliability and security.

Data is dynamic in any application—it travels between functions and modules, and to separate applications, altering the execution of the initial application as it does so. With the identification of the modules that form an application, and the components that subsequently form those modules, the path of data through an entire application can be traced. The entry points between modules and functions are the pivotal elements that affect the success or failure of the application, therefore validating data at these points is vital. Working hand-in-hand with validation is a defined response to invalid data and anomalous conditions. Many applications fail to formulate a recovery mechanism in the event of unexpected events; this often results in unstable applications that crash at the earliest sign of imperfect data.

Knowledge of the permissions and privileges required for the components to function provides important information for the application designers. Following the model of least privilege is a good design practice; it recommends the isolation and limitation of privilege in a

29

SECURE APPLICATION
DEVELOPMENT,
LANGUAGES, AND
EXTENSIONS

running application. In most cases, high privilege levels are needed very infrequently and only in isolated instances. Many applications that require elevated privileges for a small portion of functionality commit the entire application to that higher privilege level for its entire existence. This creates a hazardous environment wherein each vulnerability that is found exists in this privileged mode.

Privilege refers primarily to the several levels of authority on an operating system. At each higher level of privilege, authorized users have access to progressively more resources in the system, such as memory, other applications, hardware devices, and data. The root user in UNIX, the administrator, and the SYSTEM special account in Windows exemplify the highest level of privilege. There are often various degrees of access that provide granular access control, also. *Granular access control* allows definable access and rejection methods for the application. Files, network traffic, users, and objects can be bound to a set of explicit permissions that allow or disallow access to them.

Case Study, Phase III

The component phase analysis of our Internet commerce application looks at the individual components used in the application and their security. Entering this stage, designers should have a sense of the complete data path and the relationships between modules. The next granular step establishes the basis for the application's implementation. The goals of this analysis are to determine the privileges of the various components, a sense of organization that will be used during the implementation, and knowledge of how the implementation will occur. Here, previously determined requirements are translated into detailed implementation methods.

Designers choose a Web server and a database server at this point, based on the established requirements. In our example, an Apache Web server was chosen because it can be made to support SSL communications and has a well-documented method to interact with external applications. An Oracle database server was chosen because it provides the flexibility, scalability, and security required in the database, and also because it supports Java-based interaction. Java was chosen as the language and extension for implementing the actual Internet commerce software because it operates with the Web and database servers and supports a strong, configurable security model.

The Web server and database server are then designed by determining the most secure methods for the following components:

- Server default configuration
- Security configuration of the underlying operating system
- Privileges required to interoperate with the Java applications
- Access control components

The commerce software is organized to provide these components:

- Privilege requirements to perform its functions
- The Web server interaction and communication entry points
- User authentication and access control methods
- Session security methods to prevent impersonation of users
- The database server interaction and communication entry points

Based on this analysis and organization, it is determined that the only portion of the system that requires elevated operating system privileges is the commerce application. It also needs an internal set of privilege levels to enforce user access control and authentication. The default configurations enable only the functionality needed for operation of the system, and each operating system is security-hardened with the same minimalist approach.

The commerce application is where the majority of the security components exist. It has the responsibility of validating user credentials, setting permissions on database objects, keeping track of each user session, and having the actual intelligence required to keep the system functioning.

The commerce application needs elevated privileges only when controlling Web and database server startup and shutdown. The most secure method to perform these actions is determined to be a separate controller process that increases its privileges at the time it performs a startup or shutdown action; it then relinquishes its privileges until the next request. The controller process communicates only with the commerce application and uses authenticated messages to initiate the startup or shutdown of the system.

The commerce application will also encrypt private information before storing it in the database in order to protect user credentials and financial information. In the event of anomalous and error conditions such as invalid input data, user authentication failures, and failed communications, the design calls for a reporting system that can log this information and respond appropriately to the events.

System implementation rises naturally from the continuous analysis provided in the preceding global, organizational, and component analysis phases. The developers use the guides and procedures in place to help them write the code that maintains the high security standard established.

Secure Coding Practices

This section delves into the more technical aspects of security in the code used to implement an application, and provides guidelines to develop an enforcement process for secure implementation. The potential for vulnerabilities in an application is reduced by a strong design, but the implementation of the application seals its fate. Hard work poured into a secure design becomes inconsequential if the implementation is poorly done. It is also important to understand that the inclusion of security-related technologies or design methods does not necessarily imply or guarantee any level of security within an application. The implementation of an application and any security technology used is one of the final components that brings a high level of reliability.

Analysis in the implementation phase is the responsibility of both developers and development managers. Developers are responsible for implementing the design well, whereas managers are responsible for setting forth the process that ensures a good implementation. This can be done via standardized procedures that include documented development and coding standards, design and code reviews, and developer training with regard to security in application development. These procedures benefit the developers and applications regardless of which languages are used or the type of application developed.

The most commonly used languages today are the C programming language, Java, and scripting languages such as Perl and the UNIX shells. Each of these languages and environments can be used improperly to compromise the security of an application and the system on which it runs. The following demonstrates security issues with these languages in relation to the vulnerabilities outlined earlier in the chapter. However, this section is not a checklist for developers to follow. Instead, the development of a security-focused thought process allows for an arguably stronger coding practice.

Pitfalls by the C

The C programming languages, which include C, C++, and object-C, are the most commonly used languages and can be dangerous in unsure hands. They provide the developer with the ability to manipulate and access many parts of the system, such as memory, files and devices. This is a great strength of the C languages, but danger arises when the developer makes mistakes. C provides a high level of access to the underlying operating system, and there are few checks and balances to protect the developer. If the developer mistakenly writes data to the wrong device or memory location, the C program will do whatever the developer writes, regardless of the data or destination.

The first vulnerable area often associated with C is the buffer overflow. The following sample code demonstrates a very basic overflow:

```
char string[10];

strcpy(string, "AAAAAAAAAAAAAAA");   /* 15 "A" characters */
```

Here, 15 "A" characters are copied into the memory area for a variable string, which is declared to be a static 10-character array. The strcpy() function does exactly as directed with no regard for the size of the data being copied or the location to which it goes. A buffer overflow occurs when the 11th element is copied into the memory location, immediately following the location of the 10th element of the variable string. Now apply this principle to any input data that comes from an external source, replacing the string of "A" characters. This allows attackers to control the effects of the overflow.

The `strcpy()` function is one of several functions in C that do not perform any bounds checking and allow arbitrarily sized buffers to be copied. Other functions to avoid are `gets()`, `strcat()`, `sprintf()`, and the `scanf()` family of functions. There are updated versions of some of these functions that allow the lengths copied to be specified. These are `strncpy()`, `strncat()`, `snprintf()`, and `fgets()`. These modified functions copy only up to the number of characters specified by the length parameter. At most, *length* characters are copied from *source* into *destination*:

```
strncpy(destination, source, length);
```

> **TIP**
>
> When using the "n" versions of the string manipulation functions—`strncpy()`, `strncat()`, `snprintf()`, and `fgets()`—be sure that the length is not larger than the destination string, rather than the source string. The buffer can be overrun if the length value is larger than the size of the destination buffer.

When using pointers to buffers, instead of statically declared buffers, you need to allocate enough memory to store the values being copied. Use the memory manipulation functions, which allow you to specify length.

> **TIP**
>
> When allocating memory for string data, do not forget to add 1 to the total length, in order to accommodate for the NULL terminating character. Without a NULL terminator, the data in memory directly after the last character of the string might be considered part of the string.

These functions are not the only places where buffer overflows occur. Be sure to check that information read, copied, or written to any memory location or assigned to a variable will fit, or that the destination allocated has enough storage space.

> **TIP**
>
> To avoid buffer overflows in your code, be sure to validate input. Check the size of the data and the storage location and use manipulation functions that generate developer-specified amounts of information instead of arbitrarily long chunks of data.

Race conditions add a level of complexity to using C code. Race conditions can be exploited in two aspects of C code creation—sequencing and protection.

Sequencing refers to the order in which events occur in an application. Race conditions can result from sequencing variations between dependent events, when no checking is done between the events. This often signifies a shortcoming in any error-checking and validation routines used. If two functions normally run sequentially and the second function assumes that the results of the first are valid, then the possibility for a race condition exists. Elevated privileges, discussed in further detail in the "Operating System Interactions" section earlier in this chapter, are often targets of attack. Organization, combined with sequencing and error checking, minimizes the possibility for race conditions.

This is a bad implementation that creates a race condition:

```
increase_privs();
...
value = special_app_function(); /* requires privileges */

other_unreleated_function(); /* does not require privileges */
other_unreleated_function2(); /* ditto */

special_dependent_function(value); /* requires privileges */
...
exit();
```

Here, a couple of unsafe practices occur. The privileges of the application are elevated early in the application, but not used until later. They are also never relinquished, so most functionality executes with higher-than-needed privilege levels. Finally, the race condition is created through poor organization—dependent functions do not occur near each other. An example that solves these problems is

```
increase_privs();
value = special_app_function; /* requires privileges */
if (!validate_function(value) /* assure the safety of the value */
{
    do_error_processing(value); /* do something intelligent with the error */
}
special_dependent_function(value); /* requires privileges */
decrease_privs(); /* no longer need privileges */

other_unreleted_function(); /* does not require privileges */
other_unreleated_function2(); /* ditto */
```

Note the special validation and error processing routines that are used before passing the value to another function.

Many race conditions exist as the result of poor temporary file usage. When these files are created, they should be protected against external attack during operation. UNIX and Windows allow the developer to set the permission bits and operational flags when creating a file. Permissions should disallow access to anyone but the owner of the process. When creating the file using the open() call, set the O_EXCL and O_CREAT flags, which cause the function to return an error if the file you are attempting to create already exists. Because it is a temporary file, it should not exist prior to the need for it. If the file exists, this is a possible sign of attack. When using these methods, it is also important to check the return values of the functions and to clean up any files in the event of error conditions. The following example shows the syntax to open a file—or create one, if it does not already exist—with permissions that allow only the creator to read, write, and execute it using the S_IRWXU mode macro.

```
open("filename", O_CREAT | O_EXCL | O_WRONLY, S_IRWXU);
```

The call will fail in the event that the file exists already because of the O_EXCL flag. Also, note the unsecure filename. The static naming convention used increases the risk of attack dramatically because one component of the attack is already provided.

Due to the increased presence of temporary file race conditions and the associated insecurities, several operating systems have specific functions to create temporary files in a secure manner. The mkstemp() and mktemp() functions have been written and rewritten to solve the protection issues and the predictability problem discussed in the "Temporary Storage" vulnerability section.

Developers can also use an operating system's built-in file-locking capabilities to control access to the files. These methods control access in the fundamental kernel components.

Another component that increases reliability and can influence the security of an application is the return value. While it might seem obvious, it is important to stress the necessity of validating return values of functions. Functions often execute serially and rely on the results or data

29

from a previous function. By checking the return value of previous functions, the dependent function is protected from executing with invalid data. Even when the events are not attacks, recovering from anomalous conditions increases the robustness of the application.

This example demonstrates a poor implementation that fails to check return values:

```
n = do_string_check (string, valid_characters); /* function returns an int */
if (n == GOOD_RETURN)
{
    process_string(string);
}
```

Here, the implementation is weak because the negative case, a bad return, is never handled. A better implementation is

```
n = do_string_check(string, valid_characters); /* function returns an int */
if (n != GOOD_RETURN)
{
    special_error_processing_routine(n); /* bad value, do something */
}

process_string(string);
```

The negative return is handled by the-error processing routine, which can exit the program, request a new string, or convert the return value into a valid parameter. If the return value is good, it goes to the process routine.

TIP

The creation of reusable event and error routines provides a standard mechanism by which all applications react to various attacks and issues. Ideas for these routines include common validation methods for string and numeric values, wrapper functions to perform integrity checks, and protection mechanisms that validate variables and memory locations. Always check and process the return value of a function.

The next bit of detail involves the use of sensitive information within the application, including passwords, encryption, or any other private information. As mentioned previously, all program information exists in areas of the common pool of memory that can be subject to reading and modification by external procedures. It is beneficial to clear the memory when the information is no longer in use, in order to avoid revealing information during an attack. The most common and sufficient method to clear data, this is typically referred to as *zeroing out memory*. When stored information is no longer needed, the storage locations should be overwritten with zeros or random data to prevent an attacker from recovering the information via memory or core dumps. This procedure becomes particularly important when encryption is in use. The keys used to encrypt and decrypt messages are the most important pieces of a cryptographic system, and everything possible to protect them needs to be done.

These guidelines exemplify some of the common issues that arise in C-based applications. C is a very popular and powerful language that allows provides great flexibility to the developer, and care should be taken with its use.

A Perl of an Application

Perl is an interesting beast that combines many of the benefits of a structured programming language, like C, with the flexibility and integration of a UNIX shell. Perl allows the developer to create procedures or subroutines, define variables, and utilize applications and commands available with the operating system. These capabilities, and its strength with regular expressions and parsing, give Perl a strong presence in Web applications, system administration, and automation.

Perl programs are not generally susceptible to buffer overflows because of the weakly typed nature of its variables and declarations. Unlike C, wherein variables and memory need to be defined as a particular storage class and memory must be allocated for them, Perl does everything automatically and treats everything as string data. Take the following example:

```
#!/path/to/perl

$one = 1;
$one_s = "1";  # No different than $one
$two = $one + $one_s; # the result is 2, or "2", which are equivalent
```

In C, the variable $one would likely be declared an integer and $one_s, a string. The addition of the two elements would also result in an erroneous value. Perl does not differentiate between the different types, so $two is assigned 2, or "2"—they are equivalent in Perl. The language also does not fall prey to the memory allocation requirements that other languages exhibit. The following example is completely acceptable in Perl:

```
#!/path/to/perl
$var1 = "AAAAA";
$var2 = "BBBB";
$var2 = $var1; # $var2 becomes "AAAAA";
```

$var2 takes on the new value of five "A" characters. All variables are dynamically allocated; there is no concept of preset storage space that could be overflowed.

Perl is susceptible, however, to race conditions and the vulnerabilities associated with the execution of external programs. Care should be given to the sequencing of functions. Input validation is equally important in Perl, in order to prevent the exploitation of external applications.

29

SECURE APPLICATION
DEVELOPMENT,
LANGUAGES, AND
EXTENSIONS

Perl supports the capability to open files, similarly to C and other languages, therefore the use of temporary files should incorporate appropriate permissions and creation flags.

The use of Perl in Web-based CGI programs is also extremely popular. The greatest risks associated with its use in this environment occur during input validation and execution of external system programs from within. To protect the application, several precautions can be taken. Using the taint-check mechanisms of Perl, any variable set outside of the program will not be passed to any program run by the application. Any variables set by the tainted variable become tainted. Taint-check mode is particularly useful for avoiding vulnerabilities, wherein unchecked user variables are passed surreptitiously to programs called from the Perl application. To initialize version 5 of Perl in taint-check mode, use the following script header:

```
#!/path/to/perl -T # Run in taint-check mode
```

The next precaution is to parse input values to remove meta-characters and unwanted values. This helps protect against attacks that exploit parameter-passing to shells and other applications. The following example shows a simple routine that scans an input string for any meta-characters that might be interpreted by a program:

```
$unclean_input = &get_HTML_forms_response();
if($unclean_input =~  tr/;|`!#$&*()[]{}<>:'"//)
{
    # Print out some HTML here indicating failure
    &do_some_error_reporting();
}
```

In this case, the routine reports an error if a meta-character is found. Alternative methods replace meta-characters, or only continue if no meta-character is found.

A final precaution is the use of a shell to run other applications. As with the UNIX `system()` call and the Windows `exec()` call, the `system()` call in Perl allows the developer to run another application. The `exec()` call in Perl functions like that call in UNIX—the running process is replaced by the program indicated. These functions can be particularly dangerous when used in an environments that allow user input, such as CGI programs or system utilities. If input validation does not occur, the application can be exploited to execute arbitrary programs that can affect the system. The following example demonstrates the insecurities of using `system()` with nonvalidated input. Assume the user supplied the string `username ;/bin/rm -rf /` that became assigned to the variable `$input`:

```
system("ecommerce_app $input");
```

This effectively translates to `/bin/sh ecommerce_app username ; /bin/rm -rf /`. Assuming that the program is running with privileges, the program will execute a shell to run the e-commerce application; hit the shell semicolon, which is the command separator in a shell; and then run `rm -rf`, which erases the entire file system.

Mi Java Es Su Java

Java is a relatively recent invention in the world of distributed Internet computing. It brings to fruition the concept of platform-independent code. Java works by writing code and compiling it into a special format that is then run on Java Virtual Machines. The Virtual Machine (VM) is platform specific, but the code that runs on it is not. Java allows Web browsers and remote systems to run more complex and interactive applications. The Web browser accesses a Web site and receives a Java applet from the server. This applet then runs in the Web browser and can communicate with the originating Web server. When introduced, Java transformed static Web pages into dynamic and flowing applications. Since the early days, the use of Java has expanded into many different distributed application areas such as network management, embedded Internet appliances, and other utility functions.

Java is a fine example of a language whose developers considered security in the early design stages. The initial versions of Java had a well-documented security architecture, called the *sandbox*, that prevented the Java applet or application from accessing system resources. As use of Java began to expand, the need arose for access to system resources outside of the sandbox. The first version of the Java Development Kit provided the use of signed applets. The model describes an applet that is digitally signed to verify its creator. When the digital signature is verified, the applet is then trusted by the local system, which allows the applet access to other system resources. This digital signature method involves a fair amount of complex programming to work correctly. It is also important to note that this security model of a digitally signed Java applet is flawed. Anyone can sign an applet. An malicious applet can be signed by the attacker and downloaded by the Web browser. The Web browser effectively verifies that the malicious applet is indeed written by the attacker, and then happily executes it, to whatever result is programmed in it.

The current and second iteration of the Java security architecture is much more powerful and flexible than earlier versions. This allows Java to enter many areas of application development previously beyond its capabilities. The new Java security architecture uses easily definable security policies and access control methods that allow an applet or application to access specific resources to varying degrees. In relation to the guidelines presented here, Java designers analyzed the various interactions and vulnerabilities present with distributed Internet applications, and arrived at a model that provides high security with extreme flexibility. The use of Java security policies requires a fair amount of reading and understanding that is beyond the scope of this chapter. For complete documentation on Java and its APIs, see `http://java.sun.com`.

The Shell Game and UNIX

UNIX shells form the basis of user interaction with a UNIX system. Shells are command-line interpreters that support some level of automation and programming in the form of shell scripts. These scripts are often used to automate system tasks, perform repetitive operations, and run CGI Web applications. As with Perl, areas of potential risk are input validation, race conditions, interaction with external files and programs, and the organization of functionality.

In UNIX, privileged operations can be run by a privileged user, or they can be set to run as a privileged user. There are subtle differences between the two methods. All files in a UNIX system, including applications, have a set of attributes that include user and group ownership, and a set of permissions flags. Combined, they allow file access to be strictly controlled. Normal applications are owned by a user and, depending on the access permissions, they might be run only by the owner, by a group, or by anyone on the system. The applications inherit the privileges of the user who runs them. An application that requires root privileges can be run by a non-root user, but, at those points where higher privileges are required, it will fail. To overcome this and allow normal users to access certain privileged functions, UNIX provides the SetUID and SetGID flags. When enabled, they cause the application to run as the owner or group for that application—they set the User ID (UID) of the application to whomever owns it.

Many CGI and system programs require access to system resources and are SetUID root. This applies to compiled programs, such as C programs, and scripts, including Perl and the UNIX shells. Experienced UNIX users and developers often warn about the dangers of SetUID shell scripts that provide root privileges. As discussed earlier, input validation and race conditions are easily exploited when the script is not protected properly. When running a script as a privileged user, there is no easier way to hand over the keys to the castle than a weak shell script. Such scripts are particularly dangerous when programmed without security measures because a shell is interactive by nature. Users supply input, and the shell performs a function. Perl has many built-in checks and balances that allow safer SetUID usage.

Internet Appliances

Internet Appliances are those systems and devices whose entire purpose is Internet computing. All the design guidelines, programming language considerations, vulnerabilities, and operating paradigms discussed in this chapter are directly relevant to Internet Appliances. Internet Appliances often use common operating systems, applications, and methods to accomplish their goals. If the application in development follows this path, pay special attention to all of the information presented here. Some Internet Appliances are developed from scratch, incorporating only newly developed designs and technologies. Assessing security risk for these systems requires extra diligence. It is especially important to integrate security into a design process when starting from scratch.

Summary

Many applications are based on previously created applications and benefit from an established and exercised security architecture. New innovations have no such luxury, therefore it is vital that they begin life with strong security measures. Consideration for security should not end at the completion of the application, system, or product development cycle, however. It is a continuous process that should remain active throughout the lifespan of the application. With every new twist, turn, and feature that the application takes, sincere consideration for its effect on the remainder of the application and the environment in which it runs needs to be examined and understood. Diligence and comprehensiveness throughout the cycle is a necessity—a well-thought design can bolster the security but be undone by poor implementation, and secure code cannot secure a poor design.

The technical details involved with security require a large amount of time, experience, and exposure to grasp. An awareness of security and the ability to analyze from a security perspective allow designers, developers, and their managers to formulate questions and responses that aid the creation of a well-designed, reliable, and secure application. Security is a process, not a feature, that requires a steady but not overwhelming effort. Strive to develop with the model of least privilege necessary to accomplish a given task. Finally, always analyze the ramifications of a design or implementation decision because there is always a reaction to any action.

Appendixes

PART

VIII

IN THIS PART

Security Bibliography—Further Reading

IN THIS APPENDIX

This appendix is a book bibliography on Internet security. Many of these books were released in the last year. Some treat the subject generally, whereas others are more focused. I recommend all of them as further reading. Think of this book bibliography as the Internet security dream library.

You should look up these books on sites such as Amazon. In many cases, you will encounter customer comments, reviews, and other information. This information can help you decide which titles you actually need.

General Internet Security

Access Control and Personal Identification Systems. Don M. Bowers. Butterworth-Heinemann, 1998. ISBN: 0750697326.

Actually Useful Internet Security Techniques. Larry J. Hughes, Jr. New Riders. ISBN: 1562055089.

Advanced Military Cryptography. William F. Friedman. Aegean Park Press, 1996. ISBN: 0894120115.

Advances in Computer System Security. Rein Turn. Artech House, 1988. ISBN: 089006315X.

AIX RS/6000 System and Administration Guide. James W. Deroest. McGraw-Hill, 1994. ISBN: 0070364397.

Applied Cryptography: Protocols, Algorithms, and Source Code in C. Bruce Schneier. John Wiley & Sons, 1995. ISBN: 0471117099.

Applied Java Cryptography. Merlin Hughes. Manning Publications, 1998. ISBN: 1884777635.

AS/400 Security in a Client/Server Environment. Joseph S. Park. John Wiley & Sons, 1995. ISBN: 0471116831.

AS/400 System Administration Guide. Jesse Gamble, Bill Merrow. McGraw-Hill, 1994. ISBN: 0070227985.

Audit Trail Administration, UNIX Svr 4.2. UNIX Systems Lab. Prentice Hall, 1993. ISBN: 0130668877.

Bandits on the Information Superhighway (What You Need to Know). Daniel J. Barrett. O'Reilly & Associates, 1996. ISBN: 1565921569.

Basic Methods of Cryptography. Jan C.A. Van Der Lubbe. Cambridge University Press, 1998. ISBN: 0521555590.

Bots and Other Internet Beasties. Joseph Williams. Sams.net, 1996. ISBN: 1575210169.

Break the Code: Cryptography for Beginners. Bud Johnson, Larry Daste. Dover Publications, 1997. ISBN: 0486291464.

Building in Big Brother: The Cryptographic Policy Debate. Deborah Russell, G. T. Gangemi, Rebecca J. Duncan, Stephen T. Kent, Kim Lawson-Jenkins, Philip Zimmermann, et al. Springer-Verlag, 1995. ISBN: 0387944419.

Building Internet Firewalls. D. Brent Chapman, Elizabeth D. Zwicky. O'Reilly & Associates, 1995. ISBN: 1565921240.

Building Secure and Reliable Network Applications. Kenneth P. Birman. Prentice Hall, 1997. ISBN: 0137195842.

Cisco Router Configuration and Troubleshooting. Mark Tripod. New Riders, 2000. ISBN: 0735709998.

The Code Book, The Evolution of Secrecy from Mary, Queen of Scots to Quantum Cryptography. Simon Singh. Doubleday, 1999. ISBN: 0385495315.

The Codebreakers: The Comprehensive History of Secret Communication from Ancient Times to the Internet. David Kahn. Scribner, 1996. ISBN: 0684831309.

Codes and Cryptography. Dominic Welsh. Oxford University Press, 1988. ISBN: 0198532873.

Codes Ciphers and Secret Writing. Martin Gardner. Dover Publications, 1984. ISBN: 0486247619.

Commonsense Computer Security: Your Practical Guide to Information Protection. Martin R. Smith. McGraw-Hill, 1993. ISBN: 0077078055.

The Complete Idiot's Guide to Protecting Yourself on the Internet. Aaron Weiss. Que, 1995. ISBN: 1567615937.

Computer Communications Security. Warwick Ford. Prentice Hall, 1994. ISBN: 0137994532.

Computer Crime: A Crimefighter's Handbook. David J. Icove, Karl Icove, William Vonstorch. O'Reilly & Associates, 1995. ISBN: 1565920864.

Computer Hacking: Detection and Protection. Imtiaz Malik. Sigma Press, 1996. ISBN: 1850585385.

The Computer Privacy Handbook. André Bacard. Peachpit Press, 1995. ISBN: 32295410.

Computer Security. John M. Carroll. Butterworth-Heinemann, 1996. ISBN: 0750696001.

Computer Security. D.W. Roberts. Blenheim Online Publications, 1990. ISBN: 0863531806.

Computer Security and Privacy: An Information Sourcebook. Mark W. Greenia. Lexikon Services, 1998. ISBN: 0944601464.

Computer Security Basics. Deborah Russell and G.T. Gangemi, Sr. O'Reilly & Associates, 1991. ISBN: 0937175714.

Computer Security for Dummies. Peter T. Davis and Barry D. Lewis. IDG Books, 1996. ISBN: 1568846355.

Computer Security Handbook. R.A. Elbra. NCC Blackwell, 1992. ISBN: 1855541440.

Computer Security Management. Karen A. Forcht. Boyd & Fraser, 1994. ISBN: 0878358811.

Computer Security Risk Management. I.C. Palmer & G.A. Potter. Van Nostrand Reinhold, 1990. ISBN: 0442302908.

Computer Security: Threats and Countermeasures. K. Bhaskar. NCC Blackwell, 1993. ISBN: 1855541742.

Computer System and Network Security. Gregory B. White, Eric A. Fisch, and Udo W. Pooch. CRC Press, 1996. ISBN: 0849371791.

Computer Virus Handbook. Richard Levin. Osborne McGraw-Hill, 1990. ISBN: 0078816475.

Computer Viruses and Anti-Virus Warfare. Jan Hruska. Prentice Hall, 1993. ISBN: 0130363774.

Computers Ethics & Social Values. Deborah G. Johnson, Helen Nissenbaum. Prentice Hall, 1995. ISBN: 0131031104.

Computers Ethics and Society. M. David Ermann, Mary B. Williams, and Michele S. Shauf. Oxford University Press, 1997. ISBN: 019510756X.

Computers Under Attack: Intruders, Worms, and Viruses. Peter J. Denning. ISBN: 0201530678.

Contemporary Cryptology: The Science of Information Integrity. Gustavus J. Simmons. IEEE, 1992. ISBN: 0879422777.

Course in Cryptography. Marcel Givierge. Aegean Park Press, 1996. ISBN: 089412028X.

Cyber Crime: How to Protect Yourself from Computer Criminals. Laura E. Quarantiello. Tiare Publications, 1996. ISBN: 0936653744.

Cyberpunk Handbook. R.U. Sirius and Bart Nagel. Random House, 1995. ISBN: 0679762302.

Cyberpunk: Outlaws and Hackers on the Computer Frontier. Katie Hafner and John Markoff. Simon & Schuster, 1991. ISBN: 0671683225.

Cyberwars: Espionage on the Internet. Jean Guisnel and Winn Schwartau. Plenum Press, 1997. ISBN: 0306456362.

Crypto: When the Code Rebels Beat the Government—Saving Privacy in the Digital Age. Steven Levy. Viking Press, 2000. ISBN: 0670859508.

Cryptography Decrypted. H. X. Mel, Doris Baker, and Steve Burnett. Addison-Wesley, 2000. ISBN: 0201616475

Cryptography & Privacy Sourcebook. David Banisar. BPI Information Services, 1997. ISBN: 1579791077.

Cryptography and Secure Communications. Man Young Rhee. McGraw-Hill, 1994. ISBN: 0071125027.

Cryptography, the Science of Secret Writing. Laurence D. Smith. Dover Publications, 1955. ISBN: 048620247X.

Cryptography: Theory and Practice (Discrete Mathematics and Its Applications). Douglas R. Stinson. CRC Publications, 1995. ISBN: 0849385210.

Decrypted Secrets: Methods and Maxims of Cryptology. Friedrich L. Bauer. Springer Verlag, 1997. ISBN: 3540604189.

Designing and Implementing Microsoft Internet Information Server. Weiying Chen, Sanjaya Hettihewa, Arthur Knowles, and Paolo Pappalardo. Sams.net, 1996. ISBN: 1575211688.

Digital Copyright Protection. Peter Wayner. AP Professional, 1997. ISBN: 0127887717.

Disappearing Cryptography: Being and Nothingness on the Net. Peter Wayner. AP Professional, 1996. ISBN: 0127386718.

Disaster Recovery Planning for Computers and Communication Resources. Jon William Toigo. John Wiley & Sons, 1996. ISBN: 0471121754.

Distributed Programming Paradigms with Cryptography Applications. J.S. Greenfield. Springer Verlag, 1994. ISBN: 354058496X.

E-Commerce Security: Weak Links, Best Defenses. Anup K. Ghosh. John Wiley & Sons, 1998. ISBN: 0471192236.

E-Mail Security: How To Keep Your Electronic Messages Private. Bruce Schneier. John Wiley & Sons, 1995. ISBN: 047105318X.

Elementary Military Cryptography. William F. Friedman. Aegean Park Press, 1996. ISBN: 0894120999.

Encyclopedia of Cryptology. David E. Newton. ABC-Clio Publications, 1997. ISBN: 0874367727.

Enigma: How the German Cipher Was Broken, and How It Was Read by the Allies in WWII. Wladyslaw Kozaczuk. University Publications of America, 1984. ISBN: 0313270074.

Essential SCO System Administration. Keith Vann. Prentice Hall, 1995. ISBN: 013290859X.

Essential Windows NT System Administration. Aeleen Frisch. O'Reilly & Associates, 1998. ISBN: 1565922743.

Executive Guide to Preventing Information Technology Disasters. Richard Ennals. Springer Verlag, 1996. ISBN: 3540199284.

Fire in the Computer Room, What Now?: Disaster Recovery Preparing for Business Survival. Gregor Neaga, Bruce Winters, and Pat Laufman. Prentice Hall, 1997. ISBN: 0137543913.

Firewalls and Internet Security: Repelling the Wily Hacker. William R. Cheswick and Steven M. Bellovin. Addison-Wesley Publishing Company, 1994. ISBN: 0201633574.

Firewalls Complete. Marcus Goncalves. McGraw-Hill, 1998. ISBN: 0070246459.

Fundamentals of Computer Security Technology. Edward Amoroso. Prentice Hall, 1994. ISBN: 0131089293.

Hack Proofing Your Network: Internet Tradecraft. Syngress Media and Ryan Russell. Syngress Media, 2000. ISBN: 1928994156.

Hacking Exposed: Network Security Secrets and Solutions. Joel Scambray, Stuart McClure, and George Kurtz. McGraw-Hill, 2000. ISBN: 0072127481.

Halting the Hacker: A Practical Guide to Computer Security. Donald L. Pipkin. Prentice Hall, 1997. ISBN: 013243718.

Handbook of Applied Cryptography. Alfred J. Menezes, Paul C. Van Oorschot, and Scott A. Vanstone. CRC Press, 1996. ISBN: 0849385237.

HP-Ux 11.X System Administration. Martin Poniatowski and Marty Poniatowski. Prentice Hall, 1998. ISBN: 01310125156.

HP-Ux System Administration Handbook and Toolkit. Marty Poniatowski. Prentice Hall, 1998. ISBN: 0139055711.

Implementing AS/400 Security. Wayne Madden and Carol Woodbury. Duke Communications, 1998. ISBN: 1882419782.

Implementing Internet Security. Frederic J. Cooper. New Riders, 1995. ISBN: 1562054716.

Information Security: An Integrated Collection of Essays. Marshall D. Abrams, Sushil Jajodia, Harold J. Podell. Unknown, 1995. ISBN: 0818636629.

Information Security Management Handbook, Fourth Edition. Micki Krause and Harold Tipton. CRC Press, 1999. ISBN: 0849398290

Information Warfare: Chaos on the Electronic Superhighway. Winn Schwartau. Thunder's Mouth, 1996. ISBN: 1560251328.

An Interactive Guide to the Internet. J. Michael Blocher, Vito Amato, and Jon Storslee. Que Education and Training, 1996. ISBN: 1575763540.

Internet 1997 Unleashed. Jill Ellsworth, Billy Barron, et al. Sams.net, 1996. ISBN: 1575211858.

Internet and Intranet Security. Rolf Oppliger. Artech House, 1997. ISBN: 0890068291.

Internet and TCP/IP Network Security: Securing Protocols and Applications. Uday O. Pabrai and Vijay K. Gurbani. McGraw-Hill, 1996. ISBN: 0070482152.

Internet Besieged: Countering Cyberspace Scofflaws. Dorothy E. Denning and Peter J. Denning. Addison-Wesley Publishing Company, 1997. ISBN: 0201308207.

Internet Commerce. Andrew Dahl and Leslie Lesnick. New Riders, 1995. ISBN: 1562054961.

Internet Cryptography. Richard E. Smith. Addison-Wesley Publishing Company, 1997. ISBN: 0201924803.

Internet Firewalls and Network Security. Chris Hare and Karanjit S. Siyan, Ph.D. New Riders, 1996. ISBN: 1562056328.

Internet Security for Business. Terry Bernstein, et al. John Wiley & Sons, 1996. ISBN: 0471137529.

Internet Security with Windows NT. Mark Joseph Edwards. Duke Communications, 1997. ISBN: 1882419626.

Internet Security: Professional Reference. Derek Atkins, Tom Sheldon, Tim Petru, and Joel Snyder. New Riders, 1997. ISBN: 156205760X.

Intranet Firewalls. Scott Fuller and Kevin Pagan. Ventana Communications Group, 1997. ISBN: 1566045061.

Intranet Security: Stories from the Trenches. Linda McCarthy. Prentice Hall, 1997. ISBN: 0138947597.

A
SECURITY
BIBLIOGRAPHY,
FURTHER READING

Introduction to the Analysis of the Data Encryption Standard. Wayne G. Barker. Aegean Park Press, 1989. ISBN: 0894121693.

Introduction to Cryptology and PC Security. Brian Beckett. McGraw-Hill, 1997. ISBN: 007709235X.

Introduction to Internet Security: From Basics to Beyond. Garry S. Howard. Prima Publishing, 1995. ISBN: 1559587474.

Intrusion Detection. Rebecca Gurley Bace. New Riders, 1999. ISBN: 157801856.

Intrusion Signatures and Analysis. Stephen Northcutt, Karen Frederick, Matt Fearnow, and Mark Cooper. New Riders, 2001. ISBN: 0735710635.

Java Cryptography. Jonathan B. Knudsen. O'Reilly & Associates, 1998. ISBN: 1565924029.

Java Network Security. Dave Durbin, John Owlett, Andrew Yeomans, and Robert S. MacGregor. Prentice Hall, 1998. ISBN: 0137615299.

Java Security. Scott Oakes. O'Reilly & Associates, 1998. ISBN: 1565924037.

Java Security: Managing the Risks. MindQ Publishing, 1997. ISBN: 1575590123.

Lan Times Guide to Security and Data Integrity. Marc Farley, Tom Stearns, and Jeffrey Hsu. Osborne McGraw-Hill, 1996. ISBN: 0078821665.

Managing Privacy: Information Technology and Corporate America. H. Jeff Smith. University of North Carolina Press, 1994. ISBN: 0807821470.

Masters of Deception: The Gang That Ruled Cyberspace. Michele Slatalla and Joshua Quittner. Harper Perennial Library, 1996. ISBN: 0060926945.

Maximum Linux Security: A Hacker's Guide to Protecting Your Linux Server and Workstation. Anonymous. Sams, 1999. ISBN: 0672316706.

Microsoft Windows NT Network Administration Training. Microsoft Educational Services Staff. Microsoft Press, 1997. ISBN: 1572314397.

The NCSA Guide to Enterprise Security: Protecting Information Assets. Michel E. Kabay. McGraw-Hill, 1996. ISBN: 0070331472.

The NCSA Guide to PC and LAN Security. Stephen Cobb. McGraw-Hill, 1996. ISBN: 0079121683.

Netware Security. Doug Bierer and William Steen. New Riders, 1996. ISBN: 1562055453.

Network Intrusion Detection: An Analyst's Handbook, Second Edition. Stephen Northcutt and Judy Novak. New Riders, 2000. ISBN: 0735710082.

Network and Internetwork Security: Principles and Practice. William Stallings. Prentice Hall, 1995. ISBN: 0024154830.

Network Security. Steven L. Shaffer and Alan R. Simon. AP Professional, 1994. ISBN: 0126380104.

Network Security in a Mixed Environment. Dan Balckarski. IDG Books, 1998. ISBN: 0764531522.

Network Security: How to Plan for It and Achieve It. Richard H. Baker. McGraw-Hill, 1994. ISBN: 0070051410.

NT Network Security. Matthew Strebe, Charles Perkins, and Michael Moncur. Sybex, 1998. ISBN: 0782120067.

The Official PGP User's Guide. Philip R. Zimmermann. MIT Press, 1995. ISBN: 0262740176.

Pcweek Intranet and Internet Firewalls Strategies. Edward Amoroso and Ronald Sharp. Ziff-Davis, 1996. ISBN: 1562764225.

Pcweek Microsoft Windows NT Security: System Administrator's Guide. Nevin Lambert, Manish Patel, and Steve Sutton. Ziff-Davis, 1997. ISBN: 1562764578.

PC Security and Virus Protection. Pamela Kane. IDG Books, 1994. ISBN: 1558513906.

PGP: Pretty Good Privacy. Simson Garfinkel. O'Reilly & Associates, 1995. ISBN: 1565920988.

Practical Computer Network Security. Mike Hendry. Artech House, 1995. ISBN: 0890068011.

Practical Cryptography for Data Internetworks. Edited by William Stallings. IEEE Computer Society, 1996. ISBN: 0818671408.

Practical Intrusion Detection Handbook. Paul E. Proctor. Prentice Hall, 2000. ISBN: 0130259608.

Practical UNIX and Internet Security. Simson Garfinkel and Gene Spafford. O'Reilly & Associates, 1996. ISBN: 1565921488.

The Process of Network Security. Thomas A. Wadlow. Addison-Wesley Publishing Company, 2000. ISBN: 0201433176.

Professional NT Internet Information Server 2 Administration. Christian Gross, Michael Tracy, and Kevin Roche. Wrox Press, 1996. ISBN: 1861000480.

Protecting Business Information: A Manager's Guide. James A. Schweitzer. Butterworth-Heinemann, 1995. ISBN: 0750696583.

Protecting Your Web Site with Firewalls. Marcus Goncalves and Vinicius A. Goncalves. Prentice Hall, 1997. ISBN: 0136282075.

Protecting Yourself Online: The Definitive Resource on Safety Freedom and Privacy in Cyberspace. Robert B. Gelman and Stanton McCandlish. Harper Collins, 1998. ISBN: 0062515128.

Protection and Security on the Information Superhighway. Frederick B. Cohen. John Wiley & Sons, 1995. ISBN: 0471113891.

Public-Key Cryptography. Arto Salomaa. Springer Verlag, 1996. ISBN: 3540613560.

Risky Business: Protect Your Business from Being Stalked, Conned, Libeled or Blackmailed on the Web. Dan Janal. John Wiley & Sons, 1998. ISBN: 0471197068.

Secrets and Lies. Bruce Schneier. John Wiley & Sons, 2000. ISBN: 0471253111.

Secrets of Making and Breaking Codes. Hamilton Nickels. Citadel Press, 1994. ISBN: 0806515635.

Secure Commerce on the Internet. Vijay Ahuja. AP Professional, 1996. ISBN: 0120455978.

Secure Computing: Threats and Safeguards. Rita C. Summers. McGraw-Hill, 1997. ISBN: 0070694192.

Secure Data Networking. Michael Purse. Artech House, 1993. ISBN: 0890066922.

Secure Electronic Commerce: Building the Infrastructure for Digital Signatures and Encryption. Warwick Ford and Michael S. Baum. Prentice Hall, 1997. ISBN: 0134763424.

Secure Electronic Transactions: Introduction and Technical Reference. Larry Loeb. Artech House, 1998. 0890069921.

Securing Java: Getting Down to Business with Mobile Code, Second Edition. Gary McGraw and Edward W. Felten. John Wiley and Sons, 1999. ISBN: 047131952X

Securing Windows NT/2000 Servers for the Internet: A Checklist for System Administrators. Stefan Norberg and Deborah Russell. O'Reilly & Associates, 2000. ISBN: 1565927680.

Security, ID Systems, and Locks: The Book on Electronic Access Control. Joel Koniecek and Karen Little. Butterworth-Heinemann, 1997. ISBN: 0750699329.

Security in Computing. Charles P. Pfleeger. Prentice Hall, 1996. ISBN: 0133374866.

Security Survival: A Source Book from the Open Group. X Open Guide. Prentice Hall, 1997. ISBN: 0132666286.

Smart Card Security and Applications. Mike Hendry. Artech House, 1997. ISBN: 0890069530.

Technology and Privacy: The New Landscape. Philip E. Agre and Marc Rotenberg. MIT Press, 1997. ISBN: 026201162X.

The Ultimate Computer Security Survey/Book and Disk. James L. Schaub and Ken D., Jr. Butterworth-Heinemann, 1995. ISBN: 0750696923.

The Ultimate Windows 2000 System Administrator's Guide. Robert Williams and Mark Walla. Addison-Wesley Publishing Company, 2000. ISBN: 0201615800.

Understanding Digital Signatures: Establishing Trust over the Internet and Other Networks. Gail L. Grant. McGraw-Hill, 1997. ISBN: 0070125546.

UNIX Installation Security and Integrity. David Ferbrache and Gavin Shearer. Prentice Hall, 1993. ISBN: 0130153893.

UNIX Security. Miller Freeman. Miller Freeman, 1997. ISBN: 0879304715.

Web Commerce Cookbook. Gordon McComb. John Wiley & Sons, 1997. ISBN: 0471196630.

Web Psychos, Stalkers, and Pranksters: How to Protect Yourself in Cyberspace. Michael A. Banks. Coriolis Group, 1997. ISBN: 1576101371.

Web Security & Commerce. Simson Garfinkel and Gene Spafford. O'Reilly & Associates, 1997. ISBN: 1565922697.

Web Security Sourcebook. Avi Rubin, Daniel Geer, and Marcus J. Ranum. John Wiley & Sons, 1997. ISBN: 047118148X.

Web Security: A Step-By-Step Reference Guide. Lincoln D. Stein. Addison-Wesley Publishing Company, 1998. ISBN: 0201634899.

Who Knows: Safeguarding Your Privacy in a Networked World. Ann Cavoukian and Don Tapscott. Random House, 1996. ISBN: 0070633207.

Windows NT Security Guide. Steve A. Sutton. Addison-Wesley Publishing Company, 1996. ISBN: 0201419696.

Windows NT Security Handbook. Tom Sheldon. Osborne McGraw-Hill, 1996. ISBN: 0078822408.

Windows NT Security: A Practical Guide to Securing Windows NT Servers and Workstations. Charles B. Rutstein. McGraw-Hill, 1997. ISBN: 0070578338.

Windows NT Server 4 Security Handbook. Lee Hadfield, Dave Hatter, and Dave Bixler. Que, 1997. ISBN: 078971213X.

Windows NT Server and UNIX: Administration, Co-Existence, Integration, and Migration. G. Robert Williams and Ellen Beck Gardner. Addison-Wesley Publishing Company, 1998. ISBN: 0201185369.

Windows NT User Administration. Ashley J. Meggitt and Timothy D. Ritchey. O'Reilly & Associates, 1997. ISBN: 1565923014.

WWW Security: How to Build a Secure World Wide Web Connection. Robert S. MacGregor, Alberto Aresi, and Andreas Siegert. Prentice Hall, 1996. ISBN: 0136124097.

TCP/IP

Cisco TCP/IP Routing Professional Reference. Chris Lewis. McGraw-Hill, 1997. ISBN: 0070410887.

Demystifying TCP/IP. Paul Schlieve. Wordware Publishing, 1997. ISBN: 1556225393.

Designing TCP/IP Internetworks. Geoff Bennett. John Wiley & Sons, 1997. ISBN: 0471286435.

The Essential Guide to TCP/IP Commands. Martin R. Arick. John Wiley & Sons, 1996. ISBN: 0471125695.

A Guide to the TCP/IP Protocol Suite. Floyd Wilder and Vinton G. Cerf. Artech House, 1993. ISBN: 0890066930.

Hands-On TCP/IP. Paul Simoneau. McGraw-Hill, 1997. ISBN: 0079126405.

High-Speed Networks: TCP/IP and ATM Design Principles. William Stallings. Prentice Hall, 1997. ISBN: 0135259657.

Illustrated TCP/IP. Matthew G. Naugle. John Wiley & Sons, 1998. ISBN: 0471196568.

Implementing Ipv6: Migrating to the Next Generation Internet Protocol. Mark A. Miller. IDG Books, 1998. ISBN: 1558515798.

Inside TCP/IP. Karanjit S. Siyan, Ph.D., Nancy Hawkins, and Joern Wettern. New Riders, 1997. ISBN: 1562057146.

Integrating TCP/IP into SNA. Ed Taylor. Wordware Publishing, 1993. ISBN: 1556223404.

Internet Core Protocols: The Definite Guide. Eric A. Hall. O'Reilly & Associates. ISBN: 1565292576.

Internet and TCP/IP Network Security. Uday O. Pabrai and Vijay K. Gurbani. McGraw-Hill, 1996. ISBN: 0070482152.

Internetworking with Netware TCP/IP. Karanjit S. Siyan, Peter Kuo, and Peter Rybaczyk. New Riders, 1996. ISBN: 1562055585.

Internetworking with TCP/IP: Client-Server Programming and Applications. Douglas E. Comer and David L. Stevens. Prentice Hall, 1997. ISBN: 0138487146.

Internetworking with TCP/IP: Principles, Protocols, and Architecture. Douglas E. Comer. Prentice Hall, 1995. ISBN: 0132169878.

An Introduction to TCP/IP. John Davidson. Springer Verlag, 1998. ISBN: 038796651X.

IPNG and the TCP/IP Protocols: Implementing the Next Generation Internet. Stephen Thomas. John Wiley & Sons, 1996. ISBN: 0471130885.

IPV6: The New Internet Protocol. Christian Huitema. Prentice Hall, 1996. ISBN: 013241936X.

Mastering TCP/IP for NT Server. Mark Minasi, Todd Lammle, and Monica Lammle. Sybex, 1997. ISBN: 0782121233.

MCSE: TCP/IP for NT Server 4 Study Guide. Todd Lammle, Monica Lammle, and James Chellis. Sybex, 1997. ISBN: 078212173X.

Networking Personal Computers With TCP/IP. Craig Hunt and Mike Loukides. O'Reilly & Associates, 1995. ISBN: 1565921232.

Networking with Microsoft TCP/IP. Drew Heywood. New Riders, 1997. ISBN: 1562057138.

Novell's Guide to TCP/IP and Intranetware. Drew Heywood. IDG Books, 1997. ISBN: 0764545329.

Sams Teach Yourself TCP/IP in 14 Days. Timothy Parker. Sams Publishing, 1996. ISBN: 0672308851.

TCP/IP Administration. Craig Zacker. IDG Books, 1998. ISBN: 0764531581.

TCP/IP and the AS/400. Dan Riehl and Mike Ryan. Duke Communications, 1998. ISBN: 1882419723.

TCP/IP and Related Protocols. Uyless Black. McGraw-Hill, 1995. ISBN: 0070055602.

TCP/IP Applications and Protocols. Walter Goralski. Computer Technology Research Corporation, 1995. ISBN: 1566079519.

TCP/IP Clearly Explained. Pete Loshin. AP Professional, 1997. ISBN: 0124558356.

TCP/IP Complete. Ed Taylor. McGraw-Hill, 1998. ISBN: 0070634009.

TCP/IP for Dummies. Candace Leiden and Marshall Wilensky. IDG Books, 1997. ISBN: 0764500635.

TCP/IP for NT Server 4. Sybex. Sybex, 1998. ISBN: 0782123074.

TCP/IP Network Administration. Craig Hunt. Travelers' Tales Inc., 1998. ISBN: 1565923227.

TCP/IP Networking: Architecture, Administration, and Programming. James Martin and Joe Leben. Prentice Hall, 1994. ISBN: 0136422322.

TCP/IP Networking Protocol. Lynne G. Jolitz. Peer to Peer Communications, 1998. ISBN: 1573980072.

TCP/IP: Running a Successful Network. Kevin Washburn and Jim Evans. Addison-Wesley Publishing Company, 1996. ISBN: 0201877112.

TCP/IP: A Survival Guide. Frank Derfler and Steve Rigney. IDG Books, 1997. ISBN: 1558285644.

TCP/IP Tutorial and Technical Overview. Eamon Murphy, Steve Hayes, and Mathias Enders. Prentice Hall, 1995. ISBN: 0134608585.

TCP/IP Unleashed. Timothy Parker. Sams Publishing, 1998. ISBN: 0672311127.

Using TCP/IP. Joern Wettern and Nancy Hawkins. Que, 1997. ISBN: 0789713624.

On Netware

Bulletproofing Netware: Solving the 175 Most Common Problems Before They Happen. Mark Wilkins, Glenn E. Weadock, and K. Weadock Wilkins. McGraw-Hill, 1997. ISBN: 0070676216.

CNA Study Guide for Intranetware. Michael Moncur and James Chellis. Sybex, 1997. ISBN: 0782120989.

The Complete Guide to NetWare 4.1. James E. Gaskin. Sybex, 1995. ISBN: 078211500A.

A Guide to NetWare for UNIX. Cathy Gunn. Prentice Hall, 1995. ISBN: 0133007162.

Learning Netware 4.1. Guy Yost and John Preston. Que, 1997. ISBN: 1575760525.

Managing Small Netware 4.11 Networks. Doug Jones. Sybex, 1997. ISBN: 0782119638.

Mastering Netware 5.1. James Gaskin. Sybex, 2000. ISBN: 078212772X.

Netware 4 Made Easy. Taha. Prentice Hall, 1998. ISBN: 0132449633.

NetWare 4.X. John Preston. Que, 1997. ISBN: 1575763826.

NetWare Professional's Toolkit. Gary Araki. Advice Press, 1998. ISBN: 1889671118.

The NetWare to Internet Connection. Morgan Stern. Sybex, 1996. ISBN: 0782117066.

NetWare to Internet Gateways. James E. Gaskin. Prentice Hall, 1996. ISBN: 0135217741.

NetWare to Windows NT Complete: Integration and Migration. Arnold Villeneuve and Wayne McKinnon. McGraw-Hill, 1998. ISBN: 0079131719.

NetWare Web Development. Peter Kuo. Sams Publishing, 1996. ISBN: 1575211886.

Novell Intranetware Professional Reference. Karanjit Siyan, Joshua Ball, Jason Ehrhart, and Jim Henderson. New Riders, 1997. ISBN: 1562057294.

Novell's Guide to Creating Intranetware Intranets. Karanjit S. Siyan. IDG Books, 1997. ISBN: 0764545310.

Novell's Guide to Integrating NetWare and TCP/IP. Drew Heywood. Novell Press/IDG Books, 1996. ISBN: 1568848188.

Novell's Guide to NetWare LAN Analysis. Dan E. Hakes and Laura Chappell. Sybex, 1994. ISBN: 0782111432.

Novell's Guide to Performance Tuning Netware. Jeffrey F. Hughes and Blair W. Thomas. IDG Books, 1998. ISBN: 0764545264.

Routing in Today's Internetworks: The Routing Protocols of IP, Decnet, Netware, and Appletalk. Mark Dickie. John Wiley & Sons, 1997. ISBN: 0471286206.

Internet 101

IN THIS APPENDIX

This appendix discusses the Internet's early history. If you already know the story, feel free to skip it.

In the Beginning: 1962–1969

Our setting is the early 1960s—1962, to be exact. Jack Kennedy was in the White House, and the Beatles had just recorded their first hit single ("Love Me Do"). Americans were enjoying an era of prosperity. Elsewhere, however, Communism was spreading, and with it came weapons of terrible destruction.

In anticipation of nuclear war, the United States Air Force charged a small group of researchers with a formidable task: creating a communication network that could survive a nuclear attack. Their concept was revolutionary—a network that had no centralized control. If one (or 10, or 100) of its nodes were destroyed, the system would continue to run. In essence, this network (designed exclusively for military use) would survive the apocalypse itself (even if we didn't).

The individual most responsible for the Internet's existence was Paul Baran. In 1962, Baran worked at Rand Corporation, the think tank charged with developing this concept. Baran imagined a network in which all machines could communicate with one another. This was a radical concept that went well against the grain of conventional wisdom. However, Baran knew that centralized networks were simply too vulnerable to attack. In his now-famous memorandum titled *On Distributed Communications: I. Introduction to Distributed Communications Network*, Baran wrote

> The centralized network is obviously vulnerable as destruction of a single central node destroys communication between the end stations.

▶ The Rand Corporation has generously made this memorandum and the report delivered by Baran available via the World Wide Web. The document(s) can be found at `http://www.rand.org/publications/RM/baran.list.html`.

Baran was referring to the way most computer networks were constructed. In the old days, networks relied on mainframes. These were large, powerful machines that housed centralized information. Users accessed that information through terminals wired directly to the mainframe. Data would travel from their terminals, down the cable, and to the mainframe. The mainframe would then distribute that data to other terminals. This was a very effective method of networking but had disastrous security implications. For example, terminals could not communicate directly with one another. Hence, if the mainframe were destroyed, the network would be destroyed. This placed our national networks at considerable risk.

Baran had a simple solution: Design a network where all points could communicate with one another. In many ways, this design bore similarities to the national telephone system. As Baran explained

> In practice, a mixture of star and mesh components is used to form communications networks. Such a network is sometimes called a "decentralized" network, because complete reliance upon a single point is not always required.

Baran's proposal was thorough, right down to routing conventions. He envisioned a system whereby data could dynamically determine its own path. For example, if the data encountered a problem at one crossroads of the Net, it would find an alternate route. This system was based on certain rules. For instance, a network node would only accept a message if it had adequate space to store it. Equally, if all lines were currently busy, the message would wait until a new path became available. In this way, the network would provide intelligent data transport. Baran also detailed other aspects of the network, including

- Security
- Priority schemes (and devices to avoid network overload)
- Hardware
- Cost

Unfortunately, Baran's ideas were ahead of their time. The Pentagon had little faith in such radical concepts. Baran delivered an 11-volume report to defense officials, who promptly shelved it. As it turned out, the Pentagon's shortsightedness delayed the birth of the Internet, but not by much. By 1965, the push was on again. Funding was allocated to develop a decentralized computer network, and, in 1969, that network became a reality. The system was called *ARPANET*.

As networks go, ARPANET was pretty basic. It consisted of links between machines at four academic institutions (Stanford Research Institute, the University of Utah, the University of California at Los Angeles, and the University of California at Santa Barbara). One of those machines was a DEC PDP-10. These ancient beasts are now more useful as furniture than computing devices. However, I mention the PDP-10 here to briefly recount another legend in computer history.

It was at roughly that time that a Seattle, Washington, company began providing computer time-sharing. (This was a system whereby corporate clients could rent CPU time. They were generally charged by the hour.) The company took on two bright young men to test its software. In exchange for their services, the boys were given free dial-up access to a PDP-10. (This would be the equivalent of getting free access to a private bulletin board system.) Unfortunately for the boys, the company folded shortly thereafter, but the learning experience changed their lives. At the time, they were just old enough to attend high school. Today, they are billionaires. Can you guess their identities? The two boys were Bill Gates and Paul Allen.

In any event, ARPANET had very modest beginnings: four machines connected by telephone. At the time, this seemed like an incredible achievement. However, the initial euphoria of creating ARPANET quickly wore off when engineers realized they had several serious problems. One problem was this: They didn't have an operating system suitable to create the massive network Baran had conceived.

Fate would now play a major role. Halfway across the United States, researchers were developing an obscure operating system. Their work—which occurred simultaneously with the development of ARPANET—would change the world forever. The operating system was called UNIX.

UNIX Is Born: 1969–1973

The year was 1969, (the same year that ARPANET was established). A man named Ken Thompson from Bell Labs (with Dennis Ritchie and Joseph Ossanna) developed the first version of UNIX. The hardware was a Digital Equipment Corporation (DEC) PDP-7. The software was homegrown, written by Thompson himself.

Thompson's UNIX system bore no resemblance to modern UNIX. For example, modern UNIX is a multiuser system. (In other words, many users can work simultaneously on a single UNIX box.) In contrast, Thompson's first prototype was a single-user system and a bare bones one at that. However, I should probably define the term *bare bones*.

When you think of an operating system, you probably imagine something that includes basic utilities, text editors, help files, a windowing system, networking tools, and so forth. That's because today, end-user systems incorporate great complexity and user-friendly design. Alas, the first UNIX system was nothing like this. Instead, it had only the most necessary utilities to operate. For a moment, place yourself in Ken Thompson's position. Before you create dozens of complex programs like those just mentioned, you are faced with a more practical task: getting the system to boot.

Thompson did eventually get his UNIX system to boot. However, he encountered many problems along that road. One was that the programming language he used wasn't well suited to the task. Once again, fate played a tremendous role. At roughly that same time, other researchers at Bell Labs (Dennis Ritchie and Brian Kernighan) created a new programming language called C.

About C

C is often used to write language compilers and operating systems. I examine C here because it drastically influenced the Internet's development. Here is why.

Today, nearly all applications that facilitate communication over the Internet are written in C. Indeed, both the UNIX operating system (which forms the underlying structure of the Internet) and TCP/IP (the suite of protocols that traffic data over the Net) were developed in C. If C had never emerged, the Internet as we know it would never have existed at all.

C's popularity is based on several factors:

- C is small and efficient.
- C code is easily portable from one operating system to another.
- C can be learned quickly and easily.

However, only the first of these facts was known to AT&T Bell Labs researchers when they decided to rewrite UNIX in C. That's exactly what they did. Together, Thompson and Ritchie ported UNIX to a DEC PDP-11/20. From there, UNIX underwent considerable development. Between 1970 and 1973, UNIX was completely rewritten in C. This was a major improvement and eliminated many bugs inherent in the original UNIX system.

The Internet's Formative Years: 1972–1975

Briefly, I turn away from the on-going development of UNIX and C because, between 1972 and 1975, advances were being made in other areas. These advances would have strong bearing on how and why UNIX was chosen as the Internet's operating system.

The year was 1972. ARPANET had some 40 hosts. (In today's terms, that is smaller than many local area networks, or *LANs*.) It was in that year that Ray Tomlinson, a member of Bolt, Beranek, and Newman, Inc., forever changed Internet communication. Tomlinson created electronic mail.

Tomlinson's invention was probably the single most important computer innovation of the decade. Email allowed simple, efficient, and inexpensive communication. This naturally led to an open exchange of ideas and interstate collaboration between folks researching different technologies. Because many recipients could be added to an email message, these ideas were more rapidly implemented. From that point on, the Net was alive.

Another key invention emerged in 1974: Vinton Cerf and Robert Khan invented the Transmission Control Protocol (TCP). This protocol was a new means of moving data across the Network bit by bit and then later assembling these fragments at the other end.

NOTE

TCP is the primary protocol used on the Internet today. It was developed in the early 1970s and was ultimately integrated into Berkeley Software Distribution UNIX. It has since become an Internet standard. Today, almost all computers connected to the Internet run some form of TCP.

By 1975, ARPANET was a fully functional network. The groundwork had been done, and it was time for the U.S. government to claim its prize. In that year, control of ARPANET was given to an organization then known as the United States Defense Communications Agency. (This organization would later become the Defense Information Systems Agency.)

What remained was to choose the official operating system for ARPANET. The final choice was UNIX. The reasons that UNIX was chosen over other operating systems were complex. In the next section, I discuss those reasons at length.

UNIX Comes of Age

Between 1974 and 1980, UNIX source code was distributed to universities throughout the country. This, more than any other thing, contributed to the success of UNIX.

First, the research and academic communities took an immediate liking to UNIX. Hence, it was used in many educational exercises. This had a direct effect on the commercial world. As explained by Mike Loukides, an editor for O'Reilly & Associates and a UNIX guru:

> Schools were turning out loads of very competent computer users (and systems programmers) who already knew UNIX. You could therefore "buy" a ready-made programming staff. You didn't have to train them on the intricacies of some unknown operating system.

Also, the source was free to universities and therefore, UNIX was open for development by students. This openness quickly led to UNIX being ported to other machines, which only increased the UNIX user base.

NOTE

Because UNIX source is widely known and available, more flaws in the system security structure are also known. This is in sharp contrast to proprietary systems. Proprietary software manufacturers refuse to disclose their source except to very select recipients, leaving many questions about their security as yet unanswered.

UNIX continued to gain popularity and in 1978, AT&T decided to commercialize the operating system and demand licensing fees (after all, they had obviously created a winning product). This caused a major shift in the computing community. As a result, in a stunning move to establish creative independence, the University of California at Berkeley created its own version of UNIX. The Berkeley distribution was extremely influential, being the basis for many modern forms of commercial UNIX.

So, in brief, UNIX was chosen for several reasons, including the following:

- UNIX was a developing standard.
- UNIX was an open system.
- UNIX source code was publicly available for scrutiny.
- UNIX had powerful networking features.

UNIX and the Internet Evolve Together

Once UNIX was chosen as the Internet's operating system, advances in UNIX were incorporated into the Internet's design. Thus, from 1975 onward, UNIX and the Internet evolved together. And, along that road, many large software and hardware manufacturers released their own versions of UNIX. The most popular versions are listed in Table B.1.

TABLE B.1   Commercial Versions of UNIX and Their Manufacturers

UNIX Version	*Software Company*
SunOS & Solaris	Sun Microsystems
HP-UX	Hewlett-Packard
AIX	IBM
Digital UNIX	Compaq
Linux	Open Source—Multiple Distributors

Many of these UNIX flavors run on high-performance machines called *workstations*. Workstations differ from PC machines in several ways. First, workstations contain superior hardware and are therefore more expensive. This is due in part to the limited number of workstations built. In contrast, PCs are mass produced, and manufacturers constantly look for ways to cut costs. A consumer buying a new PC motherboard therefore has a much greater chance of receiving faulty hardware. Moreover, workstations are typically more technologically advanced than PCs. For example, onboard sound, Ethernet, and SCSI were standard features of workstations in 1989. In fact, onboard ISDN was integrated not long after ISDN was developed.

Linux is an interesting version of UNIX. It was designed to run on PC hardware and is freely available. This combination, plus the reliability of Linux, has made it an important platform for Internet servers.

> **NOTE**
>
> Technological advantages of workstations aren't always immediately apparent, either. Often, the power of a workstation is under the hood, obscured from view. For example, many workstations have extremely high throughput, which translates to blinding speeds over network connections and superb graphics performance. In fact, SGI and Sun now make machines that have absurd throughput, measuring hundreds of gigabytes per second.

High-end performance comes at a terrific price. In the past, workstations would set you back five, or even six, figures. Naturally, for average users, these machines are cost prohibitive. In contrast, PC hardware and software are cheap, easily obtainable, simple to configure, and widely distributed. However, over the past few years, workstations have dropped greatly in price and now are just slightly more expensive than PCs.

However, we are only concerned with UNIX as it relates to the Internet. As you might guess, that relationship is strong. Because the U.S. government's Internet development was implemented on the UNIX platform, UNIX contains the very building blocks of the Net. No other operating system had ever been so expressly designed for use with the Internet.

Let's have a brief look at UNIX before continuing.

The Basic Characteristics of UNIX

Modern UNIX runs on disparate hardware, including IBM-compatibles and Macintoshes. Installation differs little from installation of other operating systems. Most vendors provide CD-ROM media. On workstations, installation is performed by booting from a CD-ROM. You are usually given a series of options and the remainder of the installation is automatic. On other hardware platforms, a boot disk that loads a small installation routine into memory generally accompanies the CD-ROM.

Starting a UNIX system is also similar to booting other systems. The boot routine takes quick diagnostics of all existing hardware devices, checks the memory, and starts vital system processes. In UNIX, some common system processes started at boot and include the following:

- Electronic mail services
- General network services
- Logging and system administration services

After the system boots, a login prompt appears. Here, you provide your username and password. When login is complete, you are dropped into a shell environment.

> **NOTE**
>
> A shell is an environment in which commands can be typed and executed. A shell inter-
> preter then translates those commands to machine language for processing. In MSDOS, for
> example, the shell is `COMMAND.COM`. The user interfaces with the shell by typing commands
> (for example, the command `DIR` to list directories). In this respect, at least in appearance,
> basic UNIX marginally resembles MS-DOS. All commands are entered using the shell.
> Output of commands appears on the monitor unless you specify otherwise.

Navigation of directories is accomplished in a similar fashion to navigation of a DOS system.
DOS users can easily navigate a UNIX system using the conversion information in Table B.2.
The UNIX commands listed here operate identically or very similarly to their DOS counterparts.

TABLE B.2 Command Conversion Table: UNIX to DOS

DOS Command	*UNIX Equivalent*
`cd \<directory>`	`cd /<directory>`
`dir`	`ls -l`
`dir \directory`	`ls /directory`
`dir /w`	`ls`
`chkdsk drive`	`fsck drive/partition`
`copy filename1 filename2`	`cp filenme1 filename2`
`edit filename`	`vi filename`
`fc filename1 filename2`	`diff filename1 filename2`
`find text_string`	`grep text_string`
`format drive`	`format drive/partition`
`mem/c|more`	`more /proc/meminfo`
`move filenme1 filename2`	`mv filename1 filename2`
`sort filename`	`sort filename`
`type filename|more`	`more filename`
`help <command>`	`man <command>`

▶ To learn more about basic UNIX commands, go to `http://www.geek-girl.com/Unixhelp/`.
This archive is a comprehensive collection of information about UNIX. Or for good printed documentation, I recommend *UNIX Unleashed* (ISBN 0-672-31411-8), a title that provides many
helpful tips and tricks on using this popular operating system.

What Kinds of Applications Run on UNIX?

UNIX runs many different applications. Some are high-performance programs used in scientific research and artificial intelligence. However, not all UNIX applications are so specialized. Popular, commercial applications also run in UNIX, including Adobe PhotoShop, Corel WordPerfect, and other products commonly associated with PCs.

In all, modern UNIX is like any other platform. Window systems tend to come with suites of applications integrated into the package. These include file managers, text editors, mail tools, clocks, calendars, calculators, and the usual fare.

A rich collection of multimedia software can be used with UNIX, including movie players, audio CD utilities, recording facilities for digital sound, two-way camera systems, multimedia mail, and other fun things. Basically, just about anything you can think of has been written for UNIX.

UNIX in Relation to Internet Security

UNIX security is a complex field. It has been said that UNIX is at odds with itself, because the same advantages that make UNIX a superb server platform also make it vulnerable to attack. UNIX was designed as the ultimate networked operating system, providing you with the ability to execute almost any application remotely and transparently. (For example, UNIX enables you to perform tasks on one machine from another, even though those boxes are located thousands of miles apart.) As such, by default, UNIX remote services will accept connections from anywhere in the world.

Moreover, UNIX is an open system, and its code is publicly available. So, just as researchers can look at UNIX code and find weaknesses so can computer criminals, crackers, and other malcontents. However, UNIX is a mature operating system and over the years, many advances have been made in UNIX security. Some of these advances (many of which were implemented early in the operating system's history) include the following:

- Encrypted passwords
- Strong file and directory-access control
- System-level authentication procedures
- Sophisticated logging facilities

UNIX is therefore used in many environments that demand security. Hundreds of programs are available to tune up the security of a UNIX system. Many of these tools are freely available on the Internet. Such tools can be classified into three basic categories:

- Security-audit tools
- System-logging tools

- Intrusion-detection tools
- Encryption tools

Security-audit tools are programs that automatically detect holes within systems. These check for known vulnerabilities and common misconfigurations that can lead to security breaches. Such tools are designed for wide-scale network auditing and, therefore, can be used to check many machines on a given network (thousands, if you want). These tools are advantageous because they automate base-line security assessments. However, these tools are also liabilities, because they provide powerful capabilities to crackers who can obtain them just as easily.

System-logging tools record the activities of users and system messages. These logs are recorded to plain text files or files that automatically organize themselves into one or more database formats. Logging tools are a staple resource in any UNIX security toolbox. Often, the logs generated by such utilities form the basis of evidence to build a case against a cracker. However, deep logging of the system can be costly in terms of disk space and bandwidth.

Intrusion-detection tools are programs that automatically detect patterns that suggest an intrusion is under way. In some respects, intrusion detection tools can be viewed as intelligent logging utilities. The difference is that the logs are generated, analyzed, and acted upon in real-time.

Lastly, encryption tools allow data to be encrypted. The data might be encrypted on the hard drive so others can not read it. Data being sent across the Internet can also be encrypted, so that people cannot intercept and read the transmission.

Despite these superb tools, however, UNIX security is difficult to achieve. UNIX is a large and complicated operating system and hiring true UNIX security experts can be costly. For although these people aren't particularly rare, most of them already occupy key positions in firms throughout the nation. As a result, consulting in this area has become a lucrative business.

Moving On: The '90s Internet

So, this history of the Net is edging up on 1990. By that time, the Internet was used almost exclusively by either military or academic personnel. Casual users probably numbered several hundred thousand, if that. And the network was managed by the National Science Foundation, an entity that placed strict restrictions on the network's use. Flatly stated, it was forbidden to use the Internet for commercial purpose.

This placed the NSF in a unique position. Although the Internet was not user-friendly (all access was command-line only), the network was growing in popularity. The number of hosts had grown to some 300,000. Within months, the first freely available public access Internet server was established, and researchers were confronted with the inevitable. It was only a matter of time before humanity would storm the beach of cyberspace.

Amidst debates over cost (operating the Internet backbone required substantial resources), NSF suddenly relinquished its authority in 1991. This opened the way for commercial entities to seize control of network bandwidth.

However, the public at large did not advance. Access was still command-line based and far too intimidating for the average user. It was then that a tremendous event occurred that changed the history of not just the Internet, but the world: The University of Minnesota released new software called *Gopher*. Gopher was the first Internet navigation tool for use in GUI environments. The World Wide Web browser followed soon thereafter.

In 1995, NSF retired as overseer of the Net. The Internet was completely commercialized almost instantly as companies across America rushed to get connected to the backbone. These companies were immediately followed by the American public, which was empowered by new browsers such as NCSA Mosaic, Netscape Navigator, and Microsoft Internet Explorer. The Internet was suddenly accessible to anyone with a computer, a windowing system, and a mouse.

As more users flocked to the Net, Internet service providers cropped up everywhere. These were small, localized companies that provided basic gateway access to the general public. For $20 a month, anyone with a computer and a modem could enjoy Internet connectivity. And, it wasn't long before monster corporations (such as America Online and Prodigy) jumped on the bandwagon. This caused the Internet user base to skyrocket.

The late 1990s saw a huge rise in businesses using the Internet. Shopping on the Internet became a reality with millions, if not billions, of dollars spent across the Internet every day. New companies, such as Yahoo! and Amazon, rose out of nowhere to become huge in just a couple years. However, a lack of bandwidth remained a stumbling block for people wanting to fully utilize the Internet.

The Future

There have been many projections about where the Internet is going. Most of these projections are cast by marketers and spin doctors anxious to sell more bandwidth, more hardware, more software, and more hype. A significant number of people now have access to high-speed Internet connectivity if they are willing to pay for it. Two technologies for this have emerged: DSL (Digital Subscriber Line) and cable modem.

DSL is a high-speed phone line that ranges in speed from 128Kbps to more than 1Mbps. The problem with DSL is that the maximum speed varies depending on how far you are from the phone company central office. If you are far enough away, you cannot get DSL service at all. Also, getting a DSL line successfully installed is challenging and it often takes weeks to get the line working.

Having used both DSL and cable modem on a regular basis, my opinion is that cable modem is the far superior technology. Cable modem uses the cable TV lines that come into your home. However, some people do not have cable TV available in their area and some cable providers do not offer Internet access.

DSL providers like to claim that your neighbors slow down your cable modem access because you share the same cable line. Only on a poorly designed cable system will you notice this problem. In reality, DSL suffers from the same problem from the central office to your ISP. Therefore, this argument used by DSL providers is invalid. Your high-speed Internet connection is only as good as your provider regardless of whether you use DSL or Cable.

These technologies are always on, and people leave their computers hooked to the Internet 24 hours a day, which causes new security issues.

Additionally, many people think that these high-speed technologies will make real-time audio and video a reality on the Internet.

While decent-quality audio is usually possible, video even on DSL and cable remain problematic. Pauses are frequent, and quality is sacrificed. Faster Internet access technologies are needed to make watching movies across the Internet a reality.

The Internet is about to become an important part of many Americans' life, if it's not already. Banks and other financial institutions are now offering banking over the Internet. Within five years, this could replace the standard method of banking.

Additionally, much of the stock trading has moved from traditional brokers to the Internet. One common problem for employers is that some of their employees spend a good part of the day checking their stock prices because they can get current quotes easily. Also, the volume of "day trading" has exploded due to the Internet because it is so much easier to do now. Some have struck it rich, and others have let greed get the best of them looking for the quick, easy money.

Summary

This appendix briefly examined the birth of the Internet. Next on the agenda is the historical and practical points of the network's protocols, or methods of data transport. These topics are essential for understanding the fundamentals of Internet security.

How to Get More Information

IN THIS APPENDIX

This appendix is designed to provide you with some of the sources consulted in this book, as well as sites (or documents) that can assist you in better understanding security.

Establishment Resources

The following list of resources includes articles, papers, and tools. The majority were authored or created by individuals working in security.

Sites on the WWW

The Anonymous Remailer FAQ. This document covers all aspects of anonymous remailing techniques and tools. `http://www.andrebacard.com/remail.html`

The Anonymous Remailer List. This is a comprehensive but often-changing list of anonymous remailers. `http://www.strassmann.com/pubs/anon-remail.html`

BugNet. A site that claims to be "The World's Leading Supplier of Software Bug Fixes." `http://www.bugnet.com`

Bugtraq Archives. This is an archive of the popular mailing list, Bugtraq, one of the most reliable sources for up-to-date reports on newly found vulnerabilities in UNIX (and at times, other operating systems). `http://www.securityfocus.com/`

The Center for Secure Information Systems. This site, affiliated with the Center at George Mason University, has some truly incredible papers. There is much cutting-edge research going on here. The following URL sends you directly to the publications page, but you really should explore the entire site. `http://www.isse.gmu.edu/~csis/publication.html`

The CIAC Virus Database. This was the ultimate virus database on the Internet. It's an excellent resource for learning about viruses that can affect your platform. Though the information on this page is out of date, it provides links to all the virus database of the different commercial vendors. `http://ciac.llnl.gov/ciac/CIACVirusDatabase.html`

The Computer Emergency Response Team (CERT). CERT is an organization that assists sites in responding to network security violations, break-ins, and so forth. This is a great source of information, particularly regarding vulnerabilities. `http://www.cert.org`

Connected: An Internet Encyclopedia. This is an incredible online resource for RFC documents and related information, painstakingly translated into HTML. `http://www.freesoft.org/Connected/RFC/826/`

Criminal Justice Studies of the Law Faculty of University of Leeds, The United Kingdom. This site boasts interesting information on cryptography and civil liberties. `http://www.leeds.ac.uk/law/pgs/yaman/cryptog.htm`

Dan Farmer: Security Survey of Key Internet Hosts and Various Semi-Relevant Reflections. This is a fascinating independent study conducted by one of the authors of the now famous SATAN program. The survey involved approximately 2,200 sites; the results are disturbing. `http://www.trouble.org/survey/`

Department of Defense Password Management Guideline. This is a treatment of password security in classified environments. `http://www.alw.nih.gov/Security/FIRST/papers/password/dodpwman.txt`

Dr. Solomon's. This site is filled with virus information. Anyone concerned with viruses (or anyone who just wants to know more about virus technology) should visit Dr. Solomon's site. `http://www.drsolomon.com`

The Evaluated Products List (EPL). This is a list of products that have been evaluated for security ratings based on DoD guidelines. `http://www.radium.ncsc.mil/tpep/epl/epl-by-class.html`

Federal Information Processing Standards Publication Documents (Government Guidelines). The National Institute of Standards and Technology reports on DES encryption and related technologies. `http://csrc.nist.gov/fips/fips46-2.txt`

Forum of Incident Response and Security Teams (FIRST). FIRST is a conglomeration of many organizations undertaking security measures on the Net. This powerful organization is a good starting place to find sources. `http://www.first.org/`

General Accounting Office: *Information Security: Computer Attacks at Department of Defense Pose Increasing Risks*. A report on failed security at U.S. defense sites. `http://www.epic.org/security/GAO_OMB_security.html`

Information Warfare and Information Security on the Web. This is a comprehensive list of links and other resources concerning information warfare over the Internet. `http://www.fas.org/irp/wwwinfo.html`

InterNIC (the Network Information Center). InterNIC provides comprehensive databases of networking information. These databases contain the larger portion of collected knowledge on the design and scope of the Internet. Of main importance here is the database of RFC documents. `http://rs.internic.net`

Massachusetts Institute of Technology Distribution Site of Pretty Good Privacy (PGP) for U.S. Residents. PGP provides some of the most powerful, military-grade encryption currently available. `http://web.mit.edu/network/pgp.html`

The National Computer Security Association. This site contains a great deal of valuable security information, including reports, papers, advisories, and analyses of various computer security products and techniques. `http://www.ncsa.com/`

TruSecure IS/RECON. This is a page which advertises an interesting for-pay service. It offers a service where one can search through thousands of downloaded messages passed among hackers and crackers on BBS boards and the Internet. This commercial site is an incredible security resource. `http://www.trusecure.com/html/secsol/servprovider.shtml`

NTBugTraq. A NT/2000 specific version of Bugtraq. `http://ntbugtraq.ntadvice.com/`

A Page Devoted to ATP, the Anti-Tampering Program. In some ways, ATP is similar to Tripwire or Hobgoblin. `http://www.ja.net/CERT/Vincenzetti_and_Cotrozzi/ATP_Anti_Tampering_Program.txt`

Purdue University COAST Archive. This is one of the more comprehensive security sites, containing many tools and documents of deep interest to the security community. `http://www.cs.purdue.edu//coast/archive`

The Rand Corporation. This site contains security resources of various sorts as well as engrossing early documents on the Internet's design. `http://www.rand.org/publications/electronic/`

Raptor Systems. The makers of one of the better firewall products on the Net has established a fine security library. `http://www.raptor.com/lib/index.html`

The Risks Forum. This is a moderated digest regarding security and other risks in computing. This great resource is also searchable. With it, you can tap the better security minds on the Net. `http://catless.ncl.ac.uk/Risks`

S/Key Informational Page. This site provides information on S/Key and the use of one-time passwords in authentication. `http://www.ece.nwu.edu/CSEL/skey/skey_eecs.html`

The Security Reference Index. This site, maintained by the folks at telstra.com, is a comprehensive pointer page to many security resources. `http://www.telstra.com.au/info/security.html`

The Seven Locks Server. This is an eclectic collection of security resources, including a number of papers that cannot be found elsewhere! `http://www.sevenlocks.com/`

Short Courses in Information Systems Security at George Mason University. This site contains information about security courses. Moreover, you'll find links to a comprehensive bibliography of security-related documents. `http://www.isse.gmu.edu:80/~gmuisi/`

SRI International. This site boasts some very highbrow technical information. The technical reports here are of extreme value. However, you must have at least a fleeting background in security to even grasp some of the concepts. `http://www.sri.com/`

U.S. Department of Energy's Computer Incident Advisory Capability (CIAC). CIAC provides computer security services to employees and contractors of the U.S. Department of Energy, but the site is open to the public as well. There are many tools and documents at this location. `http://ciac.llnl.gov/`

Wang Federal. This company produces high-quality security operating systems and other security solutions. It is the leader in TEMPEST technology. `http://www.wangfed.com`

Wietse Venema's Tools Page. This page, maintained by Wietse Venema (coauthor of SATAN and author of TCP_Wrapper and many other security tools), is filled with papers, tools, and general information. It is a must-visit for any UNIX system administrator. `ftp://ftp.porcupine.org/pub/security/index.html`

WordlistsFAQ. This FAQ gives you links to many wordlists on the Internet that is useful in testing the strength of, or cracking, UNIX passwords. `http://www.hyphenologist.co.uk/wordlist/wordfaq.htm`

Reports and Publications

United States. Congress. House. Committee on Science, Space, and Technology. Subcommittee on Science. *Internet Security: Hearing Before the Subcommittee on Science of the Committee on Science, Space, and Technology.* U.S. House of Representatives, One Hundred Third Congress, second session, March 22, 1994. Washington. U.S. G.P.O. For sale by the U.S. G.P.O., Supt. of Docs., Congressional Sales Office. 1994.

General

Authentication and Discretionary Access Control. Paul A. Karger, *Computers & Security*, Number 5, pp. 314–324. 1986.

Beyond the Pale of MAC and DAC—Defining New Forms of Access Control. Catherine J. McCollum, Judith R. Messing, and LouAnna Notargiacomo. *SympSecPr*, pp. 190–200, IEEECSP. May 1990.

Computer Security: Hackers Penetrate DoD Computer Systems. Testimony before the Subcommittee on Government Information and Regulation, Committee on Government Affairs. United States Senate, Washington D.C., November 1991.

Extended Discretionary Access Controls. S. T. Vinter. *SympSecPr*, pp. 39–49, IEEECSP, April 1988.

A Guide to Understanding Discretionary Access Control in Trusted Systems. Technical Report NCSC-TG-003, National Computer Security Center. 1987.

A Model of Atomicity for Multilevel Transactions. 1993 IEEE Computer Society Symposium on Research in Security and Privacy; 1993 May 24; Oakland, California. Barbara T. Blaustein, Sushil Jajodia, Catherine D. McCollum, and LouAnna Notargiacomo (MITRE). USA: IEEE Computer Society Press. 1993. ISBN: 0-8186-3370-0.

Network Security: Protocol Reference Model and the Trusted Computer System Evaluation Criteria. M. D. Abrams and A. B. Jeng. *IEEE Network*, 1(2), pp. 24–33. April 1987.

Secure Networking at Sun Microsystems Inc. Katherine P. Addison and John J. Sancho. 11th NCSC; 1988. Baltimore. USA: NBS/NCSC: pp.212–218.

STRAWMAN Trusted Network Interpretation Environments Guideline. Marshall Abrams, Martin W. Schwartz, and Samuel I. Schaen (MITRE). 11th NCSC; Baltimore. USA: NBS/NCSC: pp.194–200. 1988 Oct 17.

Java

Microsoft: Vulnerabilities in Internet Explorer. CIAC Bulletin. May 18, 2000.
`http://www.ciac.org/ciac/bulletins/k-044.shtml`

Internet Java & ActiveX Advisor. Journal. `http://www.advisor.com/`

Java & HotJava: Waking Up the Web. Sean González. *PC Magazine*. October 1995.
`http://www.zdnet.com/~pcmag/issues/1418/pcm00085.htm`

Java as an Intermediate Language. Technical Report, School of Computer Science, Carnegie Mellon University, Number CMU-CS-96-161. August 1996.
`http://www.cs.cmu.edu/afs/cs.cmu.edu/project/scandal/public/papers/`
`CMU-CS-96-161.ps.Z`

Java Developer's Journal. `http://www.javadevelopersjournal.com/java/`

Java Security: From HotJava to Netscape and Beyond. Drew Dean, Edward W. Felten, and Dan S. Wallach. 1996 IEEE Symposium on Security and Privacy, Oakland, CA. May 1996.

Java: The Inside Story. Michael O'Connell. *Sunworld Online*, Volume 07, July 1995.
`http://www.sun.com/sunworldonline/swol-07-1995/swol-07-java.html`

Javaworld. Journal. `http://www.javaworld.com/`

NetProf: Network-Based High-Level Profiling of Java Bytecode. Srinivasan Parthasarathy, Michael Cierniak, and Wei Li. TR 622, URCSD. May 1996. `ftp://ftp.cs.rochester.edu/`
`pub/papers/systems/96.tr622.NetProf_network-based_high-level_profiling_of_java_`
`bytecode.ps.gz`

The Ultimate Java Archive.
`http://www.developer.com/directories/pages/dir.java.html`

Databases and Security

Access Control: Principles and Practice. R.S. Sandhu and P. Saramati. *IEEE Communications*, pp. 2–10. 1994.

Authorizations in Relational Database Management Systems. E.Bertino, S.Jajodia, and P.Saramati. ACM Conference on Computer and Communications Security, Fairfax, VA (1993). pp. 130–139.

Ensuring Atomicity of Multilevel Transactions. P. Ammann, S. Jajodia, and I. Ray. IEEE Symposium on Research in Security and Privacy. Oakland, CA. pp. 74–84. May 1996.
`http://www.isse.gmu.edu/~csis/publications/oklnd96-indrksi.ps`

An Extended Authorization Model for Relational Databases. E. Bertino, P. Samarati, and S. Jajodia. IEEE Transactions on Knowledge and Data Engineering, Volume 9, Number 1, pages 85–101. 1997. `http://www.isse.gmu.edu/~csis/publications/ieee-97.ps`

*Formal Query Languages for Secure Relational Database*s. M. Winslett, K.Smitth, and X.Qian. ACM TODS, 19(4):626–662. 1994.

Honest Databases That Can Keep Secrets. R.S. Sandhu and S. Jajjodia, NCSC.
`http://www.list.gmu.edu/confrnc/ncsc/ps_ver/b91poly.ps`

Locking Protocol for Multilevel Secure Databases Providing Support for Long Transactions. S. Pal, Pennsylvania State University. IFIP WG 11.3 Working Conference on Database Security, Rensselaerville, New York. August 13–16, 1995.

Messages, Communications, Information Security: Protecting the User from the Data. J. E. Dobson and M. J. Martin, University of Newcastle. IFIP WG 11.3 Working Conference on Database Security, Rensselaerville, New York. August 13–16, 1995.

Microsoft Access 2.0 Security. Tom Lucas. *PC Solutions.* `http://www.citilink.com/~jgarrick/vbasic/database/secure20.html`

The Microsoft Internet Security Framework (MISF) Technology for Secure Communication, Access Control, and Commerce. 1997 Microsoft Corporation.
`http://msdn.microsoft.com/LIBRARY/BACKGRND/HTML/MSDN_MISF.HTM`

Multilevel Security for Knowledge Based Systems. Thomas D. Garvey and Teresa F. Lunt. Stanford Research Institute, SRI-CSL-91-01. February 1991.

On Distributed Communications: IX. Security, Secrecy and Tamper-Free Considerations. P. Baran. Technical Report, The Rand Corp. Number RM-376. August 1964.

A Personal View of DBMS Security in Database Security: Status and Prospects. F. Manola. C.E. Landwehr (ed.), Elsevier Science Publishers B.V., North Holland, 1988. GTE Labs. December 1987.

A Policy Framework for Multilevel Relational Databases. Xiaolei Qian and Teresa F. Lunt. SRI-CSL-94-12. August 1994.

Role-Based Access Controls. D.F. Ferraiolo and R. Kuhn. NIST-NCSC National Computer Security Conference, Baltimore, MD (1993). pp. 554–563.

A Secure Concurrency Control Protocol for Real-Time Databases. R. Mukkamala, Old Dominion University, and S. H. Son, University of Virginia. IFIP WG 11.3 Working Conference on Database Security, Rensselaerville, New York. August 13–16, 1995.

A Security Model for Military Message System. C. E. Landwehr, C. L Heitmeyer, and J. McLean. ACM Transactions on Computer Systems, 2(3), August 1984.

Symposium on the Global Information Infrastructure: Information, Policy, and International Infrastructure. Paul A. Strassmann, U.S. Military Academy West Point and Senior Advisor, SAIC; William Marlow, Senior Vice President, SAIC. January 28–30, 1996.

Trusted Database Management System. NCSC-TG-021. Trusted Database Management System Interpretation. Chief, Technical Guidelines Division. ATTN: C11 National Computer Security Center Ft. George G. Meade, MD 20755-6000. April 1991.

Why Safeguard Information? Computer Audit Update, Elsevier Advanced Technology. Abo Akademi University, Institute for Advanced Management Systems Research, Turku Centre for Computer Science. Thomas Finne. 1996. `http://www.tucs.abo.fi/publications/techreports/TR38.html`

Articles

Accountability Is Key to Democracy in the Online World. Walter S. Mossberg. *The Wall Street Journal.* Thursday, January 26, 1995.

ActiveX Used as Hacking Tool. N. Wingfield. *CNET News.* February 7, 1997. `http://www.news.com/News/Item/0,4,7761,4000.html?latest`

Alleged Computer Stalker Ordered Off Internet. Stevan Rosenlind. McClatchy News Service. July 26, 1995.

Are Your Employees Your Biggest Security Risk? Mark Joseph Edwards. *Windows IT Security.* December 20, 2000. `http://www.windowsitsecurity.com/Articles/Index.cfm?ArticleID=16445`

Billions and Billions of Bugs. Peter Galvin. *SunworldOnline.* `http://www.sun.com/sunworldonline/swol-03-1996/swol-03-security.html`

Breaches from Inside Are Common. *Infosecurity News.* January/February 1997.

CYBERWAR IS COMING! John Arquilla and David Ronfeldt. International Policy Department, Rand Corporation. Taylor & Francis. ISBN: 0149-5933-93. 1993.

DDoS attack targets chat, Linux boxes. Scott Berinato. *EWeek*. September 5, 2000.

The First Internet War; The State of Nature and the First Internet War: Scientology, Its Critics, Anarchy, and Law in Cyberspace. David G. Post. *Reason Magazine*. April, 1996. `http://www.cli.org/DPost/X0003_ARTICLE4.html`

Gang War in Cyberspace. M. Slatalla and J. Quitner. *Wired*, Volume 2, Number 12. December, 1994. `http://www.hotwired.com/wired/2.12/hacker.html`

KC Wrestles with Equipment Theft Problem. Timothy Heider. *Kansas City Star*. February 17, 1997. `http://www.isecure.com/newslet.htm`

Network Security Throughout the Ages. Jeff Breidenbach. Switzerland (Project MAC) Association. MIT Project on Mathematics and Computation. 1994.

New York's Panix Service Is Crippled by Hacker Attack. Robert E. Calem. *The New York Times*. September 14, 1996.

The Paradox of the Secrecy About Secrecy: The Assumption of a Clear Dichotomy Between Classified and Unclassified Subject Matter. Paul Baran. MEMORANDUM RM-3765-PR; On Distributed Communications: IX Security, Secrecy, and Tamper-Free Considerations. Rand Corporation. August 1964.

Pentagon Web Sites Closed After Visit from Hacker. Nando.net News Service. December 30, 1996. `http://www.nando.net/newsroom/ntn/info/123096/info1_29951.html`

Post Office Announces Secure E-Mail. Boot. March 1997.

Secure Your Data: Web Site Attacks on the Rise! Stewart S. Miller. *Information Week*. January 29, 1996.

Security Is Lost in Cyberspace. *News & Observer*. February 21, 1995. `http://www.nando.net/newsroom/ntn/info/other/02219540865.html`

Statement Before Senate Subcommittee on Governmental Operations. John Deutch, Director, CIA. June 25, 1996.

Student's Expulsion Over E-Mail Use Raises Concern. Amy Harmon. *Los Angeles Times*. November 15, 1995. `http://www.caltech.edu/~media/times.html`

U.S. Files Appeal in Dismissed Baker Case. Zachary M. Raimi. *The Michigan Daily*. November 22, 1995.

What's the Plan? Get a Grip on Improving Security Through a Security Plan. Peter Galvin. *SunWorld Online*. September 1995. `http://www.sun.com/sunworldonline/swol-09-1995/swol-09-security.html`

Tools

Some of these tools were coded by the establishment (the legitimate security community). Others were authored by amateur hackers and crackers.

(Windows)

Cetus StormWindows. http://www.cetussoft.com/

ConfigSafe 95. http://207.8.148.186/html/products.html

DECROS Security Card. http://www.decros.cz/

Desktop Surveillance 97. http://www.omniquad.com/

HD95Protect. http://www.geocities.com/SiliconValley/Lakes/8753/

Secure4U. http://www.sandboxsecurity.com/main.htm

StopLock 95. http://www.conclusive.com/downloads/index.php

Windows Task-Lock. http://posum.com/

Windows NT

Administrator Assistant Tool Kit. http://www.aelita.com/Products/AdminAssist.htm

DumpEvt. http://www.somarsoft.com/

DumpReg. http://www.somarsoft.com/

Kane Security Analyst. http://www.intrusion.com/

NetXRay Analyzer. http://www.axial.co.uk/products/manufacturers/nai/sniffer/snifferbasic_intro.html

NT Crack. http://www.secnet.com/

NT Locksmith. http://www.winternals.com/

NTFSDOS. http://www.winternals.com/

NTHandle. http://www.ntinternals.com/

NTRecover. http://www.winternals.com/

NTUndelete. http://www.winternals.com/

PC Firewall. http://www.nai.com/

PWDUMP. ftp://samba.anu.edu.au/pub/samba/pwdump/pwdump.c

RedButton. http://www.ntsecurity.com/

RegAdmin. `http://www.ntsecurity.com/`

ScanNT Plus. `http://www.ntsecurity.com/`

Somarsoft DumpAcl. `http://www.somarsoft.com/`

Somarsoft RegEdit. `http://www.somarsoft.com/`

Virtuosity: `http://www.ntsecurity.com/`

Windows 2000 Security Tools
NOSadmin. `http://www.webmarshall.com`

Security Expressions. `http://www.securityexpressions.com`

Windows 2000 Internet Server Security Configuration Tool. `http://www.microsoft.com/Downloads/Release.asp?ReleaseID=19889`

Windows 2000 Resource Kit. `http://support.microsoft.com/support/kb/articles/q264/1/78.asp`

Macintosh Security Tools
Empower. `http://www.magna1.com/`

EtherPeek. `http://www.aggroup.com/`

InterMapper. `http://www.dartmouth.edu/netsoftware/intermapper/`

KeysOff. `http://www.blueglobe.com/~cliffmcc/products.html`

MacRadius. `http://www.cyno.com/`

Network Security Guard. `http://www.mrmac.com/`

Network Scout. `http://www.mrmac.com/`

Password Key. `http://www.cp3.com/`

Secure-It Locks. `http://secure-it.com/`

Timbuktu Pro. `http://www.netopia.com/`

Password Crackers
Claymore. A generalized password cracker for Windows. `http://www.jabukie.com/Password_Crackerz/claymore.zip`

Crack. Cracks UNIX passwords on UNIX platforms. `http://www.users.dircon.co.uk/~crypto/download/c50-faq.html`

Crack Documentation. `http://www.parkline.ru/Library/html-KOI/SECURITY/ crackfaq.txt`

Cracker Jack. Cracks UNIX passwords on the Microsoft platform. `http://www.fc.net/ phrack/under/misc.html`

Guess. Cracks UNIX passwords on the DOS platform. This utility is available everywhere. Try the search string `guess.zip`.

Hades. This UNIX password cracker is available everywhere. Try the search string `hades.zip`.

Hellfire Cracker. Cracks UNIX passwords on the DOS platform. `http://www.jabukie.com/ Password_Crackerz/hc130.zip`

John the Ripper. Cracks UNIX passwords on the DOS and Linux platforms. `http://tms. netrom.com/~cassidy/crack.htm`

Killer Cracker. Cracks UNIX passwords under DOS. `http://dafunks.9ug.com/ killercracker.html`

Qcrack. Cracks UNIX passwords on DOS, Linux, and Windows platforms. `ftp://ftp. infospace.com/pub/qcrack/`

Password NT. Cracks NT passwords. `http://www.ntsecurity.com/Services/Recovery/ index.html`

PC UNIX Password Cracker. The name of this utility says it all. This tool is hard to find; I know of no reliable locations, but you might try the name as a search string.

Pcrack (PerlCrack). Cracks UNIX passwords on the UNIX platform. `http://tms.netrom.com/ ~cassidy/crack.htm`

XIT. Cracks UNIX passwords on the DOS platform. `http://www.jabukie.com/Password_ Crackerz/xit20.zip`

ZipCrack. Cracks the passwords on Zip archives. Try the search string `zipcrk10.zip`.

Sniffers

Esniff.c. Sniffer for use on Linux machines. `http://www.esniff.com/`

ETHLOAD. Sniffs Ethernet and token ring networks. `http://www.ping.be/ethload/`

Gobbler. Sniffs in the DOS environment. This tool is good for sniffing Novell NetWare networks. `http://www.computercraft.com/noprogs/gobbler.zip`

linux_sniffer.c. Runs on the Linux platform. `http://www.rootshell.com/ archive-j457nxiqi3gq59dv/199707/linux_sniffer.c.html`

Netman. Awesome sniffer suite for use on UNIX and Windows 95. `http://www.ja.net/CERT/Software/netman/`

Scanners and Related Utilities

CONNECT. Are you looking for a vulnerable TFTP server? Try this utility. It runs on UNIX. `http://www.giga.or.at/pub/hacker/unix/`

FSPScan. This UNIX utility identifies vulnerable FSP servers. `http://www.giga.or.at/pub/hacker/unix`

IdentTCPscan. Runs on UNIX; identifies the UID of all running processes. `http://www.giga.or.at/pub/hacker/unix`

Jakal. Runs on UNIX. Scans behind firewalls. `http://www.giga.or.at/pub/hacker/unix`

NetScan Tools. Win95 port of many UNIX snooping utilities. `http://www.eskimo.com/~nwps/index.html`

Network Toolbox. Runs on Windows 95. Has many common UNIX snooping utilities and a port scanner. `http://www.jriver.com/netbox.html`

NSS. Network Security Scanner. Written in Perl, runs on UNIX. `http://www.giga.or.at/pub/hacker/unix`

SATAN. Runs on UNIX; you must have Perl. `http://www.fish.com`

Strobe. Runs on UNIX. `http://www.asmodeus.com/archive/IP_toolz/strobe/strobe.c`

TCP/IP Surveyor. Microsoft platform. `http://www.winsite.com/info/pc/win95/netutil/wssrv32n.zip/`

WhatRoute. Port of the popular UNIX utility Traceroute to Macintosh. `http://homepages.ihug.co.nz/~bryanc/`

XSCAN. Locates vulnerable X servers. `http://www.giga.or.at/pub/hacker/unix`

Destructive Devices

Avalanche. This device is yet another mail-bombing utility. Avalanche is for Windows. Try the search string `avalanche20.zip`.

Bombtrack. This is a mail-bombing utility for Macintosh.

eXtreme Mail. This utility is a mail bomber for the Windows platform. To obtain it, try the search string `xmailb1.exe`.

FlameThrower. This is a Macintosh mail-bombing utility.

Homicide. This utility is a mail bomber for the Windows platform. To obtain it, try the search string `homicide.exe`.

Kaboom. This device is an email bomber. To obtain it, try searching for the string `kaboom3.exe`.

The UnaBomber. This utility is a mail bomber for the Windows platform. To obtain it, try the search string `unabomb.exe`.

The UNIX MailBomb. This mail-bomb utility by CyBerGoAT works on all UNIX platforms. To obtain it, try the search string `MailBomb by CyBerGoAT`.

The UpYours Mail Bombing Program. To obtain this mail bomber, try searching for the string `upyours3.zip`.

Finger Clients

FFEU (OS/2). `http://hobbes.nmsu.edu/pub/os2/apps/internet/misc/ffeu101.zip`

WSFinger (Windows). `http://www.internexus.net/pub/tools/win/wsfngr14.zip`

Intrusion Detectors

Cisco Secure Intrusion Detection System. `http://www.cisco.com/`

Network Fligher Recorder. `http://www.nfr.net/`

RealSecure. `http://www.iss.com/`

Shadow. `http://www.nswc.navy.mil/ISSEC/CID`

Snort. `http://www.snort.org/`

Technical Reports, Government Standards, and Papers

The Rainbow Books and Related Documentation

The Rainbow Books set forth the U.S. government's criteria for the use and certification of trusted systems.

Computer Security Requirements: Guidance for Applying the DoD TCSEC in Specific Environments (*Light Yellow Book*). June 1985.
`http://www.radium.ncsc.mil/tpep/library/rainbow/CSC-STD-003-85.html`

DoD Password Management Guideline (*Green Book*). April 1985.
`http://www.radium.ncsc.mil/tpep/library/rainbow/CSC-STD-002-85.html`

DoD Trusted Computer System Evaluation Criteria (*Orange Book*). December 1985.
`http://www.radium.ncsc.mil/tpep/library/rainbow/5200.28-STD.html`

Glossary of Computer Security Terms (*Teal Green Book*). October 21, 1988. `http://www.radium.ncsc.mil/tpep/library/rainbow/NCSC-TG-004.txt`

A Guide to Understanding Audit in Trusted Systems (Tan Book). June 1988. `http://www.radium.ncsc.mil/tpep/library/rainbow/NCSC-TG-001-2.html`

A Guide to Understanding Configuration Management in Trusted Systems (Amber Book). March 1988. `http://www.radium.ncsc.mil/tpep/library/rainbow/NCSC-TG-006.html`

A Guide to Understanding Design Documentation in Trusted Systems (Burgundy Book). October 1988. `http://www.radium.ncsc.mil/tpep/library/rainbow/NCSC-TG-007.html`

A Guide to Understanding Discretionary Access Control in Trusted Systems (Neon Orange Book). September 1987. `http://www.radium.ncsc.mil/tpep/library/rainbow/NCSC-TG-003.html`

A Guide to Understanding Identification and Authentication in Trusted Systems (Light Blue Book). September 1991. `http://www.radium.ncsc.mil/tpep/library/rainbow/NCSC-TG-017.html`

A Guide to Understanding Information System Security Officer Responsibilities for Automated Information Systems (Turquoise Book). May 1992. `http://www.radium.ncsc.mil/tpep/library/rainbow/NCSC-TG-027.txt`

A Guide to Understanding Object Reuse in Trusted Systems (Light Blue Book). July 1992. `http://www.radium.ncsc.mil/tpep/library/rainbow/NCSC-TG-018.html`

A Guide to Understanding Security Modeling in Trusted Systems (Aqua Book). October 1992. `http://www.radium.ncsc.mil/tpep/library/rainbow/NCSC-TG-010.txt`

A Guide to Understanding Trusted Distribution in Trusted Systems (Dark Lavender Book). December 1988. `http://www.radium.ncsc.mil/tpep/library/rainbow/NCSC-TG-008.html`

A Guide to Understanding Trusted Facility Management (Brown Book). October 1989. `http://www.radium.ncsc.mil/tpep/library/rainbow/NCSC-TG-015.html`

Guidelines for Formal Verification Systems (Purple Book). April 1989. `http://www.radium.ncsc.mil/tpep/library/rainbow/NCSC-TG-014.html`

Guidelines for Writing Trusted Facility Manuals (Yellow-Green Book). October 1992. `http://www.radium.ncsc.mil/tpep/library/rainbow/NCSC-TG-016.html`

RAMP Program Document (Pink Book). March 1995, Version 2. `http://www.radium.ncsc.mil/tpep/library/rainbow/NCSC-TG-013.2.html`

Technical Rational Behind CSC-STD-003-85: Computer Security Requirements—Guidance for Applying the DoD TCSEC in Specific Environments (Yellow Book). June 1985. `http://www.radium.ncsc.mil/tpep/library/rainbow/CSC-STD-004-85.html`

Trusted Database Management System Interpretation of the TCSEC (Purple Book). April 1991. `http://www.radium.ncsc.mil/tpep/library/rainbow/NCSC-TG-021.html`

Trusted Network Interpretation of the TCSEC (Red Book). July 1987. `http://www.radium.ncsc.mil/tpep/library/rainbow/NCSC-TG-005.html`

Trusted Product Evaluations: A Guide for Vendors (Bright Blue Book). June 1990. `http://www.radium.ncsc.mil/tpep/library/rainbow/NCSC-TG-002.html`

Trusted Product Evaluation Questionnaire (Blue Book). May 1992, Version 2. `http://www.radium.ncsc.mil/tpep/library/rainbow/NCSC-TG-019.2.html`

Trusted UNIX Working Group (TRUSIX) Rationale for Selecting Access Control List Features for the UNIX System (Silver Book). July 1989. `http://www.radium.ncsc.mil/tpep/library/rainbow/NCSC-TG-020-A.html`

Selected Publications from the NCSC

Auditing Issues in Secure Database Management Systems. `http://www.radium.ncsc.mil/tpep/library/rainbow/NCSC-TR-005-4.pdf`

Computer Viruses: Prevention, Detection, and Treatment. March 1990. `http://www.radium.ncsc.mil/tpep/library/rainbow/C1-TR-001.html`

The Design and Evaluation of INFOSEC Systems: The Computer Security Contribution to the Composition Discussion. June 1992. `http://www.radium.ncsc.mil/tpep/library/rainbow/C-TR-32-92.html`

Discretionary Access Control Issues in High Assurance Secure Database Management Systems. `http://www.radium.ncsc.mil/tpep/library/rainbow/NCSC-TR-005-5.pdf`

Integrity in Automated Information Systems. September 1991. `http://www.radium.ncsc.mil/tpep/library/rainbow/C-TR-79-91.txt`

Turning Multiple Evaluated Products into Trusted Systems. `http://www.radium.ncsc.mil/tpep/library/rainbow/NCSC-TR-003.pdf`

Other Governmental Security Documents and Advisories

Augmented Encrypted Key Exchange: A Password-Based Protocol Secure Against Dictionary Attacks and Password File Compromise. 1st ACM Conference on Computer and Communications Security, pp. 244–250. ACM Press. November 1993.

Australian Computer Emergency Response Team. `http://www.auscert.org.au/Information/advisories.html`

A Basis for Secure Communication in Large Distributed Systems. David P. Anderson and P. Venkat Rangan. UCB//CSD-87-328, January 1987. `ftp://tr-ftp.cs.berkeley.edu/pub/tech-reports/csd/csd-87-328/`

Benchmarking Methodology for Network Interconnect Devices. RFC 1944. S. Bradner and J. McQuaid. `http://www.ietf.org/rfc/rfc1944.txt`

Charon: Kerberos Extensions for Authentication over Secondary Networks. Derek A. Atkins. 1993. `ftp://coast.cs.purdue.edu/pub/doc/authentication/Derek_Atkins-Charon.ps.Z`

Check Point FireWall-1 Introduction. Checkpoint Technologies Firewall Information. `http://www.checkpoint.com/products/firewall-1/descriptions/products.html`

Cisco PIX Firewall. Cisco Systems firewall information. `http://www.cisco.com/univercd/data/doc/cintrnet/prod_cat/pcpix.htm`

Covert Channels in the TCP/IP Protocol Suite. Craig Rowland. Rotherwick & Psionics Software Systems, Inc. `http://www.firstmonday.dk/issues/issue2_5/rowland/`

Crack Version 4.1: A Sensible Password Checker for UNIX. A. Muffett. Technical Report, March 1992.

A Cryptographic File System for UNIX. Matt Blaze. 1st ACM Conference on Computer and Communications Security. pp. 9–16. ACM Press. November 1993.

Daemons and Dragons UNIX Accounting. Dinah McNutt. *UNIX Review.* 12(8). August 1994.

Designing Plan 9. Rob Pike, Dave Presotto, and Ken Thompson. *Dr. Dobb's Journal.* Volume 16, p. 49. January 1, 1991.

The Eagle Firewall Family. Raptor firewall information. `http://www.raptor.com/products/brochure/40broch.html`

The Empirical Evaluation of a Security-Oriented Datagram Protocol. David P. Anderson, Domenico Ferrari, P. Venkat Rangan, B. Sartirana. University of California Berkeley, CS csd-87-350. UCB//CSD-87-350, April 1987. `ftp://tr-ftp.cs.berkeley.edu/pub/tech-reports/csd/csd-87-350/`

Evolution of a Trusted B3 Window System Prototype. J. Epstein, J. Mc Hugh, R. Psacle, C. Martin, D. Rothnie, H. Orman, A. Marmor-Squires, M. Branstad, and B. Danner. In proceedings of the 1992 IEEE Symposium on Security and Privacy, 1992.

Firewall Application Notes. A good document that starts by describing how to build a firewall. Also addresses application proxies, Sendmail in relation to firewalls, and the characteristics of a bastion host. Livingston Enterprises, Inc. `ftp://coast.cs.purdue.edu/pub/doc/firewalls/Livingston_Firewall_Notes.ps.Z`

Improving the Security of Your Site by Breaking Into It. Dan Farmer and Wietse Venema. 1995. `http://www.alw.nih.gov/Security/Docs/admin-guide-to-cracking.101.html`

C

HOW TO GET
MORE
INFORMATION

Improving X Windows Security. Linda Mui. *UNIX World.* Volume IX, Number 12. December 1992.

Intrusion Protection for Networks 171. Byte Magazine. April, 1995.

IP v6 Release and Firewalls. Uwe Ellermann. 14th Worldwide Congress on Computer and Communications Security Protection. pp. 341–354. June 1996.

Is Plan 9 Sci-Fi or UNIX for the Future? Anke Goos. *UNIX World.* Volume 7, p. 61. October 1, 1990.

Keeping Your Site Comfortably Secure: An Introduction to Internet Firewalls. John P. Wack and Lisa J. Carnahan. National Institute of Standards and Technology. Thursday, Feb 9 18:17:09 EST 1995. `http://csrc.ncsl.nist.gov./nistpubs/800-10/`

Making Your Setup More Secure. NCSA Tutorial Pages. `http://hoohoo.ncsa.uiuc.edu/docs/tutorials/security.html`

Multilevel Security in the UNIX Tradition. M. D. McIlroy and J. A. Reeds. *SWPE.* 22(8), pp. 673–694. 1992.

NCSA Firewall Policy Guide. Compiled by Stephen Cobb, Director of Special Projects. National Computer Security Association. `http://www.ncsa.com/fpfs/fwpg_p1.html`

Network Firewalls. Steven M. Bellovin and William R. Cheswick. IEEECM, 32(9), pp. 50–57. September 1994.

A Network Perimeter with Secure External Access. Frederick M. Avolio and Marcus J. Ranum. An extraordinary paper that details the implementation of a firewall purportedly at the White House. Trusted Information Systems, Incorporated. Glenwood, MD. January 25, 1994. `http://www.alw.nih.gov/Security/FIRST/papers/firewall/isoc94.ps`

On Access Checking in Capability-Based Systems. Richard Y. Kain and C. E. Landwehr. IEEE Trans. on Software Engineering Volume SE-13, Number 2 (Feb. 1987) pp. 202–207; reprinted from the proceedings of the 1986 IEEE Symposium on Security and Privacy, Oakland, CA. April, 1986. `http://www.itd.nrl.navy.mil/ITD/5540/publications/CHACS/Before1990/1987landwehr-tse.ps`

Online Firewall Buyers Guide. `http://www.icsa.net/html/communities/firewalls/buyers_guide/index.shtml`

Packets Found on an Internet. Steven M. Bellovin. Interesting analysis of packets appearing at the application gateway of AT&T. Lambda. August 23, 1993. `ftp://ftp.research.att.com/dist/smb/packets.ps`

Password Security: A Case History. Robert Morris and Ken Thompson. `http://www.alw.nih.gov/Security/FIRST/papers/password/pwstudy.ps`

Plan 9. Sean Dorward, Rob Pike, and Dave Presotto. *UNIX Review*. Volume 10, p. 28. April 1, 1992.

Plan 9: Feature Film to Feature-Rich OS. Paul Fillinich. *Byte Magazine*. Volume 21, p. 143. March 1, 1996.

Plan 9 from AT&T. David Bailey. *UNIX Review*. Volume 1, p. 27. January 1, 1996.

Plan 9 from Bell Labs. Rob Pike, Dave Presotto, and Phil Winterbottom. *Computing Systems Journal*. Volume 8, p. 221. Summer 1995.

Plan 9: Son of UNIX. Robert Richardson. *LAN Magazine*. Volume 11, p. 41. August 1, 1996.

Private Communication Technology Protocol. Daniel Simon. April 1996.

A Prototype B3 Trusted X Window System. J. Epstein, J. McHugh, R. Pascale, H. Orman, G. Benson, C. Martin, A. Marmor-Squires, B. Danner, and M. Branstad. The proceedings of the seventh Computer Security Applications Conference, December, 1991.

Rating of Application Layer Proxies. Michael Richardson. Wednesday, Nov 13, 13:54:09 EST 1996. `http://www.sandelman.ottawa.on.ca/SSW/proxyrating/proxyrating.html`

Reducing the Proliferation of Passwords in Distributed Systems Information Processing. *Education and Society*. Volume II, pp. 525–531. Elsevier Science Publishers B.V. (North Holland). 1992.

Robust and Secure Password/Key Change Method Proceedings of the Third European Symposium on Research in Computer Security (ESORICS). Ralf Hauser, Phil Janson, Refik Molva, Gene Tsudik, and Els Van Herreweghen. LNCS, pp. 107–122, SV, November 1994.

Security in Open Systems. (NIST) John Barkley, Editor (with Lisa Carnahan, Richard Kuhn, Robert Bagwill, Anastase Nakassis, Michael Ransom, John Wack, Karen Olsen, Paul Markovitz, and Shu-Jen Chang). U.S. Department of Commerce. Section: The X Window System: Bagwill, Robert. `http://csrc.ncsl.nist.gov/nistpubs/800-7/node62.html#SECTION06200000000000000000`

Security in Public Mobile Communication Networks. Hannes Federrath, Anja Jerichow, Dogan Kesdogan, and Andreas Pfitzmann. Proceedings of the IFIP TC 6 International Workshop on Personal Wireless Communications, Prague 1995, pp. 105–116.

Session-Layer Encryption. Matt Blaze and Steve Bellovin. Proceedings of the Usenix Security Workshop, June 1995.

Site Security Handbook Barbara Fraser. Update and Idraft version, CMU. Draft-ietf-ssh-handbook-03.txt. June 1996. `http://sunsite.cnlab-switch.ch/ftp/doc/standard/rfc/21xx/2196`

SQL*Net and Firewalls. David Sidwell and Oracle Corporation. `http://www.zeuros.co.uk/firewall/library/oracle-and-fw.pdf`

The SSL Protocol. (IDraft) Alan O. Freier and Philip Karlton (Netscape Communications) with Paul C. Kocher. `http://home.netscape.com/eng/ssl3/ssl-toc.html`

The SunScreen Product Line Overview. Sun Microsystems. `http://www.sun.com/security/overview.html`

The TAMU Security Package. An Ongoing Response to Internet Intruders in an Academic Environment. David R. Safford, Douglas Lee Schales, and David K. Hess. Proceedings of the Fourth Usenix UNIX Security Symposium, p. 91–118, Santa Clara, CA. October 1993. `http://drawbridge.tamu.edu/tamu-security.pdf`

TCP WRAPPER: Network Monitoring, Access Control, and Booby Traps. Wietse Venema. Proceedings of the Third Usenix UNIX Security Symposium, p. 85–92, Baltimore, MD. September 1992. `ftp://ftp.porcupine.org/pub/security/tcp_wrapper.ps.Z`

There Be Dragons. Steven M. Bellovin. To appear in proceedings of the Third Usenix UNIX Security Symposium, Baltimore, September 1992. AT&T Bell Laboratories, Murray Hill, NJ. August 15, 1992.

Undetectable Online Password Guessing Attacks. Yun Ding and Patrick Horster. *OSR*. 29(4), pp. 77–86. October 1995.

Using Screens to Implement TCP/IP Security Policies. Jeff Mogul. Rotherwick and Digital. `http://www.zeuros.co.uk/firewall/library/screend.ps`

Vulnerability in Cisco Routers Used as Firewalls. Computer Incident Advisory Capability Advisory: Number D-15. May 12, 1993 1500 PDT. `http://ciac.llnl.gov/ciac/bulletins/d-15.shtml`

Warding Off the Cyberspace Invaders. Amy Cortese. *Business Week*. March 13, 1995.

Windows NT Firewalls Are Born. Jeffrey G. Witt. *PC Magazine*. February 4, 1997. `http://www.pcmagazine.com/features/firewall/_open.htm` and `http://www.raptor.com/lib/9419.ps`

+X Window System Security. Ben Gross and Baba Buehler. Beckman Institute System Services. Last Apparent Date of Modification: January 11, 1996. `http://edessa.topo.auth.gr/~thalis/xsecurity.html`

X Through the Firewall, and Other Application Relays. Treese/Wolman. Digital Equipment Corp. Cambridge Research Lab. October 1993. `ftp://crl.dec.com/pub/DEC/CRL/tech-reports/93.10.ps.Z`

X Security. `http://consult.cern.ch/writeup/security/security_4.html`

The X Window System. Robert W. Scheifler and Jim Gettys. *ACM Transactions on Graphics.* Volume5, Number 2, pp. 79–109. April 1986. `http://www.acm.org/pubs/toc/Abstracts/0730-0301/24053.html`

Intrusion Detection

Bibliography on Intrusion Detection. The Collection of Computer Science Bibliographies. `http://src.doc.ic.ac.uk/computing/bibliographies/Karlsruhe/Misc/intrusion.detection.html`

Detecting Unusual Program Behavior Using the Statistical Component of the Next-Generation Intrusion Detection Expert System (NIDES). Debra Anderson, Teresa F. Lunt, Harold Javitz, Ann Tamaru, and Alfonso Valdes. SRI-CSL-95-06, May 1995. Available in hard copy only. The abstract is at the following address: `http://www.csl.sri.com/tr-abstracts.html#csl9506`

Fraud and Intrusion Detection in Financial Information Systems. S. Stolfo. P. Chan, D. Wei, W. Lee, and A. Prodromidis. 4th ACM Computer and Communications Security Conference, 1997. `http://www.cs.columbia.edu/~sal/hpapers/acmpaper.ps.gz`

GrIDS—A Graph-Based Intrusion Detection System for Large Networks. S. Staniford-Chen, S. Cheung, R. Crawford, M. Dilger, J. Frank, J. Hoagland, K. Levitt, C. Wee, R. Yip, and D. Zerkle. The 19th National Information Systems Security Conference. `http://seclab.cs.ucdavis.edu/papers/nissc96.ps`

Holding Intruders Accountable on the Internet. S. Staniford-Chen and L.T. Heberlein. Proceedings of the 1995 IEEE Symposium on Security and Privacy, Oakland, CA, May 8–10, 1995. `http://seclab.cs.ucdavis.edu/~stanifor/papers/ieee_conf_94/revision/submitted.ps`

Intrusion Detection Bibliography. `http://www.cs.purdue.edu/coast/intrusion-detection/ids_bib.html`

Intrusion Detection for Network Infrastructures. S. Cheung, K.N. Levitt, and C. Ko. 1995 IEEE Symposium on Security and Privacy, Oakland, CA. May 1995. `http://seclab.cs.ucdavis.edu/papers/clk95.ps`

Intrusion Detection Systems (IDS): A Survey of Existing Systems and a Proposed Distributed IDS Architecture. S.R. Snapp, J. Brentano, G.V. Dias, T.L. Goan, T. Grance, L.T. Heberlein, C. Ho, K.N. Levitt, B. Mukherjee, D.L. Mansur, K.L. Pon, and S.E. Smaha. Technical Report CSE-91-7, Division of Computer Science, University of California, Davis. February 1991.

Machine Learning and Intrusion Detection: Current and Future Directions. J. Frank. Proceedings of the 17th National Computer Security Conference. October 1994.

A Methodology for Testing Intrusion Detection Systems. N. F. Puketza, K. Zhang, M. Chung, B. Mukherjee, and R. A. Olsson. *IEEE Transactions on Software Engineering*, Volume 22, Number 10, October 1996. `http://seclab.cs.ucdavis.edu/papers/tse96.ps`

NetKuang—A Multi-Host Configuration Vulnerability Checker. D. Zerkle and K. Levitt. Proceedings of the 6th Usenix Security Symposium. San Jose, California. 1996. `http://seclab.cs.ucdavis.edu/papers/zl96.ps`

Network Intrusion Detection. Biswanath Mukherjee, L. Todd Heberlein, and Karl N. Levitt. IEEE Network, May 1994. `http://seclab.cs.ucdavis.edu/papers/bd96.ps`

A Pattern-Oriented Intrusion-Detection Model and Its Applications. Shiuhpyng W. Shieh and Virgil D. Gligor. Research in Security and Privacy, IEEECSP, May 1991.

Simulating Concurrent Intrusions for Testing Intrusion Detection Systems: Parallelizing Intrusions. M. Chung, N. Puketza, R.A. Olsson, and B. Mukherjee. Proceedings of the 1995 National Information Systems Security Conference. Baltimore, Maryland. 1995. `http://seclab.cs.ucdavis.edu/papers/cpo95.ps`

Mailing Lists

The Bugtraq List. This list is for posting or discussing bugs in various operating systems, though UNIX is the most often discussed. The information here can be quite explicit. If you are looking to learn the fine aspects (and cutting-edge news) of UNIX security, this list is for you.

> **Target:** `LISTSERV@NETSPACE.ORG`
>
> **Command:** `SUBSCRIBE BUGTRAQ` (in body of message)

Intrusion Detection Systems. This list concentrates on discussions about methods of intrusion or intrusion detection.

> **Target:** `majordomo@uow.edu.au`
>
> **Command:** `subscribe ids` (in body of message)

The NT Security List. This list is devoted to discussing all techniques of security related to the Microsoft Windows NT operating system. Individuals also discuss security aspects of other Microsoft operating systems.

> **Target:** `request-ntsecurity@iss.net`
>
> **Command:** `subscribe ntsecurity` (in body of message)

The NTBugtraq List. This list is for posting or discussing bugs in Windows NT/2000.

> **Target:** `LISTSERV@LISTSERV.NTBUGTRAQ.COM`
>
> **Command:** `SUBSCRIBE NTBUGTRAQ` *firstname lastname*

The Secure HTTP List. This list is devoted to the discussion of S-HTTP and techniques to facilitate this new form of security for WWW transactions.

> **Target:** `shttp-talk-request@OpenMarket.com`
>
> **Command:** `SUBSCRIBE` (in body of message)

The Sneakers List. This list discusses methods of circumventing firewall and general security. This list is reserved for lawful tests and techniques.

> **Target:** `majordomo@CS.YALE.EDU`
>
> **Command:** `SUBSCRIBE Sneakers` (in body of message)

The WWW Security List. List members discuss all techniques to maintain (or subvert) WWW security (things involving secure methods of HTML, HTTP and CGI).

> **Target:** `www-security-request@nsmx.rutgers.edu`
>
> **Command:** `SUBSCRIBE www-security` *your_email_address* (in body of message)

Underground Resources

2600 **Magazine.** A magazine that historically focused on phone phracking but has increasingly been following computer hacking. `http://www.2600.com/`

The alt.2600/#hack F.A.Q. The FAQ for the popular Usenet newsgroup, alt.2600. Some interesting information can be found here, ranging from wardialers to tips for covering your tracks after a break-in. `http://www-personal.engin.umich.edu/~jgotts/hack-faq/hack-faq-cp.html`

EFF Hacking, Cracking, Phreaking Archive. This is the archive of the Electronic Frontier Foundation, a non-profit organization that advocates civil liberties in cyberspace. `http://www.eff.org/pub/Privacy/Security/Hacking_cracking_phreaking/`

LHI Technologies (L0pht Heavy Industries). This group comprises some of most talented underground hackers. The archives at this site contain rare papers and reports, some of which were written by the site's proprietors. `http://l0pht.com/`

Phrack **Magazine.** A hacker e-zine that has been in existence for many years. There is a great deal of hard-core technical information in it, as well as a fascinating section called Phrack World News, which recounts cracker and hacker activities in recent months. `http://www.phrack.com`

Security Consultants

IN THIS APPENDIX

This appendix lists known security professionals from all over the world. Many provide such services to Fortune 500 companies. Consider this a miniature "Yellow Pages" of Internet security. The next time your site gets attacked by someone in Estonia, for example, you'll know whom to call.

The Listings

Some vendors provided their names, addresses, contact person, telephone numbers, and URLs, as well as a brief description of their services. Except for correction of spelling errors and cases where their address changed, their information was printed exactly as it was received. Other vendors were found on the Web or via other mechanisms.

ACROS, d.o.o. (Slovenia)

ACROS provides complete information security solutions—security systems evaluation, design and maintenance, firewalls, intrusion detection, cryptography, security policy design and maintenance, penetration testing, risk analysis and management, contingency planning, disaster recovery, mission-critical environments, security incidents investigation, and consulting.

> ACROS, d.o.o.
> Stantetova 4SI—2000 Maribar Slovenia
> Phone: +386 41 720 908
> Email: security@acros.si
> URL: http://www.acros.si

Armor Security, Inc. (U.S.A.)

Armor installs high-security physical and electronic devices to protect life and property. These include CCTV, card access systems, burglar and fire alarms, and UL-listed locks and safes.

> Armor Security, Inc.
> 2601 Stevens Avenue South
> Minneapolis, MN 55408
> Contact: Doug Wilson
> Phone: 612-870-4142
> Fax: 612-870-4789
> Email: pros@armorsecurity.com
> URL: http://www.armorsecurity.com

AS Stallion Ltd. (Estonia)

AS Stallion offers data and network security consulting and services, firewall and encryption solutions, and security evaluations and auditing.

> AS Stallion Ltd.
> Mustamae tec 55
> Tallinn 10621, Estonia
> Contact: Mr. Jyri Kaljundi, Managing Director
> Phone: 372-656-7720
> Fax: 372-656-7727
> Email: stallion@stallion.ee
> URL: http://www.stallion.ee/

ASCIItech (Canada)

ASCII Technology has solutions that address risk, including information security related to technology.

> ASCIItech
> 6497 Edwards Boulevard
> Mississauga, Ontario L5T 2V2 Canada
> Phone: 800-787-2344
> Fax: 905-564-1382
> Email: hotline@asciitech.com
> URL: http://www.asciitech.com/HTML/

AtBusiness Communications (Finland, Germany, Russia)

AtBusiness designs and implements end-to-end security solutions, including risk analysis and creation of security policies. It has experience with various security products and technologies such as strong encryption, authentication, firewalls, PKI, and VPN-solutions.

> AtBusiness Communications Oyj
> Italahdenkatu 19,
> FIN-00210 Helsinki
> Finland
> Phone: +358 9 2311 6600
> FAX: +358 9 2311 6601
> Email: info@atbusiness.com
> URL: http://www.atbusiness.com/

Atlantic Computing Technology Corporation (U.S.A.)

Started in 1994, Atlantic specializes in UNIX, Windows NT, firewalls, network security, and WAN connectivity. It currently resells seven different firewall brands.

> Atlantic Computing Technology Corporation
> 111 Founders Plaza
> Suite 900
> East Hartford, CT 06108
> Phone: 860-291-0851
> Fax: 860-291-0847
> Email: info@atlantic.com
> URL: http://www.atlantic.com

beTRUSTed (WorldWide)

beTRUSTed's goal is "to help companies to be trusted." It offers a variety of services including authentication, electronic ID, information integrity, privacy, confidential communications, and transaction validation.

> beTRUSTed
> Phone: 443-367-7150
> Email: contactus@betrusted.com
> URL: http://www.betrusted.com

Cambridge Technology Partners, Inc. (Worldwide)

Cambridge Technology Partners is a management consulting and systems integration firm. Cambridge's says its approach to information technology, network, systems security (IT) consulting, and systems integration "delivers innovative, quantifiable results to clients in unprecedented time frames…within a unique fixed time, fixed price model."

> Cambridge Technology Partners, Inc.
> 8 Cambridge Center
> Cambridge, MA 02142
> Phone: 617-374-9800
> FAX: 617-374-8300
> URL: http://www.ctp.com

Canaudit, Inc (U.S.A.)

Canaudit specializes in security auditing.

> Canaudit, Inc.
> PO Box 2110
> Simi Valley, CA 93062-2110
> Phone: 805-583-3723
> Fax: 805-582-2676
> Email: Gordon@canaudit.com
> URL: http://www.canaudit.com

CobWeb Applications (U.K.)

CobWeb specializes in Windows 95, Windows NT, network, and Web site security including encryption.

> CobWeb Applications
> 3000 Hilliswood Drive
> Hilliswood Business Park
> Chertsey
> Surrey, U.K. KT16 0RS
> Phone: +44 1972 796 031
> Fax: +44 1972 796 699
> Email: connect@cobweb.co.uk
> URL: http://www.cobweb.co.uk

Command Systems (U.S.A.)

Command Systems provides solutions including firewalls, encryption, VPN, and auditing, focusing on the Windows NT platform. Supported firewalls are Digital Altavista, Gauntlet, and Firewall-1.

> Command Systems
> Pond View Corporate Center
> 76 Batterson Park Road
> Farmington, CT 06032
> Phone: 860-409-2000
> Fax: 860-409-2099
> URL: http://www.commandsys.com

Computer Associates Services eTrust (Worldwide)

CA Services eTrust provides solutions to address companies' security needs and handles organizations of any size in any location.

> CA Services
> One Computer Associates Plaza
> Islandia, NY 11749
> Phone: 800-225-5224
> URL: http://www.computerassociates.com/

CorpNet Security (U.S.A.)

CorpNet Security focuses on performing professional security audits and assessments. CorpNet Security also has the expertise to assist with intrusion detection systems and virtual private networks.

> CorpNet Security
> Phone: 888-666-9216
> Email: info@corpnetsecurity.com
> URL: http://www.corpnetsecurity.com/

Counterpane Internet Security (U.S.A.)

Counterpane Internet Security, Inc. offers security monitoring services and help with responding to attacks.

> Counterpane Internet Security
> 3031 Tisch Way, Suite 100 PE
> San Jose, CA 95128
> Phone: 408-260-7500
> Fax: 408-556-0889
> Email: info@sj.counterpane.com
> URL: http://www.counterpane.com/

Cryptek Secure Communications LLC (U.S.A.)

Cryptek manufactures and sells network-security products for both government and commercial use that have been evaluated by the National Security Agency. Product lines include encryption, identification, authentication, access control, auditing, and integrity mechanisms.

Cryptek Secure Communications LLC

14130-C Sullyfield Circle

Chantilly, VA 20151

Phone: 703-802-9300

Fax: 703-818-3706

Email: net.info@cryptek.com

URL: http://www.cryptek.com

CygnaCom Solutions (U.S.A.)

CygnaCom Solutions, Inc. consults with the public sector, specializing in PKI, security consulting, security evaluation, and testing.

CygnaCom Solutions

7927 Jones Branch Drive

McLean, VA 22102-3305

Phone: 703-848-0883

Fax: 703-848-0960

Email: corpinfo@cygnacom.com

URL: http://www.cygnacom.com

Data Fellows (Europe, North America, Asia)

Data Fellows (aka F-Secure, Inc.) develops anti-virus and encryption products (F-Secure and F-PROT Professional product ranges).

Data Fellows

Pyyntile 7, Espoo

PL 24

02231 ESPOO

Finland

Phone: +358-9-2520 0700

Email: info@f-secure.com

URL: http://www.f-secure.com/

F-Secure, Inc.

675 N. First Street, 5th Floor

San Jose, CA 95112

Phone: (408) 438-6700

FAX: (408) 438-6701

Data Systems West (U.S.A.)

This systems integrator designs firewalls and provides implementation, security audits, policy writing, access control, network and security management, VPN, TACACS+, ICSA Web certification, application development, and e-commerce.

> Data Systems West
> 6110 Variel Avenue, 2nd floor
> Woodland Hills, CA 91367
> Phone: 800-366-4379
> Email: info@dsw.net
> URL: http://www.dsw.net

DataLynx, Inc. (U.S.A.)

This multilevel security system for UNIX and Windows NT features access control, security response, security alarms, security reporting, user account/password management, and much more.

> DataLynx, Inc.
> Phone: 858-560-8112
> Fax: 858-560-8114
> Email: sales@dli-security.com
> URL: http://www.dlxguard.com

Dataway, Inc. (U.S.A., Ireland)

Dataway provides high-availability, managed virtual private networks (VPNs) and security solutions for the financial Internet market.

> Dataway, Inc.
> 180 Redwood Street
> 3rd Floor
> San Francisco, CA 94102
> Phone: 415-882-8700
> Fax: 415-882-8787
> Email: sales@dataway.com
> 67 Lower Baggot Street
> Dublin 2
> Ireland

Phone: +353 1 676-0307

Fax: +353 1 676-0309

Email: euresales@dataway.com

URL: http://www.dataway.com

Delphi Consulting, LLC (U.S.A.)

Delphi is a Java consulting firm with experience in developing security and encryption systems.

Delphi Consultants, LLC

10000 N. Central Expressway Suite 1325

Dallas, TX 75231

Phone: 800-DELPHIS

Email: info@delphis.com

URL: http://www.delphis.com

EAC Network Integrators (U.S.A.)

EAC provides three levels of security service: intensive network and system audits, incident response (both per-incident and on retainer), and proactive security design and implementation.

EAC Network Integrators

56 Quarry Road

Trumbull, CT 06611

Phone: 203-371-4774

FAX: 203-372-4199

URL: http://www.eac.com

ECG Management Consultants (U.S.A.)

Consultants in IT management and security, ECG specializes in services to criminal justice systems.

ECG Management Consultants

1111 3rd Avenue, Suite 2700

Seattle, WA 98101

Phone: 206-689-2200

Fax: 206-689-2201

Email: ecg@ecgmc.com

URL: http://www.ecgmc.com

EGAN Group Pty Limited (Australia)

Calling itself "the professional hacker," EGAN specializes in firewall design and implementation, security audits, penetration testing, policy and standards documentation, and general Internet/Intranet network security.

EGAN Group Pty Limited

Melbourne, Australia

Phone: +61 (0)414 916 632

Email: webmaster@egan.com.au

URL: www.egan.com.au

Energis (U.K.)

Energis provides design, configuration, deployment, and management of secure Internet, intranet, and extranet services.

Energis

Contact: Sales Department

The White House, Melbourne Street

Leeds, West Yorkshire

LS2 7PS United Kingdom

Phone: +44 (0)1494 441256

FAX: +44 (0)1494 438319

Email: info@energis-eis.co.uk

URL: http://www.theplanet.net/

EnGarde Systems, Inc (U.S.A.)

EnGarde Systems offers assessment consulting and tools for network monitoring and manual intrusion investigation and response.

EnGarde Systems

4848 Tramway Ridge Drive NE

Suite 122

Albuquerque, NM 87111

Phone: 505-346-1760

FAX: 505-346-1719

Email: info@engarde.com

URL: http://www.engarde.com/

EnterEdge Technology LLC (U.S.A.)

EnterEdge offers products and tools "to help you find a complete solution to your security issues."

> EnterEdge
> 5500 Interstate North Parkway
> Suite 440
> Atlanta, GA 30328
> Phone: 770-955-9899
> Fax: 770-955-9896
> URL: http://www.enteredge.com

Ernst & Young LLP (U.S.A.)

E&Y's security professionals provide security solutions including Internet security strategy, secured commmerce, single sign-on, security assessments, auditing, penetration analysis, and security benchmarking.

> Ernst & Young LLP
> Information Security Services
> 370 17th Street, Suite 4300
> Denver, CO 80202
> Phone: 303-628-4344
> URL: http://www.ey.com

eSoft (U.S.A., U.K., Singapore)

The manufacturer of the InstaGate firewall, eSoft also conducts Internet security consulting, virtual private networking, security audits, and penetration testing.

> eSoft
> 295 Interlocken Boulevard, Suite 500
> Broomfield, CO 80021
> Phone: 888-903-7638
> Fax: 303-444-1640
> Email: sales@esoft.com
> URL: http://www.tlogic.com

Espiria (U.S.A.)

Espiria is a information security consulting services company that works in the design, implementation, assessment, and management of adaptive security solutions.

> Espiria
> 123 North Third Street
> Suite 604
> Minneapolis, MN 55401
> Phone: 612-395-6600
> Email: info@espiria.com
> URL: http://www.espiria.com

ESTec Systems Corporation (North America, Latin America, Asia)

ESTec provides auditing, assessing, managing, and designing of data security systems and information policies for companies. Current ESTec security products and services include data security management software, information protection seminars, and comprehensive network security audits.

> ESTec Systems Corporation
> 2nd Floor Suite
> 17510-102 Avenue
> Edmonton, AB T5S 1K2
> Canada
> Phone: 780-483-7120
> Fax: 780-489-9557
> Email: abnelson@estec.com
> URL: http://www.estec.com

Flavio Marcelo Amaral (Brazil)

FMA's services include encryption, proxy, access control, auditing, penetration testing, and installation of security programs.

> Flavio Marcelo Amaral
> R. CEL. Glicerio Cicero, 55
> Natal, RN 59030-040, Brazil
> Phone: 55-84-221-0007
> Email: fmca@eol.com.br

FMJ/PADLOCK Computer Security Systems (U.S.A.)

FMJ/PADLOCK is a national/international manufacturer/distributor of security lockdown and cable devices for computers and office equipment. Featuring in-house design and manufacturing, FMJ PADLOCK's line of patented lockdown devices protects servers, scanners, printers, copiers, and faxes, as well as office, medical, and scientific equipment.

FMJ/PADLOCK Computer Security Systems

741 E. 223rd St.

Carson, CA 90745

Phone: 310-549-3221

Email: info@fmjpadlock.com

URL: http://www.fmjpadlock.com

Galaxy Computer Services, Inc. (U.S.A.)

Galaxy implements various flavors of UNIX firewalls in a heterogeneous environment. Other services include penetration testing and risk assessment, client-server application security in the Windows NT environment, and its network security product, the Information Diode, an accreditable, one-way-only path from low to high networks.

Galaxy Computer Services, Inc.

10366 Battleview Parkway

Manassas, VA 20109

Phone: 703-393-1464

Email: info@gcsi.com

Gemini Computers, Inc. (U.S.A.)

Gemini products provide support for secure system applications using the Al-certified foundation of the Gemini Trusted Network Processor (GTNP) with integrated encryption. Gemini's end-to-end encryption technologies "support the legal foundation of the electronic world in compliance with applicable standards, guidelines, and laws."

Gemini Computers, Inc.

P.O. Box 222417

Carmel, CA 93922-2417

Phone: 831-373-850

Fax: 831-373-5792

Email: tft@geminisecure.com

URL: http://www.geminisecure.com

Getronics Government Services (U.S.A.)

Getronics Government Services offers the XTS-300 NSA-evaluated B3 Trusted Computer System, the Secure Automated Guard Environment (SAGE), and trusted application development services. Getronics' customers include the NSA, DoD, Army, Air Force, Navy, State Department, FBI, DOE, IRS, NATO, and the governments of the United Kingdom, Canada, and Norway.

> Getronics Government Services
>
> 7900 Westpark Drive MS 700
>
> McLean, VA 22102-4299
>
> Phone: 703-827-3000
>
> Email: webmanager@getronicsgov.com
>
> URL: http://www.getronicsgov.com

NOTE

Getronics Government Services is one of the providers of TEMPEST protection technology, which prevent eavesdropping of electronic emissions that leak from a monitor (or computer).

GlobalCenter (U.S.A.)

This ISP offers dial-up, dedicated, and server co-location services; security consulting on firewalls, security policies, encryption; virtual private networks; spam detection and cancellation; junk email filtering; and abuse prevention.

> GlobalCenter
>
> 141 Caspian Court
>
> Sunnyvale, CA 94089
>
> Phone: 800-530-6557
>
> Fax: 408-543-0074
>
> Email: sales@globalcenter.net

Global Privacy Solutions (U.S.A.)

Global Privacy Solutions provides systems for the protection and privacy of consumer electronic data and patients' medical records.

> Global Privacy Solutions
>
> Crystal Plaza, Suite N303

2111 Jefferson Davis Highway

Arlington, VA 22202

Phone: 703-418-1956

Fax: 703-418-0224

Email: info@privacysolutions.com

URL: http://www.privacysolutions.com

Graham Information Security and Management Services (Australia)

Graham Information Security and Management Services offers a wide range of security services including consulting and training on Internet, intranet, and workstation security. It specializes in cryptography, management of associated protocols and keys, access control, and user authentication and verification.

Graham Information Security and Management Services

Suite 12a Tamborine Plaza

Beacon Road

North Tamborine, Queensland, 4272, Australia

Contact: Dr. Ian G. Graham

Phone: 61 7 55452200

Email: grahamis@onthenet.com.au

URL: http://www.onthenet.com.au/~grahamis/

Grand Designs Ltd./ConfluX.net (U.S.A.)

The principals of Grand Designs Ltd. each have more than 20 years' experience in the areas of networking and software engineering, secure networking, and systems security including work for military subcontracts. Its ConfluX.net unit offers Web hosting and secure Internet access through virtual private networks.

Grand Designs Ltd./ConfluX.net

4917 Evergreen Way, Suite 10

Everett, WA 98203

Phone: 206-710-9006

Email: info@gdltd.com

URL: http://www.gdltd.com/ or http://www.conflux.net

Gregory R. Block (U.K.)

A UNIX/Windows NT security and networking consultant with 10 years of experience in the field, Block works in tiger-team analyses, firewalls, topology, design, and implementation at all levels. Finger for PGP key and mail for further information.

> Gregory R. Block
> 48A Hendon Lane
> London, N3 1TT U.K.
> Email: gblock@lemon.net

The GSR Consulting Group Inc. (Canada)

The GSR Consulting Group Inc. provides a full range of information security and disaster recovery services.

> The GSR Consulting Group Inc.
> 1255 University Street, Suite 1107
> Montreal, Quebec H3B 3W7
> Phone: 514-876-4040
> Fax: 514-876-4009
> Email: gsr@sympatico.ca
> URL: http://www.gsrinc.com/

Guardent Inc (North America, U.K.)

Guardent offers full-lifecycle security solutions.

> Guardent Inc
> 75 Third Avenue
> Waltham, MA 02451
> Phone: 888-413-4344
> Fax: 781-577-6600
> URL: http://www.guardent.com/

Hyperon Consulting (U.S.A.)

Hyperon Consulting is a high-technology company that provides Internet and electronic commerce security solutions to industry. Hyperon is CISSP certified and familiar with banking regulations.

Hyperon Consulting

3422 Old Capitol Trail, Suite 1245

Wilmington, DE 19808

Phone: 302-996-3047

Fax: 302-996-5818

URL: http://www.hyperon.com

I.T. NetworX Ltd. (Ireland)

A specialist in Internet/intranet security on UNIX and Windows NT since 1984, IT NetworX Ltd offers firewalls, penetration testing, design, consultancy, products, and freeware configuration.

I.T. NetworX Ltd.

Stonebridge House

Shankill, Co.

Dublin

Ireland

Contact: Michael Ryan

Phone: +353-(01)28 27 233

Fax: +353-(01)28 27 230

Email: webmaster@NetworX.ie

URL: www.networx.ie

Infoconcept GmbH (Germany)

Infoconcept GmbH is a Raptor Security Partner, ISS Partner, and IBM Business Partner, working in firewall installation and support, penetration testing, security consulting, and integration to the Internet.

Infoconcept GmbH

Moerscherstrasse 17-25

76275 Ettlingen

Germany

Contact: Thorsten Bruchaeuser

Phone: +49-07243-5380-0

Email: TBruchhaeuser@infoconcept.com

URL: www.infoconcept.com

INFOSEC Engineering (U.S.A.)

INFOSEC Engineering provides Fortune 500 corporations with computer and network security solutions.

> INFOSEC Engineering
>
> Phone: 978-256-4494
>
> Email: info@infoseceng.com
>
> URL: www.infoseceng.com

Infosecure Australia (Australia)

Infosecure Australia provides security policy development, security policy implementation, penetration testing, security evaluation, and computer security research.

> Infosecure Australia
>
> PO Box 7104
>
> Cloisters Square, Western Australia 6850
>
> Phone: 041 4636732
>
> Email: dave@infosecure.com.au
>
> URL: www.infosecure.com.au

Ingenieurbüro Dr.-Ing Markus a Campo (Germany)

Ingenieurbüro Dr.-Ing Markus a Campo provides many security services including security auditing, penetration tests, firewalls, network performance, consulting, and network analysis.

> Ingenieurbüro Dr.-Ing Markus a Campo
>
> Försterstr. 25
>
> D-52072 Aachen
>
> Germany
>
> Contact: Markus a Campo
>
> Phone: +49 241 / 15 80 80
>
> Fax: +49 241 / 15 80 89
>
> Email: mac.ac@t-online.de
>
> URL: http://home.t-online.de/home/mac.ac/index.htm

Integrity Sciences, Inc. (U.S.A.)

Integrity Sciences, Inc. provides consulting and software engineering services for secure networks, focusing on strong password authentication protocols that are immune to network attack.

> Integrity Sciences, Inc.
> Westboro, MA 01581
> Contact: David Jablon
> Phone: 508-898-9024
> FAX: 508-561-1953
> Email: info@integritysciences.com
> URL: www.integritysciences.com

InterNet Guide Service, Inc. (U.S.A.)

InterNet Guide Service is a consulting and coaching firm specializing in Internet strategy, security, and digital commerce. A member of NCSA, InterNet is a certified IBM firewall expert.

> InterNet Guide Service, Inc.
> 90 Stony Brook Road
> Westford, MA 01886
> Phone: 978-392-3650
> FAX: 978-392-5878
> Email: esj@inguide.com
> URL: http://www.inguide.com

D

Internet Security Systems, Inc. (ISS) (U.S.A.)

ISS is a supplier of network security assessment tools, providing comprehensive auditing, monitoring, and response software. The company's flagship product, Internet Scanner, is a leading commercial attack simulation and security audit tool worldwide.

> Internet Security Systems, Inc. (ISS)
> 6303 Barfield Road
> Atlanta, GA 30328 (Corporate Headquarters)
> Phone: 404-236-2600
> Fax: 404-236-2626
> Email: info@iss.net
> URL: http://www.iss.net

Interpact, Inc./Infowar.Com (U.S.A.)

With major corporate and governmental clients on three continents, Interpact provides security design, architecture, modeling, and penetration testing.

> Interpact, Inc./Infowar.Com
> 11511 Pine Street
> Seminole, FL 33772
> Contact: Winn Schwartai
> Phone: 813-393-6600
> Fax: 813-393-6361
> Email: winn@infowar.com
> URL: http://www.infowar.com

Jerboa, Inc. (U.S.A.)

Jerboa helps clients with UNIX, firewalls (all vendors), product reviews, consulting, topology, policy development, product integration, compatibility testing, training, seminars, business planning, Web technologies, encryption, and tunneling.

> Jerboa, Inc.
> P.O. Box 382648
> Cambridge, MA 02238
> Phone: 617-492-8084
> Fax: 617-492-8089
> Email: info@jerboa.com
> URL: http://www.jerboa.com

Karl Nagel & Company

Karl Nagel & Company's staff specializes in electronic commerce assurance and consulting services.

> Karl Nagel & Company
> P.O. Box 3255
> Manhattan Beach, CA 90266
> Phone: 310-546-6138
> Fax: 310-546-7048
> Email: info@karlnagel.com
> URL: http://www.karlnagel.com

Kinetic, Inc. (U.S.A.)

Kinetic provides Internet-related open systems and computer security consulting, UNIX security audits, firewall design, and secure off-site Web management/housing facilities.

> Kinetic, Inc.
>
> 289 East Fifth Street
>
> Suite 205
>
> St. Paul, MN 55101
>
> Phone: 651-848-0477
>
> Fax: 651-848-0478
>
> URL: http://www.kinetic.com

Learning Tree International (U.S.A.)

Learning Tree provides hands-on courses on UNIX security, Windows NT security, Internet/intranet security, and firewalls, plus more than 130 other information technology topics. A free course catalog is available by telephone.

> Learning Tree International
>
> 1805 Library Street
>
> Reston, VA 20190-5630
>
> Contact: Linda Trude
>
> Phone: 800-843-8733
>
> Fax: 800-709-6405
>
> Email: uscourses@learningtree.com
>
> URL: http://www.learningtree.com

Livermore Software Labs (Worldwide)

Network consultant LSLI is the maker of the PORTUS Secure Firewall for AIX, HP, SOLARIS, and Apple.

> Livermore Software Labs
>
> 1830 S. Kirkland Suite 205
>
> Houston, TX 77077
>
> Phone: 281-759-3274
>
> Fax: 281-759-8558
>
> Email: portusinfo@lsli.com
>
> URL: http://www.lsli.com

D

SECURITY CONSULTANTS

Lucent Worldwide Services Security Consulting (U.S.A. and UK)

Lucent Worldwide Services offers businesses a comprehensive suite, customized to meet specific business missions, needs, and objectives, while maximizing ROI and resource utilization. Support is also provided for multivendor product applications.

> Lucent Worldwide Services Security Consulting
>
> 1213 Innsbruck Drive
>
> Sunnyvale, CA 94089
>
> Phone: 650-318-1000
>
> Fax: 650-318-1001
>
> URL: `http://www.lucent-networkcare.com`
>
> Lucent Worldwide Services Security Consulting
>
> London
>
> Malvern House
>
> 14/18 Bell Street 2nd Floor
>
> Maidenhead, Berkshire SL6 1BR
>
> Phone: 44 1628 50 30 00
>
> Fax: 44 1628 50 30 01

Lunux Network Security Services (U.S.A.)

Lunux services is a consulting firm that focuses on high tech companies needing network security.

> Lunux Network Security Services
>
> Los Angeles, CA
>
> Email: `sales@www.lunux.com`
>
> URL: `http://www.lunux.com/`

Lurhq Corporation (U.S.A.)

Lurhq is a network security organization specializing in firewalls, Web-server security, electronic commerce implementations, and penetration testing.

> Lurhq Corporation
>
> 850 Hwy 501
>
> PO Box 2861
>
> Conway, SC 29526

Phone: 843-347-1075

FAX: 843-347-1076

Email: info@lurhq.com

URL: http://www.lurhq.com/

marchFIRST (U.S.A.)

This firm offers a wide range of services including enterprise security.

marchFIRST

311 S. Wacker Drive Suite 35000

Chicago, IL 60605-6621

Contact: Tucker McDonagh, Managing Director

Phone: 312-922-9200

Fax: 313-913-3020

URL: http://www.marchfirst.com

Maxon Services (Canada)

A network security systems integrator/consultant, Maxon works on Windows NT, UNIX, Cisco, Checkpoint Firewall 1, and Security Dynamics Ace Server.

Maxon Services

Contact: Eric Tremblay

8550 Marie-Victorin

Brossard, Quebec

Canada, J4X 1A1

Phone: 514-466-2422

Fax: 514-466-2113

URL: http://www.maxon.ca

Merdan Group, Inc. (U.S.A.)

Merdan Group, Inc. is a small firm specializing in security engineering services and security products.

Merdan Group, Inc

4617 Ruffner Street

San Diego, CA 92111

Phone: 800-608-6029

Fax: 858-279-8893

Email: merdan@merdan.com

URL: http://www.merdan.com

Merilus Technologies (U.S.A.)

Merilus Technologies provides solutions for connecting corporate computer networks to the Internet securely. These solutions include hardened firewalls, virtual private networking, e-commerce implementation, high-speed bandwidth allocation and shaping, and custom Linux systems.

Merilus Technologies

46165 Yale Road

Chilliwack, BC V2P 2P2

Phone: 604-792-0100

Fax: 604-792-0911

Email: sales@merilus.com

URL: http://www.merilus.com

Milvets System Technology, Inc (U.S.A.)

Specializing in UNIX and Windows NT-based systems, Milvets offers systems integration of network security products and reseller agreements with market-leading firewall vendors.

Milvets System Technology, Inc.

4600 Forbes Boulevard, Suite 104

Lanham, MD 20706

Contact: Greg Simpson

Phone: 301-731-9130

Fax: 301-731-4773

Email: Milvets@milvets.com

URL: http://www.milvets.com

MIS Corporate Defence Solutions (Holland and U.K.)

MIS Corporate Defence Solutions offers a full range of consulting services including managed security services and expert security consultancy services.

MIS Corporate Defence Solutions

MIS House

Hermitage Court

Hermitage Lane

Maidstone, Kent

England ME16 9NT

Phone: 01622 727400

Fax: 01622 28580

Email: `pr@mis-cds.com`

URL: `http://www.mis-cds.com`

Myxa Corporation (U.S.A.)

In business since 1976, Myxa is a technology-services company that deals with UNIX, client/server, and networking (intranet and Internet), including firewalls and security.

Myxa Corporation

654 Red Lion Road, Suite 200

Huntingdon Valley, PA 19006

Phone: 215-947-9900

Fax: 215-935-0235

Email: `info@myxa.com`

URL: `http://www.myxa.com`

NetraCorp LLC. (U.S.A.)

NetraCorp LLC supplies corporations with a certification level after meeting strict standards.

NetraCorp LLC

15050 W. 138th Street #3406

Olatha, KS 66063-3406

Phone: 816-898-3448

FAX: 978-285-5909

URL: `http://www.netracorp.com/`

Nett & So GmbH (Germany)

Nett & So GmbH provides services including firewalls (TIS-Gauntlet, Raptor Eagle, Firewall-1), virus scanning with firewall systems, PGP, special solutions for corporations, UNIX, and Windows NT. They are Raptor Systems certified.

Nett & So GmbH

Contact: Bogdan Pelc

Friedbergstrasse 29, 14057

Berlin, Germany

Phone: +49 (30) 3227572

Email: info@nett.de

URL: http://www.nett.de

Network Associates, Inc.

Network Associates conducts confidential network security surveys; vulnerability analysis; penetration testing; product and security policy development and review; encryption consulting; software assessments; architectural and diagnostic security analysis; and firewall configuration.

Network Associates, Inc.

Contact: Alice Westerfield

3965 Freedom Circle

Santa Carla, CA 95054

Phone: 770-492-7807

Email: consulting@tis.com

URL: http://www.nai.com

Network Security Assurance Group (U.S.A.)

The Network Security Assurance Group provides data and network security auditing, business risk assessments, incident response services, and general information security consulting.

Network Security Assurance Group

Magnificent Mile Center

980 North Michigan Avenue

14th Floor

Chicago, IL 60611-4501

Phone: 877-NSA-GROUP

Fax: 312-214-3510

Email: info@nsag.net

URL: http://www.nsag.net

Network Technology Solutions, Inc. (U.S.A.)

NTS specializes in providing management and security solutions for corporate information systems.

Network Technology Solutions, Inc.

4125 Mohr Avenue, Suite 6

Pleasanton, CA 94566

Phone: 209-839-0936

Fax: 209-839-0936

Email: nts@ntsinc.com

URL: http://www.ntsinc.com/info.html

NH&A (U.S.A.)

NH&A specializes in anti-virus, security, and network management.

NH&A

577 Isham Street, Suite 2-B

New York City, NY 10034

Contact: Norman Hirsch

Phone: 212-304-9660

Fax: 212-304-9759

Email: nhirsch@nha.com

URL: http://www.nha.com

NovaTech Internet Security (Australia)

NovaTech is an Australian Internet and Network Security Consultation firm specializing in TCP/IP networks and Secure Internet Access.

NovaTech Internet Security

P.O. Box 487

Ermingham, NSW 2115

Australia

Phone: +61 (0) 418 227646

Email: novatech@novatech.com.au

URL: http://www.novatech.com.au

D

SECURITY
CONSULTANTS

Pacificnet Internet Services (U.S.A.)

Pacificnet offers managed Internet security through co-location and custom configuration in firewalls, logging, auditing, investigation, and analysis.

Pacificnet

19725 Sherman Way, Suite 395

Canoga Park, CA 91306

Phone: 818-464-2600

Email: info@pacificnet.net

URL: http://www.pacificnet.net

Pangeia Informatica LTDA (Brazil)

Pangeia Informatica provides solutions including firewalls, encryption, VPN, access control, auditing, penetration testing, development, security free/commercial tools (like chkexploit, chk{root,demon}kit, Coordenation 2 security lists cert-br and seguranca).

SRTVS 701 Ed. Palacio do Radio II S/304

Brasilia, DF, 70340000, Brazil

Contact: Nelson Murilo

Phone: +55 61 223-5625

Email: info@pangeia.com.br or nelson@pangeia.com.br

URL: http://www.pangeia.com.br

Pentex Net, Inc. (U.S.A.)

Pentex Net, Inc. is a provider of every aspect of security, from firewalls and physical access control to penetration testing.

Pentex Net, Inc.

805 W. Oregon Street

Urbana, IL 61801

Contact: Dr. John C. A. Bambenek

Phone: 217-239-3760

Email: jbamb@pentex-net.com

URL: http://www.pentex-net.com

Predictive Systems (U.S.A.)

Predictive Systems' services include assessment with asset and risk analysis, policy development, design and implementation, public-key infrastructures, security certification, incident response, and digital forensics.

> Predictive Systems
> 417 Fifth Avenue
> New York, NY 10016
> Phone: 212-659-3400
> FAX: 212-659-3499
> URL: http://www.predictive.com

PSINet Consulting Solutions (Worldwide)

One of the world's largest provider's of end-to-end IT solutions, PSINet Consulting Solutions focuses on the middle market with a concentration in five industries: transportation, financial services, manufacturing, government/public sector, and telecommunications.

> PSINet Consulting Solutions
> 44983 Knoll Square
> Ashburn, VA 20147
> Phone: 703-726-4100
> Fax: 703-726-4200
> Email: info@psinetcs.com
> URL: http://www.psinetcs.com

R.C. Consulting, Inc. (Canada)

Providing enterprise-level security consulting for Windows NT environments, RC also hosts and moderates the NTBugTraq mailing list, dedicated to examining exploits and bugs in Windows NT.

> R.C. Consulting, Inc.
> Kenrei Court, R.R. #1
> Lindsay, Ontario, K9V 4R1
> Canada
> Contact: Russ Cooper
> Phone: 705-878-3405
> Fax: 705-878-1804
> Email: Russ.Cooper@rc.on.ca
> URL: http://www.NTBugTraq.com/

D

SECURITY
CONSULTANTS

Rainbow Technologies, Spectra Division (U.S.A.)

Rainbow Technologies' services include security and virus assessments, penetration testing, firewall verification, disaster-recovery planning, pbs and war-dialing attacks, and security-policy development.

> Rainbow Technologies, Spectra Division. (MSC)
>
> P.O. Box 6028
>
> Playa del Rey, CA 90296
>
> 8055 W. Manchester Avenue, Suite 450
>
> Playa del Rey, CA 90293
>
> Phone: 310-306-1365
>
> Fax: 310-305-1493
>
> Email: info@infoseclabs.com
>
> URL: http://www.miora.com

Ritter Software Engineering (U.S.A.)

A developer of patented and patent-pending ciphering technologies, Ritte also provides custom cipher designs, implementations, and consulting.

> Ritter Software Engineering
>
> 2609 Choctaw Trail
>
> Austin, TX 78745
>
> Contact: Terry Ritter, P.E.
>
> Phone/Fax: 512-892-0494
>
> Email: ritter@io.com
>
> URL: http://www.io.com/~ritter/

Saffire Systems (U.S.A.)

Saffire Systems specializes in secure software development, consulting, and systems integration. Saffire Systems provides engineering services (architecture, design, implementation, and testing), evaluation support services, secure network evaluations, and Windows NT security training.

> Saffire Systems
>
> P.O. Box 11154
>
> Champaign, IL 61826-1154
>
> Contact: Michelle A. Ruppel

Phone: 217-359-7763

Fax: 217-359-8753

Email: maruppel@prairienet.org

SAGUS Security, Inc. (Canada)

SAGUS offers products to secure desktops, servers, gateways, and mainframes.

SAGUS Security, Inc.

180 Elgin Street, Suite 600

Ontario, K2P 2K3, Canada

Contact: Natasha Hollywood

Phone: 888-391-9922

Email: nhollywood@sagus-security.com

URL: http://www.sagus-security.com

Schlumberger Network Solutions (U.S.A.)

Schlumberger's services include Firewall-1, penetration testing, security audits, tiger teams, encryption, virtual private networks, and Firewall-1 CCSE training.

Schlumberger Network Solutions

5599 San Felipe, Suite 400

Houston, TX 77056

555 Industrial Boulevard

Sugarland, TX 77478

Phone: 713-513-3187

Email: harji@houston.omnes.slb.com

URL: http://www.slb.com/Hub/Docs/tt/nws/index.html

SecTek, Inc. (U.S.A.)

SecTek provides services INFOSEC, COMPSEC, physical security, access control, risk assessments, penetration tests, firewall design/implementation, intrusion detection, and intranets.

SecTek, Inc.

208 Elden Street, Suite 201

Herndon, VA 22070

Contact: Bruce Moore

Phone: 703-834-0507

Fax: 703-834-0214

Email: operations@sectek.com

URL: http://www.sectek.com

Security First Technologies, Inc. (U.S.A.)

Developers of secure networks for government and industry for more than 10 years, Security First also handles B1 security, CMW, trusted operating systems, UNIX, Windows NT, secure network design and implementation, security auditing, penetration studies, authentication, and encryption software products (VirtualVault, HannaH, Troy).

Security First Technologies, Inc.

3390 Peachtree Road, Suite 1700

Atlanta, GA 30326

Phone: 404-812-6200

URL: http://www.s1.com

Security Sciences (Europe, Middle East, North America, Africa)

Security Sciences offers penetration tests and audits, privacy policy and practice reviews, and competitive analysis overview of businesses' Internet presence.

Security Sciences

Phone: 518-668-9385

Email: info@securitysciences.com

URL: http://www.securitysciences.com

Siam Relay Ltd. (Thailand)

Siam Relay Ltd. is Asia's first security consulting and electronic commerce solutions provider. Complete turnkey electronic commerce solutions are available, as well as penetration testing, network analysis, firewalls, security policies, auditing and reporting, and training.

Siam Relay Ltd.

898/6 Level 5 SV City Office Tower 2

Rama III Road

Bangkok, 10120, Thailand

Phone: +662-682-9508

FAX: 662-682-5675

Email: info@siamrelay.com

URL: http://www.siamrelay.com

Slmsoft.com (Canada)

Slmsoft.com offers ESP-Link/NSS, which can police 64,000 TCP and UDP ports, and delivers GUI-based point-and-click functionality.

Slmsoft.com

1 Yorkdale Road, Suite 600

Toronto, ON, Canada M6A 3A1

Phone: 416-787-9884

FAX: 416-789-3457

Email: `lkiervin@slmsoft.com`

URL: `http://www.slmsoft.com`

SmallWorks, Inc. (U.S.A.)

SmallWorks is a software-development and consulting group specializing in Internet security packages, including firewalls, IPSEC implementations, and high-security Internet connectivity solutions. SmallWorks developed the TACACS+, CiscoSecure UNIX Server for Cisco Systems.

SmallWorks, Inc.

4417 Ridge Oak Drive

Austin, TX 78731

Contact: Steve Bagwell, Director of Sales

Phone: 512-338-0619

Fax: 512-689-5852

Email: `info@smallworks.com`

URL: `http://www.smallworks.com`

STRATESEC, Inc. (U.S.A., WorldWide)

STRATESEC is a security provider for medium-to-large commercial and governmental organizations. It offers a broad range of services including consulting and planning; engineering and design; systems integration; and maintenance and technical support.

STRATESEC, Inc.

105 Carpenter Drive Suite C

Sterling, VA 20164

Phone: 703-709-8686

Fax: 703-709-8632

Email: `generalinfo@stratesec.com`

URL: `http://www.stratesec.com`

Sword & Shield Enterprise Security, Inc. (U.S.A.)

Sword & Shield is a security consulting firm specializing in the application of computer and network security technology.

Sword & Shield Enterprise Security

10301A Technology Drive

Knoxville, TN 37932-3342

Phone: 865-777-5500

Fax: 865-777-5599

Email: info@sses.net

URL: http://www.sses.net

Symantec Security Services (Worldwide)

Symantec Security Services provides comprehensive consulting services to organizations around the globe, including security education and training, security assessment, technology implementation, and managed security services.

Symantec Security Services

Cupertino, CA

Phone: (800)441-7234

URL: http://enterprisesecurity.symantec.com/content/services.cfm

Sysman Computers (P) Ltd. (India)

Sysman offers risk assessment, security planning, systems audit, physical security, logical security, access control, penetration testing, firewalls, and encryption.

Sysman Computers (P) Ltd.

Suite # 7, Habib Terrace, Dr. Ambedkar Road, Lalbaug,

Post Box 6023 Mumbai, India 400 012

Phone: +91-22-470-1122 Fax: +91-22-417-6207

Email: info@sysman.org

URL: http://www.sysman.org/

Sytex, Inc. (U.S.A.)

Sytex claims that the FBI is among the clients taking its hands-on network security and intrusion detection/response training. Other services include firewalls and virtual private networks, computer forensics, covert communications, and security software development.

Sytex, Inc.

22 Bailiwick Office Campus

Doylestown, PA 18901-2466

Phone: 215-348-3395

FAX: 215-348-5512

Email: webmaster@spops.sytexinc.com

URL: http://www.sytexinc.com

tec-gate.com (U.S.A.)

tec-gate.com is a consulting and technology solutions firm specializing in information security.

tec-gate.com

5001 Lincoln Drive West

Suite E

Marlton, NJ 08053

Phone: 856-797-6758

Fax: 856-797-6788

Email: info@tec-gate.com

URL: http://www.tec-gate.com

Triumph Technologies, Inc. (U.S.A.)

Triumph Technologies' Internet Security Division provides enterprise wide security services that include turn-key firewall solutions (UNIX/Windows NT), security assessments, IP addressing re/designing, and integration of specialized products, such as SMTP mail content management.

Triumph Technologies, Inc.

130 New Boston Street

Woburn, MA 01801

Phone: 781-994-3000

Fax: 781-994-3010

Email: info@ triumph.com

URL: http://www.triumph.com

Utimaco SafeWare AG(Worldwide)

Utimaco SafeWare AG provides many services, including virtual private network software for Windows 95, Windows NT, and Solaris; and strong European implementation of Crypto algorithms; and GSS authentication.

Utimaco SafeWare AG

D-61440 Oberursel near Frankfurt a.M.

Germany

Phone: + 49 (61 71) 9 17-0

Email: `info.de@utimaco.de`

URL: `http://www.utimaco.de`

Verio (U.S.A.)

Verio manages firewall services (UNIX and Windows NT), vulnerability assessment, security incident response, virtual private networking, and security awareness training.

Verio

Phone: 800-438-8374

Email: `consulting@verio.net`

URL: `http://www.nwnet.net/`

Visionary Corporate Computing Concepts (U.S.A.)

Visionary offers UNIX and firewall solutions, along with research and penetration testing, risk assessments, intrusion detection, remote system monitoring, emergency problem handling, consulting, and outsourcing.

Visionary Corporate Computing Concepts

1509 Lady Street

Columbia, SC 29201

Phone: 803-733-7333

Fax: 803-733-5888

Email: `info@vc3.com`

URL: `http://www.vc3.com`

VoteHere.net (U.S.A.)

VoteHere.net's Platinum Election System, the online voting system designed for public elections, might be the solution to the voting problems that occurred in the 2000 U.S. presidential election.

VoteHere.net
3101 Northup Way Suite 250
Bellevue, WA 98004
Voice: 425-739-2509
Phone: 888-45-SOUND
Fax: 206-329-4351
Email: info@votehere.net
URL: http://www.votehere.net

WatchGuard Technologies, Inc. (U.S.A.)

The WatchGuard Security System delivers advanced, next-generation network security with the ease of a plug-in appliance. WatchGuard calls its Firebox II platform "scalable with high-performance features for large networks, managed security services, and electronic policy distribution."

WatchGuard Technologies, Inc.
505 Fifth Avenue S. Suite 500
Seattle, WA 98104
Contact: Frances Bigley, PR Manager
Phone: 206-521-8340
FAX: 206-521-8341
Email: information@watchgaurd.com
URL: http://www.watchguard.com

D

SECURITY
CONSULTANTS

WorldCom (U.K.)

WorldCom/UUNET has developed a range of security services specifically designed to help clients use the Internet "safely and with confidence."

WorldCom
14 Grays Inn Road
London, WC1X 8HN, U.K.
Phone: +44 (0) 20 7675 5000
FAX: +44 (0) 20 7675 5711
URL: http://www.wcom.co.uk

Vendor Information and Security Standards

IN THIS APPENDIX

This appendix explains how to obtain security information from particular vendors. It also provides an annotated list of available Internet standards, known as Request for Comments (RFC) documents, that address security.

Vendor Security Information

Instead of an out-of-date list of vendor security bulletins, in this section, you will learn how to obtain the vendors' current lists of security bulletins and patches.

Any good system administrator will regularly check the security sites of the products he has or get on their security mailing lists.

Hewlett-Packard

Hewlett-Packard provides a great deal of security information. You must log in to their site to access it. The main page is `http://us-support2.external.hp.com/common/bin/doc.pl/`. Select Technical Knowledge Base after logging in.

You will see search bulletins and patches for HP-UX and MPE. HP-UX is HP's version of UNIX. MPE is an old minicomputer operating system from HP.

On HP's patch page, the best thing to do is to pick your series and OS version. Then change the box that says Search by Keyword to Browser Patch List.

For security bulletins, I recommend ignoring the links at the top of the page that only let you search the bulletins and instead find the Security Bulletin Archive. At the time of this writing, this link is at the very bottom of the page and in small print.

IBM

Unfortunately, IBM does not seem to have a good single spot for security and security patch information. What security information they have is scattered all over their Web sites.

IBM's main security page is `http://www.ibm.com/security`. This page is focused on security news and products. The library link on this page will take you to good information about security.

The main product support page is `http://www.ibm.com/support/prodsupp.html`. Each product group has its own Web page, and there is little consistency to the information by product. However, if you need security information by product, you should start at this point.

IBM's download page (`http://www.ibm.com/download`) lets you download security products, but does not focus on security patches.

IBM's Lotus division has a page known as IT Central Security Zone. It is a well-focused page covering security with the Lotus products and can be found at `http://www.lotus.com/security`.

Linux

Many Linux distributions are available, and this section presents information on security sources for some of the major distributions.

Caldera

Caldera's security advisories page is located at `http://www.calderasystems.com/support/security/`. Caldera appears to have more security advisories than any other Linux distribution. This does not mean that their Linux is any less secure. In fact, the opposite is probably true. Each security advisory tells you the packages you need to download to fix a particular security problem.

Debian

Debian does something unusual among vendors; they provide security alerts from their main Web site. On `http://www.debian.org/`, you can scroll to the bottom of the page, and the security alerts are right there. Each security alert has links to software that needs to be downloaded to patch your system.

Red Hat

Red Hat's setup for security information is as good, if not better, than that of most of the big established companies. The main support page for Red Hat is `http://www.redhat.com/apps/support/`. From this page, you can select your OS version. Under each of the version-specific pages, you will find a link to the security advisories for that version. Each security advisory has links to the new version of software that has the bugs fixed.

Red Hat has something you would never see from the major OS vendors. You can search their bug database at `http://bugzilla.redhat.com/bugzilla/` and see the currently open security bugs. From this page, click on Query existing bug reports.

You can select a particular product. If you don't, you'll get information on them all. In the status list box, you might want to add additional status information. In the summary field, you might want to put the word security. Then click Submit Query and you'll get back a list of bugs.

SuSE

SuSE is a German Linux distribution. The main security page for this Linux distribution is `http://www.suse.com/us/support/security/index.html`. From here, you can find all the security advisories. Each security advisory lists what needs to be downloaded to fix your system.

SuSE has a couple of useful mailing lists. `suse-security@suse.com` is for general security discussion. You can subscribe by sending email to `suse-security-subscribe@suse.com`. If you just want to get security announcements, send email to `suse-security-announce-subscribe@suse.com`.

Microsoft

There are many opinions on whether Microsoft does a good job of keeping on top of security issues. However, one thing you cannot fault them for is a shortage of security information on their Web site. The main security page is `http://www.microsoft.com/security/`.

From the main security page, you will find bulletins, best practices, tools, checklists, and articles. What Microsoft calls bulletins are really documents talking about patches they have out. To find out about other security issues, you need to go to a different part of their Web site—the Knowledge Base.

The Microsoft Knowledge Base is full of information on their products including security issues. The main search page for the Knowledge Base is `http://search.support.microsoft.com/kb/c.asp?ln=en-us`. Pick the product you want to find security issues about. Many searches will result in security-related articles. I recommend a simple search on just the word "security" to get started. You'll get back all kinds of security articles.

Another useful resource on Microsoft's site is TechNet, available at `http://www.microsoft.com/TechNet`. Whereas Knowledge Base is a search into a database, TechNet is more article based including many articles about security.

Sun Microsystems

Sun Microsystems has a separate Web site for their security info called SunSolve (`http://sunsolve.sun.com`). Sun takes security seriously on their site. You will find a link on the main page taking you to the security patch cluster so you can grab all the security patches for your version of Solaris as one file.

You will also see links to the latest security bulletin as well as an archive of security bulletins. These are good reading for understanding security issues related to Sun systems and Java.

You can contact Sun with security alerts by emailing `security-alert@sun.com` if you think you have discovered a new security problem. They also have a PGP key available on their Web site to use to encrypt communication with them. You can find instructions on the Sun site on how to regularly receive the Sun Bulletins via email.

RFC Documents Relevant to Security

The following list of security-related RFC documents and their locations is arranged in chronological order from the earliest to the most recently published.

RFC 912. Authentication Service. M. St. Johns. September 1984. (Discusses automated authentication of users, for example, in an FTP session.) Location: `http://info.internet.isi.edu:80/in-notes/rfc/files/rfc912.txt`

RFC 931. Authentication Server. M. St. Johns. January 1985. (Further discussion on automated authentication of users.) Location: `http://info.internet.isi.edu:80/in-notes/rfc/files/rfc931.txt`

RFC 1004. A Distributed-Protocol Authentication Scheme. D. L. Mills. April 1987. (Discusses access control and authentication procedures in distributed environments and services.) Location: `http://info.internet.isi.edu:80/in-notes/rfc/files/rfc1004.txt`

RFC 1038. Draft Revised IP Security Option. M. St. Johns. January 1988. (Discusses protection of datagrams and classifications of such protection.) Location: `http://info.internet.isi.edu:80/in-notes/rfc/files/rfc1038.txt`

RFC 1040. Privacy Enhancement for Internet Electronic Mail: Part I: Message Encipherment and Authentication Procedures. J. Linn. January 1988. (Discusses encryption and authentication for electronic mail.) Location: `http://info.internet.isi.edu:80/in-notes/rfc/files/rfc1040.txt`

RFC 1108. Security Options for the Internet Protocol. S. Kent. November 1991. (Discusses extended security options in the Internet protocol and DoD guidelines.) Location: `http://info.internet.isi.edu:80/in-notes/rfc/files/rfc1108.txt`

RFC 1113. Privacy Enhancement for Internet Electronic Mail: Part I: Message Encipherment and Authentication Procedures. J. Linn. August 1989. (Supersedes RFC 1040.) Location: `http://info.internet.isi.edu:80/in-notes/rfc/files/rfc1113.txt`

RFC 1114. Privacy Enhancement for Internet Electronic Mail: Part II: Certificate-Based Key Management. S.T. Kent and J. Linn. August 1989. (Defines privacy enhancement mechanisms for electronic mail.) Location: `http://info.internet.isi.edu:80/in-notes/rfc/files/rfc1114.txt`

RFC 1115. Privacy Enhancement for Internet Electronic Mail: Part III: Algorithms, Modes, and Identifiers. J. Linn. August 1989. (Technical and informational support to RFCs 1113 and 1114.) Location: `http://info.internet.isi.edu:80/in-notes/rfc/files/rfc1115.txt`

RFC 1135. The Helminthiasis of the Internet. J. Reynolds. December 1989. (Famous RFC that describes the worm incident of November 1988.) Location: `http://info.internet.isi.edu:80/in-notes/rfc/files/rfc1135.txt`

RFC 1170. Public Key Standards and Licenses. R. Fougner. January 1991. (Announcement of patents filed on Public Key Partners sublicense for digital signatures.) Location: `http://info.internet.isi.edu:80/in-notes/rfc/files/rfc1170.txt`

RFC 1186. The MD4 Message Digest Algorithm. R. Rivest. October 1990. (The specification of MD4.) Location: `http://info.internet.isi.edu:80/in-notes/rfc/files/rfc1186.txt`

RFC 1244. The Site Security Handbook. P. Holbrook and J. Reynolds. July 1991. (Famous RFC that lays out security practices and procedures. This RFC was an authoritative document for a long time. It is still pretty good and applies even today.) Location: `http://info.internet.isi.edu:80/in-notes/rfc/files/rfc1244.txt`

RFC 1272. Internet Accounting. C. Mills, D. Hirsh, and G. Ruth. November 1991. (Specifies system for accounting—network usage, traffic, and such.) Location: `http://info.internet.isi.edu:80/in-notes/rfc/files/rfc1272.txt`

RFC 1281. Guidelines for the Secure Operation of the Internet. R. D. Pethia, S. Crocker, and B. Y. Fraser. November 1991. (Celebrated document that sets forth guidelines for security.) Location: `http://info.internet.isi.edu:80/in-notes/rfc/files/rfc1281.txt`

RFC 1319. The MD2 Message-Digest Algorithm. B. Kaliski. April 1992. (Description of MD2 and how it works.) Location: `http://info.internet.isi.edu:80/in-notes/rfc/files/rfc1319.txt`

RFC 1320. The MD4 Message-Digest Algorithm. R. Rivest. April 1992. (Description of MD4 and how it works.) Location: `http://info.internet.isi.edu:80/in-notes/rfc/files/rfc1320.txt`

RFC 1321. The MD5 Message-Digest Algorithm. R. Rivest. April 1992. (Description of MD5 and how it works.) Location: `http://info.internet.isi.edu:80/in-notes/rfc/files/rfc1321.txt`

RFC 1334. PPP Authentication Protocols. B. Lloyd and W. Simpson. October 1992. (Defines the Password Authentication Protocol and the Challenge-Handshake Authentication Protocol in PPP.) Location: `http://info.internet.isi.edu:80/in-notes/rfc/files/rfc1334.txt`

RFC 1352. SNMP Security Protocols. J. Galvin, K. McCloghrie, and J. Davin. July 1992. (Simple Network Management Protocol security mechanisms.) Location: `http://info.internet.isi.edu:80/in-notes/rfc/files/rfc1352.txt`

RFC 1355. Privacy and Accuracy Issues in Network Information Center Databases. J. Curran and A. Marine. August 1992. (Network Information Center operation and administration guidelines.) Location: `http://info.internet.isi.edu:80/in-notes/rfc/files/rfc1355.txt`

RFC 1409. Telnet Authentication Option. D. Borman. January 1993. (Experimental protocol for Telnet authentication.) Location: `http://info.internet.isi.edu:80/in-notes/rfc/files/rfc1409.txt`

RFC 1411. Telnet Authentication: Kerberos Version 4. D. Borman. January 1993. (Weaving Kerberos authentication into Telnet.) Location: `http://info.internet.isi.edu:80/in-notes/rfc/files/rfc1411.txt`

RFC 1412. Telnet Authentication: SPX. K. Alagappan. January 1993. (Experimental protocol for Telnet authentication.) Location: `http://info.internet.isi.edu:80/in-notes/rfc/files/rfc1412.txt`

RFC 1413. Identification Protocol. M. St. Johns. February 1993. (Introduction and explanation of IDENT protocol.) Location: `http://info.internet.isi.edu:80/in-notes/rfc/files/rfc1413.txt`

RFC 1414. Identification MIB. M. St. Johns and M. Rose. February 1993. (Specifies MIB for identifying owners of TCP connections.) Location: `http://info.internet.isi.edu:80/in-notes/rfc/files/rfc1414.txt`

RFC 1416. Telnet Authentication Option. D. Borman. February 1993. (Supersedes RFC 1409.) Location: `http://info.internet.isi.edu:80/in-notes/rfc/files/rfc1416.txt`

RFC 1421. Privacy Enhancement for Internet Electronic Mail: Part I: Message Encryption and Authentication Procedures. J. Linn. February 1993. (Updates and supersedes RFC 1113.) Location: `http://info.internet.isi.edu:80/in-notes/rfc/files/rfc1421.txt`.

RFC 1422. Privacy Enhancement for Internet Electronic Mail: Part II: Certificate-Based Key Management. S. T. Kent and J. Linn. February 1993. (Updates and supersedes RFC 1114.) Location: `http://info.internet.isi.edu:80/in-notes/rfc/files/rfc1422.txt`

RFC 1438. Internet Engineering Task Force Statements Of Boredom (SOBs). Chapin and Huitema. April 1993. (Not really a security-related RFC, but so classic that I simply couldn't leave it out. Check it out for yourself. Clearly, the funniest RFC ever written.) Location: `http://info.internet.isi.edu:80/in-notes/rfc/files/rfc1438.txt`

RFC 1446. Security Protocols for Version 2 of the Simple Network Management Protocol. J. Galvin and K. McCloghrie. April 1993. (Specifies Security Protocols for SNMPv2.) Location: `http://info.internet.isi.edu:80/in-notes/rfc/files/rfc1446.txt`

RFC 1455. Physical Link Security Type of Service. D. Eastlake. May 1993. (Experimental protocol to provide physical link security.) Location: `http://info.internet.isi.edu:80/in-notes/rfc/files/rfc1455.txt`

RFC 1457. Security Label Framework for the Internet. R. Housley. May 1993. (Presents a label framework for network engineers to adhere to.) Location: `http://info.internet.isi.edu:80/in-notes/rfc/files/rfc1457.txt`

RFC 1472. The Definitions of Managed Objects for the Security Protocols of the Point-to-Point Protocol. F. Kastenholz. June 1993. (Security Protocols on subnetwork interfaces using PPP.) Location: `http://info.internet.isi.edu:80/in-notes/rfc/files/rfc1472.txt`

E

VENDOR INFORMATION AND SECURITY STANDARDS

RFC 1492. An Access Control Protocol, Sometimes Called TACACS. C. Finseth. July 1993. (Documents the extended TACACS protocol use by the Cisco Systems terminal servers.) Location: `http://info.internet.isi.edu:80/in-notes/rfc/files/rfc1492.txt`.

RFC 1507. DASS—Distributed Authentication Security Service. C. Kaufman. September 1993. (Discusses new proposed methods of authentication in distributed environments.) Location: `http://info.internet.isi.edu:80/in-notes/rfc/files/rfc1507.txt`

RFC 1508. Generic Security Service Application Program Interface. J. Linn. September 1993. (Specifies a generic security framework for use in source-level porting of applications to different environments.) Location: `http://info.internet.isi.edu:80/in-notes/rfc/files/rfc1508.txt`

RFC 1510. The Kerberos Network Authentication Service (V5). J. Kohl and C. Neumann. September 1993. (An overview of Kerberos 5.) Location: `http://info.internet.isi.edu:80/in-notes/rfc/files/rfc1510.txt`

RFC 1511. Common Authentication Technology Overview. J. Linn. September 1993. (Administrative.) Location: `http://info.internet.isi.edu:80/in-notes/rfc/files/rfc1511.txt`

RFC 1535. A Security Problem and Proposed Correction with Widely Deployed DNS Software. E. Gavron. October 1993. (Discusses flaws in some DNS clients and means of dealing with them.) Location: `http://info.internet.isi.edu:80/in-notes/rfc/files/rfc1535.txt`

RFC 1544. The Content-MD5 Header Field. M. Rose. November 1993. (Discusses the use of optional header field, Content-MD5, for use with MIME-conformant messages.) Location: `http://info.internet.isi.edu:80/in-notes/rfc/files/rfc1544.txt`

RFC 1675. Security Concerns for IPNG. S. Bellovin. August 1994. (Bellovin expresses concerns over lack of direct access to source addresses in IPNG.) Location: `http://info.internet.isi.edu:80/in-notes/rfc/files/rfc1675.txt`

RFC 1704. On Internet Authentication. N. Haller and R. Atkinson. October 1994. (Treats a wide range of Internet authentication procedures and approaches.) Location: `http://info.internet.isi.edu:80/in-notes/rfc/files/rfc1704.txt`

RFC 1731. IMAP4 Authentication Mechanisms. J. Myers. December 1994. (Internet Message Access Protocol authentication issues.) Location: `http://info.internet.isi.edu:80/in-notes/rfc/files/rfc1731.txt`

RFC 1750. Randomness Recommendations for Security. D. Eastlake, III, S. Crocker, and J. Schiller. December 1994. (Extensive discussion of the difficulties surrounding deriving truly random values for key generation.) Location: `http://info.internet.isi.edu:80/in-notes/rfc/files/rfc1750.txt`

RFC 1751. A Convention for Human-Readable 128-Bit Keys. D. McDonald. December 1994. (Proposed solutions for using 128-bit keys, which are hard to remember because of their length.) Location: `http://info.internet.isi.edu:80/in-notes/rfc/files/rfc1751.txt`

RFC 1760. The S/KEY One-Time Password System. N. Haller. February 1995. (Describes Bellcore's S/Key OTP system.) Location: `http://info.internet.isi.edu:80/in-notes/rfc/files/rfc1760.txt`

RFC 1810. Report on MD5 Performance. J. Touch. June 1995. (Discusses deficiencies of MD5 when viewed against the rates of T1 high-speed networks.) Location: `http://info.internet.isi.edu:80/in-notes/rfc/files/rfc1810.txt`

RFC 1824. The Exponential Security System TESS: An Identity-Based Cryptographic Protocol for Authenticated Key-Exchange. H. Danisch. August 1995. (Discussion of proposed protocol for key exchange, authentication, and generation of signatures.) Location: `http://info.internet.isi.edu:80/in-notes/rfc/files/rfc1824.txt`

RFC 1827. IP Encapsulating Security Payload. R. Atkinson. August 1995. (Discusses methods of providing integrity and confidentiality to IP datagrams.) Location: `http://info.internet.isi.edu:80/in-notes/rfc/files/rfc1827.txt`

RFC 1828. IP Authentication Using Keyed MD5. P. Metzger and W. Simpson. August 1995. (Discusses the use of keyed MD5 with the IP Authentication Header.) Location: `http://info.internet.isi.edu:80/in-notes/rfc/files/rfc1828.txt`

RFC 1847. Security Multiparts for MIME: Multipart/Signed and Multipart/Encrypted. J. Galvin, S. Murphy, S. Crocker, and N. Freed. October 1995. (Discusses a means of providing security services in MIME body parts.) Location: `http://info.internet.isi.edu:80/in-notes/rfc/files/rfc1847.txt`

RFC 1848. MIME Object Security Services. S. Crocker, N. Freed, J. Galvin, and S. Murphy. October 1995. (Discusses protocol for applying digital signature and encryption services to MIME objects.) Location: `http://info.internet.isi.edu:80/in-notes/rfc/files/rfc1848.txt`

RFC 1852. IP Authentication Using Keyed SHA. P. Metzger and W. Simpson. September 1995. (Discusses the use of keys with the Secure Hash Algorithm to ensure datagram integrity.) Location: `http://info.internet.isi.edu:80/in-notes/rfc/files/rfc1852.txt`

RFC 1853. IP in IP Tunneling. W. Simpson. October 1995. (Discusses methods of using IP payload encapsulation for tunneling with IP.) Location: `http://info.internet.isi.edu:80/in-notes/rfc/files/rfc1853.txt`

RFC 1858. Security Considerations for IP Fragment Filtering. G. Ziemba, D. Reed, P. Traina. October 1995. (Discusses IP Fragment Filtering and the dangers inherent in fragmentation attacks.) Location: `http://info.internet.isi.edu:80/in-notes/rfc/files/rfc1858.txt`

RFC 1910. User-Based Security Model for SNMPv2. G. Waters. February 1996. (Discussion of application of security features to SNMP.) Location: `http://info.internet.isi.edu:80/in-notes/rfc/files/rfc1910.txt`

RFC 1928. SOCKS Protocol Version 5. M. Leech. March 1996. (Discussion of the SOCKS protocol and its use to secure TCP and UDP traffic.) Location: `http://info.internet.isi.edu:80/in-notes/rfc/files/rfc1928.txt`

RFC 1929. Username/Password Authentication for SOCKS V5. M. Leech. March 1996. (Discussion of SOCKS authentication.) Location: `http://info.internet.isi.edu:80/in-notes/rfc/files/rfc1929.txt`

RFC 1948. Defending Against Sequence Number Attacks. S. Bellovin. May 1996. (Discussion of IP spoofing and TCP sequence number guessing attacks.) Location: `http://info.internet.isi.edu:80/in-notes/rfc/files/rfc1948.txt`

RFC 1968. The PPP Encryption Control Protocol. G. Meyer. June 1996. (Discusses negotiating encryption over PPP.) Location: `http://info.internet.isi.edu:80/in-notes/rfc/files/rfc1968.txt`

RFC 1969. The PPP DES Encryption Protocol. K. Sklower and G. Meyer. June. 1996. (Discusses utilizing the Data Encryption Standard with PPP.) Location: `http://info.internet.isi.edu:80/in-notes/rfc/files/rfc1969.txt`

RFC 1991: PGP Message Exchange Formats. D. Atkins, W. Stallings, and P. Zimmermann. August 1996. (Adding PGP to message exchanges.) Location: `http://info.internet.isi.edu:80/in-notes/rfc/files/rfc1991.txt`

RFC 2015. MIME Security with Pretty Good Privacy (PGP). M. Elkins. October 1996. (Privacy and authentication using the Multipurpose Internet Mail Extensions with PGP.) Location: `http://info.internet.isi.edu:80/in-notes/rfc/files/rfc2015.txt`

RFC 2040. The RC5, RC5-CBC, RC5-CBC-Pad, and RC5-CTS Algorithms. R. Baldwin and R. Rivest. October 1996. (Defines all four ciphers in great detail.) Location: `http://info.internet.isi.edu:80/in-notes/rfc/files/rfc2040.txt`

RFC 2057. Source Directed Access Control on the Internet. S. Bradner. November 1996. (Discusses possible avenues of filtering; an answer to the CDA.) Location: `http://info.internet.isi.edu:80/in-notes/rfc/files/rfc2057.txt`

RFC 2065. Domain Name System Security Extensions. D. Eastlake, III and C. Kaufman. January 1997. (Adding more security to the DNS system.) Location: `http://info.internet.isi.edu:80/in-notes/rfc/files/rfc2065.txt`

RFC 2069. An Extension to HTTP: Digest Access Authentication. J. Franks, P. Hallam-Baker, J. Hostetler, P. Leach, A. Luotonen, E. Sink, and L. Stewart. January 1997. (Advanced authentication for HTTP.) Location: `http://info.internet.isi.edu:80/in-notes/rfc/files/rfc2069.txt`

RFC 2084. Considerations for Web Transaction Security. G. Bossert, S. Cooper, and W. Drummond. January 1997. (Bringing confidentiality, authentication, and integrity to data sent via HTTP.) Location: `http://info.internet.isi.edu:80/in-notes/rfc/files/rfc2084.txt`

RFC 2085. HMAC-MD5 IP Authentication with Replay Prevention. M. Oehler and R. Glenn. February 1997. (Keyed-MD5 coupled with the IP Authentication Header.) Location: `http://info.internet.isi.edu:80/in-notes/rfc/files/rfc2085.txt`

RFC 2137. Secure Domain Name System Dynamic Update. D. Eastlake, III. April 1997. (Describes use of digital signatures in DNS updates to enhance overall security of the DNS system.) Location: `http://info.internet.isi.edu:80/in-notes/rfc/files/rfc2137.txt`

RFC 2144. The CAST-128 Encryption Algorithm. C. Adams. May 1997. (Description of 128-bit algorithm that can be used in authentication over network lines.) Location: `http://info.internet.isi.edu:80/in-notes/rfc/files/rfc2144.txt`

RFC 2179. Network Security for Trade Shows. A. Gwinn. July 1997. (Document that addresses attacks that occur at trade shows and how to avoid them.) Location: `http://info.internet.isi.edu:80/in-notes/rfc/files/rfc2179.txt`

RFC 2196. Site Security Handbook. B. Fraser, Editor. September 1997. (Updates 1244. Yet another version of the already useful document.) Location: `http://info.internet.isi.edu:80/in-notes/rfc/files/rfc2196.txt`

RFC 2222. Simple Authentication and Security Layer. J. Myers. October 1997. (Describes a method for adding authentication support to connection-based protocols.) Location: `http://info.internet.isi.edu:80/in-notes/rfc/files/rfc2222.txt`

RFC 2228. FTP Security Extensions. M. Horowitz and S. Lunt. October 1997. (Extending the security capabilities of FTP.) Location: `http://info.internet.isi.edu:80/in-notes/rfc/files/rfc2228.txt`

RFC 2230. Key Exchange Delegation Record for the DNS. R. Atkinson. November 1997. (Secure DNS and the exchanges made during a session.) Location: `http://info.internet.isi.edu:80/in-notes/rfc/files/rfc2230.txt`

RFC 2245. Anonymous SASL Mechanism. C. Newman. November 1997. (New methods of authentication in anonymous services without using the now forbidden plaintext passwords traditionally associated with such services.) Location: `http://info.internet.isi.edu:80/in-notes/rfc/files/rfc2245.txt`

RFC 2246. The TLS Protocol Version 1.0. T. Dierks. January 1999. (Describes a way to use Transport Layer Security to secure communications.) Location: `http://www.ietf.org/rfc/rfc2246.txt`

RFC 2268. A Description of the RC2(r) Encryption Algorithm. R. Rivest. January 1998. (Describes an encryption algorithm.) `http://www.ietf.org/rfc/rfc2268.txt`

RFC 2284. PPP Extensible Authentication Protocol (EAP). L. Blunk, J. Vollbrecht. March 1998. (Describes an authentication protocol for PPP.) `http://www.ietf.org/rfc/rfc2284.txt`

RFC 2289. A One-Time Password System. N. Haller, C. Metz, P. Nesser, M. Straw. February 1998. (Describes a scheme where passwords are used only once.) `http://www.ietf.org/rfc/rfc2289.txt`

RFC 2311. S/MIME Version 2 Message Specification. S. Dusse, P. Hoffman, B. Ramsdell, L. Lundblade, L. Repka. March 1998. `http://www.ietf.org/rfc/rfc2311.txt`

RFC 2312. S/MIME Version 2 Certificate Handling. S. Dusse, P. Hoffman, B. Ramsdell, J. Weinstein. March 1998. `http://www.ietf.org/rfc/rfc2312.txt`

RFC 2315. PKCS 7: Cryptographic Message Syntax Version 1.5. B. Kaliski. March 1998. (Describes the message format used in PKCS 7.) `http://www.ietf.org/rfc/rfc2315.txt`

RFC 2316. Report of the IAB Security Architecture Workshop. S. Bellovin. April 1998. (A trip report of a security workshop by the Internet Architecture Board.) `http://www.ietf.org/rfc/rfc2316.txt`

RFC 2350. Expectations for Computer Security Incident Response. N. Brownlee, E. Guttman. June 1998. (A best practices document covering dealing with security incidents.) `http://www.ietf.org/rfc/rfc2350.txt`

RFC 2356. Sun's SKIP Firewall Traversal for Mobile IP. G. Montenegro, V. Gupta. June 1998. (Describes how a device with a mobile IP address acquires access through a SKIP firewall.) `http://www.ietf.org/rfc/rfc2356.txt`

RFC 2367. PF_KEY Key Management API, Version 2. D. McDonald, C. Metz, B. Phan. July 1998. (Describes a generic key management API.) `http://www.ietf.org/rfc/rfc2367.txt`

RFC 2385. Protection of BGP Sessions via the TCP MD5 Signature Option. A. Heffernan. August 1998. (Describes an extension to TCP to secure BGP sessions.) `http://www.ietf.org/rfc/rfc2385.txt`

RFC 2401. Security Architecture for the Internet Protocol. S. Kent, R. Atkinson. November 1998. (Describes the architectural baseline for IPsec implementations.) `http://www.ietf.org/rfc/rfc2401.txt`

RFC 2402. IP Authentication Header. S. Kent, R. Atkinson. November 1998. (Describes a mechanism for authentication of IP datagrams.) `http://www.ietf.org/rfc/rfc2402.txt`

RFC 2403. The Use of HMAC-MD5-96 within ESP and AH. C. Madson, R. Glenn. November 1998. (Describes the combined use of the HMAC and MD5 algorithms as an authentication header in IPsec.) `http://www.ietf.org/rfc/rfc2403.txt`

RFC 2404. The Use of HMAC-SHA-1-96 within ESP and AH. C. Madson, R. Glenn. November 1998. (Describes the combined use of the HMAC and MD5 algorithms as an authentication header in IPsec.) `http://www.ietf.org/rfc/rfc2404.txt`

RFC 2405. The ESP DES-CBC Cipher Algorithm with Explicit IV. C. Madson, N. Doraswamy. November 1998. (Describes a confidentiality mechanism for IPsec.) `http://www.ietf.org/rfc/rfc2405.txt`

RFC 2406. IP Encapsulating Security Payload (ESP). S. Kent, R. Atkinson. November 1998. (Describes the Encapsulating Security Payload of IPsec, which provides security services.) `http://www.ietf.org/rfc/rfc2406.txt`

RFC 2407. The Internet IP Security Domain of Interpretation for ISAKMP. D. Piper. November 1998. (Describes a mapping from ISAKMP to the Internet security domain.) `http://www.ietf.org/rfc/rfc2407.txt`

RFC 2408. Internet Security Association and Key Management Protocol (ISAKMP). D. Maughan, M. Schertler, M. Schneider, J. Turner. November 1998. (Describes a protocol for establishing security associations and keys.) `http://www.ietf.org/rfc/rfc2408.txt`

RFC 2409. The Internet Key Exchange (IKE). D. Harkins, D. Carrel. November 1998. (Describes a key exchange method for the Internet.) `http://www.ietf.org/rfc/rfc2409.txt`

RFC 2410. The NULL Encryption Algorithm and Its Use with IPsec. R. Glenn, S. Kent. November 1998. (Describes the way to send data with IPsec without encryption.) `http://www.ietf.org/rfc/rfc2410.txt`

RFC 2411. IP Security Document Roadmap. R. Thayer, N. Doraswamy, R. Glenn. November 1998. (Discusses how IPsec-related specifications should be developed.) `http://www.ietf.org/rfc/rfc2411.txt`

RFC 2412. The OAKLEY Key Determination Protocol. H. Orman. November 1998. (Describes a protocol for parties to agree on a key.) `http://www.ietf.org/rfc/rfc2412.txt`

E

VENDOR INFORMATION AND SECURITY STANDARDS

RFC 2419. The PPP DES Encryption Protocol, Version 2 (DESE-bis). K. Sklower, G. Meyer. September 1998. (Describes how to use DES encryption over a PPP link.) `http://www.ietf.org/rfc/rfc2419.txt`

RFC 2420. The PPP Triple-DES Encryption Protocol (3DESE). H. Kummert. September 1998. (Describes how to use Triple-DES encryption over a PPP link.) `http://www.ietf.org/rfc/rfc2420.txt`

RFC 2433. Microsoft PPP CHAP Extensions. G. Zorn, S. Cobb. October 1998. (Describes Microsoft PPP authentication protocol.) `http://www.ietf.org/rfc/rfc2433.txt`

RFC 2437. PKCS #1: RSA Cryptography Specifications Version 2.0. B. Kaliski, J. Staddon. October 1998. (Makes recommendations of how to implement public-key cryptography based on the RSA algorithm.) `http://www.ietf.org/rfc/rfc2437.txt`

RFC 2440. OpenPGP Message Format. J. Callas, L. Donnerhacke, H. Finney, R. Thayer. November 1998. (Describes the message format used by the OpenPGP email system.) `http://www.ietf.org/rfc/rfc2440.txt`

RFC 2444. The One-Time-Password SASL Mechanism. C. Newman. October 1998. (Describes an authentication mechanism.) `http://www.ietf.org/rfc/rfc2444.txt`

RFC 2451. The ESP CBC-Mode Cipher Algorithms. R. Pereira, R. Adams. November 1998. (Describes how to use the CBC-Mode Cipher algorithms with IPsec.) `http://www.ietf.org/rfc/rfc2451.txt`

RFC 2459. Internet X.509 Public Key Infrastructure Certificate and CRL Profile. R. Housley, W. Ford, W. Polk, D. Solo. January 1999. (Gives an overview of the format of X.509 v3 certificates and X.509 v2 certification revocation lists.) `http://www.ietf.org/rfc/rfc2459.txt`

RFC 2504. Users' Security Handbook. Guttman, L. Leong, G. Malkin. February 1999. (A security handbook for the end user.) `http://www.ietf.org/rfc/rfc2504.txt`

RFC 2510. Internet X.509 Public Key Infrastructure Certificate Management Protocols. C. Adams, S. Farrell. March 1999. (Describes the protocols used for certificate management.) `http://www.ietf.org/rfc/rfc2510.txt`

RFC 2511. Internet X.509 Certificate Request Message Format. M. Myers, C. Adams, D. Solo, D. Kemp. March 1999. (Describes the Certificate Request Message Format [CRMF], used to convey a request for a certificate to a Certification Authority [CA].) `http://www.ietf.org/rfc/rfc2511.txt`

RFC 2521. ICMP Security Failures Messages. P. Karn, W. Simpson. March 1999. (Specifies ICMP messages for indicating failures when using IP Security Protocols.) `http://www.ietf.org/rfc/rfc2521.txt`

RFC 2522. Photuris: Session-Key Management Protocol. P. Karn, W. Simpson. March 1999. (Describes an experimental session-key management protocol.) `http://www.ietf.org/rfc/rfc2522.txt`

RFC 2523. Photuris: Extended Schemes and Attributes. P. Karn, W. Simpson. March 1999. (Describes extensions to Photuris.) `http://www.ietf.org/rfc/rfc2523.txt`

RFC 2527. Internet X.509 Public Key Infrastructure Certificate Policy and Certification Practices Framework. S. Chokhani, W. Ford. March 1999. (Presents a framework to be used in writing certificate policies of practices.) `http://www.ietf.org/rfc/rfc2527.txt`

RFC 2528. Internet X.509 Public Key Infrastructure Representation of Key Exchange Algorithm (KEA) Keys in Internet X.509 Public Key Infrastructure Certificates. R. Housley, W. Polk. March 1999. (Specifies fields to be used in X.509 v3 for KEA keys.) `http://www.ietf.org/rfc/rfc2528.txt`

RFC 2535. Domain Name System Security Extensions. D. Eastlake. March 1999. (Specifies extensions to DNS that validate data integrity and authentication.) `http://www.ietf.org/rfc/rfc2535.txt`

RFC 2536. DSA KEYs and SIGs in the Domain Name System (DNS). D. Eastlake. March 1999. (Describes storing Digital Signature Algorithm information in DNS.) `http://www.ietf.org/rfc/rfc2536.txt`

RFC 2537. RSA/MD5 KEYs and SIGs in the Domain Name System (DNS). D. Eastlake. March 1999. (Describes storing RSA and MD5 information in DNS.) `http://www.ietf.org/rfc/rfc2537.txt`

RFC 2538. Storing Certificates in the Domain Name System (DNS). D. Eastlake, O. Gudmundsson. March 1999. (Describes how to store digital certificates in DNS.) `http://www.ietf.org/rfc/rfc2538.txt`

RFC 2541. DNS Security Operational Considerations. D. Eastlake. March 1999. (Describes considerations for the storage of certificates and keys in DNS.) `http://www.ietf.org/rfc/rfc2541.txt`

RFC 2548. Microsoft Vendor-specific RADIUS Attributes. G. Zorn. March 1999. (Describes RADIUS attributes that apply to Microsoft systems.) `http://www.ietf.org/rfc/rfc2548.txt`

RFC 2554. SMTP Service Extension for Authentication. J. Myers. March 1999. (Describes an extension to SMTP to handle authentication.) `http://www.ietf.org/rfc/rfc2554.txt`

RFC 2559. Internet X.509 Public Key Infrastructure Operational Protocols—LDAPv2. S. Boeyen, T. Howes, P. Richard. April 1999. (Describes a protocol that satisfies some of the requirements in the Internet X.509 PKI system.) `http://www.ietf.org/rfc/rfc2559.txt`

RFC 2560. X.509 Internet Public Key Infrastructure Online Certificate Status Protocol—OCSP. M. Myers, R. Ankney, A. Malpani, S. Galperin, C. Adams. June 1999. (Describes a protocol for determining the status of a certificate.) `http://www.ietf.org/rfc/rfc2560.txt`

RFC 2574. User-based Security Model (USM) for version 3 of the Simple Network Management Protocol (SNMPv3). U. Blumenthal, B. Wijnen. April 1999. (Defines a procedure for providing SNMP message level security.) `http://www.ietf.org/rfc/rfc2574.txt`

RFC 2575. View-based Access Control Model (VACM) for the Simple Network Management Protocol (SNMP). B. Wijnen, R. Presuhn, K. McCloghrie. April 1999. (Defines a procedure for controlling access to management information.) `http://www.ietf.org/rfc/rfc2575.txt`

RFC 2577. FTP Security Considerations. M. Allman, S. Ostermann. May 1999. (Makes recommendations on how system administrators can make FTP more secure at their site.) `http://www.ietf.org/rfc/rfc2577.txt`

RFC 2585. Internet X.509 Public Key Infrastructure Operational Protocols: FTP and HTTP. R. Housley, P. Hoffman. May 1999. `http://www.ietf.org/rfc/rfc2585.txt`

RFC 2587. Internet X.509 Public Key Infrastructure LDAPv2 Schema. S. Boeyen, T. Howes, P. Richard. June 1999. (Describes the Schema used in LDAP for PKI.) `http://www.ietf.org/rfc/rfc2587.txt`

RFC 2588. IP Multicast and Firewalls. R. Finlayson. May 1999. (Discusses issues related to allowing IP multicasts through firewalls.) `http://www.ietf.org/rfc/rfc2588.txt`

RFC 2595. Using TLS with IMAP, POP3 and ACAP. C. Newman. June 1999. (Describes how to use the TLS protocol, formerly known as SSL, with the various email reading protocols.) `http://www.ietf.org/rfc/rfc2595.txt`

RFC 2617. HTTP Authentication: Basic and Digest Access Authentication. J. Franks, P. Hallam-Baker, J. Hostetler, S. Lawrence, P. Leach, A. Luotonen, L. Stewart. June 1999. (Describes how basic and digest authentication works in HTTP.) `http://www.ietf.org/rfc/rfc2617.txt`

RFC 2618. RADIUS Authentication Client MIB. B. Aboba, G. Zorn. June 1999. (Describes the SNMP MIB used by RADIUS clients for authentication.) `http://www.ietf.org/rfc/rfc2618.txt`

RFC 2619. RADIUS Authentication Server MIB. G. Zorn, B. Aboba. June 1999. (Describes the SNMP MIB used by RADIUS servers for authentication.) `http://www.ietf.org/rfc/rfc2619.txt`

RFC 2630. Cryptographic Message Syntax. R. Housley. June 1999. (Describes a syntax used for encrypting, digesting, signing or authenticating messages.) `http://www.ietf.org/rfc/rfc2630.txt`

RFC 2631. Diffie-Hellman Key Agreement Method. E. Rescorla. June 1999. (Describes how one particular Diffie-Hellman variant works.) `http://www.ietf.org/rfc/rfc2631.txt`

RFC 2632. S/MIME Version 3 Certificate Handling. B. Ramsdell, Ed. June 1999. (Describes how the S/MIME email encryption standard certificate are handled.) `http://www.ietf.org/rfc/rfc2632.txt`

RFC 2633. S/MIME Version 3 Message Specification. B. Ramsdell, Ed. June 1999. (Describes the message format for S/MIME email messages.) `http://www.ietf.org/rfc/rfc2633.txt`

RFC 2634. Enhanced Security Services for S/MIME. P. Hoffman, Ed. June 1999. (Describes security services that can be used with S/MIME.) `http://www.ietf.org/rfc/rfc2634.txt`

RFC 2659. Security Extensions For HTML. E. Rescorla, A. Schiffman. August 1999. (Describes how to embed S/HTTP negotiation into an HTML document.) `http://www.ietf.org/rfc/rfc2659.txt`

RFC 2660. The Secure HyperText Transfer Protocol. E. Rescorla, A. Schiffman. August 1999. (Specifies how the secure version of HTTP works.) `http://www.ietf.org/rfc/rfc2660.txt`

RFC 2661. Layer Two Tunneling Protocol "L2TP". W. Townsley, A. Valencia, A. Rubens, G. Pall, G. Zorn, B. Palter. August 1999. (Specifies how L2TP, a VPN protocol, works.) `http://www.ietf.org/rfc/rfc2661.txt`

RFC 2692. SPKI Requirements. C. Ellison. September 1999. (Discusses requirements of the PKI infrastructure.) `http://www.ietf.org/rfc/rfc2692.txt`

RFC 2693. SPKI Certificate Theory. C. Ellison, B. Frantz, B. Lampson, R. Rivest, B. Thomas, T. Ylonen. September 1999. (Presents the theory of PKI certificates.) `http://www.ietf.org/rfc/rfc2693.txt`

RFC 2695. Authentication Mechanisms for ONC RPC. A. Chiu. September 1999. (Describes two authentication mechanisms that can be used by Remote Procedure Call.) `http://www.ietf.org/rfc/rfc2695.txt`

RFC 2712. Addition of Kerberos Cipher Suites to Transport Layer Security (TLS). A. Mevinsky, M. Hur. October 1999. (Describes how to add Kerberos Ciphering to TLS.) `http://www.ietf.org/rfc/rfc2712.txt`

RFC 2716. PPP EAP TLS Authentication Protocol. B. Aboba, D. Simon. October 1999. (Explains how to use TLS for PPP authentication.) `http://www.ietf.org/rfc/rfc2716.txt`

E

VENDOR INFORMATION AND SECURITY STANDARDS

RFC 2726. PGP Authentication for RIPE Database Updates. J. Zsako. December 1999. (Describes how PGP authentication can be used to control updates to the IP address allocation database.) `http://www.ietf.org/rfc/rfc2726.txt`

RFC 2743. Generic Security Service Application Program Interface Version 2, Update 1. J. Linn. January 2000. (Describes updates to the GSS-API.) `http://www.ietf.org/rfc/rfc2743.txt`

RFC 2744. Generic Security Service API Version 2: C-bindings. J. Wray. January 2000. (Describes how the C programming language can access GSS-API.) `http://www.ietf.org/rfc/rfc2744.txt`

RFC 2747. RSVP Cryptographic Authentication. F. Baker, B. Lindell, M. Talwar. January 2000. (Describes how authentication can be used to protect a resource reservation system.) `http://www.ietf.org/rfc/rfc2747.txt`

RFC 2755. Security Negotiation for WebNFS. A. Chiu, M. Eisler, B. Callaghan. January 2000. (Discusses how WebNFS clients can negotiate with servers.) `http://www.ietf.org/rfc/rfc2755.txt`

RFC 2759. Microsoft PPP CHAP Extensions, Version 2. G. Zorn. January 2000. (Describes the second version of the Microsoft PPP authentication extensions.) `http://www.ietf.org/rfc/rfc2759.txt`

RFC 2773. Encryption using KEA and SKIPJACK. R. Housley, P. Yee, W. Nace. February 2000. (Discusses how encryption is done with the KEA and SKIPJACK algorithms.) `http://www.ietf.org/rfc/rfc2773.txt`

RFC 2792. DSA and RSA Key and Signature Encoding for the KeyNote Trust Management System. M. Blaze, J. Ioannidis, A. Keromytis. March 2000. (Discusses key and signature handling in a trust-management system that is Internet-based.) `http://www.ietf.org/rfc/rfc2792.txt`

RFC 2808. The SecurID(r) SASL Mechanism. M. Nystrom. April 2000. (Describes how the SecurID product can integrate with SASL.) `http://www.ietf.org/rfc/rfc2808.txt`

RFC 2809. Implementation of L2TP Compulsory Tunneling via RADIUS. B. Aboba, G. Zorn. April 2000. (Discusses implementation issues when using L2TP compulsory tunneling in dial-up networks.) `http://www.ietf.org/rfc/rfc2809.txt`

RFC 2817. Upgrading to TLS Within HTTP/1.1. R. Khare, S. Lawrence. May 2000. (Describes how a TCP connection can be upgraded to use TLS during a HTTP/1.1 session.) `http://www.ietf.org/rfc/rfc2817.txt`

RFC 2818. HTTP Over TLS. E. Rescorla. May 2000. (Describes how HTTP runs over TLS.) `http://www.ietf.org/rfc/rfc2818.txt`

RFC 2827. Network Ingress Filtering: Defeating Denial of Service Attacks Which Employ IP Source Address Spoofing. P. Ferguson, D. Senie. May 2000. (Discusses best practices that can be used to prevent denial of service attacks.) `http://www.ietf.org/rfc/rfc2827.txt`

RFC 2828. Internet Security Glossary. R. Shirey. May 2000. (Provides a glossary of Internet security terms.) `http://www.ietf.org/rfc/rfc2828.txt`

RFC 2829. Authentication Methods for LDAP. M. Wahl, H. Alvestrand, J. Hodges, R. Morgan. May 2000. (Discusses methods that can be used for authentication within LDAP.) `http://www.ietf.org/rfc/rfc2829.txt`

RFC 2831. Using Digest Authentication as an SASL Mechanism. P. Leach, C. Newman. May 2000. (Describes how to use the digest authentication method with SASL.) `http://www.ietf.org/rfc/rfc2831.txt`

RFC 2841. IP Authentication using Keyed SHA1 with Interleaved Padding (IP-MAC). P. Metzger, W. Simpson. November 2000. (Describes a method to authenticate and ensure integrity of IP datagrams using the Secure Hash Algorithm.) `http://www.ietf.org/rfc/rfc2841.txt`

RFC 2845. Secret Key Transaction Authentication for DNS (TSIG). P. Vixie, O. Gudmundsson, D. Eastlake, B. Wellington. May 2000. (Describes how to do transaction-level authentication using one-way hashing and shared secrets.) `http://www.ietf.org/rfc/rfc2845.txt`

RFC 2847. LIPKEY—A Low Infrastructure Public Key Mechanism Using SPKM. M. Eisler. June 2000. (Describes a way to get a secure channel using GSS-API and the Simple Public Key Mechanism.) `http://www.ietf.org/rfc/rfc2847.txt`

RFC 2865. Remote Authentication Dial In User Service (RADIUS). C. Rigney, S. Willens, A. Rubens, W. Simpson. June 2000. (Specifies the authentication mechanism that is used by many sites for dial-up access.) `http://www.ietf.org/rfc/rfc2865.txt`

RFC 2876. Use of the KEA and SKIPJACK Algorithms in CMS. J. Pawling. July 2000. (Discusses ways to use the Key Exchange Algorithm and SKIPJACK together with the Cryptographic Message Standard.) `http://www.ietf.org/rfc/rfc2876.txt`

RFC 2898. PKCS #5: Password-Based Cryptography Specification Version 2.0. B. Kaliski. September 2000. (Makes recommendations on how to implement password-based cryptography.) `http://www.ietf.org/rfc/rfc2898.txt`

RFC 2930. Secret Key Establishment for DNS (TKEY RR). D. Eastlake 3rd. September 2000. (Describes a way to authenticate using DNS queries using DNS resource records.) `http://www.ietf.org/rfc/rfc2930.txt`

RFC 2941. Telnet Authentication Option. T. Ts'o, Editor, J. Altman. September 2000. (Describes an option that allows Telnet to negotiate if encryption should be used and if so, which algorithm.) `http://www.ietf.org/rfc/rfc2941.txt`

RFC 2942. Telnet Authentication: Kerberos Version 5. T. Ts'o. September 2000. (Describes how Kerberos can be used to authenticate Telnet.) `http://www.ietf.org/rfc/rfc2942.txt`

RFC 2943. TELNET Authentication Using DSA. R. Housley, T. Horting, P. Yee. September 2000. (Describes how the Digital Signature Algorithm can be used to authenticate Telnet.) `http://www.ietf.org/rfc/rfc2943.txt`

RFC 2944. Telnet Authentication: SRP. T. Wu. September 2000. (Describes how the Secure Remote Password Protocol can be used to authenticate Telnet.) `http://www.ietf.org/rfc/rfc2944.txt`

RFC 2945. The SRP Authentication and Key Exchange System. T. Wu. September 2000. (Specifies the Secure Remote Password Protocol.) `http://www.ietf.org/rfc/rfc2945.txt`

RFC 2946. Telnet Data Encryption Option. T. Ts'o. September 2000. (Describes how Telnet can be used to confidentially encrypt data.) `http://www.ietf.org/rfc/rfc2946.txt`

RFC 2947. Telnet Encryption: DES3 64-bit Cipher Feedback. J. Altman. September 2000. (Describes how Triple-DES can be used to encrypt a Telnet session.) `http://www.ietf.org/rfc/rfc2947.txt`

RFC 2948. Telnet Encryption: DES3 64-bit Output Feedback. J. Altman. September 2000. (Describes how Triple-DES in output feedback mode can be used to encrypt a Telnet session.) `http://www.ietf.org/rfc/rfc2948.txt`

RFC 2949. Telnet Encryption: CAST-128 64-bit Output Feedback. J. Altman. September 2000. (Describes how the CAST-128 encryption algorithm in output feedback mode can be used to encrypt a Telnet session.) `http://www.ietf.org/rfc/rfc2949.txt`

RFC 2950. Telnet Encryption: CAST-128 64-bit Cipher Feedback. J. Altman. September 2000. (Describes how the CAST-128 encryption algorithm in cipher feedback mode can be used to encrypt a Telnet session.) `http://www.ietf.org/rfc/rfc2950.txt`

RFC 2951. TELNET Authentication Using KEA and SKIPJACK. R. Housley, T. Horting, P. Yee. September 2000. (Describes how the Key Exchange Algorithm and SKIPJACK can be used to authenticate a Telnet session.) `http://www.ietf.org/rfc/rfc2951.txt`

RFC 2952. Telnet Encryption: DES 64-bit Cipher Feedback. T. Ts'o. September 2000. (Describes how DES in cipher feedback mode can be used to encrypt a Telnet session.) `http://www.ietf.org/rfc/rfc2952.txt`

RFC 2953. Telnet Encryption: DES 64-bit Output Feedback. T. Ts'o. September 2000. (Describes how DES in output feedback mode can be used to encrypt a Telnet session.) `http://www.ietf.org/rfc/rfc2953.txt`

RFC 2977. Mobile IP Authentication, Authorization, and Accounting Requirements. S. Glass, T. Hiller, S. Jacobs, C. Perkins. October 2000. (Provides requirements that have to be supported in Authentication, authorization, and accounting to provide Mobile IP services.) `http://www.ietf.org/rfc/rfc2977.txt`

RFC 2984. Use of the CAST-128 Encryption Algorithm in CMS. C. Adams. October 2000. (Describes how to use CAST-128 in the S/MIME Cryptographic Message Syntax.) `http://www.ietf.org/rfc/rfc2984.txt`

RFC 2985. PKCS #9: Selected Object Classes and Attribute Types Version 2.0. M. Nystrom, B. Kaliski. November 2000. (Provides an object interface and attributes to public-key cryptography and LDAP directories.) `http://www.ietf.org/rfc/rfc2985.txt`

RFC 2986. PKCS #10: Certification Request Syntax Specification Version 1.7. M. Nystrom, B. Kaliski. November 2000. (Describes the syntax for certification requests.) `http://www.ietf.org/rfc/rfc2986.txt`

RFC 3007. Secure Domain Name System (DNS) Dynamic Update. B. Wellington. November 2000. (Makes a proposal on how dynamic DNS updates can be made securely.) `http://www.ietf.org/rfc/rfc3007.txt`

RFC 3013. Recommended Internet Service Provider Security Services and Procedures. T. Killalea. November 2000. (Defines what the IETF thinks ISPs should be doing with respect to security.) `http://www.ietf.org/rfc/rfc3013.txt`

E

VENDOR INFORMATION AND SECURITY STANDARDS

What's on the CD-ROM

IN THIS APPENDIX

Bastille

The Bastille Hardening Program is intended to tighten security on Linux and UNIX machines. It presently works well under Red Hat and Mandrake Linux; in its latest versions (as of 1.1.0), it can be easily enhanced to run under other distributions and UNIX systems by adding rvalues for the $GLOBAL_ variables.

Ethereal

Ethereal is a network traffic analyzer, or sniffer, for UNIX and UNIX-like operating systems. It uses GTK+, a graphical user interface library, and libpcap, a packet capture and filtering library.

Fragrouter: Network Intrusion Detection Evasion Toolkit

Fragrouter routes network traffic to elude most network intrusion detection systems.

Libnet Packet Assembly System

An API, libnet helps with the construction and handling of network packets. It provides a portable framework for low-level network packet writing and handling. (Use libnet in conjunction with libpcap, and you can write some really cool stuff.) Libnet includes packet creation at the IP layer and at the link layer as well as a host of supplementary and complementary functionality. Libnet is very handy for writing network tools and network test code. See the man page and sample test code for more detailed information.

MRTG

The Multi Router Traffic Grapher (MRTG) monitors the traffic load on network links. MRTG generates HTML pages containing GIF images, which provide a live visual representation of this traffic.

Nmap: The Network Mapper

Nmap's design allows system administrators and curious individuals to scan large networks to determine which hosts are up and what services they are offering. Nmap supports several scanning techniques such as UDP, TCP connect(), TCP SYN (half open), FTP proxy (bounce attack), Reverse-ident, ICMP (ping sweep), FIN, ACK sweep, Xmas Tree, SYN sweep, and Null scan. (See the Scan Types section for more details.)

Nmap also offers a number of advanced features, such as remote OS detection via TCP/IP fingerprinting, stealth scanning, dynamic delay and retransmission calculations, parallel scanning, detection of down hosts via parallel pings, decoy scanning, port filtering detection, direct (nonportmapper) RPC scanning, fragmentation scanning, and flexible target and port specification.

Npasswd

Npasswd replaces the `passwd` command for UNIX. It subjects user passwords to stringent "guessability" checks to decrease the chance that users will choose vulnerable passwords.

Ntop

Ntop shows the current network usage. It displays a list of hosts that are using the network and reports information concerning the IP and non-IP traffic generated by each host. Ntop can be started either in a terminal window in interactive mode or in Web mode. In the latter case, users will need a Web browser to run the program. Ntop sorts the traffic information according to host and protocol. Whenever ntop is started in Web mode (-w flag), multiple remote users can access the traffic information.

OpenSSH

Ssh (Secure Shell) logs into another computer over a network, to execute commands in a remote machine and to move files from one machine to another. It provides strong authentication and secure communications over insecure channels. It can replace rlogin, rsh, rcp, and rdist.

OpenSSL

The OpenSSL Project is a collaborative effort to develop a robust, commercial-grade, fully featured, and open source toolkit implementing the Secure Sockets Layer (SSL v2/v3) and Transport Layer Security (TLS v1) protocols. Open SL also maintains a full-strength general purpose cryptography library. A worldwide community of volunteers manages the project, using the Internet to communicate, plan, and develop the OpenSSL toolkit and its related documentation.

Scotty/Tkined

Scotty is a Tcl extension to build network management applications using Tcl (and Tk). The scotty extension provides new Tcl commands to send and receive ICMP packets, query the Domain Name System (DNS), access UDP sockets from Tcl, probe and use some selected SUN RPCs, retrieve and serve documents via HTTP, send and receive SNMP messages

(SNMPv1, SNMPv2USEC, SNMPv2C), write special purpose SNMP agents in Tcl, parse and access SNMP MIB definitions, and schedule jobs. For some OSI-folks, scotty has some optional code to parse and access GDMO MIB definitions, and to invoke CMIP operations based on the osimis/isode toolkit.

A network editor, Tkined allows users to draw maps showing their network configuration. The most important feature of Tkined is its programming interface, which allows network management applications to extend the capabilities of Tkined. Most applications for Tkined are written using scotty.

Snort

Snort is an open source network intrusion detection system, capable of performing real-time traffic analysis and packet logging on IP networks. It can perform protocol analysis and content searching/matching in order to detect a variety of attacks and probes, such as buffer overflows, stealth port scans, CGI attacks, SMB probes, OS fingerprinting attempts, and much more. Snort uses a flexible rules language to describe traffic that it should collect or pass, as well as a detection engine with a modular plug-in architecture. Snort has real-time alerting capability as well, incorporating alerting mechanisms for syslog, user-specified files, a UNIX socket, or WinPopup messages to Windows clients using Samba's smbclient.

Sudo

Sudo allows a sysadmin to give limited root privileges to users and to log root activity. The basic philosophy behind sudo is to approve as few privileges as possible but still allow people to get their work done.

TITAN

TITAN is a collection of programs, each of which either fixes or tightens one or more potential security problems in the setup or configuration of a UNIX system. Conceived and created by Brad Powell, TITAN was written in Bourne shell. Thanks to TITAN's simple modular design, anyone who can write a shell script or program can easily add to it, and completely understand the internal workings of the system.

TITAN does not replace other security tools, but, when used in combination with them, it can make the transformation of a new, out-of-the-box system into a firewall or security-conscious system significantly easier. In a nutshell, TITAN helps improve the security of the system it runs on.

YASSP

YASSP is bundle of packages to secure Solaris. The default behavior turns off most of the services, which is a suitable scenario for an external (exposed) server such as a firewall, a Web server or an FTP server. These services can be easily turned back on via a configuration file.

YASSP performs OS security tuning at various levels: turning off (networked) services, changing file owner/mode, enabling logging, tuning the network stack, changing the system parameters, and providing a coherent default environment so that administrators know what they can expect and where.

Zlib

Zlib 1.1.3 is a general-purpose data compression library. All of its code is thread safe. The data format used by the zlib library is described by RFCs (Request for Comments) 1950 to 1952 in the files ftp://ds.internic.net/rfc/rfc1950.txt (zlib format), rfc1951.txt (deflate format), and rfc1952.txt (gzip format).

Security Glossary

You will encounter many of the acronyms, terms, and names listed in this glossary as you study or implement Internet security.

802.2   An Ethernet frame format as well as a standard. Learn more here: `http://www.optimized.com/COMPENDI/EN-FrF83.htm`.

802.3 SNAP   An Ethernet frame format. Learn more here: `http://www.optimized.com/COMPENDI/EN-FrFSn.htm`.

10BASE-2   Coaxial (thinwire) Ethernet that, by default, transports data to distances of 600 feet.

10BASE-5   Coaxial (thickwire) Ethernet that, by default, transports data to distances of 1,500 feet.

10BASE-T   Twisted pair Ethernet that, by default, transports data to distances of 600 feet.

100BASE-T   Twisted pair fast Ethernet that transmits data at 100Mbps.

abuse of privilege   A violation of computer network policy or improper network access exceeding a user's authorization.

access control   Any means, device, or technique that allows an administrator to selectively grant or deny users access to a given resource, whether that resource is a file, directory, subnet, network, or server.

Access Control List (ACL)   A list that stores information on users and what resources they are allowed to access.

Active Server Pages (ASP)   A Microsoft technology for server-side programming for Web sites. Not to be confused with Application Server Providers.

ActiveX   A Microsoft technology that allows executable code to be downloaded to Web browsers and executed on the client. ActiveX has a weak security model and is a potentially very dangerous security hole.

adaptive pulse code modulation   Methods of encoding voice into digital format over communication lines.

Address Resolution Protocol (ARP)   Maps IP addresses to physical addresses.

administrator   In the general sense, a human being charged with controlling a network. In the more specific sense, the all-powerful, supervisory account in Windows NT. Whoever has Administrator privileges in Windows NT controls their network, workgroup, or domain.

Advanced Encryption Standard (AES)   The new standard for data encryption for the U.S. government. AES was selected at the end of 2000 and should be deployed by 2003. *See also* Data Encryption Standard, which AE will be replacing.

anlpasswd   A proactive password checker similar to passwd+. You can obtain it at `ftp://coast.cs.purdue.edu/pub/tools/unix/anlpasswd/`.

anonymous email   Email that is untraceable because path headers have been removed.

anonymous remailer   A machine that removes path headers from email messages, thus making the email sender anonymous. To try one out, go to `http://www.replay.com`.

ANSI C   A specification of the C programming language set forth by the American National Standards Institute.

applet   A small program for use within a Web browser environment. Written in the Java programming language, which was developed by Sun Microsystems. Applets generally enhance your surfing experience with graphics, animation, and enhanced text. They are significant from the security viewpoint because Java can flow through a firewall unfettered, unless precautions are taken to prevent it. However, by default, applets run in a security sandbox intended to prevent dangerous access.

AppleTalk   Apple Computer's networking suite that supports Ethernet and Token Ring.

AppleTalk Address Resolution Protocol   Apple's version of ARP; this protocol maps IP addresses to physical addresses.

AppleTalk Data Stream Protocol (ADSP)   Peer-to-peer streamed communication protocol for use in transporting large amounts of data over a network. (This is integrated into OpenTransport.)

AppleTalk Echo Protocol (AEP)   Apple's version of the Echo protocol; used to test the network by having a remote server echo packets you send.

AppleTalk Remote Access Protocol (ARAP)   Enabling this protocol turns your Macintosh server into a remote access server, allowing others to access your network from remote locations.

application gateways (firewalls)   These are firewall devices that disallow direct communication between the outside world and an internal network strung to the Internet. Information flows in and out using a series of proxies that filter that information along the way. Think of these as the lawyers of Internet security. The gateway speaks for both ends, without allowing direct access between them.

Application Service Providers   Companies that provide services, such as payroll services, across the Internet. Using these services requires secure connections and quite a bit of trust.

appz   Slang term. *See* warez, which means the same thing.

Ascend Inverse Multiplexing (AIM)   Proprietary protocol created by Ascend Communications (router manufacturer) for managing multiplexers. To learn more, go to `http://www.lucent.com/ins`.

Asymmetric Digital Subscriber Line (ADSL)   A high-speed, digital telephone technology that allows you to connect to the Internet at blazing speeds. ADSL is incredibly fast when you are downloading data (up to nearly 6Mbps). However, when uploading data, you are confined to as low as 64kbps. The distance from the phone company central office limits maximum speed.

asynchronous PPP   Run-of-the-mill PPP; the kind generally used by PPP dial-up customers.

Asynchronous Transfer Mode (ATM)   An ATM network is one type of network that can transfer information in standard blocks at high speed. (These are not to be confused with Automatic Teller Networks.)

attribute   The state of a given resource (whether file or directory), and whether that resource is readable, hidden, system, or other. (This is a term primarily used in reference to files on Microsoft-based file systems.) This can also refer to the state of objects in JavaScript and even HTML.

audit   Any review, independent or in-house, of existing security policies and procedures. Audits help system administrators and security personnel identify key strong and weak points in a given network's overall state of security. Audits are typically performed according to a very rigid, well-developed, predetermined plan of attack that is designed specifically for the target system.

audit trail   Logs, written documents, and other records that demonstrate the activity and use of a particular system. Audit trails are of chief importance when conducting an investigation. Without at least a minimal audit trail, a system administrator has almost no hope of catching crackers. An audit trail, in simple terms, is possibly evidence.

AUP   Acceptable Use Policy. Originally established by the National Science Foundation, AUP once forbade use of the Internet for commercial purposes. Today, AUP refers to rules a user must adhere to when using a network's services.

authenticate   Verifying a particular user's or host's identity.

authentication   The process of authenticating either a user or host. Such authentication can be simple and applied at the application level (demanding a password), or can be complex (as in challenge-response dialogs between machines, which generally rely on algorithms or encryption at a discrete level of the system).

Authentication Server Protocol   A TCP-based authentication service that can verify a user's identity. For more information, see RFC 931.

Automated Information System (AIS)   Any system (composed of hardware and software) that allows the maintenance, storage, and processing of information.

back door   A hidden program, left behind by an intruder a disgruntled employee, that allows him future access to a victim host. This term is synonymous with the more antiquated term *trap door*.

back up   To preserve a file system or files, usually for disaster recovery. Generally, backup is done on tape, floppy disk, or other, portable media that can be safely stored for later use.

bastion host   A server that is hardened against attack and can therefore be used outside the firewall as your "face to the world." These are often sacrificial.

Bell-La Padula Model   A system that utilizes access controls based on user need-to-know and data-sensitivity formulas. (For example, fewer users access sensitive data, and the procedures and mechanisms that protect that data are more stringent, as are the methods of access control and authentication associated with them.)

biometric access controls   Systems that authenticate users by physical characteristics, such as their face, fingerprints, retinal pattern, or voice.

buffer overflow   A type of attack which causes a program to overrun the end of a data storage area. The result is that the attacker can overwrite part of the program and get it to execute his code. This is primarily a problem with software written in C and C++. Other languages such as a Java are immune to it.

bug   A hole or weakness in a computer program. *See also* vulnerability.

call back   Call back systems implement security in a rather interesting way: A host connects to the server, and a brief exchange is had, after which the connection is cut. The server then calls the requesting host. This way, the server ensures that the connection was initiated from a trusted host.

Cast-128   An encryption algorithm that uses extremely large keys and can be incorporated into cryptographic applications. (You can learn more by obtaining RFC 2144.)

CERT   The Computer Emergency Response Team. CERT is a security organization, and its purpose is to assist computer networks that have been brought under attack by malicious users of crackers. They can be reached at http://www.cert.org.

certificate authority   Trusted third-party clearinghouse that is known to be reliable and secure. These clearinghouses issue security certificates and ensure their authenticity. Probably the most renowned commercial certificate authority is VeriSign, which issues certificates for Microsoft-compatible ActiveX components, among other things.

certification   There are two common definitions for this term. First, certification can refer to the result of a successful evaluation of any security product or system (certification of any product on the National Security Agency's Evaluated Products List, for example.) In this context, a product has been certified at a particular level of assurance. Still another definition is this: certification of a human being known to have successfully completed courses (and other training) that qualifies her in a particular field (such as certification as a Novell Network Engineer). *See also* NSA.

CGI-based attack   An attack that exploits vulnerabilities in Common Gateway Interface programs, usually via a World Wide Web site.

Challenge Handshake Authentication Protocol (CHAP)   Protocol that challenges users to verify their identity. The user is authenticated if the challenge is met with the right response. If not, the user is denied access to the requested resource. (This protocol is commonly used when establishing PPP sessions.) See RFC 1344 for further information.

checksum   A cryptographic value that constitutes a file's digital fingerprint. Virus scanners and audit tools use checksums to detect changes made to files (the former to check for virus attachment and the latter to check for Trojan horses).

chroot   A restricted environment in which processes run with limited access to the disk; the technique (and command) used to create such an environment (UNIX).

Common Gateway Interface (CGI)   Refers to a programming style and standard used to provide programmatic functionality to Web sites. Search engines are generally built to CGI specifications. (CGI standards are not platform specific and provide a generalized standard for any type of Web-based programming.) Perl is today's most popular language used for CGI programming. However, CGI programs can also be written C, C++, Python, Visual Basic, BASIC, and several shell languages.

COPS   Computer Oracle and Password System. A system-based tool that will scan your local host for common configuration problems and security vulnerabilities. Developed by Gene Spafford and Dan Farmer.

copy access   User privileges to copy a particular file.

crack   This can be either a noun or a verb. As a noun, crack refers to software (or any technique) used to circumvent security, including the very famous password-cracking utility Crack. As a verb, it means to breach system security or break the registration scheme on commercial software.

cracker   Someone who, with malicious intent, unlawfully breaches the security of computer systems; someone who breaks registration schemes on commercial software.

crash   The sudden failure of a system, requiring a reboot.

cyberwar   Active information warfare conducted over the Internet.

DAC   Discretionary Access Control. A system by which a central authority on a computer system or network can either permit or deny access to users, and do so incisively, based on time, date, file, directory, or machine.

data-driven attack   An attack that relies upon hidden or encapsulated data, which can be designed to flow through a firewall undetected. (Java and JavaScript can be used for such attacks.)

Data Encryption Standard (DES)   Encryption standard by IBM, developed in 1974 and published in 1977. Currently, DES is the U.S. government standard tool for encrypting non-classified data. *See also* Advanced Encryption Standard.

data integrity (file integrity)   The state of files. If files are unchanged and have not been tampered with, they have integrity. If they have been tampered with, data integrity has been breached or degraded.

DDoS   Distributed Denial of Service. A denial of service attack, which, instead of coming from a single source, comes from a large number of hosts.

digest access authentication   A security extension for Hypertext Transfer Protocol that provides only basic (and not encrypted) user authentication over the Web. To learn more, see RFC 2069.

digital certificate   Any digital value used in an authentication procedure. Digital certificates are typically numeric values, derived from cryptographic processes. (There are many values that can used as the basis of a digital certificate, including but not limited to biometric values, such as retinal scans.) *See also* biometric access controls.

DNS spoofing   A technique through which the attacker compromises a Domain Name Service server. This can be done either by corrupting the DNS cache or by man-in-the-middle attacks (in which your machine impersonates the legitimate DNS server).

DoD   Department of Defense.

DoS   Denial of service. A condition that results when a user maliciously renders an Internet information server inoperable, thereby denying computer service to legitimate users.

dual-homed gateway   Configuration or machine that supports two or more disparate protocols or means of network transport, and provides packet screening between them.

EFT   Electronic Funds Transfer.

encryption   The process of scrambling data so it is unreadable by unauthorized parties. In most encryption schemes, you must have a password to reassemble the data into readable form. Encryption is primarily used to enhance privacy or to protect classified, secret, or top secret information. (For example, many military and satellite transmissions are encrypted to prevent spies or hostile nations from analyzing them.)

Ethernet spoofing   Any procedure that involves assuming another host's Ethernet address to gain unauthorized access to the target.

firewall   Loosely, any device or technique that refuses unauthorized users access to a particular host. Minimally, a device that examines each packet and determines its source address. If that address is on an approved list, the packets gain entry. If not, they are rejected.

Flood, Floods, or Flooder   Tool or tools that overflow the connection queue of a TCP/IP–enabled system, thereby causing denial of service.

Fragmentation   The process of breaking up a large packet into small pieces to send it across a network that can only handle small packets. Often used in attacks against systems.

Frame relay   A technology that allows networks to transfer information in bursts. This is a cost-effective way of transferring data over networks because user only pay for the resources they use. (Unfortunately, users might also be sharing the frame relay connection with someone else. Standard frame relay connections run at 56kbps.)

FTP security extensions   Extensions to the File Transfer Protocol that provide authentication, integrity, and confidentiality checking for FTP-based sessions. See RFC 2228.

gigabit   1,000,000,000 bits, or 1024 Megabits, depending on who is using the term.

granularity   The degree to which one can incisively apply access controls. The more incisively a system allows controls to be set, the more granularity that system has.

hacker   Someone interested in operating systems, software, security, and the Internet generally. Also a programmer; an individual who codes for a living.

hacking   Any activity performed by a hacker.

hijacking   Seizing control of another user's session. Such attacks are rare occurrences, and when a hijacking happens, it indicates that the target's security has been breached.

HTPASSWD   A system used to password-protect sites on the World Wide Web (UNIX). Also known as *basic authentication*.

Hypertext Transfer Protocol (HTTP)   The protocol used to traffic hypertext across the Internet, and the WWW's underlying protocol.

Identification Protocol (IDENT)   A TCP-based protocol for use in identifying users. This is a more advanced and updated version of the Authentication Protocol. You can find out more by obtaining RFC 1413.

information warfare   The practice of or field of attacking another's information; a term often used in military or intelligence circles to describe the destruction, degradation, or disintegration of another's information infrastructure.

G

International Data Encryption Algorithm (IDEA)   A powerful a block-cipher algorithm encryption system that operates with a 128-bit key by default. IDEA encrypts data faster than DES and is far more secure.

Internet Engineering Task Force (IETF)   The standardization body for the Internet. The IETF's Web site is http://www.ietf.org/.

Internet Protocol Security Option   IP security option used to protect IP datagrams according to U.S. classifications, whether unclassified, classified secret, or top secret. See RFC 1038 and RFC 1108.

Internet Relay Chat (IRC)   A popular chat facility on the Internet.

Internet worm   Also called the *Morris Worm*; a program that attacked the Internet in November 1988. To get a good overview of this attack, check out RFC 1135.

intrusion detection   The practice of deploying automated procedures and applications to detect intrusion attempts. Intrusion detection typically involves the use of intelligent systems or agents.

IP   Internet Protocol.

IPSec   An encrypted form of IP. It is currently not widely deployed but might be in a few years.

IP spoofing   Any procedure by which an attacker assumes another host's IP address to gain unauthorized access to the target.

ISO   International Standards Organization.

jack in   The act of breaching the security of an Internet information server; slang term used by crackers.

Java   A network programming language, created by Sun Microsystems, that marginally resembles C++. It is object oriented and exploits the networking support built in to the Internet. It can be used to generate graphics applications, multimedia applications, and even standalone, windowed programs. However, Java is most well known for its cross-platform capabilities. Java has some security issues of its own.

JavaScript   Programming language used in Netscape and Internet Explorer environments. JavaScript was created by Netscape Communication Corporation and has support for most programmatic functions. (It is also used to generate Web pages with increased functionality, and is the cornerstone of Dynamic HTML, a new form of creating Web pages that supports many multimedia features.) It has had many security problems.

JScript   Microsoft's version of JavaScript. However, it is mostly compatible with JavaScript.

Kerberos   Encryption and authentication system developed at the Massachusetts Institute of Technology. It is used in many network applications, and works on a system of tickets and trusted third-party servers for authentication.

Kerberos Network Authentication Service   Third-party, ticket-based authentication scheme that can be (and has been) easily integrated into network applications. See RFC 1510 for more information.

keystroke capture   The act of using a Keystroke Recorder.

Keystroke Recorder   A program that surreptitiously captures keystrokes typed by an unsuspecting victim. These tools are used to steal someone's username and password.

logic bomb   Any program or code—generally malicious—that causes a system to lock up or fail.

Maximum Transmission Unit (MTU)   A user-definable parameter that denotes the largest packet that can be transmitted. Many people adjust this value and often get better performance by either increasing or decreasing its size.

MD4   A message digest algorithm used to check the integrity of files. Examine the original specification in RFC 1186.

MD5   A message digest algorithm used to check the integrity of files. Examine the original specification in RFC 1321.

NASIRC   NASA Automated Systems Incident Response Capability. An incident-tracking and response body for the U.S. government. NASIRC is located at `http://www-nasirc.nasa.gov/nasa/index.html`.

NCSC   National Computer Security Center, which is located at `http://www.radium.ncsc.mil/`.

NetBEUI   A version of NetBIOS that runs on top of TCP/IP.

NetBIOS   The protocol used by Windows to share files.

netstat   UNIX command (also available in Windows) that shows the current TCP/IP connections and their source addresses.

npasswd   A proactive password checker for UNIX that screens potential passwords before they are committed to the password file. You can obtain it here: `ftp://ftp.cc.utexas.edu/pub/npasswd/`.

NSA   National Security Agency. The National Security Agency/Central Security Service is responsible for protecting classified and unclassified national security systems against exploitation through interception, unauthorized access, or related technical intelligence threats. Find them here: `http://www.nsa.org`.

one-time password   A password generated on-the-fly during a challenge/response exchange. Such passwords are generated using a predefined algorithm, but, because they are good for the current session only, they are extremely secure.

owner   The person (or process) with privileges to read, write, or otherwise access a given file, directory, or process. The system administrator assigns ownership. However, ownership can also be assigned automatically by the operating system in certain instances.

password shadowing   A technique used to prevent crackers from capturing and cracking encrypted passwords previously stored in the /etc/passwd file. In shadowing, the encrypted password is hidden elsewhere on the drive. In the /etc/passwd file, this password is abstractly represented by a token, usually a single character.

penetration testing   The process of attacking a host from outside to ascertain remote security vulnerabilities.

Perl   Practical Extraction and Report Language. A programming language commonly used in network programming and CGI programming. Perl has features that make it exceptionally suitable for system administration tasks on the UNIX platform. Its key characteristic is its capability to convert mountains of data (such as log files) into easily readable and understandable information. (Perl also has powerful networking support and is an excellent choice if you are contemplating socket programming.)

phreaking   The process of manipulating the telephone system, usually unlawfully.

Point-to-Point Protocol (PPP)   A communication protocol used between machines that support serial interfaces, such as modems. PPP is commonly use to provide and access dial-up services to Internet service providers.

Point-to-Point Tunneling Protocol (PPTP)   A specialized form of PPP. This protocol's unique design makes it possible to encapsulate, or *wrap*, non-TCP/IP protocols within PPP. PPTP allows two or more LANs to connect using the Internet as a conduit. (PPTP is a great stride ahead of PPP because expensive, leased lines were used in the past to perform this task, which was cost-prohibitive in many instances.)

PPP Authentication Protocols   A set of protocols used to enhance security of Point-to-Point Protocol, supported at both the router and host levels. See RFC 1334 for more information.

PPP DES   A protocol that applies standard Data Encryption Standard protection to Point-to-Point links. (This is one method of hardening PPP traffic against sniffing.) To learn more, see RFC 1969.

Pretty Good Privacy (PGP)   An encrypted email program and message format created by Phil Zimmerman.

proxy   A type of firewall that has clients talk to the proxy server. Then the proxy server forwards the request to the Internet. This way, the client machine and the Internet do not talk directly, reducing the possibility of security problems.

read access   User privileges to read a particular file.

Reverse Address Protocol (RARP)   A protocol that maps Ethernet addresses to IP addresses.

RFC   Request for Comment. Request for Comments documents (RFCs) are working notes and standards of the Internet development community. They are often used to propose new standards. RFCs are generated by the *Internet Engineering Task Force*. A huge depository of RFC documents can be found here: `http://rs.internic.net`.

risk management   The field of ascertaining security risks, designing solutions, and implementing those solutions, based on a formula of need versus cost.

RSA   A public-key encryption algorithm named after its creators, Rivest, Shamir, and Adelman. RSA is probably the most popular of such algorithms and has been incorporated into many commercial applications, including but not limited to Netscape Navigator, Communicator, and even Lotus Notes. Find out more about RSA at `http://www.rsa.com`.

router   A device that routes packets into and out of a network. Many routers are sophisticated and can serve as firewalls.

SATAN   Security Administrator's Tool for Analyzing Networks. A TCP/IP port scanner that checks remote hosts for common misconfiguration problems and security vulnerabilities. An updated version known as saint is available at `http://www.wwdsi.com/saint`.

scanner   Any utility that probes remote hosts, looking for weaknesses in their security.

Secure Socket Layer (SSL)   A security protocol (created by Netscape Communications Corporation) that allows client/server applications to communicate free of eavesdropping, tampering, or message forgery. SSL is now used for secure electronic commerce. To find out more, see `http://home.netscape.com/eng/ssl3/draft302.txt`.

security audit   An examination (often by third parties) of a server's security controls and disaster recovery mechanisms.

SET   Secured Electronic Transaction. A standard of secure protocols associated with online commerce and credit-card transactions. (VISA and MasterCard are the chief players in development of the SET protocol.) Its purpose is ostensibly to make electronic commerce more secure.

shadowing   *See* password shadowing.

sharing   The process of allowing users on other machines to access files and directories on your own. File sharing is a fairly typical activity within LANs, and can sometimes be a security risk.

shell   In general, a command interpreter or any program that takes standard input and relays those commands to the system. More specifically, either one of the shells in UNIX (`csh`, `bash`, `sh`, `ash`, `ksh`, `tcsh`, or `zsh`); `COMMAND.COM` in DOS; or `CMD.EXE` in Windows NT.

shell scripts   Small programs—written in shell languages—that operate much like batch files. They are composed of various regular expression operations, pipes, redirects, system calls, and so forth.

Site Security Handbook   An excellent document that discusses basic security measures for maintaining a site. Every system administrator should have a copy. You can obtain it from RFC 2196.

S/Key   One-time password system to secure connections. In S/Key, passwords are never sent over the network and therefore cannot be sniffed. See RFC 1760 for more information.

smart cards   Small, plastic cards that house tiny microprocessors that can store data. They closely resemble credit cards, however, smart cards are more advanced than standard credit cards. Smart cards are very popular in Europe but haven't yet caught on here in the United States.

sniffer   Program that surreptitiously captures datagrams across a network. A sniffer can be used legitimately (by an engineer trying to diagnose network problems) or illegitimately (by a cracker looking to steal usernames and passwords).

sniffing   The practice of using a sniffer.

SNMP Security Protocols   Simple Network Management Protocol is used for remote management and protection of networks and hosts. There are a series of security-related protocols within the SNMP suite. You can find out about them by obtaining RFC 1352.

social engineering   The practice of tricking unwary system personnel into revealing passwords or other information about their network.

SOCKS Protocol   A protocol that provides unsecured firewall traversal for TCP-based services.

SP3   Network Layer Security Protocol.

SP4   Transport Layer Security Protocol.

spoofing   Any procedure that involves impersonating another user or host to gain unauthorized access to the target.

Telnet Authentication Option   Protocol options for Telnet that add basic security to Telnet-based connections based on rules at the source routing level. See RFC 1409 for details.

TEMPEST   Transient Electromagnetic Pulse Surveillance Technology. The practice and study of capturing or eavesdropping on electromagnetic signals that emanate from any device—in this case, a computer. *TEMPEST shielding* is any computer security system designed to defeat such eavesdropping.

time bomb   Any program that waits for a specified time or event to disable a machine or otherwise cause that machine or system to fail. *See also* logic bomb.

TCPDUMP   A utility for UNIX that captures packets. (This is a packet sniffer of sorts and is often used to obtain very detailed logs of network traffic.) The software can be found at `http://www.tcpdump.org/`.

Traceroute   A TCP/IP program that traces the route between your machine and a remote host.

traffic analysis   The study of patterns in communication, rather than the content of the communication. For example, studying when, where, and to whom particular messages are being sent, without actually studying the content of those messages. Traffic analysis can be revealing, primarily in determining relationships between individuals and hosts.

trap door   *See* back door.

Trojan (Trojan horse)   An application or code that, unbeknownst to the user, performs surreptitious and unauthorized tasks. Those tasks can compromise system security.

trusted system   An operating system or other system secure enough for use in environments where classified information is warehoused.

tunneling   The practice of employing encryption in data communication between two points, thus shielding that data from others who might be sniffing the wire. Tunneling procedures encrypt data within packets, making it extremely difficult for outsiders to access such data.

UDP   User Datagram Protocol. A connectionless protocol from the TCP/IP family. (Connectionless protocols transmit data between two hosts, even though those hosts do not currently have an active session. Such protocols are considered unreliable because there is no absolute guarantee that the data will arrive as intended.)

UID   *See* user ID.

user   Anyone who uses a computer system or system resources.

user ID   In general, any value by which a user is identified, including his username. More specifically, and in relation to UNIX and other multiuser environments, any process ID—usually a numeric value—that identifies the owner of a particular process. *See also* owner and user.

Virtual Private Network (VPN)   VPN technology allows companies with unsecured connections to form a closed and secure circuit between themselves over the Internet. In this way, such companies ensure that data passed between them and their counterparts is secure (and usually encrypted).

virus   Self-replicating or propagating program (sometimes malicious) that attaches itself to other executables, drivers, or document templates, thus infecting the target host or file.

vulnerability   This term refers to any weakness in any system (either hardware or software) that allows intruders to gain unauthorized access or deny service. Also called a *hole*.

WAN   Wide Area Network.

warez   Stolen or pirated software, often traded on the Usenet network.

worm   A computer program (not necessarily malicious) that replicates, spreading itself from host to host over the network. Worms sometimes consume significant network resources and are therefore possible tools in denial of service attacks.

write access   User privileges to write to a particular file.

INDEX

SYMBOLS

0-day exploits, 465

A

abuse of privilege, 828
acceptable use policies,
  615-617
access control, 90, 828
  back door Trojan horses, 358
  policies, 611-615
  requirements assessment, 679
  software, 380-381, 411-416
access devices, 638-640
account lockout, 441
accuracy of coverage, IDSs,
  233
ACL (Access Control List), 828
ACROS, 762
Active Directory, 390
Active Setup download vulnerability, 395
ActiveX, 828
adaptive pulse code modulation, 828
addresses
  hiding email addresses,
    150-158
addressing IPv4, 66
administrative collaboration,
  631

administrative security policies,
  615-616
Administrator Assistant Tool
  Kit, 404
Administrator's Pak, 404
administrators
  responsibilities, 828
  training, 43-44
Adobe Acrobat, 31
ADSL (Asymmetric Digital
  Subscriber Line), 830
ADSP (AppleTalk Data Stream
  Protocol), 829
AEP (AppleTalk Echo Protocol),
  829
AES (Advanced Encryption
  Standard), 828
AIDS Trojan horse, 358
AIM (Ascend Inverse
  Multiplexing), 829
AIS (Automated Information
  System), 830
Allaire ColdFusion, 12-13
allies, 91-100
America Online, 558
AMI Decode password cracker,
  274
Amidecod utility, 379
Analog, 250
anlpasswd, 829
anomaly-based IDS, 229
anonymous email, 557, 829
anonymous remailer, 829
ANSI bombs, 361
ANSI C, 829

S

Other Related Titles

Maximum Linux Security
Anonymous
0-672-32134-3
$44.99 US/$67.95 CAN

Linux Programming Unleashed, Second Edition
Kurt Wall
0-672-32021-5
$49.99 US/$74.95 CAN

Red Hat Linux System Administration Unleashed
Thomas Schenk
0-672-31755-9
$49.99 US/$74.95 CAN

Java Security Handbook
Jamie Jaworski
0-672-31602-1
$49.99 US/ $74.95 CAN

Drew Haywood's Windows 2000 Network Services
Drew Haywood
0-672-31741-9
$49.99 US/$74.95 CAN

Sams Teach Yourself TCP/IP, Second Edition
Joe Casad
0-672-32085-1
$24.99 US/$37.95 CAN

Linux Socket Programming
Sean Walton
0-672-31935-7
$49.99 US/$74.95 CAN

Software Testing
Ron Patton
0-672-31983-7
$39.99 US/$59.95 CAN

Embracing Insanity: Open Source Software Development
Russell C. Pavlicek
0-672-31989-6
$29.99 US/$44.95 CAN

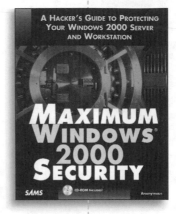

Maximum Windows 2000 Security
Anonymous
0-672-31965-9
$49.99 US/$74.95 CAN

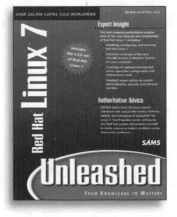

Red Hat Linux 7 Unleashed

0-672-31985-3
$49.99 US/$74.95 CAN

SAMS
www.samspublishing.com

All prices are subject to change.

Installation Instructions

The companion CD-ROM contains security tools and all the examples developed in the book.

Windows 95, Windows 98, Windows Me, Windows NT, and Windows 2000 Installation Instructions

1. Insert the CD-ROM disc into your CD-ROM drive.

2. From the Windows desktop, double-click the My Computer icon.

3. Double-click the icon representing your CD-ROM drive.

4. Open the readme.txt file for descriptions and installation instructions for the individual software products.

Linux and Unix Installation Instructions

These installation instructions assume that you have a passing familiarity with UNIX commands and the basic setup of your machine. As UNIX has many flavors, only generic commands are used. If you have any problems with the commands, please consult the appropriate man page or your system administrator.

1. Insert the CD-ROM in the CD drive.

   If you have a volume manager, mounting of the CD-ROM will be automatic. If you don't have a volume manager, you can mount the CD-ROM by typing
   `mount -tiso9660 /dev/cdrom /mnt/cdrom`.

   NOTE: `/dev/cdrom` is typically used on Linux systems to describe your first CD-ROM device. UNIX and variants can use different device nomenclature to describe your CD-ROM drive. `/mnt/cdrom` is just a mount point, but it must exist when you issue the `mount` command. You can also use any empty directory for a mount point if you don't want to use `/mnt/cdrom`.

2. Open the readme.txt file for descriptions and installation instructions of software products.